RY

HUNGARY
pest

R U M A N I A

Danube

BLACK SEA

be

rade

VIA

SERBIA

BULGARIA

Sofia

ALBANIA

MACEDONIA

GREECE

AEGEAN

TURKEY

Athens

SAMOS

PELOPONESE
(MOREA)

LEROS

COS

DODECANESE

RHODES

C. Matapan

KYTHERA

CYPRUS

CRETE

Tobruk

Benghazi

Y A

The Italian Campaign
1943-45

The Italian Campaign 1943-45

A Political and Military re-assessment

G. A. Shepperd

Arthur Barker Limited
5 Winsley Street London W1

940.5421
Sh4i
95627
Jan.1976

S B N   213 76404 0

Printed in Great Britain by
Morrison and Gibb Limited, London and Edinburgh

Contents

Illustrations

MAPS

**Except where otherwise stated the photographs are reproduced by kind
permission of the Imperial War Museum**

Introduction

BY FIELD MARSHAL LORD HARDING, GCB, CBE, DSO, MC

As far as I am aware Colonel Shepperd has produced the first complete account of the Italian Campaign in the Second World War to appear in print and I count it an honour to have been asked to write an introduction to his book.

I am not able to comment from first-hand experience on the events of 1943, but from January 1944 when I joined Alexander's headquarters as his Chief of Staff until the end of the fighting when I found myself in command of the British and American forces in Venezia Giulia with responsibility for the controversial port of Trieste, I was closely in touch with the events which Colonel Shepperd describes, and have been impressed by the accuracy and balance which characterises his work.

He has produced a readable and workmanlike study in which he does justice to the courage and endurance of the troops of many nations who fought their way to final victory in Italy and the skills of the German Armies they defeated; gives due credit to the contribution made by all three fighting services without minimizing the dominant part played by air power; brings into focus the interplay of operational, strategic, political, national and personality considerations all of which had their bearing on the conduct of this campaign; and last but not least in importance, puts the Italian Campaign into proper perspective in relation to the global situation of the time and its impact on the future. To achieve this balance and perspective must have called for infinite perseverance in research and judgement in the selection of the material available. I only hope that the reception of his work will bring Colonel Shepperd the reward he deserves for the time and devotion he has given to it.

A review of the Italian Campaign with its varied controversial issues gives food for thought on many aspects of the conduct of military operations and the pursuit of political aims in war on an allied basis with all the related problems of conflicting interests, misunderstandings stemming from prejudice or ignorance of geography and history, clash of personalities, and the confusions and contradictions to which all human activities of a corporate nature are prone.

Out of this welter of problems I would like to comment on two: the first is purely operational or tactical in the military sense as exemplified in the Battle for Rome. The second is primarily strategic with a strong political overlay and concerns the diversion of forces from Italy to the South of France.

ix

INTRODUCTION

A study of Allied Military Operations in Italy from the landing at Salerno to the hold-up at Cassino disclosed three factors of paramount tactical importance in the conduct of offensive land operations in Italy. They were the terrain, the weather and most important of all the exceptional skill of the German command in the manipulation of troops on the battlefield in blocking operations. The conclusion of this study was that despite the overwhelming superiority in the air, in armour and artillery enjoyed by the allies it would be necessary to attack on a broad front to pin down the enemy and to assemble a superiority of three to one in infantry on the frontage of attack to obtain penetration and maintain momentum.

This was the concept on which operation Diadem was based and in spite of immense administrative difficulties overcome largely by the skill and determination of General Sir Brian Robertson (now Lord Robertson of Oakridge) the necessary concentration was obtained between Cassino and the west coast of Italy and the Battle for Rome was won. This need for great superiority of numbers of men on their feet with weapons in their hands which they can use effectively applies to any form of fighting, and even to police operations where the enemy or the quarry enjoy immunity from capture through mobility and independence of fixed lines of communication and supply.

The diversion of troops from Italy to the South of France in the autumn of 1944 was, in my opinion, the biggest strategic blunder of the war, an even greater mistake in the light of subsequent events than the diversion of forces from the Western Desert to Greece in 1942, also done for political reasons and in all conscience bad enough. By the time this operation was launched it had become perfectly clear that Hitler was obsessed with hanging on everywhere that German troops were placed. The only purpose achieved by operation Anvil was to manoeuvre the German forces in the South of France back to positions in direct defence of the German homeland to which Hitler should have withdrawn them anyhow if he had been in his right mind. On the other hand had the Allied Armies in Italy not been weakened and their advance lost momentum by this diversion it is not too much to claim that Vienna, which is not in the Balkans as seems to have been thought in Washington at the time, would have fallen to Allied rather than Russian Arms with all that that would have implied. No more need be said.

Yet to me the true value of Colonel Shepperd's work lies in the integrity of his writing which establishes beyond dispute that the troops who responded so bravely and consistently to Alexander's inspiring leadership not only most worthily upheld the traditions of the nations they represented, but together made an outstanding contribution to the final and total victory of the Allies in the Second World War.

Foreword

The Mediterranean area has been described as a crossroads and this is as true in our century of intercontinental sea and air travel as it was in ancient times when the sea received its name. Historically the Mediterranean has been the source of our Western civilization, a meeting point of great religions and of conflicting ideologies, an area long accustomed to the incursions of invading armies and the passage of naval squadrons seeking to dominate the sea and land routes. Sicily and the southern part of the Italian peninsula, jutting out to divide the Mediterranean, are particularly vulnerable to attack by sea. The Athenian expedition to Syracuse, the Pyrrhic expedition in aid of Tarentum, the Carthaginian operations around Eryx in the third century BC, and the Norman occupation of Sicily point to the early use of seaborne assault in this area. In spite of Italy's long and vulnerable coast lines, however, the traditional route of the invaders attracted by the wealth of the northern and central provinces has been overland across the mountains. From this direction the Alps themselves have never formed an effective barrier and in particular to the north-east the passes leading down towards the rich plains of the Po valley are easy to negotiate, while the valleys themselves tend to converge at their exits and assist the concentration of an invading army and this was the route that led the Goths to the sack of Rome in 407 AD. To break out across the Alps from the south, however, is a different matter with the ring of mountains dominating the approaches from the northern plains. The difficulties of the terrain even in the north-east are well illustrated by the failure of the many offensives against the Austro-Hungarian forces on the River Isonzo between April 1915 and the disastrous battle of Caporetto two and a half years later.

The military history of peninsular Italy has been shaped by two physical characteristics; the Apennine mountain range that divides the country down its length and the numerous rivers that plunge down from the snow-capped peaks to cut across the narrow coastal plains. These natural barriers inhibit large-scale military movement except on the established coastal roads, particularly in winter when the rivers are often in spate. In addition the extensive mountainous areas, themselves formidable barriers, favour the defence and operations launched against 'the grain of the country' invariably prove both slow and costly.

With the advent of long-range aircraft, Italy, between the two world wars, became a communication centre on many air routes. From a strategic point of view, however, the development of air power changed the whole situation as regards the sea routes through the Mediterranean. This fact was quickly demonstrated by the Axis Powers when, after the Allied withdrawal from Greece and the fall of Crete, the Mediterranean was closed to Allied naval convoys for the Middle East and the island fortress of Malta could only be maintained by great sacrifice of men and ships. The efforts of the Axis to extend this stranglehold on the Mediterranean by an advance to the Suez Canal inevitably resulted in the bitterly fought out Desert campaign and the long haul by the Allies back to Tripoli and beyond.

In point of time this account of the Italian Campaign starts with the decision at Casablanca to mount a great amphibious operation against Sicily with the object of re-opening the Mediterranean. These plans were soon expanded to include an advance to the Italian mainland with the object of knocking Italy out of the war and capturing the Foggia airfields from whence Allied bombers could reach hitherto inaccessible areas of eastern and southern Germany. 1943 saw the end of Hitler's grandiose offensive strategy. On the Eastern Front his armies were in retreat and in the Mediterranean both the African coastline and Sicily had been lost. After the fall of Mussolini and the Italian surrender Hitler's only strategy was to fight for the ground he held. Obsessed with the importance of the Balkans, he saw the island outposts in the Aegean and guarding the Peloponnese, together with the defence line across peninsular Italy, as a single front to be held at all cost. The Western Allies however were faced with more complex decisions. Global war demanded a global strategy. Operations in the Mediterranean were now whittled down to fit in with plans for the war in the Pacific, operations in Burma and the requirements of the cross-Channel invasion that Stalin was constantly calling for.

This attempt to cover such a wide spectrum has brought several problems in presentation. In the space of a single volume only the broad pattern of operation can be described and accounts of the exploits of individual units must perforce be left in the able hands of the regimental historians. Similarly limitation of space has meant that many of the smaller towns and villages have had to be omitted from the maps and it has only been possible to indicate the principal physical features. Place names are given in the form considered most easily recognizable by those who took part in the campaign. Some inconsistencies are difficult to avoid. Allied accounts speak of 'Anzio', while German writers use 'Nettuno'. To the men of Cassino there can be only one Castle Hill but a Monte Maggiore is seemingly met in every major defence line.

This then is the story of plans made within the frame of global conflict, the story of a campaign fought out in a land that has seen war in all its forms through the centuries, the story of a slow and desperately contested advance the length of a country that had never before been totally overrun from the south. It is the story of amphibious assaults, bitterly opposed and thrown back to the very beaches, and of allied air power, playing a dominant part ahead of the two armies struggling towards the northern plains. The campaign was fought under conditions that, in spite of the many advances in technology, equipment and material that emerged during the Second World War, were to test the training, endurance and qualities of the fighting men to their limit. Such aspects will long continue to demand close study.

1
Strategies in Conflict

War situation early in 1943: Axis position in Europe: Battle of Atlantic:
The Air War: Hitler's Strategy, Mussolini's Doubts, Stalin's Objectives:
Second Front: Aid to Russia: Casablanca and Global Strategy: Churchill
flies to Turkey: Planners' Problems: Ships *v* Divisions *v* Industry: Third
Washington Conference: Churchill meets Eisenhower.

CHRONOLOGY COVERING CHAPTERS 1 AND 2

1943	14–23 Jan	Casablanca Conference (SYMBOL) to plan Allied Strategy for 1943.
	23 Jan	Eighth Army enters Tripoli.
	30 Jan	Dönitz becomes C-in-C of German Navy.
	31 Jan	German surrender at Stalingrad.
	Feb	Heavy sinking of Allied merchant shipping in Atlantic.
	9 Feb	Japanese resistance ends on Guadalcanal.
	14 Feb	Russians occupy Rostov.
	17 Feb	Tedder given command of all Allied Air Forces in Middle East and North Africa.
	Mar/Jul	Battle of the Ruhr.
	5 Apl	Americans join up with the Eighth Army in North Africa.
	May	Forty-one U-boats sunk in North Atlantic and Bay of Biscay.
	3 May	Eisenhower decides on plan for landing in Sicily (HUSKY).
	6 May	Final advance in Tunisia.
	12–25 May	Third Washington Conference (TRIDENT).
	13 May	Tunisian Campaign ends.
	18 May	Bombing of Pantelleria starts.
	22 May	Dönitz withdraws his submarines from the North Atlantic.
	11 Jun	Pantelleria surrenders. Allies switch air attack to Axis airfields in Sicily and Italy.

The decision to follow up the clearing of the Axis forces from North Africa by an invasion of Sicily was taken at the Casablanca Conference (SYMBOL) in January 1943 and plans to carry the attack to the mainland of Italy emerged from the Third Washington Conference (TRIDENT) between President Roosevelt and Winston Churchill in May 1943, and so the Italian Campaign was born.

The Japanese attack on Pearl Harbour had taken place eighteen months previously and the American nation, shocked by the disaster and determined on full retribution, were now mobilized against the Axis Powers. With the spread of Nazi advances barely contained, the Allies, strengthened by the industrial resources and manpower of the USA, faced the problems of global war; a war which must be fought largely on exterior lines of communication with long ocean routes to be protected and vast distances to be overcome. Churchill's record of this period, from the entry of the USA into the war to the spring of 1943 – *The Hinge of Fate* – concludes with a chapter 'Italy the Goal' which describes his flying visit to confer with General Eisenhower in North Africa immediately after the TRIDENT Conference in Washington. It was here that the decision over Italy was sealed. Churchill wrote, 'Here then we end this Volume, which describes the turning point of the Second World War. The entry of the United States into the struggle after the Japanese assault on Pearl Harbour had made it certain that the cause of freedom would not be cast away. But between survival and victory there are many stages. Over two years of intense and bloody fighting lay before us all. Henceforward however the danger was not destruction but stalemate.' To overcome this stalemate a grand strategy was needed.

In fact the SYMBOL and TRIDENT Conferences themselves were a turning point in bringing about a 'new look in Strategic Planning' by the Allies. The earlier struggles for survival against the German and Italian Armies in Europe and Africa and the Japanese forces in the Pacific and Far Eastern theatres had left little scope for anything but stop-gap measures. Now the climate of the war had been tempered by the American successes in the naval and air battles of the Coral Sea and Midway, by the battles of El Alamein and the Allied landings of Operation TORCH in French North Africa and by the dramatic and vital defence by the Russians of Stalingrad. But how to avoid stalemate and what of the future when the Axis Powers were defeated and the exhausted combatants faced the rebuilding of their devastated countries?

3

The thoughts of the Allied leaders could now turn to a broader concept of military strategy and plans for a proper integration of the material and man-power resources of the Allies. Indeed planning in both respects was now vital to the Allies. All the time, however, the political problems, which must in-evitably result from this unprecedented slaughter and destruction and from the changing frontiers, hung as a cloud over the still distant goal of military victory. In the second half of January 1943 Churchill and Roosevelt were planning, at Casablanca, a joint strategy for the three theatres of war in Europe, the Pacific, and in the Far East. Planning where to hold fast and where and when to attack on land and sea and in the air.

Hitler now no longer had the resources in men and material to achieve strategic mobility on the grand scale. The bold eastward thrusts of 1942 at the Caucasus and the Suez Canal had been halted and turned back. Plans to capture Malta had never been attempted. The disaster of Stalingrad was only days away. General von Thoma, the Nazi commander of the Afrika Korps, when captured in Libya, had been sufficiently disillusioned to remark to General Montgomery 'the Germans are convinced they have lost the war'. Count Ciano at the time of the Allied landings in North Africa foresaw that 'Italy will become the centre of attack by the Allies in the offensive against the Axis' and a month later he wrote '1943 will be the year of the Anglo-Saxon effort. Mussolini considers that the Axis must have the greatest possible number of Divisions in order to defend itself in Africa, in the Balkans and perhaps even in the West.' At the same time Hitler made a significant remark in conversation with Admiral Raeder saying he must 'first of all prevent a collapse on any front where the enemy could substantially injure home territory'.[1] Both Axis Powers were now forced on to the defensive. Hitler's game of Grand Strategy was played out. The days of sweeping advances, of blitzkrieg from the air and deep armoured penetrations on land were over. The defence of 'Fortress Germany' was now the only card left and, as Hinsley wrote, 'To defend Fortress Germany against ever lengthening odds; to refuse retreat on any front until it became unavoidable, as the only method of ensuring Germany's defence; to prolong the struggle for as long as possible, even when the defence of Germany broke down – these were the only thoughts which guided him. He had no other strategy.'[2]

In the Battle of the Atlantic Hitler's U-boats had suffered very heavy losses in the second half of 1942 and Admiral Dönitz's prediction earlier in the year that the U-boats still had a chance of forcing a stalemate was now overcome by events. Air support, new tactics, new equipment (including acoustic homing torpedoes) must be developed, but these would take time and could only be palliatives. An entirely new type of U-boat, with increased underwater speed, was urgently needed. In September of 1942 Admiral Raeder was given 'complete freedom to take all decisions concerning experimental and mass production' to this end, but he had to announce as early as December that 'the new type could not be operational in any numbers until 1944 at the earliest'.[3] In fact by the end of the war in Europe the six or seven new type U-boats completed were still not operational.

In the air the 1,000 bomber raid on Cologne had opened the real bomber offensive against Germany. At the turn of the year the British front-line bomber strength was an average of 78 medium and 261 heavy bombers, but now the four-engined Lancasters were becoming available. These were the only aircraft in the world capable of carrying the 22,000-lb. 'Grand Slam' bomb. In January 1943 Lancasters were used in an attack by 388 aircraft on Berlin, using the new pathfinder techniques. Unfortunately owing to unfavourable weather over the target area the damage was scattered, but the Germans could no longer have any illusions of what was in store for them. Similarly the raids on Genoa, Turin and Milan during the last three months of 1942 had far-reaching results on Italian production and in particular on civilian morale in the Northern Provinces.

Discontent among the Italian generals, loss of faith in German omnipotence, and a serious loss of morale in the Services and amongst the Italian people as a whole must all have been evident to Mussolini. Count Ciano at the time of TORCH was certain the Allies would next strike at Italy – Churchill, indeed had said so in the House of Commons – he recorded in his diary. The state of the Italian Army in January 1943 is summed up in Mussolini's remark 'they do not make war with the "fury of the fanatic" but rather with the indifference of the professional'.[4] Indeed the Duce was in a cleft stick as Antonescu, the Rumanian Head of State, suggested that both Rumania and Italy should make contact with the Allies to establish a defence against the bolshevism of Europe. Ciano comments 'let us not bandage our heads before they are broken, but let us look at the situation realistically and remember charity begins at home'.[5] The Duce refused Antonescu's offer saying 'the Danube is not the route we must follow', but did not protest at Ciano saying openly 'we should try to make some direct contact'. Meanwhile the Italian Generals quarrelled amongst themselves. General Ambrosio told Ciano that the Commander-in-Chief, General Cavallero, 'consorts with the Germans, and steals all he can'. 'How far did the Duce intend we go' he asked, being convinced the Germans would lose the war. How seriously the Italian leaders regarded the situation is underlined by a report by Colonel Lucca (the Italian Military Attaché in Ankara) reporting that he was now convinced that Italy should make a separate peace with Russia.

At about the time of the Casablanca Conference Mussolini still held up the mask of Axis solidarity and reaffirmed his decision to march with Germany to the end. But in private he 'listened to General Anio who was convinced 1943 would witness the collapse of Germany and believes we must begin to think of our (Italy's) own affairs'.[6] The following day (22 January) the Duce was faced with the German communiqué reporting the rout at Stalingrad –

the worst news of the war. With the Germans in Russia in retreat everywhere and Tripoli about to fall he lashed out at Rommel, saying he had manoeuvred to save German forces at the expense of the Italians. The Axis partners were indeed beginning to understand each other!

Before we consider the situation as it was known to the British and American planners preparing for the SYMBOL Conference, however, we should examine the attitude and aspirations of the other Allied partner, Russia. It is here indeed that many of the strong political undercurrents that tend to dominate the whole of the Italian Campaign have their birth. Looking back twenty years after VE Day Alan Bullock wrote, 'After the fall of France we were up against an enemy too strong for us to defeat with our own resources. We won the war – and only could have won it – as allies of the United States and Russia. It was not, however, an alliance on equal terms: the most important result of the Second World War was to leave the United States and USSR as the only undisputed great powers in the world.'[7] Two men saw this possibility only too clearly, Churchill and Stalin. Throughout the darkest days of the war Stalin never lost sight of his objectives. 'He was clear on restoring the great Russia of the Tsars, both in the Far East and in the west. The "aspirations" of the Pan-Slav days, the claims of the Straits, and the determination to dominate Central Europe became actual as the liberated areas were occupied by the Russians, whose hands were left free by Anglo-American commitments elsewhere. Stalin was perfectly clear where these Anglo-American commitments should mainly lie – in the west, and specifically through the speedy opening of a second front at the nearest convenient point on the continent opposite England. . . . The last thing he wanted was a diversion of Anglo-American strength towards his hitherto undeclared sphere of influence in the Balkans.'[8] Indeed any delay in opening a Second Front in the West brought the strongest reaction from Stalin. His was virtually a one-element strategy, land warfare on the grand scale. It was extremely difficult to convince him of the problems of opening a Second Front in 1942 or indeed in 1943. For instance in May 1942 there were only sufficient landing craft to lift 4,000 men a day, and during the critical stages of the Battle of the Atlantic there were totally inadequate resources of men and material available for the mounting and launching of any major combined operation from the United Kingdom.

General Eisenhower, newly appointed Chief of War Plans Division, War Department General Staff, in April 1942 presented plans for a major cross-Channel assault early in 1943. He even visualized a holding assault, to form a bridgehead in the late summer of 1942, if it was felt absolutely necessary to take pressure off the Russians. The Americans wanted to get on with the war in Europe, so that they could concentrate on the defeat of Japan. They had agreed to giving the European theatre priority, and they were convinced that within that theatre their aims would best be served by a military policy of concentration of effort. Towards the end of May, Molotov came to London to press for a Second Front but he had to be told that the Allies could not commit themselves to attempting this in 1942. In the middle of July twenty-three out of twenty-four merchant ships of an Arctic convoy, taking war material to Archangel, were sunk. Convoys to Russia had to be suspended until the conditions of ice-packs and perpetual daylight had passed. Churchill's telegram to Stalin explaining this decision brought a 'rough and surly answer' which ended, 'taking fully into account the present position on the Soviet-German front, I must state in the most emphatic manner that the Soviet Government cannot acquiesce in the postponement of a Second Front in Europe until 1943'.[9] But at this very moment Britain and America had agreed that there could be no cross-Channel attack in 1942 and that the landing in North Africa should take place 'not later than 30 October'.

Churchill immediately made plans to meet Stalin to explain the British and American plans and viewpoint, and on 12 August, in the Kremlin, the two great war leaders met face to face for the first time. For Churchill, who fiercely stood his ground, it was a personal triumph. In reporting the result of the meeting to the War Cabinet and the President he concludes, 'Now they know the worst, and having made their protest are entirely friendly; this in spite of the fact that this is their most anxious and agonising time. Moreover, Stalin is entirely convinced of the great advantages of TORCH and I do trust that it is being driven forward with superhuman energy on both sides of the ocean.'[10] But the week after Churchill left Moscow Stalingrad was invested and by the end of the month the Panzer Divisions were threatening the Grozny oilfields. In September the Black Sea port of Novorossisk fell and the all-out assault on Stalingrad had begun. Stalin's urgent appeal to Roosevelt for a minimum delivery of 500 fighters, 8,000 tanks and vast quantities of ammunition came at the moment when the Western leaders had just decided to suspend the sailing of the October convoy to Murmansk for the sake of mounting TORCH. There just were not enough ships and escorts for the Atlantic and Pacific operations, let alone to re-open and step-up the Arctic supply route to Russia. Nor indeed were planes and tanks to spare in such excessive numbers. For the moment the Allied effort in the Mediterranean had to take priority. How then could the West help Russia at this critical moment? The only immediate action that seemed practicable was to establish an Anglo-American bomber force in the Caucasus, which was the only part of the land front in the East that could be reached. This proposal had first been mentioned by Churchill in Moscow in mid-August. He suggested (in a letter to Roosevelt at the end of the month) dispatching a British force of nine fighter squadrons, three light and two medium bomber squadrons, and that the Americans should send one heavy bomber group which was already in the Middle East, together with an air transport group of at least fifty planes. General Marshall opposed the plan saying that the force

7

could not be operational in the Caucasus until the end of January 1943. Roosevelt, however, was faced in October with joining Churchill in telling Stalin that convoys to Murmansk must be suspended on account of TORCH and was anxious to 'sugar the pill'. He therefore backed Churchill's proposal and agreed to the force being dispatched to the Caucasus early in 1943. Encouraged by apparent Soviet interest, the Western Powers made plans to get a token force on the ground to reconnoitre the area and on 13 October decided to send a mission to Moscow to arrange this as soon as the Soviet Government had accepted the offer. A month later, although there was still no word of Soviet intentions, the mission led by Air Marshal Drummond arrived in Moscow from Cairo. 'It quickly became evident that the Soviet Government had no intention of accepting the offer of an air force in the Caucasus, Soviet representatives proposed instead that, in place of an air force, Great Britain and the United States should send planes to the Soviet Union – in addition to those already scheduled to be sent.'[11] The reasons given were that the effect of sending an Anglo-American Force would be to reduce lease-lend supplies, the force would be restricted to one area and the aircrews would find conditions too primitive. 'The Soviet representatives made the mission aware, moreover, that the Soviet Government did not want Allied soldiers to fight alongside Soviet soldiers or in Soviet territory . . . fraternization might have a "deleterious political effect" and the presence of Allied forces in the Caucasus "might give a future hold on or near their oil resources".'[12]

Three weeks elapsed before the Soviet Government made a formal proposal, this time saying crews could be sent with the planes to fight in Soviet units. This proposal was equally unacceptable, as the mobilizing of American air units would in the first place be slowed down and units already organized would have to be broken up. The President was still unwilling to abandon the project and in a personal approach to Stalin in mid-December offered a concession on the question of the command of the force. Stalin's reply was brief and to the point – the crisis was now over and the main fighting would be on the central front. He would be glad for planes, especially fighters, but he had enough pilots and crews.

Was this astonishing incident typical of Russia's attitude to the Western Powers, and if so, how much of their suspicion and fear of the British and American motives was inspired by Stalin himself? Colonel Jacob (later Lieutenant-General Sir Ian Jacob), who had accompanied Churchill and Alanbrooke to Moscow in August 1942, wrote on the day they left, 'I don't believe that it is possible to make friends with a man like Stalin in the sense that we understand friendship. The thing that impressed me most about Stalin was his complete self-possession and detachment. He was absolute master of the situation at all times and appeared to be cold and calculating. . . . All his life he has been a revolutionary fighting for his own position.'[13] A week later in Cairo, Alanbrooke recorded his impressions of Stalin, whom he had just met for the first time. 'A crafty, brilliant, realistic mind, devoid of any sense of human pity or kindness. Gives one an uncanny feeling to be in his presence. But undoubtedly a big and shrewd brain with clear-cut views as to what he wants and expects to get.'[14] This then was the man who did not join the other two war leaders at Casablanca where the pattern of Western strategy for 1943 was to be decided.

The Prime Minister and the President were accompanied by the Service Chiefs of Staff and planning advisers of their respective countries. The British team, led by General Sir Alan Brooke, had made careful preparation. Their policy was clearly formulated and their plans worked out in considerable detail. They felt the successes at Alamein and of the TORCH landings must be reinforced. The clearing of North Africa would lead to the re-opening of the Mediterranean and 'the British and American land, sea, and air forces would strike from the springboard where they were already deployed at the exposed underbelly of Hitler's Europe – the point where the Axis was most vulnerable. It would break the crumbling morale of Italy, throw the Balkans into a ferment, and, possibly, bring Turkey into the war. No time should be allowed to the enemy forces in the Mediterranean basin to recover, and help should be afforded Russia by keeping them continuously engaged.'[15] The British proposed that the bombing of Germany should be stepped up and, as bases became available in Africa and later in Sicily and Italy, bombers could strike at Southern Europe. In the Pacific holding operations only should be undertaken to permit considerably larger forces than could be available in 1943 to be trained and assembled for cross-Channel operations in 1944. Alanbrooke's calculations were based on a realistic assessment of the Western Allies' present and future resources, not only of men and material but of the availability of shipping, assault vessels and, in particular, of landing craft.

The opening of the Mediterranean would release over a million tons of shipping capacity to Britain alone, but this would only offset the losses in the Atlantic during 1942. The vital requests for escort vessels had practically stopped the production of landing craft throughout 1942, but if the battle against the U-boats in the Atlantic could be won by the summer of 1943 (and the successes of the last three months justified this view) then the shipbuilding programme could be geared to the requirements of both the Pacific and the cross-Channel attacks. The American Joint Chiefs of Staff, although less well prepared for the conference, were at least agreed that Germany must first be disposed of, but they doggedly held to the view that a cross-Channel attack was the sole strategy to achieve this end. They regarded operations in the Mediterranean theatre as a possible trap, if the Axis should counter-attack through Spain, and also an unjustified drain on the Allied resources which would contribute nothing to the defeat of Germany in particular. Indeed they suspected the British of attempting to further their own imperialistic interests in the Eastern Mediterranean. The British Chiefs of Staff were prepared for this view as Sir John Dill, their representative in Washington who was attending the conference, had 'explained that the main factors which loomed large in American eyes were first a general fear of commitments in the Mediterranean, and secondly a suspicion that we did not understand the Pacific problem and would not put our backs into the work there once Germany had been defeated. Thus although the Americans were honestly of the opinion that Germany was the primary enemy, they did not see how quite to deal with her, especially as they felt that there were great and urgent tasks to be done in Burma and the Pacific.'[16]

General Marshall, still pressing for an early cross-Channel attack, considered that operations in the Mediterranean would retard the concentration of American troops in the United Kingdom. 'Every diversion or side-issue from the main plot acts as a suction pump.'[17] The President was more easily convinced of the need to defer any cross-Channel assault to the summer of 1944 on logistic grounds. But equally he was prepared to defer major decisions on a Mediterranean strategy. In fact immediately before the conference he had been prepared to adopt a 'wait and see' policy on both counts. Admiral King, who was largely responsible for operations in the Pacific, was anxious to ensure that sufficient forces should be available in that theatre to prevent the Japanese consolidating their position. General Marshall wished to solve the problem by an allocation of 70 per cent of the Allied resources to the Atlantic theatre and 30 per cent to the Pacific, which the British pointed out was an unusual approach to war strategy. Detailed discussions amongst the Combined Planners on the resources required for the Pacific were complicated by American Naval representatives' attitude that, 'The Pacific was a US theatre, and that it was nobody else's business what was done there. Anyway the US Navy had made their plans for 1943, and didn't intend to alter them. He was quite prepared to say what they were, but he would not go into detail on the resources they required. All he would say was that they could be done with the resources allotted to the Pacific, in which he included everything earmarked but still in the USA.'[18] Admiral King was firmly against the building-up of even larger forces in North Africa without any immediate prospect of their useful employment. In this he was in full accord with Churchill, who several weeks previously had observed, 'I never meant the Anglo-American army to be stuck in North Africa. It is a spring-board and not a sofa.'

General Alanbrooke replied to the American view with a masterly survey of the war situation in which he contended that the Japanese were now on the defensive in the Pacific. His case, he suggested, was unanswerable – until the U-boats were beaten the shortage of shipping must remain a 'stranglehold on all offensive operations'. The twenty-one divisions available in 1943 could not succeed in a cross-Channel attack. The Germans were too strong in

France and none of their troops would be diverted from the Eastern Front. But by the Allies striking across the Mediterranean the Germans would be forced to 'deploy and keep deployed large forces to defend an immense stretch of coastline and hold down the restless peoples of Southern and South-Eastern Europe. By doing so and knocking Italy out of the war, the Allies would leave Germany by the end of the year some fifty-four divisions and 2,200 aircraft short of her minimum requirements for holding her present Russian front and garrisoning the West against the major cross-Channel attack which the Allies would be able to launch by 1944.'[19] Largely as a result of the CIGS's brilliant exposition the conference was able to get down to detailed work. This resulted in a report on 'the conduct of the war in 1943' which as regards the Mediterranean theatre gave two objectives for 1943. (a) The occupation of Sicily with the object of (i) making the Mediterranean line of communication more secure (ii) diverting German pressure from the Russian front (iii) intensifying the pressure on Italy. (b) To create a situation in which Turkey can be enlisted as an active ally.'[20] This was set against the primary task of the defeat of the U-boats and 'the heaviest possible air offensive against German war effort' from United Kingdom bases while cross-Channel invasion forces would be built up. Pressure on Japan would be maintained, but without prejudice to the need to defeat Germany first. In agreeing this report the two Allied leaders, among other points, emphasized the need for an early attack on Sicily, during the favourable June moon period. Although the final reports stopped short of plans for the invasion of Italy, much had been settled and an overall strategy for 1943 had emerged. As far as the Mediterranean theatre was concerned a clear instruction was given to General Eisenhower, who was appointed Supreme Allied Commander, to clear North Africa and carry out Operation HUSKY, the seizure of Sicily. For this operation three British commanders would be appointed, General Alexander, Admiral Cunningham and Air Marshal Tedder. On learning news of the Casablanca meeting, Ciano wrote in his diary, 'it seems a serious thing – very serious indeed. I neither share nor approve the easy ironies of our press.'[21] Not for much longer would 'Mare Nostrum' shield the shores of Fascist Italy. But while the President's formula of 'unconditional surrender', announced at Casablanca, served the US Military Staffs as their military objective, there was no proper decision as to what should be done after HUSKY.

Churchill flew on from North Africa to confer with the Turkish President with the object of persuading him to accept arms and aid and throw in his lot with the Western Powers. Churchill explained that the defeat of Italy would lead to the Allies making 'contact with the Western Balkans and with the highly hopeful resistance maintained both by General Michailovitch in Serbia and the partisans in Croatia and Slovenia'. Regarding Russia he felt that both Stalin and Molotov sought 'a peaceful and friendly association with the Western Powers' and that 'Russia would concentrate on reconstruction for the next ten years'.[22] The Turkish Prime Minister, however, felt that Russian Imperialism, the possibility of which had been mentioned by Churchill, was a real threat and that it was necessary for Turkey to be very prudent. They regarded Europe already as 'full of Slavs and Communists' and were convinced that if Germany was beaten Europe would turn to Communism. Military discussion then followed and Alanbrooke records 'we . . . covered a great deal of ground, and have, I think, got them definitely working towards fulfilling our hopes of ultimately coming to our assistance. But they have got a long way to go before they can be considered a really efficient force, and how we are to provide them with the necessary equipment in spite of their poor communications is a mystery.'[23] The talks resulted only in a military agreement against the contingency of Turkey entering the war.

From the British point of view the next few months were full of anxiety. The U-boat attacks were intensified. Russian operations were largely suspended by the spring thaw. The African Campaign had slowed down, and after the Japanese withdrawal from Guadalcanal the Americans were embarking on new Pacific ventures that were to make increased demands on men and material far beyond the priorities laid down at Casablanca. Furthermore Churchill was still pressing for an early date for HUSKY and probing for means to bring about a cross-Channel assault in 1943. In March 1943, with the improving weather conditions, the U-boats sank half a million tons of Allied shipping, mainly in the North Atlantic. But unremitting countermeasures, and a building programme that added two million tons of shipping in the first six months of 1943, began to swing the balance in favour of the Allies. The opening of the Mediterranean to Allied convoys right through to Alexandria in May 1943 added a further two million tons of available shipping, through the avoidance of the long Cape route. In spite, however, of this improvement in the availability of shipping, the movement overseas of US troops was not going quite as planned for the first half of 1943. The Allied planners at Casablanca had visualized 527,200 US troops being allotted to the main operational theatres. There was shipping, however, for only 496,844. With the need to speed up the North African operations reinforcements for this theatre were increased from 184,000 to 292,385 men, and instead of a planned figure of 79,200 the Pacific theatre received 121,581 men. The buildup in the United Kingdom for the cross-Channel attack, later given the code name OVERLORD, should have been 250,000 men during this period, but arrivals by June 1943 had dwindled to 65,830 men. The result was that the USA contribution to any cross-Channel attack in 1943 could be only six divisions. It was now quite obvious that no major assault of the Atlantic Wall could be launched in 1943.

Pressure on the British planners was mounting; the North African campaign must be finished, and HUSKY planned and, although the cross-Channel assault was postponed until 1944, the preparations demanded ever-increasing efforts. Special equipment and techniques had to be developed; complex training in amphibious assault and inter-service co-operation had to be organized in considerable detail; special air force groups for direct support of the divisions landing in France had to be formed and trained. In the Far East the Americans were pressing for a campaign to re-open the Burma road. Dominating all the calculations was the unpredictable toll of U-boat attacks on the Atlantic convoys and the grave shortage of landing craft.

In the air the Battle of the Ruhr had started. The RAF heavy bomber force was now much stronger and was using much improved radar target-finding techniques. After the end of March the American Flying Fortress groups began active participation in the bombing programme with daylight sweeps. The night raids by the RAF bombers were now striking deeper into Germany, where more and more effort had to be put into defensive measures.

But although Hitler was now forced on to the defensive and Mussolini was looking over his shoulder to save what he could of a crumbling regime, the Axis was still extremely strong. In Europe, Asia and the Pacific enormous areas were held in an iron grip. No solution on land could be achieved in Europe until the two Western Sea Powers, in support of Russian land power, had sufficient shipping and assault craft as well as trained and equipped land, sea and air forces to strike deeply and surely at the vitals of the Axis strongholds. But where and when should these blows fall? It was important that this should be decided soon. At the end of April 1943 Churchill proposed an urgent meeting with Roosevelt and on 12 May TRIDENT, the Third Washington Conference between the two leaders, opened. Tunis had fallen on 9 May and by the time the conference started a quarter of a million Axis troops had surrendered and the Tunisian Campaign, which had cost the British 50,000 casualties, out of an Allied total of 70,000, was over.

In Washington the American planners were better prepared than at Casablanca, but they were still haunted by a fear of stalemate in Europe and regarded operations in the Mediterranean as a side-issue which would interfere with the early defeat of Germany. The US Army Planning Staff warned their Joint Chiefs of Staff that they should take a firm stand against the continued pouring of US resources into the Mediterranean theatre after HUSKY, lest the cost in time and money of defeating Japan became almost prohibitive. The American planners in 1943 were having a good deal of difficulty over manpower requirements keeping pace with their evolving global strategy. Industry, geared to the concept of the USA serving as the 'Arsenal of Democracy', was beginning to hit full production, this in turn limited the manpower available for the Armed Services. Expert advisers had insisted, late in 1942, on a ceiling for the Armed Forces of ten and a half million, which at 7·8 per cent of the population compared unfavourably with both German and British figures of 10·9 per cent and 8·2 per cent respectively. Faced with

13

global war the US Joint Planners as late as November 1942 were talking in terms of three hundred and thirty-four divisions being required by December 1944, which, together with the requirements of the Navy, Marine Corps and Coast Guards, would involve thirteen million men in the services. Sombre economies had to be achieved and the strategic coat cut with far less flare.

Thus in April 1943 the Joint Planning Staff were recommending, for both 1943 and 1944, an army troop basis goal of just under eight and a quarter million men and one hundred divisions. Faced with such economies 'the Army staff were all the more reluctant to accept plans that might dissipate the combat forces in being or prevent the husbanding of a strategic reserve. Unless overall strategy embodying the principles of concentration were made sufficiently firm and manpower and production requirements for victory were definitely tied to it, the staff feared the disarrangement of the American economy and a stalemate in the war.'[24] The year 1944 would in fact be the peak of both US war production and the mobilization and training of their armies. Britain was already fully extended in both respects. Meanwhile it was essential to keep the USSR, who still contained the bulk of the German forces, in the war, and it was against Russia that the Germans were expected to resume the offensive. The US planners argued, therefore, that events on the Eastern Front and the effectiveness of the Combined Bomber Offensive were the two critical factors in considering what action should follow HUSKY. They were prepared to admit that limited offensives in the Mediterranean could contain strong Axis forces and might release some pressure from the Russians, but there was still the need to build up the assault forces for cross-Channel attack in 1944 and for all-out operations to ensure the defeat of Germany in 1945. If Russia became ineffective the 'Pacific Alternative' should be applied and all the Allied efforts turned against Japan after securing their position in Europe and the Mediterranean. General Marshall was much impressed by an argument that Russia could best be supported by the Allies avoiding all further Mediterranean operations, concentrating the maximum forces in England for a knock-out blow in 1944, and meanwhile relying on air bombardment to maintain the offensive against Germany. But the US Joint Chiefs of Staff were still undecided about a Mediterranean policy and felt they should at least be prepared to discuss any British proposals for following up HUSKY, but only if the forces committed were a reduction from those already in the area and only as an emergency measure to relieve pressure on Russia. They also felt that they should refuse to take part in any operations in the Eastern Mediterranean. Any proposal in this direction would be an unjustified diversion and difficult to put over to the American people, as well as being likely to rouse Russian suspicions over the Dardanelles. If the British pressed a Mediterranean policy to the point where the early defeat of Germany and the ultimate defeat of Japan were prejudiced, then they were to be told that the American Government would reverse the Casablanca decisions and the Pacific war would be given first call on all American resources.

In opening the conference the President approached the Mediterranean question with caution. He wanted Italy knocked out of the war after HUSKY, but not by committing large armies in Italy. He suggested an air offensive from bases in Sicily, or the southern tip of Italy, would equally draw off German forces from the Russian front. On the other hand he pressed hard for a decision on a cross-Channel attack in the spring of 1944. The Prime Minister, however, saw the elimination of Italy from the war as 'a great prize' with far-reaching results. Germany would then be quite alone and Turkey might grant bases from which the Ploesti oilfields could be bombed and the Aegean cleared. Germany would be forced either to give up the Balkans, which they could hardly afford to do, or to replace the occupation force of twenty-five Italian divisions. These replacement German divisions would have to come from the Russian front. Furthermore the elimination of the Italian Fleet would release British warships and carriers for either the Indian Ocean or the Pacific. Churchill felt the best way of helping Russia at this point was by knocking out Italy, to force the Germans to occupy the Balkans. In any case, now that the cross-Channel attack was put off until 1944, any inaction by the large forces in North Africa, where the British alone had thirteen divisions, over the intervening seven or eight months, would have a serious effect on the Russians.

The conference lasted fourteen days. An overall strategy covering all theatres had to be agreed. Admiral King constantly pressed for more priority for the Pacific war. Concessions had to be made by both sides before any agreed statement could be prepared. The strategic priorities would be the same; unconditional surrender of the Axis in Europe first; simultaneously pressure would be maintained on Japan, but any extension of these operations must be approved first by the Combined Chiefs of Staff; after the defeat of the Axis in Europe the Allies would turn on Japan with their full resources. In the detailed list of undertakings in support of this overall strategy no definite recommendation was made on an invasion of Italy.

Churchill records, 'the best I had been able to get was the following resolution by the Combined Chiefs of Staff: that the Allied Commander-in-Chief North Africa will be instructed, as a matter of urgency, to plan such operations in exploitation of HUSKY as are best calculated to eliminate Italy from the war and to contain the maximum number of German forces. Which of the various specific operations should be adopted, and therefore mounted, is a decision which will be reserved to the Combined Chiefs of Staff.'[25] Knowing that the Americans favoured limiting any such operation to the capture of Sardinia, Churchill made a last-minute appeal to Roosevelt to allow General Marshall to accompany him to Algiers to discuss the matter with Eisenhower, the commander now charged with making the choice. At Eisenhower's North

African headquarters Churchill spoke frankly and eloquently. Insisting he had no intention of interfering with the launching of the cross-Channel attack in 1944, he stressed the need to exploit any opportunity arising out of the fall of Sicily, which he forecast would be by 15 August. Eisenhower later wrote, 'He was fearful that we would interpret our mission in such a narrow fashion as to stop short with the capture of Sicily regardless of circumstances. Since a normal part of every battle is maximum exploitation of victory, I was personally in doubt as to just what the Prime Minister expected or desired. However, he did not propose in my hearing any campaign on a major scale, with the Balkans, or even northern Italy, as a minimum objective. He seemed honestly concerned in the quick capture of southern Italy, but, so far as I know, no more, at that moment.'[26] Both the American generals were still suspicious of British motives in pressing for an assault on the Italian mainland, but after further discussions an agreement was reached which, as Eisenhower wrote, 'in effect, left exploitation of the Sicilian operation to my judgment – but expected me to take advantage of any favourable opportunity to rush into Italy – and which emphasized the great value of the Foggia airfields. Since a major port was necessary to sustain us in Italy, the city of Naples was named as the other principal locality desired by the Allies.'[27] As yet there was no clear-cut decision, and as the US Official Historian puts it, 'General Marshall had won his way on postponing a final decision'.[28] But as Churchill has said, 'the hinge had turned'.

2
Setting the Stage

Geographic and climatic conditions: Planning starts: Hitler's and Mussolini's views on Allied intentions: Air cover the key: Pantelleria: Allies gain air supremacy: Comparison of Naval forces: Axis Command structure and forces: Problems of defending Sicily: Allied Command and forces for HUSKY: Administrative factors: Allied Intelligence successes.

At this point it is appropriate to consider briefly the geography of both Sicily and Italy. The area consists of four regions, the southern slopes of the Alps, the Po valley, the long peninsula divided by the central spine of the Apennines, and the islands of Sicily, Sardinia and Corsica. The Alps, stretching for 650 miles from Trieste to the Riviera, tend to isolate Italy from Europe, but form less of a barrier than do the Pyrenees in separating Spain from France. The easiest passes are in the north-east, where for instance, the road from Udine to Laibach does not rise above the 1,500-foot contour. The peninsula tends to divide the Mediterranean, being set across the main sea and air route. Sicily itself is only ninety miles from the coast of Africa.

The Apennine range of mountains not only encloses the Po valley from the south but divides the peninsula down its whole length. On the Adriatic side the mountains run close to the coast and have a steep face to the sea. On the western side the mountains fall rather less precipitously, but the coastal strip, particularly in the south is still very narrow. In the central area between Rome and Pisa a depression separates the mountains from the coast. The Apennines are formed of a very rough limestone and are a serious barrier to communications. Not only do they restrict movement up the peninsula to a narrow coastal strip on either side, but they are the source of innumerable rivers and streams flowing in rocky valleys. These valleys quickly flood with the winter rains.

In the Abruzzi district due east from Rome and north of Naples, the mountains are so high that they are snow-capped for several months of the year. On the western side of the Apennines the rivers tend to be longer, and those in Central Italy flow along the depressions for some distance before breaking out to the Tyrrhenian Sea. Apart from the River Po in the north, only the Tiber and Arno rivers are navigable, and then only during the rainier months. Steamers can reach Rome on the Tiber and boats can navigate for about sixty miles further, but boats alone can navigate on the Arno and only as far as Florence.

In spite of its extensive coastline the peninsula is very short of both natural harbours and shelter for ships. This is most evident on the Adriatic coastline, where between Venice and the artificial harbour of Brindisi there is only inadequate harbourage in the Bay of Ancona. Moreover, the coastline between Fano and Termoli is formed of low cliffs. Further south the naval base at Taranto is constructed from a lagoon. On the west coast Spezia has a good harbour, but at Naples ships must use the roadstead in the Bay.

Sicily similarly lacks natural harbours. Palermo faces an open bay and the harbour at Syracuse is artificial. Other ports in Sicily are Catania and Messina which is the largest in the island.

The mountainous backbone of the Italian peninsula forces the centres of population on to the coastal plains. These are narrow and subject to flooding and through these plains must pass the main road and rail communications. In order to cross the high and rugged mountains of the central Apennines the roads must follow the deep river valleys that cut into the mountain ranges. In this manner main roads link Florence and Rome with Ancona, and Rome through Aquila and the Aterno valley with Pescara.

Further south the Apennines are broken up into groups of hills and coast-to-coast road links are easier. Incidentally, the area round Foggia, reclaimed from swamp, had been developed as an important series of military airfields.

The mountains of northern Sicily, dominated by the huge volcano of Etna, consist of a series of ridges with a steep face to the Tyrrhenian Sea, but more gentle slopes to the south. Again highways must keep to the coast. Good roads connect Palermo, Catania and Agrigento.

The Po valley has a central European climate with hot summers, cold winters and a fairly even rainfall. The climate of Peninsular Italy is comparable to that of north-west Europe in winter but to the Sahara in summer. Winters are mild and wet, and summers hot and dry, and throughout the year the skies are clear and sunny. The east coast is colder than the west and frost occurs everywhere, but rarely in the south. The central Apennines have cold winters and often heavy falls of snow, although the peaks are not snow-covered throughout the year. Generally speaking rainfall in the peninsula is moderate, for instance 32–33 inches a year in Naples and Rome. The long hours of sunshine, however, cause a high rate of evaporation bringing summer droughts, except in the mountain regions of the central Apennines. Rain falls in short sharp showers, often of several inches at a time and accompanied by thunder. The wettest months are October to December, with drought in July and August. Southern Italy and Sicily have a truly Mediterranean climate. June to August are months of drought, and the rainfall is more spread through to the spring, with October and January being the wettest months.

The following table gives mean temperatures of the four main areas for January and July:

	Mean temperature in ° F	
	Jan	July
Milan	34	75
Rome	44·6	76·1
Naples	47	76
Palermo	51	76·3

Sicily and parts of the south are subject, especially in the spring, to the

Sirocco, a wind carrying dust which blows off the Sahara. This brings excessively high temperatures; for instance a noon temperature of 110° F (95° F at midnight) has been recorded at Palermo. Italy in the main is an agricultural country suffering, however, from the conflicting needs to drain marshes on land subject to flooding and to irrigate extensively during the months of drought.

The Po valley not only contains Italy's main industrial development, and the majority of the hydro-electric power stations, but for centuries has been intensively cultivated. In the peninsula the principal crops on the coastal areas are vines, olives, maize and some wheat, and in the south and Sicily wheat and citrus fruits are grown. Regarding natural vegetation, there are deciduous forests of sweet chestnut and oak above the 3,000-foot contour line and on the coastal plains evergreens such as stone pine, evergreen oak, cyprus and olive trees with an undergrowth of evergreen shrubs such as myrtle, oleander and laurel. Many mountainous areas are very bare and barren. Extensive areas in southern Italy and the majority of south-eastern Sicily, in particular the plains of Catania and the Pachino peninsula, are malarious areas. Malaria is also endemic in many coastal areas in North Africa.

Planning for HUSKY started early in February 1943, immediately the decision to invade Sicily was taken at Casablanca. Five months were available for setting up the operation, and the detailed work was done with great thoroughness and care by a special Allied staff, known as Force 141, working in a commandeered school outside Algiers. At this time, as a member of General Alexander's staff has remarked, the invasion of Sicily 'was a mere pendant to the African Campaign, designed to open the Mediterranean as a safe passage to the Far East'.[1] As we have already seen, the Americans were against further major commitments in the Mediterranean. Indeed at the Algiers meeting early in June, General Marshall had even expressed regrets over the North African Campaign, telling Alanbrooke that 'he still felt the occupation of North Africa had been a mistake in that it diverted our effort from Europe'.[2]

Meanwhile Hitler was witnessing the final frustration of all his hopes in Africa. The failure of the Italians in the final battles in Tunisia only added to his earlier fears for an Allied breach of the southern boundaries of his 'Fortress Europe'. Some months earlier, at the end of 1942, both Hitler and Admiral Raeder had thought an assault through the Aegean on the Balkans would be the next Allied move in the Mediterranean and for some time his naval advisers had been urging the occupation of the Iberian Peninsula which was also regarded as a possible line of advance by the Allies.

Again in the spring of 1943, both Admiral Dönitz and Field Marshal Kesselring had urged the occupation of Spain as 'the best way of bringing relief to the Mediterranean situation'. General Franco, however, firmly stuck to his policy of neutrality and without his co-operation any move into

21

Spain was impossible. Hitler just had not got the resources to seize and hold down the country by force. Now, with Tunisia about to fall, Hitler saw an assault on Italy as an immediate threat. But where would the assault be made? Which of the islands occupied as outposts of the Axis' southern defences would be chosen as a stepping stone for an Allied thrust against the mainland? Without the strength to counter-attack by land through Spain, or to stop an invasion fleet at sea, or in its ports of embarkation, Hitler now had to think in terms of defending his vital interests in south-eastern Europe from where he obtained essential raw materials for Germany's war economy. Essential supplies of grain, timber, oil and minerals all came from this area, which was also the route for Turkish supplies of copper and other minerals. Consequently Hitler was particularly sensitive to any Allied threat against Greece or the Balkans, and while an invading force must first cross the difficult mountainous regions, ahead lay the plains that led to the heart of Germany. In the words of the American official historians, 'Hitler expected the Allies to land in Greece or the Balkans, and his reasoning was sound. Both areas were more important to the German economy than Italy. The populations were friendly to the Allies. An Allied invasion would supplement pressure, force the dispersal of Axis troops over widely separated areas, and forestall a Russian occupation of the Balkans.'[3]

The Italians naturally had a rather more parochial view; their Commando Supremo, General Ambrosio, saw the capture of Sardinia as a preliminary to a landing in southern France and a gateway to the Po valley. The whole of Italy and parts of southern Germany would come within range of air attack and the Italian Fleet would be bottled up in the Tyrrhenian Sea. Mussolini, however, thought the Allies' main attack would be in the eastern Mediterranean and that the seizure of Sicily would be a preliminary objective, to open the Mediterranean and prevent the passage of the Italian Fleet through to the Ionian or Adriatic Seas. In any event the southern coastlines were threatened and the outposts of islands became the first line of defence. A glance at a map of the central Mediterranean shows the extent of the problem that faced the German General Staff and their reluctant Italian allies.

The capture of Tunisia enabled the Allies to move their air forces to a position from which they not only dominated the Sicilian Straits but threatened both Sardinia and Sicily. The key to the seaborne assault was the effective range of fighter cover. Only Malta was within single-seater fighter range of the southern part of Sicily. With the lifting of Malta's siege at the end of 1942, the island was rapidly developed to become the most important air base in the whole of the Mediterranean and a new landing strip on the neighbouring island of Gozo was rapidly constructed by American engineers. By June 1943, 600 first-line aircraft were based on Malta, supported by the latest fighter control and radar installations. The fighter cover, however, from Malta alone was still considered insufficient, so the Allies turned their attention early in May to the Axis-held fortified islands of Pantelleria and Lampedusa. Both were held in strength by the Italians. Pantelleria had an airfield and underground hangars with a capacity of eighty fighters. The island also had many caves and grottoes used for refuelling Axis submarines and torpedo boats. Both islands had radar stations and observation posts which denied the Allies any chance of tactical surprise in crossing to Sicily.

General Eisenhower decided to reduce the islands by air bombardment, supplemented by naval gunfire, to be followed by seaborne assault. Heavy bombers of the North-West African Strategic Air Force were joined by bombers and fighters of the Desert Air Force and set about reducing the defences of Pantelleria. Although the Axis air strength in the central Mediterranean at this time came to 2,374 planes, only 1,276 of these were serviceable and these were scattered over a wide area from Italy to Pantelleria and Sardinia to Greece. The Allies estimated that only about 900 Axis planes were on, or within range of, Pantelleria. The air bombardment opened on 9 May and the Navy started shelling the island on 13 May. The final efforts came between 6–10 June with a round-the-clock bombardment, culminating with the release of 1,500 tons of bombs on 10 June. By 11 June 5,600 sorties had been flown and 6,570 tons of bombs had fallen on the island and the Italian garrison had had enough. The arrival of a British landing force (3 Infantry Brigade Group), with strong air and naval support, clinched the matter. Soon after mid-day on 11 June, 11,100 Italians and 78 German troops surrendered. The Allied bombers and warships immediately turned on Lampedusa which survived the attack for twenty-four hours, after which the Commander decided to surrender the island to the pilot of an Air/Sea Rescue Swordfish who had made a forced landing on the air strip. That evening the whole garrison of 4,600 Italian troops succeeded in formally surrendering to a landing party from the Coldstream Guards. These successes led some exponents of air power to claim that no defensive position or ground force could stand up to prolonged and continuous air attack. While the damage on Pantelleria to the port, town, roads and telephone communications were extensive the defences were damaged but not destroyed. Fewer gun positions had been hit than had been expected. The underground hangars were intact and less than 200 of the garrison had been killed. Furthermore the conditions were exceptionally favourable to the Allies. The Italians had made little attempt to camouflage their position and the gun crews were not prepared to stand and fight it out. The troops lacked battle experience and felt isolated and even abandoned. In fact over 500 German troops had left Pantelleria just before the attacks started and the Axis air forces failed even to check the air and naval bombardments. During the first eleven days of June only 250 enemy aircraft were seen by the Allies and of these 57 were shot down. With the loss of their two advanced radar stations and airfields

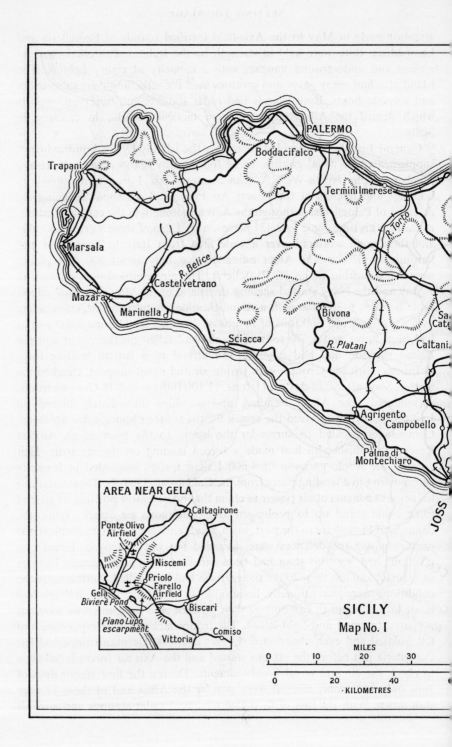

Trapani

PALERMO

Boddacifalco

Termini Imerese

Marsala

R. Belice

Castelvetrano

Mazara

Marinella

Bivona

Sa
Cate

R. Platani

Caltani.

Sciacca

Agrigento
Campobello

Palma di
Montechiaro

JOSS

AREA NEAR GELA

Caltagirone

Ponte Olivo
Airfield

Niscemi

Priolo
Farello
Airfield

Gela
Biviere Pond

Biscari

*Piano Lupo
escarpment*

Comiso

Vittoria

SICILY

Map No. I

MILES

| 0 | 10 | 20 | 30 |

| 0 | 20 | 40 |

· KILOMETRES

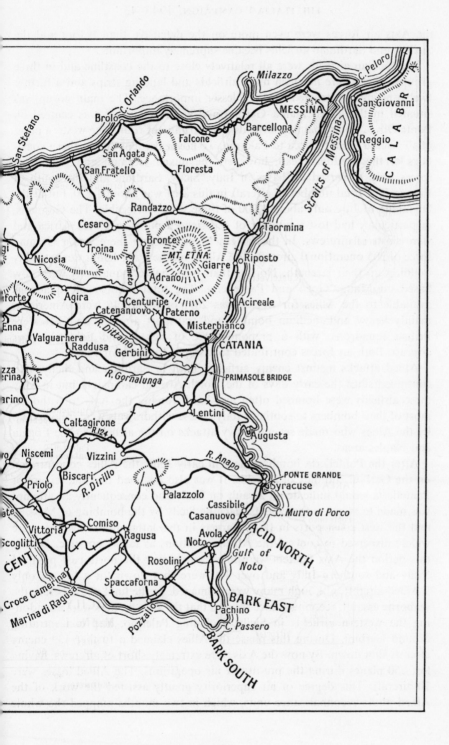

the Axis air forces were even more on the defensive than before and the Sicilian and Sardinian airfields became supremely important.

The Sicilian airfields were all relatively close to the coastline and in three groups. There were nineteen main airfields and landing strips and a further twelve newly constructed fields of lesser importance. The main group was situated in the area Catania–Gerbini and a further group was centred on Ponte Olivo. The remaining airfields were strung out round the western point of the island from Sciacca to Palermo. To cover the lengthy northern coast-lines of the Mediterranean, however, the mixed German and Italian air forces were dispersed on bases in Italy, Sicily, Sardinia and the south of France. The total number of aircraft in this area was about 1,850, but at the beginning of July only about 1,000 of these were serviceable. The Germans, in particular, had lost a number of experienced pilots in North Africa and were short of aircrews. In the eastern Mediterranean there was a German force of 305 operational aircraft. The Allies, on the other hand, were steadily building up their strength. No less than forty fighter squadrons were now based on Malta, Gozo and Pantelleria. The total number of squadrons available to the Allies for HUSKY was 267; of these 146 were American, mainly heavy and medium bomber and transport aircraft, and 121 were British squadrons, with a preponderance of fighter and fighter-bomber aircraft. Both air forces contributed to a single Tactical Air Force.

Allied attacks against enemy airfields, both in Sardinia and Sicily, had continued since the early days of the North African campaign, but in May these airfields were bombed often and hard, forcing the Axis to withdraw most of their bombers to southern Italy. These withdrawals were followed up by the Allies who made several heavy attacks on the airfields in the Foggia and Naples areas.

After the Pantelleria bombardment in early June, the Allies concentrated on the Gerbini complex of airfields. It was also assumed that the seizure of Pantelleria would indicate an assault on Sicily and consequently an attempt was made to stop reinforcements reaching Sicily by the bombing of Messina and the west coast ports in Italy. Targets in this latter area, however, were widely dispersed to conceal the Allied intentions as far as possible. During this period the Axis fighters were most active over the north-east point of Sicily and southern Italy and over 100 were shot down for a loss of only 7 Allied aircraft, although many were damaged. In the final phase before the seaborne assault, reconnaissance showed that the Axis fighters were abandoning the western airfields in Sicily, including Palermo, and concentrating around Gerbini. During this phase the Allies claimed a further 139 enemy aircraft shot down. By now the Axis were extremely short of aircrews, having lost 250 planes during the pre-HUSKY air operations. The Allied losses were 70 aircraft. This degree of air superiority greatly assisted the work of the Allied photo-reconnaissance units, which in two months mapped the whole of Sicily's 10,000 square miles and kept a close watch on the Italian Navy and the various supply ports, as well as a regular check on the enemy airfields over a wide area.

Having failed to keep open the supply routes to Tunisia in the last stages of the North African campaign, the heavier elements of the Italian Navy had withdrawn to Spezia and Taranto. Their effective strength at the time of HUSKY was:

Battleships	6	Torpedo Boats	16
Cruisers	7	Escort Vessels	27
Destroyers	32	Motor Torpedo	
Submarines	48	and Gunboats	115 (about)

In addition there were 18 German U-boats in the Mediterranean. Inactivity and the defeats at Taranto and Matapan, together with losses during TORCH had seriously sapped the morale of the Italian Navy. Realizing the true state of affairs, the Germans insisted on placing their own officer 'advisers' on board, in the hopes that these not inconsiderable naval forces could be used rather more effectively.

Admiral Cunningham's orders to the Allied fleets recognized the low state of morale in the Italian fleet but stressed 'if it is ever going to fight, it must fight now in defence of its country . . . and that it is strategically well placed to do so'.[4] By comparison the Allies had not only greater strength in fighting ships but battle-tested and experienced crews of the highest morale. In addition the Allies were assembling large convoys of specially constructed landing ships and smaller landing craft. For instance, the Landing Ships Tank had a displacement of 1,500 tons and were 328 feet long and crossed the Atlantic on their own bottoms, with the smaller Landing Craft Tank on their decks. The first convoys bringing troops and stores from America sailed as early as 28 May. By the beginning of July, sufficient naval covering force, transports, landing ships and craft were converging on the Gulf of Sirte and the Sicilian Straits from the Clyde, Alexandria, Port Said and the North African ports as far afield as Oran and Algiers. Nearly 2,500 naval vessels and landing craft were to carry 115,000 British Empire and over 66,000 American assault troops on the largest amphibious operation that had ever been mounted in the history of warfare. Indeed the number of troops and craft involved were only exceeded in the Normandy landing if the follow-up formations are taken into account.

Forced on the defensive, both in the air and on the sea, the Axis commanders could only hope to stop a landing by the use of ground forces, and it is appropriate at this stage to examine both their channels of command and the disposition of their forces in the defence of Sicily. Both the dictators, and Hitler in particular, liked to keep a tight hold over their operational commanders at a low level. It was Hitler's habit to superimpose over the normal command structure his own personal liaison officers, often with their own signal communications set-up. The situation in Italy was further complicated by the fact that while the Commando Supremo felt bound to insist on retaining operational control of both German and Italian forces on the mainland and the islands, Hitler and his Generals equally attempted to maintain control through German staff officers and liaison officers at each level down to formation headquarters. Knowing the inherent weaknesses of the Italian military machine the Germans more or less insisted on retaining their own channel of command in this manner. In mid-June Field Marshal Kesselring was the German Commander-in-Chief, South. As theatre commander he had control of all German armed forces in Italy, and in fact was Hitler's personal representative on all questions concerning the conduct of the war in the central and western Mediterranean. The command of the German Second Air Force, for which Kesselring had also been responsible, now passed to Field Marshal von Richthofen who became responsible for the Luftwaffe squadrons and their entire ground organization, as well as the majority of the German anti-aircraft units in Italy. The forces in Sicily were under Sixth Army, whose commander was the sixty-six-year-old Italian General Guzzoni. Guzzoni had been in retirement for two years after failures in Albania. In theory Guzzoni had a unified command and received his orders from General Ambrosio and the Commando Supremo; in practice the German formation commanders more often turned to Kesselring's headquarters for their instructions. Kesselring tried to stiffen up the Italian command structure by establishing a mixed German and Italian Staff at Commando Supremo, with his own Chief-of-Staff General Westphal holding a key position, but his greatest problems were trying to reconcile the somewhat conflicting demands of German Commanders and Italian prerogatives and trying to combat Italian pessimism on defending Sicily.

Kesselring felt the Allies would limit their objectives to the effective range of land-based fighter cover and that they would strike at Sicily rather than at Sardinia – possibly as a prelude to an advance, across the Italian mainland, on the Balkans. The German troops were disposed accordingly; one division in Sardinia; a weak brigade in Corsica; a reinforced division in South Calabria and two divisions in Sicily, one of which was in the process of forming. Strong flak forces were assembled in Sicily and Calabria, especially around Messina through which all reinforcements were passing. As for reinforcements, it is worth noting that by the beginning of July a further four German divisions were moving into southern Italy. In the third week of June General von Senger und Etterlin was sent by Hitler to Sicily as his personal liaison officer to the Sixth Army and made responsible for the defence of the island. It is evident from von Senger's account of his interview, when he was briefed by the Fuehrer, that 'Hitler was already reckoning with the early defection of Italy, blaming it on the "machination of the Court, Society, the General Staff, etc." ',[5] and was weighing the chances of the German forces in Sicily acting alone, without calling on the Italians. Over lunch, served privately in his own house, General Warlimont expressed the view 'that in the event of a major Allied attack it would be best to transfer the mass of the troops from Sicily to the mainland'. Also in private, Field Marshal Keitel was equally sceptical and von Senger records his view 'that it would not be possible to keep the scanty German forces together as a mobile reserve in the interior of the island or in its eastern sector. The nature of the mountain roads, and the enemy's air superiority would preclude all movement of troops during daylight.'[6]

Three days later (25 June) von Senger reported to Kesselring in Rome and found him over-optimistic. Kesselring's appreciation of the situation was not accepted by von Richthofen who thought Sardinia would be the 'thrust point' and moved his defences to that island.

The next day Kesselring, von Senger and Guzzoni met at Sixth Army headquarters at Enna to review the island's defence plans. In spite of Kesselring's apparent optimism, which was largely based on his low opinion of the Allies' training for amphibious operations, the situation in Sicily was far from rosy. Kesselring found the Italian construction work 'mere eyewash' and their positions and tank obstacles 'so much gingerbread'. Steps had already been taken to move in German Pioneers and construction material to strengthen the coast defences, in particular to strengthen the improvised Italian coast batteries. Incidentally the Italians wanted these batteries sited well back and the German military advisers wanted them well forward – the argument, in fact, was never resolved!

Guzzoni had plenty of troops but was desperately short of artillery and particularly short of supplies. The daily needs for the civilian population and military units was 8,000 tons of supplies of all kinds. Only 1,500 to 2,000 tons a day were being shipped. The effect on the civilian population in particular was very serious. The rationing system had broken down completely and civilian morale was at rock bottom. The shortage of artillery for the Army was acute; for instance, Guzzoni could only mount one anti-tank gun for each five miles of coastline. However, as Kesselring later commented, 'on the maps everything was in order'.[7] The Italian XVI Corps held the eastern sector and the XII Corps the western sector. Each had two field divisions totalling about 60,000 men. In addition there were five static (or coastal) divisions, totalling about 40,000 men, which consisted of low-quality troops with inadequate scales of equipment. The coastal divisions held extensive sectors; for instance the 206 Coastal Division was responsible for sixty miles of coastline between Syracuse and Licata. The only complete German division on the island at this date was 15 Panzer Grenadier Division, reconstituted from the remains of the Afrika Corps. This division was stationed as a mobile counterattack force in the central portion of the island. A second German division, the 'Hermann Göring' was on its way. In addition the Luftwaffe ground organization and the German supply and administrative troops added a further 30,000 men. With these 'static' troops von Senger did his best by forming strongpoints based on the anti-aircraft battery positions. Battle Commanders were appointed for all the troops in any particular locality, but as he later wrote, 'the so-called alarm units, into which (the Luftwaffe ground troops, etc.) were to be formed, could not be regarded as fit for operations, for they were not mobile'.[8] In all, the Italians had about 315,000 and the Germans 50,000 troops on the island. It was, however, with the role of the two German and four Italian Field Divisions that Kesselring and Guzzoni were concerned. Guzzoni wished to keep the two German divisions together in the eastern sector, based on the Caltanissetta District, as a strong mobile reserve. The Italian Field Divisions were to be more forward in positions where they could fight delaying actions. The German theory, however, was to concentrate all available fire on the enemy at the moment of landing, if possible while they were still in their landing craft. In fact, Kesselring made it quite clear to the two German Divisional Commanders that whatever the Sixth Army Commander ordered they 'must go into immediate action against the enemy the moment you ascertain the objective of the invasion fleet'.[9] This forward policy was to a degree supported by the consideration that, without air cover and on the mountain roads of the interior, the German mobile columns would be forced to move by night. But there was not sufficient mobile strength to counter-attack a number of simultaneous landings. Kesselring was in a cleft stick. He certainly could not rely on the Italian Coastal Divisions stopping a landing and the ability of their Field Divisions to counter-attack successfully was problematic. Nor could he possibly afford to commit the German divisions right up in the coastal defences, where they might well be subjected to direct bombardment. So, contrary to Guzzoni's wishes, Kesselring arranged for the German troops to be divided into several mobile reserves positioned in line with the Italian Field Divisions.

The 15 Panzer Grenadier Division was moved by slow marches, from the eastern sector which they had thoroughly reconnoitred, to the area of Salemi at the western point of the island. The Hermann Göring Division, formerly a parachute division which was in transit from the mainland, moved into position near Caltagirone. Kesselring was worried that if the assault first came in the east this sector might become isolated and he advised Guzzoni that reserves would have to be brought over from the west in such a contingency. As the Hermann Göring Division was seriously below strength, only having two infantry battalions and an armoured regiment, the 15 Panzer Grenadier Division loaned a Regimental Group which came under the Hermann Göring Divisional Commander in the Catania area.

Time was running out, however, and the Axis forces were beset with problems on all sides. Their administrative depots had been concentrated in the western sector, where they had been extensively used for supplying the troops in Tunisia, and some of these now had to be re-sited in the Enna area. There was also a serious shortage of transport and to achieve any degree of mobility the 15 Panzer Grenadier Division had to resort to a shuttle service. One Regimental Group of the Hermann Göring Division was also not mobile and in the event of operations it was to be motorized by using transport from supply columns, which was normally fully occupied on other tasks. General von Senger complained bitterly about the inadequacy of the signal communications. The task he was expected to perform required a fully equipped Corps Headquarters and he only had one General Staff Officer and a single wireless set that he had borrowed from one of the German divisions. Consequently, at Sixth Army Headquarters, he was completely out of touch with Rome and Oberkommando der Wehrmacht, the German High Command. The only link the Germans in Sicily had with the mainland was a Luftwaffe telephone network along the coast, with a cable across the Straits of Messina. Even more serious, however, was the complete lack of co-operation between the Regia Aeronautica and the Luftwaffe. 'No uniform system of air-to-air or ground-to-air signalling, or of aircraft safety and weather reporting procedure had been introduced and the ill-assorted partners had throughout shown a marked tendency to keep their own signal codes a closely guarded secret from each other. Only when the campaign was almost over and the situation desperate was any improvement made in this, the most important factor in the operation of a modern air force.'[10] The naval problems faced by the Axis were more fundamental and in many ways simpler. With German representation limited to a few U-boats, the Italian Admirals were free to make their own decisions.

At Allied Headquarters the Commander-in-Chief, General Eisenhower, had a strong team of experienced commanders for each of the services. The battle for air supremacy over Sicily and the Central Mediterranean had started even before victory came in Tunisia and throughout had been under the direction of Air Chief Marshal Sir Arthur Tedder. The North-West African Air Forces taking part were commanded by Lieutenant-General Spaatz, USA. The Tactical Air Forces, consisting of US XII Air Support Command, the Desert Air Force, and a Tactical Bomber Force were commanded by Air Marshal Sir Arthur Coningham. The Strategic Air Force was commanded by Major-General Doolittle, USA. Other components included the Troop Carrier Command, Coastal Air Force and Photo Reconnaissance Wing. Air Vice-Marshal Sir Keith Park commanded at Malta and Air Chief Marshal Sir Sholto Douglas at Middle East Air Command, both playing a major part in the preparatory phases and in covering the sea and air passage of the assault forces. All these forces were under Tedder's command and in spite of the multiplicity of headquarters 'dotted over thousands of miles between Malta and Algiers the degree of unity and therefore of success can only be described as remarkable'.[11]

The Allied Naval Forces were under the command of Admiral of the Fleet Sir A. B. Cunningham, who established his headquarters at Malta. The

Eastern Task Force was commanded by Vice-Admiral Sir Bertram Ramsay, RN, and the Western Task Force was under Vice-Admiral Hewett, USN. The naval forces available for the HUSKY operations are given in the following table.

NAVAL FORCES FOR OPERATION HUSKY

Class	British	American	Other Nations
Battleships	6	—	—
Fleet Carriers	2 (97 Aircraft of Fleet Air Arm)	—	—
Cruisers	10	5	—
Anti-Aircraft Ships	4	—	—
Fighter Direction Ships	2	—	—
Monitors	3	—	—
Gunboats	3	—	2 Dutch
Minelayers	1	3	—
HQ Ships	5	4	—
Destroyers	71	48	6 Greek 3 Polish
Escort Vessels	35 (2 Royal Indian Navy)	—	1 Greek
Minesweepers	34	8	—
Landing Ships Infantry	8	—	—
Major Landing Craft	319	190	—
Minor Landing Craft	715	510	—
Coastal Craft	160	83	—
Submarines	23	—	1 Dutch 2 Polish
Miscellaneous Vessels	58	28	—
Merchant Ships, Troop Transports and MT ships	155	66	7 Dutch 4 Polish 1 Belgian 4 Norwegian
Totals	1,614	945	31

Exercises were carried out at the end of May in the Red Sea and the Gulf of Aquaba and later many of the ships of the Eastern Task Force carried out rehearsals with the assault troops embarked.

The Allied Ground Force Commander, General Sir Harold Alexander, established his headquarters near Carthage with a small tactical HQ on Malta. The British Eighth Army was commanded by Lieutenant-General Sir Bernard Montgomery and consisted of 13 Corps (5, 46, 50 Divisions) and 30 Corps (51, 78 and 1 Canadian Divisions, together with 231 Independent Brigade and 1 Airborne Division). Seventh Army was commanded by Lieutenant-General

George Patton with II Corps, consisting of the American 1, 3, 9 and 45 Infantry Divisions, 2 Armoured Division and 82 Airborne Division. The Corps Commander was Lieutenant-General Omar Bradley. Training in combined operations was hampered by shortage of time and of landing craft and had to be carried out in a number of different areas. The two divisions (5 and 50 Divisions) coming from the Middle East carried out simulated landing exercises, known as 'Dryshod', in the desert, and took part in some incomplete rehearsals with the Navy in the Gulf of Aquaba. The Canadian Division, who were coming from UK, unfortunately had to cancel their exercises on the Ayrshire coast owing to bad weather. The remaining divisions, including the American 45 Division who had been training in Chesapeake Bay before leaving the USA, held exercises along the North African coast, but these were much hampered by the shortage of landing craft.

The movement problems in mounting the operation was greatly complicated by several factors. Firstly, when planning started the various commanders were still fully engaged in the Tunisian battle. Secondly, the forces were widely dispersed from the USA to the Levant. Thirdly, the distribution of the necessary shipping and craft to the various mounting ports had to be started in motion very early, even before the Mediterranean was opened and certainly before the operational plans were completely firm.

The administrative factors at this stage are particularly important. In early 1943, when the planners started work, an accepted doctrine for amphibious operations was that sufficient major ports, capable of maintaining the total forces to be landed, must be captured within forty-eight hours. The landing of supplies over the beaches was only regarded as a temporary expediency for the interim period. Thus the early plans for HUSKY were based on a consideration of the three main Sicilian ports, Messina, Catania and Palermo. The early capture of Messina was considered out of the question. It was estimated that Catania could handle the supplies for four divisions and, if developed, possibly for up to six divisions. Palermo could handle the tonnage required for the whole force. Palermo, however, was situated near the limit for air cover and remote from the eastern group of airfields, the early capture of which was vital to the overall tactical requirement. Thus for a time the planners considered that a simultaneous attack on the south-eastern and western parts of the island would be required in order to seize both Catania and Palermo. Any alternative would involve administrative risk. About this time, however, the DUKW started to arrive in the Mediterranean theatre, a large quantity having been specially ordered from the USA towards the end of March. The potential of this amphibious truck, which was capable of ferrying ammunition and stores from ship to shore and driving straight on to supply points inland, was increased by the fair weather conditions in July and by the fact that there was no tide to compete with. Acceptance of the feasibility of 'beach maintenance', i.e. the supply of a large proportion of the force over the beaches for a prolonged period, was a key factor in the evolution of the final plans for the assault.

A good deal of study had already been going on in all theatres of the problems of organizing beach supply. This resulted in the formation of Beach Groups or 'Bricks' which consisted of a headquarters and the necessary personnel, vehicles and equipment for labour, engineer work, signal duties, anti-aircraft and general defence, as well as elements for the recovery and repair of vehicles, and ordnance and medical detachments. A Beach Group was allocated to each major landing area with the sole role of organizing and defending the beaches. These groups made a major contribution to the success of the operations. It was not intended that Sicily should be built up as a supply base, nor was Malta to be turned into an advanced base although it was used as a staging post for some reinforcements and for forward reserves of supplies and ammunition for the Eighth Army. Consequently the administrative plan could be kept extremely simple and could be based on the existing arrangements and lines of communication on the North African coastline. The overall plan for the assault was finalized on 3 May. In June the loading of the ships started. Only the devoted work of the planners and administrative staffs in preparing the loading schedules early, and keeping them revised at each change of plan, enabled the convoys to sail on time and with all the multitudinous stores and supplies of a modern army stowed in their correct order and quantities.

Several aspects of Allied Intelligence work are worthy of note. The excellent work of the photo-reconnaissance squadron over many months enabled detailed maps of the whole 10,000 square miles of the island to be prepared, showing many up-to-date details of recent German efforts to improve the defences, gun-positions, etc.

Practically nothing, however, was known about the beaches themselves. Small landing parties, known as Combined Operations Pilotage Parties, were carried by submarine at night to positions close inshore where a dinghy would be launched so that soundings could be taken, and if possible a reconnaissance made of the beach itself and its exits. These parties, however, could not always land and it was important to discover which beaches had steep enough gradients for landing craft to beach themselves close to the foreshore, to reduce to a minimum the dangerous interval that must be covered by men and vehicles wading ashore. Sir David Hunt tells how this problem was solved. 'A mathematical formula (was devised) whereby the slope of the beach could be ascertained from the interval between the crests of waves in certain wind conditions. This interval showed up plainly in parallel lines of white on air photographs.'[12] The Allied Intelligence staffs were also able to build up a remarkably accurate picture of the enemy order of battle and unit locations through the simple device of examining mail passing through Cairo to the seven hundred thousand Italian prisoners of war held in the Middle East,

India and South and East Africa. Letters from relatives still serving in the Italian forces often gave the address of the writer and in many cases disclosed where the unit was serving. Even where Italian military censorship had scored out this information, means were found to remove the indian ink and later replace it before sending the letter on to its destination. The information about the Italian dispositions obtained in this way was to prove remarkably accurate.

3

Sicily – The Landings

3
Sicily—The Landings

Concentration or Dispersion: Final Plans Decided: Opposing Forces Compared: Cover Plan: HUSKY Plans Outlined: The Convoys Assemble: The Storm: The Airborne Landings: Assault from the Sea: Progress on D-Day and Axis Reactions: The Fight for Gela: Situation on 12 July: Seventh Army Changes Direction: Casualties 9–12 July.

1943	June	Allied air forces pound Axis airfields in Sicily and Italy.
	29 June	General Eisenhower considering proposals for invasion of toe of Italy and Sardinia.
	2 July	Allied air forces attack Sicilian and Italian ports and step up attacks on airfields.
	9 July	Final pre-invasion bombing and airborne parachute and glider operations on Sicily.
	10 July	HUSKY – the landings.
	11 July	Americans counter-attacked at Gela. American parachute reinforcements suffer heavy losses.
	12 July	Eighth Army meets stubborn resistance at Priolo. Seventh Army given fresh axis of advance.

The first Allied plan for the invasion of Sicily was drawn up in February 1943, being based on the broad directive decided upon at the SYMBOL Conference. This proposed simultaneous assaults, each in two phases, on the south, eastern and western sectors of the island. The British were to land at Avola-Pachino–Pozzallo, and Gela, with objectives the ports of Syracuse and Augusta and the airfields of Pachino, Comiso and Ponte Olivo. Simultaneously the Americans would land at Sciacca and Marinella with objectives the airfields in this area, in particular at Castelvetrano, which were to be used to furnish air cover for the main landing on D + 2 at Palermo. The following day the British would follow up with landings in the Catania area to capture that port and the Gerbini group of airfields. Throughout February and early March the battle in Tunisia gave General Alexander little time for any detailed study of these plans, but he was already thinking of concentrating his forces against the south-eastern corner of the island. At this point he was advised by his staff that the port facilities in the south-east were inadequate and that the early capture of Palermo and Catania was vital to the maintenance of the force of ten divisions, which was considered necessary to insure the capture of Sicily. The enemy strength at this time was estimated to be eight divisions.

General Alexander then turned his attention to the air situation. The extent of air cover would be roughly a line from Catania to Trapani, but both these points would be at extreme range for fighters. He arrived at the conclusion that the British assault on the eastern side of the island would be too dispersed and would need strengthening. Air Marshal Tedder insisted that the Ponte Olivo airfields should be captured early and in this he was supported by Admiral Cunningham who was anxious for the safety of the mass of ships which would be standing close inshore. Consequently an extra division from the Middle East was phased in to strengthen the assault in the south-east and the planners continued to work on the original plans with only minor modifications. At the end of April the battle in Tunisia was reaching its conclusion and on 29 April the Allied commanders were finally able to meet in Algiers. General Leese straightaway weighed in with the Eighth Army view that, under the existing plans, their assault was too widely dispersed. His proposal was that both armies should land on the south-eastern tip of the island; the British at Avola and the Americans on the Pachino peninsula. It is noteworthy that General Montgomery had thought it necessary to press, in a signal to General Alexander five days previously, for the landings to be concentrated both in time and place. At the conference General Leese's proposals were immediately opposed by both Tedder and Cunningham. Tedder pointed out that no less than thirteen landing grounds would be left in enemy hands and that he could not guarantee to neutralize them all. As Alexander later wrote in his dispatch, 'On the existing plan it was impossible to reconcile these conflicting points of view'. General Eisenhower called a further conference for 2 May where General Montgomery presented his views in person. Alexander himself was unable to get to Algiers owing to bad flying weather. The following day Eisenhower endorsed Montgomery's proposals and Alexander issued a plan based on the strategic concept of a concentrated assault on the south-eastern corner of the island, but avoiding any close bunching of the two armies. The Eighth Army was to land in the Gulf of Noto and also astride the Pachino Peninsula with two divisions in each area. A Commando Brigade and an Air Landing Brigade Group (glider-borne) would be used on the right flank in the area of Syracuse. The Seventh Army would land three divisions on a seventy-mile stretch of the Gulf of Gela between Scoglitti and Licata, preceded by parachute troops which would secure vital high ground a few miles from Gela itself. The American divisions would have to be maintained over the beaches and the use of the Pantelleria airfield facilities became a vital requirement, as both the Gerbini airfield complex as well as other airfields in the south-west were outside the immediate ground objectives. Eisenhower had already been under attack by the Combined Chiefs of Staff who sought to launch a modified assault immediately the battle in Tunisia died down. He had to point to the unpalatable fact that he only had, at this time, sufficient landing craft for one division and only enough assault craft for a regimental combat team! His view was that 'an attack with less than two divisions (was) too great a risk',[1] and that later more craft would be available. So only hours before the final collapse of the Axis in Tunisia the decision was taken that D-day would be 10 July, and the commanders and staffs turned to their task of planning in detail a combined operation that ultimately built up to an Allied strength in Sicily of 217,000 men in the US Seventh Army and 250,000 men in the British Eighth Army.

In justification of the unusually prolonged period of planning it must be remembered that, as a combined operation, HUSKY exceeded anything so far attempted in the history of modern warfare. The Allied commanders, however, unlike the defenders of Sicily were a closely integrated team. They were served by a devoted staff where inter-service and inter-allied co-operation was of the highest order. As for the two Allied armies, Alexander later wrote in his dispatch, 'Seventh Army was certainly fast-moving and hard-hitting and it undoubtedly owed these qualities to the leadership of its Commander (General Patton). General Montgomery was also a commander in whom I had every trust and confidence. He and his Eighth Army had served under my command since August 1942.' Eighth Army included 'in addition to the veteran desert formation the splendid 1 Canadian Division, trained to a hair in the United Kingdom and eager and confident for battle. I also welcomed 78 Division, the most experienced of First Army's Divisions.'[2] Throughout the planning phase the Allies calculated that the garrison in Sicily would be considerably reinforced as soon as the Axis lost North Africa. Ignoring the coast divisions, it was estimated that the enemy would have not less than six Italian and two German field divisions operational in the island by the beginning of June. This in fact proved to be an overestimate. Nevertheless there were some 315,000 Italian and 50,000 German troops in Sicily when the assault took place, and after the battle began a further 40,000 German reinforcements were brought in by sea and air from the mainland. The morale and fighting qualities of the Italians was admittedly low but they were expected to fight better for their homeland than they had in the desert campaigns. With the Germans no chances could be taken. So in addition to the need for a sound strategic plan of assault, every effort must be made to mislead and deceive the two Dictators and their commanders as to the point of attack.

The cover plan evolved by the Allies aimed at persuading the Axis that the immediate Allied objectives were Sardinia and the Peloponnese, so that the Axis would maintain and even reinforce their forces in Sardinia, southern France and throughout the Balkans. The story of the 'planting' of a body, dressed as a Royal Marine officer and carrying secret instructions from the War Office to General Alexander, is well known. The document showed an attack on Sicily to be a feint to screen a main assault on Sardinia and suggested that General Wilson, the Commander-in-Chief Middle East, should similarly attack the Dodecanese as a feint for an assault on the mainland of Greece. The ruse was dramatically successful. Three days after a British submarine had dropped the body off the Spanish coast, word was received in London that Axis agents had intercepted the 'secret' instructions. This resulted in the OKW on 12 May ordering reinforcements into Sardinia 'and the best German Armoured Division then available, the 1st, made a hasty journey from France to the southern Peloponnese where it took up antiinvasion position on the beach facing the island of Crete'.[3]

While it had been accepted that the capture of Pantelleria would underline the seriousness of the Allied threat to Sicily, air action right up to the time of the assault landing followed a broad pattern that could be construed as being equally preparatory to an attack on the other island outposts. Orders for the air operations covered four main phases:

(a) Sustained air operations to paralyse or destroy the enemy air forces over a period immediately preceding D-day.

(b) Close air cover to the convoys at sea.

(c) During the assault landing phase, the protection of the ships lying off-shore and the attack by day and night of the beach defences.

(d) Finally, once the armies were established ashore, the closest co-operation above and behind the battlefield.

The air situation between the fall of Tunis and the beginning of July has already been outlined in Chapter 2 and the final phase of pre-HUSKY air operations opened on 2 July (D−8). The enemy fighters, particularly those of the Luftwaffe, were now concentrated on the Gerbini complex and came under attack from the heavy bombers of the Strategic Air Force and IX Bomber Command. The medium bombers of the Tactical Air Force took over responsibility for airfields in the west of the island and Ninth Air Force largely concentrated on airfields in southern Italy. These attacks were planned with great skill. 'Areas containing a number of fields were divided into sectors for a specific assignment to definite formations of planes. On some occasions heavy attacks would be laid on all but one or two fields in a given area, and then when the enemy diverted his fighters to the unscathed fields the Allies followed with a concentrated blow on them. Attempts by the Luftwaffe to use widely dispersed satellite strips were countered by mass strafing and fighter-bomber attacks . . . a follow up with fragmentation bombs added immeasurably to the effectiveness.'[4] Fragmentation bombs were principally used at the start of this phase as being most effective against aircraft on the ground and, as D-day approached, 500-lb demolition bombs were used to destroy the airfield installations. Meanwhile the attacks on Sardinia continued and, in accordance with the cover plan, attacks were also made at the end of July on airfields in Greece and Salonika.

As far as Sicily was concerned, Gerbini and seven of its twelve satellites were unusable by D-day, and of the remaining airfields Comiso and Boddaci-falco were unusable and Castelvetrano had been abandoned. The smaller airfields in Sicily and those in Sardinia were largely neutralized, 'only Sciacca and Trapani/Milo being fully operational. Photo-reconnaissance indicated that approximately half of the enemy's Sicily-based planes had been driven from the island to the mainland and by the close of the HUSKY operations Allied personnel had counted approximately 1,000 enemy aircraft abandoned or destroyed in Sicily.'[5] During the week of concentrated attack on their airfields the Axis fighters had been goaded into the air with the result that they lost 250 planes against an Anglo-American loss of 70 aircraft. In the air Allied planes dominated the sky over Sicily and all was now ready.

The naval plan for the movement of the convoy was very carefully designed to mislead both as to the date of the attack and the destination of the assault convoys up to the last possible moment. Sir Andrew Cunningham's objects were tersely described as 'the safe and timely arrival of the assault forces at their beaches, the cover of their disembarkation, and subsequently their support and maintenance'.[6] The routing of the convoys was arranged to conform to the normal through-Mediterranean shipping movement. In addition strong naval forces appearing in the Ionian Sea would suggest an attack on Crete or Greece. Similarly the movement of naval forces in the western Mediterranean would produce the impression that the American Army in North Africa was about to attack Sardinia or Corsica, preparatory to a landing in southern France. These movements in fact also placed the Allied battleships where they could best protect the convoys from any interference by the Italian fleet. A heavy covering force was to assemble to the north of the Gulf of Sirte during the day before the actual landings and lighter forces would protect the exposed northern and western flanks of the assembly areas. A further link with the cover plan was a demonstration off western Sicily, including the bombardment of Trapani. This in fact succeeded in drawing off one of the four German battle groups moving back across the island. Apart from the action of the covering forces described above, strong naval and air escorts had to be provided for the protection of the convoys as they passed along the African coast and during the actual assaults. This protection had, of course, to be provided throughout the whole period of operations and the problem became more and more complex as protection was needed for the follow-up convoys, as well as for returning convoys, and for other ships while actually discharging supplies over the beaches. Meanwhile the immediate problem was to land some 115,000 British and Empire troops and 66,000 American troops, together with their fighting equipment, vehicles, ammunition and stores. Moreover the units and formations were actually assembling not only from ports in North Africa and the Middle East but from as far away as Britain and America.

As already mentioned 45 Division left America on 28 May. The ships of this convoy were to join up with others already assembled at Oran and Algiers where six assault and follow-up convoys would be formed to carry Seventh Army and all its assault craft and supplies. The convoys at Oran sailed on 4 July and were followed almost immediately by the main assault convoys assembled at Algiers; 45 Division would land on a twelve-mile stretch of beach astride Scoglitti (CENT beach) and 1 Division (less one regiment) would land at Gela (DIME) and 3 Division at Licata (JOSS). On their flank would be a floating reserve of one regiment each of tanks and infantry, with reconnaissance and artillery units from 2 Armoured Division and an infantry regiment (from 1 Division) plus anti-aircraft and field artillery and engineer units; 9 Division and 82 Airborne Division (less four battalions) stood by in North Africa as Army Reserve. The parachute drop inland from Gela was to be carried out by 505 Parachute Infantry Regimental Combat Team reinforced by an extra battalion. All these troops were American.

Eighth Army convoys from Alexandria and Port Said carried 5 Division, 3 Commando and 50 Division (ACID North), 231 Independent Infantry

Brigade (BARK East) and 4 Armoured Brigade. The four convoys in this group sailed between 3 and 9 July. 51 Highland Division and 23 Armoured Brigade embarked at Sfax and Tripoli in three convoys which sailed on 8 and 9 July. The assault infantry sailed in two convoys of Landing Craft Infantry from Malta between 1500 hours 9 July and early 10 July. All these troops were destined for BARK South. 1 Canadian Division, plus 40 and 41 Royal Marine Commando and an Anti-Aircraft Brigade, left the Clyde in five convoys between 20 June and 1 July and sailed direct to BARK West. 78 Division remained in Army Reserve in North Africa and a further infantry division, 46 Division, was also standing by in reserve. An Air Landing Brigade of 1 Airborne Division was to land in gliders to capture the bridge over the River Anapo south of Syracuse and to assist in the capture of the town.

So far we have seen the development of the fight for air superiority and the assembly of the convoys, and the subsequent routing and destination of the various assault forces. While we have also seen the evolution of the overall plan and the decision to land the two armies side-by-side in the south-eastern part of the island, we must now look beyond the beaches and study the tasks that awaited the Corps and Divisional Commanders in thrusting inland. Indeed, the selection of the assault beaches, and the immediate objectives inland, together with plans for the development of the land battle formed part of a single pattern. 13 Corps as 'right of the line' were undoubtedly in a key position. 5 and 50 Divisions were to land on a three-brigade front between Cape Murro di Porco and a point just south of Noto. On the Cape itself was an important coastal battery which would be assaulted by the Commandos. Four hours previously (between 2200 and 2230 hours 9 July) 1 Air Landing Brigade Group in gliders would land and capture the Ponte Grande over the River Anapo and deal with coastal batteries and a nearby seaplane base all in this area. 5 Division's objective was to capture Cassibile and then advance north on Syracuse and Augusta. 50 Division would capture Avola and a plateau which dominated the coast road, so as to protect the beach head from the west and south-west. As regards 30 Corps, 231 Brigade Group on landing would protect the right flank and patrol towards Avola. 51 Division, on a four-battalion front, would land astride the Pachino Peninsula and capture the town. On the left 1 Canadian Division and the two Royal Marine Commandos would protect the left of the British front and seize the Pachino landing ground, which was to be brought into use urgently. 30 Corps' objective was the road Noto–Rosolini–Spaccaforna and subsequently to seize the high ground overlooking the road centres of Palazzolo and Ragusa. At Ragusa 1 Canadian Division would join up with II Corps. In the second phase 13 Corps were to secure bridgeheads over the River Simeto and capture Catania. 30 Corps after relieving 50 Division in the beach-head area would thrust forward on the road axis Palazzola–Vizzini.[7]

Seventh Army was divided into two forces. II Corps with 45 and 1 Infantry Divisions, together with Rangers and some tanks, had the task of capturing the airfields at Ponte Olivo, Comiso and Biscari, and then to join up with the Canadians at Ragusa. The parachute drop by 505 Regimental Combat Team aimed at capturing the high ground overlooking 1 Division's beaches and the vital Ponte Dirillo over the River Acate.

The second force was on the Seventh Army's left. Here 3 Infantry Division, reinforced with two armoured regiments, on landing at Licata, had the task of capturing the town and airfield. It is of interest to note that 4th Moroccan Tabor of Goums (Berber infantry with French officers and NCOs at battalion strength) would land on D+5 and be attached to 3 Division.

In support of the landings there was a floating reserve consisting of the remainder of 2 Armoured Division and a Regimental Combat Team from 1 Division. A further reserve of 9 Division and the remainder of 82 Airborne Division stood by in North Africa.

The Seventh Army task in the second phase was to seize a line from Vizzini–Caltagirone–Mazzarino–Campobello–Palma di Montechiaro. These objectives were very different than those given to the Americans under the original plan to seize Palermo, but the plans were now firm and it only remained to use the remaining weeks and days before D-day to prepare for the assault.

At each level the plan had to be broken down, subordinates briefed, units trained, and weapons, equipment, vehicles and all the multitudinous stores of all kinds assembled and checked and loaded. Much would depend on the right priority being given in the loading tables. Every man, every gun, every vehicle and every box of ammunition or stores must be landed on the right beach at the right time and in exactly the right sequence. It was fortunate that the staffs had done much of the preliminary work in preparing the loading tables while waiting for the assault plan to be finally decided.

In early July the Italian and German staffs estimated that 90 per cent of the Allied troops and practically all their landing craft were massed in the central Mediterranean and that this indicated a landing on Sardinia, but most likely on Sicily. To Guzzoni the signs were almost conclusive: Sicily was the target. The weather was favourable and so was the phase of the moon (by 10 July there would be no moon visible) and so he issued a preliminary warning to his troops. On both 4 and 5 July the movement of convoys and the assembly of hospital ships was reported. This convinced Guzzoni that an attack was imminent and on 8 July he ordered the port facilities in the west and south of the island to be prepared for demolition. Further convoy movements were spotted by the Luftwaffe during the morning and late afternoon of 9 July and reports kept on coming in during the night of convoys off the south-east corner of the island. At 1900 hours Guzzoni issued a preliminary alert and at 2200 hours the full alert.

Receiving the reports of the Allies' convoy movements on 9 July, Hitler ordered the German 1 Parachute Division in France to stand by to move to Sicily. This move could be completed in five days.

The weather on the morning of 9 July had in fact broken. The wind blowing from the west began to rise, and with it the sea, and by early afternoon had reached forty mph. As the convoys turned north in the late afternoon the wind and the seas struck on the beam. Landing craft slowed down and began to straggle. Many ships lost their places in their convoy. Seasickness began to affect the crowded troops, especially in the small Landing Craft Infantry. With the rolling of the heavily loaded ships, many cargoes shifted and speeds and courses had to be changed. This all resulted in delays of up to an hour in the arrival of the convoys in their offshore assembly areas and many ships hove-to seriously off station. At about the time Guzzoni issued the preliminary alert, Eisenhower and Cunningham were listening to the latest meteorological forecast. This gave indications of an improvement in the weather during the night. The decision was quickly taken: to proceed as planned. As Eisenhower later wrote, 'my feeling was that, even if the forces on the southern coast should find it necessary to delay landing, those on the east would surely get ashore and we would have less confusion and disadvantage than would result from any attempt to stop the whole armada. But the evening wore on and the wind velocity increased alarmingly. There was nothing we could do but pray, desperately.'[8] Overhead in the half light flew the Dakotas (C-47s) with the American paratroopers and the tugs and gliders carrying the men of 1 Airborne and for them the high winds were even more serious.

The British glider force of 1,200 men of 1 Air Landing Brigade were carried in 127 Waco gliders (maximum load 14 men) and 17 Horsas (taking 30 men). The tugs were provided by 109 American C-47s and 35 British Albemarles and Halifaxes. The RAF planes had towed the Horsas out from England the week previously and these British pilots of both tugs and gliders had considerable experience. The American C-47 pilots and the glider pilots for the Wacos, however, only had three weeks for training together. Unfortunately 'some of the glider pilots had not advanced beyond the first solo stage of instruction at the time of their arrival in Africa'.[9] Although 1,800 night flights were practised, there were further difficulties as many of the tug pilots themselves were not fully trained for night flying. This factor, combined with the difficulties of towing a heavily loaded glider in a high wind and coming under heavy flak probably for the very first time, brought disastrous results.

Of the 137 gliders that were towed in along the Gulf of Noto, 69 were released too soon and fell into the sea; 56 more were scattered over the whole south coastline, some many miles off target. Only twelve gliders carrying less than 100 men landed in or near the landing zone – these had, in fact, all been brought in by the experienced RAF tug pilots. By dawn eight Officers and sixty-five other ranks held the Ponte Grande and the remainder of the small but resolute force had over-run a nearby coastal battery. Unfortunately the pilots of the American transport aircraft on Seventh Army front were facing similar conditions. Their navigational problems were aggravated by having to follow a complicated route so as to avoid the shipping lanes. The force flying through the night was a considerable one, 226 C-47s with 2,781 paratroopers and 891 equipment packs to be dropped. For many pilots the conditions were too difficult and some became completely lost, while those who succeeded in keeping on course found the dropping zones obscured by smoke and fires from the preliminary air bombardment. The division found itself scattered all over south-eastern Sicily – '33 sticks landed in Eighth Army area: 53 round Gela and 127 inland from the 45 Division beaches'. Only one battalion landed relatively intact but found itself twenty-five miles from its proper dropping zone. By dawn less than 200 men had assembled on the high ground of Piano Lupo. The remainder of the division 'were roaming through the rear areas of the coastal defence units, cutting enemy communication lines, ambushing small parties and creating confusion among enemy commanders as to where exactly the main airborne landing had taken place'.[10] Some Italian units, not expecting such an apparently large-scale airborne operation, are reported as having withdrawn as much as ten miles. The general confusion of the defenders was increased by the widespread dropping of hundreds of parachute dummies.

H-hour for the seaborne assault was 0245 hours 10 July: a moment of time fixed in the minds of thousands of Allied troops. For all it was the culmination of months of training; for some it meant the sudden grinding shudder of the assault craft hitting the beach; for many more following in the larger craft with the guns and tanks and vehicles it was a time of suspense, of waiting to get ashore. On the naval ships standing offshore the gun crews stood by to open fire on the coastal batteries. Fighter squadrons were waiting to start their patrols, the fighter-bombers were standing by to take off every thirty minutes throughout the day to strike at the approach roads to the beaches. In the darkness thousands of men waited. It was a moment of almost unbelievable silence.

The Eighth Army assaults went in just about on time, although swell caused some delays it also helped some of the smaller craft over the offshore sand-banks. Tactical surprise was achieved everywhere and what little resistance that came from the coastal defence units was quickly overcome. Some coastal batteries and field artillery started shelling the beaches but were quickly silenced by naval gunfire. The American landings were rather more affected by the gale and high seas and the three task forces arrived somewhat disorganized. The landing of 45 Division had to be delayed an hour but the other two landings were not seriously behind schedule. The Western Task Force had been exposed to the full force of the westerly winds and had much difficulty in hoisting out and launching their landing craft. Unfortunately contact had also been lost with a control vessel and when the craft were launched they found they had a much longer run-in than planned. The first wave touched down at 0430 hours on the extreme left, beyond Licata, and was followed by other assault elements of 3 Division, who were now landing in daylight (first light being 0415 hours). The infantry pressed forward with the support of naval gunfire and by 0630 hours tanks and guns were coming ashore. In the centre the 1 Division landings got in well before first light but the right-hand regiment did not really get going off the beach until a cruiser and destroyer succeeded in silencing the Italian mortar and artillery fire. The two regiments landing near Gela got very early support from the naval guns and made better progress. On Seventh Army right the landing of 45 Division ran into serious delays. The convoy had been much dispersed on arrival and the rough sea and heavy swell added to the confusion. Some of the assault craft had been ready on time, but, when the time of the landing was put back an hour, found themselves having to circle for almost three hours before being released for their run-in. In one transport it took nearly four hours to launch the assault craft for the first wave and generally there was great difficulty in assembling craft anywhere near their proper positions. The first waves of the division finally succeeded in landing about 0440 hours, although some craft touched down a considerable distance from the planned beach and the leading troops found themselves scattered over twelve miles of coastline. Luckily the defences in this area were not strong and the landings met with little resistance.

In spite of the difficulties caused by the weather conditions, especially on the American beaches where a number of landing craft got stranded on sandbanks in the heavy swell, the Allied ground forces continued to build up steadily over the beaches and at about 1000 hours the situation was as follows: on Eighth Army right the small airborne force still held the Ponte Grande bridge and continued to do so for nearly eighteen hours with great heroism; 13 Corps had been delayed by some shelling of their beaches but held Cassibile and Casanuova and had a footing in Avola and Noto; 30 Corps after meeting only half-hearted resistance had captured their beaches by 0545 hours and by 0730 hours were starting the rehabilitation of Pachino airfield, which was ready for use five hours later. On the Seventh Army front the battalions were starting to thrust forward and at about 1000 hours elements of 45 Division had reached S Croce Camerima and a point four miles short of Vittoria, as well as the area of the Ponte Dirillo. In the centre, 1 Division held the road junction at Piano Lupo and the airfield and town of Gela. On the left, in 3 Division area, Licata was being cleared and the leading battalion held the coast beyond for eight miles, with columns penetrating inland for up to five miles.

The Allied fighter cover was designed to give all beaches continuous protection for the first two and the last one and a half hours of daylight, and in addition from 1030-1230 and 1600-1700 hours, while in rotation two of the beaches would be covered between these times. Also a complete fighter wing was held in reserve for any emergency conditions. The limiting factor was in fact airfield facilities and not aircraft. The first Axis aircraft appeared over the assembly area, already thick with shipping, at about 0430 hours. In the American sector a destroyer and minesweeper were sunk, but in the British sector serious air attacks did not develop until later in the day. Before dealing in more detail with these attacks, however, it is as well to recall that through their concentrated attacks on the Axis air forces in the preliminary operations the Allies had achieved virtual air supremacy. The general situation was that the advance inland and the discharge of follow-up units and stores went unchecked and, almost more important, in the early hours of daylight on D-day the amount of detailed information available to Guzzoni from air reconnaissance was negligible. The telephone communications, which were already poor, had been seriously dislocated by the previous nights' bombing and the scattered American paratroopers were cutting every line they could find; so it is hardly surprising to find that it was 0500 hours on 10 July before reports of the parachute drops, and the glider landings at Augusta, reached the Italian Sixth Army Headquarters. About the same time the Hermann Göring Division reported twenty transports unloading off Gela.

General Conrath, commanding the Hermann Göring Division, in fact first heard of the American landings from Kesselring's Headquarters in Italy and in accordance with a pre-arranged plan his divisions had begun to move forward at 0400 hours. Colonel Schmalz's battle group was in action against the British early in the morning, but practically no intelligence reached Sixth Army from that flank. With little else to go on, Guzzoni faced up to the known threat at Gela. The 15 Panzer Grenadier Division, who had only just succeeded in assembling in the western sector, were told to move back to Canicatti and Caltanissetta as best they could with inadequate transport. At the same time Guzzoni ordered the Livorno Division, augmented by two Italian airfield mobile groups, and the Hermann Göring Division to make a co-ordinated attack on the landings at Gela. These orders never reached General Conrath whose division was already assembling for a two-pronged attack through Priolo and Biscari. Owing to poor communications the Italian attack was completely unco-ordinated but succeeded in reaching the outskirts of Gela and Piano Lupo. Here the attacking tanks came under heavy fire from several warships and were forced back with losses. An unsupported infantry attack by the Italians on the west of Gela was thrown back with exceptionally heavy losses. US Rangers, using captured field guns, helped turn defeat into rout and by noon the town was firmly in American hands. By 1400 hours, General Conrath had succeeded in getting his troops in position, five hours later than planned. His tank regiment, supported by infantry, advanced south from Niscemi, while a strong infantry force with some Tiger tanks struck south-west from Biscari, so as to sweep in on the flank of the main tank attack. The main German tank attack was checked by American naval gun-fire in the Piano Lupo area where the 16 Infantry Regiment put up a magnificent resistance, while the 180 Infantry held the German infantry on the other flank. The failure of the Tiger tanks to get forward resulted in General Conrath relieving their commander on the spot. The Germans then put in a second and much better co-ordinated attack with the Tiger tanks leading and broke through to the coast road. This very dangerous situation was somewhat restored by 3rd Battalion 180 Infantry counter-attacking and forcing the Germans back towards Biscari. At nightfall the Germans held Ponte Olivo airfield with a strong tank force and strong positions south of both Niscemi and Biscari. In the early afternoon, as the threat to 1 Division area developed, General Patton ordered 2 Armoured Division and 18 Regimental Combat Team, from the floating reserve, to land on the beaches at Gela. When the reconnaissance party got ashore, however, they found the selected beaches were mined and other beaches had to be used. This change of plans and the consequent confusion over orders was only one of the difficulties that now arose. As the German counter-attack developed, the shelling of the beaches intensified and air attack on the restricted beach heads and massed shipping standing offshore became more persistent. Disembarkation continued throughout the night but by daylight on 11 July only ten tanks had been landed and these were all bogged down in soft sand. Four extra battalions of infantry, however, were ashore and moving up towards the high ground beyond the Gela airstrip.

On the Eighth Army front there had been steady progress throughout the remainder of 10 July. On the right, 5 Division had occupied the plateau overlooking Cassibile and relieved the gallant survivors at the Ponte Grande in the afternoon. This fine forced march ended with the division entering Syracuse at 2100 hours. 50 Division were established north-west of Noto by the early evening and 30 Corps had cleared the whole of the Pachino Peninsula. So far, on the British front the enemy mobile columns, including the Italian Napoli Division at Vizzini, had held back and opposition had been fairly light. The following day 13 Corps pressed on up the east coast. Marching in the intense heat, contact was made with elements of the Napoli Division at Priolo, halfway to Augusta. 30 Corps started to advance inland on the axis Palazzolo–Vizzini and on the left the Canadians were in contact with the Americans at Ragusa. General Guzzoni was still very much in the dark. Communications with the east-coast defences were so ineffective that orders for Group Schmalz and the Napoli Division to attack beach heads south of Syracuse only went out an hour before the port itself was captured. By this time British Eighth Army held over forty miles of coastline and was well established inland.

Completely unaware of the extent of the Eighth Army operations, Guzzoni turned again to the American landings. At about 2000 hours on 10 July he

General Montgomery and Lieutenant General Freyberg with the Italian General Messe after the Axis surrender in North Africa, 13 May 1943.

Invasion of Sicily. Scene off Avola 10 July with an LST approaching the beach head.

Plain of Catania. A 6 pr anti-tank gun position, July 1943.

Capture of Centuripe. The German tank is a Panzer Mark III, August 1943.

gave orders for a coastal division to counter-attack towards Licata. At Gela he judged he had the best chance of success. No armour had been met so far and the Hermann Göring Division was poised close to the narrow beach head. Guzzoni's plan was for a co-ordinated attack to start at 0600 hours, 11 July. The Hermann Göring Division, in three columns, would thrust down on Gela from the east and the Livorno Division, also in three columns, would attack from the west. Returning from the Italian XVI Corps Headquarters to his command post, General Conrath received similar orders to counter-attack Gela from Kesselring, who was completely out of touch with Guzzoni and convinced that only the German troops were capable of effective action. During the night the news of the fall of Syracuse came through and Guzzoni realized the extent of the British threat. General Conrath was given further orders. As soon as his attack at Gela showed signs of success he was to turn off east and advance on Comiso and Palazzolo. This move would knock out the 45 Division beach head at Scoglitti and enable the Schmalz Group to rejoin the division. Thus re-united the Axis divisions were to strike a hard blow at the British. Meanwhile the Livorno Division, assisted by 15 Panzer Division, would 'destroy' the Americans at Licata. On the map these plans looked splendid, but 1 Division anticipated the German attack at Gela with a night attack towards the Ponte Olivo airfield and Niscemi. Although this attack did not stop Conrath's tank columns swooping down and across the plain east of Gela, the American infantry were able to bring heavy fire on one part of the Italian columns. As the Italians advanced all three columns came under heavy field artillery and mortar fire and were halted before they reached the railway line on the outskirts of Gela. At this point the cruiser *Savannah* opened fire and five hundred 6-inch shells crashed down on the unfortunate Italian infantry. This clinched the matter and the Livorno Division ceased to be an effective formation. Meanwhile, Conrath's centre tank column had forced the Americans right back on to the edge of the Piano Lupo escarpment. The American infantry with only bazookas and light howitzers were in a very precarious position. At this critical moment anti-tank guns, only now coming off the beaches, were rushed forward and enabled the feature to be held. The German infantry attack from Biscari, the third prong of their advance, by now had reached the Ponte Dirillo over the Acate River. Here they were taken in the flank by a strong body of paratroopers who had made a forced march from Vittoria. The success of this flank attack distracted the attention of Conrath from the battle, which was now developing in the plain of Gela. Here the main German tank attack was within two thousand yards of the shore and, seeing his tanks firing on the supply dumps and landing craft, Conrath signalled that 'pressure by the Hermann Göring Division has forced the enemy to re-embark temporarily'. General Guzzoni was elated and confirmed the prearranged plan for the Division to turn east. But the German tanks never reached the beaches. Field artillery coming ashore in DUKWs came into action on the edge of the dunes over open sights. Four of the stranded American tanks at last got off the soft sand. Infantry guns were ferried across the Acate River and every soldier in the beach head added his fire to the guns that now pounded the German tanks. With a third of his tank force destroyed or disabled and unsupported by his infantry column, which was now under artillery and naval gun-fire, Conrath called off the attack at 1400 hours and withdrew the remnants of his tanks to the foothills south of Niscemi.

Guzzoni now decided to pull back the Hermann Göring Division to Caltagirone, ready for an advance on Vizzini against the British the following day. Before these instructions were issued, however, von Senger had seen Conrath and told him to carry out the original plan of striking across the path of 45 Division. Conrath, however, hearing of the heavy losses to his infantry column (who were still heavily engaged at 1900 hours) chose to comply with Guzzoni's orders and withdrew by stages on Caltagirone, which he did not in fact reach until the night of 13 July.

Throughout 11 July the Axis air forces had made repeated attempts to attack the beach heads and massed shipping. 198 Italian and 283 German planes had been committed and particularly heavy attacks were made in the Seventh Army area. These attacks succeeded in sinking a transport and blowing up an ammunition ship and, during two particularly prolonged attacks, forced many of the transports to weigh anchor and disperse. The last of these concentrated attacks occurred at 2150 hours and it was almost an hour before the bombers were driven off, through the combined efforts of the Allied fighters and the anti-aircraft gunners on shore and aboard the circling ships. The confusion caused by this raid was to have tragic consequences.

Early on 11 July General Patton had decided to reinforce the Gela front by parachuting in 504 Combat Team, consisting of two battalions of paratroopers plus airborne artillery and engineers, the same night. The landing zone was to be the Gela-Farello airstrip and the route the same as two nights before. General Ridgway, commander of 82 Airborne Division, had previously failed to get a guarantee from the Navy that an air corridor over the sea would be cleared in the event of follow-up airborne operations. Obviously the planes would have to pass directly over shipping which was now assembled round the whole of the south-eastern portion of Sicily. He was assured, however, that 'if a follow-up air transport movement followed certain designated routes and made its last leg overland, the withholding of friendly naval fire could be guaranteed'.[11] In addition to the instructions based on this agreement, sent out from Allied Force headquarters, General Patton sent out at 0845 hours 11 July top priority orders that all units, and particularly the anti-aircraft gunners, should be told to expect the planes at about 2330 hours that night.

On their flight over the sea the force of two thousand paratroopers in 144

C-47s was in fact fired on as it passed over Allied shipping north of Malta, but fortunately the fire was from light weapons and no damage was done. On reaching the coast at Marina di Ragusa the formations turned north-west along the coastline as planned. The leading flight arrived over the dropping zone five minutes early at 2240 hours. The last of the enemy bombers had in fact only just been driven off, but at this moment all was calm and the sticks came floating down on to the airstrip. The second flight was about three miles behind, passing over the Biviere Pond, when a lone machine-gun opened up. Within moments the coastline was ablaze with anti-aircraft gun-fire, with the inshore craft adding their fire to the inferno above the beach heads. Only the first flight that had dropped their sticks a few minutes early escaped. 'The slow-flying, majestic columns of aircraft were like sitting ducks.'[12] Each successive formation that attempted to complete their approach run seemed to draw even more intense fire. Some pilots turned back, many dropped where they could, even into the sea, or turned east to drop over the British zone. The 'gauntlet' of fire now extended right along the coastal corridor and pilots who succeeded in reaching land and dropping their sticks still had to face the 'deadly hail of fire rising from the ships' as they turned for home. On shore and at sea control over the anti-aircraft gunners was lost. The Army Air Corps historian indeed records that 'some of the returning planes remained under fire for as much as twenty miles after they had left Sicily'.[13] Twenty-three aircraft were lost, more than half of the remainder were badly damaged. The 504 Combat Team suffered 229 casualties during the drop, and the next morning the force assembled at the landing zone amounted to one scratch rifle company and the equivalent of a battery of light howitzers. By the late afternoon of 12 July a total of 555 all ranks had been collected; the remaining 1,200 men were scattered over sixty miles of territory from Gela to the east coast. The subsequent inquiry into this disastrous operation was inconclusive. Lack of time for the issue of orders; lack of co-ordination between the services; a breakdown in communications; routing over an active battle front; all were named as contributory factors. General Ridgway was more definite – the lessons learnt with such deplorable loss of life must 'provide a basis for the belief that recurrence can be avoided'.[14]

On 12 July the Schmalz group of the Hermann Göring Division were fighting hard in the area of Priolo to check the British advance on Augusta. These counter-attacks were beaten off with naval and air support and 5 Division took Augusta that night. Meanwhile 30 Corps had reached Palazzolo with orders to advance on the axis Vizzini–Caltagirone the following day. The main British effort was to be an attack on 13/14 July from the Lentini area to break into the plain with the object of capturing Catania by 16 July. In the American sector the situation was steadily improving. At Gela the Americans mounted determined counter-attacks and by 13 July they held the airfield areas of Comiso, Biscari and Ponte Olivo, and 3 Division had pushed on as far as Canicatti. To give 30 Corps room to continue their sweep towards Caltagirone and Valguarnera, and avoid a clash with 45 Division's advance, General Alexander gave this road axis to the Canadians, as the main task of Seventh Army in the forthcoming phase was to prevent enemy reserves moving eastwards against the left flank of Eighth Army. This was an unpopular decision for General Patton who felt his troops were well placed to strike deeply inland in the same area. His instructions now were to pivot Seventh Army on its left flank, which was now about 15 miles short of Agrigento, and strengthen his grip on the central part of the island. On balance, casualties between 9–12 July were very much in the Allies' favour. The Italians had lost 132,000 men, including many prisoners of war, and the Germans 32,000 men. The Allied casualties were under 20,000. As far as the Allies were concerned the operations were developing as planned.

4
Sicily – The Door Jambs

German Reinforcements Dispatched: Axis Commanders in Disagreement: Parachutists at Primasole: The Etna Line: Capture of Palermo: Centuripe and Troina: Fall of Mussolini: Hitler's Reactions: Ambrosio's Delaying Tactics: Success of German Evacuation: Comparison of Casualties: Lessons of the Campaign.

1943	11 July	Hitler decides to dispatch reinforcements to Sicily.
	13 July	British parachute operations at Primasole Bridge.
	14 July	Naples and other ports bombed to stop supplies and reinforcements for Sicily.
	15 July	Patton forms Provisional Corps to clear western Sicily.
	16 July	Axis withdrawal to Etna Line. Alexander issues new directive.
	17 July	Eisenhower considering various alternatives for invasion of Italy.
	18/19 July	Hitler meets Mussolini at Feltre in northern Italy.
	22 July	Palermo captured – first supply ships berth 28 July.
	25 July	Fall of Mussolini – Badoglio takes over.
	31 July–3 Aug	78 Division storms Centuripe.
	1–6 Aug	Germans make stand at Troina. US 1 and 3 Divisions heavily engaged.
	6 Aug	Fall of Adrano – Germans in retreat from Catania line.
	8 Aug	American amphibious landing near Agata; Kesselring orders evacuation from Sicily.
	9 Aug	5 and 50 Divisions attack east of Etna.
	11 Aug	Germans start evacuation. Montgomery regroups in preparation for invasion of mainland.
	14 Aug	Quebec Conference (QUADRANT) opens.
	17 Aug	German evacuation complete – Allies enter Messina.

As late as 9 July, as we have seen, Hitler still thought Greece was the main objective, with possibly Sicily and Calabria being used as a springboard. The 29 Panzer Grenadier Division was now just north of Cosenza, the 26 Panzer Division in the area of Salerno and the 16 Panzer Division near Bari. Under the XIV Panzer Corps the German formations were to co-operate with the Italian Seventh Army in opposing an Allied landing in southern Italy. On 11 July Hitler decided to reinforce Sicily with 1 Parachute Division flown in from France. Headquarters XIV Panzer Corps, together with 29 Panzer Grenadier Division, would cross from the mainland as soon as possible. General Hube, the Corps Commander, would take command of all German units in the island. On the same day the First Secretary at the Italian Embassy in Berlin wrote, 'the news from Sicily is worse. The battle by now is considered lost. Silence from Rome over the most disturbing questions. No instructions at all.'[1] While the Italians longed for peace, Hitler tightened his grip over the situation and, with a cynical eye on Mussolini's waning power, retained 3 Panzer Grenadier Division and a complete Corps Headquarters (LXXVI) in the vicinity of Rome. He had already decided to ensure German control of the operations and the rapid dispatch of reinforcements, although not unexpected by the Allies, was to have an almost immediate effect on the development of the campaign. Kesselring flew in to consult with Guzzoni and von Senger on 12 July and to weigh up the situation. The same evening the first German parachute reinforcements landed south of Catania. Kesselring later wrote, 'My flight to Sicily yielded nothing but a headache' and he continued by briefly setting out his appreciation of the situation. He considered that the west of the island 'had no further tactical value and had to be abandoned', and the eastern part 'on an extended bridgehead round Etna could only be held for a short time'.[2] A third division, he felt, was urgently needed to consolidate this line. Kesselring claims that he had to persuade Hitler to transfer the whole of the 29 Panzer Grenadier Division immediately and blames the dilatoriness of the OKW for later retaining a part of the division in Calabria. General von Senger, however, sees Kesselring's insistence on accelerating the arrival of 29 Panzer Grenadier Division as an over-optimistic attempt to regain the initiative. Both he and Guzzoni were opposed to this reinforcement; they felt an early evacuation was inevitable and that the arrival of more troops would only make this more difficult. On his return, on 13 July, Kesselring telephoned to General Jodl. He reported that the situation was critical and that there was no longer a chance of counter-attacking the bridgeheads. The best thing, he said, was to fight for time, especially as he considered the loss of Sicily would seriously affect Italian determination to continue the war. Jodl told Hitler that he did not think that Sicily could be held for long, but Kesselring's view prevailed. So long as Mussolini was in power Hitler would support him, moreover Hitler's doctrine was to fight for every inch of territory occupied by German troops. Hube was ordered 'to delay the enemy advance as much as possible and bring it to a halt in front of Etna along a defence line running approximately from San Stefano via Adrano to Catania'.³ Hube was also given instructions, which were to be kept from the Italians, that he was to take over complete control, as unobtrusively as possible, of all operations in the Sicilian bridgehead. General Jodl added his own private instructions; Hube was to conduct the operations with a view to saving as much of the German force as possible. This too was to be kept from the Italians.

German suspicions that the Italians were 'looking over their shoulder' were well founded. Five days later (18 July) Mussolini sent a long telegram to Hitler saying, in effect, that Italy was exhausted by war and had had enough. Hitler's reaction was automatic: he would go and see Mussolini immediately and convince him of ultimate Axis victory. Once Mussolini's full support was ensured more German reinforcements would be offered. The meeting took place at Feltre in northern Italy at very short notice. Hitler opened the conference and spoke for two hours. He blamed the Italian ground staff for the disastrous losses of aircraft in Sicily. As to the defence of Italy, Hitler said he could not guarantee to hold any line south of the northern Apennines. It would be better to fight in Sicily and this was why he had already sent reinforcements there. If the Italians would support this policy and send two additional divisions to Sicily and southern Italy, the Germans would do the same, as well as reinforcing the flak defences at Messina. Mussolini, who was a sick man, kept silent. In private, his staff urged him to speak out and seize the opportunity of telling Hitler the truth; that the Italian people would not stand much more. This Mussolini would not do. The conference finished where it had started. Hitler demanded a pledge that Italy would stand and fight in Italy. On the way back from the conference to the airfield, Keitel made it clear to Ambrosio that Hitler's demands also meant an Italian guarantee of reinforcements and supplies, as well as complete freedom for Kesselring to put the south of Italy into a proper state of defence. Ambrosio in his turn made no promises, saying the matter must be decided by Mussolini. Such was the atmosphere of mutual mistrust that neither was prepared to speak openly; both indeed had too many secrets to guard.

Meanwhile the main Eighth Army thrust for Catania opened, on the evening of 13 July, with the dispatch of Commando and Parachute forces to seize the bridge at Lentine and the Primasole Bridge over the Simeto River, some seven miles short of Catania. The Commando units landed and seized the Lentine Bridge, removing the charges, but were driven off by a heavy German counter-attack. The attack on the Primasole Bridge by 1 Parachute Brigade involved a considerably larger force and a great deal of careful planning. At sunset on 13 July, 1,900 parachutists in 126 Dakota aircraft with anti-tank guns and their crews in 19 gliders (towed by RAF Halifaxes and Albemarles) assembled on North African landing strips between Kairouan and Sousse, south of Tunis. The route from Malta onwards was supposed to have been cleared but, in the light of the three-quarter moon, the compact formations found themselves flying over more and more Allied ships. Unfortunately the Luftwaffe had been making sporadic attacks since sundown on the massed ships off the south-east corner of the island and soon the Allied Transport Squadrons came under heavy fire from the friendly ships below. In the haze the gunners did not see the recognition signals fired above, some did not wait to see. 'Such a greeting was as unnerving as it was unexpected,'[4] and many pilots got seriously off course so that, on turning north-east near the Cape, they strayed into the five-mile-wide danger zone where the ships unloading immediately opened fire, or, having taken evasive action, found themselves over enemy-held ground where they were met with what appeared to be a wall of anti-aircraft fire. 'Twenty-seven aircraft carrying parachute troops lost their way, nineteen returned to base without dropping their passengers, and ten Dakotas, one Halifax and three Albemarles were shot down.'[5] Only thirty-nine aircraft succeeded in dropping within a mile of the bridge. Other sticks of parachutists were dropped as far away as the slopes of Etna twenty miles off target. Some unfortunate plane-loads were ordered to jump while the aircraft were still over the sea. Soon after 0215 hours on 14 July a small party of an officer and about fifty men seized the bridge without great difficulty. Throughout the night parties of British parachutists moved in on the bridge from the surrounding countryside where they had been scattered on dropping. At dawn Brigadier Lathbury, who had already been wounded, set about preparing for the inevitable German counter-attack. His force for the defence of the north end of the bridge now amounted to two hundred and fifty all ranks and three anti-tank guns. To the south of the bridge, part of the Brigade had been given the task of capturing three hill features which dominated the approaches from that direction. The first of these objectives was held by a separate body of about two hundred and fifty men, which was all that could be collected from a complete battalion that had left North Africa the night before. The Germans, however, had also chosen the night of 13/14 July to drop the redoubtable 4 Parachute Regiment as reinforcements for the Catania sector. Some of the sub-units were in fact dropped on the same landing zones chosen by the British – consequently the first counter-attack came in south of the bridge instead of from the north as expected. Throughout the day the Germans attacked from both the north and the south with increasing ferocity and by evening the surviving defenders had been forced back to the south end of the bridge and were virtually without ammunition. Brigadier Lathbury ordered the remnants of his force to fall back, as soon as it was completely dark, on the covering party to the south, who themselves had been heavily attacked on three sides. All that day 50 Division with 4 Armoured Brigade had been fighting desperately to reach the bridge. At one point Augusta was temporarily lost and strong enemy forces in the area of Catania were only forced back by an outflanking tank attack. Finally, during the early hours of 15 July, the leading battalion of 50 Division, supported by tanks, reached the survivors of 1 Parachute Brigade who were still holding out in a position covering the southern end of the bridge. A tank and infantry attack to regain the bridge failed, but that night the infantry succeeded in crossing the river under cover of darkness and at dawn on 16 July the bridge was captured. It was, however, not until the following day that a shallow bridgehead could be consolidated on the north bank of the river. British casualties in the five days' fighting for the bridge amounted to 450.

The violence of the German counter-attacks was an indication of their realization that the Eighth Army advance on the direct coast road to Messina must be delayed at all costs to allow time for the occupation of the Etna line. The Hermann Göring Division was already deployed to cover the line of the River Dittaino, but 15 Panzer Grenadiers only started reconnoitring the western part of the Etna position on 16 July. Eighth Army by now were advancing on a wide front against increasing German resistance. In the centre 51 Division was up to the south banks of the Dittaino and 231 Brigade were north of Raddusa in contact with the remnants of the Livorno Division. The Canadians had taken Piazza Armerina and were fighting their way towards Enna, which was held in strength by 15 Panzer Grenadiers. On 15 July Patton set up a provisional corps, consisting of 3 Infantry Division and 82 Airborne Division and 4 Tabor of Goums, to operate on his left flank. With the remainder of his forces under II Corps he struck north towards Enna and Sante Caterina, in an attempt to contain the Germans who were moving back across the Seventh Army front. While these operations were developing, the German XIV Panzer Corps Headquarters and infantry and tank reinforcements were starting to arrive, and it was clearly the Germans' intention to cover Messina by holding the Etna line. This tactic would also deny the Allies the use of the airfields around Catania. The difficulties facing Alexander were formidable. The whole of the Messina peninsula was mountainous with extremely poor roads and the southern slopes of Etna dominated the plain between Gerbini and Catania. Moreover, the narrow coastal strip to the east of Etna was not only completely overlooked from steep ridges, that descended like an opened fan towards the sea, but was itself ideal defensive country. Here there were innumerable stone walls enclosing vineyards and olive groves which gave admirable cover for infantry and guns, as well as concealment for tanks in ambush positions. To an attacking force flank movement was impossible and tanks and vehicles were largely confined to the coast road itself. For the Allies speed was essential, for if given any breathing space the Germans would take full advantage of the natural strength of the Etna positions. General Alexander's new directive of 16 July sought to bring the Eighth Army's left column round north of Etna on two axes, Leonforte to Adrano and Leonforte to Troina and Randazzo. At the same time a strong attack was directed on Catania on the Army's right flank. The Seventh Army was to protect the rear of the attack and seize Enna, and then cut the east-west road at Petralia.

In spite of the almost continuous bombardment of the routes into the Catania sector by the Allied air forces, the Hermann Göring Division had now been reinforced by no less than six battalions of parachutists and two 'fortress' battalions rushed over from Calabria. Consequently the attack by 50 Division across the Simeto River on the night of 17/18 July 'met very strong resistance, and made little progress. The ground on this front was open but intersected with watercourses which made difficult the employment of our armour.'[6] On 19 July General Montgomery switched his attack to the left towards Misterbianco, but 5 Division met the same heavy resistance. Now 51 Division advanced (on 20 July) across the Dittaino River towards the Gerbini airfields, only to be thrown back on 21 July. Meanwhile the Canadians were making some progress, 'but it was now clear that Eighth Army would not have the strength to encircle Etna on both sides against the strong resistance of the Germans'.[7] The Canadians were therefore ordered to advance on Leonforte and then turn east to Adrano. Also on 20 July 78 Division was ordered forward from North Africa. The task of striking wide round the north of Etna was now given to Seventh Army and, as a preparatory move, General Patton was instructed (on 18 July) to press on after the capture of Petralia to cut the northern coast road and mop up the whole of the western part of the island. Unfortunately by this time 15 Panzer Grenadiers had succeeded in extracting themselves and, having scrambled across Seventh Army front, were now in action against the extreme left of the Eighth Army. General Patton executed this wide sweeping manoeuvre with considerable dash. Palermo was reached on 22 July and the coast road was cut at Termini Imerese the following day. Although the Italians put up little resistance (36,000 prisoners were taken during these operations) it was a considerable feat for the American infantry columns marching under a sweltering sun. The port of Palermo was quickly opened to supply the American divisions, and to keep up the pressure on the north coast road Patton brought in his reserve division (9 Division) direct by sea to Palermo. With a fresh division now in position on both flanks, Alexander fixed 1 August as the date for the final drive on Messina by the two armies.

In the central sector the Canadians and 231 Brigade reached Agira by 28 July and the following night 78 Division with a Canadian Brigade attacked and captured Catenanuovo and, fighting their way on, crossed the Dittaino River. Ahead was Centuripe, a hill town set on a very high rocky pinnacle and approached by only one steep and twisty road. Centuripe itself was the key to the whole Adrano position and the capture of Adrano would in turn force the Germans to withdraw from the whole of the Catania sector of the Etna line. On the night of 1 August the 78 Division attack went in, to be met by fanatical resistance from troops of the Hermann Göring Division and 3 Parachute Regiment. For over thirty-six hours the battle was fought out in the steep cobbled streets and shattered houses, until finally the town was taken on the morning of 3 August and the German survivors withdrew back over the Salso River. As Alexander wrote in his report, 'The storming of Centuripe was a particularly fine feat and its effects were widespread, for from that time the front once more became fluid. In face of the threat to Adrano the enemy position became untenable.'[8] With four divisions Montgomery struck at the German line from Catania to Adrano and 'with the fall of the latter (on 6 August) the main defence line across north-eastern Sicily was broken and the enemy was now in retreat in all sectors'.[9] On the Seventh Army front Patton had pressed his divisions to the limit, using both the coast road and the parallel road through Gangi and Nicosia. The two leading divisions were relieved every few days and on 3 August the situation was that 3 Division was advancing east from San Stefano towards San Fratello and 1 Division was meeting increasingly fierce resistance in its attempts to take Troina.

Aerial reconnaissance had previously reported much activity in the area of Cesaro, but only troop movement through Troina, which was thought to be lightly held. In fact Seventh Army were now right up against 29 Panzer Grenadiers, holding the coastal sector at San Fratello, and strong elements of 15 Panzer Grenadier Division astride Route 120 through Troina, which was the key to the whole sector. The hill formations in this area were such that movement off the road was extremely difficult and the last two and a half miles of the approaches to the town itself were dominated by features that could be held by relatively small forces and which gave excellent observation against any outflanking movement. The initial attack at regimental strength was thrown back and bitter fighting continued for four days (until 6 August) before General Hube decided to withdraw to a shorter line. 'Troina . . . was one of the most fiercely fought smaller actions of the war. The enemy launched twenty-four separate counter-attacks during the battle.'[10] On the coast road 29 Panzer Grenadier Division had put up an equally stubborn resistance. General Hube, however, hoped to gain a week by a phased withdrawal to a shorter line from Giarre (on the east coast) across Etna to Randazzo and Cape Orlando, with 29 Panzer Grenadier Division holding on to San Fratello as long as possible. Bringing up the fresh 9 Division, Patton captured Cesaro on 8 July and a brilliantly mounted small amphibious operation, put in behind the German lines, led to the capture of Santa Agata. In the central sector Randazzo was now the key. The decision to evacuate Sicily had by now been taken and through Randazzo ran the last lateral road connecting with the two coast roads to Messina on which many units must withdraw.

The overthrow of Mussolini on 25 July, coming only ten days after Hitler's decision to reinforce Sicily, not only caught the Allies unprepared but 'came as a complete surprise to Hitler'.[11] Urgent decisions were needed. The following day a conference was called at Hitler's headquarters. All the Service and Party Chiefs were present. Rommel, who had been appointed C-in-C of the whole of the South-Eastern theatre, with command of all German and Italian forces in the area, had arrived in Greece only two days before to inspect the defences and was hurriedly flown back from Salonika. Hitler's first reaction to the news of Mussolini's fall was disbelief that he had resigned voluntarily – he must be found and restored to power; Rome must be seized by a swift blow and the King, Marshal Badoglio and the entire Cabinet kidnapped. Hitler in his anger even considered seizing the Vatican and only the intervention of Goebbels and Ribbentrop dissuaded him from these extreme measures. Rommel advocated a withdrawl from Sicily, Sardinia and southern Italy to enable northern Italy to be held in strength. After the conference he wrote, 'we can expect Italy to get out of the war, or at the very best the British to undertake further landings in northern Italy' and when the Italian Minister Farinacci arrived to tell Hitler to 'expect Italy to make armistice proposals in a week or ten days' he comments 'the British may then land at Genoa and Leghorn'.[12] Hitler met the situation with ruthless determination to take over complete control in Italy, retaining if possible the co-operation of the Italians but otherwise by force. Rommel would take over Army Group B. The two divisions already moving towards the Italian frontier would be reinforced by four more from France. II SS Panzer Corps, of two SS Panzer Divisions, would be withdrawn from the Eastern Front and join Rommel's command. Meanwhile, the Alpine passes would be taken over by troops from a Mountain Training School near Innsbruck. General Student was to be dispatched to take over command of the two divisions in the Rome area, seize the capital and arrest the government. Mussolini must be found and liberated and Hitler personally chose Captain Skorzeny for this secret mission. The moment Student was ready to seize Rome, Rommel would take command of all the troops in north Italy and Kesselring would pull out from Sardinia, Corsica and Sicily and join Rommel in the north. Southern Italy would be abandoned and Kesselring's command in Italy would fold up. Kesselring received precise instructions, through a naval officer dispatched to Frascati on 26 July, to stop all reinforcements to Sicily and to prepare to evacuate all air force units from the three islands. He was also ordered to concentrate the 16 and 26 Panzer Grenadier Divisions, which were still on the mainland, so as to be ready to move north. Kesselring was also told to send all the aircraft he could find to bring 2 Parachute Division from France to Rome to take part in the coup. The King, backed by Badoglio and Ambrosio, took good care to deceive the Germans as far as possible as to their real intentions and maintained a front of continued alliance and co-operation with the Germans. Kesselring, optimistic and trusting by nature, was completely taken in and reported back to the OKW advising a cautious handling of the situation. He argued that military action against Rome would completely destroy any good will remaining between the Axis partners and, furthermore, would so disrupt the lines of communication that his forces in the south might get cut off. He felt it would be better to exploit the Italians' apparent willingness to receive German units and fight it out with the Allies. If he received reinforcements he felt he could hold all Italy as well as the Balkans. Although Hitler suspected Badoglio of 'planning treason' he only now began to suspect just how far matters had gone, and that the proposed conference between the King and the Fuehrer had only been suggested to give the Italians a chance of trying to persuade Germany to join them in seeking a joint peace with the Allies. Soon, however, he became convinced that Allied peace negotiations were under way; so he decided to play along with Kesselring's suggestions, if only to help allay Italian suspicions and their (very understandable) reluctance to open their frontiers to the considerable German forces now moving towards the passes. For several days, while the OKW completed their plans, this cat-and-mouse game was played out in the Chancelleries and Supreme Headquarters of the crumbling partnership.

Kesselring's efforts to move in more divisions as reinforcements, as had earlier been requested by the Commando Supremo, were now frustrated by 'difficulties over railway congestion' or 'shortage of rolling stock'. Tension on the frontier mounted, but Badoglio was still playing for time to foster his prime intention of making 'the Germans realize Italy's plight and the need for a common effort to terminate the war'.[13] So Ambrosio was told quite bluntly to avoid any action that would bring the German and Italian armies into open conflict. Consequently, when the OKW moved units forward into Italy on their own transport, without waiting for rail facilities, the advance of Army Group B was unopposed by the frontier posts and by 2 August the German formations were beginning to fan out over northern Italy. Within another four days 2 Parachute Division was concentrated near Rome. The Germans explained this apparent haste to bring in reinforcements by pointing out that 'the political changes in Italy might encourage the Allies to use an estimated thirteen to fifteen available divisions on the Ligurian or north Adriatic coasts. OKW therefore thought it prudent to provide for the security of all forces by moving divisions first into the north, then into the south.'[14] The Italians, sensitive to the proximity of the fresh German divisions to their northern naval bases and seeking both to reduce the threat to Rome and to have some kind of shield against an Allied invasion, pressed the Germans to move their divisions further south. In reply OKW proposed a co-ordinating conference on 6 August at Tarvis. Meanwhile the Commando Supremo continued to co-operate somewhat warily, both in the defence of Sicily and in preparation for an invasion of the south of Italy.

At this very moment the Italian emissaries D'Ayeta and Benio were in contact with the Allies through diplomatic channels in Lisbon and Tangiers. While General Ambrosio was in Badoglio's confidence, the Army Chief of Staff, Roatta, knew nothing of these moves. Roatta's genuine protestations of good faith further deceived Kesselring, who still advocated the Axis holding what was left of Sicily and thereby tying down up to twelve Allied Divisions. Kesselring argued that, in any event, premature action against Rome and the Government would force an immediate withdrawal from Sicily and the South. What he needed urgently was at least three more divisions to guard against Allied landings in Calabria, Puglia and the bays of Naples and Salerno. General Jodl took the completely opposite view, that had earlier been put forward by Rommel, and proposed an immediate withdrawal to north Italy. Hitler, however, was intent on rescuing Mussolini and wished the pretence of good faith towards the Badoglio Government to be kept up. While Hitler was prepared to send reinforcements to the south of Italy, equally he could not decide to withdraw from Sicily. On these notes of uncertainty and mutual mistrust the Tarvis Conference opened, with the two countries represented by their respective Foreign Ministers and Chiefs of Staff.

The Italians tried to get agreement that their troops should be brought back from France and the Balkans and also tried to force a discussion on the redeployment of the German forces in Italy away from Rome and the naval bases, but Keitel would not listen to their arguments. The Italians were in reality playing for time to see how the Allies reacted to their overtures. In the end nothing was decided. The Germans gave nothing away and, in their anxiety, the Italians gave formal acceptance of the German moves through the frontier passes. Thirty thousand German troops had in fact passed through the Brenner Pass alone. Rommel was not deceived by the Italian proposals which he describes as 'a delaying action' and on 7 August he noted that the Italians were reinforcing their troops on the Brenner, while on the following day he recorded in his diary that the Italians had set up road blocks in the area of Spezia 'to prevent German troops occupying the naval base'. Ambrosio's worst fears were being realized. Germany obviously intended keeping Italy in the war at pistol point. To Hitler the defence of Germany was all that mattered and Ambrosio saw his country becoming one vast battlefield. Ambrosio now speeded up the redeployment of Italian divisions, the early moves of which had been spotted by Rommel. An Alpine Division was ordered back from Calabria to reinforce the Brenner. Two divisions were ordered from Turin to the Spezia area. More troops were sent to Rome with orders to guard the city against German interference. In Ambrosio's opinion the situation was critical and, with the King's approval, Roatta, who at first objected, was told to issue precise orders that all military posts, and civilian and military installations, must be safeguarded against German attack. If the Germans attacked first, commanders were to bring their troops into action immediately, otherwise this would only be done on orders from Roatta's Headquarters. On 9 August Rommel wrote in his diary, '10.45 hours General von Vietinghoff reported back from the Fuehrer, having been given command of both corps in southern Italy. The Fuehrer intends to evacuate southern Italy and "will not be happy until the divisions in southern Italy and Sicily are standing south of Rome". He does not anticipate a British landing in southern Italy (because of the malaria danger). He no longer trusts the Italian promises. Co-operation between Kesselring and von Vietinghoff will probably not be easy, as Kesselring's idea is to put as many German troops down south as possible.'[15]

On 8 August Patton's Seventh Army took San Fratello and Cesaro. Eighth Army took Bronte and was eight miles north of Catania, trying to break through on the coast road. General von Senger saw Kesselring and impressed on him the seriousness of the situation. Kesselring could no longer justify his optimistic arguments for drawing out the campaign. Hube was ordered to evacuate his troops in accordance with the plans that had been completed seven days previously. Westphal was to tell the Commando Supremo what was happening and Jodl told Hitler, presenting the decision as a *fait accompli*. Guzzoni considered fighting on alone with what was left of the mobile divisions, but received orders to conform to the German plan and pull back to Calabria. As far as the Germans were concerned, the night of 11 August would be the first of five nights during which their forces would be ferried over the straits. The Germans were taking no chances at Messina. By now there were about 500 guns mounted to protect the crossings from air and sea attack. An inter-service command was organized under Colonel Baade, and included ten batteries of coastal defence guns and 350 anti-aircraft (dual purpose) guns, including some borrowed from 15 Panzer Grenadier Division. A ferry service on four routes was organized with thirty-three naval barges, twelve Siebel (10-ton flat-bottomed) ferries, thirteen lighters and small landing craft and seventy-six motorboats. Each night 8,000 German troops were to be ferried across, but the evacuation of tanks, guns and equipment was to continue round the clock. As regards vehicles, the German units left Sicily with more than they brought in, having taken what they wanted from their Allies! The Italians themselves had started pulling out troops as early as 3 August. On 10 August, Guzzoni handed over to General Hube and moved his Headquarters across to the mainland, where he took over responsibility for the defence of part of Calabria. His troops were to follow as best they could on four routes independently of the Germans. The only means of crossing left for the Italians was one train ferry (taking 3,000 men on each trip), two small steamboats and four motor rafts. Heavy equipment could only cross on German craft if space was made available.

On 11 August Jodl and Rommel discussed the urgent problem of ensuring German operational control in Italy. Owing to the delicate political situation Rommel's headquarters still had not crossed the frontier and Jodl at first proposed that Rommel should now assume command in the north. Rommel, however, got agreement that the time had come for him to take complete charge over all Axis troops in Italy. At the Fuehrer's conference that evening Rommel's plan was approved; this was to continue delaying actions in Sicily and meanwhile 'to construct four defence lines (1) Cosenza–Taranto (2) Salerno (3) Cassino (4) a rearward line in the Apennines'.[16] Although Hitler now realized 'that all the Italians were doing was trying to gain time so as to get out of the war in the end', he was still intent on the release of Mussolini and the reinstatement of Fascism. Jodl and Rommel were therefore sent off to Bologna, which they reached on 15 August, to confer with General Roatta. Rommel, having been warned he might be poisoned or seized by the Italians, took along a company of Grenadiers. Jodl wanted to know why Italian divisions had been hurriedly withdrawn from France and others moved up from the south of Italy. He insisted that in any case German supply lines must be under German control. By this time both sides were in no doubt as to the intentions behind the German troop dispositions and occupation programme in Italy. During the conference Roatta would not give an inch of ground and, when the discussion was finally brought round to the grouping of German and Italian forces for the defence of the country, his proposal was to reinforce Sardinia and the south of Italy with the maximum number of German divisions with Commando Supremo in overall command. Perhaps he knew the Germans would never agree to this. The conference was a complete failure. The last grains of sand were running out and only days remained to the uneasy partnership.

In Sicily, by 13 August, 50 and 51 Divisions of Eighth Army were advancing from Riposto on the east coast road against determined resistance from the Hermann Göring Division. In the central sector 9 Division had captured Randazzo, with the assistance of 78 Division operating to the south of the town, and Floresta. In the north, 3 Division, supported by a seaborne landing, had nearly succeeded in cutting off part of 29 Panzer Division at Brolo and were now coming up against the first of Hube's three phased stop lines about Falcone. The Germans had no difficulty in holding these three lines, which were laid out to allow for a night withdrawal of about ten miles to a shorter line across the peninsula. The Allied advance was now forced on to the two narrow coast roads. These were heavily mined in numerous places and some parts, of several hundred yards in length, were completely blown away. In one particularly narrow stretch of the coast road, where on the sea side there was a sheer drop to the sea and on the inland side high cliffs, the Germans had blown thousands of tons of rock from the cliff face to fall on about four hundred yards of the road which was completely blocked. A Canadian tunnelling unit was urgently flown out from England and, in an astonishingly short time of about four days, achieved a tunnel right through the rock and re-opened the road.

The focus was now on the Straits of Messina. Here the evacuation routes had only two and a half miles of water to cross and were concentrated in the area between Messina harbour and Cape Peloro, about five miles to the north. Admiral Barone, the Italian naval commander on the spot, estimated that the coastal and dual-purpose guns ranged on this strip of sea totalled 150 at the height of the evacuation. Captain Roskill, the British Naval historian, comments that this is probably an under-estimate, adding that any warship entering the area would also be in range of a large number of smaller calibre guns making the task of protracted patrols quite suicidal. The problem of attacking the Straits from the air was somewhat different but no less difficult. The flak defences around the Messina crossing were of such concentration and intensity as to inhibit low-flying attacks. Heavy bombers could fly above much of the defensive fire but their capacity to even check the flow of men and equipment, embarking in small craft and crossing from a number of insignificant harbours and loading hards, depended upon the attack being almost continuous and very carefully co-ordinated. A week before the evacuation really got under way Alexander asked about naval and air plans to attack the obvious escape route through Messina. Admiral Cunningham said the operation of light craft at night in the Straits would be intensified and suggested the Air Force should operate 'without let or hindrance' over the whole of the Straits, and 'as the coast batteries are mopped up it will be possible for surface forces to operate further into the Straits'.[17] Tedder agreed and wanted operations started at once; so consultations between the various air commands began. Air Marshal Coningham's appreciation at this time was that evacuation would be mostly by night and that considerable air opposition would be met with over the Straits. Thus the problem was rather to prevent night crossing when 'only a positive physical barrier, such as the Navy can provide, would be effective'. At the beginning of August General Doolittle's heavy bombers of the Strategic Air Force were excluded from the operations over Messina, as the whole force was to be used against communications and airfields in Sardinia, Calabria and further up the peninsula as far as the Lorenzo marshalling yards near Rome. These attacks, of course, were intended to pave the way for the Allied assault on the mainland. This embargo on the use of the heavy bombers at Messina was lifted between 5 and 9 August, when three daylight raids were made by Flying Fortresses on Messina harbour. These attacks were supplemented by night bombardment using Wellingtons, flying an average of eighty-five sorties each night on Messina itself and the harbour. By 14 August Alexander felt the evacuation had really begun, but by now the Strategic Air Force was too deeply committed to their programme against targets on the mainland and only medium and light bombers, together with some fighter and fighter-bomber squadrons, were released to help the Tactical Air Force in their round-the-clock attacks. Indeed the Tactical Air Force had only received orders the day previously 'that evacuation is held to have begun and that all sorties were to be directed against ships, barges and beaches',[18] but by the evening of that day 15,000 Germans, with much of their transport, and a considerable number of Italians had already crossed. The night attacks by the Wellingtons caused some disruption on the shorter routes and after 13 August German troops were ferried over during daylight, while on the longer routes crossing continued by both day and night. The Germans indeed were completely mystified by the absence of heavy bomber attacks by day and made full use of the situation. Colonel Baade's massed anti-aircraft guns threw up such an intensive fire that it was described as being 'heavier than the Ruhr'. In consequence the mounting efforts of the Tactical Air Force brought very meagre results. As an example of the effort being made, 270 fighter-bomber and 47 medium bomber sorties were flown on 16 August. From figures subsequently given by the Axis, fifteen craft were sunk and six damaged between 3–16 August. Allied claims for the same period were twenty-three craft destroyed and forty-three hit. On the night 16 August an American patrol entered Messina. Before the two converging Allied columns entered the city the following morning, however, the last ferry had left and a well-planned and skilfully conducted operation had resulted in the evacuation of 39,569 German troops with 9,605 vehicles, 47 tanks and 94 guns, together with 17,000 tons of ammunition. These figures are as reported by Field Marshal Kesselring, but some authorities put the number of Germans who escaped from Sicily as high as 60,000. In addition about 62,000 Italians, with some of their guns and vehicles, succeeded in escaping over the Straits.

The Axis casualties on all counts during the thirty-nine days of the land campaign amounted to 164,000. The total German casualties are estimated at 32,000 and the Italians lost about 132,000 men, the majority of whom became prisoners of war. The total Allied casualties were 31,158. During the actual land campaign 15 Army Group battle casualties were under 20,000, about 9,000 in the Eighth Army and 8,375 in Seventh Army. In the air the Allies had achieved a very high degree of air supremacy with relatively low losses. Including the preparatory bombardment of the Sicilian airfields, the Allied air forces lost less than 400 planes. The Axis lost a total of 1,850 aircraft, 740 of which were destroyed in the air, and over 1,100 (including 600 aircraft of the Luftwaffe) were strewn all over Sicily having been destroyed or damaged on the ground. In a telegram to London on 18 August Tedder underlined the high degree of co-operation achieved between the Allied air forces. 'The outstanding feature of the whole operation was the ability of two air forces – American and British – supported by certain French and Polish units, operating from mainland and island bases covering a front of some 2,000 miles, to integrate their operations and achieve the intense concentration of effort which contributed vitally to the success of the whole operation.'[19] There is no doubt that the intensive air assault on the Axis airfields and installations in the weeks before D-day brought high dividends. The Axis air strength was so reduced when the assault went in that on D−1 and D-day only twelve ships were lost. The Allies had been prepared for losses of up to 300 ships in this period.

The pattern of air operations developed by the Allies for Sicily were later to be used again both in the Mediterranean and European theatres. First the launching of an offensive against enemy airfields and lines of communication; then the protection of the seaborne passage and assault and of the beach heads themselves; followed by the isolation of the battlefield by attacks on communication centres, combined with direct support of the land battle. As the campaign developed the Strategic Air Force would again stretch out to pound the enemy airfields and communications in preparation for the next move forward. In Sicily two lessons were learnt the hard way. On the Seventh Army front no close air support was used during the first forty-eight hours of the landing and no close support missions were actually flown until 13 July. The total absence of close air support against the German tank attacks at Gela caused a good deal of bitterness among the GIs fighting to keep their foothold on the beaches. As a result of this experience the cumbersome methods for calling for air support, which led to delays and many missions being cancelled, were improved and light bomber squadrons were added to the American Tactical Air Component. Secondly, it must be acknowledged that during the evacuation period, which resulted in such a high proportion of the *élite* Axis forces escaping to the mainland, only half of the total strength of the North African Strategic Air Force was employed against the evacuation targets and then only in a very limited manner. Admittedly the bombing of Italian cities at this time must have helped the Italian Government make up its mind that they ought to get out of the war quickly, and this long-range bombing equally fitted in with General Eisenhower's plans for an advance to the mainland, but the fact remains that a very high proportion of the German troops in Sicily escaped and it can be argued that a better co-ordinated and full-strength air assault against the evacuation points in the Straits of Messina, both by day and night, might have brought higher dividends in the long run. The physical separation of the principal Allied headquarters at the end of the Sicilian campaign undoubtedly made proper co-operation extremely difficult. Tedder has commented: 'I do not think that the separation of the Commanders-in-Chief between the mainland and the island (of Malta) seriously affected our co-ordination. Nevertheless, there was no doubt that it was undesirable for us to be separated for long periods. This was particularly the case now that the landings were established, when we were all so anxious to push on with the next move, or rather, to follow up hard. Since 13 July I had been trying to get Alexander to come back with his Heads of Departments so that his headquarters could once again become a live organization with whom we could do business.'[20]

The airborne operations were a great disappointment to the Allies. It is significant, however, that the Axis commanders took almost the opposite view. The widespread pockets of determined paratroopers and glider-borne forces on the night before the landings caused considerable confusion and destroyed many of the remaining means of communication. Unlike the Germans, who after Crete never used their parachute troops in their prime role again, the Allies were not disheartened in their efforts to develop their airborne forces, although Eisenhower at one point seriously considered recommending that the airborne divisions should be broken up. There is no doubt that the lack of training of many tug and glider pilots, combined with complicated routes, were major factors contributing to the failure to land the airborne troops with any kind of cohesion. The insistence of the naval forces that they fire at all aircraft within range at night is indeed understandable when one recalls the desperate battles to get the convoys through that had been fought not only in the Mediterranean but in the Pacific and the Atlantic. The lesson that emerged was that much more time was needed to plan and co-ordinate routes, so that all naval and ground forces were properly briefed and warned of the arrival overhead of the troop-carrying squadrons. After the war an interesting comment was made by General Student on the extra-ordinary coincidence of the German Parachute battalions dropping on virtu-ally the same landing zone in the Primasole Bridge area during the British glider-borne attack. General Student had in fact proposed dropping two parachute divisions to counter-attack the beach heads. 'But Hitler turned this down – Jodl in particular was against it. So the 1st Parachute Division was merely flown to Italy . . . and soon sent on to Sicily – for use as ground troops to reinforce the scanty German forces which were there when the Italian troops began to collapse *en masse*. The Division was flown by air in successive lifts and dropped behind our front in the eastern sector south of Catania. I had wanted them to be dropped behind the Allied front. The first contingent was dropped about three kms behind our front . . . and landed almost simultaneously with the British parachute troops.'[21]

As already mentioned the Allied naval forces suffered remarkably small losses. Nineteen German U-boats and forty-five Italian submarines were in the Mediterranean when HUSKY started. In the three weeks from D-day onwards, U-boats sank four British merchantmen and two American LSTs and damaged two cruisers and three merchantmen. During the same period three U-boats were sunk by Allied destroyers and patrol boats. The Italian Navy were less successful as no Allied merchantman was sunk by an Italian submarine during the whole of 1943 and ten of their submarines were sunk or captured. The enemy air attacks were more serious. During July eight Allied ships were lost (total tonnage 54,306 tons) from air attacks. These losses mainly fell on the Eastern Task Force, which between D-day and the end of the month lost three landing craft and six merchantmen (totalling 41,509 tons), sunk in or near the assault area, while a fleet carrier, several destroyers together with four landing craft and three merchantmen were damaged by air action. During the same period the Western Task Force 'lost a destroyer, a minesweeper, two LSTs and a merchant ship (7,176 tons) sunk and a few transports, minesweepers and LSTs damaged – mostly superficially by near misses'.[22]

The American Navy, in particular, were critical of the lack of tactical bomber support and close fighter patrolling over the assault areas, but it must be remembered they had the worst of the storm conditions in landing and almost immediately faced serious counter-attacks. There is little doubt that after the initial landing period the Germans were far more sensitive over the Catania front; hence the far heavier losses from air attack suffered by Admiral Ramsay's ships. The overall picture, however, was that Allied air power so dominated the whole area of operations that, as Admiral Cunningham wrote in his dispatch, it appeared 'almost magical that great fleets of ships could remain anchored on the enemy's coast within forty miles of the main aerodromes with only such slight losses . . . as were incurred'. A feature of the campaign was the effective use of naval gun-fire against land targets. The successes of the American warships against the German tank attack at Gela have already been mentioned. On the British sector some two hundred calls for gun support were answered by British bombardment ships during HUSKY, the fire from the two 15-inch monitors being particularly demoralizing to the enemy.

As regards Allied strategy during the development of the campaign, the decision by General Alexander to develop a two-pronged attack on the Etna positions and give the Caltagirone–Leonforte route to the Canadians, which necessitated the pulling back and diverting of 45 Division from their direct route towards Enna, has been much criticized. Up to this point (12/13 July) the campaign had developed as planned, with Eighth Army set on the rapid capture of Catania and the Gerbini complex and the Seventh Army linking up with and protecting the left flank of Eighth Army. Alexander's intention was to seize the road centres of Enna and Caltanissetta and follow this with a drive on Nicosia with the object of splitting the island in half. At this point the Germans reinforced their Catania front and were intent on getting their Panzer columns back to the Etna line. General Bradley felt that he was well placed to advance directly on the Enna road centre, using Route 124 for 45 Division with 1 Division on its left. Both armies in fact were seeking to apply pressure on a swing door hinged on the Catania coastal road. Lord Montgomery has supported his left hooks from this hinge saying, 'to persist in the thrust towards Catania would have meant very heavy casualties and I was by no means convinced that success would follow this expenditure of life. Furthermore I did not wish to blunt the weapon when it was clear that much hard fighting lay ahead on the mainland of Europe. The object could be achieved with less loss of life by operating on the Adrano axis with the added advantage that on that flank we would be in close touch with our American Allies.'[23] General Eisenhower's comment is of interest. 'Montgomery's operations on the east coast had begun auspiciously and for a few days it looked as if Alexander's hopes might be realized. But by the time Montgomery was ready to assault the natural defensive barriers running from Mount Etna to the sea the enemy had brought up too much strength. The chance for a *coup de main* passed if it had ever existed . . . thereafter the northward path of the Eighth Army was fully as difficult from the terrains viewpoint as the eastern advance on their left of the Seventh Army. In addition the Eighth Army had to overcome the preponderance of enemy strength . . . I believed then and believe now a headlong attack against the Mount Etna position with the resources available in the middle of July would have been defeated.'[24] The road pattern in the centre of the island must have made any decision on the employment of the American divisions in the area north or east of Enna at this stage extremely difficult from an administrative point of view. The decision to clear the west of the island and use Palermo to supply Seventh Army's advance on a two-road axis was an obvious solution. The two American seaborne landings ahead of their advance on the north coast road were very successful and it has been suggested that such 'end runs' might have been employed on the Eighth Army flank. Captain Roskill, however, points out that 'north of Catania the coast becomes so precipitous and the few beaches have such poor exits that it was scarcely possible to land or deploy a substantial assault force'.[25] An added difficulty would have been the disengaging of the necessary troops, already committed on a wide front. Captain Roskill argues, however, that greater use might have been made of raids by 'comparatively small forces to harass and discourage the traffic on the coastal road and railway'. In fact two such operations were planned but later cancelled and the one landing that was made, on 15/16 August, was too late to be of value.

On the administrative side the Allies were very well served. Maintenance over the beaches was particularly successful and the rate of discharge was higher than anticipated. The DUKWs proved a marked success. The Germans carried out very extensive bridge, road and rail demolitions. As has already been mentioned, whole sections of the coast road, particularly where it was built *en cornice*, were blown into the sea or blocked for hundreds of yards by large quantities of rock fall. The work of the Allied engineers in competing with the demolitions, in bridging extensive gaps and mending the communications, in dealing with minefields and literally thousands of booby-traps was brilliantly carried out. Excellent work was also done by the movement staffs and transportation units in speedily opening up the ports. The landing and dispatch of the follow-up convoys was arranged by a special inter-service staff called 'Ferry Control' and the experience gained proved invaluable for the future. This special staff set-up was the forerunner of 'Build-up Control Organization' which was so successfully employed for the Normandy operations. From a medical point of view the most serious problem was the incidence of malaria. During the campaign the losses from this disease affecting the two Allied Armies rose to the alarming total amounting to the effective strength of two divisions and exceeded those from battle casualties, as the following table shows:

Losses by	Seventh Army	Eighth Army
Malaria	9,892	11,590
Battle Casualties	8,375	9,000 (approx.)[26]

The Director of Medical Services at Eisenhower's Headquarters, from whose report these figures were taken, pointed out that many cases developed in the concentration areas in North Africa. Many men had to be left behind and nearly a thousand cases developed in the first fortnight after the landings in Sicily, being of North African origin. In Sicily itself the Lentini and Catania plains were intensely malarious areas. Battle conditions made it difficult to take proper precautionary measures and in fact a number of units did not have mosquito nets included early enough in the landing tables. Subsequent investigation shows that many units had failed 'to realize the importance of malaria-prevention among combatant personnel and as a result precautions were not fully observed'.[27] Resulting from this report the War Department of both the Western Allies issued orders, on a world-wide distribution, setting out the preventive measures to be taken in future and making formation commanders responsible for taking the necessary action, as well as stressing that 'freedom from malaria depends largely on discipline'.

Regarding the Axis strategy in Sicily, Lord Montgomery dismisses this in one sentence as 'faulty to a degree'. Kesselring continued to maintain that a forward policy was correct. In his memoirs he wrote, 'Positions in depth were an indispensable complement to coastal fortification . . . concentrated fire against the enemy at his most vulnerable points, i.e. against unloading transport ships, approaching landing craft and men who had just disembarked, still appeared to be the best method of defence. In fighting from depth local reserves must be so strong and so close that they could immediately equalize their own repulses. The first main reserves must be brought forward so near to the coast that they could move up into their battle areas as far as possible in the hours of darkness.'[28] General von Senger, however, is extremely critical of this doctrine that the assault troops could be 'thrown back into the sea', which he considered 'reflected a deep-rooted weakness in the German military intellectual tradition'. He points out that most German leaders 'could think only in terms of land operations, not in the three-dimensional terms of forces of all arms'. Thus, they 'over-estimated the value of coastal defences', and had 'an exaggerated idea of the difficulties of landing by an enemy possessing air and sea supremacy'.[29] The invader, he points out, has a good chance of achieving surprise and can be helped ashore by the naval guns and, in the case of Sicily, overwhelming air superiority. Kesselring rightly pays tribute to the skill of General Hube's delaying actions, which resulted in his extricating such a high proportion of the German troops and evacuating them successfully to the mainland. General von Senger points out that in Sicily 'there was never any question of defence in depth', owing to the lack of field divisions as distinct from static coastal formations. 'Consequently the six mobile divisions were kept together as mobile reserves in two large groups near the coast – one in the west the other in the east.'[30] The near-success of the counter-attack at Gela is sufficient proof of the wisdom of von Senger's orders regarding the initial employment of the two German Panzer Divisions. The American official historians end their study of the campaign in Sicily with the following comment, 'The campaign in Sicily that led to the capitulation of Italy proved several things. Like the invasion of North Africa the Sicilian landings showed that Axis-held Europe was vulnerable to amphibious and airborne attacks. It demonstrated the superiority of Allied weapons and equipment. It illustrated the resourcefulness and skill of the German foot soldier who despite numerical and technological inferiority demonstrated once again the fundamental importance of terrain and its use in a struggle between ground forces. It gave the American field commanders in Europe experience and particularly with respect to the British ally a maturity not achieved before. Most of all the Sicilian campaign by making possible the Italian surrender, marked a milestone on the Allied road to victory.'[31]

5

The Crossroads

Allied Priorities and Shortages: Shipping: Landing Craft: Manpower:
Conflicting viewpoints on Mediterranean Operations: Stimson reports:
OVERLORD plans emerge: Preparations for a Show-down: QUADRANT decisions:
Hitler's plans: Italians negotiate Armistice.

1943	25 July	Mussolini overthrown.
	26 July	Combined Chiefs of Staff agree to Eisenhower planning amphibious attack at Salerno (AVALANCHE) as soon as possible, but using existing forces.
		Churchill sends Roosevelt 'Thoughts on the Fall of Mussolini'.
		Hitler issues Directive No. 48.
	2 Aug	Eisenhower recommends seizure of 'reasonable bridge-head in Calabria prior to AVALANCHE.
	5 Aug	General Morgan's outline plan for OVERLORD reaches Washington.
	14 Aug	Allied Conference at Quebec (QUADRANT) until 24 August.
	15 Aug	Eisenhower issues outline plan for AVALANCHE.
		General Castellano reaches Madrid and starts negoti-ations for Armistice with Allies.
	16 Aug	Eisenhower decides to cross Straits of Messina between 1–4 September and date for AVALANCHE as 9 September.
	17 Aug	German evacuation of Sicily complete.
	18 Aug	Combined Chiefs of Staff tell Eisenhower to send representatives to Lisbon to negotiate Italian surrender terms. Secret meetings continue in North Africa and Sicily.

The capture of Sicily may rightly be regarded as the culmination of the Allied efforts to clear the Axis from North Africa and re-open the Mediterranean. From a planning point of view, however, the Allies were now at the 'crossroads in the war'.[1] The collapse of Italy was imminent and the situation should be exploited to achieve the maximum damage to Germany. This brought the whole question of a Mediterranean policy *vis-à-vis* a cross-Channel attack right into the open. Any continued uncertainty on Allied objectives in Europe would make the task of the planners almost impossible. Many priorities must be decided urgently if shortages of shipping, landing craft and men were to be brought into balance. Between the fall of Mussolini and the invasion of the Italian mainland six vital weeks elapsed. The decisions taken during this time were to have far-reaching effects not only for the campaign in Italy but for the development of the whole Allied strategy in the west right up to VE Day.

On 9 August, the day when Kesselring decided to order the evacuation of Sicily, the Allied war leaders and their advisers started to assemble for the QUADRANT Conference in Quebec. The purpose of this conference was to set out the full offensive strategy for the Allies in Europe and a limited offensive strategy in the Far East. In the Battle of the Atlantic the situation was steadily improving. For instance, by comparison with March 1943 when 477,000 tons of merchant shipping were sunk and only 12 U-boats destroyed, in July 1943 the Allies lost only 123,000 tons and on the other hand no less than 37 U-boats were sunk. By the autumn only individual U-boats were reaching the convoy routes. Increased numbers of escorts were now available and air cover was becoming more and more effective. The Allies were in fact negotiating with Portugal for facilities in the Azores, so that long-range land-based aircraft could stretch out over a vital central area of the North Atlantic. By mid-October Flying Fortresses began operating. 'Thus after more than four years of war could reliable air cover at last be provided over the whole Atlantic north of 30 degrees North; while the escort carriers looked after convoys using the more southerly routes.'[2] The combined results of naval and air co-operation, of more escorts, better air cover and improved tactics were dramatic. In September and October of 1943 out of 2,468 merchant ships that sailed in sixty-four convoys only nine were lost and twenty-five U-boats were sunk in mid-ocean, thirteen of these U-boats being sunk by shore-based aircraft. The air attacks against German industry in the Rhur were being pressed home both by night and by day. The American daylight sorties with large formations of Flying Fortresses were, however, meeting increasing numbers of German fighter squadrons and mounting losses became a matter of serious concern. More and more of the American effort became diverted to attacks on German fighter aircraft production. This in fact was a diversion from the overall Allied bombing policy, known as POINTBLANK, which had been agreed in Washington in May, but it was to have a far-reaching effect in bringing about increased Allied air superiority in the European theatre of operations.

At the time of the QUADRANT Conference there were many problems of supply to be brought into balance and the British historian John Ehrman points out that 'four main shortages threatened to limit the offensive strategy: merchant shipping, assault shipping, transport aircraft, and, in the case of the British, men'.[3] A shortage of merchant shipping indeed remained a problem throughout the war and affected in particular the British, who had to think not only of the needs of military operations but also of the vital necessity to maintain both the population of the United Kingdom and its war industries through imports, as well as providing the many needs for overseas countries. The varying requirements under these three heads were difficult both to plan and to resolve. From a military point of view there was growing pressure in America to allocate more and more shipping for the war in the Pacific, while the requirements for OVERLORD, particularly in coastal shipping and small tankers, were placing an added strain on the construction programme. Allied successes in the Battle of the Atlantic were only just beginning to ease the situation. In the long term the effect of the reduction in sinkings would be felt, but from an immediate point of view shortages appeared in every planning forecast, only to be resolved after economies and adjustments had been laboriously worked out and agreed time and time again, according to the changing pattern of operations and the war economies of the two Western Allies. After the summer of 1943 military operations in fact were not to suffer from a lack of merchant shipping but to the planners the fear of shortages remained a potent factor in all their calculations.

The shortage of assault ships and craft was an even greater factor likely to restrict offensive operations. The need to construct merchant ships and escort vessels had forced the British to employ their shipbuilding yards on this vital task, while the boatyards, and later factories, were used to construct the specially designed smaller assault and landing craft. The Americans, with their considerably greater shipbuilding resources, were meanwhile able to put into production the larger landing ships, which had a more conventional construction, as well as a proportion of the landing craft. In Britain, so long as the great shipyards could not take over any of the programme, only just over 1,000 landing craft could be produced annually. In America, as soon as it was decided not to invade France in 1943, the priority for assault shipping had been reduced, with the result that the figures for July 1943 were only 51,000 tons compared with 106,000 in February. The seriousness of the situation is seen when the estimated requirements for OVERLORD came to be considered at the QUADRANT Conference in August and it was estimated that only 64 per cent of the LSTs, 77 per cent of the LCTs and 31 per cent of the LCI (L) required for the operation would in fact be available. The British construction programme was already stretched almost to the limit and, although some of the big shipyards were brought in, it became obvious that, unless American production could fill the gap in time for the ships to be fitted out and assembled and the crews trained, the OVERLORD plan would have to be modified. This grave shortage of assault shipping and craft of all types now became an almost dominant factor in operational planning and was to have a particular significance in the Mediterranean. Shortages of transport aircraft were to have a similar restricting effect on British operations in the Far East but in Europe the situation was not really serious. The Americans had always given priority to the production of air transports and already had somewhat over-insured in the Mediterranean. The growing requirements for the cross-Channel attack, however, resulted in a number of squadrons being moved out of this theatre to take part in OVERLORD.

In the summer of 1943 the Americans were becoming increasingly concerned with manpower problems as over-mobilization into the armed forces had begun to hit their economy. A special committee, under a Colonel Maddocks, was set up to recommend how many divisions were needed to ensure victory first against the Axis in Europe and then against Japan in the Pacific. As a result of the committee's report it was decided in mid-June that only the eighty-eight divisions then fully mobilized (and two others already authorized) would in fact be needed at the moment, although the American planners considered that this figure might have to be raised to a hundred divisions, according to the course of operations on the Russian front and the success of the Allied bombing offensive in Europe. In accordance with this recommendation the US War Department set about achieving a number of economies and in July 1943 the strength of the US Army was cut back to a total of 7,686,000. The result of these decisions was that after the summer of 1943 the army planners became increasingly conscious of the point of balance between mobilization, production, and strategic plans and as their official historian records, 'the question of whether ninety divisions was enough was to plague the War Department leaders down to the very end of the war. Henceforth problems of reserves and narrow margins of safety would become the nightmare to disturb planners' dreams – problems all the more aggravated for them in 1943 by the threat of an unsettled strategy and consequent drain of the precious stock of manpower in indecisive undertakings in secondary theatres . . . henceforth US strategic planners would be more and more insistent on precise agreements on magnitudes and timings and less and less willing to accept "agreements in principle" of the 1942 variety.'[4]

In Britain it was not so much a question of redeployment of available manpower but of scraping the barrel. At the beginning of 1943 Britain had 4,105,000 men and women in the armed forces and 22,056,000 engaged in war production, out of a population of 48,400,000. By June the Services and Ministries of Supply and Aircraft Production were bidding for an additional 1,912,000 men and women. In spite of cutting back on air and civil defence and by making adjustments between the Munitions departments the War Cabinet was told there would still be a deficit of 71,000, excluding civil defence requirements, at the end of the year. Britain now had 4,800,000 men and women in its armed forces, an unprecedented figure of just over 10 per cent of the population, and at the same time had slightly increased the labour force. This had only been achieved by cutting civil defence and by applying extremely severe restrictions on the manufacture or provision of everything not directly contributing to the war effort. The standard of living of the workers and civilian population alike had now been reduced just about as far as the Government and the public could take it. 'By the end of this year,' the Minister of Labour stated, 'the mobilization of the nation will be practically complete.' If the war in Europe dragged on the British would face a grave shortage of manpower. America equally feared any state of stalemate in Europe. The American people would hardly stand for it and wanted to get on with defeating the Germans, so that all their strength could be turned against Japan with the least delay.

In London on 18 July Alanbrooke saw Eisenhower's cable to the Combined Chiefs of Staff recommending that as soon as Messina was taken he would cross to the mainland and make a landing at Salerno, with the object of seizing the port of Naples and cutting off the southern part of the peninsula. At the Chiefs of Staff meeting the next day a direct attack on Naples was discussed but Alanbrooke notes, 'air cover bad and dependent on carriers; also put forward by joint planners with only three divisions, quite inadequate. Rate of build-up also slower than that of the Germans.' The same evening a new appreciation for an attack on Naples was under discussion and he wrote, 'we shall have a busy time to knock into some shape to wire out to Eisenhower, and to bring Marshall along with us without frightening him out of the Mediterranean'.[5] Marshall, however, had stuck to his word that a follow-up attack on Italy could be made, providing the British operations ended soon enough and the build-up for the cross-Channel attack was not prejudiced, so he agreed to the proposed landing at Salerno. The British Chiefs of Staff, however, saw the implication of the TRIDENT decisions to pull back a number of landing craft to the UK and send others to Burma at an early date and pressed for these moves to be halted and for extra carriers and assault craft to be allocated to the Mediterranean, so that Eisenhower could mount a much

Salerno. American infantry moving into the hills above the plain, September 1943.

The docks at Naples showing German demolitions, October 1943.

The Volturno. Gun crews moving a 5.5 medium gun from a flooded position, October 1943.

Tehran Conference. Marshal Stalin, Voroshilov, President Roosevelt, General Sir Alan Brooke, Mr Churchill, Admiral Leahy, November 1943.

stronger seaborne attack while the Axis forces in Italy might still be in a state of confusion. The Germans were already in serious trouble on the Eastern front and the Russian counter-offensive near Orel was making ground. The time was ripe for a determined and immediate assault by the large Allied forces already poised and in position. General Marshall, however, was not prepared to change his stance. The decisions taken two months before must stand. So Eisenhower was told that four American and three British divisions would be withdrawn by the end of November, plus three American heavy bomber groups. Moreover 'in the third week of October the Mediterranean was due to lose 80 per cent of its LSTs and LSIs and two-thirds of its landing craft within the next six weeks'.[6] As Alexander wrote on 24 July, 'a very disappointing wire from American Chiefs of Staff. Marshall absolutely fails to realize the strategic treasures that lie at our feet in the Mediterranean and hankers after cross-Channel operations. He admits that our object must be to eliminate Italy and yet is always afraid of facing the consequences of doing so. . . .'[7] The next day came the news of the fall of Mussolini. Early decisions were vital if the Allies were to take advantage of the situation. As we have seen Hitler at this time was prepared to abandon the Italians and the whole of southern Italy including Rome itself, only holding a line from Pisa across the Apennines to Rimini. But three weeks were to elapse before the Allies reached Messina and by then the negotiations for an Italian armistice had only just begun. The Germans had meanwhile assembled fifteen divisions on Italian soil with another four *en route*.

The day after Badoglio took over power, Churchill sent Roosevelt a long paper entitled 'Thoughts on the fall of Mussolini' and Hitler issued 'Directive Number 48, Command and Defence Measures in the South East'. Hitler's appreciation of the situation in the first paragraph of his directive is of interest. 'The enemy's measures in the Eastern Mediterranean, in conjunction with the attack on Sicily, indicate that he will shortly begin landing operations against our strong line in the Aegean, Peloponnese–Crete–Rhodes, and against the west coat of Greece with offshore Ionian islands. Should the operations of the enemy extend from Sicily to the mainland of southern Italy, we must also reckon with an assault on the east coast of the Adriatic, north of the straits of Otranto. The enemy's conduct of operations is also based on the bandit movement, which is increasingly organized by him in the interior of the south-east area. Turkey's neutrality is at present beyond question, but needs continuous watching.'[8] The directive continued with detailed orders for the strengthening of the defences of Greece and the destruction of bandit gangs in Greece, Serbia, and Croatia. Churchill's summing-up of the situation and how it should develop covers a rather broader canvas but points clearly to areas in which Hitler was particularly sensitive. Dealing first with essential surrender terms involving the whole of the Italian armed forces which covered Corsica, Sardinia, the Dodecanese, Corfu and the Riviera together with Yugoslavia, Albania and Greece and with special mention of the Italian fleet and a discussion on the liberation of Allied prisoners of war, Churchill forecast fighting breaking out between the Germans and the Italians, particularly in the south. The Allies, he felt, should do all they could by sending troops and air support to help 'in procuring the surrender of the Germans south of Rome. When we see how this process goes we can take a further view about action to be taken north of Rome. We should however try to get possession of points on both the east coast and west coast railways of Italy as far north as we dare. And this is a time to dare!' Churchill continued by pointing to the advantages to the Allies of airfields in Italy 'on which we can base the whole forward air attack on south and central Germany' an area previously out of range of air attack from Great Britain. He continued, 'It will become urgent in the highest degree to get agents, commandos and supplies by sea across the Adriatic into Greece, Albania and Yugoslavia. It must be remembered that there are fifteen German divisions in the Balkan peninsula of which ten are mobile. Nevertheless, once we have control of the Iberian peninsula and the Adriatic and the Italian armies in the Balkans withdraw or lay down their arms it is by no means unlikely that the Germans will be forced to withdraw northwards to the line of the Sava and the Danube, thus liberating Greece and other tortured countries.' He also pointed out that 'Italian capitulation' would have a 'profound effect' on Bulgaria, Rumania and Hungary and that now was the time to put 'the strongest pressure on Turkey to act in accordance with the spirit of the alliance'.[9] Ten days before, Churchill had written to General Smuts, 'Not only must we take Rome and march as far north as possible in Italy but our right hand must give succour to the Balkan patriots. In all this there is great hope provided action is taken worthy of the opportunity. I am confident of a good result and I shall go to all lengths to produce the agreement of our Allies, if we have not ample forces to act by ourselves.'[10]

On 27 July Eisenhower proposed an early landing at Salerno with the object of getting a division into Naples as soon as possible, only 'to be told by his planners that it would be logistically impossible for lack of assault craft and carriers to land there before the second week in September. Even a crossing to the mainland across the narrow Messina straits would not be practicable for another four or five weeks.' But although the British Chiefs of Staff on their 'own initiative had ordered the whole of their disposable force in the Mediterranean basin to stand by in readiness for immediate operation against Italy their American colleagues still refused to commit more than the scheduled proportion of resources to that sea'.[11] Alanbrooke later wrote 'success breeds success in these cases and the ball was at our feet . . . what was wanted was to knock all the props from under the Germans in the defence of the Mediterranean: let them alone to bear the full burden'. He pointed out that the German forces 'distributed round the perimeter of Europe' were 'served by the most perfect east and west railway system in existence . . . reinforced by the autobahn system of roads' whereas 'the German north and south communications were, however, nothing like as efficient comprising only one double line of railway through the leg of Italy and one through the Balkans to Greece. Our strategy had now become a delicate matter of balancing. Our aim must be to draw as many divisions as possible from the English Channel and to retain them in Southern Europe as long as possible. When arguing with Marshall I could never get him fully to appreciate the very close connection that existed between the various German fronts. For him they might have been separate wars – a Russian war on one side, a Mediterranean war on another and a cross-Channel one to be started as soon as possible.'[12] In the middle of July the seventy-five-year-old American Secretary for War Henry Stimson was in England inspecting American troops and at the same time keeping an eye on the planning for the cross-Channel assault. Both he and Marshall had served on the Western Front in 1918 and he was not only an ardent admirer of his service colleague but convinced 'that the whole of the Allied effort against Germany should be concentrated on the western front'. While he was in London he saw the OVERLORD planners, and he reported back to the President that 'Lieutenant-General Morgan was very frank in stating his fears of delays which might be caused by getting too deep into commitments in the Mediterranean . . . Barker (US Army Deputy to General Morgan) who explained the details of the plans to us shared the same fear'.[13] Stimson also had several frank discussions with the Prime Minister. Much to Churchill's delight Marshall's agreement to the Salerno landings had just been received and he assumed that the remainder of his Italian policy was equally accepted. Knowing that Marshall had only agreed to the Salerno landing 'to hasten the completion of the Italian adventure', Stimson not only pressed this view but telephoned Marshall for confirmation and subsequently repeated the conversation to Churchill. 'The effect was disastrous. Argument on strategic matters was meat and drink to the Prime Minister and he embarked on an impassioned disquisition that confirmed Stimson's worst fears.'[14]

Early in August the British delegation to the conference in Quebec sailed in the *Queen Mary* from the Clyde and on the first day out, 6 August, the Chiefs of Staff were at work discussing how best to present the Mediterranean situation to the American Chiefs of Staff. Alanbrooke's diary reads, 'Decided to relate the actions in this theatre to the requirements in northern France . . . to admit of an invasion, in my mind it is all so clear and palpable that the policy we must pursue is to complete the elimination of Italy, profit from the situation by occupying as much of Italy as we require to improve bombing facilities of southern Germany, and to force a withdrawal of German forces from Russia, Balkans and France in order to face the Italian threat. If we pin Germany in Italy she cannot find enough force to meet all her commitments.'[15] The same day Alanbrooke was studying General Morgan's plans for the cross-Channel attack which had just been finished in time to be discussed at the forthcoming conference.

Across the Atlantic the American planners were also studying General Morgan's proposals and taking great care to mark out the ground on which they could take their stand at the forthcoming meeting with their British Allies. General Marshall feared particularly that the scale of Allied operations in the Mediterranean theatre might 'escalate' to the point where not only the limited offensives in the Pacific would be affected but where they might even begin to take precedence over the main cross-Channel assault (now called OVERLORD). With the arrival of General Morgan's outline proposals for OVERLORD the time for decision had come and the time also for a 'show-down' with the British. But the President's support would be needed and, before leaving for Quebec, Marshall and the President met (on 9 August) to discuss their 'line of action' at the QUADRANT Conference. Roosevelt referred both to OVERLORD and the forthcoming operations in the Mediterranean. While he was insistent on OVERLORD 'he felt the planners could make more of the opportunities in the Mediterranean, although he did not wish to have any- thing to do with an operation into the Balkans nor did he ever intend to agree to a British expedition in that area that would cost the United States vital resources such as ships and landing craft necessary for other operations. He was in favour of securing a position in Italy to the north of Rome and taking Sardinia and Corsica thereby posing a serious threat to southern France.'[16] With this in mind he proposed replacing the seven battle-tested divisions, that were being withdrawn from Eisenhower's command to the United King- dom, with seven fresh divisions from the United States. General Marshall saw this as likely to affect the build-up for OVERLORD but promised to 'have a critical review made of the logistical factors involved' and the army planners produced a report the same day.

In May, at the TRIDENT Conference, a build-up of 1,300,000 US troops had been promised for the cross-Channel attack. The planners estimated there would be sufficient ships and men available in addition to lift 100,000 more men either to the United Kingdom or to some other theatre. Meanwhile the requirements of OVERLORD and the Combined Bomber Offensive 'called for over 1,400,000 US troops by 1 May 1944. Seven fresh divisions could be put into the Mediterranean theatre but would not reach there before June 1944 and the planners felt that the ships and men could be better employed 'to ensure a well-balanced force in the United Kingdom'.[17] The following day Marshall presented this view to the Joint Chiefs of Staff, pointing out that Eisenhower had accepted the reduction of his forces by seven divisions and that if these were replaced they 'would in reality constitute an expeditionary force available for use in the Balkans'. He felt, moreover, 'the President was opposed to operations in the Balkans and particularly in US troops' partici- pation in them on the grounds they represented an uneconomical use of shipping and also because of the political implications involved'.[18] Admiral King naturally supported this view as he saw the operations in the Pacific being seriously affected by any diversion of shipping to the Mediterranean. The same day Stimson, who had just returned from his tour of inspection, went to lunch with Roosevelt. He took with him a short memorandum setting out four recommendations based on his report which the President had already studied. In brief the four points were: firstly, because Churchill and Alanbrooke were 'frankly at variance with such a proposal' (for a cross-Channel attack) the operations should not be mounted under a British commander. Secondly, the 'pinprick warfare' represented by the British theory of a 'series of attritions in Northern Italy, in the Eastern Mediterranean, in Greece, in the Balkans, in Rumania and other satellite countries' would not fool Stalin. Both nations were pledged to a proper Second Front and the American staff believed that Germany could only be defeated 'by massing the immense vigour and power of the American and British nations under the overwhelming mastery of the air . . . to cover our subsequent advance in France'. Thirdly, Roosevelt's Government 'must assume the responsibility of leadership in the great final movement of the European war' . . . because there was no time 'to confer again' and 'we cannot afford to begin the most dangerous operation of the war under half-hearted leadership which will invite failure or at least disappointing results'.[19] Fourthly, Marshall, whose name had been put forward by the British eighteen months previously, should command the cross-Channel attack. Roosevelt accepted the conclusions immediately and shortly afterwards the two statesmen were joined by the Joint Chiefs of Staff to discuss the forthcoming conference in Quebec. When the President said he understood that 'the Prime Minister currently favoured operations against the Balkans', Stimson pointed out that Churchill 'had disclaimed any wish to land troops in the Balkans but had indicated that the Allies could make notable gains in that area if the Balkan people were given more supplies and that it was the British Foreign Secretary, Mr Anthony Eden, who wanted to invade the Balkans'. To this the President added that the British Foreign Office did not wish the Balkans to come under Soviet influence . . . and wished 'to get to the Balkans first'! He did not believe 'that the USSR wished to take over the Balkan States . . . but to "establish kinship with other Slavic people" ', and he himself was opposed to Balkan operations, declaring that it was 'unwise to plan military strategy based on a gamble as to political results'. This resulted in a decision that the seven divisions due to leave Eisenhower's command for the United Kingdom would not be replaced, note being taken that Eisenhower had forecast that he would still be able 'to conduct the proposed operations in Italy, capture Sardinia and Corsica, and have fourteen divisions available for an invasion of southern France in coordination with OVERLORD'.[20] Admiral King then suggested that if the British insisted upon abandoning OVERLORD, or postponing it indefinitely, the United

States should abandon the project. The President replied with the optimistic view that the United States itself could if necessary carry out the cross-Channel operation. General Marshall, however, pointed out the fact that fifteen British divisions were already available in the United Kingdom. 'In no other place in the world, he maintained, could fifteen divisions be put into an operation without entailing great transportation and supply problems.'[21] The President and his service advisers were now ready to speak with one voice. OVERLORD would be the main Allied effort against Germany. It would be launched under an American commander with, if possible, a preponderance of American troops 'from the first day' and any major change of plan or divergence of effort which would inevitably result 'in dislocation of the American war effort' would be unacceptable.

Four days later (14 August) the conference opened and the Chiefs of Staff of the Western Allies sat down together for full-scale discussions on the war strategy. On the 19 August they were joined by the President and the Prime Minister, who meanwhile had spent several days together at the President's retreat, Hyde Park, above the Hudson River. Churchill had devoted a great deal of time during the voyage over to studying General Morgan's plans for OVERLORD and in particular he examined very carefully the technical problems involved in the use of the artificial MULBERRY harbours and PHOENIX and GOOSEBERRY breakwaters and other special equipment and devices which would enable the invasion forces to be supplied over open beaches. As he later wrote, 'I was very well satisfied with the prospect of having the whole of this story presented to the President with my full support. At least it would convince the American authorities that we were not insincere over OVERLORD and had not grudged thought or time in preparation.'[22] Churchill was delighted to hear his host speak so ardently for the build-up of an overwhelming American force in Britain and Europe 'and readily agreed to Roosevelt's proposal that the command should be given to Marshall (although in fact he had already promised it to Alanbrooke). In exchange the British would be given supreme command in the Mediterranean and South-East Asia.'[23] But while these private discussions on OVERLORD were going on and Roosevelt's mind was set on an inflexible attitude towards any extension of operations in the Mediterranean, Churchill was engaged in setting down his own ideas on Allied war policy. 'Should Naples be captured (Operation AVALANCHE) in the near future we shall have a first-rate port in Italy, and other harbours, like Brindisi and Taranto, will fall into our possession thereafter. If by November our front can be established as far north as the Leghorn–Ancona line the landing craft in the Mediterranean will have played their part. A detachment would be required from the landing fleet for amphibious turning movements such as we have seen in Sicily for minor descents across the Adriatic, and for operations such as ACCOLADE (the capture of Rhodes and other islands in the Aegean) . . . Although I have frequently spoken of the line of the Po or of the Alps as being desirable objectives for us this year in Italy, it is not possible to see so far at present. A very great advantage will have been gained if we stop at the Leghorn–Ancona line. . . . From such a position we could by air supply a fomented rising in Savoy and the French Alps, to which the young men of France would be able to rally, and at the same time with our right hand we could act across the Adriatic to stimulate the Patriot activities in the Balkan peninsula. It may be necessary for us to accept these limitations in order that the integrity of Operation OVERLORD shall not be marred.' Churchill later wrote 'the immediate point on which my mind was focused was to procure the invasion of Italy as the natural consequence and exploitation of our victory in Sicily and Mussolini's fall'.[24]

Before the first plenary session of the conference was held on 19 August the respective Chiefs of Staff and the planners spent five days on a series of discussions, which were then presented as a full report on future strategy for the remainder of 1943 and 1944. The Americans were prepared for a show-down on the question of giving full priority to the build-up for OVERLORD. The British, who had already spent a good deal of time and thought examining the implications of the choice of the assault area and the technical problems involved, were in this respect better prepared to take a wider view of the operation in relation to the European theatre as a whole. Far from opposing Marshall's view that OVERLORD should be the main Allied offensive for 1944, Alanbrooke welcomed the proposal for a more rapid build-up of forces for the assault and 'urged that, in order to widen the initial assault, for which the planners had been allowed smaller naval assault forces even than Sicily, 25 per cent more landing craft should be allocated'.[25] This, however, was not accept-able to the Americans as it would restrict their operations in the Pacific where nine-tenths of the assault craft available to the Allies were concentrated. Alanbrooke then reiterated the three conditions on which General Morgan had based his plans for OVERLORD. (1) The reduction of German fighter strength, (2) The restriction of German strength in France and the Low Countries and German abilities to bring in reinforcements during the first two months, and (3) the solution of the problem of beach maintenance.[26] This reopened the whole question of operations in Italy and the withdrawal of the seven divisions. The British view was that by the containment of German forces in this theatre and through the use of suitable Italian airfields, if possible in the north, the Allies would best achieve the first two of the conditions required for the success of OVERLORD. Marshall, however, stuck to his inflex-ible policy for over-riding priority to be given to the OVERLORD build-up. Any change from the troop allocations agreed in May would dislocate shipping and supply arrangements. The alternative was to rely on the Combined Bomber Offensive and leave a single reinforced US Corps in the United Kingdom to take part in an 'opportunistic' cross-Channel attack. Such a re-casting of strategy, he pointed out to the British, might lead to a possible reorientation of American offensive efforts towards the Pacific.[27] Alanbrooke comments on this particular session, 'I entirely failed to get Marshall to realize the relation between cross-Channel and Italian operations and the repercussions that the one exercises on the other. It is quite impossible to argue with him as he does not begin to understand a strategic problem. He had not even read the plans worked out by Morgan for the cross-Channel operation, and consequently was not even in a position to begin to appreciate its difficulties and requirements. The only real argument he produced was a threat to the effect that if we pressed our point, the build-up in England would be reduced to that of a small Corps and the whole war reorientated towards Japan.'[28] It is interesting here to note that the US Assistant Chief of Staff Operations Division, Major-General Handy, and Major-General Hull, Chief of Operations Division Theatre Group, had both submitted plans within the last month for an all-out effort in the Mediterranean as an alternative to OVERLORD. Hull's analysis, written in mid-July, seems to have been based on practical grounds in that reinforcement of the Mediterranean operations was inevitable and the Allies would then become committed to making their main effort in that theatre. Handy's proposal, submitted on 16 August, was put up only as an alternative 'if the British Chiefs of Staff refused to back OVERLORD wholeheartedly'[29] and understandably received little consideration from the American Joint Chiefs of Staff, who shared Marshall's view on absolute priority being given to OVERLORD. The same day, however, Alanbrooke once again set about trying to close the gap between the British and American viewpoints and records that the morning session was followed by a 'small session with all secretaries and planners removed. Our talk was pretty frank. I opened by telling them that the root of the matter was that we were not trusting each other. They doubted our real intention to put our full hearts into the cross-Channel operation next spring, and we had not full confidence that they would not in the future insist on our carrying out previous agreements irrespective of changed strategic conditions. I then had to go over our whole Mediterranean strategy to prove its objects which they had never fully realized, and finally I had to produce countless arguments to prove the close relation that exists between cross-Channel and Italian operations. In the end I think our arguments did have some effect on Marshall . . .'[30]

When Roosevelt and Churchill joined the conference on 19 August a compromise 'was in the making' although, as Chester Wilmot remarks, 'it was too late to extract the full advantage from the Italian situation', for, as Marshall himself reminded the conference, 'the greatest limiting factor on all the prospective Anglo-American operations was the shortage of landing craft. Had landing craft been available . . . the Anglo-American forces could already have made an entry into Italy.'[31] As the discussions developed, it became clear that the American view on the Mediterranean theatre basically was to limit the forces to those already agreed at TRIDENT, although the operations envisaged included the elimination of Italy and the occupation of at least the southern part of the peninsula, the seizure of Sardinia and Corsica and the launching of an operation in southern France in conjunction with OVERLORD. The British, however, wanted some leeway to ensure success in the Mediterranean as a necessary requisite to the success of OVERLORD and 'saw great danger in accepting rigid commitments for the Mediterranean – a strait jacket likely to jeopardize the Allied cause in the whole European-Mediterranean area'.[32] The final report of the Combined Chiefs of Staff was agreed on 24 August. As far as the war against Japan was concerned, plans were made for limited operations over the next six months such as the capture of the Gilbert and Marshall Islands and advances in New Guinea, together with operations in Upper Burma and the build-up of air routes aimed at supporting China. As regards the war in Europe, however, the decisions taken at QUADRANT were far-reaching and the strategic pattern finally agreed became the blueprint for the final defeat of Germany. Dealing first with the U-boat war, of which there were 'encouraging reports', the anti-U-boat attacks were to be stepped up by sea and air and included the use of the Azores. 'The defeat of the Axis in Europe' was then dealt with in some detail under a number of headings. The bomber offensive against 'the German military, industrial and economic system', lines of communication, and fighter strength was to be 'a prerequisite to OVERLORD and continue to have highest strategic priority'. OVERLORD was to be the principal Allied effort against the Axis in Europe with target date 1 August 1944, with provision for a balanced force 'in readiness for an opportunistic cross-Channel move into France', together with an alternative plan to attack southern Norway if for any reason the launching of OVERLORD became impossible. Those paragraphs of the report that dealt with the Mediterranean theatre follow in full.

Operations in Italy
14 (a) First Phase. The elimination of Italy as a belligerent and establishment of air bases in the Rome area, and, if feasible, further north.
(b) Second Phase. Seizure of Sardinia and Corsica.
(c) Third Phase. The maintenance of unremitting pressure on German forces in Northern Italy, and the creation of the conditions required for OVERLORD and of a situation favourable for the eventual entry of our forces, including the bulk of the re-equipped French Army and Air Force into Southern France.

Operations in Southern France
15 Offensive operations against Southern France (to include the use of trained and equipped French forces) should be undertaken to establish a lodgement in the Toulon-Marseilles area and to exploit northward in order to create a diversion in connection with 'Overlord'. Air-nourished guerilla operations in the Southern Alps will, if possible, be initiated.

Air Operations

16 (a) Strategic bombing operations from Italian and Central Mediterranean bases, complementing 'Pointblank'.

(b) Development of an air ferry route through the Azores.

(c) Air supply of Balkan and French guerillas (see paragraph 17 below).

Operations in the Balkans

17 Operations in the Balkan area will be limited to supply of Balkan guerillas by air and sea transport, to minor Commando forces, and to the bombing of strategic objectives.

Garrison requirements and Security of Lines of Communication in the Mediterranean

18 Defensive garrison commitments in the Mediterranean area will be reviewed from time to time, with a view to effecting economy of force. The security of our lines of communication through the Straits of Gibraltar will be assured by appropriate dispositions of our forces in North-West Africa, so long as there remains even a remote possibility of the Germans invading the Iberian Peninsula.[33]

As regards the Mediterranean theatre, these plans were in the nature of a compromise as, although the Americans' intention was that only the forces allocated in May at the Third Washington Conference would be available, the British at least established the relationship between the Mediterranean operations and OVERLORD. The door was kept ajar by the phrase 'except insofar as these may be varied by decisions of the Combined Chiefs of Staff'. It seems doubtful, however, if the Americans set much store by this clause in view of General Bradley's comment that 'the British had successfully wiggled through another loophole'.[34]

While the Allied war leaders had been in conference in Quebec, Eisenhower had been kept busy with pressing diplomatic and operational plans for the Italian surrender and the invasion of the mainland. About the middle of August there were sixteen German divisions in Italy. Half of them were in the north under Rommel, two were around Rome and six were in the south under Kesselring, while considerable reinforcements were available in France. Before the conference ended the landings on the toe and at Salerno were in preparation and the decision to seize Sardinia and Corsica 'as a second priority' had been taken. Churchill wrote 'it was exactly what I had hoped and striven for. Later it was proposed to land an airborne division to capture the airfields south of Rome. This also we accepted . . .'[35] Churchill regarded these decisions as 'highly satisfactory' but before he left Quebec he learned from General Whiteley, a British officer who had arrived from Eisenhower's headquarters, that the Allied force landing at these two points would not be built up to twelve divisions before 1 December. He immediately wrote (26 August) to General Alexander, 'I cannot understand why two and a half months will be required to get ashore, or why it should be necessary once we

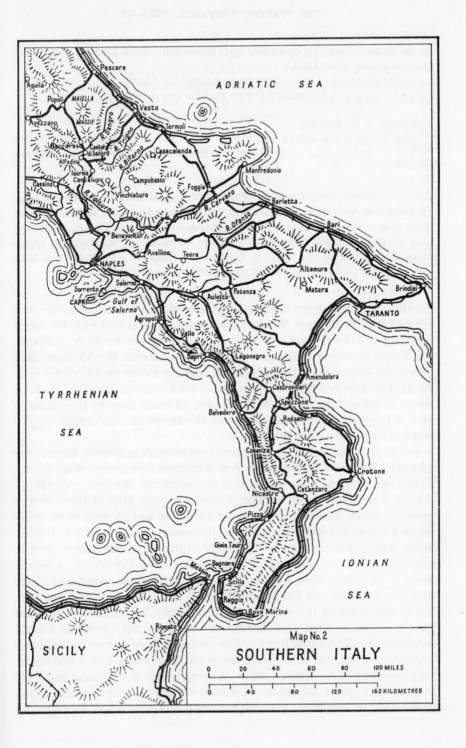

Map No. 2

SOUTHERN ITALY

0   20   40   60   80   100 MILES

0   40   80   120   160 KILOMETRES

have obtained an effective port and bridgehead at AVALANCHE to march all the BAYTOWN divisions through Calabria instead of sending some at least of them round the sea'. Such a slow build-up, he wrote, opened 'dangers of the gravest kind'. Apart from the political implications of not being able to help the Italians in Rome, there was the danger that the Germans would have time to assemble a very much stronger force than the Allies. The effect of the forthcoming withdrawal of seven Allied divisions and 80 per cent of the landing craft from Eisenhower's forces was now becoming only too obvious. Churchill, on his return to England, set in motion measures to correct what he described as 'this administrative failure' by arranging for the re-equipping of 1 Armoured Division and for the early move of 4 Indian Division, the New Zealand Division and two Polish divisions to Italy. As he later wrote, 'in the early days of October a hundred thousand men were added to General Alexander's army. Had this not been achieved a disaster might easily have occurred for the Germans were arriving in strength.'[36]

This, however, is jumping ahead and it is now necessary to consider briefly the political moves by Italy and Hitler's plans immediately prior to the Allied invasion of the mainland. By the middle of August Hitler had a firm grip on the northern part of Italy. Rommel had established the head-quarters of Army Group B at Lake Garda and had five infantry divisions and two Panzer divisions under his immediate command. If and when the Italians defected, plans were ready for German formations to take over from the Italians in France and throughout the Balkans. 'Important installations and positions in Italy were to be seized; the Italian fleet was to be captured; and German forces were to take up new defensive positions.'[37] At this point, Hitler in fact was still very concerned about the possibility of an Allied landing in the Balkans. In July and August six further German divisions were dispatched to the south-eastern European theatre to bring the total to eighteen. When Kesselring, however, tried to get reinforcements sent to southern Italy 'in view of the strategic importance of these regions as a springboard to the Balkans', Hitler preferred to listen to the more cautious Rommel who advocated a withdrawal to the line of the northern Apennines. The plan (which would only be effective on orders from the OKW) should Italy collapse was for Rommel to secure the northern frontier and the Apennine passes, while Kesselring pulled back towards this line, 'disarming the Italian army and crushing any resistance'. Sardinia would be evacuated and the troops transferred to the mainland and Rommel would assume command over all German forces in Italy as soon as Kesselring's withdrawal was complete. Kesselring's objections to this plan 'prompted (him) to submit his resignation on 14 August but Hitler refused to accept it'.[38] In the middle of August, however, the situation began to alter very much to the detriment of the Allies. Sixty thousand German troops had crossed from Messina with the majority of their equipment and by 22 August General von Vietinghoff, commanding the newly formed German Tenth Army, had XIV Panzer Corps of three divisions assembled in the Gaeta–Naples–Salerno area and the LXXVI Panzer Corps with two divisions and elements of a third in Calabria and Apulia. Hitler still, however, planned to pull back, first to positions about Rome and then to the northern Apennine line, in the event of the Allies landing in support of an Italian defection. He was determined on a successful withdrawal of his troops in the south, where he saw the possibility of Allied landings near Rome or in the Naples–Salerno area or at Apulia, although he would not allow Kesselring to send reinforcements to the latter area. The most likely areas for a landing were regarded as Naples and Salerno and Tenth Army would hold these with at least three mobile divisions. 'Only mobile forces were to remain in southern Calabria and they would execute a fighting withdrawal to the north. In case political development made a continuation of the fight in southern Italy impossible the Tenth Army would fall back to the Rome area.'[39] There is little doubt from Hitler's plan to abandon the whole of the south of Italy that he over-estimated the strength of the Allied attack on the mainland. Although he was prepared for the attack and in fact made a sound appreciation of the most likely points of attack, his plan was still related to his intention of ensuring the safe withdrawal of all the German forces in the south right back to a line from Massa, south of Spezia, across the Apennines north of Florence to Pesaro. 'He was even prepared, at the worst, to pull back to the line of the Po; at least he hoped to stand on a line Grosseto–Perugia–Ancona, through the Apennines to the south of Lake Trasimene. All of such plans, of course, ceded Rome in the course of the retreat.'[40]

If the Germans were deceived as to Allied strength, the Italians deceived themselves over the ability of the Allies to land outside the range of land-based fighter cover. From the start of the negotiations for an armistice between Italy and the Allies, General Castellano was principally concerned with plans to throw off the German yoke. His very first words to Eisenhower's representative on arrival in Lisbon were that 'he had come to discuss the question of how Italy could arrange to join the United Nations in opposition to Germany'. From his point of view it was not a question of 'unconditional surrender' but of an active partnership in saving as much of Italy as possible. Castellano was in fact chief of the planning department at Commando Supremo and gave the latest German appreciation of the four most likely places where the Allies might land as 'Calabria; the area from Salerno to Gaeta; the Rome area, particularly Civitavecchia; and the Genoa–Spezia area. They would not attempt to defend Calabria but they would resist strongly on the beaches themselves any attempt to land in the other three areas.' General Castellano was not slow in offering some advice from Marshal Badoglio who urged the Allies to 'land somewhere in the Leghorn area with a force of not less than fifteen divisions. He added that it would be useful to land a similar force of about the same strength on the other side of Italy near Ancona, so that the two together would make a strategic pincers.'[41] With landing craft for three divisions and Leghorn three hundred miles outside the range of fighter cover, this suggestion can only underline the Marshal's complete lack of understanding of amphibious operations, shared also by the Germans who feared landings near Rome or Spezia. Sir John Hunt, who, as an intelligence officer on Alexander's staff, had a ringside view of the negotiations for the Italian armistice, comments, 'the result of this funda-mental misconception was that we were throughout at cross-purposes with the Italians. Castellano was always demanding to know what our plans were for invading his country and we were always telling him to wait and see, while maintaining that we should of course, invade in great force.'[42] The Allies insisted that first the surrender terms must be signed and then the day before the invasion of the mainland a simultaneous announcement of the armistice would be made, but in the meantime the Italians would not be told the date or place of the invasion. This of course did not suit the Italians, who feared the consequences of German action when the armistice terms were broadcast and Castellano pressed hard for the announcement to be made after the Allies had landed and made some progress. In the end, the armistice terms were signed some hours after units of Eighth Army had crossed the straits of Messina and the broadcast of the armistice terms was made, as agreed, the night before the Salerno landing but under somewhat dramatic circumstances as will be related later.

6
Plans in Jeopardy

Strategic Alternative for the Allies: Naples the objective: Salerno chosen: Flexibility of planning: German dispositions: Allied bombing tactics: Naval plans in difficulty: Parachutists for Rome: Castellano signs Armistice terms: Eighth Army crosses at Messina: Badoglio dickers: Rome drop cancelled: Italy Surrenders.

1943	27 July	General Mark Clark, Commanding Fifth Army, appointed to make plans to seize Naples.
	16 Aug	Plans for landing at Calabria (BAYTOWN) issued.
	17 Aug	Fifth Army comes under command Fifteen Army Group.
	18 Aug–2 Sept	Allied Air Forces make 4,500 bombing sorties against rail and road communications on Italian mainland.
	22 Aug	General von Vietinghoff in command of German Tenth Army in Southern Italy.
	3 Sept	Eighth Army crosses Straits of Messina.
		Castellano signs surrender terms.
		82 Airborne Division planning to land near Rome on 8 September.
	4 Sept	General Alexander alerts 1 Airborne Division for capture of Taranto on 9 September.
	5–6 Sept	AVALANCHE assault forces start passage by sea.
	7 Sept	Major-General Taylor reaches Rome on secret mission.
	8 Sept	231 Brigade land at Pizzo.
		82 Airborne Division drop on Rome cancelled.
		Eisenhower broadcasts announcement of Italian surrender.
		Kesselring issues orders for offensive action against Italian forces.
		Italian battle fleet sails from Spezia for Malta during the night.

In broad terms Allied planning for a landing on the mainland of Italy started on 3 June immediately after the discussions held in Algiers between Churchill, Marshall and Eisenhower. As the pace of operations quickened, more and more responsibility for planning, hitherto undertaken in London or Washington, devolved on the theatre commander. Eisenhower's task in this instance was not an easy one. The decision taken at the TRIDENT conference the week before gave Eisenhower freedom as to choice of objective with one hand but took away much of his striking power with the other. General Alexander comments 'here were no geographical objectives pointed out but two desiderata, one political (the elimination of Italy) and the other, the containing of the maximum number of German divisions, from its very nature indefinable. It is essential that this directive be constantly borne in mind, for it continued to rule all strategy in Italy right up to the final surrender of the German armies in the field, and the campaign can only be rightly understood if this is firmly grasped. The campaign in Italy was a great holding attack. The two parts of the directive aim at the same purpose: the diversion of German strength to a theatre as far removed as possible from the vital point, the Channel coast.'[1]

For the autumn of 1943 a number of possible strategies were open to the Allies and a brief examination of these will illustrate how the pattern of operations about to be described was finally decided upon. The elimination of Italy from the war would result in the loss to the Axis of some sixty divisions or about two million men. Thirty-two of these divisions were stationed in the Balkans and seven in southern France, together with a number of additional anti-aircraft and coast defence units. Germany would have to replace these straight away, especially in the Balkans where there was already considerable unrest and partisan activity. Alexander, however, remarked in his dispatch that 'lower category formations including foreigners and satellites' could be used for occupation duties and that the problem would still remain of holding down a number of German divisions well away from the OVERLORD area. The invasion of Sardinia and Corsica could be discounted, as this would not necessarily bring about the collapse of Italy and would tend to draw German forces into France rather than away from it. An attack on the south of France at this stage would have a similar effect. Hitler rightly feared an Allied invasion of the Balkans from which he drew vital supplies for his war industries and where the Allies might link up with the Russian advances. Alexander regarded this as 'the best alternative' to an invasion of Italy, but points to

99

three difficulties: (a) to insure air cover it would be necessary to break into the 'outer ring of islands', a difficult operation in autumn, (b) the terrain is even worse than in Italy, (c) the available landing craft would soon be drastically reduced. This last factor in effect was the over-riding one from a military point of view, as without a large force of carrier-borne aircraft and many more landing craft than were available it would have been impossible to achieve a break-in and advance through the islands. Alexander adds 'a final argument against this course was that the United States government was most reluctant to become involved in a Balkan campaign'.[2] Stalin and Roosevelt were certainly of one mind on this point, if for different reasons. By a process of elimination, or shall we say by comparison with these alternatives, an assault on the Italian mainland seemed the best course of action, if only as being the only sure way of knocking Italy out of the war. As for the question of holding down German divisions, the Allied appreciation of the situation on Italy's capitulation was that Hitler could hardly afford to give the Allies a free run throughout the country, although as we have seen he was prepared to abandon virtually the whole of the peninsula to make sure of a strong defence line blocking the road to Germany itself. The general opinion was that, apart from securing the Alpine frontier, Hitler would deny the Allies the use of the Italian airfields as long as possible and would certainly use strong forces to hold the Allies away from the industrial areas of northern Italy. An advance into Italy thus seemed the best strategy to serve the dual require- ments of eliminating Italy and holding down a number of German divisions at a distance from the OVERLORD area. This having been decided, Eisenhower's planners had to face up to the difficulties of invading Italy from the south. As we have seen the terrain of peninsular Italy, with its mountainous spine and narrow coastal plains containing numerous rivers, makes any advance from the south very difficult. 'Military operations must . . . commence on one or both flanks of the mountains, and must continue along them in virtual independence of each other, or proceed into the mountains themselves against formidable natural obstacles. Only flanking attacks from the sea can relieve the difficulties of a frontal attack.'[3] It was therefore appreciated that the Allies would be forced to fight on narrow fronts and through country which favoured the defence. The Germans also had the advantage not only of operating on interior lines but also of having good communications and administrative facilities in the north of Italy, which it was estimated could support many more divisions than the Germans were likely to deploy there. Advancing up the peninsula the Allies on the other hand would have limited communications and considerable administrative difficulties. 'There was thus a danger in 1943 that a large effort might be compressed into a narrow front, where the defence held great advantages over the attack, and where in conse- quence the enemy might contain the Allies instead of the Allies containing the enemy.'[4] Eisenhower, however, could not look too far ahead, especially in the knowledge that he would soon lose some of his best divisions and most of his landing craft. At least he held the initiative as to the point of attack and enjoyed command of the sea and in the air. These factors, the planners believed, should balance out the inherent difficulties of the terrain in peninsular Italy. Although a landing in Italy was now accepted as the logical course of action, from a planning point of view, much depended on how HUSKY and the political situation in Italy developed. General Alexander records that 'the result of the first few days' fighting in Sicily brought a breath of actuality into the process of planning – and with it a full gale of optimism'.[5] Allied casualties had been light and few landing craft had been lost. Moreover it seemed obvious that the Italian army was unlikely to put up any serious resistance to a landing on the mainland, while the civilian population would probably welcome the Allies as liberators as had happened in Sicily. In the early days after the Sicilian landings, Alexander made plans to land in Calabria, even before the capture of Messina, using reserves standing by in North Africa. 78 Division, however, had to be brought in against the Etna line and, without the use of the port of Catania, the plan had to be abandoned. It was about this time (17 July) that Eisenhower and his three senior commanders really got down to selecting a number of alternative landing operations, to take advantage of the foreseeable political and operational developments. These preliminary plans visualized various landings on the toe or at Taranto and included the use of Naples, after the capture of the port as the result of an advance by land from southern Italy. Detailed planning for this particular operation was in the hands of Fifth Army commanded by Lieutenant-General Mark Clark. Since being formed late in 1942, Fifth Army had been almost continuously involved in planning and training for amphibious operations; for landing near Gibraltar, in the event of Spanish hostility, then in Sardinia, or at Taranto and now to reinforce through Naples. Since the fall of Mussolini and with Italy's capitulation within sight, Eisenhower and his commanders were now prepared to take greater risks and were anxious to strike as far up the peninsula as possible. So on 27 July General Clark was directed to prepare plans for seizing the port of Naples as a base for further operations. The target date was to be 7 September and outline plans were to be ready by 7 August. This was considered the earliest date because all the landing craft were engaged in maintaining the operations in Sicily, which were not likely to end before mid-August. Also time had to be allowed to repair and refit any damaged craft before they were used in the forthcoming amphibious operations against the mainland. At this stage it was still not decided whether the landings in Calabria or in the vicinity of Naples would be the major effort. Montgomery considered that both 10 and 13 Corps would be required in the direct assault across the Straits of Messina and for the time being only VI Corps, consisting of one armoured, two infantry and one airborne division under Fifth Army, were earmarked for the attack on Naples.

Uncertainty as to German intentions and moves to reinforce the southern provinces, combined with the fluid political conditions throughout Italy, demanded a good deal of flexibility as to Allied plans. So it was decided that 10 Corps would be allotted sufficient landing craft to allow it to be used in either operation. The decision to cross to Calabria in advance of the Naples landing had already been taken and, as we have seen, 1 Canadian and 5 Division had been withdrawn from the operations in Sicily and placed under 13 Corps Headquarters to prepare for the assault across the Straits. Meanwhile, beaches had to be chosen and detailed plans drawn up for the more ambitious operation aiming at the capture of Naples, which was given the code name AVALANCHE. Time was running short, however, if the assault force was to be ready to take full advantage of the rapidly deteriorating political situation in Italy. Meanwhile the plums were Naples and Taranto and from the Navy's point of view the sooner the Straits of Messina were opened the better.

As in the case of the invasion of Sicily air cover was the key. As there 'was no possibility of getting the necessary aircraft carriers for the theatre',[6] planning had to be based on the operational range of land-based fighters. In the case of the Spitfires, this was a radius of 180 miles from the most advanced Sicilian airfields at Milazzo and Messina. Naples and Taranto themselves were just, but quite definitely, beyond the range of effective fighter cover. In the toe of Italy south of a line Amendolara–Belvedere there were five enemy fighter fields, the most important being at Reggio and Crotone. The prior capture of these would allow seaborne assaults north of Naples but equally allow time for the Germans to bring considerable reinforcements into the area. Inland from the coast, between the mouth of the Volturno River and Naples, was 'one of the few plains along the west coast of Italy not dominated by nearby mountains, a fact which would permit the rapid deployment of large forces and the full use of our armour . . . the beaches were unsuitable for landing and in parts obstructed by off-lying sand-bars'. In the Gulf of Salerno, however, there were twenty miles of beaches 'undoubtedly the best for an assault on the whole west coast',[7] with gradients which allowed the landing craft to come close inshore and with good sea approaches. Moreover the enemy fighter airfields at Montecorvino, which were only three miles inland, would take four fighter squadrons once captured. This was an important factor as it was estimated that some 600 German and Italian day fighters and 50 German night fighters were stationed on airfields in the Naples and Foggia areas. The disadvantage of the Salerno area, however, lies in the fact that the coastal plain is enclosed by a ring of mountains from two to ten miles inland which gave the Germans excellent observation and positions commanding the plain. Also any direct advance on Naples was blocked by the rocky spur of Mount Picentini, through which there were two difficult passes in narrow and easily defended gorges. However, a landing at Salerno was 'the furthest north and the nearest to Naples' that could be covered from the air. Owing to the shortage of landing craft, the initial seaborne assault had to be limited to three divisions, with a floating reserve of one regimental combat team. In addition, three American Ranger battalions and two British Commandos were included in the assault phase. Although two airborne divisions had been allotted to Fifth Army, there were unfortunately only sufficient aircraft to lift one division and 82 US Airborne Division was nominated. General Clark initially planned to land his airborne troops east and south of Mount Vesuvius, where they could delay reinforcements from Naples or Rome and hold the two passes mentioned above. The mountainous terrain and treacherous air currents around Mount Vesuvius, however, made low-altitude approach for aircraft extremely hazardous and, coupled with these factors, there were known to be strong anti-aircraft concentrations sited in the area as part of the defences of Naples. So this plan had to be abandoned. Still intent on protecting the landings from the strong German forces assembled in central Italy, General Clark then proposed dropping a regimental combat team of parachutists to seize and blow up the bridges over the Volturno at Triflisco, Capua and Cancello, some forty miles from the Salerno bridgehead area. Major-General Ridgway the divisional commander was pretty lukewarm about this proposal at first but the plan was backed by both Spaatz and Tedder. The importance of the coastal strip inland from the Gulf of Gaeta and of the Volturno crossings was obvious and, as we shall see later, Kesselring was convinced that this would be the most likely area for an Allied amphibious landing. As Alexander later wrote, however, 'this drop was subsequently cancelled, to the great detriment of the operations'.[8]

By 16 August a balance between the two operations, BAYTOWN, the landing in Calabria, and AVALANCHE had been decided and outline plans issued. Two divisions of Eighth Army would cross the Straits between 1–4 September and 10 Corps would be allotted to Fifth Army for the assault at Salerno on 9 September. The overall strength of the landing forces and the dates were dictated by the shortage of landing craft; this was the best that could be done under the circumstances. Three weeks only remained before the date for AVALANCHE. On both sides this was to be a period of intense activity. For the German troops evacuated from Sicily this meant reorganization and redeployment and they achieved both with their usual skill and efficiency. For the Italians there were the uncertainties of political upheaval, fear and mistrust of their Axis allies and the dread of the Allied bombing raids and in the background the secret negotiations with the Western Powers. For the Allies there was little time left. The pre-invasion air assault had to begin immediately and the refitting and loading of the ships and craft had to be completed while the maintenance of the formations in Sicily still went on. Compared with HUSKY the plans for all three services were complicated. Sea lanes had to be swept of mines, fighter strips had to be hastily constructed in the Milazzo area and large quantities of gun ammunition had to be moved up for the bombardment over the Straits. In his report Alexander comments on the result of aiming at extreme flexibility in the planning, 'It is fair to say that few operations of war of this magnitude have been so distinguished by the speed with which they were mounted and the shortness of the time between the decision to undertake the invasion and its launching. This speed was made possible by the flexibility of strategy permitted by the nature of amphibious operations and the geographical configuration of the theatre and it was encouraged by the challenge of a constantly changing military and political situation.'[9] But there is more than forethought required for the planning of large and complex operations of war and while special praise must go to the unit and formation staffs, who day by day kept abreast of the changing pattern for the various assaults, little could have been achieved but for the tremendous spirit of inter-Allied and inter-service co-operation that united the whole of Eisenhower's command. During the negotiations of the surrender terms General Castellano was able to give Eisenhower's staff a forecast of the German intentions, so far as these had been disclosed at the Roatta conference in mid-August, together with fairly detailed information on the disposition of their forces. As we have seen, Hitler was determined to hold the northern Apennines or at least the line of the River Po. According to the Allied strength, he hoped to stand on a forward line from Grosseto through Mount Amiata to Perugia and Ancona and 'finally if the circumstances and relative strength were particularly favourable, an attempt would be made to stand south of Rome on the line Gaeta–Isernia–Vasto . . . a line which the Italians had already surveyed, and defences were already being prepared at certain places'.[10] Consequently, at the beginning of September we find considerable German forces in the north, where Rommel's Army Group B contained eight infantry and two armoured divisions (including one and a half in Sardinia and Corsica), supported by well-developed lines of communication and administrative facilities. In the south, Kesselring had eight divisions. XI Flieger Corps, commanded by General Student, came under his own control in the general area of Rome; 3 Panzer Grenadier Division was around Viterbo and 2 Parachute Division on the coast near Ostia. The remaining divisions were formed into two corps under Tenth Army, XIV Panzer Corps, commanded by General Hube, was centrally placed with the newly formed 16 Panzer Division covering the Gulf of Salerno, while the Hermann Göring Division and 15 Panzer Grenadier Division were in the Naples area refitting after the withdrawal from Sicily. Further south, LXXVI Panzer Corps, commanded by General Herr, had 29 Panzer Grenadier Division (from Sicily) and the newly formed 26 Panzer Division in Calabria. This latter division was based on the isthmus of Catanzaro and had no tank regiment; one tank battalion never arrived in Italy and the other was north of Rome with 3 Panzer Grenadier Division. 1 Parachute Division was placed at Altamura in Apulia. These dispositions of course fitted in with the German appreciation of the most likely areas for Allied landings and with their policy for holding their strength back in the north, where they were particularly sensitive of the possibility of landings near Genoa, Spezia and in the Rome area. The area Gaeta–Naples–Salerno was also considered and landings here would again be opposed. In Calabria delaying tactics only were considered practicable. The strength of the forces near Salerno were obviously of particular importance to the Allies and here we find the Germans had two divisions covering Naples and the beaches further north on either side of the Volturno, and only moved over a third, 16 Panzer Division, from Apulia to Salerno late in August. This division consisted of four battalions of infantry and a battalion of tanks, plus reconnaissance and engineer battalions, and it had the task of holding over thirty miles of coastline. It arrived in the area only a week before the Allied attack.

Even before the operations in Sicily were ended the Allied air forces were turning their attention to the interdiction of the railway system and to airfield attacks in Italy. The intention of this intensive bombing programme 'was to isolate the German Division in Southern Italy and drive what remained of the Luftwaffe from its landing grounds'.[11] Heavy attacks had already been made at Rome and Naples and now the Foggia marshalling yards and other yards and railway junctions as far north as Pisa were attacked. These attacks against the communication system and airfields were pressed on without any pause between the two campaigns. This meant that the heavy and medium bomber squadrons and their fighter escorts and indeed all the ground crews that serviced the squadrons were involved in continuous operations. Between 18 August and 2 September the bomber operations, including those by the fighter-bombers, against communications 'had grown to more than 4,500 sorties with around 6,500 tons of bombs dropped'.[12] The results were dramatic. Marshalling yards and rail communications throughout the peninsula had been so damaged that movement by rail south of Naples–Foggia 'was practically at a standstill' and further north was seriously reduced. The only serious attack by the Luftwaffe had been a raid on Bizerta on 17 August by a strong force of about a hundred JU88s, sinking an LCI and damaging three other vessels and causing some 240 casualties. Among the casualties in this raid was Lieutenant-General Horrocks, the Corps Commander of 10 Corps, who was seriously wounded and had to be relieved by Lieutenant-General McCreery. Although the Axis bomber squadrons were pushed back into central and northern Italy, the German fighter squadrons based on the Foggia complex of airfields were still very active. Here a low-flying attack on 25 August by 276 P38s, with an escort of Lightnings, dropped 240 tons of 500-lb. general-purpose and 20-lb. fragmentation bombs in thirty minutes on four airfields. Forty-seven German planes were destroyed and thirteen damaged. After this attack there was a sharp decline in the number of Allied bombers lost to enemy fighters. Previously, as high an average as forty fighters at a time had attacked the Allied bombers during daylight. By September the Luftwaffe was down to about 600 planes in Italy, Corsica, Sardinia and southern France. Of these a third were of low serviceability and the Luftwaffe was only able to fly between fifty and a hundred sorties a day in the whole area. All the Germans could do in the air was to save their strength against the expected Allied landings. Meanwhile the air operations in direct preparation for AVALANCHE were being stepped up. Tedder records that 'for ten days the Mediterranean air forces had been preparing the way. After a raid by Wellingtons on Salerno itself during the night of 31 August/1 September the fires could be seen for sixty miles around. On 2 September we began the systematic bombardment of marshalling yards, while the light bombers busied themselves in attacking troop concentrations, gun emplacements, and an army headquarters. One raid produced a violent explosion believed to be due to a hit on an ammunition dump. From the following day, we attacked enemy airfields consistently. Other assaults were made on bridges and roads and rail bottlenecks.'[13]

While Eisenhower looked to the air force to stop the concentration of re-inforcements in the Salerno area, the strength of heavy bombers for AVALANCHE was considerably less than for HUSKY, owing to the withdrawal of three B24 Liberator Groups which left only four B17 Fortress Groups and two B24 Groups, both of which were under strength. Eisenhower had in fact asked the Combined Chiefs of Staff at the end of July for the loan of an extra four heavy bomber groups for a month to five weeks. This proposal, however, was turned down owing to the critical stage of the day battle over Germany and the administrative problem of moving four thousand ground personnel and an enormous quantity of equipment. It was estimated that this move might take a month 'during which time the squadrons would operate at much reduced efficiency'.[14] Now the situation would be even worse than before as Eisenhower was told that three Wellington squadrons would be withdrawn on 15 September. This would not only reduce the total heavy bomber force by a third, compared with HUSKY, but the withdrawal of the Wellingtons would reduce the night bomber force by more than a third and this was considered a very serious matter. So serious in fact that Tedder 'with deep reluctance' challenged the decision to withdraw these squadrons. The result-ing interchange of signals between himself and Portal at least kept the door open until it was finally agreed to 'see how events unfolded'. Every day the difficulties of mounting AVALANCHE increased – first a shortage of landing craft – now a serious reduction in the bomber force. As Tedder signalled to Portal at the time, 'there is a tendency to consider the Italian chicken as being already in the pot, whereas in fact it is not yet hatched'.[15]

Eisenhower's negotiations over the Italian armistice were also running into difficulties. Castellano arrived in Rome with the Allied terms of surrender on

27 August and four days later he returned by air via Sicily. Although in the meantime Badoglio and the King had decided to accept the terms, Castellano was only prepared to discuss 'the methods by which the Italian change of side was to be made most smoothly. The Italians were now getting extremely worried about the German reaction. German troops continued to pour into Italy, and they were afraid that they would not be able to defend themselves when the surrender was announced.'[16] Time was now getting very short. Within a couple of days the Eighth Army would cross at Messina. Soon the Germans would be able to estimate the likely strength of any amphibious assault, even if they were still in doubt as to the point of attack.

The naval preparations equally were made in conditions of frustration and uncertainty. When the Liberator squadrons were withdrawn Admiral Cunningham signalled to the First Sea Lord, 'I believe that we can and shall succeed, but only if we go flat out. If we whittle away our resources now to build up OVERLORD our chances of success will be greatly reduced, and if AVALANCHE fails OVERLORD may be stillborn.' The Admiralty had in fact taken early action to build up the naval covering forces in preparation for landings on the Italian mainland. Within three days of the Combined Chiefs of Staff approving Eisenhower's plans they had arranged the dispatch of a fleet carrier (to replace the carrier damaged during HUSKY) and four escort carriers (taken off Atlantic convoy duty) plus an aircraft repair ship to reinforce the Mediterranean fleet. In addition, the Admiralty ordered ten large troop-ships, which had returned to the United Kingdom after HUSKY, to sail immediately back to the Mediterranean.

Meanwhile the Americans stuck to the letter of the TRIDENT agreement and refused to operate a 'standstill' on ships and craft being moved out of the Mediterranean, so for the moment the British were left on their own 'to mitigate the thinness of the forces left to General Eisenhower as best they could from British resources'.[17] At the end of July Vice-Admiral Hewitt was appointed to command the naval forces for AVALANCHE and planning got under way. Within a couple of weeks the pattern of operations was beginning to take shape and both Eisenhower and Cunningham were getting extremely worried over the adequacy of the forces available. At Cunningham's request the Admiralty replaced two cruisers damaged during HUSKY and ordered the modern battleships HMS *Howe* and *King George V* to remain temporarily under his command. Cunningham was also allowed to retain forty-eight LCTs that, but for his 'standstill' request, would already have returned to Britain. Although Cunningham's requests in the main were met by the Admiralty, acting on their own initiative, the Combined Chiefs of Staff at the QUADRANT conference on 20 August ordered ten American LSTs to sail from the Mediterranean for India and countermanded the 'standstill' on British shipping movements out of the Mediterranean. As Captain Roskill, the official British Naval historian, points out, 'these decisions were to produce unfortunate consequences on operations in the Aegean'. Indeed he also records his opinion that, 'had the Admiralty not met the naval needs so fully the narrow margin by which operation AVALANCHE was finally successful might well have disappeared'.[18] The naval forces involved in the assault and follow-up convoys together with the covering force for AVALANCHE are summarized in the following table and a comparison with a similar table for HUSKY (see p 32) clearly shows the shortage of ships and particularly of landing craft that faced Eisenhower and his commanders.

NAVAL FORCES FOR AVALANCHE 9 SEPTEMBER–13 OCTOBER
COVERING FORCES AND ASSAULT CONVOYS

Class	British	American	Other Nations
Battleships	4	—	—
Fleet Carriers	2	—	—
Escort Carriers	4	—	—
Light Carriers	1	—	—
Cruisers	7	4	—
AA Ships	1	—	—
Fighter Direction Ships	2	—	—
Monitors	2	—	—
Gunboats	—	—	1 Dutch
HQ Ships	1	1	—
Destroyers	40	17	2 Greek
			3 Polish
			2 French
Escort Vessels	38	41	—
Minesweepers	6 and 27 Craft	9 and 12 Craft	—
LSI (and Transports) (a)	5 (Transports)	24	1 Polish
LST (b)	57	63	—
LCI	54	74	—
LCT (c)	60	30	—
Coastal Craft	13 (Trawlers)	2 (Tugs)	—
Miscellaneous Vessels	5 (Tankers)	31	—
Submarines	—	—	—
Hospital Ships	3	—	—
Total	332	308	9

(a) Most of the Transports and landing ships also took part in the follow-up convoys.
(b) Figures for LSTs, LCIs and LCTs are based on Morrison. Roskill shows no distinction between British and American.
(c) In addition there were 19 support landing craft divided between the two assault areas.

The naval plans had to provide for five separate landings at Salerno; Rangers and Commandos on the left flank; two British divisions, 46 and 56 Divisions, with first objectives Salerno itself and the Montecorvino airfield;

36 US Division at Paestum to seize the high ground commanding the coastal plain. Further convoys were required for the floating reserve, 45 US Division, and the follow-up force, 1 Armoured and 34 US Divisions and 7 Armoured Division. The assembly and routing of no less than fifteen separate convoys and their escorts had to be arranged and co-ordinated. Not only was there little time for detailed planning but changes in orders had to be catered for right up to the last moment. The Northern Attack Force carrying the two British divisions would mostly sail from Tripoli, under the command of Commodore Oliver, RN. The Southern Attack Force for the landing at Paestum would sail from Bizerta, Oran and Algiers under Rear-Admiral Hall, USN. 'In all some 700 large and small warships, merchantmen and landing craft of a great multiplicity of types took part.'[19] A number of follow-up convoys had also to be planned. The first of these was of fifteen MT ships due to arrive in the assault area on 11 September, while the first troop-ship convoy of thirteen ships was due on 21 September. It was hoped that the troop-ships would unload in Naples, but as we shall soon see all the ships had to discharge over the Salerno beaches.

On 21 August, nine days after the outline plan for AVALANCHE was issued, General Clark advanced 'H' hour by thirty minutes and most of the convoy orders had to be altered. The convoy timetables in fact were very complex, this was mainly because all the landing craft and small escort vessels had to refuel at ports in northern Sicily *en route* for the bay of Salerno. Now a further problem arose. A number of enemy minefields were discovered at a late date in the Gulf of Salerno itself. The transports would now have to lower their landing craft from nine to twelve miles offshore to give the mine-sweepers a chance of clearing these fields and the whole of the intricate time-table for the assault had to be revised. A further change of plan resulted in a number of landing craft having to be diverted to ferry units of the Eighth Army across the straits of Messina. When he eventually issued his orders on 29 August, Commodore Oliver hoped that 'a combined operation will never again have to be concerted in such conditions'. In the end verbal orders had to be passed down to ensure that every ship's captain and commander of a landing craft group was properly briefed on the latest change of plan, and Captain Roskill comments, 'that very few misunderstandings actually arose is a tribute to the care and skill with which this was done'.[20] Each convoy was given some close escort but in addition a strong British covering force, called Force H, under the command of Vice-Admiral Willis, was to be provided from Malta and consisted of four battleships and two fleet carriers. This force originally included four British cruisers under Commander Agnew but, as we shall see, they were temporarily diverted for an unusual and dramatic task. Each attack force for AVALANCHE included a special fire support group. In the northern assault area this was provided by three cruisers, an anti-aircraft ship, a monitor and a number of destroyers, all from the Royal Navy.

For the southern assault area, fire support was provided by four American cruisers and a British monitor. In an attempt to achieve surprise there was to be no preliminary naval or air bombardment, but elaborate plans were made to use the fire of these support groups once the landings had gone in. Unfortunately there was a shortage of air observation planes, so much would depend on the early setting up of observation posts on shore. In the British sector it was hoped to bridge this gap by the employment of rocket batteries, mortars and guns mounted in special landing craft. Before we leave the naval plans, mention must be made of a small diversion group consisting of an American destroyer, a British gunboat and twenty-seven motor torpedo boats, launches and air-sea rescue craft. This force was sent to demonstrate in the Gulf of Gaeta and off the mouth of the River Volturno. Unfortunately the only result achieved was the somewhat tardy surrender of the small island of Ventotene.

Eisenhower was determined to announce the armistice before and not after AVALANCHE. Something had to be done to bolster the Italian Government's faltering morale and convince them of the overwhelming strength of the Allied attack on the mainland. Eisenhower decided to land the 82 US Airborne Division near Rome, providing Badoglio would guarantee that 'the armistice is signed and announced as desired by the Allies; that the Italians will seize and hold the necessary airfields and stop all anti-aircraft fire; that the Italian divisions in the Rome area will take action against the Germans'.[21] A senior officer with experience of airborne operations was to be secretly dispatched to Rome on 7 September and plans were made to fly in part of the division to four airfields near Rome at 2130 hours the following night. The remainder of the division would follow on succeeding nights and ammunition and heavy weapons would be brought in up the Tiber from a beach head established at Ostia by landing craft. Several squadrons of Spitfires and American P40 fighters were to be flown in to assist in the defence of the airfields. Armed with this proposal Castellano once more flew back to report to Badoglio. This extremely risky operation was of course at the expense of the AVALANCHE plans, as there were only enough aircraft for the one airborne division and the drops or landings would have to be done on successive nights. The proposition, however, put some heart into the Italians and Castellano was back in Sicily on 2 September. Finally, after a further delay of some thirty-six hours, he eventually received authority to sign the military terms of surrender. As a matter of interest these instructions from Badoglio were passed over 'a special wireless set designed for spy work', that Castellano had been given in Lisbon and which was operated in Rome by a British parachute officer released from an Italian prisoner of war camp.

At 0430 hours on 3 September, the day that General Castellano signed the surrender terms, the leading troops of Eighth Army landed on the Italian mainland. General Montgomery had been preparing for this attack well before operations in Sicily ended. A reconnaissance party had landed during the night of 27/28 August at Bova Marina to find the place deserted but other parties landing at later dates had not returned, so the plans for Operation BAYTOWN, as the crossing of the Straits was called, went ahead on the assumption that the landings would be opposed by elements of 29 Panzer Grenadier Division and possibly of 26 Panzer Division who were reported to be holding the 'toe'. Having obtained some extra landing craft, the original plan for an assault by only four battalions was changed to allow 13 Corps to attack on a two-divisional front. 1 Canadian Division would be on the right and 5 Division on the left and the crossings would be made directly over the Straits immediately north of Reggio. The whole of 30 Corps artillery was deployed around Messina and included eighty medium and forty-eight heavy guns loaned by Seventh Army. A heavy air attack was also laid on to deal with targets further inland. Finally, two Commandos and 231 Infantry Brigade Group were held ready at Riposto in Sicily 'for mounting seaborne hooks along the north coast of the "toe" as required'.[22] At the southern entrance to the narrows, fifteen British warships, including two cruisers, closed in to bombard the defences at Reggio. In the mountainous country close above Messina the guns to cover the crossing were massed row upon row. As the leading waves of some 300 assault and landing craft, together with a number of the recently developed 'Rhino' ferries, sailed out across the narrow straits, it seemed to observers looking down from the heights above on to the narrow strip of sea and the slow-moving lines of little craft, that they were spectators at an exercise, rather than witnesses to the re-entry by an Allied army into the mainland of Axis-dominated Europe. But as the guns opened fire any sense of unreality was shattered by the crash of the mounting barrage. On the opposite shore a great pall of smoke began to form, to rise and thicken and drift out towards the approaching lines of assault craft, which soon completely disappeared from sight in the swirling dusty cloud. Apart from some long-range shelling, which was quickly dealt with from the air, the landings were unopposed. A single German regiment had been left to hold seventeen miles of coastline but had retired in the face of the all too obvious strength of the assault. Italian coastal units surrendered at the earliest opportunity. Throughout the day no contact was made with the Germans and by nightfall the line San Stefano–Scilla had been reached. That night commandos landed at Bagnara and got in behind the German rearguards. The leading elements of 5 Division soon joined up with the commandos but found such heavy demolitions had been carried out that only infantry on foot could enter the town. The terrain in fact was admirably suited to such delaying tactics, as movement off the roads was virtually impossible for wheeled vehicles. As Montgomery comments 'the roads in Calabria and southern Italy proper twist and turn in mountainous country and are admirable feats of engineering; they abound in bridges, viaducts, culverts and even tunnels and thus offer unlimited scope to military engineers for demolitions and road blocks of every conceivable kind'.[23] The Germans, with their customary skill and thoroughness, took full advantage of these conditions and were able to delay the advance of the Eighth Army with little difficulty and relatively weak rearguards.

13 Corps' initial objective was the narrow neck at Catanzaro and by noon on 6 September Gioia Tauro had been captured and the Canadians had been switched to the southern coast road to try and speed up the advance. In an attempt to pinch off some of the German withdrawal, the Corps Commander, General Dempsey, sent 231 Brigade Group round by sea to land at Pizzo early on 8 September. This assault in fact coincided with elements of 29 Panzer Grenadier Division pulling out along the coast road, which was only a few yards inland from the beaches on which the Brigade was about to land. The approach of the landing craft, whose only naval escort was a monitor and two gunboats, was met by artillery shelling and dive bombers. During the run in this critical situation was dramatically changed by the commander of one of the LSTs beaching his ship, which by now was burning furiously, at full speed. 'A bulldozer burst open the jammed bow doors, the ramp was dropped and mobile guns rushed ashore.'[24] The engagement continued in and around Pizzo all day but during the night the Germans slipped away up the coast road. The leading Brigades of 13 Corps reached the line Catanzaro to Nicastro about thirty-six hours later (10 September) having advanced a hundred miles in seven days, in the face of considerable difficulties in getting the fighting vehicles and essential supply echelons forward over the heavily damaged and mined roads. Eighth Army was now getting very strung out and the rate of advance was also slowing down, owing to the slow build-up across the Straits of urgently needed lines of communication units and transport columns.

In the meantime Eisenhower was having trouble with Badoglio over the announcement of the surrender terms, which it had been agreed they would jointly make at 1830 hours on 8 September. On the morning of that very day Eisenhower was conferring with his Commanders-in-Chief, at his advance headquarters near Carthage, when two radio messages were brought in. The first was from General Taylor who had reached Rome early the previous night. Here he had seen General Carboni, who commanded the Italian troops in Rome, and had set before him the plan and conditions for the landing of 82 Airborne Division. Cardoni painted the most depressing picture imaginable. He claimed that 12,000 German troops were in Rome and 36,000 nearby. His own troops had practically no ammunition and no petrol and he could not guarantee to hold the airfields. Faced with this virtual veto of the plan, General Taylor insisted on speaking to Badoglio. The meeting took place in the early hours of the following morning and the Marshal not only confirmed Carboni's assessment of the situation but got back on to his old tactics of pleading for time. He wanted the announcement of the armistice to be delayed; he also wanted the parachute drop to be delayed and in any case he must be told where the seaborne landing would take place. Badoglio made it clear that 'it is no longer possible to accept an immediate armistice as this could provoke the occupation of the capital and the violent assumption of the government by the Germans'. He ended the interview by trying to persuade General Taylor to return to Sicily to present his views and in his presence wrote out a signal for transmission to Eisenhower containing the passage quoted above. General Taylor somewhat naturally concluded that the Italians were both unable and unwilling to co-operate and that, in face of the reported German strength in and around Rome, the parachute drop must be cancelled. His recommendation to this effect was contained in the radio message handed to Eisenhower, who had no option but to send General Lemnitzer by air (no other means would have been in time) to countermand the orders for the airborne operation on Rome. General Lemnitzer arrived only just in time. As his plane touched down at Licata sixty-two planes had already taken off, loaded with airborne troops, and were circling into formation. The second radio message was from Badoglio himself. This had been sent on from the main headquarters in Algiers where 'the staff, thrown completely off balance, radioed the Combined Chiefs of Staff for instructions at the same time that they forwarded the original message (to Eisenhower)'.[25] On reading the message from Badoglio Eisenhower was furious. Already thoroughly put out by the matter having been referred to Washington, he 'demanded to be led to a telephone to speak with his Chief of Staff in Algiers . . . dictating on the spot a remarkably incisive telegram to be sent forthwith to Marshal Badoglio. He reminded the Marshal that his accredited representative had signed the terms of the armistice and had undertaken on his behalf that they would be carried out. Whatever happened it was his intention to make the broadcast as arranged at 6.30 pm that night.'[26] The wretched Castellano, who had meanwhile been sent for, was curtly told what had happened and dismissed 'to spend the rest of the day in the greatest anxiety'.[27] Much indeed was at stake, as the convoys for AVALANCHE were already north of Sicily and as soon as it was dark would turn towards Salerno itself. The convoys were sailing through narrow swept channels in mined waters and could not possibly turn back. On the assumption that the Italian Fleet would act on the surrender terms in a matter of hours, plans had meanwhile been made to dispatch the British 1 Airborne Division to Taranto, where the Italians had already agreed to hand over the port intact. The division was already embarked on four British and one American light cruisers and a fast 2,600-ton minelayer and this force would be at sea before the time for the broadcast, as the intention was that their arrival at Taranto should coincide with the Salerno landings. No reply came from Badoglio and at 1830 hours Eisenhower went on the air over Radio Algiers and the world learned that the Italian Government had surrendered its forces unconditionally. Ten minutes later the text of Badoglio's proclamation went out in English and shortly afterwards in London and Washington the news was released through Reuters. Almost the first to learn the news were Roatta and Westphal, who were discussing joint measures to meet the Allied invasion. Since about 1800 hours, Badoglio, with several of his Ministers and Service Chiefs, had been in conference with King Victor Emmanuel. It was no longer a question of playing for time, or of making clandestine military plans for the defence of Rome, or even of discussing these plans with the Allies. Eisenhower's telegram had been quite explicit. Some of those present claimed it was an attempt to compromise them with the Germans, others feared German reprisals and wanted Badoglio to be dismissed, so that the government could disclaim responsibility for the armistice negotiations. General Ambrosio and Gariglia, the Foreign Minister, now saw that the country was trapped between the Allies and the Germans, both of whom would turn on them without hesitation. The news of Eisenhower's broadcast brought the argument to an abrupt conclusion. Badoglio offered no solution. The King himself decided – it was impossible to change sides again. The armistice must be accepted. So at 1945 hours, an hour late, Badoglio's voice was heard on Radio Rome reading the announcement. Within the hour Kesselring issued codeword ACHSE for the German troops to attack and disarm the Italian forces and to seize Rome.

Up in the north, the Italian battle fleet at Spezia slipped away in the early hours of 9 September, but the considerable Italian Army forces made little or no move to prevent the Germans taking over key points throughout the whole of the vital industrial area. Even the city of Milan 'with a strong garrison of regular troops and an allegedly turbulent and liberty loving proletarian population surrendered to a small force of SS troops'.[28] The half-hearted resistance by the five Italian divisions in and around Rome was quickly smashed by the German 2 Parachute Division, with the assistance of reinforcements rushed in from 3 Panzer Grenadier Division. Further south, the Germans moved equally efficiently and overnight the Italian garrisons of many coastal defence positions, including those at Salerno, were disarmed and the defences taken over. While the Allies had hoped that the announcement of the surrender would confuse and embarrass the Germans and that many Italian units would resist, in the end, the situation may well have had the opposite result. The uneasy Axis partnership was ended. The Germans knew now where they stood. Accustomed to operating in alien countries, they may even have felt a sense of relief. The years of frustration and compromise and of pretence were over. Now the Italians would have to obey orders and not be giving them, while the Germans could get down to the business of war with greater efficiency and under conditions they really understood.

American self-propelled gun supporting the British attack on Monte Camino, December 1943.

An RAF Baltimore bombing the road from Avezzano to Pescara.

Spitfires taking off from a captured airfield near Naples. In foreground a wrecked ME 109.

Admiral Troubridge, General Lucas and Major-General Penny on board HMS *Bulolo* off Anzio, 22 January 1944.

7

Attrition at Salerno

Salerno and the German defences: Fifth Army plan and the landings: Effect of Naval and Air support: A new weapon: Allied reserves committed: The Panzers close in: The fight for Battipaglia and Persano: The crisis in the bridgehead: Parachute reinforcements: Alexander sees for himself: The Bombers join in: Taranto landing and Eighth Army advance: The link up: Kesselring pulls out.

1943	9 Sept	Fifth Army (10 and VI Corps) assault landings at Salerno. 1 Airborne Division lands at Taranto.
	10 Sept	Eighth Army ordered to increase pressure on Germans withdrawing from Calabria.
	11 Sept	13 Corps (Eighth Army) push forward light forces. Brindisi falls to 1 Airborne Division. Germans start evacuation of Sardinia. Italian Fleet reaches Malta – Germans sink *Roma en route*.
	12 Sept	Critical situation in Salerno beach heads.
	13 Sept	US Parachute reinforcements dropped in VI Corps area.
	13–16 Sept	In Aegean British units from Middle East occupy Islands of Kos, Leros and Samos.
	14 Sept	Allied air forces fly maximum sorties in direct support at Salerno. 82 Airborne Division drops reinforcements and also behind German lines at Avellino. 7 Armoured Division starts arriving in 10 Corps area. 1 Airborne Division enters Bari. 5 Division concentrating at Belvedere.
	15 Sept	5 Division reaches Sapri. HMS *Valiant* and *Warspite* join naval bombardment forces. Germans at Salerno turn to defensive. Alexander gives Volturno crossings as next objective.
	16 Sept	5 Division in contact with VI Corps bridgehead. 1 Canadian Division in contact with 1 Airborne Division (from Taranto).

	Kesselring orders phased withdrawal from Salerno positions.
	Fifth Army increases pressure to break out from bridgehead.
17 Sept	VI Corps attack at Altavilla held – Germans pull out overnight.
	Eighth Army begins general advance northwards, reaching Auletta–Potenza on 19 September.
18 Sept	Fifth Army enters Altavilla, Persano and Battipaglia.
	Sardinia surrenders to Allied landing party.

So far we have seen AVALANCHE in almost a political context. When Eisenhower's voice was heard announcing the Italian capitulation the troops sailing towards the Salerno beaches were jubilant, but immediately afterwards the senior officers were warning their units that the armistice made no difference to the plan for the assault, which must be carried out on the assumption that the landings would be opposed. Fifth Army's task, the early capture of Rome, was not an easy one. As we have seen, the beaches at Salerno were good and there was plenty of room for dumps to be built up by the Beach Maintenance Groups to support the subsequent advance. There is no doubt, however, that the terrain generally speaking favoured the German defenders and an examination of the area shows how certain physical features helped determine the pattern of the battle for the beach head that raged for a week. The principal exit from the Salerno plain towards Naples is by Route 18 and the railway which cross the mountains by the Cava Gap. There is a further rail and road link running north from Salerno to Avellino. Subsidiary roads from Maiori and Amalfi also cross the mountainous Sorrento peninsula. The early capture of Salerno itself, and of these passes and routes north, was obviously vital to any plan for a rapid advance on Naples after the landing. The beaches stretch south from Salerno for about twenty-six miles as far as Agropoli, near which Route 18 and the coastal railway line enter the plain from the south. The plain is roughly triangular in shape with its long base on the coastline and is divided by the Rivers Sele and Calore, which join about five miles inland from the coast. Just below the junction of the two rivers, Route 18 crosses the River Sele at the Ponte Alla Scafa and continues to swing inland as far as Battipaglia. A further main road (Route 19) and rail link from the south and 'heel' of the peninsula enters the plain at its furthest point from the sea, crosses the River Sele at Ponte Sele (which is twelve miles inland from the coast) and passing below Mount Eboli joins Route 18 at Battipaglia. Battipaglia itself is the principal road and rail centre in the northern part of the plain and is six miles from the coast. Roads from the north serve both Battipaglia and the village of Eboli and between Eboli and Ponte Sele these roads strike south across the plain, following the river valleys towards Ponte Alla Scafa. The southern end of the plain is closely overlooked from Mount Soprano and Mount Scittani. Here the foothills close in round Capaccio and also dominate the roads leading down on to the plain through the valleys either side of these two mountains. The implications of this pattern of road communications become only too

117

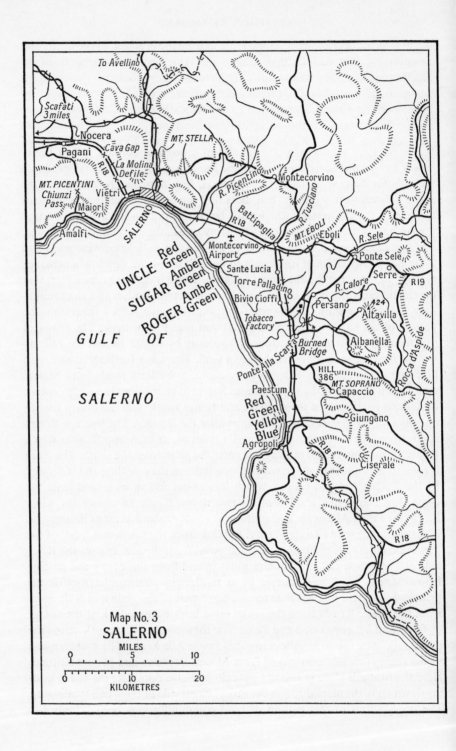

Map No. 3
SALERNO
MILES
0 — 5 — 10
KILOMETRES
0 — 10 — 20

obvious as the operations developed inland from the beaches. In the meantime, however, we can deduce that, before the Allies could advance from the Salerno beaches, they would not only have to capture Salerno itself and the passes to the north but also the communication centre at Battipaglia and the Montecorvino airfield, in addition to a sufficiently large beach-head area to protect themselves, by the occupation of the Ponte Sele area, from forces advancing on Route 19. The Allies would also have to protect themselves from interference by forces entering the plain from the south, or the south-east, and this could only properly be achieved by seizing the high ground opposite Paestum, from Agropoli right round to Altavilla. This would stop any flank attack along Route 18 from the south and also any approach along the roads that climb up from the valley of the upper Calore River to cross into the southern part of the plain. From the German point of view, the ring of mountains gave plenty of concealment and splendid observation over the Gulf and the beaches and the whole of the plain. The holding of Battipaglia was of particular importance. Not only was it the key to the northern beaches but it covered the valley routes which led straight down into the central plain. In fact, if Altavilla (and the Point 424 feature), Persano and Battipaglia were held, reinforcements arriving by Route 19, in particular, could be switched over the Ponte Sele to many parts of the plain.

The 16 Panzer Division had arrived from Bari about the 29 August and had concentrated in the Eboli–Battipaglia area. Some Italian defences were taken over straight away and anti-invasion exercises held. On the announcement of the armistice the Germans immediately disarmed their former allies and took over a number of the Italian coast defence positions. The divisional sector stretched from the Sorrento peninsula to Agropoli. An engineer battalion was posted on the Sorrento peninsula. One Panzer Grenadier Regiment was allotted the area from Salerno to the River Sele and another the remainder of the coastline down to Agropoli. The Panzer Regiment was at Battipaglia. Encouraged by the Germans the Italians had laid some minefields on the beaches and the Germans themselves had done a certain amount of wiring-in of machine-gun posts and digging tank traps. Although the Germans had not had time to develop and fortify the beach defences to any major extent, and were still engaged in taking over Italian gun positions when the landings took place, they had taken great care to reconnoitre the area thoroughly. Within hours of the announcement of the armistice the beach defences were manned and covered by well-sited machine-gun positions and several mobile batteries of 88-mm guns in the hills behind Battipaglia. In accordance with their doctrine of striking as hard as possible at any invading force at the moment of landing, small groups of tanks were moved up close behind the actual beach defences. '*Alarmzustande* II'[1] had been ordered at 1600 hours 8 September by the division when a report was received that thirty-six ships with destroyer escorts had been sighted twenty-five miles south of Capri. Whether the final warning of 'imminent invasion' was given or not in the Salerno sector is not known – certainly the forward troops were active through the night taking over from the Italians and settling into previously reconnoitred positions. When the first wave of Allied troops landed they were ready.

The Fifth Army plan was to use two British divisions on the left. 46 Division would capture Route 18 and Salerno itself, while 56 Division was directed on the Montecorvino airfield, Battipaglia and Ponte Sele. 10 Corps boundary would be the River Sele. On the right 36 (US) Division under VI Corps was given the task of landing at Paestum and blocking the southern and eastern approaches into the plain, by seizing the high ground between Agropoli and Altavilla. This division was commanded by Major-General Dawley, who planned to land three regimental combat teams which would fan out on to a frontage of nearly twenty-five miles. On the left of his front the hill feature Point 424 was over twelve miles cross country from the landing beach. The special Ranger and Commando force, whose task was to capture the passes over the Picentini range, came under Lieutenant-General Sir Richard McCreery, commanding 10 Corps, and consisted of three battalions of Rangers, who would land at Maiori to seize the broad Nocera–Pagani pass, and the two British Commandos who would land at Vietri Sul Mare, seize the Cava Gap (through which the road and railway ran to Naples) and attack Salerno from the west. General Clark was eventually allotted a few extra landing craft which he used to carry a floating reserve. This consisted of one regimental combat team from 45 (US) Division and another from 82 Airborne Division. Follow-up troops were 7 Armoured Division and 3 and 34 (US) Divisions, together with the remainder of 45 Division and 82 Airborne Division, plus a field artillery brigade and a tank battalion which formed the remainder of VI Corps. Of the three assault divisions 'only 46 Division had had much previous experience in action and that experience had been occasionally unlucky; 56 Division had had only a few days' fighting on the Enfidaville line in Tunisia, with varied success; 36 Division was entirely inexperienced'.[2] Much would depend on these three divisions, as it was known that there were at least six good German divisions south of Rome, and unless Fifth Army could get firmly established ashore and land the follow-up formations quickly, the German rate of build up would soon give them a numerical advantage over the invasion force. In an attempt to achieve tactical as well as strategic surprise, the Allied command decided not to carry out any preliminary bombardment, either from the sea or the air, to soften up the beach defences.

On the extreme left the three Ranger battalions, under Lieutenant-Colonel Darby who had distinguished himself at Gela, met no opposition at Maiori and within three hours all their supplies and equipment were ashore and the leading units were in possession of the Chiunzi Pass, looking down on the road and railway running north from Salerno and the road centre of Nocera. The two Commandos under Brigadier Laycock also landed on time (0330 hours on 9 September), after a shore battery had been silenced by naval gun-fire, and by 0600 hours had reached the La Molina defile against increasing resistance. In Vietri itself, mortars and machine-guns were now firing on the beach and the Germans were only evicted after two hours' fighting. When the Commandos pressed their attack into the outskirts of Salerno they found the German engineers had already started blowing up the port installations. While the landing by the Rangers and Commandos had been virtually unopposed, it was quite a different matter in the two main assault areas.

The approach of the two attack forces had been uneventful, although the naval covering force, probably mistaken for an invasion convoy, had been attacked the previous night by forty torpedo-bombers. This attack was successfully driven off by an intense anti-aircraft barrage and by night fighters. As the convoys reached their assembly areas, the minesweepers went ahead to sweep channels for the passage of the assault and landing craft. On the British sector, as early as 0121 hours, as the LSTs were getting into position some 8 miles offshore, preparatory to lowering the assault craft, they came under fire from 88-mm guns. Closely following the minesweepers, three British destroyers posted themselves within a mile of the beaches and immediately opened fire on the German gun positions, while Rear-Admiral Conolly, in USS *Biscayne*, laid a smoke-screen to cover the forming up of the assault waves. As the craft ran in to the beaches, gunboats moved up to take over from the destroyers and the specially converted 'rocket' craft discharged a salvo of 790 rockets on to each beach, with the object of breaching the minefields which it was correctly assumed had been sown on the beaches themselves. The rockets intended for Uncle Green beach fell on Sugar Amber and troops from 46 Division, who had been told to follow the placing of the rockets, found themselves the wrong side of a stream and crowding one of 56 Division's beaches. These two battalions, through this mishap, became separated from their vehicles and supporting weapons and suffered serious casualties when attempting to join up with their brigade. No proper beach head at Uncle Green was cleared for a considerable time and landing craft attempting to discharge guns and vehicles were met with accurate gun-fire, causing more confusion and heavy casualties to the point that 'although Green beach was never lost, nothing could be unloaded there throughout D-day'.[3] The assault waves on the Roger sector landed 1,500 yards south of the correct beach, which at daybreak was found to be under direct fire from an 88-mm battery. 'A support boat . . . closed the shore at full speed, firing machine-guns and mortar, and silenced the battery, which was later knocked out for good by a destroyer.' The Germans quickly spotted the confusion in the centre of the Corps front and the heaviest shelling and dive bombing was concentrated on the Uncle beaches and roadstead. A number of LSTs were damaged and there were serious delays to the unloading of guns and vehicles. For instance, an LST beaching on Uncle Green 'at 0745 when the front line were only 150 yards inland'[4] was shelled for over an hour, suffering eleven direct hits and a number of casualties. In the other two sectors on Sugar and Roger beaches, in spite of shelling and some dive bombing, the LST convoys were able to start beaching at 0600 and 1030 hours respectively and by nightfall no less than thirty-eight of these 'invaluable ships' had discharged direct on to the beaches and were already sailing south in two convoys to collect the follow-up units. The cruisers supporting the main landings of 10 Corps had a good deal of difficulty in making signal contact with their forward observation officers and were unable to play much part in the D-day fighting, but the eight destroyers steaming up and down only a mile offshore, the seven landing craft converted to mount 4·7-inch guns and the monitor played a decisive part in silencing German batteries and on several occasions broke up tank attacks. In particular, a strong tank column attempted to break through on the right flank of 56 Division but was driven off by the fire of a destroyer. The German mobile guns were not only well-camouflaged but elusive, as they quickly moved to fresh positions as soon as they were spotted. The combination of naval bombardment and the use of smoke-screens, not only saved the offshore shipping from heavy losses, but enabled the build-up on at least two of the assault beaches to be kept up throughout the day. The naval guns gave vital support to the troops fighting their way forward on shore, especially on several of the beaches where there was insufficient space to bring into action all the supporting artillery which was being landed. As the beaches became more and more congested, the difficulties of the leading brigades increased and the move forward of anti-tank guns, now urgently needed, was considerably delayed. In spite of the naval gun-fire, German mobile batteries and some railway guns near Salerno kept up the shelling of the roadsteads and beaches all day. Inland, the leading brigades were slowly fighting their way forward but the ground was difficult and broken up. Cultivated fields, hedgerows, dykes, small rivers, flooded areas and narrow lanes both slowed down and channelled any infantry advances, which were met by carefully sited machine-guns and small groups of tanks working right forward. When darkness fell none of the attacks had penetrated more than three miles inland. The Montecorvino airfield was firmly held by the Germans. British patrols entering Battipaglia had been forced back by tanks and infantry. On the left, patrols of 46 Division were close to Salerno, but on the right of 56 Division there was a considerable gap between the British and the Americans, of something over five miles.

Intent on achieving tactical surprise, the Southern Attack Force made no arrangements for destroyers to close on the beaches in support of the assault waves. Support craft fitted with rocket projectors were included in the convoys but were only to be used if the first waves came under heavy gun-fire. The assault went in on time, in spite of difficulties in clearing a minefield close to the assault craft lowering position. The two regimental combat teams landed abreast on four adjacent beaches which were all correctly identified. 142 RCT was on the left and 141 RCT on the right. 143 RCT was to follow over a beach which would be decided later. As the first waves ran in to the shore, to the north the British naval guns could be heard but ahead there was an 'unnatural' silence over the American beaches. Colonel Starr, the Fifth Army historian, describes the moment of beaching. 'The tense quiet did not last long. The troops came in, and as though on signal the Germans opened fire with artillery, machine-guns and mortars. Machine-guns had been emplaced among the dunes, but much of their fire was too high to produce casualties. It was still dark, and the invading troops, impressed with the unhealthful state of the beach, cut paths through or crawled under the wire and dashed inland to find protection among the sand-dunes. From there they could go about the task of destroying the machine-gun and mortar crews near the beach. The hostile fire of artillery, mortars and machine-guns from positions further inland was heavy. A few of the landing craft were hit; others were forced to turn back. Confusion was added when some coxswains attempted to change direction and go around the hostile fire. Others started to return to their mother ships; some simply milled about.'[5] The troops landed in the first wave fought their way doggedly but slowly inland towards their initial objectives and against stiffening resistance. Four further organized waves should have followed them closely but as daylight approached the shelling and mortar fire on the beaches and approaching craft intensified. To the south, tanks had moved close up to the shore and, together with a number of machine-guns, were firing directly on the beaches and craft. The result was serious; 'two of the four beaches had to be closed for several hours, and when craft were diverted from them to the other two beaches they became very congested'.[6] About an hour after sunrise, at about 0530 hours, urgently needed field guns loaded on DUKWs began to land. In the subsequent two hours 'no fewer than 123 DUKW landings were made on the American beaches – a remarkable achievement'.[7] An attempt was made at about 0630 hours to land thirty tanks from six LCTs on Blue beach, but the craft were prevented from beaching by heavy gun-fire and having suffered casualties and damage the LCTs withdrew. With supporting fire from a destroyer the tanks were eventually landed under fire on Red beach seven hours later.

Once again the Germans concentrated most of their gun-fire on the centre beaches and determined attacks by strong groups of tanks were made against the beaches from soon after daylight until well into the afternoon. The early attacks came from the south and one group of about 15 Panzer Mark IVs kept the 141 Regiment 'pinned down near the beaches most of the day'.[8] Three strong tank attacks developed from the north between about 1030 and 1300 hours, when about twelve to fifteen tanks on each occasion attempted to break through to Paestum. But although one of these attacks got within a mile of the beaches they were all halted by the combined efforts of the gunners ashore, the infantry using bazookas and even rifle and hand grenades, and the naval guns of Admiral Davidson's support group. Altogether about fifteen German tanks were knocked out in these attacks. The first ship in action was the British monitor HMS *Abercrombie*, firing at 25,000 yards with the assistance of a spotting aircraft. *Abercrombie* unfortunately struck a mine and had to withdraw the same evening.

The difficulties on the American beaches increased as the day wore on, and in an attempt to relieve some of the congestion, a new beach was opened during the afternoon two miles further up the coast. The naval operation order catered for fifty LCTs to be diverted from the northern area, as soon as they were unloaded, to assist in unloading in the American area. 'This hope proved far too optimistic. Commodore Oliver himself possessed too few LCTs to unload all his ships; some had broken down and, for lack of spare parts, could not be repaired, while others were damaged.'[9] Only sixteen were transferred on D-day and eleven on 10 September. Thirty-two LSTs were due to beach at Paestum on 9 September, but unswept mines, the closing of two of the beaches, incorrect loading and acute congestion on shore so delayed the operations that the ships were not all cleared until the night of 11/12 September. On Red beach 'a veritable mountain ridge of boxed ammunition and bales of supplies lined the water's edge and extended several feet into the sea. Landing craft could not even find room to let down ramps.'[10] The real trouble, however, was the determined resistance ashore, combined with the fact that the German air attacks were largely concentrated against the American beaches. By nightfall, however, 36 Division had reached their initial objective, except on the right, where 141 Regiment had been pinned down all day. From Paestum a salient running east included Capaccio and the foothills of Mount Soprano at Point 386 and then ran parallel to the coast, at about three miles inland, to a point on Route 18 short of the Ponte Alla Scarfa which was held by the Germans.

Owing to the heavy bombing attacks on their airfields and a shortage of petrol, which was aggravated by the bombing of the railway communications, the Luftwaffe was at a serious disadvantage, in spite of the fact that their bases were so much nearer to the battlefield than those of the Allied air forces. We have already seen that the Luftwaffe had been powerless to stop the approach of the convoys. Serious attempts were made to attack the shipping, waiting to unload, by some thirty to forty Focke-Wulf 190s, but the Germans were unable to intervene effectively in the land battle. The Allied air plan to cover the beaches was for the carrier-force Seafires to cover the period from dawn to 0830 hours and again from 1830 hours till dusk, when RAF Beaufighters based on Sicily took over. During the day the Seafires also protected the anchorages from the north. On D-day the Seafires flew 265 sorties, with an average patrol strength of twenty aircraft, and did sterling work, although they were not fast enough to stop 'tip and run' tactics by fast German fighter-bombers. Over the beaches, throughout D-day, shore-based squadrons from as far away as Gerbini kept up continuous patrols, flying from 175–220 miles to reach the battle area. Mustangs flew as low cover with Lightnings and Spitfires above. With long-range tanks the Spitfires could remain over the area for twenty-five minutes. On D-day the Allied shore-based fighters flew almost 700 sorties to cover the beaches and offshore shipping. Unable to break through this cover by day, the Luftwaffe concentrated more and more on night raids and attacks on the shipping, using two new types of bomb against which the Allied ships had no real defence. Both of these new glide bombs were fitted with rocket boosters and were carried under the wings of Dornier 217s. After the glide bombs had been launched from a height, and at some distance, they were directed on to the target visually by radio control. Their range was three and a half and eight miles respectively and they reached speeds in excess of 550 mph. The smaller of these new weapons was in the form of a miniature monoplane with a wing span of 11 feet and carried an explosive charge of 1,100 lbs. The larger had stabilizing fins and carried a considerably greater charge, being designed to pierce armour plating. The smaller type had first been used against escort groups operating in the Bay of Biscay on 27 August with limited success, as they were vulnerable to concentrated close-range anti-aircraft fire. Off Salerno, however, there were many favourable targets for these new weapons, especially the heavier armour-piercing type (FX1,400) which was first used on 11 September. If released at 18,000 feet, this bomb was travelling at 800 feet per second at the end of its trajectory and it could neither be shot down by gun-fire nor avoided by manoeuvring, especially in the congested waters of the assembly areas. On 11 September the American cruiser *Savannah* was seriously damaged by a glide bomb, while *Philadelphia* was badly shaken by a near miss. The same day HMS *Uganda* was hit and had to be towed to Malta. Five days afterwards the British battleship HMS *Warspite* was attacked by three glide bombs, one of which penetrated the boiler room. The *Warspite* eventually reached Malta under tow.

This account of D-day at Salerno would be incomplete without mentioning once again the part played by the Allied warships in support of the fight on shore for the beach heads. On the British sector, gun-fire from destroyers materially aided the actual assault and throughout the day any enemy battery that was spotted or tank that moved in the open was immediately engaged. On the American sector there was no naval gun support for the assault but HMS *Abercrombie* was in action by 0825 hours. By 0914 hours the cruiser *Savannah* was in touch with her shore fire control party and firing on a railway-mounted battery and later in the morning drove off a concentration of tanks at a range of 17,450 yards. By now the flagship *Philadelphia* and several destroyers of Rear Admiral Davidson's fire support group were all in the fight. The two cruisers and three of the destroyers between them fired over 1,800 shells during the first day at Salerno. A special word of praise is due to the pilots of the SOC spotter planes which were flown off the cruisers and also for the work of the Mustang (P51s) reconnaissance squadron whose aircraft, flying in pairs over the beaches (one spotting and one as top cover), also directed the naval gun-fire.

Overnight the Germans switched their meagre forces to attack 10 Corps and on 10 September 36 Division was able to press forward and 179 RCT landed from 45 Division's floating reserve. On the right, 141 Infantry were able to reorganize and move up to block the approaches from the south on a line Agropoli–Cicerale. In the centre, patrolling extended as far east as Monteforte and the upper Calore River. On the left, battalions held Albanella and the ridge to Rocca d'Aspide preparatory to an attack on Altavilla, which, together with Point 424, was captured the following day against light opposition. While further reserves were landing, the 179 Infantry were put in late on 10 September in a two-pronged attack between the Sele and Calore Rivers to seize the Ponte Sele. The right columns were driven back by tanks and engineers holding the crossings of the Calore north of Altavilla and during the night of 11 September were back on the La Cosa Creek. The left column almost reached the Ponte Sele but was taken in the rear by a strong tank and artillery counter-attack launched due south from Eboli and Persano. These two American battalions were virtually cut off and forced to pull back to a position north-east of Persano. Meanwhile, the 157 Infantry crossed the Ponte Alla Scafa and advanced up Route 18 and up the right bank of the River Sele, to try to relieve the situation at Persano. Over the river from Persano, on a dominant ridge, five large stone buildings made up a tobacco factory and had been fortified and occupied by a strong German tank and infantry force, which successfully stopped any further outflanking move by the 157 Infantry. At the end of the third day's fighting VI Corps held the high ground from Agropoli to Point 424, but on the left 45 Division (now complete and under Major-General Middleton) was held by determined German forces, strongly entrenched both in the tobacco factory and Persano itself. Furthermore, movement northwards over the plain was under direct observation and fire from artillery positions in the foothills of Mount Eboli. The German counter-attack towards Persano had in fact been made by elements of the 29 Panzer Grenadier Division from Calabria and Field Marshal Kesselring describes the situation at this point. 'The fighting on the beaches of Salerno, despite the Allies' overwhelming air superiority, their tremendous naval gun-fire and our numerical weakness, went better than I had dared hope. By a stroke of luck on 11 September the first elements of the 29th Panzer Grenadiers, coming up from Calabria, though suffering from a shortage of petrol were able to counter-attack on the left wing. They were soon followed by the bulk of the division and the 26th Panzers. On the right wing a counter-attack was delivered by the 15th Panzer Grenadiers, those parts of the "Hermann Göring" division which were ready to move following hard on their heels.'[11]

The heaviest fighting on 10 and 11 September was on 10 Corps front. On the extreme left, the Rangers held strong positions on Mount di Chiunzi against holding attacks and extended their hold by the capture of Mount Pendolo. On 11 September the Rangers were reinforced by an infantry battalion with supporting arms switched from the southern sector. North of Vietri and astride Route 18 the Commandos and several units of 46 Division, which had captured Salerno on 10 September, advanced into the pass but were halted after fierce fighting with elements of 3 Panzer Grenadier Division. This German division had quickly dealt with the situation in Rome and, together with the advance guards of the Hermann Göring Division, were trying to break through from the north. On the heels of the 46 Division's entry into Salerno came a British naval port party to open the harbour. The German gunners, however, had the range exactly and it was never possible to use the harbour until after the final German withdrawal. On the British sector the German pressure was steadily increasing. General von Vietinghoff appreciated that time was vital to allow the northern passes to be held and for a strong counter-attack force to be assembled. The Hermann Göring Division were now coming into the line alongside 16 Panzer Division. Although 46 Division held Route 18 and Salerno, their beach head was still only about two miles wide at the northern end of the bay and their positions generally were dominated by German batteries on a 2,000-foot-high ridge, overlooking the whole of their sector. On D-day the Germans had been forced to withdraw from Battipaglia itself by the intensity of the naval bombardment and artillery shelling. Overnight a battalion of 167 Brigade occupied the town. The German reaction was violent. At dawn a strong counter-attack came in with two battalions of infantry supported by tanks. Heavy fighting continued all day in the town and nearby tobacco factory, which, like the one near Persano, had been made into a strongpoint. Just before dusk the Germans brought up more tanks and finally recaptured the town. 56 Division's plans now were to attack in strength. 167 Brigade (in a night attack) was to cut the road between Battipaglia and Eboli; while 201 Guards Brigade recaptured Battipaglia itself and seized the factory. On the left 169 Brigade advanced from the Montecorvino airfield area to capture a hill feature about two miles north of Route 18. 'On the left the attack was successful . . . in the centre the Guards fought their way into the streets of Battipaglia but on the right the 167 Brigade met an impenetrable defence, and there (the) attack was held from the start.'[12] The fight for Battipaglia continued throughout 11 September and most of the following day, but by now the Germans had weighed up the situation and appreciated that 56 Division had little in reserve. So they decided, on the evening of 12 September, to strike through and round the town with a well-planned counter-attack, mounted by 29 Panzer Grenadier Division headed by forty tanks. The British were driven out of the town with heavy loss and the situation became extremely dangerous. Engineer and Pioneer units working on the beaches were brought into the line, which was finally held about 3,000 yards south-west of the town with the right-hand Brigade drawn back to Santa Lucia. The Divisional Reconnaissance Regiment held an extended front reaching out towards the American sector.

On 10 and 11 September the Allied land-based fighters had flown 1,250 sorties and the Seafires 400, while over 1,100 sorties had been flown by the bomber force, which continued to strike at communications and airfields inland. In the first three days of AVALANCHE the Allies destroyed forty-four German aircraft in the air and a number on the ground, for the loss of twenty-four of their own aircraft. The Allies had hoped to use the Montecorvino airfield as early as 10 September but, although the airfield was captured on 11 September, German shelling made it quite impossible for aircraft to land or take off. By now the operational strength of the carrier-borne Seafires 'had become seriously reduced, for a sustained air effort could not be kept up by carriers for more than 48 to 72 hours and landing accidents had become frequent'.[13] In fact ten Seafires had been lost and thirty-two damaged, mainly in deck landing crashes. On 12 September the surviving twenty-six Seafires were flown on to an emergency landing strip at Paestum, from which they operated successfully for the next three days. After this date the carrier force was withdrawn. American engineers had in fact started building an emergency strip as early as the evening of D-day, but were driven off to another site by the German shelling. This new strip was started early on 10 September and within twenty-four hours a 3,800-yard runway had been levelled out, involving the filling of drainage ditches and felling of trees to clear the approaches and the provision of sufficient hard standings for a complete fighter squadron. On the British sector an emergency strip was also ready on 11 September at Tusciano and forty-eight hours later two more strips had been constructed, one in each sector.

On the evening of 11 September Clark, after visiting the two Corps, was sufficiently optimistic about the way the build-up of Fifth Army was going to signal to Alexander 'that he would soon be ready to launch an attack northwards through Vietri towards Naples'. At this time he was quite unaware that the drop on Rome had not taken place. General Alexander, however, was very conscious of the dangers ahead. On the afternoon of 10 September he signalled to General Montgomery that 'it was of the utmost importance that he should maintain pressure upon the Germans so that they could not move forces from his front and concentrate them against AVALANCHE'.[14] Meanwhile more fighting troops were needed in the bridgehead. On 11 September, after getting permission from the Chiefs of Staff, Alexander intercepted eighteen LSTs about to leave for India and dispatched them with reinforcements. The battleships *Warspite* and *Valiant* were ordered at full speed to the Gulf, and orders were given for the strategic bomber force to be switched to direct support of the land battle. An account of the landing at Taranto and of the advance by Eighth Army of 300 miles in seventeen days will be given later, so that the story of the dramatic events of the next four days at Salerno may follow directly on from this short account of the assault and early battles for the bridgehead. As General Alexander later wrote, 'the Germans in their counter-attacks had been working under definite limitations of time. They had, deliberately, broken contact with Eighth Army in order to fling the troops coming up from Calabria against Fifth Army but they could not ignore Eighth Army's advance beyond a certain date.'[15]

By 12 September, Kesselring had assembled a high proportion of the fighting troops of five Panzer Grenadier divisions to reinforce the original 16 Panzer Division at Salerno. He had now assembled a force, that included some 600 tanks and mobile guns, for the single purpose of halting Fifth Army while there was still time, and if possible throwing it back into the sea. Kesselring's troops were well placed to exploit the dangerous situation caused by the two bridgeheads never having been joined up. In the north it would be relatively easy to contain any British attempt to break through the mountain passes, and there were troops to spare for strong flank attacks from the direction of Avellino and the town of Montecorvino and down the Tusciano creek. The salient the Germans held south-west of Battipaglia now gave them room for manoeuvre, although the town itself was so full of rubble that vehicles could not pass through. Attacks from this direction would further threaten the British on their more exposed flank. Down in the centre of the valley, at Persano, the Germans held a strong forward position dominating a gap between the two Corps, which was the weakest point in the whole of the Allied positions. At the head of the valley, von Vietinghoff had now concentrated 16 Panzer Division, still an effective force in spite of its losses in the fight for the beaches, and the whole of 26 and 29 Panzer Grenadier Divisions. The time had come to divide the Allies and strike at their weak and exposed inner flanks. The first moves came in the north where, in conjunction with the recapture of Battipaglia already described, the Hermann Göring Division had attacked 46 Division with tanks down the road from Avellino, while on the Allied left flank an attempt was made to dislodge the Rangers in their mountain positions above Maiori. Both attacks were beaten off. The following day (13 September) a strong attack, which made some progress, was launched south from Nocera and three battalions attempted to reach Salerno from the east. These attacks were combined with renewed German pressure on the Battipaglia sector with a thrust on the evening of 13 September down either bank of the Tusciano, in an attempt to drive a wedge between the two British divisions. This attack was beaten off; but forty-eight hours later the Germans attacked the same positions and also launched an attack from the tobacco factory. Again the attacks were held and eventually driven back. The following day, on the right of 56 Division, a battle group from 16 Panzer Division succeeded in breaking through in several places. The situation was restored by concentrated artillery fire and a determined counter-attack by a squadron from 23 Armoured Brigade, whose Crusaders charged the attacking infantry and drove off the much heavier armoured German Mark IV tanks. The fighting in the Battipaglia sector, throughout the whole of this critical period, had been at close quarters and almost continuous, with German tanks and infantry probing for any weakness in the British positions. Initially short of tanks, 10 Corps brought forward any artillery to hand, regardless of type or calibre, to stop the Panzers. The naval guns of the Support Group broke up many attacks, and on 14 September the tactical and strategic air forces were launched in strength to pound the German positions. It was again on 14 September that urgently needed tank reinforcements started moving up from the beaches, with the arrival of the leading elements of 7 Armoured Division. As we shall see, after studying the events from 12–14 September in the American sector, the decisive period in the battle for the Salerno beach head was ending.

While 12 September had seen 167 Brigade driven out of Battipaglia with such losses that it had to be relieved, in the American sector there had been both gains and losses. 'On the left of VI Corps, elements of 45 Division drove the enemy out of the tobacco factory, with the help of gun-fire from *Philadelphia*, captured Persano and advanced inland.'[16] Some progress was also made along Route 18 and the railway line as far as Tre Palladino. Point 424 was also captured but a German counter-attack retook both this feature and Altavilla itself. Conscious of the German pressure at Battipaglia and of the gap between the two Corps, General Dawley reinforced his left flank and the positions east of Persano overnight. The next morning, 13 September, a force of three battalions (under Colonel Martin) again attempted to recapture Altavilla; but after heavy fighting lasting most of the day, during which one of the battalions was surrounded, the majority of the force was withdrawn under cover of darkness to a defensive line on the La Cosa Creek. On the left, the main German counter-attack, launched at about 1530 hours, had penetrated to below the junction of the Sele and the Calore. Strong tank and infantry attacks by both 26 and 29 Panzer Grenadier Divisions, advancing from the direction of Eboli and Ponte Sele, had retaken the tobacco factory and Persano and driven straight on down between the two rivers making for a 'burned' bridge, flanked by a ford across the Calore, only just over five miles from the beaches between the mouth of the Sele and Paestum. Strong German infantry attacks protected the flanks of this armoured thrust and mobile guns were now as far forward as Persano and joining in the attack. Although the bridge itself was damaged and ditches on either side of the track leading to it somwehat limited the manoeuvring of the leading German tanks, the situation was extremely serious. General Clark later wrote, 'at this point we were certainly at the mercy of Kesselring, provided he massed his strength and threw it at us relentlessly'.[17] The German attack at this point was virtually through to the gun lines, as the only troops facing them across the Calore (at about 1830 hours) were two battalions of field guns. With their positions already under fire, the two commanding officers rallied every available driver and mechanic and 'stripping their gun crews to the minimum',[18] set them to dig in and hold the gentle slope down towards the 'burned' bridge and ford. Even the artillery headquarters bandsmen were armed and rushed up to hold a nearby hill, dubbed by General Clark 'Piccolo Peak'. As the Germans attacked to force a crossing over the ford the two artillery battalions opened fire and, aided by the handful of riflemen and machine-gunners on the slopes below, held and gradually wore down successive attacks until the Germans wavered. With the arrival at sunset of part of a further battery of field guns, the Germans finally broke off the attack and pulled back. The engagement had lasted about an hour and the American gunners at the 'burned' bridge had fired just under 4,000 rounds to defend the crossing. Although a complete breakthrough had been narrowly averted, the situation was still critical. Many units had been badly mauled and much ground had been lost. It was obvious that the only chance of holding the bridgehead was to concentrate every available man and weapon on a very much shorter line, which would join up with the La Cosa Creek defence positions already mentioned. This line was not naturally strong and was overlooked from the high ground at Altavilla, but it was the only possible stop line 'for what might well have become a last stand . . . there was nothing else to fall back on'.[19] That night 600 paratroopers of 82 Airborne Division dropped (with only one casualty) south of the River Sele to reinforce VI Corps at the most critical point of their defensive line. The request for these reinforcements had been flown straight to Sicily, where General Ridgeway laid on the operation at an hour's notice. On this occasion orders for the withholding of anti-aircraft fire during the drop were obeyed explicitly. 'The following night 1,900 more paratroopers were successfully dropped in the same zone.'[20]

The following day (14 September) was the last day when German reinforcements arrived; these were part of 26 Panzer Grenadier Division from the south and a further battle group of 3 Panzer Grenadier Division from the north. All day the Germans continued their attacks south and west of Persano, in places succeeding in breaking the line temporarily and infiltrating some tanks and infantry. As the beaches were now under heavy artillery fire, Admiral Hewitt ordered all unloading to be stopped. By dusk, however, all the attacks had been beaten back. In this phase of the battle, naval gun-fire played a significant part. Von Vietinghoff himself records that 'the advancing troops had to endure the most severe heavy fire that had hitherto been experienced, the naval gun-fire from at least sixteen to eighteen battleships, cruisers, and large destroyers lying in the roadsteads. With astonishing precision and freedom of manoeuvre, these ships shot at every recognized target with very overwhelming effect.'[21] On VI Corps front the artillery of the two Divisions fired just under 10,800 rounds on 14 September.

In the air the whole effort of both the strategic and tactical air forces was concentrated on the battlefields, and on 14 and 15 September 3,400 sorties were flown in direct support of the land battle. Road and rail communications into the area were heavily attacked and the towns of Battipaglia and Eboli virtually obliterated, while fighters and fighter-bombers patrolled the bridgehead attacking any movement of tanks or vehicles that could be spotted. The Luftwaffe were powerless to stop these attacks and concentrated on tip-and-run sorties against the battleships and other shipping in the bay. The intensity of the bombing achieved by the Allied air forces between 12-15 September is shown by the total of 3,000 tons dropped, while 'the actual target areas had received an average bomb density of 760 tons per square mile'.[22] Referring to a raid by 126 Wellingtons on the night of 14/15 September, 'when the road from Battipaglia to Eboli was buried beneath 237 tons of bombs', Lord Tedder remarks, 'this was the greatest effort yet made by night bombers in this theatre. It was also the justification for the request we had put to Portal for the retention of the three Canadian Wellington Squadrons.'[23] The same night (14/15 September) a parachute battalion of 82 Airborne Division was dropped in the Avellino area to add to the disruption of communications into 10 Corps sector. This drop was less successful than those made behind VI Corps line where lighted ground signals could be used. Although pathfinder techniques were used (dropping a small party in advance to guide the aircraft to the dropping zone) the radio transmitter and signal lamps used were inadequate, and owing to the mountainous country the drop had to be made at 3–5,000 feet instead of 600 feet. Only fifteen out of the forty planes succeeded in dropping their parachutists near the correct zone and most of the equipment was lost in the vineyards and surrounding woods. The remainder of the force (of 600 men) were scattered as far as twenty-five miles from their objective. A small party, however, did succeed in damaging the main road bridge at Avellino. In all, 118 men of the battalion were killed or captured and it was several weeks before all the small scattered parties made their way back to the Allied lines.

On the morning of 15 September General Alexander arrived in Salerno bay in a destroyer to visit both Corps. During his tour he learned that Admiral Hewitt the previous day had been asked by General Clark to prepare emergency plans for re-embarking either the British or, more likely, the Americans and transferring them to the other Corps' beach. Commodore Oliver, in command of the Northern Attack Force, had already 'protested that to re-embark heavily engaged troops from a shallow beach head was certainly impracticable, and would probably prove suicidal'.[24] Oliver had insisted that General McCreery should be told of the plan. The latter had also opposed the whole idea in no uncertain terms. After General Alexander's visit nothing more was heard of the 'quite impossible suggestion to transfer the American beach head to the British sector. Happily by that evening – 15 September – the crisis was over.'[25] The following day Alexander sent a long and reassuring message to Churchill, who had stayed on in America after QUADRANT to have further talks with the President and was now on his way back by sea. Describing the measures taken to reinforce the bridgehead, Alexander added, 'I have also been able to cheer them up and issue certain directions, of which the following are most important. Hold what we have gained, at all costs consolidating key positions by digging, wiring, and mining. Reorganize scattered and mixed units and formations. Form local reserves and as strong a mobile reserve as possible. Inform troops of rapid approach of Eighth Army and flow of reinforcements now arriving day and night.'[26]

By 15 September the *Valiant* and *Warspite* had arrived and by that evening the latter was adding the fire of her fifteen-inch guns to the general naval bombardment of the German positions. More direct air support was now becoming available, as both British and American squadrons moved on to airfields in southern Italy. On 16 September the three cruisers arrived from Tripoli and disembarked the British infantry reinforcements they had brought over. Two days later (18 September) 3 US Infantry Division started disembarking, having been rushed over from Sicily. On 15 September the Germans were seen digging in in many areas. Two attacks were launched against the British sector early on 16 September, but the Americans on the extreme right of the Army front were able to advance towards Point 424 and Altavilla, which was taken for the third time on 18 September. On the same day the infantry of 7 Armoured Division entered Battipaglia without resistance. Kesselring writes 'on 16 September in order to evade the effective shelling from warships – I authorized a disengagement on the coastal front with the express proviso that the Volturno line, to which the Tenth Army intended to fall back, must not be abandoned before 15 October'.[27] This is only half the story. By 16 September the leading patrols of Eighth Army were in contact with the Americans near Vallo and by 19 September the two leading divisions occupied Auletta and Potenza and the Germans were in retreat back to the Volturno. Alexander comments, 'throughout the battle the Eighth Army were advancing rapidly from the toe of Italy and working their way round the rear of the German defences. I think it was this threat more than anything else, that caused the Germans to pull out.'[28]

The army casualties reported by General Clark for the first seven or eight days of the battle of Salerno are: 10 Corps, 2,446 killed and wounded and 1,561 missing; VI Corps, 1,078 and 589 missing. Considering the number of naval ships involved and the fact that the Luftwaffe largely concentrated on attacking the Allied warships, the naval losses were remarkably small. 'One British and three American destroyers, one American fleet minesweeper, two British LSTs, two LCIs and seventeen LCTs of both nations, three American merchantmen and one British hospital ship were the principal losses attributable to the enemy; and about another seventy vessels, ranging from battleships and cruisers down to landing craft, were damaged.'[29]

In the air, the Allied strength was clearly demonstrated. During the critical days 12–15 September the Allied air forces flew over 6,000 sorties, while the Luftwaffe was rarely seen over the battle area. For instance, on 16 September, when HMS *Warspite* was seriously damaged by glider bomb attacks, only about 120 Luftwaffe sorties were seen over the whole battle area. In the period from 1–15 September, which covered both BAYTOWN and AVALANCHE, the Allies flew approximately 17,500 sorties and dropped 10,000 tons of bombs. Two hundred and twenty-one Luftwaffe planes were shot down for a loss of eighty-nine Allied planes. These figures do not disclose the Luftwaffe losses on the ground. For instance in two day-attacks against the Foggia airfields (17–18 September) the Allies destroyed or damaged nearly 300 Luftwaffe planes and gliders on the ground.

To see the advance of Eighth Army we must go back a few days. At dusk on 9 September, the cruiser force with 1 Airborne Division embarked sailed into Taranto harbour, where they were met by Italian pilots and berthed immediately. The landing was unopposed but was marred by the British minesweeper (HMS *Abdiel*) being sunk at her berth by a mine with the loss of 150 men. As soon as the port was secured, the plan was to bring in 78 Division from Sicily, when landing craft were available, and 8 Indian Division who would sail direct from the Middle East. All three divisions would then come under 5 Corps Headquarters, which was already standing by to move to Taranto. Meanwhile, General Alexander was anxious that 13 Corps, which had reached the Catanzaro–Nicastro line, should maintain maximum pressure on this front in support of AVALANCHE. As we have already seen, Eighth Army's Lines of Communication were much extended and there was not enough transport to support the advance of large formations. General Montgomery immediately sent forward light forces, which reached Castrovillari and Belvedere late on 11 September, and the same day the port of Crotone was secured undamaged. The plan was to concentrate 5 Division at Castrovillari and the Canadians at Spezzano and Rossano, but this would take 4–5 days owing to the maintenance difficulties. The main operational difficulties remained 'the extensive demolitions, which demanded ever-increasing resources in engineers and engineering material'.[30] Meanwhile, every effort was made to move squadrons of the Tactical Air Force over to the 'toe' of Italy, where they would be in range of the Salerno beach head. As the situation at Salerno deteriorated, Eighth Army redoubled their efforts to speed up their advance. On 14 September, 5 Division pushed a brigade forward to Sapri and the following day, when extra ferry craft and transport companies became available, 5 Division's patrols were sent towards Vallo, where contact with the Americans was made on 16 September. These patrols successfully by-passed rearguards of 26 Panzer Grenadier Division, who were pulling back from north of Lagonegro. Auletta was captured by 5 Division and Potenza by the Canadians on 19 September. The Canadians were already in contact with patrols from 1 Airborne Division from Taranto and the leading elements of 78 Division were about to land at Bari. In seventeen days, 13 Corps had advanced 300 miles on roads that were blocked and the bridges blown every few miles. The engineering problems had been enormous and the difficulties of supplying the force became progressively more acute as the lines of communication lengthened. Initially supplied through Sicily and across the straits, Eighth Army was operating very much on a shoestring from the start, especially as absolute priority for supplies and stores of all kinds was being given to Fifth Army. Engine assemblies needing repair had to be sent right back to Egypt and replacements were slow in coming forward, consequently the transport resources dwindled at the time when they were needed most, before the ports in the 'heel' could be opened. Even then, ships diverted from Sicily were found to be loaded in bulk to stock depots in Sicily and not to meet the urgent and particular demands of the forward units. To begin with, the Airborne Divisions landed at Taranto were even worse off as they had to rely on the Italians for both transport and supplies. All these administrative difficulties only underline the fact that, compared with HUSKY, the landings on the mainland were mounted very much against the clock and with insufficient craft to build up forward dumps behind Eighth Army's advance.

Regarding the battle for the Salerno bridgehead, there is little doubt that the close support of the naval guns turned the scales in the Allies' favour in the early days of the landing. The high degree of Allied air superiority enabled the British and American warships to operate day after day in restricted areas and close inshore without crippling losses. At the critical stage of the German counter-attacks, the combined effect of concentrated aerial bombing and heavy and accurate naval gun-fire finally convinced Kesselring that he could not reach the sea. General Alexander remarks, 'my conclusion is that if the navy and the army had not enjoyed air superiority at Salerno the operation would have failed'.[31] But the battle was not just won by the fighters and the warships and the bombers. On the plain of Salerno it was a battle of attrition, fought out by depleted units and small groups of men who, no longer able to advance, fought back hour by hour against an equally determined enemy – an enemy who could watch every move from the hills above and who was set on one object alone, the destruction of the bridgehead. On land it was a very close fight indeed, and there is little doubt that many of Fifth Army's difficulties stemmed from their failure to seize

135

more than shallow beach heads in the initial stages of the battle. Admiral Hewitt was only one of several senior Allied officers who condemned the decision not to employ heavy naval and air bombardment to neutralize the defences prior to the assault. This was the main lesson learned at Salerno; unfortunately it had to be learned the hard way.

The German view, in retrospect, both of Westphal and Kesselring, is that, if two Panzer Divisions from the north (asked for on 9 September) had been sent immediately, they would have reached the Salerno battle-field by 13 September and could have tipped the scales against the Allies. The fact remains, however, that on the very day of the Salerno landings, Hitler, but for the announcement of the Italian surrender, would have issued an ultimatum that the Italian army should make a stand in the south with the German Tenth Army concentrated in their rear (probably in the Rome area) as a counter-attack force.[32] Hitler's mind was set on holding the northern Apennines and Rommel probably feared landings well up the coastlines, at least north of Rome or in the Ancona–Pescara area. Consequently Kesselring's southern policy received no support, although, as we shall see, Hitler's preoccupation with the security of the Balkans soon led him to change his mind.

8
Hitler Decides

Fate of Italian army and Allied prisoners of war: von Senger evacuates Sardinia and Corsica: Kesselring's defence lines and Hitler's decision: Alexander's directives: Shortage of landing craft: Eighth Army re-groups: Naples taken: Fight for Termoli: The weather breaks: Volturno crossings: Mount Camino and the Mignano Gap: Alexander calls a halt: Strategic Bomber Offensive and Fifteenth Air Force.

1943	*Fifth Army*	*Eighth Army*
11–18 Sept	Germans successfully evacuate Sardinia and Corsica.	
21 Sept	General Alexander issues outline plans for future operations (revised plans issued 29 October).	
22 Sept		8 Indian Division lands from Africa. Part of 78 Division lands Bari to drive on Foggia.
26 Sept	10 Corps still trying to break out. 82 Airborne Division lands Maiori.	
29 Sept	Complete instrument of Italian surrender signed by Badoglio and Eisenhower on HMS *Nelson*.	
1 Oct	King's Dragoon Guards enter Naples.	13 Corps occupy Foggia.
2/3 Oct		Commandos capture Termoli, Germans react strongly.
3 Oct	34 Division takes Benevento.	36 Brigade of 78 Division lands 3/4 October.
5/6 Oct	10 Corps reaches River Volturno.	Fierce fighting for bridgehead at Termoli (Irish Brigade land evening 5 October).

1943	*Fifth Army*	*Eighth Army*
7 Oct		Germans in retreat to line of River Trigno.
12/13 Oct	Fifth Army assault crossings over River Volturno.	
14 Oct		Canadians take Campobasso and Vinchiaturo on 14 October.
25 Oct	Fifth Army established north of Volturno.	
27 Oct		78 Division fails to expand bridgehead across Trigno, weather deteriorating.
1 Nov	US Fifteenth Air Force formed	to operate from Italian bases.
2 Nov	10 Corps reach River Garigliano.	Main assault of Trigno positions – night of 2/3 November.
5 Nov	Attack on Mount Camino and Winter Line for next 10 days.	Germans pursued through Vasto.
8 Nov	General Alexander orders Fifth Army plan amphibious operation on west coast.	78 Division reaches heights overlooking River Sangro.
15 Nov	Fifth Army attacks called off and ordered re-group.	

While the Salerno battle was being fought out 600,000 Italian troops in the Balkans, Greece and Crete were disarmed, virtually without resistance. Keitel's orders were that volunteers willing to fight in German units would be accepted, but all other Italian troops would be made prisoners of war for forced labour. In Occupied France and north Italy some 500,000 Italian troops just disappeared into thin air and all that Rommel's subordinate commanders could round up was some 40,000 who were sent to Germany. In the Rome area and further south all Kesselring attempted, after crushing weak resistance to his occupation of the capital, was to disarm the Italian troops and send them home. Few Italians volunteered to fight on with the Germans, a notable exception being a number from the Italian 184 Parachute Division. By the end of the war the total Italian strength fighting on the German side only amounted to one Mountain and three Infantry Divisions. In Sardinia and Corsica, General von Senger, who had been sent there by Hitler after leaving Sicily, succeeded in evacuating by air (and finally by lighters and Siebel ferries), practically the whole of his command of about one and a half divisions and air force units totalling 30,000 men. This was achieved in spite of some resistance by the Italians, a landing by Free French units and Allied air attacks.

Another kind of evacuation had been started by the Germans within hours of the Italian defection. This was to seize and transport to Germany in heavily guarded trains thousands of Allied prisoners of war held in camps in northern Italy. Many camps were surrounded before the occupants realized what had occurred, but of some 75,000 British prisoners of war at least 10,000 escaped and in Churchill's words, 'mostly helped by the local populations with civilian clothes, were guided to safety, thanks to the risks taken by members of the Italian Resistance and the simple people of the countryside'.[1] Many of these men escaped into the mountains and made their way in small parties south in the hopes of reaching the advancing Allies. One of these parties was led by Lieutenant-Colonel Denis Gibbs, whose diary records the adventures in marching 625 miles from the valley of the Po, through some of the most mountainous country in Europe, to a crossing over the River Volturno held by 5 Division. The march was achieved in fifty-three days. Towards the end of September, 'Kesselring issued a series of orders threatening death or imprisonment to Italians for failing to surrender fire-arms to the Germans or to the local police, killing or injuring German soldiers, hiding or helping Allied personnel, disobeying the orders of the German forces, hindering their work, slackness in their own work, distribution of enemy leaflets and possession of wireless transmitting sets'.[2] Gibbs's diary records the help and many acts of kindness unhesitatingly given by the Italians, but also vividly describes the fear and dread of the Germans shown by those unfortunate enough to have had actual contact with their former allies. After their escape, Gibbs and his party reached a small mountain village north of Rome well after dark on 25 October. 'It was the first time and I hope it will be the last that we have ever entered a village at night with the intention of feeding and staying there. Owing to being late and night catching us we could not find out anything about the village before entering it. We only knew that there was no other village for a long way and we did not want to have to spend the night out. We found everyone scared stiff of the Germans. Apparently the Boche, according to villagers' statements had surrounded it and searched it a few nights ago, in the early hours of the morning. Some of the inhabitants told us that the Germans did this every night, a thing which was most unlikely to be true. I tried my very best to explain that if the Boche had searched, it was most unlikely he would come back to this same village for a long time. But no, they were too panic-stricken to listen. They ran at the sight of us, they pushed us out of their houses, saying did we want to get them all shot, and the women wept and wailed. . . . The Germans have the people exactly where they want them in this district and one can visualize their propaganda working towards the forcing of fugitives to give themselves up for want of food and for lack of a place to lay their heads. The village folk think they will all be slain and their homes burnt if we are found in the village or near it.'[3]

As early as 12 September Kesselring had outlined to von Vietinghoff his task of delaying the Allied advance and of holding the Volturno line until at least 15 October. Kesselring had already mapped out two defensive lines south of Rome, the most southerly ran through Mignano and was to be in a state of defensive preparation by 1 November. This was called the Bernhardt or Winter Line. The other line was based on the River Garigliano and Monte Cassino and became known as the Gustav Line. Kesselring, it will be remembered, had received no reinforcements from the north and could only hope that von Vietinghoff's Tenth Army would hold the Allies while these two defensive positions were prepared. On the Adriatic flank General Heidrich and his already depleted 1 Parachute Division was the only force now left to face the advance of 78 Division that had landed at Bari. Kesselring still thought the Allies could be stopped south of Rome and, from his point of view, everything would turn on the success of the delaying actions during Tenth Army's withdrawal and the release of reinforcements from Rommel's Army Group in the north to help hold the main positions mentioned above. But while Kesselring was issuing orders for a phased withdrawal he was also trying to work out what would be the next move by the Allies. His appreciation sent back to the OKW on 15 September was that, having captured the air bases at Foggia, the Allies would turn towards the Balkans, making no attempt to move into central or northern Italy. This view was held by both Rommel and Hitler, while Dönitz supported Kesselring's belief that, 'a prolonged defence of southern Italy would delay an Allied attack against the Balkans'.[4] When the suggestion was made that extra troops for the defence of the Balkans would have to result from pulling back to the northern Apennines, Kesselring pointed out that the Winter Line could be held with less troops than would be needed further north and that the Allied bombers would be held further back from the industrial targets in southern Germany and northern Italy. Kesselring also argued that, should the Allies withdraw forces to take part in an invasion of the Balkans, a counter-offensive might well result in the recapture of the Foggia air bases at the moment that they would be most needed by the Allies. Rommel probably still feared amphibious landings well up the Italian coastline and was already preoccupied with the recapture of Trieste and Fiume from the Slovenes, who had moved in on the heels of the Italian surrender. Both Hitler and the OKW, however, were beginning to link the Italian and Balkan theatres more and more in their minds and to see that a withdrawal to north Italy would place the Allies in a very central and favourable strategic position. They feared that they themselves might even be forced to pull back from Greece to achieve the necessary concentration for the defence of their own frontiers. This Hitler would not even contemplate. Consequently he was more and more drawn towards Kesselring's viewpoint. On 4 October he went so far as to order Rommel to send Kesselring two divisions and supporting artillery. Meanwhile Major Otto Skorzeny had discovered that Mussolini was held captive in a ski lodge on the inaccessible Gran Sasso in the central Apennines. A daring landing by German paratroopers in gliders caught the Italian guards napping. Mussolini was flown out in a flimsy Storch aircraft which had to take off over a cliff with both Mussolini and Skorzeny crammed into the fuselage, the pilot only just succeeded in levelling the aircraft out after a drop of several hundred feet. The rescue took place on 12 September and within forty-eight hours the now listless and emaciated Dictator reached Hitler's headquarters. The following day Hitler issued Orders of the Day proclaiming that Mussolini had 'resumed the supreme direction of Fascism in Italy. . . . On 18 September the Duce broadcast from Munich and the Italian Social Republic was born.'[5] It has been suggested that Hitler's decision to hold Rome was also connected with the political need to bolster the puppet Fascist regime. Whatever considerations finally decided Hitler, the fact remains that Kesselring's view prevailed and in an order of 6 November he was given supreme command over the whole Italian theatre of operations, with the designation of Commander-in-Chief South West and of Army Group C. Rommel left three weeks afterwards as Hitler's personal representative to inspect the western coastal defences. The troops in North Italy came under Kesselring's command as the German Fourteenth Army. Although Hitler played the hand, the cards had been stacked by Kesselring and for once his optimistic views were accepted.

On 21 September General Alexander issued a broad directive for an advance in four phases. Firstly, the line Salerno to Bari was to be consolidated; secondly, Naples and the Foggia airfields were to be secured. Objectives for the third phase were Rome and its airfields and the communications centre at Terni, with the further objectives given as Leghorn, Florence and Arezzo. These plans must be seen, however, against a pretty sombre background. The decisions taken in May still stood. Eight divisions, about 150 bombers, most of the troop-carrying aircraft, 80 per cent of the landing ships and two-thirds of the assault craft would soon leave the theatre. The recent decision to establish a strategic bombing force at Foggia as soon as possible meant an additional maintenance requirement, nearly as great as for the whole of the Eighth Army, to be brought in through the same east coast ports. Meanwhile there were immediate administrative problems to be faced. Naples was still not available as a supply port for the Fifth Army and the switch over of Eighth Army's maintenance to Taranto and Brindisi was only just beginning to operate and reserve stocks were practically exhausted. The most vital problem, however, and one which was controlled by the availability of shipping, was the need for a reasonably fast build-up of the Allied forces in Italy to contain the nineteen German divisions already in Italy (and it was hoped to draw more into that country) and indirectly to hold down, by the threat of further landings, many of the fifty-odd divisions spread from southern France to the Balkans. Towards the end of October the Allies had eleven divisions facing Kesselring's force of nine divisions but in north Italy there were now fourteen more, and it would not be until February 1944 that the Allies could hope to build up to anywhere near this total. The shortage of shipping and landing craft was now the limiting factor in every plan and every calculation. In the plans being formulated at the end of October for the advance on Rome two amphibious flank attacks were visualized; by a brigade group on the east coast and by at least a division with armour on the west coast. There were insufficient landing craft for simultaneous attacks and not nearly enough for the divisional attack. Nor were there enough craft to complete the build-up of formations already in Italy. As late as the first week of November 2,500 urgently needed vehicles for Fifth Army were still waiting to be shipped over from Bizerta. In addition, the programme for establishing the strategic bomber force in Italy was already lagging behind for want of shipping space. Eventually, after repeated appeals to the Combined Chiefs of Staff, permission was finally given (about 5 November) for fifty-six British and twelve American LSTs to remain in the theatre until 15 December. An acute shortage of shipping resulting in serious administrative problems, a virtual ban on any but minor amphibious outflanking assaults, and a slow build-up of forces on the mainland, this is the background against which the operations over the next three months will now be described.

The first phase of these operations was the natural result of Kesselring's decision to withdraw to and hold the line of the Volturno and the Biferno until 15 October. To give as much time as possible for the destruction of the port of Naples, von Vietinghoff kept most of his strength south of the Apennines and, as no reinforcements from the north were forthcoming, had little left to oppose Eighth Army on his left flank. On 24 September the position at Salerno was sufficiently stabilized for Montgomery to start regrouping for a drive up the east coast, the first objective being the airfields at Foggia. The port of Brindisi would not be operating for another three days and Taranto, where 8 Indian Division had started landing on 22 September, was still involved with troop convoys. The same night, elements of 78 Division and detachments of 4 Armoured Brigade landed at Bari and within thirty-six hours were approaching the River Ofanto. This advance on the coast coincided with the Canadians and 1 Airborne Division closing in on Altamura, which the Germans abandoned on 23 September, and a follow-up of this withdrawal through Canosa. The Germans pulled out of Foggia on 27 September and 13 Corps reported the whole of the Gargano peninsula clear by 1 October. Eighth Army regrouping at this stage placed 13 Corps in the lead, with 78 Division on the right and 1 Canadian Division on the left, supported by 4 Armoured and 1 Canadian Tank Brigades. 5 Corps was at the moment in reserve and contained 5 Division, 8 Indian Division and 1 Armoured Division, the latter being due to leave for the United Kingdom towards the end of November.

On Fifth Army front the Germans were forced to hold the Sorrento peninsula and its passes to give time both for the destruction of the port of Naples and for the withdrawal of their divisions moving back through the mountains and across the plain to the Volturno. 10 Corps attempting to break out towards Naples were faced by the Hermann Göring Division, with detachments from the 3 and 15 Panzer Grenadier Divisions, holding well-prepared positions. VI Corps were swinging round on a wide arc through the mountains towards Teora and Avellino with the object of capturing Benevento. Making skilful use of demolitions and small covering parties in the difficult and mountainous country, 16 Panzer Division was able to cause considerable delay with little risk to their own withdrawal. Fifth Army's attack started on 23 September and on the right Teora was entered on 26 September and Avellino on 30 September, after a night attack by 3 Division. 10 Corps had been attacking through the passes for four days against stubborn resistance between Cava and Mount Stella but now the German positions were threatened by the outflanking movements inland. On 26 September 82 Airborne Division was landed by LCIs at Maiori to reinforce the Rangers, who still held their positions overlooking Nocera. Threatened now on both flanks, the Germans were forced to give way on the whole of 10 Corps' front. 23 Armoured Brigade passed through 46 Division to lead 7 Armoured Division straight towards Naples. On 29 September the bridge at Scafati was captured before it could be blown and to speed up the advance three more temporary bridges were thrown across the river. Working along the coast road 82 Airborne Division was well up with the advance columns but the first Allied troops to enter Naples early on 1 October were Armoured patrols from the King's Dragoon Guards. Much damage had been caused by Allied bombing and the sewage system had entirely broken down. Before they left the Germans did 'their utmost to wreck all public utilities, including electricity, transportation, and water'.[6] This was not all, however, as the water system had been deliberately polluted, the city's priceless archives burnt and several public buildings mined with delayed action bombs, timed to cause the maximum loss of life to the civilian population. Other time-bombs were placed in barracks and buildings likely to be used as military headquarters, in several cases causing heavy casualties. The Germans' main concern, however, had been to destroy the port facilities. 'Fires were burning along the waterfront, access to every pier and mole was blocked by wrecks, and on the bottom of the harbour vessels, cranes, trucks and even an occasional locomotive were obscenely piled.'[7] The Allies, however, had already dealt with this kind of situation at Bizerta and Salerno, though not on such a scale. A hand-picked team from the Royal Navy and US Army Engineers, US Navy fire fighters and a New Zealand hydrographic unit moved in with remarkable results. By 18 October, 5,000 tons of cargo a day were being discharged through the port and 'by the end of the year, more Allied tonnage was being discharged in Naples than the maximum official capacity of the port before the war'.[8] Before the Salerno beach head was closed down, towards the middle of October, two US destroyers were sunk by U-boats, one in the bay and one off the North African coast while escorting a convoy bound for Salerno. In the first of these two actions there was heavy loss of life. Naval casualties over the whole AVALANCHE period were:

	Killed	Missing	Wounded
US Navy	296	551	422
RN	83	—	43

Although the Germans had abandoned Naples they were still able to slow down Fifth Army advance, particularly in the mountainous district on VI Corps front. General Lucas, the new corps commander, tried unsuccessfully to pass 45 Division advancing from Benevento, round the flank of the German positions on the upper Volturno. After some sharp engagements with the German rearguards Fifth Army reached the general line of the Volturno about 6 October on a forty-mile front. In the last few days the weather had

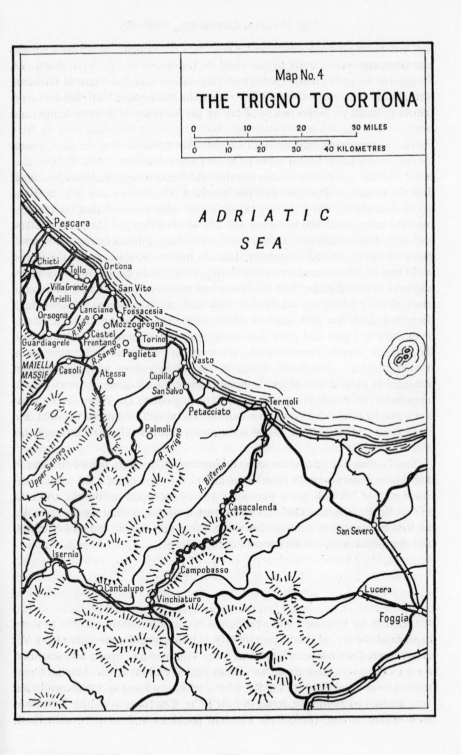

Map No. 4

THE TRIGNO TO ORTONA

0   10   20   30 MILES
0   10   20   30   40 KILOMETRES

ADRIATIC

SEA

Pescara

Chieti
Tollo   Ortona
Villa Grande   San Vito
Arielli
Orsogna   Lanciano   Fossacesia
              Mozzogrogna
Guardiagrele   Castel   Torino
                Frentano
         R. Sangro   Paglieta
MAIELLA   Casoli   Atessa   Vasto
MASSIF   Cupilla
                  San Salvo
R. Moro
                Petacciato   Termoli
              Palmoli
Upper Sangro   R. Trigno
              R. Biferno

              Casacalenda
                          San Severo
Isernia
              Campobasso
Cantalupo   Lucera
    Vinchiaturo
                        Foggia

145

broken bringing cold winds and heavy rain. Overnight, roads became impassable and many units found all their transport, except for a few jeeps, bogged down in the mud. These conditions caused General Clark to postpone the attack across the river by three days, to the night 12/13 October. This pause gives us an opportunity of taking up the story of Eighth Army once more.

The administrative difficulties of Eighth Army were still acute and General Montgomery knew that a rapid advance in strength was out of the question until the east coast ports were operating fully and proper maintenance areas had been set up. He had also just received Alexander's directive that the capture of Rome was 15 Army Group's next objective and that the task for Eighth Army would be to secure the lateral road Pescara to Avezzano. The country ahead consisted of a narrow coastal plain intersected by major river lines at about ten-mile intervals. Inland, the mountains rose steeply with swift-running streams and rivers in deep gorges. Tanks could only manoeuvre along the coastal plain, 'but here trees and intensive cultivation also favours the defence by limiting the field of view and the effectiveness of weapons'.[9] In winter the rivers were often in spate and the lower reaches flooded. Moreover there was only one good road along the coast, with the nearest main axis of advance some forty miles to the flank running up through the Apennines. Under these circumstances it was obviously necessary to have sufficient ammunition and engineer and bridging materials well forward for a series of opposed river crossings taken head on. The immediate tactical problem, however, was to secure the Foggia area so that the airfields could be brought into use by the tactical air forces and the recently formed Fifteenth Strategic Air Force.

The Germans were known to be taking up positions on the River Biferno and Montgomery sent 78 Division straight off up the coast road to seize the small port of Termoli, some two miles west of the mouth of the river. On the left flank, 1 Canadian Division was directed on the communications centre of Vinchiaturo in the mountains some forty miles south-west of Termoli. During the advance 5 Corps would occupy the general area Foggia–Canosa–Barletta. On 2 October the leading troops of 78 Division were within twenty-five miles of Termoli. 'The going was slow: enemy aircraft caused casualties as they harried the advancing columns, there were continual diversions to avoid the craters, and in the first four miles three bridges had been demolished that had to be repaired before the advance could be continued.'[10] The early capture of the lateral road Termoli–Campobasso would materially help Fifth Army operations towards Naples and the Volturno and speed was essential. So 3 Commando, now down to 180 all ranks, and 40 Royal Marine Commando, plus a Special Raiding Squadron, making a force of 1,000 men in all, were embarked at Manfredonia in four LCIs. The force sailed on 2 October with orders to land behind the German positions and seize Termoli itself.

Naval support at Anzio, showing HMS *Spartan* in action. In background landing craft and ships waiting to beach.

Field-Marshal Kesselring gives orders by telephone for the attack on the Allied beach head at Anzio. Field-Marshal Baron von Richtofen stands in the centre foreground, Westphal on extreme right.

General von Senger assisting the Abbot of Cassino into a staff car at XIV Corps battle headquarters at the time of the evacuation of the Monastery, February 1944.

Cassino town after the bombing attacks 15 March 1944. Castle Hill is outlined against the smoke on the right.

There was only one inadequate chart for the entire flotilla and owing to the speed of the advance no air photos were available. Little was known of the German dispositions, except that no armour had been met on the Foggia plain and that troops of 1 Parachute Division were on the high ground north of the Biferno, from where they could also dominate the lateral road. The voyage of 120 miles had to be made without naval escort. In spite of several craft grounding on an uncharted sand-bank near the mouth of the river the landing west of the town achieved complete surprise. By dawn on 3 October the whole force was ashore without opposition. The town was taken by 1800 hours after fierce fighting around the railway station. The Germans lost 130 killed and 200 prisoners out of a force of about 600. Brigadier Durnford-Slater later wrote, 'during the fighting General Heydrich, the German para-troops divisional commander, slipped out of the town on foot. He kindly left his car behind, a 1939 Horch, long, low, black and very fast. 3 Commando found it, cleaned it up and presented it to me. It has always struck me as extraordinary how the news of a battle sometimes fails to spread. Throughout the morning, German supply lorries kept coming in from the north. 40 Commando ambushed twelve of these at a northern cross-road, greeting each vehicle with long Bren bursts until it ran off the road and overturned, often in flames.'[11] The coast road bridge across the river had, of course, been blown but the leading brigade of 78 Division, who reached this point during the morning, got a battalion across by wading and in small boats, together with some anti-tank guns on rafts. By dusk a folding boat bridge had been built and part of the Divisional Reconnaissance Regiment and a Regiment of Field Artillery were over the river. It was obvious, however, that the Germans were preparing for a strong counter-attack and throughout the morning the commandos had been engaged in laying ambushes for German mobile columns probing towards the town and in setting up a perimeter defence. As the day wore on, more and more British infantry moved into positions round the town and a further brigade was landed by sea during the night 3/4 October. The situation, however, was becoming extremely critical. In the rapid advance all the bridging equipment had been used up and the division's own Bailey bridge had been taken for railway repair. Until this could be got back no tanks could get across the river to support the infantry. There was also a shortage of gun ammunition and regiments were down to 200 rounds per gun, as supply through the ports was not yet functioning properly. On top of all this the weather broke and torrential rain fell continuously for eighteen hours. The temporary bridge was swept away and what little transport the division had (most of it still being back in Sicily) was completely bogged down. Overnight more anti-tank guns had been landed but even carriers were unable to get them forward through the mud to the units on the perimeter.

The reports of the commando landing reached Tenth Army while Kessel-ring was actually at their headquarters. He immediately ordered 16 Panzer

Division to cross from their positions opposite Fifth Army and attack the Termoli bridgehead at the earliest moment. At the army headquarters, however, something went wrong and about four hours were lost before Kesselring discovered the division had not even started to move. The result was, 'the division arrived belatedly on 4 October and was thrown in piecemeal'.[12] Early on 4 October 36 Brigade, which had landed overnight, and the Reconnaissance Regiment of 78 Division, started to move outwards to expand the bridgehead across the river and around Termoli. The Germans' reactions became more and more violent as groups of Mk IV tanks and fresh infantry arrived on the scene. The German shelling was now greatly increased and remarkably accurate. An observation post hidden in the church tower of Termoli was unfortunately only discovered later. During the night 4/5 October the fighting became confused. An attack by the Argylls to seize high ground three miles west of the town was halted and at dawn the battalion found themselves in an extremely exposed position. Still there was no heavy bridging equipment and the Sappers were struggling under shell fire to make a ford that the tanks could use. Six Shermans succeeded in getting over but four were knocked out. The Argylls had lost 5 officers and 150 other ranks and found themselves forced back into a brickworks, which by now was being heavily shelled. As the morning wore on the German tanks closed in upon the depleted units and the Royal West Kents were down to eighty men. The ground was so wet that anti-tank guns could not be moved. Field gun ammunition was almost exhausted and lorries bringing up more had to negotiate no less than seven crossings, 'at each of which the bridge was blown and at each of which the diversions climbed down and up a steep and slippery slope – almost impassable for the lorries of the RASC and the divisional artillery regiments which had rear-wheel drive only'. For twenty-four hours the engineers had been working under shell fire and in pouring rain to build the Bailey bridge so that the tanks could cross. At 1440 hours on the afternoon of 5 October the bridge was finished and the Sherman tanks started to cross and come into action. Five out of nine tanks were knocked out but 'these first five Shermans . . . had prevented the enemy from coming in to make the kill he expected, and at dusk that night came the real turning point in the battle'.[13] Two squadrons of the Canadian Tank Regiment crossed the bridge and the Irish Brigade started landing 300 men an hour from seven landing craft, which had just sailed into Termoli harbour. During the night the Germans tried to break through into Termoli and at one point the Lancashire Fusiliers were forced to withdraw in the face of a heavy combined infantry and tank attack. The attack was finally halted with the aid of heavy artillery concentrations. On 6 October General Evelegh struck back with an attack south, parallel to the road, using tanks followed by the Buffs. This attack at first met stiff resistance from a number of anti-tank guns and German tanks. Meanwhile in the Termoli sector the Irish Brigade, assisted by tanks, attacked with great *élan*

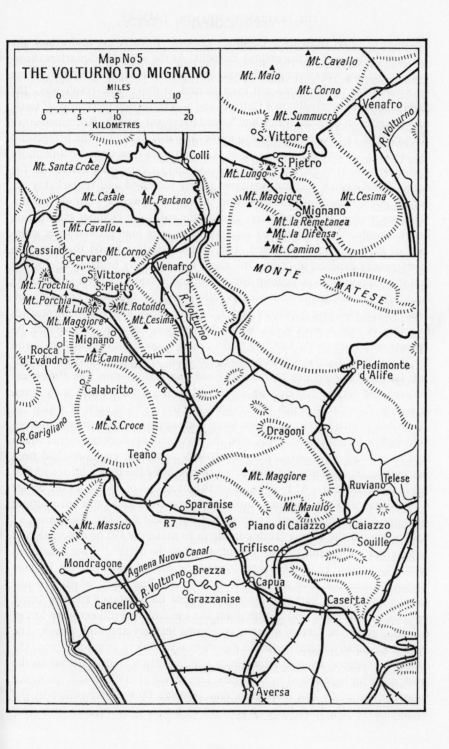

THE VOLTURNO TO MIGNANO

Map No 5

MILES
0 ... 5 ... 10

KILOMETRES
0 ... 5 ... 10 ... 20

Inset (top right):

Mt. Cavallo
Mt. Maio
Mt. Corno
Venafro
Mt. Summucro
R. Volturno
S. Vittore
S. Pietro
Mt. Lungo
Mt. Maggiore
Mt. Cesima
Mignano
Mt. la Remetanea
Mt. la Difensa
Mt. Camino

Main map:

Colli
Mt. Santa Croce
Mt. Casale
Mt. Pantano
Mt. Cavallo
Cassino
Cervaro
Mt. Corno
Venafro
S. Vittore
S. Pietro
Mt. Trocchio
Mt. Porchia
Mt. Rotondo
Mt. Lungo
Mt. Cesima
Mt. Maggiore
R. Volturno
Mignano
Rocca d'Evandro
Mt. Camino
MONTE
MATESE
Calabritto
R6
Piedimonte d'Alife
R. Garigliano
Mt. S. Croce
Dragoni
Teano
Mt. Maggiore
Ruviano
Telese
Sparanise
Mt. Maiulo
R7
R6
Piano di Caiazzo
Caiazzo
Mt. Massico
Souille
Triflisco
Mondragone
Agnena Nuovo Canal
Brezza
Capua
R. Volturno
Cancello
Grazzanise
Caserta
Aversa

and recaptured the brickworks and pressed home their attacks astride the coast road towards Vasto. In this climax to the battle the Germans lost eight tanks and suffered heavy casualties. Losses in the Irish Brigade were surprisingly light. This attack eased the situation for the Buffs and 'by nightfall the battle of Termoli was over, and the enemy was withdrawing from every point of the peninsula, leaving our hold on Termoli secure and the road to Pescara open'.[14] Over the last two days Spitfires and P40s flew 950 sorties in direct support of the land battle and against road movements as far back as Isernia. Such raids as the Luftwaffe made were concentrated on any shipping standing offshore and the Allied transport vehicles struggling up the coast road with gun ammunition and supplies. Two British destroyers arrived off Termoli on 6 October and joined in the bombardment of the German positions.

On Eighth Army's left the Canadians had been having a tedious and frustrating struggle against demolitions and skilfully conducted rear-guard actions during their advance up Route 17 into the mountains. There was now a considerable gap between the army's two lines of advance and 5 Division was brought forward, under 13 Corps, and captured Casacalenda on 13 October and Vinchiaturo the following day. With the Germans withdrawing back to the line of the River Trigno, the Foggia airfields were secure and Eighth Army could now pause for regrouping and 'to establish (the) administrative facilities on a firmer base before advancing to contact the main German winter line on the Sangro'.[15]

On the western side of the Apennines the winter line ran through Mignano, where Route 6 climbed up to what was known as the Mignano Gap. This area was about thirty miles north of Capua, the junction point between VI and 10 Corps preparing to cross the Volturno. Although Hitler's decision to stand south of Rome had still not been taken, Tenth Army had already been promised two extra divisions. The 94 and 305 Infantry Divisions were expected to be in position by 1 November and von Vietinghoff had already been told to hold the line of the Volturno till 15 October. East of Capua the river ran through 'a well-cultivated valley through country that is hilly and thickly wooded'.[16] Minefields were sown at crossing points and covered by anti-tank guns and artillery. Battle groups from 26 Panzer Division, 3 Panzer Grenadier Division and the Hermann Göring Division were placed in some depth, in a counter-attack role between the Matese mountains and Route 6. Below Capua the river meanders through an open plain dominated by Monte Massico. The river itself, in this area, was a definite obstacle, being 150–300 feet wide between banks from 12–30 feet high and backed by levees 10–15 feet high. These levees had been built to check flooding and gave excellent defilade positions. The river itself was about six feet deep and no fords could be found. Owing to the heavy rains movement across the open plain was extremely difficult off the main roads. The sector was held by a line of company positions found by 15 Panzer Grenadier Division and part of the Hermann Göring

Division. There was little depth to the position but good observation for several miles across the river and machine-guns and mortars were right forward, dug in to the sides of the levee.

General Clark's plan was to attack with the six divisions that were already lined up south of the river. The main effort by VI Corps would be made by 3 Division east of Triflisco. 34 Division would cross between Caiazzo and Souille supported by 45 Division, who were already north of the Calore River tucked in below the Matese mountains. On 10 Corps front, in the open coastal plain, General McCreery decided to attack on as wide a front as possible, in the hopes that a breakthrough could be made by 46 Division on the extreme left at the mouth of the river. Here it was planned to bring in a battalion of tanks by LCTs to land north of the mouth of the river in support of the division. Here also naval gun-fire could be effectively used. In the centre, 7 Armoured Division would make a holding attack towards Brezza, while 56 Division attacked below Capua with 167 Brigade. A diversionary attack would be made by 201 Guards Brigade near the rather obvious crossing point below Triflisco. On the night of 12/13 October the Allied artillery opened up and the troops closed up to the river line over the sodden fields and along tracks deep in mud. On the right, the Guards Brigade advanced under an intense barrage and a company got across the river but the position was un-tenable, being outflanked from high ground above Triflisco, and had to be abandoned before daylight. 56 Division's main attack below Capua was observed forming up. The fields were so waterlogged that a single road had to be used and there was little cover. The Germans even counter-attacked across the river at dusk. In spite of this interference and a good deal of shelling, the Oxfordshire and Buckinghamshire Light Infantry made repeated attempts to cross in assault boats but suffered such severe losses that the attack was called off before midnight. The Queen's Brigade of 7 Armoured Division similarly met fierce resistance and at first were unable to cross. After repeated efforts, including using a wire rope to haul themselves over in the flat-bottomed assault boats, a small bridgehead was seized, but by dawn less than a company was over the river. The timing and artillery support for these attacks probably led the Germans to believe this was the main assault, as on the VI Corps' front the attacks went in two or three hours later. Near the mouth of the river 46 Division, however, crossing in silence and without any artillery barrage, achieved surprise. Three battalions were over by 0130 hours 13 September and were reinforced by a further two battalions before dawn. The tanks and some guns were safely landed north of the river's mouth but were unfortunately halted by a minefield. Fire from 88-mm guns stopped further landings by sea after it became light. On the 13 October 15 Panzer Division made repeated attacks on 46 Division using tanks and infantry. The Foresters on the right between Cancello and Grazzanise suffered considerable casualties and had to be relieved by the York and Lancasters. Overnight two minefields were cleared and a further squadron of tanks landed and a number of anti-tank guns were ferried across the river. Six battalions with a strong force of tanks were now in position across the river and the Panzers pulled back, leaving the bridgehead secure. The Queen's Brigade, meanwhile, had gradually got a foothold and had built a ferry at their crossing point. On 14 October they were pressing forward against accurate shell and mortar fire. 56 Division still could not force a crossing at Capua.

On VI Corps' front the attack by 3 Division also started with a feint near Triflisco at midnight on 12/13 October. Following a heavy artillery bombardment two battalions crossed the river a couple of hours later without difficulty and, meeting only small arms fire, made for Monte Maiulo. A crossing further upstream met considerable resistance but by dusk 13 October 3 Division held Monte Maiulo and the hills above Piano di Caiazzo. Further reinforcements crossed during the night and by now three bridges, one carrying 30 tons, had been built. The crossing by 34 Division had started off well with the troops wading across, although one battalion was pinned down by artillery and machine-gun fire until the following afternoon. The river on VI Corps' front was still up to 200 feet wide but only about three to five feet deep. There were good covered approaches through vineyards and orchards and along sunken roads and tree-lined streams. Caiazzo was captured overnight 13/14 October and on the right an advance was made towards Ruviano. By 14 October 34 Division had built two bridges in the face of a good deal of shelling, as much of the river in this sector was under direct observation from high ground to the north-east. Meanwhile 45 Division had taken Telese and by the 14 October was pressing forward over the Telese Creek towards the middle Volturno Valley. 3 Division's advance on the left flank of the Corps front was now dangerously exposed and General Clark shifted the Corps boundary to give 56 Division the use of the bridge that had been built at Triflisco. On the 15 October 201 Guards Brigade crossed to secure the American flank and an outflanking attack was also made from north of the river to clear the Germans from opposite Capua. The following day a crossing south-west of Capua was successful, both Capua and Brezza being cleared before nightfall. A bridge near Grazzanise and a tank ford that was discovered nearby were now brought into use. By now Fifth Army was building up fast in the bridgeheads and the advance of 3 Division in the centre was threatening the main artillery positions on the slopes of Monte Maggiore. The Germans could no longer hold on to the river line but Tenth Army had successfully carried out its task of holding the river until 15 October. Kesselring later wrote, 'Vietinghoff and his brilliant operations chief, Wentzell, carried out the retirement in exemplary fashion and forced a delaying action on the Volturno till 16 October. It was not until two days later that the Allies began the crossing of the river.'[17] This is hardly in agreement with the fact that, by the evening of 18 October, 46 Division had forced a crossing over the Agnena Nuovo canal, 3 Division was in

Dragoni and 45 Division was on the point of capturing Piedimonte d'Alife. The weather conditions, however, were now so bad that Fifth Army's advance on a thirty-mile front could only make slow progress and it was quite impossible to break through the German rear-guards.

Ahead lay a very complex pattern of mountains and rivers. As Route 6 leaves the valley of the lower Volturno to climb towards Mignano it gradually swings round to a north-westerly line, passing through the town of Cassino and below the famous monastery. The Rivers Rapido and Garigliano establish a water line running roughly north and south between Cassino and the sea. East of the two rivers is a range of broken and rugged mountains which start as the divide between the Rapido and the upper Volturno and end on the coast at Monte Massico. The line of the Allied advance up Route 6 thus required a deliberate attack in to the 'waist' of this mountainous divide, at a point just below where the two river lines are roughly parallel and only some twelve miles apart, in order to pass through the Mignano Gap and across the valley to Cassino. The narrow valley which forms the gap itself is virtually ringed by a complex of mountains consisting of Mount Cesima (often referred to as Point 1170), Mounts Sammucro, Lungo and Rotondo which dominate the valley from the north, while to the south lie Mounts Maggiore, La Difensa and Camino. This latter group of mountains 'formed the southern anchor of the Winter Line proper'.[18]

As Fifth Army wheeled slowly to the north-east they found the Germans' tactics in withdrawal had changed. The demolition programme was even more intense. Bridges and culverts on both main and secondary roads had been systematically destroyed. Many buildings in villages had been demolished to block the narrow streets. Both Teller and 'S' mines had been sown at road junctions and on the verges and along the banks of streams. Likely bivouac areas were mined and booby-trapped. Instead of covering road blocks with mobile guns, small parties of infantry were now used well forward, covered by mortars and artillery. Machine-gun teams were often left behind in villages after they had been abandoned. Tanks and all kinds of self-propelled guns, six-barrelled Nebelwerfers and the ten-barrelled version mounted on a half-track were now being used. The cumulative effect of these tactics was to slow down the Allies' advance considerably. On 25 October 7 Armoured Division took Sparanise and 56 Division reached Teano on 30 September and Roccamonfina the following day. 46 Division with the help of tanks attacked along the coast below Mount Massico and by 2 November elements of both 7 Armoured Division and 46 Division reached the Garigliano. By 3 November 34 and 45 Divisions were east of the Volturno facing the loop of the river opposite Venafro and both 3 Division and 56 Division were approaching Mount Camino. On Fifth Army right 34 and 45 Divisions crossed the river on the night of 3/4 November and for ten days fought their way into the mountains above Venafro. Although the peaks of Mounts Corno and Santa

Croce were eventually taken, the momentum of the attack petered out against German positions that had been blasted into the solid rock and which were covered by heavy defensive artillery fire. On 5 November 56 and 3 Divisions had attacked into the 'hill mass' of Camino. 201 Guards Brigade took Calabritto early on 7 November and after an eight-hour climb seized part of a ridge that led up to the crest of Camino itself. Every attempt to advance into the mountains was met by accurate and heavy cross fire. In five days' fighting the already depleted infantry companies had lost up to half their strength. Improvised mule trains were formed but were insufficient to maintain the forward units, and whole battalions had to be used to carry up supplies and ammunition to the forward positions, perched precariously on the exposed rocky outcrops.

In the centre, 3 Division had advanced into the gap. 'A local failure of the Panzer Grenadiers'[19] gave the Americans possession of Point 1170 and then allowed Mount Rotondo to be attacked from the flank. Although this attack failed, a second attack, made in fog on 8 November, reached the crest which was held against several counter-attacks. An attack on La Difensa on 5 December continued for ten days. 'Along the top of the mountain there was nearly a mile of sheer cliff, fifty or sixty feet high, and with perfect observation the enemy could bring fire to bear from all his weapons. Only porters could supply the regiment, and as in many cases men needed both hands for climbing, they could carry very little at a time. . . . It took six hours to carry down the wounded.'[20] The men of Fifth Army had been in continuous action since 9 September. Casualties had been heavy and reserves had already been absorbed. The problem of supplying the forward units in the mountains and the sodden valleys had become acute. On 15 November General Alexander called a halt. The frost-bitten and exhausted men of 56 Division were withdrawn from Camino and 3 Division pulled back from the equally exposed positions below La Difensa. It would now be the turn of Eighth Army, whose advance from Termoli into the Winter Line on the Adriatic front will shortly be described. Before doing so, however, some mention should be made of the Allied use of the Foggia and other airfields in support of the Combined Bomber Offensive, this being one of the principal objects of the landings on the Italian mainland.

When the target priority was laid down for the Combined Bomber Offensive by RAF Bomber Command and the US Eighth Air Force the short-term or 'intermediate' aim was the reduction of the German fighter strength. This took absolute priority over the 'long-term' attacks on the U-boat yards and bases and the German aircraft industry and other essential war industries and oil supplies. Attacks on the German oil supplies were, in fact, 'contingent upon attack against Ploesti from the Mediterranean'.[21] The techniques of the two bombing forces operating from Britain were of course quite different. The British concentrated on night bombing and the Americans on daylight attacks. As the offensive developed, however, the Fortress groups had to reach out further and further to attack essential industrial plant in Prussia, southern Germany and even Poland. There was already a shortage of long-range fighter escorts and many of the targets were now even beyond the range of the P47s which, with extra belly tanks, had a theoretical range of 375 miles but could not operate effectively as escorts much beyond 300 miles, and it was not until March 1944 that P51s with extra tanks could properly match the range of the daylight bombers.

A raid on the ball-bearing plants at Schweinfurt on 14 October illustrates the degree of resistance met by the bombers. A total of 291 B17s took part, all carrying extra fuel tanks for the round trip of 900 miles. Some 240 miles from the British coast the escorting fighters had to turn back and the Fortresses were on their own until they were back again over the Channel on the return journey. For over 600 miles they were harassed by the Luftwaffe. Wave after wave of fighters, including many twin-engined planes equipped with rocket projectiles, attacked the bombers and twenty-eight Fortresses were lost before they reached the target. Although the attack was exceptionally effective it was not decisive and caused only a temporary set-back in production. The Eighth Air Force lost 60 B17s and crews, and 138 aircraft were damaged, 17 being beyond reasonable repair. German records show their own losses on this day, over the whole Western Front, were 38 fighters lost and 20 damaged in combat. This raid was the climax of six days' fighting by the Eighth Air Force and included four attempts to break through the German defences by unescorted bombers. The result was the loss of 148 bombers and their crews and, as far as daylight operations were concerned, air superiority over Germany had temporarily been lost. The development of the Foggia complex and other airfields in southern Italy, Sardinia and Corsica thus became a matter of urgency, as essential targets in southern and eastern Germany and in many of the satellite countries, as well as parts of southern France and northern Italy, could be more easily reached from Italian airfields. Operations from Italy were seen as one of the principal means of overcoming the 'autumn crisis' in the CBO programme which, in relation to the approaching date of OVERLORD, must somehow be accelerated and intensified. Between the end of October 1943 and the turn of the year, British and American engineer and airfield construction groups in Italy, Sardinia and Corsica had 'completed or were in process of completing construction on more than forty-five airfields. The work ranged from repairs and drainage to building paved or steel-plank runways as much as 6,000 feet in length.'[22] Oil pipelines were built, the principal being from Manfredonia to Foggia capable of supplying 160,000 gallons of 100-octane fuel a week, and a special supply base was opened at Bari.

All this intensive activity made heavy demands on shipping space and transport but served the dual purpose of achieving the move forward of the air support components of the North West African Air Force, as well as bomber groups of Twelfth Air Force, and the creation on 1 November of the Fifteenth Strategic Air Force. This newly formed bomber force was commanded by General Doolittle and operating from the Italian bases would work to the CBO directives and also assist when possible the land battle in Italy. The Fifteenth Air Force was initially formed by taking six heavy bombardment groups, five medium and four fighter groups from XII Bomber Command. The intention, however, was to build up rapidly with fifteen new bomber groups by March 1944. At the end of December the strength of Fifteenth Air Force was 4,872 officers and 32,867 men. While the aircraft strength in December was only 564, this was increased in January 1944 by three groups of B24 heavy bombers, three groups of B26 medium bombers and 42 bombardment wing (mediums) totalling some 356 aircraft. By the end of June Fifteenth Air Force had an operational strength of nearly 1,200 heavy bombers. Bad weather and the demands of the land campaign in Italy limited the operations of Fifteenth Air Force strategic bombers until well into 1944, when they began to play a major part in the CBO programme. Many vital targets could now be covered. For instance fifty-one industrial plants producing crude and synthetic oil would now be within range of heavy bombers based on Foggia. The estimated production of these fifty-one plants was 76 per cent of Germany's total production amounting to nearly twelve million tons of fuel a year. As Tedder later wrote, 'the establishment of airfields in southern Italy had initiated a new phase of the war'.[23] In January 1944 Tedder, Doolittle and Spaatz went to England to join the OVERLORD team and the Allied air forces in the Mediterranean were now commanded by General Eaker. The Fifteenth Strategic Air Force was taken over by Major-General Twining and the Tactical Air Force consisting of XII Air Force and the Desert Air Force was commanded by Major-General Cannon.

9
Winter Line

Eighth Army strikes first: Battle of River Sangro: German reinforcements arrive: Ortona reached: Air Battle continues: Kesselring holds fast on Winter Line: Fifth Army attacks into the mountains: Mount Camino and San Pietro: French Expeditionary Corps arrives.

1943	Fifth Army	Eighth Army
22 Oct		Crossing of the River Trigno (to 3 November).
28 Oct		13 Corps operation from Vinchiaturo to capture of Isernia (on 4 November).
8 Nov		78 Division reaches River Sangro.
15 Nov	Fifth Army regrouping.	
16 Nov		78 Division seize bridgehead over Sangro.
18 Nov	II Corps (General Keyes) takes over centre sector (3 and 36 Divisions).	
19 Nov		Battle of River Sangro (to 3 December).
24 Nov	General Clark issues plans for assault on Winter Line (to start 2/3 December).	13 Corps capture Castel Alfedena.
25 Nov	Plans for landing south of Rome (Operation SHINGLE) approved.	
2 Dec	Battle of Monte Camino (to 9 December).	New Zealand Division captures Castel Frentano.
7 Dec	Battles for San Pietro (continue to 17 December).	8 Indian and 78 Divisions reach River Moro (Canadians cross on 10 December).
8 Dec	French units start taking over in VI Corps area (in action on 26 December).	
20 Dec		Canadians in Ortona (finally captured on 28 December).

| 1943 | *Fifth Army* | *Eighth Army* |

24 Dec   Announcement of United Command for Mediterranean Theatre of Operations (under General Wilson).

29 Dec   Raid by 9 Commando north of mouth of River Garigliano.

While Fifth Army was fighting its way forward from the Volturno to the Mignano gap, Eighth Army was facing up to the other end of the Bernhardt Line which ran through the mountains north of Isernia down to the San Salvo ridge and Vasto on the coast. In front of this was the River Trigno. Some twenty miles to the rear of these positions was the German Winter Line based on the River Sangro and the forward slopes of the great Maiella massif. Facing Eighth Army was LXXVI Panzer Corps, consisting of 26 Panzer Division and 29 Panzer Grenadier Division together with 16 Panzer Division and 1 Parachute Division, both of which had been seriously mauled in the Termoli fighting. The Allies aimed at capturing Rome and the task of Eighth Army, as outlined by General Montgomery, was to seize the high ground north of Pescara and then to strike south-west through Avezzano in support of a co-ordinated attack by Fifth Army, which could be supplemented by an amphibious landing south of the Tiber. Although firm plans had to await the Combined Chiefs of Staff's decision about retaining the fifty-eight landing craft until mid-December, this was the pattern of operations formulated by Alexander to 'keep the enemy on his heels'.[1] Eighth Army was already re-grouping and with the winter weather closing in earlier than expected the advance was ordered as soon as possible. The plan was for 13 Corps (1 Canadian and 5 Divisions) to attack on 28 October on the axis Vinchiaturo–Isernia as a diversion to the main assault by 5 Corps (78 Division and 8 Indian Division) up the coast road on the night of 30/31 October. All started well and in a preliminary action 78 Division succeeded in getting a battalion across the River Trigno on 22/23 October. Some two miles ahead, across a 'wooded undulating plain', was the San Salvo ridge and the main German positions and there were high hopes of establishing a strong force across the river in preparation for the main attack. At this moment the weather finally broke and heavy rain fell for days on end. The clay banks of the river, which is very broad near the coast, turned to mud. Movement by vehicles off the road became impossible. Attacks to enlarge the bridgehead on 27 and 28 October failed and the diversionary attack on Cantalupo was postponed for thirty-six hours, but 'in spite of the weather, difficult country and demolitions'[2] 5 Division captured Cantalupo on 31 October. The weather was 'atrocious' and on this flank the country was extremely broken with the strongly fortified mountain villages resolutely held by 26 Panzer Division. German shelling was increasing and becoming very effective. 'The hard ground made it impossible to dig in, and the sole means of protection was to build sangar-like shelters as in the fighting on the north-west Frontier of India in pre-war days.'³ Mules were now increasingly used for carrying machine-guns and heavy equipment, as well as for maintaining companies on the rocky outposts. Isernia was taken on 5 November.

On the coast the main attack was mounted in strength and with some care to deceive the Germans. The assault was preceded by the shelling of Vasto and Cupello by two destroyers and a number of motor torpedo boats to simulate preparations for a seaborne landing, while on the left Bofors guns using tracer and a machine-gun battalion fired as if in support of an attack well inland. On the right 78 Division advanced straight for the village of San Salvo. Major-General Evelegh, the divisional commander, had insisted that the anti-tank gun carriers and supporting Sherman tanks should be got across the river before the infantry advanced from the bridgehead He also arranged for thirty DUKWs to land extra gun and tank ammunition north of the mouth of the Trigno. On the coastal flank the Germans fought hard for the San Salvo railway station and the expected tank battle developed in the olive groves around the town itself, which changed hands before 16 Panzer Division were forced to withdraw during the night. At dawn on 4 November the attack continued and with good artillery support the infantry and tanks reached the outskirts of Vasto which together with Cupello fell overnight. On the left, 8 Indian Division, which 'distinguished itself in this its first engagement',⁴ took the hill village of Tufillo after hard fighting and cleared Palmoli to reach the lateral road from Vasto on 5 November. 'There were prepared defence positions both in Vasto and Cupello and it was pretty obvious that orderly as the enemy's withdrawal had been, it had been made earlier and more swiftly than he had intended.'⁵ Keeping on the axis of the coastal road 78 Division now had 11 Armoured Brigade leading the pursuit and by 9 November the south bank of the Sangro had been reached and cleared as far as Paglieta. Inland, 8 Indian Division, working across the grain of the country, made slower progress but by 19 November it too was facing the German Winter Line across the river. In 5 Corps' sector a steep escarpment gave good observation of the far bank of the river and of the German positions beyond. Below the escarpment was the river itself, some 300-400 feet wide with many channels and already in flood. With heavy rain in the mountains the level of the river rose alarmingly by five or six feet in a day, making it a formidable obstacle which could only be forded in a few places with the greatest difficulty. On the north bank a flat plain extended for about 2,000 yards ending in a steep escarpment 'rising abruptly some hundred and fifty feet'; beyond this was further high ground and the two fortified villages of Fossacesia and Mozzagrogna. This vital coastal sector was held by 65 Infantry Division, equipped only with horse transport, which had recently arrived from the north. In the mountain sector further inland 1 Parachute Division was holding an extended front. The 305 Grenadier Division, also from the north, covered the junction between Eighth and Fifth Armies west of Isernia. A third division, 94 Grenadier Division had also arrived and was on the Garigliano. The arrival of three fresh divisions had enabled Kesselring to pull out the Hermann Göring Division and the 3 Panzer Grenadiers for a much-needed rest. The persistent Fifth Army attacks up Route 6, however, had caused him to switch both 26 Panzer Division and 29 Panzer Grenadier Divisions from the Adriatic flank to take their place. With the decision now taken to stand on the Winter Line, Kesselring, as theatre commander, was busy inspecting the positions and arranging the placing of extra mountain and infantry formations who were already moving south. With a shortage of armour on the Russian front the OKW had decided to send 16 Panzer Division from Italy and when the battle of the River Sangro started it was already on its way. Its place was to be taken by 26 Panzer Division on their relief by 44 Infantry Division. Unfortunately the relief arrived late and 26 Panzer Division once again found itself making a forced march over the mountain passes to get into a fight that was already half lost.

General Montgomery's appreciation briefly was as follows. An attack by 13 Corps through Castel di Sangro to Popoli would outflank the Sangro positions but would be tied to two minor roads which were liable to blocking by snowdrifts and separated by high mountains. 'There would be great maintenance problems and the conditions of cloud and mist in the mountains would virtually preclude the use of our air power.'[6] In the centre, an attack down the axis of the road Atessa to Casoli would threaten the coastal sector but 'it would have been difficult if not impossible to mount a major attack on this axis because of the extremely poor communications south of the river'.[7] An attack on the coastal sector, however, could be mounted quickly and with full artillery support through being served by a good main road; naval gun support would also be possible and the flying conditions the 'best available'. With the onset of winter conditions time was running out as unless the attack could follow a dry spell, of at least forty-eight hours, the movement of tanks and guns would be impossible. The plan was to deceive the Germans into thinking the main thrust would come from Eighth Army's western flank and 13 Corps was ordered to start operations aiming at the capture of Roccaraso. Meanwhile 2 New Zealand Division would relieve 8 Indian Division in the centre, except for one brigade who would remain in forward positions until the last moment to deceive the enemy. The task of the New Zealanders was to attack north from Atessa as a diversion, while the main attack would be made on a narrow front by 78 Division and 8 Indian Division, with objectives the line Ortona–Lanciano with target date 20 November. The orders were for 78 Division to seize a bridgehead and 8 Division to break into the line. Then 78 Division was to come into the lead again and exploit to Pescara. Simultaneously the New Zealanders would strike across the river at Chieti. The main attack would be supported by 400 guns as well as a number of squadrons of the Tactical Air Force and several destroyers.

Near the coast, battle patrols were soon over the river and for about a week, up to 15 November, dominated the plain as far as the escarpment. In addition to gaining valuable information these patrols successfully cleared a number of tracks which had been mined. In some cases this patrolling was done by specialists. 'All activities were controlled by one officer, who was allotted a proportion of men from each company who were used for nothing else. They put in raiding parties, smaller parties to draw fire and otherwise reconnoitre the German strength and dispositions and protective patrols for the Sappers' and tanks' own reconnaissances.'[8] But everything depended on the weather. Unfortunately the heavy rain persisted and the patrols could no longer cross each night and much of their work was lost as the Germans quickly relaid the minefields. With the river rising there was now no chance of getting tanks and vehicles across and the plan of attack had to be modified. As a first step a bridgehead over the river must be seized. For two days, from 20–22 November, 78 Division struggled in the rain and mud to extend their limited hold on the plain the other side of the river but further rain again halted operations. 8 Indian Division was now brought up on the left of 78 Division. The infantry already held most of the plain on a front of some 10,000 yards but very few anti-tank guns or heavy weapons could be got across the river. Surprise as to the point of attack was now virtually lost. The New Zealanders, however, were ordered to launch their attack across the river on a two-brigade front on 28 November, the date now chosen for the main attack which had already been postponed three times owing to the weather. 27 November was a fine day and 4 Armoured Brigade got 100 tanks across the river and many carriers and anti-tank guns also crossed to join up with the forward infantry. The following day was again fine and the assault went in at 2130 hours. 8 Indian Division soon reached Mozzagrogna. The supporting tanks, however, were held up by demolitions and, after a German counter-attack with tanks and flame-throwers at dawn, fierce fighting continued around the village all day. On the second night (28/29 November) the village was captured. By noon 29 November 4 Armoured Brigade got through the village and with the close co-operation of the infantry moved outwards along the ridge. As was expected, the main German positions were sited on the dominating feature and every inch was contested. The German 65 Infantry Division, however, was now being heavily shelled and bombed and machine-gunned from the air. From 28–30 November the Tactical Air Force bombers and fighter-bombers flew 1,200 sorties against key points in the German positions and so dominated the battle area that, according to a German officer, 'counter-attacks were impossible'.[9] General Montgomery judged the time had come to pull out all the stops. 78 Division was given the task of clearing Fossacesia and 8 Indian Division was ordered to attack along the ridge from Mozzagrogna towards

Castel Frentano. 78 Division's plan was simple and very effective. On 29 November a battalion with tanks captured the village of San Maria and Li Colli, a spur close above Mozzagrogna. In this area the Irish Brigade and a tank regiment were assembled. Before this force advanced early on 30 November, however, another brigade had formed-up in the plain and then withdrawn from behind a smoke-screen. The Germans assumed the smoke was to cover an attack from this direction and concentrated the fire of their artillery on the plain. At this moment the main attack by the Irish Brigade went in straight down the ridge towards the village of Fossacesia and the coast road beyond. Behind a heavy barrage the tanks, closely followed by the infantry, advanced over ground the Germans had thought impassable. By mid-day Fossacesia fell and by 1600 hours the attack reached the sea. In the centre of 5 Corps' front 8 Indian Division had beaten off a counter-attack by the leading elements of 26 Panzer Division, who were now being committed piecemeal on their arrival in the battle area. By the end of the day 8 Indian Divison held the high ground overlooking Castel Frentano and were in touch with the New Zealanders, who themselves were across the river in some strength. By now more German reinforcements were being thrown into the battle and on 1 December 90 Panzer Grenadier Division started arriving from Venice to take over the coastal sector. 65 Infantry Division, which had suffered heavy casualties, was given a few days' rest but was soon back in the line opposite the New Zealand Division, whose advance was already being op-posed by several Parachute battalions and elements of 26 Panzer Division. After seven days of dry weather, rain again delayed operations and while a high-level bridge at Paglieta was being completed Montgomery regrouped to strengthen the right flank. 78 Division, 'which had suffered 10,000 casualties in the last six months',[10] was relieved by 1 Canadian Division and placed in 13 Corps Reserve. On 4 December 5 Corps was on the line of the River Moro and 2 New Zealand Division was approaching Orsogna and Guardiagrele. Operations in the mountains were now virtually at a standstill owing to the weather. The New Zealand attacks on Orsogna on both 7 and 14 December had been held and 5 Division, together with 13 Corps Headquarters, was moved down to fill the gap between 8 Indian Division and the New Zealand Division.

By 10 December 1 Canadian Division had a bridgehead over the Moro and was advancing towards Ortona. In an action at the Berardi crossroads a last-ditch stand by 90 Panzer Grenadiers resulted in the remnants of this division being decimated and the formation was not back in the line for nearly six months. German resistance was meanwhile strengthened by the arrival of 334 Infantry Division from Genoa. In the coastal sector whole villages had been converted into strongpoints. When the Canadians entered Ortona on 20 December the town had to be cleared, or rather blown-up house by house, against violent resistance by parachute units. Intense fighting for Ortona continued for a week and Montgomery later wrote, 'the Canadian troops were quite magnificent and in the end out-fought the Germans'.[11] But the cost was high. During December the total casualties in the Canadian Division were 164 officers and 2,101 men. Further inland 8 Indian Division took Villagrande on 22 December and 5 Division took Arielli the following day. The Germans, however, still held the hill village of Orsogna which, perched high on its crags, was a natural fortress, although it was partially outflanked by the New Zealand Division which had succeeded in capturing some high ground to the north-east. Since crossing the Sangro the New Zealand Division, however, had suffered over 1,600 casualties and the defences of Orsogna proved too strong. Eighth Army had broken into but not through the Winter Line. In his dispatch General Alexander wrote, 'the difficult "ridge and furrow country" of the Molise offered few chances of a decisive success to an army attacking as Eighth Army had always done, across the grain of the country. The further north we pushed our advance the more numerous and close together were the river lines.'[12] Hitler's decision to release reinforcements from the north had tipped the scale. There was no longer any chance of a breakthrough to Pescara and the road to Avezzano. Kesselring notes that 'after particularly stiff fighting from 6–13 December there followed a lull on this wing'. The winter had now set in and during December 78 Division had 113 cases of exposure and five men died from the bitter cold. For over a week at the turn of the year the main dressing station for 5 Division was cut off by heavy snowfalls. The New Zealanders reported that at least six men were needed to bring each stretcher case back through the difficult mountainous country in the snow or driving rain. In the plains below men and vehicles daily sank deeper into the mud and slush.

On 31 December General Montgomery handed over to Lieutenant-General Sir Oliver Leese and left for England to take command of 21 Army Group. In his personal message to Eighth Army, Montgomery paid tribute to the support of the Allied Air Forces writing, 'I am also very sad at parting from the Desert Air Force. This magnificent air striking force has fought with the Eighth Army throughout the whole of its victorious progress; every soldier in this army is proud to acknowledge that the support of this strong and powerful air force has been a battle-winning factor of the first importance. We owe the allied air forces in general, and the Desert Air Force in particular, a very great debt of gratitude.'[13] In spite of the deteriorating weather, the Allied air effort during December resulted in over 27,500 effective sorties, which included 4,500 sorties by the Strategic Bomber Force with 10,500 tons of bombs dropped. As conditions became more static the Allied Air Forces began to give more attention to marshalling yards and communications. While the Luftwaffe withdrew many of their bombers to take part in attacks on Britain, the combined efforts of their ground air defences brought increased losses to the Allies. During December the Allies lost 209 planes with

544 damaged, mostly by flak and ground fire. During the month some 285 German planes were destroyed. It is of interest to note that from 9 September to the end of November, Allied Air Force battle casualties per month averaged 7·69 per thousand men compared with 6·33 in the two armies in Italy. At the end of the year the Allied Air Forces in the Mediterranean theatre totalled 315,000 men and 7,000 effective aircraft. As more and more squadrons and ancillary air force units were moved to Italy, the build-up of Fifteenth Army Group suffered increasingly on account of the overall shortage of shipping and it was the end of November before Fifth Army were in any way ready to continue their attacks to break through into the Liri Valley.

Although the goal was still Rome the task for the Allies was equally to draw into the fight the maximum number of German divisions. Alexander's plan, as we have seen, was to lead off with the Eighth Army drive on the Adriatic side of the mountains, while Fifth Army reorganized and received reinforcements for a breakthrough on Route 6. The divisions that had fought their way forward from Salerno to Mignano, however, were not only tired but considerably reduced in strength. For instance, many British infantry battalions in 10 Corps had lost two-thirds of their officers and over half their men. Although units were receiving reinforcements, time was needed before they could be properly absorbed as part of the fighting machine and, owing to the need for building up the OVERLORD forces, units in the Mediterranean never received their proper scale of reinforcements. Furthermore the time-table for replacing the divisions on their way back to England was very tight. 1 US Armoured Division had only just started disembarking at Naples, while 2 Moroccan Division, the first of four divisions forming the French Expeditionary Corps, was due to arrive in the first week of December. Reinforcements already with Fifth Army were a Regimental Combat Team held back from 82 Airborne Division and 1 Special Service Force, comprising six battalions of specially trained Canadians and Americans. Fifth Army, now on a forty-mile front was, however, facing several fresh German Divisions. The Hermann Göring and 3 Panzer Grenadier Divisions had been pulled back for a well-earned rest and two fresh divisions had been brought in. The 94 Grenadier Division was on the coast with 305 Grenadier Division on the other flank in the mountains covering the junction between the two Allied armies. In the centre were two mobile divisions, 29 Panzer Grenadiers and 44 Grenadier Division, the latter replacing 26 Panzer Division. 5 Mountain Division was expected to arrive in December. With three fresh divisions in position and encouraged by the successfull halting of the Fifth Army attacks earlier in November, Kesselring now hoped to hold the Winter Line indefinitely. Previously he had visualized the main defence would be made on the Gustav Line further to the rear in this sector. It will be remembered that the Gustav Line was based on the Rivers Garigliano, Gari and Rapido as far as Cassino and then on the forward slopes of the mountains running straight up into the remote passes of the Central Apennines and down the other side to the Maiella massif and the coastal plain below, where the Eighth Army advance from the Sangro was slowly being halted. These positions, which were 87 miles in length, passed across the narrowest part of the peninsula. The conventional use of the term 'line' is misleading; 'the entire line was a belt of defences in depth without a single key. There was no opportunity for a brilliant stroke that could break it. Each mountain had to be taken, each valley cleared and then there were still more mountains ahead and still another line to be broken by dogged infantry attacks.' In the forward, or Winter Line, positions the Germans held the Maggiore–Camino hill masses, the exits to the Mignano gap, Mount Sammucro and beyond this a 'tangled mass of mountains nine miles wide between the Rapido and the Volturno valleys stretched north from Mount Sammucro past Venafro to the main ridge of the Apennines'.[14]

The weather had completely broken. The bitter cold and heavy rain now added to the difficulties of operating in mountainous country and the rain and mud restricted the supply routes forward from Naples over the few main roads, which were still under repair after extensive demolitions. In the forward areas there were still not enough mules to carry the supplies and ammunition into the mountains. But with every day that passed the fortifications in the Gustav Line were being strengthened and, regardless of the weather and administrative difficulties, the Germans must be allowed no respite. General Clark commented, 'there was only one sector on which we could move in strength; that was on either side of Mount Camino, beyond which lay the Liri river-valley leading to the Italian capital. To reach the Liri valley we first had to drive the Germans off the Camino hill-mass, which included Mount Lungo, Mount La Difensa, Mount La Remetanea, Mount Maggiore, and a little town called San Pietro Infine.'[15] In mid-November the Allies stood within ten miles of the mouth of the Liri valley. It was to be six months before they could break through beyond Cassino.

The penetration of the Winter Line was to be achieved in three phases; firstly the capture of Monte Camino and the other dominant features south of Route 6; secondly the capture of Monte Sammucro combined with a drive from Colli towards Atina; then only after these operations had been completed would II Corps advance into the Liri valley with 1 Armoured Division ready to pass through into the lead. The attack on the Camino hill-mass was mounted by 10 Corps from the south, followed by an attack from the north-east by 1 Special Service Force and part of 36 Division. Attempts were made to deceive the Germans into thinking that a seaborne landing would be made in the Gulf of Gaeta north of Garigliano. Naval forces were assembled in Naples and Mondragone and dummy batteries were set up and targets zeroed around the town of Gaeta. A feint attack was also made towards

San Pietro and the bombing programme included many targets that would fit in with an assault landing north of the river. A gallant but abortive attempt to seize Calabritto by two battalions of 46 Division, made overnight on 1/2 December, succeeded in providing sufficient flank protection for the main attack on Mount Camino to be made by 56 Division the following night as scheduled. From 1630 hours on the previous afternoon 925 guns, including 24 8-inch howitzers, fired 165,000 rounds on the German mountain positions, while 274 bombing sorties were made on 2 December and 612 on the following day. It was difficult, however, for pilots to achieve accuracy in the bad weather and mountainous terrain. The Allied artillery equally had much difficulty with improvised range tables and in getting the necessary elevation to fire on to and over the high mountains. The guns themselves became embedded in the mud and could only be moved by being winched out. 56 Division attacked with two brigades and during the night both attacks made good progress. On the right, the easterly end of the ridge that had held the attack by 201 Guards Brigade about a month before was reached by dawn. The position was retaken by troops of 15 Panzer Grenadiers and held by them for three days against repeated attacks. The other brigade attack, however, made good progress round the western slopes of the mountains and, as a result of this threat, the crest of Mount Camino was reached late on 6 December. Within three days Rocca d'Evandro had been captured and the western part of the Camino hills had been cleared down to the Garigliano. To the north-east, 1 Special Service Force, in a night assault over extremely difficult ground, took La Difensa before dawn on 3 December but were driven back from Mount La Remetanea the following day. After four days' fighting La Remetanea was finally captured. The occupation of these two features was the key to the Maggiore ridge. This was successfully taken by 142 Infantry from 36 Division and held against several counter-attacks. Colonel Starr comments on the problem of supply at this stage. 'Operation Raincoat was very properly so named, for rain fell on 2–4 December and made the trails impassable even to mules. Two companies of the 141 Infantry and half of the 142 Infantry were required to carry supplies for troops on La Difensa and Maggiore. The round trip of three miles from a point near Mignano to Mount Maggiore consumed twelve hours. Air drops were attempted but were defeated by poor visibility, poor recovery grounds, and the proximity to enemy positions.'[16]

Phase two of the offensive aiming at opening Route 6 by the clearing of Mounts Sammucro and Lungo now started. Between these dominating features the road ran through a valley only a mile wide with the little village of San Pietro lying north of the road amongst 'rocky orchard-covered terraces'. II Corps' plan was to envelope the two features and avoid the valley. The extensive slopes and hill features of Mount Sammucro needed special attention and three battalions were ordered to launch a double-pronged attack, supported by Rangers who would attack a feature further to the north. The assault was to be made on the night of 7 December. Early the following morning 1 Italian Motorized Group, a force of four infantry battalions with field and anti-tank regiments, would assault the bare rocky slopes of Mount Lungo from the south-east. The two most northerly American attacks on Mount Sammucro itself went well. After close fighting early on 8 December the actual crest was taken and held against a fierce counter-attack later in the morning. The Rangers also reached their objective but were subsequently thrown back. The position, however, was retaken at dawn the following day (9 December) and successfully held against counter-attacks put in by 71 Panzer Grenadier Regiment of 29 Panzer Grenadier Division for the next four days. The other attack along the southern slopes of Mount Sammucro was a different story. Crossing the start line a mile east of San Pietro at 0620 hours 8 December, the leading battalion of 143 Infantry was halted by intense artillery, mortar and machine-gun fire after an advance of 400 yards. A second battalion got no further. The Allied guns were now turned on to shelling the village all night and to supporting further attacks which continued throughout 9 December. The result was insignificant gains and the infantry were finally pulled back. The Italian attack was equally abortive. The Group had assembled on 7 December. Unfortunately several of the men were so anxious to announce to their former allies what was in store for them the following day, for deserting their comrades in the African campaign, that they crawled out during the night to shout taunts and threats in the direction of a battalion from 15 Panzer Grenadiers holding the slopes of Mount Lungo. There was now little chance of surprise being achieved. The following morning at 0550 hours the German positions were shelled for thirty minutes but before the attack could develop a heavy fog closed in over the mountains 'like a huge smoke-screen'. The advancing infantry battalions were met by a storm of machine-gun and mortar fire. In spite of heavy casualties they continued in their attempts to advance, now with the support of the whole of the Corps artillery. By noon the attack was called off. The fighting so far had been inconclusive, as the Germans still held Mount Lungo and sufficient of the western slopes of Mount Sammucro to stop any advance towards San Pietro or into the valley through which ran Route 6. General Walker now proposed to exploit the limited successes achieved north of the crest of Sammucro with an attack early on 15 December, to be followed by the main effort on San Pietro at noon (using tanks if possible) and a further attempt on Lungo after dawn on 16 December. To the north, two battalions, including one of parachutists who were to relieve the Rangers, met very stiff resistance and in two days' fighting were unable to reach their main objective. One of these units was now reduced to 155 men. The main infantry and tank attack along the lower slope of Sammucro started at 1200 hours 15 December. 'The terrain, however, proved to be extremely difficult for tank operations.

The narrow road was mined and the ground on either side was a series of rock-walled terraces three to seven feet high, covered with olive trees and scrub growth. Stream beds, gullies, and accidents of terrain prevented cross-country operation. Trees limited visibility to about 25 yards and rain had made the ground very soft.'[17] By the end of the day only four tanks returned to their assembly area and twelve had been lost, destroyed or disabled. The advancing infantry had met a terrible concentration of fire and for eight hours fought to gain only a few yards. At 0100 hours the attack was renewed but without artillery support, as all communications had been destroyed. Attacking with grenades, a few men reached the village but by now one of the battalions was down to 120 men and, in spite of further attempts shortly after dawn, the surviving infantry were back on their start line by mid-afternoon 16 December. Nothing, it seemed, could shift the 15 Panzer Grenadiers from San Pietro. The attack on Mount Lungo however had been well prepared. On both 12 and 13 December several features to the west had been captured and on the night of 15/16 December a simultaneous attack was made from this direction and from the slopes of Mount Maggiore. This pincer movement resulted in the majority of the German positions being over-run by daybreak. The subsequent Italian attack cleared the remainder of the mountain by early afternoon 16 December. Early that evening a furious counter-attack struck the battalion holding the slopes of Mount Sammucro north of the San Pietro–Venafro road and continued to about midnight. Patrols early on 17 December found San Pietro abandoned and the relieving force gone. Further to the north, in the mountains west of Venafro, VI Corps had been mounting limited attacks to stop German reinforcements being switched against the II Corps operation and to try to reach the upper Rapido valley. In this rocky mountainous area broken by ravines only very limited advances were made on the roads towards Atina and St Elia.

In mid-December 2 Moroccan Division relieved 36 Division. A few days later the Moroccans were in action and by 17 December had captured Pantano and the northern slopes of Mount Casale. On their left, 45 Division took Mount Cavallo on 22 December, roughly handling the German 5 Mountain Division who were caught taking over from 305 Division in this sector. Early in January 3 Algerian Division took over from 45 Division. General Juin commanding the French Expeditionary Corps now took over this sector and VI Corps was withdrawn to prepare for an operation that had been under consideration for some time, a landing immediately south of Rome (operation SHINGLE) which was intended to coincide with Fifth Army's break out into the Liri valley. These plans, however, should be seen within the context of further meetings between the Allied war leaders that had just taken place in Cairo and Teheran to decide Allied strategy for 1944. These conferences were known by the code names SEXTANT and EUREKA.

10

Politics and Strategy

British views on Mediterranean strategy: Tito's Partisans: Greece split: The Aegean and Turkey: Dodecanese operations fail: Argument at Mena House: Shortage of landing ships: Priority for Chiang Kai-shek: Stalin plays his hand: BUCCANEER off: ANVIL decided: President Inonu prevaricates: Command decisions: SHINGLE agreed.

1943	
19 Oct–2 Nov	Tripartite conference of Foreign Ministers in Moscow.
27 Oct	Eisenhower submits outline study of a landing (or threat) in South of France in support of assault phase of OVERLORD.
6 Nov	Combined Chiefs of Staff agree to LSTs being held temporarily in Mediterranean.
16 Nov	Dodecanese operations, which opened mid-September with landings on Aegean Islands, end with German recapture of Leros.
22–28 Nov	SEXTANT conference in Cairo – opening stage.
28 Nov–1 Dec	EUREKA conference in Teheran.
3–7 Dec	SEXTANT conference re-assembles and reaches agreement on OVERLORD and ANVIL (Landing in south of France).
4–7 Dec	Inconclusive discussions with President Inönü of Turkey.
5 Dec	Roosevelt cancels BUCCANEER.
6 Dec	Eisenhower appointed Supreme Commander for OVERLORD.
17 Dec	Eisenhower requests more assault shipping for ANVIL.
28 Dec	Date for SHINGLE (landing at Anzio) decided as 22 January 1944. Departure of LSTs from Mediterranean again delayed.
30 Dec	Assault shipping starts leaving Indian Ocean for Europe.

Before outlining the SEXTANT and EUREKA conferences it is necessary to examine briefly, as far as the Italian Campaign is concerned, the political and strategic developments in the Mediterranean theatre as a whole since the fall of Italy. Throughout the autumn the effects of the fighting in Italy on the southern Balkans and countries in the eastern Mediterranean was being closely studied by the British planners. The fall of Italy had put the Balkans into a ferment and continued unrest would tie down a number of German divisions. The planners also considered there might be the need to apply pressure elsewhere in the Mediterranean if the Germans withdrew right back in Italy and refused to commit strong forces at a distance from the Normandy assault area. The areas of possible operations were Yugoslavia, Greece and the Aegean.

By the end of October the Communist guerilla 'partisans' under Tito amounted to some 220,000 men and controlled to a great extent over half of Yugoslavia. Both the partisans and the less-influential Serbian Nationalist 'Cetnick' guerilla bands were being supplied by the Allies with arms and equipment. Between October and December 1943 only 125 tons of material were air dropped but over 2,000 tons were landed by naval coastal forces, mainly on the Dalmatian Islands. The establishment of a bridgehead at Durazzo had been under consideration for some time, although the Chiefs of Staff stressed it must 'not in any way, prejudice our main effort in Italy. We must guard against being drawn into a fresh campaign with inadequate forces.'[1] The fighting in Italy for the Winter Line, however, left no margin to the Allies for this venture and at the same time the situation in Yugoslavia was also changing. By the end of September the Germans had succeeded in regaining control of Istria and most of the Dalmatian coast. During October and November no less than fifteen German divisions were engaged in Slovenia, Macedonia and the Islands, with the result that the partisans were forced back into the central mountains. Here the inconclusive fighting continued until March 1944 when the Germans finally accepted that they would never beat the guerillas on their home pitch. In Greece also there were rival resistance movements but with political instead of racial allegiances. Serious fighting broke out between the two factions, the Communists and the Republicans, early in October and continued until February 1944. So in Greece there was no real opportunity for British intervention at this time. Operations in the third area, the Aegean, were directly connected with the whole question of Turkey. The capture of the sea and air bases in the Dodecanese would allow the Allied naval forces to dominate the Aegean and their bombers to attack communications throughout the Balkans. The key was Rhodes with its naval and air base. There was also an important naval base at Leros and a 'complementary' air base on the island of Cos. In September 1943, Crete was garrisoned by one German and one Italian division, while a further German division and two Italian divisions occupied Rhodes and the other islands. At an appropriate moment it was hoped to persuade Turkey to join the Allies and a phased programme of British support, should she enter the war, had earlier been agreed. The Allied plans catered for some fifty RAF squadrons, together with several anti-aircraft and anti-tank regiments, to be moved in, and the intention was that these would be followed by two armoured divisions. The maintenance of these forces, however, would depend on the Aegean being opened so that the Allies could use the port of Smyrna. British plans to land a force of about two brigades to capture Rhodes were set back by Eisenhower's refusal (in August) to release ships and planes while the Salerno landing was being planned and were finally frustrated by the subsequent decision by the Combined Chiefs of Staff in Quebec to send five (out of eight) landing ships, held temporarily in the Middle East, to the Indian Ocean. Thus, at the announcement of the Italian surrender, all that could be done was to parachute in a small party on to Rhodes to contact the Italians and to try and persuade them to overpower the German garrison, pending the arrival by sea of an Allied stiffening force of a tank battalion and two fighter squadrons. The Italian commanders argued the matter for two days before attacking the Germans who by then were thoroughly prepared. The fight was short and sharp and left the Germans in complete control of the island by 13 September. Meanwhile landings by units of a British infantry brigade were being made on Cos, Leros and Samos and a number of smaller islands. As no landing craft were available, the force was carried on destroyers and small coastal craft and consequently no heavy equipment or supporting artillery could be landed.

Both Dönitz and the Army Commander-in-Chief Balkans were prepared to evacuate Crete and the islands, but Hitler, always sensitive to any threats to the south-east, took the opposite view. Within days about eighty additional aircraft, mostly long-range bombers, arrived to bring the strength of the Luftwaffe in the eastern Mediterranean at the end of September to 362. Rhodes and Crete both possessed two good airfields apiece and were only 70 and 150 miles respectively from the island of Cos. The British squadrons on Cyprus were 350 miles away and without specialized equipment it had proved quite impossible to develop adequate landing strips on either Cos or Leros. Churchill pressed Eisenhower to do everything possible to support these operations in the Aegean and Tedder moved ten long-range bomber squadrons to the Benghazi-Gambut area to operate against airfields on the Greek mainland and on both Rhodes and Crete, as well as against shipping in the Aegean At Churchill's insistence plans to assemble a force to land on Rhodes were pressed forward. Holding units and reserves stationed in the Middle East would make up roughly a division. Eisenhower would send part of an armoured brigade and a small air force element, consisting of a group of troop-carrying aircraft and six long-range fighter squadrons. Three landing ships, some landing craft and ten cargo ships, almost all from the central Mediterranean, were all that could be scraped up to transport the force. Unfortunately the long-range fighter squadrons were not ready to operate from Gambut, well situated just east of Tobruk, until 6 October. It was too late now to stop the Germans landing by sea back on Cos early on 3 October. A parachute landing quickly followed and within 36 hours the island was retaken. Churchill's plea for nine large landing craft to be held back for six weeks and his offer to fly out to Tunis himself to meet General Marshall and thrash the matter out on the spot gained no support from Roosevelt, who replied, 'with a full understanding of your difficulties in the Eastern Mediterranean my thought . . . was that no diversion of force from Italy should be made that would jeopardize the security of the Allied armies in Italy, and that no action towards any minor objective should prejudice the success of "Overlord" '.[2] Eisenhower was told to call a conference of all three Service Commanders-in-Chief of both the Mediterranean and Middle Eastern theatres. This took place in Tunisia on 9 October. Eisenhower's view was that, 'detachments from the Italian command were not warranted and that we could and would do nothing about the islands. These islands (in his judgment) while of considerable strategic importance did not compare in military value to success in the Italian battle.'[3] His opinion went unchallenged and the decision was reported to the Combined Chiefs of Staff. On the following day the long-range fighters were withdrawn to continue their escort duties with the strategic bombers operating from Tunisia. Leros and Samos, however, were still holding out in face of mounting air attacks and, in spite of attempts by the Royal Air Force to maintain air patrols over the sea approaches, the Royal Navy were suffering heavy losses in maintaining the garrison. Unless the garrisons were maintained entirely by submarine, the only answer was to move at least six squadrons of fighters to Turkish bases in south-west Anatolia. The matter was now referred to the Allied Foreign Ministers in conference in Moscow. Opinions were divided. The Americans wanted Turkey to remain neutral. The Russians desired her immediate entry into the war. Finally it was decided to ask for immediate Turkish help over the air bases. After ten days' negotiations the Turkish Government (on 15 November) somewhat reluctantly agreed on a policy of 'co-belligerency'. But fearing heavy German reprisal attacks they would neither lend the bases, nor consider entering the war, without a guarantee of the support of forty Royal Air Force squadrons at the moment they declared war. The move of such a large air component obviously could not be arranged in a matter of days and the British could not agree to the Turkish demands. Meanwhile Leros was retaken on 16 November after four days' bitter fighting and before the end of the month the remaining islands had been recaptured by the Germans or evacuated. British army losses were 4,800 men and the Royal Air Force lost 115 aircraft during the operations. The Germans probably lost about 4,000 men and about 21,000 tons of shipping. The British and Greek naval losses in the Aegean over the last two months had been severe. Six destroyers, two submarines and ten coastal craft were lost and four cruisers and four destroyers had been damaged. In Churchill's opinion, however, the Turkish negotiations were still wide open and operations in the Aegean presented the best means of tying down the Germans if Rome fell early in 1944. Under these conditions the Germans might well decide to pull back from the Balkans to the River Sava and the Danube. Eisenhower, on the other hand, was studying yet another 'diversionary' operation that had been suggested at the Quebec conference – a landing in the south of France to coincide with the OVERLORD assault and with the object of holding down German reserves in south and central France. These then were some of the plans and problems that were shortly to be discussed by the Allied war leaders in the conferences that were about to take place.

The British planners took the view that recent events showed up the dangers of an inflexible strategy tied to the decisions made at Quebec. Alexander had pointed out late in October that it was vital for the twenty-five German divisions in Italy to be 'kept on their heels' and the Americans saw the validity of this argument. There were, however, no plans to ensure that the German divisions in south-east Europe would be held down during and immediately after the OVERLORD landings. The QUADRANT decisions indeed stultified any efforts to this end. Taking a broader view than their American allies the British Chiefs of Staff sought to modify the QUADRANT decisions to achieve a more realistic insurance policy for OVERLORD, without altering the premium to be paid in the Mediterranean. What was needed was a degree of flexibility in the plans and perhaps some change of emphasis and even a delay of six to eight weeks for the date of OVERLORD. Their argument was that 'the existing policy was wasting resources which could otherwise be used profitably in support of a modified policy. The campaign in Italy was hanging fire, and operations in the Aegean were starved for the necessary troops; but divisions remained idle in North Africa and Sicily awaiting their transfer to England for an operation in some six months' time. The fate of the Dodecanese hung in the balance, and with it that of Turkey; but the necessary assault shipping was engaged partly in ferrying an air force to Italy for which the airfields did not yet exist.'4 There were three requirements; a unified command for the Mediterranean; the diversion of some forces to secure the Dodecanese as a base for a more flexible strategy with limited forces; and the retention of sufficient LSTs, already needed for the next stage in Italy, on which this broader strategy would depend. The real danger lay in the removal of the sixty-eight LSTs due to sail for England on 15 December. The British argued that if these LSTs left the Mediterranean the initiative would pass and the Allies themselves might be contained in Italy, while elsewhere the Germans would be free to reallocate their divisions long before the date for OVERLORD. It was with this in mind that the Chiefs of Staff argued, 'our policy is therefore clear; we should stretch the German forces to the utmost by threatening as many of their vital interests and areas as possible and, holding them thus we should attack wherever we can do so in superior force'.[5] In outline the proposals regarding future action in the Mediterranean were:

(a) Command in the Mediterranean to be unified.
(b) Operations in Italy should aim at securing the Pisa–Rimini line.
(c) Aid to the partisan and irregular forces in Yugoslavia, Greece and Albania should be stepped up.
(d) Turkey should be brought into the war before the end of the year.
(e) The Dardanelles should be opened as soon as possible.
(f) Everything possible should be done to weaken the German powers of resistance in the Balkans and 'promote a state of chaos and disruption in the satellite Balkan countries'.

Finally if OVERLORD had to be delayed this should be accepted. These arguments were not merely a plea for more flexible plans for the Mediterranean operations but for a less rigid attitude towards the date for OVERLORD, as the British Chiefs of Staff saw the direct link between the two theatres. If the operations in the Mediterranean were allowed to enter a 'blind alley' OVERLORD itself might be endangered. These proposals, however, alarmed the Joint Chiefs of Staff in America, who regarded them as further attempts to indulge in 'sideshows' which would endanger OVERLORD and might even divert Allied forces from the war against Japan. Thus the British proposals that aimed at holding down considerable German forces, largely by the threat of attack at a number of vital points and without any overall increase in the forces allocated to the Mediterranean, were seen in an entirely different light by their American allies. Indeed, a week before the conference opened in Cairo, Marshall gave his opinion at a joint Chiefs of Staff meeting with Roosevelt and Hopkins present that, 'the British might like to "ditch" OVERLORD now in order to go into the Balkans'.[6]

Churchill had hoped to have private talks between the British and Americans in Malta to discuss the Mediterranean before the SEXTANT conference opened. Roosevelt, who earlier in the year had failed to arrange a private meeting between himself and Stalin, preferred to go straight to Cairo. Here the Mena House Hotel and nearby villas had been prepared for the meetings which would continue from 22 November to 7 January, with a break in the middle for the EUREKA conference in Teheran between 28

177

November and 1 December 1943. From the British point of view the sequence of the agenda for SEXTANT further underlined the basic differences in strategic outlook between themselves and the Americans. The latter, it was now evident were determined to preserve a policy of non-participation in operations in the eastern Mediterranean. On Roosevelt's insistence Chiang Kai-shek was invited to attend from the start of the conference, with the result that discussions on operations in South-East Asia were dealt with before OVER-LORD and the Mediterranean and largely occupied four out of the five sessions held before the conference adjourned to meet Stalin. The Americans were very anxious to keep China in the war, intending to make use of their manpower and later on establish their own bases in China itself. The proposal was to launch operations across the Chindwin to coincide with a drive by Chinese forces in North Burma. These land operations would be supplemented by an amphibious assault (named BUCCANEER) on the Andaman Islands. Unconvinced of the value of the Chinese contribution to the war in South-East Asia and conscious of the fact that the Americans were now proposing to allocate landing craft for BUCCANEER, that they had refused to use either for OVERLORD or in the Mediterranean, the British did not wish to get heavily involved in these operations. Churchill anyhow favoured a landing against Sumatra and was opposed to linking the land and sea attacks. The Generalissimo, after several changes of heart, eventually agreed to Chinese support in North Burma, making at the same time great play that BUCCANEER should be mounted as an essential part of the strategic plan. Alanbrooke later commented, 'we should never have started our conference with Chiang; by doing so we were putting the cart before the horse. He had nothing to contribute towards the defeat of the Germans, and for the matter of that uncommonly little towards the defeat of the Japanese.'[7]

When the conference eventually got round to discussing European strategy the British straight away reiterated the argument that had been submitted earlier in the month. The Chiefs of Staff pointed out that everything really depended on the availability of landing craft. If sixty-eight LSTs were held back in the Mediterranean until 15 January 1944 three separate amphibious operations could take place; a landing on the west coast of Italy, to aid the capture of Rome, in December 1943 or early January 1944; a landing on Rhodes in February 1944 and BUCCANEER in March 1944. But this programme would mean a postponement of OVERLORD until about 1 July 1944. If OVER-LORD was not to be postponed one of these operations would have to be abandoned. While the conference eventually agreed to the British proposals by 'tentatively' adopting them as a basis of discussion with the Russians, the Americans required certain safeguards. They certainly stood firm on BUCCANEER and also insisted that, if it turned out that the Russians were determined to force Turkey into the war, they would not agree to supplies and troops being diverted from other operations to achieve this end. The

Aerial view of the Cassino battlefield looking across the Monastery (M) and Hangman's Hill (H) over the valley of the Liri towards Pontecorvo and the mountains beyond. Castle Hill (C), Route 6 and the Railway Station are indicated with arrows. Snake's Head Ridge is in the deep shadow to the right of the Monastery.

General Anders inspecting a unit of 2 Polish Corps.

Build-up of supplies at Anzio in preparation for the Allied advance.

Goumiers on the march.

likely Russian attitude to these various proposals was almost impossible to gauge. During the Foreign Ministers' talks in Moscow the Russians had stressed the urgency of pressing forward preparations for invading France, which had been promised for the 'spring' of 1944. The possible use of Swedish air bases and the advantages of Turkey's entry into the war had both been raised by the Russians on this occasion, Vyshinsky adding that the latter event would cause the withdrawal of fifteen German divisions from the Eastern Front. The Russian offensive had gone well and their armies were within sixty miles of the Polish border and were even nearer to Rumania. The Russians, however, were very sensitive to any apparent let-up by their allies. This was evident from Marshal Voroshilov's complaint (on 11 November) that since the beginning of October the Germans had been able to withdraw four divisions from both France and the Balkans and two from Italy and send them to the Eastern Front. The Americans concluded that the Russians at Teheran might well back the British proposals for a more active policy in the Eastern Mediterranean. Furthermore they saw these proposals as prejudicing both OVERLORD and their plans for South-East Asia.

When the conference moved to Teheran the position briefly was that the Americans were determined to avoid involvement in the Balkans and, in order to insure the launching of the amphibious attack on the Andamans, they were prepared to accept a postponement of OVERLORD. In fact the inviolability of an early OVERLORD had already been compromised as the President had made a private agreement with Chiang Kai-shek over BUC-CANEER. 'Roosevelt's confidence in his own skill as a diplomat and his trust in Stalin's intentions were to have a marked effect on the outcome of the discussions at Teheran. The first meeting was a private one attended only by Roosevelt, Stalin and their interpreters. The two leaders discussed the world situation at large, and the President made it clear that he had ideas about the conduct of the war and the structure of the peace which did not entirely coincide with those of the British Prime Minister. Sensing a desire on Roosevelt's part to appear independent of Churchill's influence, Stalin proceeded to stimulate it. At the beginning of the conference he proposed that Roosevelt should act as Chairman at all sessions, and that evening invited him to move from the American Legation to the Soviet Embassy.'[8] On each of the three days a plenary session was held in the Soviet Embassy. The first session opened with the President outlining the proposals for the Pacific and South-East Asia, after which he dealt with the more immediate problems of OVERLORD and the Mediterranean. In the latter connection Roosevelt outlined a number of possible operations, 'an increased drive into Italy, an operation from the North-East Adriatic, operations in the Aegean, and operations from Turkey'.[9] Also, as Harry Hopkins records, 'the President also informed the Marshal of the plans for landings in southern France'.[10] In this introductory survey the President showed how the shortage of landing craft and the operations already being contemplated in the Mediterranean would mean a postponement of OVERLORD until May or June. While Churchill has recorded his delight at the suggestion for an attack from the head of the Adriatic through the Ljubljana Gap towards Vienna, the mention of plans for a landing in the south of France must have surprised the British Chiefs of Staff. A landing in the south of France, originally mooted at Quebec in August, had hitherto been regarded only as a possible diversionary operation. Eisenhower's preliminary report had been 'cautious and not entirely favorable'[11] and had been accepted by the Combined Chiefs of Staff only as a basis for further planning, with the object of holding down two German mobile divisions either by 'deceptions or attack' on the actual day OVERLORD was launched, but not before. Such an operation, General Morgan had earlier pointed out, could only be complementary to the main task of tying down sufficient German forces outside France, to prevent the move of major reinforcements against OVERLORD during the first two months after the assault. After the President had spoken Stalin was invited to give his opinion as to how the Western Allies could be of greatest help to the USSR. Stalin dealt briefly with the Pacific, saying that as soon as Germany was defeated Russia would join the Allies against Japan. Regarding Europe, what he wanted above all else was a strong cross-Channel attack on 1 May. Any dispersal of forces to other points would be a mistake. The Balkans, he pointed out, were a long way from France; Turkey wasn't worth worrying about and he wasn't concerned over the opening of the Dardanelles. As for Italy, the country was easily defended and a breakout across the Alps was almost impossible. Stalin stressed that the best thing to do was to concentrate on OVERLORD but in his experience attacks should be made from several directions. Therefore he suggested closing down operations in Italy, even before the capture of Rome, and landing six divisions in the south of France two months before OVERLORD. Churchill strongly stressed the British view concerning operations in the eastern Mediterranean. Stalin agreed that two to three divisions might be profitably employed in the capture of the Dodecanese and in aiding Turkey but he was firmly against any diversion from OVERLORD. Roosevelt pointed out that operations in the eastern Mediterranean would result in OVERLORD being delayed from two to three months. Finally, in spite of Churchill's complaint regarding the arbitrary date of 1 May for OVERLORD, the military staffs were asked to examine the possible timings for a landing in the south of France on the assumption that OVERLORD would be launched on that date.

The next morning Leahy, Marshall, Voroshilov, Portal and Alanbrooke held an inconclusive discussion. Marshall was at pains to explain the difficulties over landing craft, pointing out that in the Pacific five separate operations were in progress, with four more planned for January 1944, and that all of these required considerable numbers of landing craft. Voroshilov continued to insist OVERLORD must be launched on 1 May and that, except for a landing

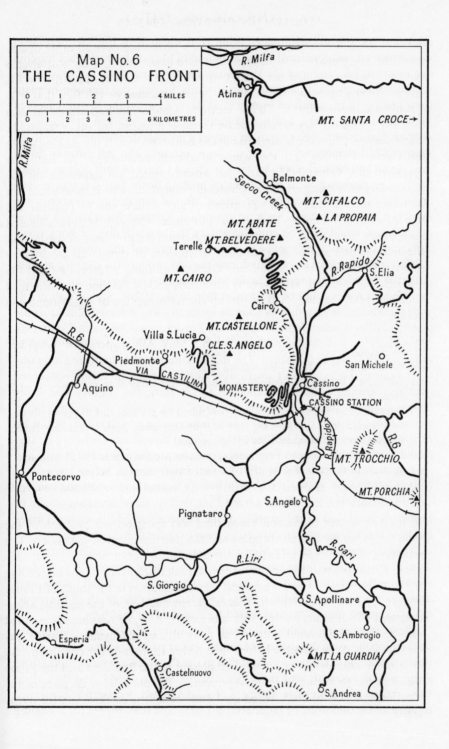

Map No. 6
THE CASSINO FRONT

0 1 2 3 4 MILES
0 1 2 3 4 5 6 KILOMETRES

R.Milfa

Atina

MT. SANTA CROCE →

R.Milfa

Belmonte

Secco Creek

MT. CIFALCO
▲ LA PROPAIA

MT. ABATE
MT. BELVEDERE ▲

Terelle

R. Rapido
S.Elia

MT. CAIRO

Cairo

MT. CASTELLONE

Villa S.Lucia

CLE.S.ANGELO

San Michele

Piedmonte
VIA CASTILINA

R.6

MONASTERY

Cassino

Aquino

CASSINO STATION

R.Rapido

R.6

MT. TROCCHIO

Pontecorvo

MT. PORCHIA

S.Angelo

Pignataro

R. Gari

R.Liri

S.Giorgio

S.Apollinare

S.Ambrogio

Esperia

MT. LA GUARDIA

Castelnuovo

S.Andrea

in the south of France, OVERLORD must take preference over all other operations. In the plenary session later that afternoon Stalin, with Roosevelt's support, merely restated the same two points. As Alanbrooke wrote in his diary, 'Americans supported his view, quite unaware of the fact that it is already an impossibility'.[12] In the morning Alanbrooke had argued in vain that any let-up in Italy would release German divisions for other fronts. In the afternoon Churchill again laid out the British proposals for pinning down the Germans throughout the whole of the Mediterranean. As both the President and General Marshall had already stated, all depended on the availability of landing craft and Churchill pointed out that if these could not be found no Mediterranean operations of any scale would be possible and this included any landings in the south of France. Although Stalin considered such details immaterial, at Churchill's suggestion the problems of sorting out the timings and scope of operations in support of OVERLORD were again referred to the military committee. The next morning Alanbrooke and the other British Chiefs of Staff were at work early and by the time the Combined Chiefs of Staff met they had drawn up the following list of suggestions and points.

(a) An operation shall be mounted for the south of France. Timing and scope to be decided later – may be after 'OVERLORD'.
(b) We advance in Italy to Pisa–Rimini line.
(c) We assist partisans in Yugoslavia, but no forces other than commandos to be used.
(d) Operations in Aegean are entirely dependent on the entry of Turkey into war. In any event no more landing craft will be kept away from 'OVERLORD' for the specific purpose of operations in the Aegean.
(e) In view of (b), we must keep landing craft in Mediterranean till 15 January.
(f) Because of (e) earliest date of 'OVERLORD' cannot now be before 1 June.
(g) Is 'BUCCANEER' affected by Marshal Stalin's statement about Russia coming in against Japan once Germany is out?[13]

In the subsequent discussion much time was spent on the question of the time-tables for the assault shipping and the postponement of OVERLORD. The retention of sixty-eight LSTs in the Mediterranean would mean the postponement of OVERLORD to 15 May (by American calculations) or 1 June (according to the British figures) and it emerged that the landings in the south of France could only be by one division. This raised the question of the possible abandonment of BUCCANEER to provide more craft. Also, as Alanbrooke pointed out, Stalin's 'conditional promise' of a simultaneous Russian offensive was very unlikely to be possible before June owing to the weather conditions. So after much argument it was agreed to present to the President and the Prime Minister the following formula, representing the unanimous decision of the Combined Chiefs of Staff, based on 1 June being the earliest date for OVERLORD.

(a) That we should continue to advance in Italy to the Pisa–Rimini line. (This means that the sixty-eight LSTs which are due to be sent from the Mediterranean to the United Kingdom for OVERLORD must be kept in the Mediterranean until 15 January.)

(b) That an operation shall be mounted against the south of France on as big a scale as landing craft permit. For planning purposes D-day to be the same as OVERLORD D-day.

(c) To recommend to the President and Prime Minister respectively that we should inform Marshal Stalin that we will launch OVERLORD during May, in conjunction with a supporting operation against the south of France on the largest scale that is permitted by the landing craft available at the time.[14]

In the words of the American official historian, Maurice Matloff,

the conference now moved swiftly to a close. On the afternoon of 30 November Roosevelt, Churchill, and Stalin accepted the report of the Anglo-American Staffs. Stalin agreed to time his offensive on the Eastern Front to coincide with the launching of the attack in the West in May 1944. The President promised that he and the Prime Minister would take up the matter of a supreme Allied Commander and make a decision within the next three or four days.[15]

It was also agreed that a further attempt would be made to try and persuade Turkey to enter the war.

Commenting on Churchill's part in the discussions, Arthur Bryant remarks 'together he and Brooke had averted what might well have led to the worst disaster in British – and American – military history'.[16] Alanbrooke's assessment of Stalin is of interest; 'he has a military brain of the highest calibre. Never once in any of his statements did he make any strategic error, nor did he ever fail to appreciate all the implications of a situation with a quick and unerring eye.'[17] Yet Stalin gave no support to the British proposals which were designed to pin down even more German forces and ensure the success of OVERLORD. Instead he backed an operation in the south of France which, if launched two months ahead of OVERLORD, as he suggested, might well have resulted in an Allied defeat and would certainly have resulted in exceptionally heavy Allied casualties, without necessarily contributing to the success of OVERLORD. Admittedly Stalin had no experience of the complexities of amphibious operations and to the Russians OVERLORD represented the long-delayed opening of a Second Front, so it could be argued that Stalin would naturally support the proposed landing in the south of France, particularly as it was presented as a direct contribution to the cross-Channel assault. Stalin, however, never lost sight of the political factor and, whatever may have been his military appreciation of the value of a landing in the south of France, there is little doubt now that he also saw these operations as a means of drawing the Allied forces in the Mediterranean away from the Balkans and south-east Europe. Commenting on the Russian attitude to the conference Alexander Werth has written, 'the Russians were going to get their real Second Front at last. It was on this note – which caused immense satisfaction in Russia – that the victorious but very hard year of 1943 ended for her. A year that had carried the Red Army all the way from Stalingrad and the Caucasus to Kiev and beyond. Over two-thirds of the German-occupied territory had been liberated. But it was still a long way to Berlin. Perhaps Stalin was not bluffing when he said at Teheran that the Red Army was growing war-weary, and that it needed something to encourage it. The Teheran communiqué did it.'[18]

While Roosevelt and Churchill remained in Teheran to spend a day discussing with Stalin the political aspects of Germany's defeat before returning to Cairo, the Combined Chiefs of Staff reassembled at Mena House to study the immediate problem of relating the available assault craft to the operations now decided for 1944 in Europe. To their dismay it was announced that the President would have to leave Cairo on 7 December so there was no time to be lost. Landing craft were required for four landing operations to take place within six months, SHINGLE in a matter of weeks, BUCCANEER in March, OVERLORD and ANVIL at the end of May, all had to be catered for. The British argued that, on the present distribution of landing craft, there would only be sufficient to lift one and a half divisions for ANVIL and that anyhow the allocations for OVERLORD only allowed an initial assault by three divisions, which would be less than employed for HUSKY. Furthermore, there was still the chance of Turkey entering the war and there would be absolutely no margin for supporting operations in the Aegean in this eventuality. In simple terms BUCCANEER should be cancelled and the British assault craft returned to the Mediterranean or replaced by the Americans. It was also important that any possible Turkish entry into the war should not take place before the middle of February 1944. The joint planners were told to produce urgently the estimated figures for ANVIL, with an initial assault of not less than two divisions and with a follow-up by sea of possibly eight more, and a world-wide survey of assault shipping was put in hand. Meanwhile the Americans stood by BUCCANEER. At a planning session held on 4 December Churchill presented his arguments. ANVIL must be based on a two-division assault and on this scale there would in the meantime be sufficient landing craft for SHINGLE and, if necessary, for operations in the eastern Mediterranean. Churchill made it clear, however, that these plans depended on BUCCANEER being cancelled, especially in view of Mountbatten's revised requirements for over 50,000 troops and extra aircraft carriers for this particular operation. He pointed out that, with Stalin's promise to enter the Pacific war on the defeat of Germany, the need for Chinese bases was diminished and anyhow he felt that 'Chinese continuation in the war was not so dependent on BUCCANEER as upon the supplies China received over the Hump'.[19] At this point the President began to weaken in his resolve to keep his word to Chiang Kai-shek and on 5 December BUCCANEER was called off and the Generalissimo informed.

Owing to the postponement of OVERLORD, Admiral King was able to make a 'significant contribution to the pool of assault shipping by arranging for all new landing ships and craft, completed in the United States between 1 March and 1 April, to be sent to Europe instead of to the Pacific'.[20] This involved a total of an extra twenty-five LSTs and sixty-six landing craft. Plans for ANVIL, however, had not been completed and when they became available it was found that this contribution of craft diverted from the Pacific still did not meet the new requirements, which proved to be an additional twenty-six LSTs and eighty-eight landing craft for OVERLORD, over and above the allocation agreed at Quebec, plus an additional forty-one LSTs, thirty-one LCTs and six LSI (L)s for ANVIL.[21]

Meanwhile an invitation had been sent to President Inönü to join the Prime Minister and the President in Cairo on 4 December. The Turkish approach to any involvement in the war, however, was extremely cautious, as they feared an immediate German attack which might seriously damage their country. The Americans were lukewarm about the whole affair and were certainly not prepared to agree to any diversion of effort from any other operations already planned. British offers of military assistance were, however, discussed and it was finally agreed that some 2,000 British technicians would be moved quietly into the country to prepare for the arrival of seventeen RAF squadrons and anti-aircraft and armoured units as soon as any declaration of war was made. If on 15 February the Turks sent word that they would not accept this force the whole plan would be dropped. If they accepted and the necessary landing craft could be found, an assault on Rhodes would be mounted in March by two British divisions, one of which would be made up of garrison troops, found from the Middle East. After much hesitation President Inönü in the end agreed to refer these proposals secretly to his National Assembly. While all these plans were being discussed and pressed forward Roosevelt had announced his decision that Eisenhower would command the Allied forces for OVERLORD and a unified command for the whole of the Mediterranean had also been agreed upon. Within the next few days the following appointments were agreed. General Sir Henry Maitland Wilson would be Commander-in-Chief in the Mediterranean, with Lieutenant-General Devers, US Army, as his Deputy. General Alexander remained to fight the land battle from the newly titled Headquarters Allied Armies in Italy. Admiral Sir John Cunningham took over as Commander-in-Chief Allied Naval Forces to relieve Admiral of the Fleet A. B. Cunningham, who had been appointed First Sea Lord. Lieutenant-General Eaker became Commander-in-Chief Mediterranean Allied Air Forces.

The SEXTANT/EUREKA conferences have a special significance in any account of the strategic development of the war in Europe. The plans for the main effort by the Western Allies against Germany were now in step with those of Soviet Russia. The balance of Allied resources between Europe and the Pacific were more clearly in perspective. Before Teheran and Cairo many strategies had been considered and now the pattern was decided. With plans interlocked and an agreed time-table the immediate task came into sharp focus. One of the most urgent tasks was the re-allocation of landing craft, now that ANVIL was tied in with the date for OVERLORD. There was also the urgent need to overcome the stalemate developing in Italy. It will be remembered that a month previously Alexander had set in motion plans for landing a single division at Anzio, with the object of seizing the Alban hills to coincide with Fifth Army's arrival near Frosinone in their drive for Rome. In mid-December Fifth Army was still fighting in the Mignano Gap and as the extra landing craft were due to leave for the United Kingdom by 15 January the plans for this landing had to be cancelled. In the meantime, however, Alexander was working on a new plan. The landing would now be made in sufficient strength (two divisions reinforced with armour) 'to hold its ground by itself for a longer time than we had previously considered'.[22] The objectives would be the same – to seize the Alban hills and cut Route 6, thus forcing Kesselring to abandon his Cassino positions. Churchill, although seriously ill with pneumonia and confined to his bed in Eisenhower's villa in Carthage, took an active part in furthering this proposal. If a two-division landing at Anzio was to be mounted, fifty-eight LSTs must be held back and this might pre-judice OVERLORD, if the latter was launched in early May. Operations to capture Rhodes would have to be abandoned. In a series of telegrams to London and Washington Churchill paved the way. He was not alone in his appreciation of the problems and it was at this time that both Eisenhower and the Chiefs of Staff began to consider a date about 3 June as the most favourable moon period for the launching of OVERLORD. At a conference held on Christmas Day Eisenhower and his commanders agreed the new proposals for SHINGLE. Three days later Churchill received Roosevelt's approval to the retention of the necessary LSTs for the reinforced landing at Anzio on about 20 January but on the understanding that the Teheran agreement on OVER-LORD was honoured. Two days later assault shipping started to leave the Indian Ocean for Europe and, as we shall later see, three special LSTs arrived in the Mediterranean in time to load the first follow-up troops for Anzio. The problem now emerged, however, that there would be insufficient shipping to maintain the divisions once they had landed and it was not until 8 January that the planners could resolve the intricate calculations and decide the date for the SHINGLE operation as 22 January. The shortage of landing craft, how-ever, was to plague the planners for months to come and indeed bring a postponement to the date for ANVIL that would hardly have been accepted when that operation was written into the Allied strategic plans only a few weeks previously at Teheran.

11
Two Rivers

Kesselring abandons Winter Line: Gustav Line described: Orders for SHINGLE and the drive for Rome: Clark reinforced from Eighth Army: Garigliano crossed: Rapido held: British threat to coastal flank: Kesselring commits reserves: San Angelo crossing repulsed.

1944	2 Jan	Alexander gives target date for SHINGLE 20–31 January.
	3 Jan	General Juin and French Expeditionary Corps take over VI Corps area.
	3–11 Jan	5 Division transferred from Adriatic to 10 Corps.
	4–15 Jan	Fifth Army fights forward to Gustav Line.
		Germans finally withdraw after loss of Mount Trocchio.
	12 Jan	Alexander issues directive aiming at capture of Rome.
		Orders issued for VI Corps landing at Anzio.
	17–20 Jan	10 Corps' operations to cross lower Garigliano open.
		5 and 56 Divisions seize bridgeheads and make good initial progress.
	19–20 Jan	46 Division's abortive attempts to cross upper Garigliano.
	20–22 Jan	II Corps opens first battle of Cassino.
		36 Division's crossings of lower Rapido astride San Angelo fail.
	21–22 Jan	Kesselring launches strong counter-attacks against 10 Corps' threat to outflank southern sector.
	22 Jan	SHINGLE – VI Corps lands at Anzio.
	24 Jan	Battle of Cassino continues with 34 Division attacking across Rapido north of Cassino and French Expeditionary Corps' preparations complete for drive through mountains.

On New Year's Eve a heavy snow-storm in the Abruzzi mountains brought the fighting on Fifth Army front to a temporary standstill. It was not until 5 January that II Corps resumed the attack down Route 6. Having lost ground in the mountains and control of the Mignano Gap, the Germans were still holding the line of the River Peccia through Mount Porchia and north to Mount Maio (1,259 metres, not to be confused with Mount Maio 940 metres in the Liri Valley) and Monna Casale. Centrally placed, Mount Trocchio dominated the plain between the Peccia and the Rapido south of Route 6. 1 Special Service Force led off with an attack on Mount Maio, which was captured on 7 January and held for three days against fierce counter-attack. Meanwhile 34 Division captured San Vittore and pressed forward to take Cervaro on 12 January. In the centre, 46 Division, supported by part of 1 Armoured Division, captured Mount Porchia in the face of reinforcements rushed up from the Hermann Göring Division. Ahead was the huge isolated hill of Mount Trocchio. This bare and rocky feature was less than two miles east of the Rapido and was now untenable owing to the advance of 34 Division. In the mountains the French Expeditionary Corps were approaching Mounts Santa Croce and La Meta and by 15 January the German resistance east of the Rapido was virtually ended. But time had been gained to fortify the Gustav Line. The fighting withdrawal had been skilfully conducted. In six weeks' fighting Fifth Army had lost 16,000 casualties. XIV Panzer Corps, which had been under the command of General von Senger since October, was now safely ensconced in prepared positions of tremendous natural strength.

The valley of the Liri, as far as Ceprano, is a broad depression some ten miles wide and about twenty miles in length, which runs roughly east and west parallel to the coast and some fifteen miles inland. Towards the eastern end the Rapido flows down from the mountains to join the River Gari, into which the Liri itself discharges. All three rivers now become the Garigliano, which continues southwards to the gulf of Gaeta through a fairly wide plain. The Garigliano is overlooked by rising ground and low hills on both sides. The River Milfa, which like the Rapido rises in the Abruzzi mountains, passes through a natural basin about Atina to join the Liri in the western part of the valley. If within this pattern of river valleys the mountains are now shaded in it will be seen that the Aurunci mountains, and in particular Mount Maio (940 metres) and the high ground around Castelforte, guard the crossings of the Garigliano. North of the Liri valley a range of exceptionally high and rugged mountains run south-west from the spine of the Apennines, about Mount Petroso, between the valleys of the Rivers Rapido and Milfa through Mount Cairo to end at Monte Cassino. Monte Cassino, itself topped by the massive buildings of the famous monastery, completely dominates the little town below, the valley of the Rapido to the east and the valley of the Liri to the south. Route 6 passes immediately below Monte Cassino along the northern edge of the Liri valley. On the flat plain below Monte Cassino and only a few hundred yards from the Rapido stood the little town of Cassino with its railway station further to the south, the other side of Route 6. Behind the town stood 'a rocky 300-foot knoll, the Rocca Janicula, crowned with the remains of a mediaeval castle. This knoll, which was to become better known as Castle Hill, seemed to crouch at the foot of the larger mountain like a watch dog, and the saddle of rock which links them is the start point of the shortest, though the most strenuous, way of climbing the mountain.'[1] From the town a motor road zig-zags up Monte Cassino, finally to reach the monastery. Short of the crest this route passes behind a distinctive cone-shaped feature that guards the south-east part of the summit and this became known as Hangman's Hill. Four miles north-west of the monastery the range of mountains has risen to meet the great bulk of Mount Cairo (1,669 metres). Beyond this the Belvedere Hill (720 metres) overlooks the Secco creek, a tributary of the Rapido, and the road from S Elia to Belmonte and Atina. To the north, the Gustav Line follows the rising mountains through Mount Cifalco and on to the highest peak above Castel di Sangro and then down to the Maiella massif on the Eighth Army front.

The key to the line facing Fifth Army was the mountain range culminating with the completely dominating Monte Cassino which gave perfect observation over the valleys of the Rapido and the Liri. Von Senger took over on this front when the Allies were still facing the Volturno. Work on both the Bernhardt and the Gustav Lines was already in progress. In the end the German engineers had three months in which to prepare the defences. North of Cassino town the Rapido had been dammed and the valley flooded for several miles. Both banks of the river were mined. In the more open country of the Liri valley, buildings had been fortified and guns and tank turrets dug in, protected with concrete and steel and carefully camouflaged. 'Cassino town was heavily fortified. Buildings were turned into strongpoints. Cellars and ground-floors were reinforced. Tanks were concealed inside some of the larger buildings. Tunnels and connecting trenches were constructed between a cellar strongpoint on one side of the road and a shelter on the other. Many buildings, strong in themselves, were made stronger by the inclusion of a bunker or pill-box inside.'[2] It was on and around Monte Cassino itself and the mountain positions to the north, however, that the engineers and the working parties showed the full measure of their skill and ingenuity. Gun emplacements were blasted out of the solid rock and protected with steel and concrete. Machine-gun and mortar positions were carefully sited and prepared in ground which naturally afforded both concealment and protection. Alongside each position caves, either natural or dynamited, had been prepared and strengthened. These sheltered the defenders not only against the bitter winter conditions but from air or artillery bombardment. In front of the positions wire entanglements and mines were sited in any gully or ravine that was not directly covered by fire. Acknowledged as one of the most formidable defensive positions in Europe the Cassino sector was now manned against the inevitable Allied assault. On 2 January General Alexander decided that the target date for the landings at Anzio would be between 20–31 January. His instructions to Fifth Army were to 'make as strong a thrust as possible towards Cassino and Frosinone shortly prior to the assault landings to draw in enemy reserves which might be employed against the landing forces and then to create a breach in his front through which every opportunity will be taken to link up rapidly with the seaborne operation'.[3] Ten days later the overall plan for 'the Battle of Rome' gave Fifth Army the task of forcing a German withdrawal north of Rome and inflicting maximum losses in the process. Eighth Army would launch a holding attack to prevent reinforcements being moved across. The time-table for Fifth Army was very tight. Following the preliminary operations through S Elia and the capture of Mount Trocchio, which have already been described, General Clark was faced with mounting a major assault on the Gustav Line within a week. 5 Division was brought across from Eighth Army to join 10 Corps, which would lead the attack by crossing the lower Garigliano and driving towards Ausonia and S Giorgio. This attack would start on 17 January and the following day II Corps would assault across the Rapido on either side of S Angelo. Four days later VI Corps would land at Anzio. With this deadline for SHINGLE there was little time for preparation. The two attacks must follow immediately on the weary battles that had finally penetrated the Winter Line. While the Allies had suffered heavy casualties, von Vietinghoff's divisions also were seriously under strength and when the time came to occupy the Gustav Line along its whole length there were few German reserves left. On paper the opposing forces were evenly balanced. The Allied armies in Italy amounted to eighteen divisions and six brigades, the equivalent of about twenty divisions. Of these ten to twelve were now drawn up facing the Gustav Line and a further three committed to SHINGLE. The German forces consisted of some thirteen divisions in central Italy under Tenth Army and about eight more in northern Italy under Fourteenth Army, three of these latter divisions were still in the process of forming. In the German XIV Panzer Corps' area and south of Rome there were two reserve divisions. These were the 29 and 90 Panzer Grenadier Divisions, the latter having been withdrawn from the Adriatic front. Von Senger had already noted the weakness of his right flank but as reserves were invariably kept under Army Group control he could only await the turn of events. The Anzio landing has been called 'the gamble that failed'.[4] It was conceived as the stroke that would open the road to Rome and the men of Fifth Army facing von Senger's equally weary troops across the Garigliano and the Rapido made ready with a good heart.

In the air the Allies had very much a free hand and only the weather limited their operations. The estimated operational strength of the Luftwaffe in the whole of the Mediterranean theatre was now about 550 planes and the nearest heavy bomber force was some fifty JU88s in Greece and Crete and about sixty heavy bombers of various types in southern France. North of Naples the Allies had constructed three new airfields, bringing the total in this area to nearly a dozen. All were crammed with the planes of XII Air Support Command and the Tactical Bomber Force. Allied air operations concentrated mainly on isolating the Anzio area from both the north and the south. North of a line Pisa–Florence strategic bomber attacks were ordered, on 10 January, on marshalling yards and airfields but owing to a misunderstanding the attacks only started on 16 January. South of Florence, communications were under air attack from 2 January by medium and tactical bombers. From 1–22 January the Mediterranean Allied Air Force dropped 5,400 tons of bombs on road and rail communications, as well as on airfields to drive the German fighters northwards from the Anzio area. Perugia, the main base for the German long-range reconnaissance aircraft, came in for special attention. On 19 January the airfield was successfully attacked by a small force of twenty-seven B24s, with the result that it was out of use for the next four vital days. On Fifth Army front, in the first three weeks of January, XII Air Support Command flew 4,500 sorties in offensive patrols and against communications between the Army front and the Rome area. At this stage Luftwaffe sorties were only about eighty a day, mostly 'escorted fighter-bomber attacks on targets close behind the Allied lines'.[5] With over 4,000 aircraft, of which 3,000 were operational, it seemed to the Allies there was little danger of SHINGLE failing for lack of air support. There was still, however, the need to draw into the Cassino area as many of the German Tenth Army's divisions as possible and, before describing the landing by VI Corps at Anzio, we must turn back to the crossings of the Garigliano and the Rapido that were launched a few days before.

On the extreme left, 5 Division moved up during the night 15/16 January into the coastal sector astride Route 7. Great care was taken to keep their presence secret, as the crossing was to be made silently and without any artillery preparation. During the previous week gun positions had been dug and ammunition dumped by night and carefully camouflaged, so that 5 Divisional artillery could support the crossings by 56 Division in the Castel-forte area on the right. The Garigliano is fast flowing and unfordable throughout its length and near its mouth dangerous currents and the width of the

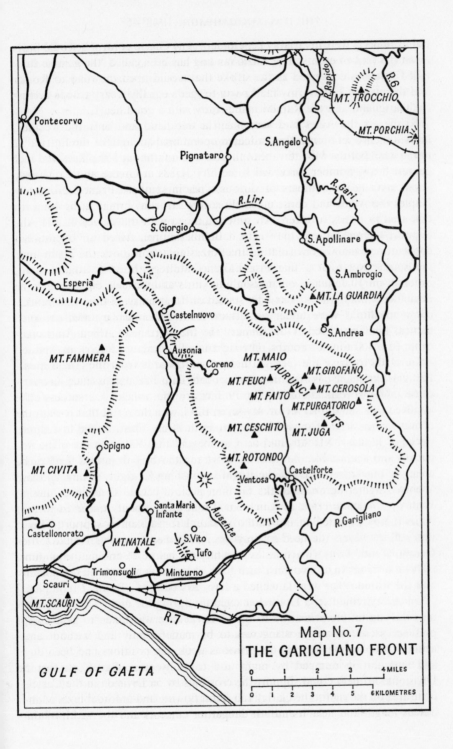

Pontecorvo

R. Rapido

MT. TROCCHIO

R. 6

MT. PORCHIA

S. Angelo

Pignataro

R. Liri

S. Giorgio

R. Gari

S. Apollinare

S. Ambrogio

Esperia

MT. LA GUARDIA

Castelnuovo

S. Andrea

MT. FAMMERA

Ausonia

Coreno

MT. MAIO

MT. FEUCI

AURUNCI

MT. GIROFANO

MT. FAITO

MT. CEROSOLA

MT. PURGATORIO

MT. CESCHITO

MT. JUGA

MTS

Spigno

MT. ROTONDO

MT. CIVITA

Ventosa

Castelforte

R. Garigliano

Santa Maria
Infante

R. Ausente

Castellonorato

MT. NATALE

S. Vito

Tufo

Trimonsuoli

Minturno

Scauri

MT. SCAURI

R. 7

GULF OF GAETA

Map No. 7
THE GARIGLIANO FRONT

0   1   2   3   4 MILES

0   1   2   3   4   5   6 KILOMETRES

193

river increase the difficulties of a crossing. The plan was for the Royal Scots Fusiliers to be embarked in DUKWs and landed some 2,000 yards behind the German lines west of the mouth of the river. The attack was planned for 2100 hours 17 January. A small party to guide the DUKWs in with landing lights touched down too late to achieve a co-ordinated landing. Many DUKWs completely lost direction in the darkness and the anti-tank guns, that later were so urgently needed, were landed back on the wrong side of the river. Betrayed by the phosphorescence of the sea, the first wave of infantry came under heavy shell fire 200 yards from the shore. Already hampered by the confused landing, the leading troops almost immediately found themselves in a large minefield covered by heavy small arms fire from the nearby Argento feature. By now the divisional artillery was helping the infantry forward and by dawn the battalion had penetrated 1,000 yards but with heavy loss. On the right a direct crossing over the river at Pontafiume suffered serious losses, 'the north bank was riddled with anti-personnel mines, so concentrated that the battalion's taping was quite inadequate' and the minefields were 'well covered by spandaus firing on fixed lines and mortar defensive fire'.[6] With daylight the shallow bridgehead came under observed artillery fire, restricted in intensity only by the shortage of ammunition available to the German gunners. The right-hand brigade of 5 Division crossed east of the railway and one of these crossings achieved complete surprise. By 0800 hours the Wiltshires were through Tufo but after a sharp counter-attack had to withdraw to high ground east of the village. A crossing in the centre of the divisional sector, however, ran into serious trouble through the boats being carried forward to the wrong position. This resulted in surprise being lost and the troops had to cross behind the Wiltshires using the few boats still serviceable. Artillery support for the brigade attack had to be delayed ninety minutes, but the Royal Inniskilling Fusiliers, advancing close behind the barrage, cleared the German positions with the bayonet, taking many prisoners still sheltering in their 12-foot-deep dugouts and an important salient was captured to the east of Tufo. The problem now was to build bridges in full view of the German gunners, as otherwise only rafts and ferries could be used to move across the urgently needed tanks and anti-tank guns. The first bridge to be completed (early on 19 January) was hit and temporarily closed within a few hours, while 'a class 30 bridge on Route 7 (completed 20 January) could only be used at night'.[7]

Crossing behind a heavy barrage 56 Division made good progress except on the left. Here many boats were sunk by cross-fire and the left-hand battalion was forced back to the river line near the upper railway bridge. By 19 January the Division held a line from Hill 413–Ventosa–Castelforte and the high ground to the east. By now 5 Division had recaptured Tufo and taken Minturno and the following day (20 January) the Division held both Mount Natale and Tremensuoli and was preparing to attack S Vito. At 2100 hours

19 January 46 Division attacked across the Rapido east of S Ambrogio. Launching their assault boats into the swift currents two battalions of the Hampshires made three separate attempts to cross. On one flank the boats were swept away in mid-stream and a cable broke after only five men had crossed. The other battalion succeeded in getting thirty men across but the head of water prevented the boats from returning. The next day dense fog hindered any further attempts to cross and the operation had to be called off. In the coastal area, however, the Germans had been taken by surprise. There were now ten battalions across the Garigliano, well placed to strike north through the Ausente valley. Visiting the German 94 Division's sector on 18 January von Senger saw that without tank support this front could not be held. From General Steinmetz's battle headquarters von Senger telephoned direct to Kesselring requesting the immediate support of the two Panzer divisions held in reserve, and Kesselring agreed. Von Senger writes, 'I was pretty confident of achieving a tactical success by throwing in these divisions. The counter-attack struck the enemy at the moment when, from long experience, the impetus of his attack was bound to slacken.'[8] Sensing the danger of an assault by 46 Division separating 15 Panzer and 94 Division, von Senger directed 29 Panzer Grenadier Division down through Ausonia on Castelforte, while 90 Panzer Grenadier Division were sent south to attack astride Route 7 to restore the situation on the coastal area, where 5 Division threatened to turn the German flank. 90 Panzer Grenadier Division arrived piecemeal and were unable to launch a co-ordinated counter-attack but succeeded in preventing further penetration near the coast. Some ground north of Minturno was retaken by the Panzers and the high ground of Tufo changed hands four times. Between 21–23 January 29 Panzer Grenadier Division made numerous counter-attacks in the Castelforte area. Heavy fighting ensued and part of 40 Royal Marine Commando was brought in to reinforce the centre brigade of 56 Division. German losses were mounting and on 24 January the counter-attacks were halted, with the Germans in possession of Mount Rotondo, Castelforte and the northern slopes of Point 413. In the next three days General McCreery regrouped and brought in 46 Division to attack Mount Juga on 27 January, while 5 Division attacked Mount Natale. By the end of the month both objectives were taken and Mount Purgatorio as well. Further attacks in the Castelforte sector, however, had to be broken off and 10 Corps bridgehead became stabilized. With the removal of 56 Division, as reinforcements for Anzio, 10 Corps went on the defensive. Between 17 and 31 January the Corps had suffered 4,152 casualties.

Almost halfway between the Liri and Cassino the village of S Angelo stands on a steep forty-foot-high cliff a little back from the Rapido. The river in this sector is from twenty-five to fifty feet wide and at least nine feet deep, fast flowing between vertical banks anything from three to six feet high. It was in this area that General Clark planned to break the German line and pass through part of 1 Armoured Division and at least one follow-up infantry division towards Piedmonte and Aquino. Such a move would envelop the Cassino positions from the south-west. The actual crossing of the Rapido was to be made by 36 Division. The 141 Regiment would attack at an 'S' bend north of S Angelo and the 143 Regiment south of the village, using two crossing points. The three assaults were spread over some 4,000 yards of front. The Rapido in this sector follows a particularly winding course with many well-defined loops. Consequently, the forward defences did not follow the west bank of the river but were drawn back to allow a belt of cross fire to be built up from a series of positions, set back from the river in a zig-zag pattern. 15 Panzer Grenadier Division had been to great pains to fortify this sector. Not only were the defences sited in depth for several hundred yards but liberal use had been made of steel pill-boxes, dug-in tank turrets and concrete bunkers concealed in hedgerows and hummocks. Deep dug-outs, many of them reinforced, gave immunity to the defenders from both shelling and bombing. Both banks of the river were heavily mined and the defensive posts were protected by double apron wire fences and a number of mines fitted up as booby-traps. S Angelo itself had been largely demolished to cover over concreted bunkers which were sited inside buildings and the Allied bombing had only succeeded in piling up more rubble, making these strongpoints impervious to shell fire. The plan catered for 34 Division to simulate an attack against Cassino town as a diversion and for the whole of II Corps' artillery to pound the German defences for thirty minutes to cover the move forward of the assault troops to the line of the river. The crossings were ordered for 2000 hours, which would be two hours after dark. The divisional orders rigidly set out the various timings and assembly areas. One regiment had to move forward two miles from its assembly area and the other fully a mile to reach the river line. It was inevitable that some of the preparations in the assembly areas would have to be done in daylight if the regiments were to launch their boats on time. The result was that virtually all surprise was lost. Fully alerted and with a very fair idea of the likely lines of approach and crossing points, the Germans brought fire down on the American infantry columns almost as soon as they started out from their assembly areas towards the dumps, where the boats and other equipment were to be picked up. In addition to the assault boats over 200 heavy wooden boats and large rubber dinghies, together with fifty sections of 'catwalk', had to be carried forward. All this unwieldy and heavy equipment was needed by the engineers for improvised floating footbridges. On the right, the 141 Regiment moved out from their assembly area at 1800 hours and while they were actually forming up in boat parties at the dump, at about 1900 hours, the first white flares went up from the German lines to illuminate likely crossing points. From now on shelling and mortar fire increased and even more serious still the passage through the minefields on the near bank of the river could not be followed safely, as the tapes had been cut or blown away by the shelling. In several places the Germans had also laid fresh mines. The assault went in nearly an hour late and by 2100 hours a few boat-loads of men were across. The whole area round the crossing point was now under artillery, mortar and small arms fire, while *nebelwerfers* steadily pumped shells on to the tracks leading up to the crossing point. For nearly seven hours the engineers struggled in thickening fog to erect and launch footbridges. Finally at 0400 hours 21 January a single footbridge (out of five) was successfully launched and two companies crossed. With daylight, however, the shelling and direct fire on the crossing point intensified and the whole of the follow-up battalion was withdrawn back to the assembly area.

Although one of 143 Regiment's crossings south of S Angelo achieved an initial success the other was a complete failure. On the regiment's right two companies got a foothold on the west bank but lost a number of men at the crossing point. When two footbridges were launched successfully (by 0500 hours 21 January) the remainder of the battalion crossed but by 0700 hours found themselves forced back into a loop of the river and facing tanks and self-propelled guns. A divisional order to stand firm came too late and by 1000 hours the officer commanding, on his own initiative, had withdrawn the remnants of the battalion back across the river. Further to the south, the third assault crossing was never launched. 'Engineers leading the boat group became lost in the dense fog and strayed into a minefield where the rubber boats were destroyed. Both infantry and engineers were badly disorganized. By the time [the] battalion commander could restore order and bring up footbridges, enemy artillery again prevented a successful effort. Before daybreak the assault companies were back in their original positions.'[9] During the morning of 21 January a regiment of 71 Grenadier Division took over the northern end of 15 Panzer Grenadier Division's front and a reconnaissance battalion closed in on the thinly held 141 Regiment's bridgehead. When 36 Division resumed their efforts to cross during the afternoon they came under even heavier fire. Assisted by smoke, 143 Regiment achieved limited bridgeheads and made desperate efforts to build them up during the night but casualties were mounting. On the right, all the boats and the footbridge had been destroyed and three out of four of the company commanders killed or wounded. At the most southerly crossing point a penetration of 500 yards was achieved early on 22 January but the flat ground was swept by fire and the whole area was being shelled from batteries on Monte Cassino. To the north, 141 Regiment had penetrated some 1,000 yards across the river on 21 January. Although a concentrated attack had been planned for 1400 hours, no reinforcements could cross for a further seven hours owing to the difficulty in getting boats and equipment forward. Moreover the crossing point itself was still under direct machine-gun fire right up to the early hours of 22 January. Although the reserve battalions now crossed before dawn, they not only lost many men in doing so but found themselves in a narrow and restricted area, from which all cover had been systematically cleared, and were pinned down by accurate shelling and cross fire. While a footbridge had been successfully launched, attempts to start building a Bailey bridge under the cover of fog and later smoke proved an impossible task, as the German artillery and mortars had the range precisely. By 1600 hours 22 January the troops fighting on the west bank were completely cut off, all the boats and bridges having been destroyed, together with the field cables and the few remaining wireless sets. At about this time the regimental commander, seeing the situation was hopeless, requested a smoke-screen and orders to withdraw. These were refused as maps at the divisional command post showed approximately six battalions across the river. A German counter-attack was repulsed with heavy loss but by the time darkness fell the firing west of the river line had died down and the resistance of the two decimated battalions had been crushed. A handful of survivors swam back through the icy water of the Rapido during the night. In less than three days' fighting 36 Division lost nearly 1,700 men, including practically all the company commanders of the regiments committed at the crossings.

Many factors contributed to this 'costly failure', some have been mentioned already. The failure of 46 Division's attack and the absence of any proper diversion at the time of the crossings, resulted in 36 Division facing the concentrated fire of the massed German guns and *nebelwerfers* in the whole of the central sector. II Corps artillery, on the other hand, were seriously hampered by poor visibility and the early and almost complete breakdown of communications with the forward troops, many wireless sets having become damaged even before the crossing points were reached. From the German viewpoint, as von Senger has commented, 15 Panzer Grenadiers were well dug in on ground that suited their tactical methods and put up 'a completely successful defence. At that time neither 15 Panzer Grenadiers nor the Corps fully realized the extent of the enemy's failure; it was not until the US Congressional Enquiry into the costly attack by the US 36 Division that the facts came to light. The German commanders paid little attention to this offensive for the simple reason that it caused no particular anxiety.'[10] Early on 22 January the SHINGLE landings went in. Two German reserve divisions had been drawn into the fighting south of Cassino but on this front, except in 10 Corps' area, the Allied attacks had been beaten back. With the chances of an early breakthrough receding much now depended on the thrust and initiative of General Lucas who was in command at Anzio.

12

The Albano Road

Plans and forces for SHINGLE: Maintenance problems: Bridgehead secured:
Results of RICHARD: von Mackenson moves south: Lucas prepares to move:
The 'Factory': Rangers ambushed: Salients and Counter-attacks: Hitler's
tactics: The Fly-over: Truscott takes over: Harmon's Force: Kesselring's
second offensive held: Analysis of casualties: Difficulties of Air Support:
Comments and lessons.

1944

22 Jan	VI Corps lands at Anzio. By midnight 36,000 men and 3,000 vehicles ashore.
25 Jan	General Lucas starts limited attacks to enlarge bridgehead.
	Regimental Combat Team 45 Division lands.
27 Jan	General Alexander orders full-scale operations aiming at Velletri.
29 Jan	Remainder 45 Division and 1 Armoured Division (less Combat Team B) now complete.
30 Jan–2 Feb	VI Corps attacks to break out of bridgehead against steadily increasing German resistance.
2 Feb	General Clark orders bridgehead to be prepared for defence.
	1 SSF arrives as reinforcements.
3–11 Feb	1 Division salient on Albano Road driven back.
3 Feb	168 Brigade of 56 Division lands as reinforcements (remaining brigades arrive 9 and 18 Feb).
16–18 Feb	Von Mackensen's first offensive halted on final bridgehead line in area of 'fly-over'.
17 Feb	General Truscott appointed Deputy Corps Commander (assumes command of VI Corps on 23 February).
19 Feb	VI Corps' last reserves committed under General Harmon.
25 Feb	18 Brigade arrives from Egypt. Germans assemble further reinforcements.
28 Feb–3 Mar	Second German offensive fails to penetrate 3 Division front.
2 Mar	Allied bombers intervene in battle for bridgehead.
4 Mar	Kesselring orders defensive containment of bridgehead.

199

While the air preparations for SHINGLE were already under way, the naval plans were completed in twelve hectic days at Admiral Cunningham's advanced headquarters in Naples and the orders went out on 16 January. Excellent photographic coverage was available and beach reconnaissance parties only confirmed what was already known that, while the beach head area was ideal strategically, the beaches themselves were difficult with poor gradients and several minefields to seaward. Rear-Admiral Troubridge, in charge of the Northern Task Force, later reported that the British beaches which had a gradient of 1:120 were 'the worst in his experience'.[1] Above the water line the sand was soft and the exits through the dunes were poor. 3 Division was to be landed about four miles south of Anzio on 'X Ray' beach, while two Brigade Groups from 1 Division and the SS Brigade of two Commandos landed just beyond some steep sandy cliffs about five miles north of the town. This was called 'Peter' beach. Three battalions of Rangers were given the task of seizing the port of Anzio itself. A parachute drop behind the beaches was planned but cancelled two days before the landing. The (504) Parachute Infantry joined the Rangers' attack. The remainder of 1 Division formed a floating reserve and the follow-up troops were to be 1 Armoured Division, less the combat command waiting at Cassino, and 45 Division. Although aerial photographs showed numerous defences in the area of the Anzio beaches, these were known to have been built largely for training purposes by the Italians and there was little indication of their being occupied. The picture presented by Allied Intelligence was that the coastal area at this point was very lightly held. Consequently it was decided to land at 0200 hours, with a waning last quarter moon rising an hour later, which gave about four hours for the beach head to be occupied before dawn. As only light opposition was expected there would be no preliminary bombardment, but a LCT (R) with 798 rocket tubes was allotted to each of the three landing points to fire their 'spectacular' salvoes on to the beaches a few minutes ahead of the first assault wave.

The composition of both convoys was as shown in the Table on page 203.

It is interesting to compare the total of warships and landing craft with those provided for the landings at Sicily and Salerno. In the case of SHINGLE 'there was an acute shortage of the modern type of LST fitted with six pairs of davits for carrying assault landing craft. As only fourteen of this type could be provided (four for the British assault force and ten for the American),

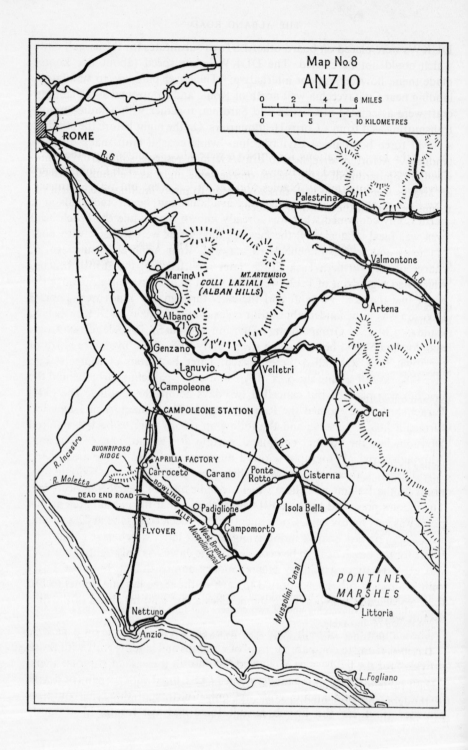

Map No. 8

ANZIO

0 2 4 6 MILES
0   5   10 KILOMETRES

ROME

R.6

R.7

Palestrina

Valmontone

R.6

Marino

MT. ARTEMISIO
COLLI LAZIALI
(ALBAN HILLS)

Artena

Albano

Genzano

Lanuvio.

Velletri

Campoleone

Cori

CAMPOLEONE STATION

R.7

BUONRIPOSO
RIDGE

APRILIA FACTORY

R. Incastro

Carroceto

Carano

Ponte
Rotto

Cisterna

R. Moletta

BOWLING

DEAD END ROAD

ALLEY

Padiglione

Isola Bella

FLYOVER

West Branch
Mussolini Canal

Campomorto

PONTINE
MARSHES

Mussolini Canal

Nettuno

Littoria

Anzio

L. Fogliano

DUKWs were placed on board other LSTs as substitutes for the assault craft which could not be carried. The DUKWs' slow speed (about five knots) made them, however, a poor alternative.'[2] The cover plan was to simulate a landing near Civitavecchia well north of Rome and troops and some landing craft were assembled in Corsica and Sardinia, together with a radio station transmitting as if from a Corps Headquarters. On the night before the landing a naval force bombarded Civitavecchia, 'while coastal craft made dummy landings'.[3] A further diversion to draw German reserves south from Rome was the bombardment of Terracina on the same night as the landing. Allied air attacks were fitted in with this cover plan to imply landings well north of Rome or even on the south of France.

NAVAL FORCES FOR SHINGLE
ASSAULT CONVOYS 22 JANUARY 1944

Class	British	American	Other Nations
Cruisers	3 (a)	1	—
AA Ships	2 (b)	—	—
Gunboats	—	—	2 Dutch
HQ Ships	1	1	—
Destroyers	12 (a)	10	2 Greek
Escort Vessels—Motor Launches and Scout Craft	8	32	—
Minesweepers (with Auxiliaries)	12	10 and 17 craft	—
LSI (and transports)	3 and 4 Transports	—	1 Polish Transport
LST	68	14	2 Greek
LCI	35	54	—
LCT	42	7	—
Landing Craft for Salvage and Repair Duties	5	9	—
Coastal Craft	2 Tugs 4 Trawlers (c)	2 Tugs	—
Miscellaneous	3	—	—
Submarines (Beacon)	2	—	—
Hospital Ships	4	—	—
Totals	210	157	7

Notes

(a) The British diversionary bombardment forces of one cruiser and several destroyers operating off Civitavecchia and of two cruisers and four destroyers off Terracina are not shown on this table.

(b) One AA ship and one Transport each embarked a US Army Air Force Fighter Direction Team.

(c) Converted for anti-submarine or minesweeping duties.

The problem of maintaining the force once ashore required considerable forethought and presented special difficulties. With the number of landing craft first allocated, it would have only been possible to land three days' maintenance (of supplies and ammunition) with the assault troops, while a further seven days' was carried in supply ships. Owing to the shallow gradients of the beaches, the British beach in particular being quite unsuitable for landing stores, DUKWs and pontoons would have to be used for ferrying stores from the LSTs. This was a very slow process. Unless the port was available early in the operation a serious maintenance problem would present itself. In the end, extra landing ships were found and fifteen days' maintenance loaded on about twenty-four LSTs, several LCTs and four Liberty ships. The LSTs carried some 700 trucks and second line vehicles together with 100 DUKWs all fully loaded. By this means the force would be virtually self contained on landing and for a time independent of the conventional beach or port maintenance set-up. Follow-up convoys were similarly organized. A pool of American trucks was assembled at Naples and every three days four Liberty ships and about fifteen LSTs, carrying in all 500 pre-loaded trucks, would sail for Anzio. On arrival the trucks would drive direct to dumps or gun lines while empty trucks were embarked for the return trip to Naples. As will be seen later on, this novel method of 'door-to-door' delivery proved most effective under the extremely difficult conditions that developed in the beach head. Room had also to be found in an early convoy for 1,000 tons of expanded (steel) sheets with which to construct a fighter airstrip. When the loading tables were finally issued some 50,000 men and over 5,000 vehicles had been found a place in the craft that were now assembling in the Bay of Naples.

There was practically no time for landing rehearsals or combined training. The British troops carried out a landing on the Salerno beaches with 'partial success', although the proper number of craft was not available. 3 Division's rehearsal on the same beaches, held on 17/18 January in particularly rough weather, 'was a near disaster'. The Navy's choice of landing beach was unfortunate. The correct number of ships failed to turn up. General Truscott's report on the exercise pulled no punches. 'No single battalion landed on time or in formation. Transports were so far offshore that assault craft required up to four and a half hours to reach the beach. Four DUKWs, carrying anti-aircraft guns were swamped, and it appears that at least five others, carrying howitzers, were lost. No single element was landed in hand and on its correct beach. Some beaches were missed by as much as 1,000 yards. No anti-tank weapons, artillery or tank destroyer guns were ashore by daylight. No tanks were landed. Ship to shore communications were defective, if not totally lacking.'[4] When the count was taken it was found that some forty DUKWs had been swamped, with the loss of a number of 105-mm howitzers and anti-tank guns and a quantity of signal equipment. An unforeseen result of these unfortunate accidents was that a number of DUKWs due to take part in 10 Corps and 36 Division's crossings over the Garigliano and Rapido Rivers were not available. Admiral Lowry promptly issued stringent orders to his ships' captains that at Anzio they were to close the shore to within three and a half miles. On General Clark's orders a conference was immediately held between the various force commanders 'to do what they could to straighten out the landing routine'.[5] There was no time for any further rehearsal and on 21 January the two assault forces assembled off the Gulf of Naples and set course for their 110-mile run to a point west of Ponziano Island, from where they would make their final approach.

Kesselring had been in fear of another Allied landing for some time and troops not employed in the Gustav Line were placed on the coast at the more vulnerable points. Fifth Army Intelligence estimated that some fifteen thousand German troops were positioned sufficiently near to the Anzio beaches to oppose the landings and consolidation of the beach head. After 10 Corps' attack across the Garigliano, against which Kesselring committed his two divisions in immediate reserve, all that remained near the coast between the Tiber and Terracina in the third week of January were three engineer companies, some reconnaissance troops, and two weak battalions pulled out for rest. One of these battalions was billeted in and about Anzio and the other near Cisterna. Apart from minor coastal artillery gun positions there were no other German troops within twenty-five miles of Anzio. But this did not mean that Kesselring had made no plans to counter a landing. In December an 'alarm plan' with the code-word 'Richard' had been carefully worked out so that formation headquarters and units, wherever they were in Italy, knew what to do in the event of an Allied landing in any one of a number of named areas. Without the troops to counter-attack immediately a landing took place, Kesselring could only hope to delay an advance from the beach head while a counter-attack force was being assembled. To both Alexander and Kesselring time was the key factor.

The voyage of the assault convoys, made in perfect weather, went unobserved. This was undoubtedly due to the fact that no Luftwaffe long-range reconnaissance aircraft could take off after the successful bombing of the airfields at Perugia. At midnight the assault ships were hoved to in a dead calm sea with haze limiting visibility to 300 yards. After an 'alert' on the three preceding nights the few troops manning beach defences had been given a night in billets and apart from one or two coastal guns the defences were unmanned. The landings achieved complete tactical surprise. During the approach the minesweepers had much difficulty in clearing the channels and the task was not properly finished. On 'Peter' beach it was two hours before mines on the beach itself could be cleared to allow DUKWs to come ashore. By 0800 hours the port had been captured intact and by late afternoon was taking both landing ships and craft for the unloading of guns and heavy equipment. By mid-day the three forces had joined up and were firmly established ashore and by midnight 22/23 January over 36,000 men and some 3,000 vehicles were ashore. Casualties in VI Corps were about 150. The Luftwaffe had been slow to react and the first air attacks came from about six Messerschmitt dive bombers at about 0900 hours. This and subsequent raids sank an LCI and set fire to some vehicles. Altogether the Luftwaffe flew only about 50 sorties over the beach head during the whole of D-day. Allied fighters flew 635 patrols and claimed seven enemy aircraft shot down and seven damaged for the loss of three aircraft. A further 600 sorties were flown by the bomber force, who were continuing their attacks on communications leading to the bridgehead.

Some twenty-five miles ahead, almost due north, lay the Alban hills, possession of which would cut all road and rail communications south to the Cassino front. The railway centre and town of Campoleone lay more than halfway to this objective. The refusal of Kesselring to denude the Cassino front in the face of the threat to his rear, however, put paid to any ideas of an early link up of the two wings of Fifth Army. The ground to the immediate front of VI Corps had been reclaimed and resettled by the draining of the Pontine marshes. 'Low swampy bog land, formerly nothing but a breeding ground for malarial mosquitoes, had been converted into an area of cultivated fields, carefully drained and irrigated by an extensive series of canals and pumping stations.'[6] Immediately north of Anzio and Nettuno was a boggy, scrub-covered and thinly wooded area, interspersed with bare open fields, which had been left untouched. Through this ran the road from Anzio to Carroceto and the modern community centre at Aprilia dubbed the 'factory' about ten miles from Anzio, Campoleone four miles further on, and Albano on Route 7 which was twenty-two miles from Anzio. On this road, seven miles from Anzio, a road from Padiglione crossed by a fly-over and later joined the coast road near the mouth of the Moletta River. In the flat ground this fly-over and the railway embankment at Campoleone station gave observation over the surrounding fields. North of the fly-over the ground became more undulating and rose gradually towards the Alban hills and the western slopes of the Lepini mountains which overlooked Cisterna. To the east, the reclaimed land was bounded by the main Mussolini canal which drained into the sea. Built to drain the northern part of the Pontine marshes, a smaller western branch of this canal flowed down from east of the 'factory' and then turned across (at Padiglione) to join the main canal about eight miles inland. This western branch of the canal was a poor obstacle but the Mussolini canal itself was 170 feet wide with steep banks and, running through marshy land, gave some protection against a German advance from this flank. The western part of the reclaimed area was bounded by the Moletta River, the principal of a number of shallow streams and drains half full of water which meandered and twisted through an area deeply cut into gullies. This area became known as the 'Wadi' country. Some of the gullies were as much as fifty feet deep into the subsoil and everywhere they were narrow and with precipitous banks, carrying shallow streams by devious and complex routes towards the sea. With the winter rains the whole plain was waterlogged and the drainage ditches showed the water level only a few feet down. In the highly cultivated areas, in particular, attempts to dig in were largely frustrated and until the ground later dried out, protection from shelling or bombing could only be got by sandbagging above ground.

By the evening of 23 January the bridgehead was well established on a twenty-five-mile front. On the right, the positions followed the Mussolini canal and its western branch as far as Padiglione and then across to the fly-over and on to the Moletta River and the coast. The only opposition had come from elements of the Hermann Göring Division on the Mussolini canal. Although the British beaches were now abandoned, the unloading of guns and heavy equipment speeded up as eight LSTs and a number of craft could be handled through the port each day. The Liberty ships were now being off-loaded by LSTs acting as lighters, or by some of the 400 DUKWs that were available.[7] At dusk on 23 January one of the hospital ships and a destroyer were sunk in an air attack. In spite of gales on 24 and 26 January the landings of pre-loaded lorries continued smoothly. By 29 January VI Corps had nearly 70,000 men ashore, with 508 guns, 237 tanks and 27,000 tons of stores. By now the bridgehead and the port were coming under accurate shell fire from guns closing in round the perimeter and the Luftwaffe attacks were increasing in strength. Two JU88 groups had arrived from Greece and Crete and others were brought back from attacking London, bringing the German bomber strength within reach of Anzio up to 200. An attack by over 100 bombers at dusk on 29 January sank a cruiser and a Liberty ship. The following day Fifteenth Air Force achieved a considerable success in an attack on Luftwaffe airfields in the Udine area, north-west of Trieste. A force of American bombers flying high made a normal approach and were plotted on the German radar net. At the moment that the Luftwaffe fighters were about to take off to intercept, P47s, that had flown across the Adriatic below the radar screen to arrive ahead of the bomber force, attacked and achieved complete surprise. Nearly forty German aircraft were destroyed for the loss of two P47s. American bombers now dropped 29,000 fragmentation bombs and destroyed an even greater number of planes on the ground. The total Allied losses were six bombers and three fighters. For the whole operation it was claimed that about 140 German aircraft had been destroyed in the air or on the ground.[8] This Allied success considerably reduced bomber raids against the bridgehead, but in their attempt to stop the arrival of reinforcements the Allied air forces were less successful. Both the heavy and medium bombers continued their attacks against rail and road communications but with only limited success. This was mainly due to bad flying conditions which between 24 January and 4 February stopped or seriously hampered flying on nine out of the twelve days. Earlier attacks had not been sufficiently effective and the result was that the Germans were able to keep at least one railway line to Rome open and found few roads or bridges seriously damaged.

Although Kesselring had earlier reported to the OKW (at 0600 hours 22 January) that a landing directed at Rome had been made, it was 0820 hours before the exact area was reported by a fighter pilot sent out on patrol. Following the issue of code word 'Richard', Kesselring's immediate concern was to check an Allied thrust inland by a mobile force. Flak batteries from the Rome area under General Ritter von Pohl were ordered to set up an anti-tank screen as far south as possible. Meanwhile German troops were on the move from near and far and were thrown into the line as they arrived. Kesselring recalls, 'what followed in those days was a higgledy-piggledy jumble – units of numerous divisions fighting confusedly side by side'.[9] Nevertheless, the force was growing stronger every day and by the end of the month, with General von Mackensen in command, the force included 180 tanks and a considerable number of guns deployed round the bridgehead. On Tenth Army front, as we shall later see, the Gustav Line was still intact and there were troops to spare to throw into the battle at Anzio. The build-up of German forces over the first twenty-four days is shown on the following table:

BUILD-UP OF GERMAN FORCES AGAINST ANZIO BRIDGEHEAD

Already in Area

Near Anzio	A weak battalion from 29 Panzer Grenadier Division withdrawn for rest.
Cisterna Area	Part of a tank regiment and some artillery from Hermann Göring Division, withdrawn for rest.

Stop Gap Units

By 23 January	Flak batteries from Rome area under General von Pohl: Elements 3 Panzer Grenadier Division (*en route* to Adriatic front): A regiment from 15 Panzer Grenadier Division (from Cassino).
23–24 January	Elements 4 Parachute Division (from Perugia).

Fourteenth Army and other reinforcements

Complete before 29 January	Headquarters Fourteenth Army (advance elements arrived 25 January): Headquarters 1 Parachute Corps (from Garigliano front): Lieutenant-General Schlemmer took command at Anzio late on 22 January – see below.
By 30 January	Remainder Hermann Göring Division (from Garigliano) plus three battalions 1 Parachute Division (from Adriatic): Remainder 3 Panzer Grenadiers (from Adriatic): 26 Panzer Division (from Adriatic): 65 Infantry Division (less one regiment) from Genoa: 362 Infantry Division as Army Reserve (from Rimini).

By 1 February	Headquarters LXXVI Panzer Corps (from Adriatic).
By 4 February	715 (Motorized) Infantry Division from south of France.
By 10 February	114 Jäger Division (from Yugoslavia).
Before 16 February	Remainder 29 Panzer Grenadier Division (from Garigliano): Lehr Regiment of three battalions (from Doberitz): Battle Group 16 SS Panzer Grenadier Division: 1027 and 1028 Panzer Grenadier Regiments, each of two battalions (all from Germany).

Many units were under strength but the total force opposing the bridgehead on 16 February was the equivalent of nine divisions – approximately 92,000 men. 'The command structure built up very rapidly. General von Mackensen reported to Kesselring on 23 February and was put in overall command. Lieutenant-General Schlemmer the Commander of 1 Parachute Corps had already arrived to co-ordinate the placing of units arriving from north Italy and "performed the remarkable feat of welding this heterogeneous mass of fighting men into a corporate, coherent military entity".'[10]

General Lucas, having made good the initial bridgehead line by the evening of 23 January, decided to consolidate his position, build up supplies and wait for reinforcements. So six days passed, by which time 1 Armoured Division (less Combat Command B) and 45 Division had landed. Meanwhile operations to enlarge the bridgehead were started by both 1 and 3 Divisions. 3 Division attacked towards Cisterna between 25 and 27 January but was halted three miles short of the town. Attacking straight up the Albano road, 1 Division took the 'factory' on 25 January after a stiff fight with 3 Panzer Grenadiers. This advance, however, was held one and a half miles further up the road, about halfway to Campoleone. General Alexander, who had visited the bridgehead shortly after the landing, on 27 January ordered General Clark 'to press the advance with the utmost energy before the enemy reinforcements could arrive'. As the arrival of 45 Division was imminent, he 'suggested that all efforts should now be concentrated on full-scale co-ordinated attacks to capture Cisterna and Campoleone followed by a rapid advance on Velletri'.[11] After inspecting the Fifth Army drive into the mountains and across the Rapido, General Clark set off for Anzio by motor torpedo boat on 28 January and narrowly escaped being killed when a minesweeper opened fire in the semi-darkness as they approached the channel leading to the port. Having conferred with Lucas and urged him 'to speed up his attack towards Cisterna, a town we wanted to include in our defensive line' it was decided to make a 'major effort'[12] on 30 January. General Lucas now adjusted his forces which amounted to four divisions. In the centre, the Rangers were relieved by 1 Division Reconnaissance Regiment in the Campomorto area and the flank positions of the bridgehead were taken over by 45 Division.

General Lucas planned to use the Rangers to lead an attack by 3 Division to get astride Route 7 at Cisterna and then exploit towards Velletri, while 1 Division would attack straight down the Albano road to gain the high ground above Albano and Genzano. 1 Armoured Division was ordered to move round the left flank of the British attack and seize the high ground above Marino on the western slopes of Colli Laziali. There would be no preliminary artillery preparation but comprehensive plans were made for artillery and direct air support during these attacks. Naval gun support and a smoke-screen to be laid by air were also arranged. Major-General Penney, command-ing 1 Division, planned to maintain the impetus of his attack by first breaking through the German covering positions north of Carroceto and the factory, in a night attack starting before midnight 29/30 January, to seize a line about 1,000 yards north of the 'factory' and then to pass a fresh brigade through for the second phase. This divisional attack was linked with the armoured attack on the left. When the night attack went in the Guards Brigade almost im-mediately ran into serious resistance at a strongly fortified road block and as daylight came hull-down tanks and self-propelled guns inflicted heavy losses on the leading troops. After the whole brigade and a regiment of tanks had been committed the objectives were cleared by noon 30 January and 3 Brigade passed through. By nightfall two battalions 'were digging in on high ground south of Campoleone railway line'.[13] After a night of almost continuous shelling the attack was resumed, supported by tanks, but all efforts to gain ground across the railway embankment were beaten back, in spite of strong artillery support. Campoleone remained in German hands. On the left, 1 Armoured Division, who had supported this engagement, found themselves in most difficult soft ground broken with deep gullies and were unable to take up the advance.

Towards Cisterna the Rangers had made a night approach up a drainage ditch leading from the western branch of the Mussolini canal to within half a mile of the town. Here the columns were ambushed in the open fields by a strong force from 1 Parachute Division supported by mobile guns. Attempts to relieve the Rangers failed and by noon a tank attack sealed their fate. Of 767 men from the two battalions who took part in the venture only six escaped, most of the remainder being taken prisoner. The main attack by 3 Division had followed up the Rangers' attempt at a *coup de main* and 'gained the high ground overlooking Ponte Rotto and the village of Isola Bella (by the afternoon of 30 January) at the cost of heavy casualties'.[14] A diversionary attack by 504 Parachute Infantry Regiment also failed to reach Route 7 on the right. The American attack was renewed on both 31 January and 1 February but German resistance was increasing and the American battalions were becoming exhausted. Anticipating an armoured counter-attack, as 26 Panzer Division had been identified on his front, General Truscott ordered his men to dig in where they stood. In three days the divisions had gained

General Leese, General Juin and General Alexander before the summer offensive 1944.

General von Mackensen, bending over map, inspecting coastal fortifications in Northern Italy, May 1944

German six-barrelled Nebelwerfer battery captured intact in the Hitler Line, May 1944.

General Clark with General Truscott (extreme right) mount the steps to the Capitol in Rome, June 1944.

about two to three miles but since landing 3 Division had lost 3,131 men and twenty-six tanks and self-propelled guns. With the bridgehead still very limited and now coming under a good deal of artillery fire, General Alexander ordered the launching of a fully co-ordinated Corps attack on Cisterna, to be followed by the capture of Campoleone and extension of the left flank to the River Incastro. 1 Special Service Force now arrived and took over the Mussolini canal positions, releasing the whole of 45 Division to be positioned on the left flank. Plans were also made to land 168 Brigade of 56 Division as reinforcements. The time for a bold Allied thrust was passed. Now the weather took a hand. Continual rain and low cloud hampered both ground and air operations. The German strength was increasing steadily. On 2 February General Clark ordered the whole bridgehead to be prepared for defence. The Germans had suffered considerable losses including 1,485 prisoners but VI Corps casualties now totalled nearly 6,500 men and the infantry and tank battalions in particular were seriously depleted.

Kesselring now saw the opportunity to develop his plans. With the Allied naval forces engaged in maintaining the troops at Anzio there was no longer a threat to the long coastline elsewhere. Eighth Army had been reduced to reinforce the Cassino front so German reserves could also be taken from the Adriatic positions with safety. Moreover Fifth Army attacks on the Gustav Line were being successfully held. Fearing Allied naval gun fire, Kesselring discarded the idea of attacking the bridgehead from the north and concentrated on plans to attack down the Albano to Anzio road, which gave him the best chance of splitting the defences. But first the salient almost touching Campoleone must be nipped out. Von Mackensen now had his troops organized into two corps; 1 Parachute Corps held from Albano to the Moletta River with 4 Parachute Division and 65 Infantry Division; LXXVI Panzer Corps controlled the remainder of the front with a mixed force of about five divisions. 3 Panzer Grenadiers were astride the Albano road, with 715 and 71 Infantry Divisions linking with the Hermann Göring Division on the Mussolini Canal. 26 Panzer Division was in corps reserve. At 2300 hours 3 February a pincer attack by 3 Panzer Grenadier and 71 Infantry Divisions (both strongly reinforced) went in against the British salient. The British infantry were now under attack from three sides and fierce fighting continued throughout the night. As daylight came 1 Division were confident they could hold their positions but a German attack, infiltrating from the west, made ground. By 1000 hours 4 February 3 Brigade, reinforced with a parachute battalion, holding the narrow salient facing Campoleone were cut off. General Lucas counselled withdrawal but was reluctant to commit his armoured division in support. Major-General Penney had nothing left for the necessary counter-attack. At this critical stage 168 Brigade, who had providentially arrived straight from the Cassino front less than twenty-four hours beforehand, at Penney's insistence was launched into the battle. At 1600 hours the

London Scottish and 46 Royal Tank Regiment swept forward with great *élan* and cleared a corridor up the road. In heavy rain and under shelling all the way the weary survivors of 3 Brigade started back, covered by heavy concentrations of fire from VI Corps' guns. What had seemed certain annihilation had now become a deliberate withdrawal by men dropping from fatigue but instinctively closing their ranks and turning once again to face the enemy. Although now short of anti-tank guns and tanks, that had had to be abandoned bedded deep in the mud, 'the Brigade was still intact as a fighting organisation'.[15] The line now ran about a mile north of Carroceto and the 'factory'. 'British casualties had been extremely heavy, totalling 1,400 killed, wounded and missing in the action.'[16] German probing attacks near Cisterna over the next three days resulted in the recapture of Ponte Rotto but the main threat remained in the 'factory' area. This area was a communications centre, the possession of which would enable the Germans to concentrate their armour rapidly for an attack down the road towards Anzio. The whole of 1 Division was now holding the salient from Padiglione north to the 'factory' and Carroceto and thence a lay back position along the Buonoriposo ridge, for about two miles south-west towards the lateral road from the fly-over. To the rear, every available man was working on a final beach-head defence line from the Moletta across the fly-over to the Mussolini Canal. Behind this line in the sparse wooded area and back into the open fields the Allied batteries stood in rows, in places wheel to wheel. Dumps and hospitals were sited wherever space could be found. Deserters and aerial photographs indicated an imminent German attack down the road to Anzio. 168 Brigade held the vital 'factory' area, while the Guards held Carrocetto. Von Mackensen saw no reason to alter his previous successful pincer attack. 65 Infantry Division would attack the Buonoriposo ridge from the west and 3 Panzer Grenadier Division the 'factory' from the east. Soon after dusk on 7 February the Germans started infiltrating on the west of the ridge position and by midnight fierce and confused fighting had broken out in the whole of this sector. In the Guards' sector, west of Carroceto, the Grenadiers and the Parachute battalion mustered twenty-nine and forty-five men respectively. Attacks against the 'factory' had been beaten back and Major-General Penney gave the two weak battalions from 3 Brigade and a tank squadron the task of recapturing Buonoriposo ridge. This counter-attack was pressed home with the utmost gallantry for nearly ten hours. As the light failed the survivors of the attacking force fell back. Machine-guns on the slight rise of the ridge and accurate German artillery concentrations had taken a terrible toll. Practically all the officers and NCOs had been killed. There was nothing now left to stop the Germans cutting the road again. General Lucas refused to release troops from the corps reserve. No staff officer from Corps visited the divisional area to see their plight. 1 Division was on its own and, considerably weakened by two weeks' fighting, its situation was critical.

The next day von Mackensen renewed his attacks on the same pattern. Heavy mortar and artillery fire pounded the shrinking salient and then the infantry started infiltrating between the positions. The Panzer Grenadiers were now in the 'factory'. Quickly laying mines and bringing forward anti-tank guns, the Germans successfully beat off a counter-attack by 1 Armoured Division, many of whose tanks became bogged down as soon as they left the road. An Allied air attack by 200 bombers and fighter-bombers struck at Campoleone but failed to influence the immediate battle around Carroceto, where the Guards were virtually surrounded. At 0500 hours on 10 February General Penney 'reported that his division [which had lost half its strength] could not hold without the help of a counter-attack by fresh troops who would have to take over much of the front'.[17] In the three days' fighting the Germans had employed more than twenty battalions. With the support of VI Corps artillery and limited air strikes (bad weather from 9–12 February practically stopped flying) the British line was straightened and two battalions from 45 Division were brought up either side of 3 Brigade. The survivors of the Guards Brigade came into divisional reserve. The success of this withdrawal was undoubtedly due to the heavy and extremely accurate concentrations put down by the Allied guns. On both 11 and 12 February 45 Division and 1 Armoured Division counter-attacked towards the 'factory' but without success and once more the Germans attempted to break the front of 3 Brigade, but neither side gave ground. By 15 February 1 Division was out of the line with their front now held by two brigades of 56 Division (the remaining brigade had not yet arrived) and part of 45 Division. The number of guns now lined up in VI Corps bridgehead was 432 firing 25,000 rounds a day to which the Germans replied with perhaps 1,500 rounds per day.[18] Von Mackensen's main blow, however, was still to come. This assault, supported by two subsidiary attacks, would again be made down the road to Anzio. This time the whole weight of Fourteenth Army, now considerably reinforced by troops from France and Germany, would be thrown into the attack. Bohmler writes, 'But the milestone still showed ten miles to Anzio. Aprilia and Carroceto had been only the curtain raisers; the main battle was still to come and the overwhelming material superiority of the enemy and the determination of his troops left no room for optimism. The German attacking divisions had a hard task before them. The Allied High Command had correctly interpreted the action at Aprilia and Carroceto as the opening moves of an impending general offensive.'[19]

Hitler now intervened and, on seeing the plan, ordered the attack to be made on a much narrower front than had been proposed by von Mackensen and placed his favourite infantry demonstration regiment, the Lehr Regiment, in the van. The equivalent of six divisions was assembled for the attack which would be made as soon as possible. When the Lehr Regiment arrived there was no time for the necessary detailed reconnaissance of the ground for a night assault and the attack consequently was ordered for 0630 hours 16 February. 45 Division now had two regiments astride the Albano road and the third regiment holding the more central sector towards Carano. The remainder of the Corps' right flank was held by 3 Division and 1 Special Service Force on the canal. 56 Division, still short of a brigade until 18 February, was on the left of 45 Division, with an American engineer battalion holding the lower part of the River Moletta. The considerably weakened 1 Division and 1 Armoured Division were in reserve about five miles north of Anzio. Behind the Lehr Regiment von Mackensen had formed up 114 Light Division to the east, 715 Grenadier Division in the centre, and 3 Panzer Grenadiers with part of 4 Parachute Division to the west. The attack would go in straight down and astride the Anzio road. 26 Panzer Division and 29 Panzer Grenadier Division stood by to exploit the breakthrough. New type Mark VI Tiger and Mark V Panther tanks had been specially brought from Germany. Hitler's latest 'secret' weapon, a miniature tank filled with explosives and fired electrically from a distance, was to be used for the first time and his orders made it clear the Allies were to be driven into the sea. At 0600 hours on 16 February the German guns opened up on the whole of the central sector. Half an hour later a number of diversionary attacks developed in six different areas and attacks of not more than two company strength probed 3 Division's front. Two rather more determined attacks were successfully beaten back by 56 Division on the other flank. The first main effort was launched by 715 Grenadier Division supported by tanks to soften up 45 Division. Using Carroceto and the 'factory' as a screen and supply point, small groups of tanks would suddenly emerge to fire at almost point-blank range at the forward positions and then withdraw before artillery fire could be effectively brought down on them. South-east of the 'factory' German infantry penetrated down two creeks towards Padiglione. The fighting continued inconclusively all day with fairly heavy losses on both sides. Attacks coming in astride the road, where German shelling was heaviest, followed the same pattern but by the evening 45 Division's front, although dented, was still holding. The German artillery were now engaged on a major counter battery effort, particularly against 45 Divisional artillery. The Nettuno airstrip from which a few fighters had been able to operate in daylight, came under accurate fire and had to be abandoned. For some time German long-range guns and bombing attacks had been focused on trying to prevent the landing of supplies at Anzio. Now air raids increased and on 16 February reached a peak of 172 sorties in the day. A landing craft was sunk and a landing ship damaged, while on shore an ammunition dump was blown up, otherwise these attacks achieved poor results. By comparison XII Air Support Command flew 468 medium-light and fighter-bomber sorties in direct support, mainly on 45 and 56 Divisional fronts. Before midnight on 16 February German infantry attacked down the Anzio road and nipped out a company of 157

Regiment holding a key position covering the road. Fourteen survivors were eventually extracted after a counter-attack by tanks screened by smoke had driven off German tanks advancing from the flank. A dangerous gap was now developing between 157 Regiment and 179 Regiment who were in position east of the road. The Germans immediately struck to widen the gap. Dive bombers led an assault shortly before 0800 hours 17 February, when approximately three Grenadier regiments with about sixty tanks and several battalions of infantry swung south-east against the 179 Regiment. This attack, which again received support from the Luftwaffe who dive-bombed and machine-gunned the American positions, made ground against all efforts to form a line and by noon the regiment was forced back to the 'dead-end' road, only 1,500 yards north of the final beach-head line. A wedge two and a half miles wide and a mile deep had been punched in the centre of 45 Divisional front.[20] The whole weight of the Allied corps and divisional artillery together with four batteries of 90-mm anti-aircraft guns and the fire from two cruisers was now brought down in an attempt to stop the breakthrough. Three companies of tanks from 1 Armoured Division were brought forward and the whole XII Air Support Command was launched against the German assaults on the 45 Divisional front. The bombers alone flew 531 sorties and 1,100 tons of bombs were dropped on the immediate approaches through Campoleone and on the 'factory' and targets on the Albano road.[21] Von Mackensen now launched his carefully assembled reserves and during the afternoon the Lehr Regiment attacked with tank support. Belying their reputation, the Lehr Regiment made a poor showing and failed to achieve the expected break into the American lines. Fourteen battalions of German infantry working with a number of tank groups, however, were now committed. The co-operation between the German infantry and tanks was excellent and their concerted attacks reached the junction of the 'dead-end' road. West of the Anzio road a battalion of 157 Regiment was now virtually surrounded. A counter-attack by a regiment of 1 Armoured Division failed to regain the ground lost east of the road. British 1 Division, leaving 3 Brigade as Corps reserve, now came forward to hold the overpass. As the depleted battalions took up their positions on the lateral road on a two-mile front once again they were fighting with their backs to the sea and practically nothing behind them. When Major-General Penney was wounded Major-General Templer took command and co-ordinated the defences of both 56 and 1 Divisions. At this point General Truscott was ordered to Corps headquarters as deputy commander. General Eagles, commanding 45 Division, now put in a night attack in an attempt to cut off the head of the German salient from both flanks. Unfortunately the attack was not in sufficient strength and failed. Throughout the night 17/18 February the German infantry worked forward, strengthening their hold on the shoulders of the salient. At dawn the German attacks east of the road and towards Padiglione started once more. By mid-morning 179 Infantry were back on the final stop line and the left of 3 Division's front was under heavy attack. 45 Division and 1 Division were now holding the final bridgehead defences side by side and under heavy attack. The Allied artillery took tremendous toll of the German attacks. Flying conditions, however, were so poor that only 150 direct support sorties were made by XII Air Support Command. During the withdrawals of the past few days many anti-tank guns had had to be abandoned embedded in the mud and the British and American units astride the road were at a serious disadvantage. German tank losses, however, had been heavy and their infantry were very tired. On 3 Division's left twelve German tanks were only halted at a blown bridge. From late afternoon into the night the attacks continued to come in on the whole of 45 Division's front and against the fly-over. Near the fly-over the Loyals beat back an attack in hand-to-hand fighting. Here, to the east of the fly-over on the lateral road, the fighting reached its greatest intensity. All day German infantry and tanks had attacked across this last 1,000 yards of flat ground which gave no cover. The embankments of the fly-over itself were honey-combed with command posts and artillery observation posts which, from this slight elevation, could look out over the flat ground in front. The torn and twisted girders and great gaps where whole sections of the embankment had been blown away by shell fire bore testimony to the attempts of the German gunners to deprive the Allies of this vital point of observation. As the German attacks developed they were met by a storm of shells which inflicted terrible losses but still small groups of infantry continued to advance, now to meet the machine-gun, mortar and rifle fire of the thin ranks holding the lateral road.

At Corps Headquarters Truscott was trying to persuade General Lucas to throw in his reserves. There was little left but now was the time to throw in all that remained. 169 Brigade of 56 Division was actually in process of land-ing. 3 Division could spare a regiment and 45 Division still had one battalion uncommitted. These troops with an infantry battalion and some tanks from 1 Armoured Division would make a sizeable force. Lucas still hesitated but Clark, who was present during the discussion, supported the plan.[22] Major-General Harmon was given a composite force from 3 Division and 1 Armoured Division, which was assembled near Padiglione. His orders were to attack early on 19 February straight up the diagonal road known as the 'bowling alley' towards Carroceto. In the meantime every man in the bridgehead area was to be given his place for a last-ditch stand. On the left, a force under General Templer, mainly found from 169 Brigade, would attack north from the fly-over to join up with the battalion of 157 Regiment now completely cut off. Late on the night 18/19 February there had been a slight lull near the fly-over, then at 0400 hours on 19 February the Germans attacked again. A company of the Loyals was overrun. The rest of the battalion fought on. The crisis had come and the Germans seemed within an ace of breaching the line. Intense concentrations from the Allied guns were crashing down just ahead of the lateral road. '2nd Brigade ordered all their men who could fire a weapon to be hurried forward: storemen, cooks, and drivers grasped their rifles and grenades, men of the dock operating companies left their derricks and came up the Anzio road. And then, quite suddenly, the Germans' attack cracked.'[23] As the daylight came, the defenders on the fly-over and the lateral road peered out across the shell-torn fields but no fresh attacks came in. Von Mackensen had thrown in his last reserves; the German infantry had had enough. To the right, a smoke-screen began to drift across and heavy concentrations of gun-fire were crashing down on the 'bowling alley'. General Harmon's counter-attack had started. By the afternoon this attack had penetrated some 2,000 yards into the German salient and caused a good deal of confusion. In the Loyals' sector the situation had been restored. Pockets of Germans were surrendering and several hundred prisoners were taken. The counter-attack by 56 Division had to be postponed, as the heavy equipment for 169 Brigade could not be landed in time. The American counter-attack, however, had thrown the Germans off balance and Harmon's scratch force was now drawn back from the open ground to the bridgehead line. A battalion from 169 Brigade, on 21 February, succeeded in extricating 200 survivors out of the 800 men of 157 Regiment that had been cut off west of the road. Now the relieving force found itself isolated in the caves and wadis where the Americans had fought and died since early on 17 February. In this difficult and broken country patrols could disappear without trace and there was no fixed line. Most of the relief force was lost.

By now Lucas had been relieved of command of the Corps and Truscott took over. 'General Evelegh, who understood the Americans as well as Truscott understood the British, became Deputy Corps Commander.'[24] Truscott was to prove an outstanding commander and confidence between the Allies was quickly restored. Between 16–20 February VI Corps suffered 3,400 casualties and a further 3,000 over the next five days. In spite of a steady flow of reinforcements, returns on 20 February showed that units in the bridgehead were 20,000 below their proper establishment. VI Corps was reinforced on 25 February by 18 Brigade from Egypt. Although beaten back the Germans had not given up and by 28 February Kesselring had scraped up roughly the equivalent of a further division. Bitterly disappointed at the earlier failures, Hitler ordered the resumption of the offensive. Again the attack must be on a narrow front and this time was aimed at Cisterna. The original date was 25 February but foul weather caused a postponement of four days. On 28 February a diversionary attack was put in on the British sector but the Germans suffered serious losses and the attack was not pressed home. The following day the German artillery switched to 3 Division's front and three weak divisions of the Panzer Corps, including 362 Infantry Division, attacked south from Cisterna. General Truscott was ready. 3 Division had been reinforced with extra anti-tank guns and a battalion from 1 Armoured Regiment. New minefields had been laid particularly on all the roads and tracks leading in to the bridgehead. The German attack never really got going. Kesselring was under no illusions as to the weakness of the effort. He hoped only to drive back the Allies to the original bridgehead line on the west branch of the Mussolini canal. The main German thrust was checked on the minefields and by the Allied artillery and twenty-one tanks were lost. Fighting continued on 1 March but on a reduced scale, with a number of small attacks spread over the whole of the eastern sector. On 2 March with reasonably good flying weather, the medium and fighter-bombers were joined by 350 Liberators and Flying Fortresses. Altogether 800 bomber sorties were made and 600 tons of bombs dropped on and around Cisterna, Carroceto, Campoleone and Velletri and along the actual front. But Kesselring's mind had already been made up. Late on 1 March he called the offensive off and by 4 March the Germans were digging in where they stood.

For over seven weeks the troops of VI Corps were invested in the bridge-head at Anzio. Between 22 January and 22 May the VI Corps battle casualties at Anzio were over 25,000 and even greater losses were suffered from exposure, exhaustion, trench feet, etc. The approximate figures for the 'non battle' casualties were 26,000 in the US Forces and 11,000 amongst the British Forces. In the four days 16–20 February VI Corps' casualties were 414 killed, 1,982 wounded, 1,025 missing and 1,637 'non battle' casualties, a total of 5,048 casualties from all causes. British casualties from January to March were 1,308 killed, 6,125 wounded, 5,510 missing and 5,698 'non battle' casualties, a total of 18,641 in all.[25] In the first thirty days after the landing, British units lost an average of 27 per cent and American units 17 per cent of their strength. After the war Kesselring estimated his total casualties at Anzio as 40,000 of which 5,000 were killed. The Allies took some 4,500 German prisoners.[26] British naval losses at Anzio were two light cruisers, three destroyers, a hospital ship, three LSTs and a LCI sunk, with 429 battle casualties amongst the crews. The US Navy suffered 326 battle casualties and lost five landing craft and one LST, two minesweepers and two Liberty ships sunk. The large majority of these losses resulted from aerial bombing attacks and the use of glide bombs directed from high ground overlooking the road-stead. Attacks by German and Italian E Boats (who themselves suffered many losses) on Allied shipping off Anzio resulted only in the sinking of one LST. A mass attack by twenty-three Marder 'human torpedoes' on 20/21 March was a complete fiasco. Not a single Allied ship was lost and ten Marders were sunk or captured. The remainder out of the total force of forty were withdrawn from the Mediterranean. Naval bombardment by Allied warships was freely given whenever called for. For instance *Brooklyn* fired 580 rounds of eight-inch shells on 9 February and up to the end of February nearly 20,000 shells had been fired at shore targets by the British cruisers and destroyers alone.

During the entire period of the German counter-attacks five cruisers, two gunboats and every available destroyer engaged German troop and tank concentrations and mobile batteries. According to a German war diary this naval bombardment 'contributed greatly to halting the drive towards (the) beaches'.[27]

A disappointing feature of the fighting at Anzio, taking into account the fact that the Allies had air superiority, was the lack of direct air support. Apart from the obvious bad weather factor, this was almost entirely due to the refusal by the US Army Air Force to recognize the need for and the value of a proper communication system, with controllers on the actual battlefield linked to special squadrons allocated to direct support. The two Fighter Direction Teams embarked on naval vessels were not kept supplied with adequate information on the movement of friendly aircraft and achieved little. The Senior Air Officer on *Biscayne* had no signal link with Air Head-quarters on land, no air plot and was divorced from both Fighter Direction Teams. General Truscott, whose proposals for air support procedures 'similar to the shore fire-control parties for naval gunfire support'[28] had been turned down, was particularly critical of the cumbersome procedure insisted upon by Allied Air Headquarters. Mention has already been made of the timely intervention by the Mediterranean Allied Air Forces during the critical period of the German counter-attacks. Generally speaking, however, the bomber squadrons were tied to the 'independent' CBO programme and the inter-diction of communications. Air doctrine at this time also advocated sustained mass bombing attacks on clearly defined targets, as were about to be attacked at Cassino, but the employment of such tactics in a defensive battle was a new concept. General Eaker commented, in retrospect, that the effect of bad weather on the obviously vital air co-operation had not been given sufficient thought. General Arnold noted that 'no systematic complete and enduring isolation of the battlefield was possible without more night operations than had been employed'. He also 'pointed out that the air forces did not always concentrate their available air power so as to hit selected areas with sustained mass attacks'.[29] Many lessons were learned from the air operations at Anzio. Not the least of these was the need for very clearly defined aiming points for heavy bombers engaged in close support. Squadrons were constantly being diverted from the CBO operations to take part in what can only be described as purely defensive operations against the German counter-attacks. With the opposing ground forces closely locked in battle in restricted areas these air operations were difficult to plan and execute. Nevertheless, in spite of the bad weather and the other difficulties, the Mediterranean Allied Air Forces made a tremendous contribution to the Anzio battle. The successful fighter pro-tection of the bridgehead alone required an average of 450 defensive fighter sorties each day. The weary troops of VI Corps and the crews of the ships standing offshore at least had this tangible proof that the air forces were meeting their commitments to the full. Under the energetic direction of von Richthofen, the Luftwaffe, although completely outnumbered at Anzio, employed what strength it had to support the German counter-attacks and to harry the Allied shipping. A special Luftwaffe battle headquarters was established in the Alban hills under General von Pohl who co-ordinated the air strikes with his extensive flak layout.

In early March the first phase of the battle of Anzio was over. The operation had offered high hopes to both sides. Churchill saw the landing as directly leading to the early fall of Rome. After the containment of the Allied bridgehead, Hitler clearly hoped for a dramatic victory to offset the long months of withdrawal and defeat. On both sides failure led to controversy both on the strategic value as well as the conduct of the operations. It is important to set the Allied landings and the German counter-attacks in the larger frame of the opposing strategies in the Mediterranean theatre at the beginning of 1944. Hitler had decided to stand on the Gustav Line and to end the withdrawals that had started at El Alamein fourteen months earlier. Thus he did not hesitate to send reinforcements the moment the extent of the landings at Anzio were appreciated. Since Salerno the Allied advance on Rome had been progressively slowing down and Churchill regarded the reinforced VI Corps landing at Anzio as vital to the whole Mediterranean campaign in 1944. The shortage of shipping and the holding back of divisions in North Africa for the ANVIL landings on the south of France, however, seriously limited Alexander's ability both to increase the rate of the initial build-up and to furnish sufficient reinforcements for a break out, in the face of the unexpectedly strong and rapid German concentration against the bridgehead. Originally the landing was planned to cut the line of retreat of the German Tenth Army after the Allies had penetrated into the Liri valley. With the need to return landing craft for OVERLORD this concept had to be modified and it became necessary to plan for the landing of a considerably stronger force which could hold on for an indeterminate period, although it was hoped that the threat to his rear would force von Vietinghoff to weaken his main front and thereby enable Fifth Army to break through at Cassino. Alexander took pains to ensure that the two divisions landing at Anzio would at first be self-sufficient both in transport and supplies. As we have seen, fifteen days' maintenance and a considerable quantity of extra ammunition was loaded in the D-day convoy, while other convoys arriving every three days would quickly build up stocks at three times the rate of likely expenditure. In orders issued on 2 January 'the objective of VI Corps was defined as to cut the enemy communications and threaten the rear of German XIV Corps'. Three days later, plans were initiated to 'land in the first follow-up convoy a mobile, hard-hitting force from 1 United States Armoured Division and 45 Infantry Division. Later the remainder of these divisions was to follow'.[30] A force of 110,000 men with extra transport, ammunition and stores of all kinds was now involved in an amphibious operation which would be launched in poor weather conditions and with barely sufficient landing craft for the initial assault by two divisions. The paradox now emerges. To carry out his task General Lucas should seize and hold the Alban hills but initially only two divisions would be ashore and the build-up in the bridgehead, both of men and materials, could only proceed as fast as the weather and limited shipping resources allowed. In addition, emphasis had been placed on the need to land additional stocks of ammunition and supplies of all kinds, in case the link up with Fifth Army from the Cassino front was seriously delayed. The initial German resistance at Anzio had been estimated at about a division (29 Panzer Grenadiers plus four Parachute battalions and some tank and anti-tank units) but it was hoped that the Allied Air Forces would effectively delay reinforcements from reaching the area. General Lucas was told that at least 29 Panzer Grenadiers had been drawn into the battle on the Garigliano but the Allied bombers failed to produce the expected degree of 'interdiction' of the communications leading to the bridgehead. At the time of the landings, Allied Intelligence esitmated only two German divisions would reach the bridgehead from north of Florence by 6 February. General Lucas, it seems, was thoroughly imbued with a 'Salerno outlook' and never really believed in the concept of SHINGLE. He expected to have to fight his way ashore and could not adjust himself when the landing achieved complete surprise. He expected to be facing early counter-attacks and, it seems, could see no further ahead than the seemingly inevitable and violent German assault that would threaten his base. He later wrote 'the only thing that ever really disturbed me at Anzio, except, of course, my inability to make speedier headway against the weight opposing me, was the necessity to safeguard the port. At any cost this must be preserved as, without it, the swift destruction of the Corps was inevitable.'[31] While Alexander pressed, on 27 January, for 'full-scale co-ordinated attacks to capture Cisterna and Campoleone followed by a rapid advance on Velletri',[32] Clark's original orders had been left vague requiring only an advance 'on' the Alban hills. Yet in an earlier outline plan for SHINGLE issued by Fifth Army, in November 1943, the early capture of the Alban hills had been regarded as 'vital to secure a limited force landed in the beach head'.[33] When Lucas had finally assembled four divisions and was ready to advance on 30 January he found the Germans prepared and in sufficient strength to prevent any break out. On the afternoon of the landing, Kesselring toured the Anzio front and later wrote 'as I traversed the front I had the confident feeling that the Allies had missed a uniquely favourable chance of capturing Rome and of opening the door on the Garigliano front. I was certain that time was our ally.'[34] His Chief of Staff, General Westphal, comments, 'at the moment of the landing the only troops available south of Rome for the initial defence, apart from a few auxiliary coastal batteries, were two battalions. That was all! Otherwise there was absolutely nothing on hand to oppose the enemy on the same day. The road to Rome was open, and an audacious flying column could have penetrated to the city. Moreover, this breathtaking situation persisted for two days after the landing, before the German counter measures could take effect.'[35] Although taken completely by surprise Kesselring once again succeeded in extricating himself with great skill. A number of factors were in his favour. The remarkable resilience of his troops and the flexibility of his command organization and anti-invasion instructions all played a great part. The partial failure of the Allied air forces to seal off the area, strengthened his determination to hold the Gustav Line at all costs. So far as the VI Corps delays in making an early concerted effort to advance 'on' the Alban hills is concerned, this obviously gave Kesselring time to contain the bridgehead without weakening his main front or at any time considering abandoning the Gustav positions. Alexander makes the point that 'the Alban hills are really a massive mountain terrain, much more difficult to gain and maintain than can be apparent from maps. And to have secured the hills and kept open the line of communication to Anzio would not have been an easy task.' On the other hand he holds to his view that General Lucas 'missed his opportunity by being too slow and cautious. He failed to realize the great advantage that surprise had given him. He allowed time to beat him.'[36]

After von Mackensen's counter-attack had failed someone had to explain the true facts to Hitler. General Westphal was given this unenviable task and his conclusions as to the causes of the German failure at Anzio are summarized as follows:

(a) The direction of the attacks was too obvious.
(b) There was inadequate ammunition to silence the Allied artillery.
(c) The German armoured formations were tied by the 'muddy ground' to the roads and causeways 'where they presented excellent targets'.
(d) The Allies had air supremacy.
(e) The restricted front of the attack (six kilometres) proved disadvantageous.

As Westphal told Hitler, 'after five years of war the troops had become exhausted to a frightening degree. The heavy losses had seriously handicapped the commanders of all ranks. For instance it was now only seldom possible really to co-ordinate the fire of the various weapons.'[37] Still not satisfied, Hitler sent for twenty officers of all ranks and arms to report on conditions in Italy – he got the same answers. Although the shortage of men and ammunition and the superiority of the Allies in the air applied equally to the German Tenth Army, the defensive operations around Cassino, as will now be outlined, effectively blocked the Allied advance. At Anzio both sides were exhausted and nearly two months were to elapse before the break out took place and the capture of Rome was finally achieved.

13

Shadow of Cassino

Clark continues attempts to break through: Attacks switch to north of Cassino: French successes: General Freyberg and the New Zealand Corps: Snake's Head Ridge: Three weeks' bad weather: Bombs and Craters: Castle Hill and the Railway Station: Alexander plans spring offensive.

1944	24 Jan	10 Corps penetration across Garigliano stabilizes.
	24 Jan–12 Feb	34 Division attack across Rapido north of Cassino.
	25–31 Jan	French Expeditionary Corps drive results in capture of Mounts Cifalco, Belvedere and Abate.
	25 Jan	5 Canadian Armoured Division joins 13 Corps (Eighth Army Area).
	2–7 Feb	36 Division move to Monte Castellone sector.
	5–12 Feb	II Corps continues attack north of Cassino.
	6 Feb	New Zealand Corps takes over sector south of Route 6 releasing 36 Division.
	8 Feb	78 Division ordered from Adriatic sector to join New Zealand Corps. Deep snow delays arrival until 17 February.
	12 Feb	New Zealand Corps relieves II Corps north of Cassino.
	15 Feb	Monastery bombed. 4 Indian Division commence attacks on Point 593.
	16–17 Feb	Air support diverted to Anzio where German counter-attack threatens beach head.
	18 Feb	New Zealanders lose Cassino railway station. 4 Indian Divisional attack fails north of Cassino. Torrential rain and snow postpone further attacks (scheduled for 24 February) until mid-March.
	28 Feb	Alexander plans regrouping for major offensive.
	15 Mar	Allied heavy bombers and artillery reduce Cassino town to rubble as prelude to New Zealand Corps attack.
	15–22 Mar	Bitter fighting in Cassino sector and New Zealand Corps dissolved.
	2 Apr	Alexander decides strategy for spring offensive.

Linked with the crossing of the Garigliano, the opening phase of the first battle of Cassino consisted of several separate but co-ordinated Allied attacks, an advance into the mountains in the north by the French Expeditionary Corps, an assault over the lower Rapido by 36 Division and the attack by 34 Division and the French Expeditionary Corps north of Cassino. These latter operations which lasted from 24 January to 12 February will now be described. Originally it was planned that the attacks would be spread over a much wider front and would include the resumption of 10 Corps operations in the coastal sector. The withdrawal, however, of 56 Division as reinforcements for Anzio caused this part of the plan to be abandoned. On the right flank of Fifth Army the French Expeditionary Corps had already made a start towards Mount Croce but had been driven off some of the foothills. General Juin was a strong advocate of avoiding any direct assault on Monte Cassino and of thrusting first for the Atina basin. From here the whole of the central sector would be threatened and the 'Senger Barrier' reserve line across the Liri valley would also be outflanked. Conscious of the weakness of 5 Grenadier Division and of the fine quality of the French mountain troops, Kesselring was particularly sensitive to any move by the French Corps but at this moment his reserves were committed against 10 Corps on the lower Garigliano bridgehead and he could only await events. His problem was solved for him. Clark originally supported Juin's plans for a drive on Atina but at the last minute changed his mind and turned the wide outflanking movement into a short right hook towards Mount Belvedere, Abate and Terelle with the object of cutting Route 6 near Piedmonte. This attack, which was to be led by 3 Algerian Division, was linked with orders for 34 Division, supported by two tank battalions, to cross the Rapido north of Cassino and advance on Mount Castellone with a similar object of reaching Piedmonte. Another column from 34 Division would attack Cassino town from the north. Action by the shattered 36 Division was confined to a demonstration opposite S Angelo.

Kesselring was already moving troops from the Adriatic front to Anzio. The Adriatic sector of the Gustav Line was fortified in considerable depth and if necessary he was prepared to give some ground. General Leese's divisions in Eighth Army were seriously depleted and quite incapable of forcing a breakthrough. Any lesser action would fail to bring back German divisions, so Alexander decided to reinforce at Cassino by cutting down Eighth Army to a holding force. 2 New Zealand Corps was formed under

General Freyberg with the New Zealand Division and 4 Indian Division, which had recently arrived from the Middle East. This move was carried out with as much secrecy as possible and the New Zealanders relieved 36 Division on the lower Rapido sector on 6 February. Two days later orders were given for 78 Division to join the New Zealand Corps but owing to heavy snowfalls they did not arrive on the Cassino front until 17 February. Von Senger's XIV Panzer Corps who were responsible for the southern half of the Gustav Line was stretched almost to the limit. In the line from north to south were

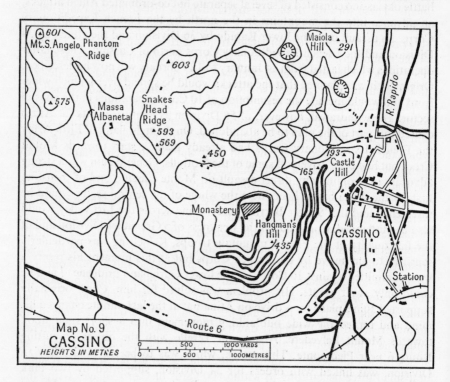

5 Grenadier Division, down as far as Mount Belvedere, 44 Grenadier Division (the Hoch und Deutschmeisters) under General Franck who held the remainder of the mountain positions down to the Monastery and also Cassino town. 15 Panzer Grenadier Division held the Liri valley and 94 Infantry Division, supported by 90 Panzer Grenadiers, stood opposite the British 10 Corps in the coastal sector. At first von Senger had no reserves but, as the battle developed, 90 Panzer Grenadier Division were pulled back from the coastal sector to a central position behind Monte Cassino. Here two parachute battalions were also posted. The re-formed 71 Grenadier Division, newly arrived in Italy, were due to relieve the 15 Panzer Grenadier Division and were deployed a regiment at a time as they arrived. The first regiment was

sent to bolster the Cassino sector itself and the second was used to counter-attack in the Belmonte valley.

The attack by 34 Division was made at what von Senger considered to be the weakest point of his front but the German positions were still protected by formidable obstacles, indeed worse than those met by 36 Division. Many ditches and both banks of the river were extensively mined and a good deal of wire extended for up to 3–400 yards west of the river line. Fields of fire had been cleared and tree stumps three feet high left to hinder tank movements. These forward obstacles stretched from just south of Cairo village right down to Cassino town. To the rear, a series of pill-boxes and fortified stone houses covered the approaches from the river itself right up to the base of the mountains, from where every daylight movement for miles across the plain could be closely watched. Below S Elia the Rapido had been diverted and 'the entire plain, already soggy from heavy rains, was thus turned into a quagmire impassable to armour except by the construction of corduroy roads'.[1] The 34 Division plan was for one regiment to make the initial crossing and seize a feature (Hill 213) about 2,200 yards west of the Rapido, after which the other two regiments would carry out the divergent attacks already mentioned. Preceded by a thirty-minute concentration by the corps artillery, the leading regiment started crossing the river at 2200 hours 24 January. It was not until after midnight on 25 January, however, that the three battalions were established on the west bank and no tanks had crossed. On 26 January two battalions reached Hill 213 but were forced back to the river by nightfall. Attempts to advance on Cassino town failed. Plans were now made to pass a fresh regiment with tanks through the small bridgehead still holding out. This attack was launched early on 27 January, after an hour's artillery preparation and a heavy barrage, but only resulted in four companies of infantry and four tanks crossing the river. The tanks were soon knocked out but some of the infantry reached Hill 213 before dawn on the following day, only to withdraw under the impression that the position could not be held after daylight. An attack further upstream by another battalion, led by a French guide, resulted in a small force penetrating to within 800 yards of Cairo village. Using this new crossing point three battalions with tanks were launched on the original objectives early the following morning, 29 January. Considerable difficulty was experienced in getting the tanks across and nine hours elapsed before a fresh force of twenty-three tanks, advancing down a dry river-bed, joined the infantry attack. By 21 January Hill 213 and Cairo village had been captured and held against counter-attack.

Initially the French were more successful. Advancing at dawn on 25 January, the Algerian Division, ignoring the strongly held Mount Cifalco position, advanced on Le Propaia and then swung west to capture Mounts Belvedere and Abate on 26 January. The Le Propaia positions briefly changed hands and Mount Abate was retaken by the Germans on 27 January but the

Algerians still firmly held on to Mount Belvedere. From Mount Cifalco von Senger was able to look down on the whole 'arc' of this spirited and audacious penetration and was much impressed by the French colonial troops, 'who lived up to their reputation by fighting most stubbornly without regard for losses'.[2] Launched from near S Elia the Algerians were faced first with crossing a broad flooded area and then the wire and minefields protecting the high wall ahead, before storming the peaks of Belvedere and Abate, some 3,000 feet above the foothills. After penetrating the forward positions, the attack into the mountains was made with incredible dash and was skilfully developed to make good use of the re-entrants and spurs leading down to the valley of the Secco, a tributary of the Rapido which fell down from Belmonte. Having crossed the valley, the Algerians climbed up again to work round the dominating position on Belvedere. The loss of Mount Abate, however, put paid to any immediate opportunity for driving south towards Piedmonte. With 2 Moroccan Division largely committed against the 5 Grenadier Division further north, the Algerian Division's penetration was halted. The German artillery observation posts on Mount Cifalco were now bringing down heavy fire on to the supply route through the Belmonte valley and on the approaches to S Elia and the chances of any rapid reinforcement of the French success were receding. General Clark ordered forward a Regimental Combat Team from 36 Division but this was attached to 34 Division and used on the inner flank of the French advance. The plan was to use this extra regiment to gain elbow-room for an attack on Mount Castellone. The transfer was ordered on 26 January but the move was not completed until the night of 30/31 January. The attack made little progress but the Algerians retook Mount Abate on 31 January. Von Senger considered this move by the French to be the most serious threat on his whole front. Part of 71 Infantry Division had already been thrown in to halt the advance south of Belvedere and now Colonel Baade with a regiment from 90 Panzer Grenadier Division at last succeeded in recapturing Mount Abate and blocking the road to Terelle. To the south, the remainder of 71 Infantry Division and elements of 3 Panzer Grenadier Division were stiffening up the defences of Cassino town and the heights above. It was this area of six square miles around the Monastery that now acted as a magnet for the Allies, who were beginning to realize the extent of the German build-up at Anzio and the possibility of stagnation on both of Fifth Army's fronts.

The focus was always the Monastery and Monastery Hill, guarded by seemingly inaccessible features to the north and over a dozen hills and pinnacles, including Hangman's Hill and Castle Hill, that overlooked the town and the eastern approaches. Faced with the urgent need to press their attack, 34 Division reached the crest of Mount Castellone under the cover of fog on 1 February and then turned south towards Colle S Angelo. By 3 February two battalions were advancing along a ridge that became known as the

Snake's Head towards Point 593, only one and a half miles from Route 6. This feature was held by a German parachute battalion that had been rushed over from the Adriatic front. To the north, the Panzer Grenadiers under Colonel Baade effectively held the line Colle S Angelo to the slopes of Mount Castellone. On the inner flank, between 31 January and 3 February, an American regiment with tank support was attempting to break into Cassino town from the north but, coming under heavy fire from Castle Hill and well-fortified blockhouses and buildings, suffered heavy losses and only reached the northern outskirts of the town. For the next three days 34 Division launched a series of desperate efforts to cross the final ridges towards Monastery Hill and enter the town itself. Further elements of 1 Parachute Division had now arrived and the men of this *corps élite* had gradually taken over key positions around the Monastery.

With the arrival of the New Zealand Corps, Clark now switched the remainder of 36 Division to take over in the Castellone sector and relieve the whole of 34 Division for a final effort to take the Monastery Hill. This attack was to be preceded by the capture of Albaneta Farm, near Point 593, on the night of 7 February. This would be followed by the assault on Monastery Hill, co-ordinated with a further concerted effort to penetrate into the town the following day. A German counter-attack from Point 593 anticipated the opening move and, to take advantage of darkness, the main attack against Monastery Hill was advanced by two hours, to 0400 hours 8 February. For three days 34 Division struggled to reach the final crests, only to be beaten back by cross fire from numerous machine-guns covering every ridge and accurate mortar fire that sealed every gully. Units of 36 Division were now hurried into the battle but German counter-attacks effectively stopped even local advances, with the exception of a very limited penetration near Castle Hill. On 11 February General Keyes ordered one last effort by the exhausted troops of II Corps. The objectives for both divisions were the same, Albaneta Farm and the Monastery. In spite of the failures of the last few days, Alexander agreed to this final effort. If it succeeded the New Zealand Corps could be launched into the Liri valley and the original plans for linking up with VI Corps might come off. Part of 4 Indian Division stood by to advance via Terelle through the mountains to exploit towards Piedmonte, or, if II Corps' attack failed, they were ordered to continue the drive south against Monastery Hill. The remainder of the New Zealand Corps prepared to take up the pursuit straight up the Liri valley. The attack on Albaneta Farm was repulsed with serious losses. Colonel Starr records that after beating off two counter-attacks by the Panzer Grenadiers two of the American battalions involved in the action could only muster a combined total of twenty-two officers and one hundred and sixty men. Early on 12 February Colonel Baade launched a heavy counter-attack, supported by every gun within range, against the Castellone area. A critical situation lasted until the late afternoon before the

Panzer Grenadiers were finally beaten off. The attack against Monastery Hill never properly got under way. A violent snow-storm, followed by torrential rain, on 11 February reduced visibility to a few yards and the units of II Corps were now utterly exhausted. The infantry companies were so seriously under strength that drivers and clerks were hastily organized into 'ad hoc' units to act as reserves. Major-General Kippenberger, recently promoted to command the New Zealand Division, later wrote, 'the Americans had battled since January with a stubbornness and gallantry beyond all praise, but they were fought out. Some of the eighteen battalions in the line had lost 80 per cent of their effectives and they were utterly exhausted. When relieved fifty men had to be carried out on stretchers. It was our turn.'[3] The German divisions had similarly suffered considerable losses. Even at the start of the battle many infantry battalions had been down to a hundred men led by their battalion commanders 'in the forward front line as if they were mixed assault companies and the divisions engaged in the main battle area were losing fighting strength at a daily rate of one or two battalions'. Faced with a desperate shortage of infantry, the Germans resorted to bringing in supply and signal units and even artillery units from the rear areas. These, however, were expediencies of desperation and generally unsatisfactory. Von Senger remarks 'a modern division is too complicated to undergo organizational changes on the battle-field (and units) unaccustomed to infantry fighting were usually "eaten up" much sooner than the regular infantry'.[4]

This indeed was a critical moment for both sides. Von Mackensen was about to launch his 'all out' offensive at Anzio and for the moment no further reinforcements could be sent to the Cassino front. General Wilson was still confident that the vital breakthrough could be achieved at Cassino. This must now be done by the New Zealand Corps and plans were immediately made for a resumption of the offensive. The operations which followed and which extended over the next weeks are often called the Second Battle of Cassino. In outline the directive given to Freyberg was for 4 Indian Division to attack through the salient captured by 34 Division (north-west of the Monastery), while the New Zealand Division seized a bridgehead over the Rapido south of the town. The two points of this pincer movement would join and a mobile force would be launched up Route 6. Following roughly the pattern of previous attempts, this particular battle has been the subject of controversy every since, owing to the decision to bomb the monastery itself as a prerequisite to the infantry attack. Only those who fought under its shadow or in the valley below the awesome bastion of Monte Cassino can truly know how the Monastery itself dominated the minds and lives of the men who fought on the road to Rome. As Alexander reported, 'this famous building had hitherto been deliberately spared to our great disadvantage but it was an integral part of the German defensive system mainly from the superb observation it afforded'.[5] The bombing of the Monastery was regarded by

Major-General Tuker, who commanded 4 Indian Division, as a matter of military necessity. A commander's first duty is always to his troops and Freyberg, who was convinced that the building was being used by the Germans, supported Tuker's request. General Clark discussed the proposal with Keyes and several of the regimental commanders who had been involved in the earlier attacks and was unconvinced. It was left to Alexander to make the decision. Eighteen years afterwards his opinion that the bombing was a military necessity was unaltered. He wrote, 'it was necessary more for the effect it would have on the morale of the attackers than for purely material reasons . . . when soldiers are fighting for a just cause and are prepared to suffer death and mutilation in the process, bricks and mortar, no matter how venerable cannot be allowed to weigh against human lives . . . in the concept of the Cassino battle, how could a structure which dominated the fighting field be allowed to stand?'[6] A warning was sent so that the Abbot with the remaining monks and a number of refugees could be evacuated. From a purely military point of view the consequences of the bombing of the Monastery were bitterly disappointing. In the piled rubble of the historic building, previously 'neutralized' on Kesselring's orders, the Germans now had a 'mighty commanding strongpoint which paid for itself in all the subsequent fighting'.[7]

The ground attacks were to be launched as soon as possible, as news from Anzio was worsening. The immediate task was to relieve 34 Division in their positions north-west of the Monastery and it was here the first delays were encountered. A brigade group of the Indian Division was ordered forward during the night 10/11 February. The experiences of the leading battalion (1 Royal Sussex) illustrates some of the reasons. Using borrowed American four-wheel-drive vehicles, as their own transport was useless in the deep mud and rutted tracks, the battalion reached S Michele on the plain north of Mount Trocchio. On the way up two trucks with all their reserve mortar ammunition and grenades crashed over an embankment and were lost. The next day was spent in trying to assemble a mule train. Only a third of the required number of animals were available. That night the battalion marched across the sodden fields to cross the river and climb to the slopes of Mount Castellone. Here they were shelled continuously for five hours. In the afternoon the battalion was ordered to attack Mount Belvedere. Fortunately the fact that the French were firmly ensconced there was realized in time. That night the battalion was to take over from the Americans on Snake's Head Ridge. The situation maps showed their forward positions, which was also the jumping off point for the forthcoming attack, as Point 593. 'On that ridge, which they were soon to know so well, were four American Battalions belonging to three different brigades and two different divisions, but each battalion was reduced to only a hundred strong and was completely exhausted when relieved by the Royal Sussex. The battalion made a two-hour climb up a narrow mountain track to carry out the relief. They found that the Americans were not holding Point 593, as originally supposed, but were just below it – which made all the difference.'[8] At dawn the battalion found itself holding 400 yards of a narrow ridge overlooked from Mount Cairo to their rear and from the Monastery Hill 1,000 yards to the east. The German positions on Point 593 were only seventy to eighty yards away. In the hard rocky ground only shallow sangars could be built and here the men huddled with only a solitary blanket against the bitter cold and waited for the orders for the attack, which was now postponed until 16 February. The difficulties of supply were acute. From S Michele mule trains were faced with a circuitous seven-mile march and scramble up narrow paths which took five hours. To reach the forward positions porters alone could climb the last few hundred yards up the narrow paths. Every night the route was shelled steadily and many mules and men were lost. The Snake's Head Ridge was in the form of a dog leg, with the short end leading to within 400 yards of the Monastery. Point 593, at the elbow, effectively covered any advance from the narrow assembly area, alongside the Royal Sussex, now occupied by 16 Punjabis and 2 Gurkhas of 7 Indian Brigade. To take the direct route to Monastery Hill 'would entail crossing a chaos of slopes, gullies, ravines, boulders, gorse thickets and shattered walls where shells had churned up the terracing. On the whole the approach along Snake's Head seemed the lesser of the two evils, but Point 593 would have to be taken.'[9]

The divisional plan was for 7 Brigade to attack on this axis, followed by a second brigade which would either reinforce the attack or pass through to take the Monastery. The whole of the third brigade would have to be employed as porters to maintain the other two in action. The problem seemed not so much how to maintain the momentum of the attack as how to achieve the initial impetus. With the leading battalion virtually pinned to the ground and the narrow line of approach overlooked from three directions there could be no proper deployment and certainly no chance of turning towards Monastery Hill until Point 593 had been captured. Shortly after 0930 hours 15 February the familiar sound of friendly bombers flying high was heard but a few minutes afterwards bombs began to fall all around the area. The bombing came as a complete surprise to the forward brigade as they had been told it had been planned for the following day. To the Royal Sussex it meant only one thing, the attack on Point 593 would certainly be ordered within a matter of hours. The bombing attack had originally been planned for 13 February but had been delayed owing to bad weather. Now the first groups of Fortresses were over the target. Some squadrons had flown all the way from the United Kingdom to join in. Before the day was out 254 heavy and medium bombers had dropped 576 tons of high explosive on to the Monastery and Monte Cassino. Between the raids heavy artillery poured shells on to the entire area. The Monastery suffered considerable damage but, built into the solid rock, much of the massive walls still stood, grim witness to the faith and skill of past generations of men who, over seventeen centuries, had three times before seen the abbey destroyed. One German comment is, 'Colonel Schulz's paratroopers were hanging by their eyebrows to literally the last slopes before the Via Casilina. Had the Allies dropped their bombs on these positions instead of on the Monastery, they could have by-passed the Monastery without a qualm, particularly as it was completely dominated by the height to the north-west of it.'[10] So it remained to 4 Indian Division to assault this 'dominating height' that had been marked on the Fifth Army maps as their own forward positions. Soon orders came through to the Royal Sussex to attack Point 593 that night. The grenades and mortar shells lost five days before had not been replaced. Patrolling had been impossible and the exact German positions could only be guessed at. The task was given to the company already in position. The men moved very slowly with the utmost care. Any stumble or stone dislodged on the steeply rising ground would betray the advance, which for fifty yards seemed to be undetected. But the German paratroopers were alert and at twenty-yards' range opened fire. The defenders seemed to have unlimited supplies of grenades and at this close range checked every attempt to work round their positions. The last few yards up the steep and rocky slopes were never crossed. With the few grenades collected from the whole battalion used up and half the company killed or wounded, the attack was called off. To have remained in the open in daylight would have meant the sacrifice of the remainder of the company. The Commanding Officer of the Royal Sussex was then ordered to put in a battalion attack the following night 16/17 February. The timing of the attack was based on the expected arrival of a mule train with the urgently needed grenades. When the porters eventually arrived nearly an hour late, it was found that half the grenades requested had been lost when a number of mules were killed in the shelling coming up the supply route. The only artillery support possible at such close quarters was neutralizing fire on two features 800 yards to the flank. Several shells, however, unfortunately fell on the leading companies as they crossed the start line causing a good deal of confusion. A diversionary attack to the right of the Snake's Head Ridge 'at once ran into trouble. Just in time they stopped on the edge of a forty-foot precipice not indicated on the map. There was no way round by the right, so they edged leftwards, and then found themselves faced with a crevice fifteen feet deep and twenty feet across.'[11] From the far side of this formidable obstacle accurate spandau fire and grenades now pinned the company to the ground. The main attack on the left of the ridge drove into the German positions after several machine-gun posts had been silenced by individual acts of gallantry. In the confused fighting several parties gained the main feature and even penetrated beyond it. In the darkness and confusion one party fell down a precipice and another was overpowered in a grenade battle with German reserves hurrying forward. The battle had now lasted some two hours and the reserve company was committed. In the centre, with mounting casualties and few grenades left and ammunition running out, the situation was critical. The Germans fought with the utmost determination and seemingly had an inexhaustible reserve of grenades. One fresh company of the Royal Sussex remained. This had originally been detailed for the immediate consolidation of Point 593 on its capture, so as to hold the feature against counter-attacks. This company 'was sent in as a last resort, but it came up against the deep crevice that had halted the one on the right, and at the same time it was caught in a murderous cross fire'.[12] The remnants of the four companies were eventually withdrawn. In two nights' fighting twelve out of fifteen officers and 162 out of 313 men had been lost and the 'preliminary objective' of Point 593 remained firmly in German hands. The two-fold problem of supplying more than about a brigade and the serious lack of suitable jumping-off positions in this mountainous forward area now determined the pattern for an attack on the following night (18/19 February), using the whole resources of the New Zealand Corps. A fresh battalion, with the Royal Sussex under command, was now ordered to take Point 593. Two hours after the attack two battalions of Gurkhas would pass through some 400 yards to the left and storm the Monastery. At the same time 2 New Zealand Division would cross the lower Rapido in the area of the railway station and drive in to the Liri valley, while a further Indian brigade attacked north of Cassino town to pin down the defences.

The assault on Point 593 met with the same result as the previous attacks. During nearly five hours of bitter and confused fighting small groups of the Rajputana Rifles and the Royal Sussex reached the heart of the defences and survived several counter-attacks. By dawn, however, the Germans had dealt with these pockets and still held the vital half-acre of shaggy crest and the remnants of the two battalions found themselves pinned to the ground, only yards short of their objectives. On the left, one of the Gurkha battalions had struck downhill towards a feature only 300 yards short of the Monastery but almost immediately came under heavy cross and converging fire which sealed their only approach to the objective. A little to the left again the second Gurkha battalion moved towards a fold in the ground below the north wall of the Monastery. Beyond this 'false crest' aerial photographs had shown a belt of scrub which seemed unlikely to prove a serious obstacle to men accustomed to mountain warfare. The scrub was in fact a thorn thicket that had been heavily sown with anti-personnel mines and numerous booby-traps fitted to trip wires. Beyond the belt of scrub the Germans lay in wait with concealed machine-gun and bombing posts close up to the hidden minefield. Met by a shower of grenades the leading platoon of the Gurkhas immediately charged into the scrub and were blown up almost to a man. The casualties were disastrous. In fifteen minutes twelve officers and 138 men were lost in fruitless attempts to reach the defenders. The survivors fought on and the reserve companies were committed in an abortive attempt to outflank the German positions, but by dawn both Gurkha battalions were held pinned, only a little ahead of their original start lines. The massive shell of the Monastery towered above. Every movement brought mortar and machine-gun fire and there was little chance at the moment of renewing any attacks from this direction. Major-General Kippenberger similarly had difficulty in deploying the New Zealand Division in any strength. The only quick means of getting tank and supporting armour across the Rapido near to Cassino was to make use of the railway causeway. No attack on a broad front could be attempted owing to the floods and the causeway was mined and breached in several places. The Maori Battalion was given the task of seizing the railway station which was on the far side of the river, and holding it while the causeway was repaired. Once the tanks were over, a reinforced brigade would cross and drive south to open up the valley route. Every available gun, together with the machine-guns and mortars of the whole division, would keep the Cassino defences under fire. The attack went in on the night 17/18 February and reached the railway station but the Maoris found themselves holding a very limited area. In spite of superhuman efforts the engineers still had one gap in the causeway to fill when daylight exposed the whole operation to the full fury of the massed *nebelwerfers* and guns on Monastery Hill. Firing smoke the Allied gunners screened the causeway and the station for nearly ten hours. The three New Zealand Field Batteries fired the remarkable total of nearly 17,000 rounds of smoke and 7,000 HE shells. Guns became too hot to touch. A three-ton lorryful of ammunition was being fired off by a battery in eight minutes. Transport columns were sent back as far as Teano to bring up more and more ammunition as the day wore on. By mid-afternoon a counter-attack by 15 Panzer Grenadiers, led by tanks and approaching under cover of the smoke, retook the station and drove the New Zealanders back from the causeway and across the river. The battle had ended with a wedge driven into the German positions north of the town but was a decided victory for the defence.

With only one fresh division (78 Division) in hand, General Alexander now decided to use completely new tactics. At the suggestion of General Cannon, commanding the Tactical Air Forces, it was decided to see what the air arm could do to pave the way for the resumption of the offensive. It was also obvious that the twenty-one Allied Divisions would need reinforcing if any progress was to be made against the German build-up in Italy, that now totalled twenty-four divisions, of which nineteen were engaged south of Rome. Major Allied reinforcements could not be assembled and ready for an offensive before mid-April and meanwhile the situation at Anzio was critical and the attacks on the Gustav Line must continue. The stalemate in Italy had become a matter of growing concern both in London and Washington, where General Arnold argued that the 4,000 Allied aircraft in the Mediterranean had made little positive contribution to the ground battle. Pursuing this view a stage further, Arnold pointed out that, if properly applied, this amount of air power would mean that some 2,900 aircraft could take part in the ground offensive for limited periods. In terms of sorties and bomb loads this meant 5,600 sorties and 6,200 tons of bombs a day. His argument was that the air arm could blast a way through the German defences but the army must be ready to exploit the situation and regain the initiative on the ground. The impressive figures quoted above of course did not take into account the grave shortage of shipping in the Mediterranean and the tremendous supply problems of bombing offensives on this scale. On both sides of the Cassino front the weary troops braced themselves for the inevitable resumption of Allied attempts to break through towards the Anzio bridgehead, which was now effectively sealed off by von Mackensen's Fourteenth Army. There was little chance of the attackers being able to take 'corresponding offensive action' in conjunction with the massive air attacks now suggested to General Wilson by the Joint Chiefs of Staff. As we have seen, Alexander was already thinking on the same lines and proposing to employ a large bomber force against Cassino town. These plans were now pressed forward. General Eaker, however, was not very hopeful of the result. Nothing had been achieved through the bombing of the Monastery, the weather was now even worse and so were the floods in the valley which would seriously affect the Army's mobility. He felt, moreover, that the ground forces were in poor shape to take full advantage of any mass air attack.

During February the US 88 Infantry Division had landed in Italy and a battalion was sent forward to take over on Mount Castellone. Apart from this additional unit the Allied front was now held by the French Expeditionary Corps, the New Zealand Corps and 10 Corps. II Corps which was much in need of rest and reinforcement was brought into reserve. By now all three regiments of the German 1 Parachute Division were concentrated in the Cassino area and in the hills to the north and west. The takeover from 90 Panzer Grenadier Division was carried out gradually and by 26 February General Heidrich was in command as far as the southern slopes of Mount Cairo. Two parachute battalions occupied the town itself, with the exception of the small area in the northern suburbs which had been captured by 34 Division. General Freyberg's plan was linked with a major effort by the Allied air forces, supplemented by the fire from every available gun, to smash Cassino town and neutralize the German positions covering it. Following this bombardment 6 New Zealand Infantry Brigade with an armoured regiment would take the town and Castle Hill from the north, covered by 4 Indian Division holding the mountain positions. 5 New Zealand Brigade would cross the lower Rapido and pinch off the town from the south with an attack through the railway station. At this point 4 Indian Division would take over the Castle Hill area and pass on to seize Monastery Hill and cut Route 6. In essence the plan was to roll up the German positions one by one from the north, while 78 Division and the American Armoured Divisional Group stood by to open up the Liri valley by a thrust astride S Angelo. The plan was based on two assumptions, firstly that the air bombing would enable the town to be taken with few losses, and secondly that the massed artillery would saturate the defences on the remainder of the Cassino battlefield. The main difficulties envisaged again stemmed from the approaches being completely overlooked from Monastery Hill and the fact that the main line of attack from the north would be enfiladed by the German positions in strong bunkers built into the forward slopes of the hills overlooking the town. It was hoped that the massed guns would neutralize these defences, while the smoke from the bombing should cover the initial attack. Regarding the weather factor, three dry days were required before tanks could be used on the floor of the valley and the air force needed good visibility. In fact the date and hour of the attack was to be decided solely on these two counts. By 21 February the orders had gone out and three days later the troops stood ready. At this point the weather broke and for three weeks the infantry, huddled in exposed positions, suffered the full force of winter gales, snow and freezing rain. From day to day the operation was postponed and consequently the units were held in their assembly positions without relief or respite from shell and mortar fire. In the mountains the supply problem was acute. The mountain tracks became coated with ice and men and mules often disappeared into precipitous gullies without trace. Struggling porters lost touch in the darkness, only to be caught in the open in daylight. After about a fortnight of these appalling conditions the weather began to improve somewhat and on 14 March the long-delayed signal went out that the air attack would take place the next day.

Before dawn the New Zealanders were withdrawn 1,000 yards back from the town and at 0830 hours the aerial bombardment started. For three and a half hours 275 heavy and 200 medium bombers pounded Cassino with over 1,000 tons of bombs. The target area was 1,400 by 400 yards and although the mediums claimed 90 per cent accuracy, only about 500 tons of bombs overall struck the town, as the heavy bombers were far less accurate. During the afternoon the weather again began to deteriorate and further attacks by heavy and medium bombers were cancelled. Only the light and fighter-bombers were able to get in below the overcast and continue the assault on the south side of the town, the railway station and the slopes of Monastery Hill. The bombing attacks destroyed the town. Cassino was now a mass of rubble, with only the shells of buildings standing. The attack had been opened by the medium bombers and by the time the Fortress squadrons approached a heavy pall of smoke and dust increased their aiming difficulties. Many bombs in this latter stage of the attack were seriously off target, some falling on the forward Allied gun positions and as far back as Corps Headquarters, while others caused a number of large craters on the outskirts of the town.

In the town itself the scene was one of utter desolation. The streets were filled with rubble and shattered masonry, interspersed with huge craters as much as fifty feet across. In all directions collapsed buildings, with jagged walls alone marking their sites, were evidence of the tremendous blast effect of the 1,000-lb. bombs. At noon, as the last bombers wheeled away, the gunners took over. Directly supporting the two divisional attacks of the New Zealand Corps were 420 guns, about half of which were 25 pounders or American 105s, and the remainder of heavier calibre. Estimates of the total number of Fifth Army guns employed on the whole front are 610 and 890, this latter figure probably includes anti-aircraft and anti-tank guns not directly concerned in the huge programme of supporting fire. The New Zealand Corps gun areas have been described as suddenly becoming 'a vast and highly active volcanic region'[13] as the artillery support programme started. Targets on Monte Cassino were soon lost from view as smoke and dust rose up from the town, where a creeping barrage on an 800-yard front traversed the town from north to south. Commencing with fifteen minutes on the first line the barrage lifted 100 yards every ten minutes. The barrage was timed from 1200 to 1410 hours but in fact was extended to 1530 hours, as it was obvious the infantry could not keep up. The southern edge of the town was again shelled at 1730 hours for thirty minutes. Meanwhile, concentrations, harassing fire and smoke were being put down on Monte Cassino and every other conceivable trouble spot. In eight hours nearly 190,000 shells poured down on to Monte Cassino, the town and the intervening hill features.

Promptly at 1200 hours the leading New Zealand battalion, supported by tanks, moved up behind the barrage into the town, detaching a company to assault Castle Hill. Slowly the three companies made their way over the rubble and at first made good progress. One column of tanks was halted at a huge crater, too wide to span with their bridging tank. The other tank column only reached the outskirts of the town after superhuman efforts, with the crews working with pick and shovel and often under heavy fire. As the afternoon wore on resistance in the town slowly halted the advance. Two companies of the German parachutists had suffered heavy losses in the bombing but it was now evident that the majority of the remainder of the defenders were very much alive. Emerging from concreted cellars and manning reinforced pill-boxes, machine-gunners and snipers were now met at every turn. Months of preparation of the defences now bore fruit. Strongpoints in specially shored-up buildings were linked through cellars and tunnels with alternative positions, often on the other side of the street. Small pockets of resistance now formed in the rear of the New Zealanders. Fighting was at such close quarters that often the Germans held one floor of a building, while the New Zealanders occupied another. By about 1700 hours Castle Hill had been captured but the attack through the town was held near to Route 6 in the centre of the town. A company of the follow-up battalion was now sent in but the impetus of the New Zealand attack had been lost. Fighting with great tenacity the paratroopers held out in strongpoints and amongst the shattered buildings. Each position had to be taken with the bomb or the bayonet. Still no tanks could be got across the craters or through the rubble and artillery support was impossible, as only a few yards separated each side in the fight for a mound of rubble, a corner of a demolished building or a cellar held by men who fought back for every yard of ground. At last at dusk the remainder of the follow-up battalion moved forward. Their objective was the railway station right through the town. By 2100 hours, after it had taken them three hours to cross the last 650 yards in pitch darkness, they reached Route 6 in the centre of the town. The whole of their advance had been made in torrential rain. The craters began to fill with water. The engineers continued with their now almost hopeless task of making a passage for the tanks but the break in the weather was the last straw and no tanks entered the town that night. Too late now a third battalion was brought up. In the continuous downpour the infantry wireless sets just 'packed up' and now there could be no cohesion to the infantry attack.

Behind the New Zealanders came 5 Indian Brigade, forcing their way in the darkness down the single road which was jammed with troops and tanks. By midnight a battalion of the Essex Regiment had taken over on the outskirts of the town and sent a company to relieve the New Zealanders on Castle Hill. By 0300 hours 16 March a further company seized the lower hairpin bend of the road leading up to the Monastery, some 300 yards above the Castle. Behind the Essex came the Rajputana Rifles. Heavily shelled as they reached the town, only a single company climbed up to attack the second hairpin bend and was driven back to the Castle, where they were joined by a second company of the same battalion. The 9 Gurkhas was already advancing to attack Hangman's Hill with two companies in the lead. One of these companies was ambushed and unable to reorganize before dawn and the other company disappeared into the darkness. The remainder of the battalion now formed a perimeter in the rear of Castle Hill. Dawn on 16 March brought bitter fighting. Through gullies and ravines German reinforcements were fed forward to the area round Castle Hill and, by way of Route 6 round the base of Monastery Hill, into the town itself. The approaches into the north of the town were now under heavy mortar and shell fire and in the town itself the hand-to-hand struggle continued. During the afternoon the New Zealand gunners were just about to shell Hangman's Hill when figures were seen just below the crest and a faint wireless signal confirmed the 'electrifying' news that the company of Gurkhas, that had been believed lost, were in possession. That evening the remainder of the Gurkha battalion debouched from Castle Hill to consolidate the vital position on Hangman's Hill, while the Rajputanas made for a covering position further north near the second hairpin bend. Fighting their way forward it took the Gurkhas eight hours to reach their isolated company. Although the Rajputana Rifles were thrown back by a dawn counter-attack the Gurkhas held their ground. By the evening of 17 March it was vitally necessary to get supplies through to the Gurkhas but the approaches to Castle Hill itself were now under fire from German paratroopers who had infiltrated into the northern outskirts of the town. Porters carrying supplies forward suffered heavy casualties in reaching the Castle and in the end two companies of the Rajputanas had to fight their way through to Hangman's Hill carrying as many of the loads as they could. The Rajputanas were now unable to return from Hangman's Hill before dawn. An attempt to drop supplies by air the following day failed.

During this fighting Allied tanks advanced up Route 6 to reach the outskirts of Cassino and the New Zealand infantry in the town had advanced in places beyond Route 6. An infantry battalion with tanks was now launched south from the edge of the town to capture the railway station on 17 March. But still one-third of the town was firmly held by the German paratroopers and fierce fighting took place throughout 18 March, principally in an attempt to dislodge positions below Castle Hill. 4 Indian Division now sent forward a fresh battalion to take over the Castle, while the Essex Regiment moved up to make a co-ordinated attack with the Gurkhas from Hangman's Hill. From Monastery Hill fire continued to pour down on every Allied movement in Cassino and its approaches. Orders were now given that during the night 18/19 March supplies would be carried forward to the Gurkhas and the relief on Castle Hill would be effected by 0400 hours 19 March. The Essex Regiment would then move forward and the attack would be made at dawn. The tortuous uphill route to the Castle, however, was dominated by the Germans and under fire from several directions and it was midnight before any of the relief force reached the Castle. Several hours now passed while the involved relief took place, as positions at the lower hairpin bend had also to be taken over. Consequently the Essex Regiment was very late starting on the long trek to Hangman's Hill. Shortly before dawn, when the garrison in the Castle only numbered 150 men, the German guns, mortars and machine-guns suddenly opened up on the Castle itself and the surrounding hillside. A battalion of paratroopers overwhelmed the hairpin bend positions and swept on to the Castle. With reckless gallantry the paratroopers endeavoured to climb the walls and grenades showered into the courtyard. The attack was beaten back after hand-to-hand fighting and heavy losses on both sides. Three further attacks were beaten off. In this action 1,500 mortar bombs had been fired by the defenders and over 8,000 rounds of machine-gun ammunition. The Allied guns and every mortar, machine-gun and tank within range joined in with the defensive fire to halt the German paratroopers again and again. Now only three officers and sixty men remained to defend the Castle. About noon some Gurkha reinforcements reached the Castle but German paratroopers were infiltrating from the edge of Cassino town right up to its walls.

'During the afternoon a party of eight Germans led by an officer managed to insert a demolition charge under the buttress of the northern battlements. The explosion breached the walls, burying two officers and twenty men of A Company of the Essex. As the Germans leapt through the gap they were riddled. One wounded paratrooper crept in to surrender. He stated that out of 200 men launched in the dawn assault only forty remained on their feet.'[14] Sending a stretcher-bearer under the white flag, the Germans now requested a thirty-minute truce to allow them to pick up their wounded and this was arranged. During the truce a number of the Essex Regiment were dug out from under the collapsed wall by the defenders in the Castle. One further attack was beaten off by the Allied gunners. The delay in the reliefs the previous night and this series of German counter-attacks, however, had put paid to the attempt on the Monastery. The companies of the Essex Regiment had in fact been so late in starting for Hangman's Hill that they were only halfway across by day-break. Some men turned back to help defend the Castle but few reached its walls. The remainder went on up the bare slopes in full view of the enemy. Only seventy-five men reached the Gurkha positions. The attack on the Monastery had already been put off until 1400 hours but there were now too few men to make the attempt and the Essex were ordered back to the Castle that night. Few succeeded in returning. Some turned back to Hangman's Hill, the German outposts took the others.

In spite of these reverses the mobile diversionary force, consisting of an Indian reconnaissance squadron and a mixed force of forty Sherman and light tanks, set out early on 19 March, using a tank track that had been constructed with great skill by the engineers. Their task was to penetrate through the mountains right round to the rear of the Monastery Hill position. It was hoped that if this diversionary force reached a position from which effective fire could be brought on the Monastery the attack from Hangman's Hill would reach the crest. Encircling Point 593 and breaking through a thinly held reserve position the tanks passed into a narrow defile with steep sides that led straight towards the Monastery walls. This bold move came as a complete surprise to the Germans and thoroughly upset the local commander who anticipated a co-ordinated infantry attack. But there were no infantry with the tanks and not enough to press the attack from Hangman's Hill and so the opportunity was lost. The column now met a hastily laid minefield and the way was blocked in the narrow defile by a brewed-up vehicle. The heavy tanks could not negotiate the steep slopes but the light tanks pressed forward firing on Albaneta Farm. The defile was now covered by mortar and machine-gun fire. More parties of German infantry were closing in on the tanks and attacking them with mines and grenades. After twelve tanks had been lost the force was ordered to withdraw under cover of darkness. The diversion had been carried out with gallantry and ingenuity but the lack of supporting infantry gave no flexibility to the plan. 19 March proved to be the decisive day of the battle. The Germans still held Monastery Hill and parts of the town and had only just failed to cut the narrow 'bottleneck' to the Castle. The Gurkhas still held on to their positions on Hangman's Hill but were now virtually isolated. From almost the first day of the battle the German artillery, mortars and machine-guns had been co-ordinated to a remarkable degree. This concentrated and accurate fire that was brought down on every Allied advance had slowed down and finally halted the attack towards the Monastery. In addition, General Heidrich had been steadily reinforcing the parachute battalion in the town and was now infiltrating groups of paratroopers down from the hill positions, to try to link up with the detachments still holding parts of the northern edge of the town. His obvious intention was to cut off Castle Hill completely. In reply General Freyberg sent forward a fresh battalion from 78 Division to take over the Castle. The following night a two-battalion attack to regain the lower hairpin bend was halted by fresh minefields and concentrated fire. Encouraged by this success, the Germans now launched a further strong attack downhill against the Castle early on 21 March but they were beaten back with the help of the Corps artillery. Attempts were now made by the Indian divisional engineers to lay minefields and wire in a corridor up to the Castle. This move brought an immediate reaction and General Heidrich launched his last reserves at the Castle at dawn on 22 March. The Allied gunners were again ready and the attack 'disintegrated with heavy loss'. The troops on both sides were now utterly exhausted and on 22 March, with no possibility of a breakthrough, the New Zealand Corps offensive was called off. The following night the Gurkhas were withdrawn from Hangman's Hill and 4 Indian Division was relieved by 78 Division. Two days later 13 Corps took over command of the Cassino sector and the New Zealand Corps was dissolved. So ended the first battle of Cassino which had lasted for two months. From 16 January to 31 March, Fifth Army's casualties on this front were 52,150. Over 30,000 of these casualties were incurred in the fighting on the Gustav Line. In the short time they were in action at Cassino the New Zealanders suffered no less than 1,655 casualties and in the last phase of the battle the New Zealand Corps lost 2,106 men. During this phase of the battle the staggering total of nearly 590,000 shells were fired by the Allied gunners in eleven days. After the bombing of Cassino town the Allied medium and heavy bombers turned once again to attacking the enemy communications well to the north. The principal targets for the fighters and fighter-bombers were the German gun positions on the heights above the battlefield against which 500 sorties were made. 154 sorties by A36s were flown in four days to air-drop supplies on Hangman's Hill but only a few parachutes fell near enough for their loads to be recovered by the Gurkhas. Weak Luftwaffe forces made brave efforts to support the defenders of Cassino, about 150 sorties being flown on both 19 and 24 March, but the attacks accomplished little and the Germans lost forty-two planes against ten Allied fighters lost.

The result of
Allied air
attacks on a
railway line
near Florence,
July 1944.

Gurkhas before
an attack near
Coriano, Sep-
tember 1944.

German position in the Gothic Line, showing extent of field of fire.

Near Isola with the Polish Corps, a 75mm. 'pack' Howitzer and mule transport, February 1945.

From the start of the battle the Allies were facing political pressure to capture Rome and later faced the urgent need to relieve the Anzio bridgehead. The winter weather conditions seriously limited the effectiveness of the Allied air forces and virtually put a stop to tank movement. The fighting on the Winter Line had given the Germans sufficient time to fortify the Gustav Line and reap full benefit from the natural strength of the Cassino positions. When Fifth Army finally drew up to the Gustav Line it had to be attacked immediately as SHINGLE was about to be launched. The first phase of the battle, from the Allied point of view, suffered from a lack of reserves to exploit the success by 10 Corps. The subsequent attacks in the central sector were not only rigidly held to the original time-table but lacked the necessary strength and were widely dispersed. When 10 Corps' attack slowed down the Germans were able to switch their meagre reserves and defeat the other attacks in detail. Having only poor-quality mountain troops themselves, the Germans were very impressed by the excellent showing of the French Expeditionary Corps and feared a breakthrough into the Atina basin and a drive via Terelle towards either Roccasecca or Piedmonte. As we have seen Clark turned the thrust by the French Expeditionary Corps, which started off so well towards Atina, into a short right hook. In neither case, however, was there sufficient concentration of forces or any reserves to punch a hole in the German positions. From this stage onwards the Allied command seemed drawn to Monte Cassino as if by a magnet. The attack on Point 593, following the bombing of the Monastery, was so similar to the earlier attempts that there could be no surprise and owing to the difficulties of the ground it could not be made in sufficient strength to offset this grave disadvantage. Down on the plain the floods and winter conditions deprived Fifth Army of the use of their strong tank forces to help the infantry consolidate a bridgehead across the Rapido. Furthermore, the concentration of German artillery and *nebelwerfers* around Monte Cassino largely prevented bridge-building operations. It has been argued that the bombing of the Monastery should have been followed up immediately by an infantry attack. It was, however, the German positions on Point 593 and the nearby features that held the attack by 4 Indian Division from the north and these positions were sufficiently far from the Monastery to avoid destruction. The destruction of the Monastery indeed served only to present the men of 1 Parachute Division with ready-made shelters and many positions for weapons of all calibres, which later played a major role in stopping the attacks by 2 New Zealand Corps on Cassino town and Hangman's Hill. The attacks by the New Zealand Corps in the last phase of the battle at least had an original plan, being launched on a different axis and to a different overall design than previous attacks. But there were too many 'ifs'. The weight of bombs on Cassino was intended to destroy the town and in fact practically all the anti-tank guns and infantry support weapons were buried by the bombing. A great number of the garrison, however, dug themselves out from deep cellars and tunnels and emerged in time to deny the passage of the relatively weak infantry attack that followed the bombing. The fact that the garrison had not been overwhelmed by the air attack was not appreciated soon enough. As it was, insufficient reinforcements were sent in and they were sent in too late. Again the Allies were prevented from using their tanks, this time by the enormous bomb craters, which quickly filled with water when the torrential rain started, and by the piled rubble which filled every street through the town. This latter result of the bombing should have been foreseen from the experience of the fighting in Sicily. Both the bombing and the artillery concentrations on Cassino were overdone and made the task of the New Zealand Division immensely more difficult. If the town had fallen earlier the attack on the Castle and Hangman's Hill would have stood more chance of success. If the German paratroopers had not infiltrated back into the northern edge of the town the supply route up to the hill positions would have been more secure. Finally it is fair to say that if any other division of the German Army had been holding Monte Cassino and the town the battle might well have gone the other way. The German 1 Parachute Division may well be proud of their achievements at Cassino.

The Allied winter campaign achieved one very important result. Twenty-three German divisions, including some of their best troops, had been held down in what had now become a secondary theatre by an offensive mounted without any superiority of numbers and with both the terrain and the weather conditions favouring the defence. Long before the first battle of Cassino was ending Alexander was planning his spring offensive. Dry weather and clear skies should favour the Allies and for the breakthrough into the Liri valley he laid his plans carefully. This time he aimed to achieve the maximum concentration, particularly in infantry, at the point of attack. The plan involved a considerable regrouping and was decided at a conference at Caserta on 28 February. Regrouping started as soon as the Cassino battle was called off and on 2 April Alexander explained his plans to the two Army Commanders. Over a month was to pass before all was ready and the timing of the operation, which was given the code name DIADEM, became closely linked with the date of the Normandy landings.

14

Plans for Deception

Wilson's directive: Both sides regroup: Allied reinforcements arrive: STRANGLE: Dummy tanks and night moves: Alexander's plans: Kesselring's fears: Clark's doubts: Massed guns launch DIADEM: Juin opens up the Valley.

CHRONOLOGY COVERING CHAPTERS 14 AND 15

1944	19 Mar	Directive issued for air operations STRANGLE to start.
	end Mar	Both Kesselring and Alexander commence regrouping their forces and Allied reinforcements start arriving.
	19 Apr	General Wilson's proposals for continuation of Italian campaign agreed.
	During Apr	Allied shipping and landing craft leave Mediterranean to take part in OVERLORD.
	9 May	RAF and Eighth Air Force bombers commence attacks on German airfields in France.
	early May	German reorganization of Cassino sector.
	11 May	Battle of Liri valley opens. Heavy fighting for Eighth Army bridgeheads south of Cassino.
	12 May	First Polish attack on Monte Cassino abandoned after bitter fighting.
	13–14 May	French break through Gustav Line and capture Ausonia. Goumiers launched through Aurunci mountains. American II Corps in coastal sector start to gain ground.
	16 May	Eighth Army advance into Liri valley. Kesselring orders withdrawal from Cassino.
	17 May	Second Polish attack suffers heavy losses. Monastery falls early 18 May.
	18 May	36 Division starts move to Anzio. II Corps advance continues along coast.
	19 May	Unsuccessful attempt on Eighth Army front to rush Hitler Line.
	22 May	French break through Hitler Line south of River Liri.
	23 May	Co-ordinated attack on Hitler Line by Canadians who seize bridgehead over River Milfa 24 May. VI Corps at Anzio open attack to break out from bridgehead, Cisterna falls 25 May.

25 May	Fifth Army and Anzio forces join up. Fall of Valmontone imminent. Clark orders change of direction of attack by VI Corps.
26 May	10 Corps follow up German withdrawal from Mount Belmonte.
30 May	Eighth Army reach Arpino and Frosinone in battle for Velletri.
	36 Division penetrate gap in German positions on Mount Artemisio.
	Loading of assault troops for OVERLORD starts (complete 2 June).
2 June	Germans abandon Valmontone. II Corps attacks towards Rome on Route 6.
4 June	Elements of 88 and 1 Armoured Divisions enter Rome. Eighth Army regroups to take up pursuit as soon as roads clear.
	Eisenhower postpones OVERLORD by 24 hours.
5 June	Defeated German Tenth and Fourteenth Army withdrawing on both sides of Tiber with Allies in pursuit.
6 June	21 Army Group lands in Normandy.

As the date for OVERLORD drew closer the need to hold down as many German divisions as possible well away from the Normandy coastline became the predominant factor in Allied Mediterranean strategy. The Allied planners were still in great difficulty over the shortage of landing craft, especially to meet the increased need of OVERLORD. Consequently, when General Wilson sought a directive from the Combined Chiefs of Staff in late February that the Italian Campaign should be given 'over-riding priority over all existing and future operations in the Mediterranean', the only proviso that they made was that he should continue to plan for amphibious operations to assist OVERLORD. The Combined Chiefs of Staff indicated that the most obvious choice would be a landing in the south of France but this must be without prejudice to operations in Italy and they promised to review the situation on 20 March.

From a political point of view the battle for Rome had to continue. Strategically Kesselring's armies must be brought to battle and the airfields near Rome were needed by the Allies to supplement those in Corsica and relieve the congestion around Naples. The immediate task was clear and General Alexander's plan for redeployment and for the spring offensive were already taking shape. What was now to be decided was Allied strategy after the capture of Rome. Which would help Eisenhower most; to continue the offensive up Italy 'indefinitely'; or to switch to a landing in the south of France? Wilson recommended the continuation of operations in Italy, at least as far as the Pisa–Rimini line. This policy would tie down at least those German forces already committed in Italy. Also the forces available to the Allied Armies in Italy, as the unified command was now called, would be concentrated rather than dispersed. This latter factor was important to the Strategic Bomber Force, as an extension of the area of operations away from Italy to the south of France might well interfere with their ability to intervene in northern France at the time of OVERLORD. Wilson therefore recommended that the proposed landing on the south of France should be cancelled and that he should 'carry through the battle in Italy to include the capture of Rome and its airfields (and) thereafter to concentrate on intensive operations up the mainland of Italy'. So that he would be free to carry out local amphibious operations and feints, Wilson proposed an allocation of 'an assault lift of one division plus, on a shore-to-shore basis together with extra resources for commando operations'.[1] After nearly a month's delay Wilson's proposals were agreed on 19 April by the Combined Chiefs of Staff, although they

247

instructed him that the threat of a landing on the south of France was to be retained as part of the Allied strategic plan for the Mediterranean. Meanwhile Major-General Patch, US Army, had been appointed to command the US Seventh Army to plan for this contingency. As the planners explained to General Wilson they wanted to retain 'the maximum flexibility' in the event of the Germans making a voluntary withdrawal, although to Wilson it seemed almost certain that Kesselring would stand and fight. Throughout the winter Kesselring had been receiving reinforcements at the rate of 15,000 men a month and with a total of twenty-three divisions which included a good proportion of armour and an increased allocation of assault guns he was reasonably confident of meeting Hitler's demand to hold the Gustav Line and at the same time prevent any advance from Anzio. The defence of Cassino and the denial of Rome to the Allies had both become matters of great prestige in Hitler's mind. The result was that German strategy in Italy became shackled and the Germans allowed the Allies to play on their fears of a further outflanking landing in the vicinity of Rome. Kesselring at this time complained that Goebbels's taunts and sneers at the Allies' lack of initiative at Cassino and Anzio were likely to 'goad' them into changing their tactics of cautious advance and limited objectives. Kesselring indeed found it necessary to send Westphal to explain to Hitler and the OKW some of the difficulties of the 'strait jacket' in which he found himself. Briefly these were that against Allied superiority on land, sea and in the air he could not stop 'invasions' without defence in depth. Secondly, Allied predominance in heavy artillery generally held the German counter-attacks. Finally, Allied air superiority denied him freedom of operation, except 'under special weather conditions or with a specially favourable ground layout'. Kesselring was also concerned about 'the economic necessity of making (the Italian) theatre of war basically self-sufficient'.[2] Presumably this was a recognition of the increasing difficulty of moving men and supplies in the face of the Allied attacks on communications.

As soon as the battle of Cassino died down and the Anzio bridgehead was safely contained, the Hermann Göring Division was sent to Leghorn to re-form before moving to France. The 162 Infantry Division, recruited from Soviet Turcomans, took over the Tuscan coast and other 'white Russian' units were sent as reliefs to the Adriatic coastal sector. Reserves were now formed behind the two main fronts by pulling back the mobile divisions and thinning out the infantry positions as far as possible. Parallel with this preliminary regrouping, work on a number of defensive positions in depth and on switch lines was hurried on. The Senger Line, which joined Mount Cairo with Piedmonte and Pontecorvo on the Liri, was extended down to the coast at Terracina. In this latter sector, however, the terrain again was difficult and mountainous and there were few permanent defences. This line was now given the name 'Adolf Hitler'. Later it was to suffer yet another change of name to 'Dora' shortly before it was captured! Appreciating that the Hitler

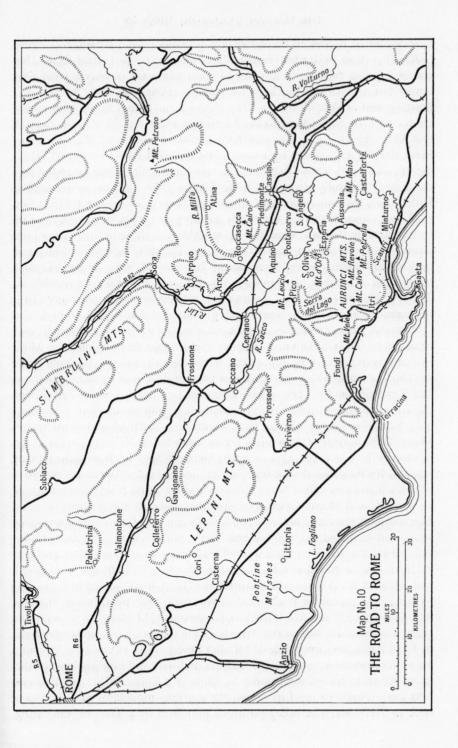

R. Volturno

Mt. Petroso

Cassino

Atina

Piedimonte

Mt. Maio

R. Milfa

Roccasecca

Mt. Cairo

Pontecorvo

S. Angelo

Ausonia.

Mt. Revole

Castelforte

Arpino

Aquino

S. Oliva

Esperia

Mt. Calvo

Sora

Arce

Mt. Leucio

Pico

Mt. d'Oro

Mt. Petrella

Scauri

Minturno

R.82

Serra
del Lago

AURUNCI MTS.

Itri

Gaeta

R. Liri

Ceprano

R. Sacco

Mt. Vele

Fondi

SIMBRUINI MTS.

Frosinone

Ceccano

Prossedi

Terracina

Priverno

Subiaco

Palestrina

Valmontone

Gavignano

LEPINI MTS.

Colleferro

Cori

Littoria

L. Fogliano

Cisterna

Pontine
Marshes

Tivoli

20

30

R5

R6

Anzio

Map No. 10

THE ROAD TO ROME

ROME

R7

MILES

10

KILOMETRES

10

20

0

249

Line would be useless in the event of a break out from Anzio, Kesselring ordered work to be started during March on the 'C' or Caesar Line. This was a stop line running from coast to coast and was not only a good deal longer but also lacked much of the natural strength of the Gustav Line. Starting west of Pescara on the River Saline it ran across the Apennines via Celano and Avezzano down to the Alban hills and on to the western flank of the Anzio beach head. The southern sector thus covered Rome and in particular the approaches by Route 6 and the road Palestrina–Tivoli. Here the engineers and labour battalions concentrated their efforts on improving the already naturally strong positions. Similarly the work of improving the Hitler Line, the construction of which had been going on since December 1943, was concentrated on the sector covering an advance through the Liri valley. Here the defences were now comparable with those of the Gustav Line where it covered the entrance to the valley. Extensive wire, minefields and tank obstacles were covered by numerous concrete pill-boxes and dug-in tank turrets and a number of deep dug-outs had been concreted or reinforced. The approach to the Hitler Line up the Liri valley was over open and fairly flat country, and with the warm spring weather the untended crops in the fields around Aquino effectively screened many of the defences from ground observation. The German dispositions indicated that they expected the Allies to attack south of Cassino but exactly where and when they could only guess at. The Luftwaffe was quite unable to provide adequate air reconnaissance and Kesselring and his commanders remained very much in the dark about the Allied intentions and were constantly worrying about another landing near Rome or further north. They were also concerned about where the French Expeditionary Corps might attack and whether airborne troops might be used in the Liri valley. One thing the Germans were fairly confident about was that the Allies would not try again at Cassino, unless the attack was part of a much stronger offensive. With superb observation from Monte Petrella on one side and Monte Cassino on the other and with the majority of their four hundred guns and *nebelwerfers* able to fire into the valley, where over seventy six-barrelled *nebelwerfers* and heavy mortars were sited down in the valley itself, this southern flank seemed reasonably secure from frontal attack. As the focus for Allied attacks had moved south to Cassino von Vietinghoff had adjusted his dispositions accordingly. The Adriatic sector and the line as far as the Apennine peaks at Alfadena was held by General Hauck's 'Gruppe' with 305 and 334 Infantry Divisions and 114 Jäger Division in that order. On the south side of the Apennines the mountain positions were held by 5 Mountain Division, while 44 Infantry Division and 1 Parachute Division were concentrated around Monte Cassino and were still holding parts of the town. All these troops were under LI Mountain Corps. XIV Panzer Corps held the entrance to the Liri valley, the Aurunci mountains and the coast back to Terracina. The valley positions were held by a 'Gruppe' consisting of a regimental group detached from 305 Division plus a regiment of 15 Panzer Grenadiers. The Aurunci mountain sector was held by 71 Infantry Division supplemented by three battalions from 44 Division, holding a long sector covering Mount Maio down to the Ausente creek, while 94 Infantry Division held the coastal sector down to Scauri. The remainder of 15 Panzer Grenadier Division was in Corps reserve and watching the coastline. 90 Panzer Grenadier Division were in Army reserve. Opposite VI Corps at Anzio von Mackensen still retained eight divisions. Both LXXVI Panzer Corps and 1 Parachute Corps contained three divisions, while 29 Panzer Grenadiers and 92 Infantry Division were held in Army Reserve. The remainder of Army Group 'C' area, covering northern Itlay, the Riviera and parts of Yugoslavia, was garrisoned by a single corps of seven divisions, four of which were in Italy.

Between the end of March and early May several fresh Allied formations arrived from North Africa and the Middle East in support of the new directive given to General Wilson. These reinforcements were the US IV Corps Headquarters and 85 Infantry Division, the British 6 Armoured Division, the South African 6 Armoured Division, three extra armoured brigades, 10 Indian Division and the Moroccan 1 Motorized Infantry Division. The British 1 Armoured Division (less 18 Brigade already at Anzio) and the US 91 Infantry Division were expected to arrive in Italy in early June. Two British Infantry Divisions (46 and 56) returned to the Middle East for rest and re-fitting. Before he could achieve the necessary concentration of forces at the vital points of attack Alexander had to carry out extensive regrouping. This had to be executed with great secrecy and involved the move round of a very large proportion of the troops in the forward positions. 5 Corps consisting now of 4 and 10 Indian Divisions with two armoured brigades and other reinforcements, remained in the Adriatic coastal sector but were directly under command of General Alexander's Headquarters, so as to relieve Eighth Army of their administration. 2 Polish Corps (3 Carpathian and 5 Kresowa Divisions and an armoured brigade) temporarily took over the whole of the mountain positions on both sides of the Apennines, releasing the French Expeditionary Corps. The French Expeditionary Corps and II Corps (85 and 88 Divisions plus 1 Armoured Group) under Fifth Army then went in side-by-side opposite the Aurunci Mountains in the coastal sector which had originally been captured by 10 Corps. IV Corps' Headquarters and 36 Division were kept in Fifth Army Reserve ready to move to Anzio if needed. 10 Corps, consisting of 2 New Zealand Division, a South African Motor Brigade, 24 Guards Brigade, a British Parachute Brigade and two cavalry armoured regiments together with the Italian Motorized Group, then took over the whole of the mountain sector from the Polish Corps, which slipped into concealed assembly positions on the right of 13 Corps. 13 Corps remained in the Liri valley, which was to be the main point of attack, and here were assembled 6 Armoured Division, 4 and 78 Divisions and 8 Indian Division. 1 Canadian Corps consisting of 1 Canadian Division, 5 Canadian Armoured Division and 25 Tank Brigade were in reserve.

The Allied deception plan was simple and designed to play on German fears of another landing near Rome. In fact barely sufficient landing craft remained in the Mediterranean to maintain the troops at Anzio. A beach group moved to Salerno and the area was fully equipped with Canadian Corps signs. Canadian wireless detachments were assembled in the same area, transmitting as if at least two divisions were under training. 36 Division, in Fifth Army reserve south of the Volturno, transmitted on the same frequencies to represent further formations undertaking intensive training. The Royal Navy then carried out signal exercises in Salerno Bay to simulate practice landings by a large force. The attention of the Germans was now drawn to the beaches at Civitavecchia by the activities of beach reconnaissance parties and extensive aerial photography of the area. While this deception was developing, activity and wireless traffic opposite the Gustav Line was carefully controlled to complete the picture that at least three divisions had been withdrawn to undergo training for an amphibious operation and that this was timed for 15 May. Elaborate precautions were taken over the whole period of regrouping to conceal the troop movements and concentrations actually taking place. On one road over a mile of vertical screens were erected to prevent vehicle movement being observed from the Monastery. Using broken rocks and stone chips lying everywhere after the intensive shelling, jeep and mule tracks were constructed up into the mountains for the supply of the Polish divisions and concealed by camouflage nets strung from trees. Troop movement was done by night straight into concealed concentration areas. Many units were only brought forward at the last possible moment but rear parties, together with vehicles, were still left to continue normal activity in their old areas. Quantities of dummy tanks were mocked up in wood and canvas and left in the old areas when the armoured units went forward to their new assembly positions. New tracks constructed down to the river were worked on at night and covered with brush-wood well before dawn each day. New gun positions and the many forward dumps that had to be prepared were camouflaged with the greatest care. Finally, in the vital 13 Corps area training programmes and reliefs were arranged, simulating a purely 'inactive' defensive role extending well beyond the actual D-day for the offensive. The Navy were unable to play much active part in the deception plans, except through their obvious presence off Anzio and in the Bay of Naples. During April shipping and landing craft, amounting to no less than 46 LSTs, many LCTs, DUKWs and LCIs, earmarked for OVERLORD had to leave for the United Kingdom. By early May the naval bombardment forces were reduced to Admiral Mansfield's flagship, the light cruiser HMS *Dido*, the American cruisers *Brooklyn* and *Philadelphia* and a handful of destroyers. In preparation for the offensive and to cater for the extra troops expected in Anzio, which would bring the total there to seven divisions by the second week in May, the Navy made prodigious efforts during March and April to build up stocks in the beach head, making the maximum use of the landing craft before they left for OVERLORD. In March 158,274 tons were landed and 97,658 in April, by which time it was difficult to find space on shore for further dumps. Dumping, however, continued at a high rate throughout May and a further 131,424 tons of stores were landed, it being the intention to supply Fifth Army by sea through the port at Anzio once their advance got going. In nineteen weeks the Navy had landed no less than 523,358 tons of stores, which was a remarkable achievement.

Examples have already been given of the Allied air operations against communications throughout the campaign. What was now called the 'interdiction' of enemy communications had been closely studied by the Allied Air Commanders and also by Professor Zuckerman, a British scientist who was making a special study of bombing strategy. So far attacks on communications had concentrated on rail centres and in particular on marshalling yards. Results had been encouraging during the advance from the toe of Italy, as the rail communications in the south of the country had to pass through very few centres such as Naples and Rome. The relative failure of the Air Forces at the time of the Anzio battles to prevent large-scale movement of German troops and supplies caused the Allied Air Commanders to seek for reasons other than that of bad weather. It was seen that the blocking of marshalling yards, of which there were over 150 in Nazi-occupied Italy, was really beyond the capacity of the bomber force, large as it was. Furthermore, less than half the weight of bombs was needed for the destruction of a bridge compared with the blocking of a marshalling yard; moreover it often took longer to repair the bridge, especially in difficult terrain, than to restore the flow of traffic through the yard. This led the planners to consider the effect of simultaneous attacks on both types of target, starting with the principal rail centres in northern Italy, through which the men and supplies must enter the country, and working right forward to the area of ground operations, where road communications and transport would also be attacked. The whole operation, given the code name STRANGLE, was seen as a concerted effort by all types of aircraft to disrupt the German lines of supply, to the point where they could not maintain their two armies in the face of the coming Allied offensive. The area of operations for the medium bombers was the rectangle of rail communications south of the line Pisa–Florence–Pontassieve, thence south down the mountain route to Arezzo–Orvieto–Orte. A fighter group was moved to Corsica to attack both rail and road targets in the northern part of this area. The light and fighter-bombers of XII Air Support Command and the Desert Air Force were given the area south of the line Terni–Montalto di Castro back to the battle area at Cassino and were also charged with attacking the Persaro, Ancona, Perugia links from the Adriatic line of communication. The strategic bombers were given the task of attacking marshalling yards in northern Italy, although priority was still being given to the Combined Bomber Offensive, Operation POINTBLANK. The principal difference between this plan and previous attempts at interdiction was that the whole fighter-bomber force was brought in to supplement the work of the medium and heavy bombers. These operations were to prove a significant experiment in the employment of tactical air power. Fighter-bombers could fly in conditions unsuitable for the medium bombers and were effective not only in disrupting stretches of open railway track but in attacking motor transport, after the Germans found themselves forced to move their supplies by road rather than by rail. These tactics were developed to achieve a policy of 'simultaneous interdiction' and of attacking whole sections of railway line including the yards, bridges, tunnels, defiles and open tracks. As the operations developed against the railway system, the Germans turned more and more to road transport on which the tactical air forces now concentrated. The overall effect was gradually to slow down and reduce the delivery of supplies to the fighting formations. The one weak link in the operation was a shortage of night bombers. Medium bombers of the Strategic Air Force were switched to night attacks on ports but there were not enough to maintain attacks on communications generally on a 'round the clock' basis. Nevertheless, it was estimated that although the German forces in Italy were receiving deliveries of nearly 4,000 tons of supplies a day this would fall short by up to 1,500 tons of their daily requirement, once they were involved in major operations. While rationing could be applied under conditions of static defence and it was believed that a ten-day supply of fuel had been built up in the forward zone, it was hoped there would be little chance of the Germans getting supplies forward quickly once the battle started. As more and more motor transport became tied up on the supply routes, the Germans felt the shortage of vehicles for moving reserves and supplies in the forward area. When in a desperate attempt to meet the situation motor transport was used in daylight substantial losses resulted, with the Allied fighters and fighter-bombers claiming some 1,800 vehicles destroyed or damaged before the offensive actually started. After the battle started the Germans faced the full effect of STRANGLE and their carefully hoarded reserves of fuel and ammunition and other stores were quickly expended and reinforcements from the north just did not arrive in time to stop the breakthrough. Owing to the shortage both of transport and of petrol many units had to march for long distances and were often under air attack, arriving in the battle area thoroughly disorganized and having lost equipment and vehicles. The shortage of petrol is exemplified by reports that many German tanks were seen on the march being towed by oxen.[3] The Strategic Air Force's contribution to STRANGLE was some 5,000 tons of bombs on marshalling yards and port installations, this includes

1,300 tons in one raid on Toulon harbour. The real credit, however, for the success of STRANGLE must go to the Tactical Air Force squadrons, which in the last month before the ground offensive opened flew 22,000 sorties. The lessons of STRANGLE are simply these; an air force engaging in interdiction operations, even on this scale, could not by itself force an enemy to withdraw but it could create the situation where his army would become increasingly handicapped in the face of heavy and prolonged ground attacks. Furthermore, an orderly withdrawal would be prejudiced through loss of mobility and lack of supplies and providing the ground attack was pressed the withdrawal could become a rout. The defeat of the enemy thus depended upon each arm making its proper contribution. Secondly, the Zuckerman theory of concentration on one type of target was an over-simplification. The whole pattern of a communications system had to be studied in its geographic and military context and the denial of supplies and reinforcements to the enemy depended more on a widespread and simultaneous disruption of his lines of communication than on attacks against any single link in the chain. A further conclusion was that, under conditions of air supremacy, once the ground attack gained momentum the best use of tactical air power was against the enemy supply routes rather than close support targets.

In mid-April General Clark was ordered back to Washington to report to Marshall, who wanted 'to know what chance there was that (the Allies) would reach Rome before the cross-Channel invasion started'.[4] When the plans for the spring offensive were first outlined earlier in the month, General Alexander had not known the date for OVERLORD, but the operations in Italy were now carefully timed with a view to the capture of Rome just before the Normandy landings. The date for the opening of the offensive was now fixed for 2300 hours on 11 May. The intention was 'to destroy the right wing of the German Tenth Army; to drive what remains of it and the German Fourteenth Army north of Rome; and to pursue the enemy to the Rimini–Pisa Line, inflicting the maximum losses on him in the process'.[5] Eighth Army was ordered to break through in the Liri valley and advance on the general axis of Route 6 to the east of Rome, while a simultaneous attack by Fifth Army would strike at the Ausonia defile and advance parallel to Eighth Army but south of the Rivers Liri and Sacco. At the appropriate moment General Truscott's force at Anzio would attack on the axis Cisterna–Cori and to cut Route 6 at Valmontone, thus preventing the supply and withdrawal of Tenth Army. Only then was it visualized that the thrust to Rome and beyond would be made by both armies. The boundaries allotted gave the Americans the honour of entering Rome, while the other Allies would by-pass the city on either side. Anxious to prepare both for an early collapse of the Gustav Line as well as for a delay in the advance up the Liri valley, General Clark discussed with Truscott four alternative plans for the employment of VI Corps in their attack from Anzio. Apart from the attack on Valmontone, he proposed an

255

attack almost due east on Sezzi, to aid the advance of Fifth Army, and two other attacks directly towards Rome through Campoleone or Ardea up the coast. Detailed plans for all four attacks were prepared with great attention to secrecy and the obvious difficulties of road control in the confined beach-head area. These VI Corps plans received the approval of Fifth Army Head-quarters at the end of April. Shortly afterwards, on 5 May, General Alexander visited the beach head and Truscott takes up the story. 'With some measure of pride, I explained to him the details of our plans, and the extent of our preparations. General Alexander, charming gentleman and magnificent soldier that he was, let me know very quietly and firmly that there was only one direction in which the attack should or would be launched, and that was from Cisterna to cut Highway 6 in the vicinity of Valmontone in the rear of the German main forces. He had, he said, reserved to himself the decision as to when he proposed to initiate it. After he left that afternoon, I reported our conversation to General Clark.'[6] Clark saw this as an attempt to 'run' his army and complained to Alexander on the telephone. Two days later the objective of the attack was again discussed and Alexander reaffirmed his views that 'the Valmontone attack would result in the capture of a large number of German prisoners'. It is evident, however, that Clark had reservations. He later wrote, 'if (the plan) succeeded the Germans' main forces would either be caught in a pincer, or, as was far more likely, avoid capture by withdrawal northwards along a number of suitable axial roads that ran east of Rome. The trouble with this plan was that in order to get to Valmontone the beach-head forces would more or less by-pass the Alban hills, leaving the enemy holding high ground that was vital to us if we were to enter Rome.'[7] Soon after this conversation Alexander issued orders that VI Corps were to be ready to attack any time after 15 May but in his written orders Clark stuck to his option for any one of the four plans for a break out. Orders for the attack by Eighth Army were issued by General Leese verbally in a series of conferences with his Corps Commanders. 13 Corps was given the task of securing a bridgehead between Cassino and the River Liri, of isolating the town, which would subsequently be cleared, and joining up with the Poles. 2 Polish Corps had the special task of isolating the Monte Cassino feature from the north, so as to dominate Route 6 and join up with 13 Corps, after which they would take Monastery Hill. At this point 13 Corps would have opened up Route 6 and the Poles would be directed against the Hitler Line north of Route 6. The task of 10 Corps holding the right flank was to make a diversionary attack towards Atina. 1 Canadian Corps stood ready to assist 13 Corps or to pass through, according to how the situation developed. 6 South African Armoured Division was also in army reserve ready to exploit the breakthrough. The strength on this part of the front was between six to seven Infantry Divisions and three Armoured Divisions.

Fifth Army occupied a thirteen-mile front opposite the extreme southern flank of the German Tenth Army and faced very different terrain to that opposite the Eighth Army in the Liri valley. The only through route westwards towards Rome was the coastal Route 7 which for more than half the distance between the two wings of Fifth Army ran straight across the Pontine Marshes from Terracina to Cisterna. North of this road lay a series of mountain ranges up to fifteen miles wide and running north-westwards for some forty-five miles to join up with the Alban hills. First came the formidable mass of the Aurunci Mountains with Mounts Maio and Petrella guarding the Ausonia Gap leading towards Pontecorvo. Behind Mount Petrella some ten miles of extremely rugged peaks had to be negotiated before reaching the north-south road from Pico to Itri and Fondi which separated the Aurunci from the Ausoni Mountains. More widespread and not quite so high, this latter range lay right across the line of any advance north from Terracina and dominated the approaches to the extreme southern sector of the Hitler Line running from Terracina through Fondi. Further west again and north of the Pontine Marshes lay the Lepine Mountains which extended as far as the Velletri–Valmontone Gap. Between the Ausoni and Lepini Mountains roads ran south-west from Frosinone and south-east from Valmontone through Priverno and Sezze and south to the Pontine Marshes and Route 7. Apart from these widely separated north-south links between Routes 6 and 7, the road communications in this whole mountainous area were so poor that the Germans considered the ground too difficult for any major advance westwards through the area. They therefore continued to concentrate their defensive preparations on that part of the Hitler Line that covered the Liri valley from Aquino to Pontecorvo and S Oliva. General Clark defined Fifth Army's task 'to advance with both Corps abreast, secure the Ausonia defile and advance south of the Liri River to cut the Pico–Itri road'.[8] The French Expeditionary Corps was given the task of capturing Mount Maio, opening the Ausonia Gap and then advancing straight through the mountains to cut the Pico–Itri road and in particular to capture Monte d'Oro which overlooked Pontecorvo. II Corps would meanwhile advance on the line Mount Civita–Castellonorato and Mount Scauri to reach Itri. These attacks would be launched simultaneously with the attacks by Eighth Army. Clark proposed using six infantry divisions and three tabors of Goumiers, holding back only 36 Division in reserve. The French Expeditionary Corps, which now totalled 99,000 men, provided four of these infantry divisions and the 12,000 Goumiers.

On 13 April von Senger put in a report to Tenth Army forecasting with some accuracy that the next Allied attempt to breach the Gustav Line would probably come in the southern part of his Corps' sector. Four days later both he and von Vietinghoff were ordered back to the Fuehrer's headquarters on the Obersalzberg to receive decorations and to attend, together with many other senior officers, a course on *Weltanschauung*. After this dose of 'spiritual education' von Senger went on leave and von Vietinghoff decided to start his leave on 11 May. Meanwhile General Westphal, Chief of Staff to Kesselring, was taken ill and von Senger's own Chief of Staff had also been sent on leave by the Deputy Corps Commander. None of these four officers were present at their headquarters on 12 May. As we have already seen the decision had been taken that XIV Corps' front should be shortened and the Deputy Corps Commander broke up 15 Panzer Grenadier Division into penny packets, instead of holding the division centrally between Fondi and Pico as had been intended. The adjustment of the Corps boundary, giving LI Mountain Corps the responsibility for Monte Cassino and the valley as far as the River Liri, also thoroughly upset von Senger's well-organized arrangements for co-ordinating the whole of the Corps Artillery. This reduction of the front of course meant that there were no longer some six to eight divisions under a single commander, who would have enough troops to form local reserves and the freedom to switch units to threatened areas. These adjustments to the boundaries and troops in the southern sector of the Gustav Line presum-ably were made on Kesselring's orders and were to have far-reaching effects when the battle started. Kesselring undoubtedly was much concerned with the Allied threat of a further landing, probably north of Rome, and the possible use of airborne troops in the Liri valley. Consequently he placed the Hermann Göring Division north of Leghorn, the 29 Panzer Grenadier Division near Viterbo, the 92 Infantry Division on the coast between Civita-vecchia and the mouth of the Tiber and the 26 Panzer Division west of Valmontone, all primarily in an anti-invasion role. 90 Panzer Grenadier Division were stationed immediately west of Velletri, again close to Rome, but with the special responsibility of defeating the anticipated airborne drop on Frosinone. The 3 Panzer Grenadiers on the Anzio perimeter were also given an anti-invasion role. After a good deal of deliberation, Kesselring, who feared a thrust from the Anzio bridgehead towards Valmontone, finally agreed on von Mackensen's advice that the 362 Division, which did not have a particularly good battle record, should continue to hold Cisterna. Here the positions were strong and 362 Division were directly supported by the Lehr Regiment, now recovered from their mauling, and two independent Panzer Grenadier Regiments. As for an Allied attack between Cassino and the sea, Kesselring's appreciation was that his four divisions, well entrenched and in strong positions, were sufficient to hold the six Allied divisions that he be-lieved were facing them in this sector. The latest appreciation by the Corps Commander was that an Allied attack might be expected about 24 May. On 11 May General Feuerstein, commanding the LI Mountain Corps, was still engaged in reorganizing the Cassino sector that he had recently taken over. Headquarters 44 Infantry Division was moving down from the mountains to take over command of the mixed force of five battalions in the valley and reliefs were taking place on Monte Cassino that same night. Not wishing to draw attention to these moves, the German gunners towards evening ceased firing at the same time as the Allied harassing fire died down for a similar reason. For an hour or so there was an unnatural silence until the Allied artillery again opened up harassing fire on 'routine' targets. On Tenth Army front everything seemed quiet and normal. As the reliefs moved forward to Cassino and the alarm posts in the valley settled down to their night-long vigil, the Allied guns suddenly opened fire with a violent counter-battery programme, as well as heavy concentration on the forward German infantry positions. Caught in the open 44 Infantry Division staff turned back; there could be no hand over that night. It was 2300 hours on 11 May and the BBC time-check had been the signal for 2,000 guns to open fire. The battle of the Liri valley had started. Alexander's Allied Armies in Italy had achieved complete strategic and tactical surprise.

Over a month previously General Juin had formulated his plans for operating in the Aurunci Mountains and wrote, 'Le succès de la manoeuvre du CEF dépend essentiellement du facteur *Vitesse*; la rupture de la première position ennemie ayant été réalisée, il s'agira d'arriver rapidement et en force là où l'ennemi compte se redresser, et de le battre avant qu'il n'ait eu le temps de regrouper ses moyens et de s'asseoir'.[9] His subsequent orders were for 4 Moroccan Mountain Division on the left to break through at Castelforte and 2 Moroccan Infantry Division to seize Mount Maio on the right. 3 Algerian Division would be in support and both attacks would start at 2300 hours 11 May. At dawn 12 May 1 Motorized Infantry Division would attack up the left bank of the Garigliano through S Andrea to capture the La Guardia feature. Initially, the four tabors of Goumiers, reinforced by a Moroccan Mountain Regiment and a Regiment of Mountain Artillery, totalling 12,000 men and 4,000 animals would remain in reserve concealed east of the river. On the narrow Fifth Army front 600 guns had been massed to support the French Expeditionary Corps and the II Corps' attack on their left and in the first twenty-four hours fired some 174,000 rounds into the German battery positions and defences. The effect of the initial concentrations at H hour were such that no German artillery or mortar defensive fire was met during the first forty-five minutes of the advance. By this time the Moroccan infantry were through the forward defences to take Mount Faito and the Cerasola hill within the hour. On 12 May attempts to widen this gap and advance on Mount Maio met with violent reactions and a counter-attack by a battalion from 15 Panzer Grenadiers, which halted several battalions of French infantry forming up to assault Mount Feuci and caused heavy losses. The following morning 2 Moroccan Infantry, under General Dody, captured both Mount Girafano and Mount Feuci and by the middle of the afternoon was firmly established on Mount Maio and held the key to the whole sector. As soon as Mount Girafano fell, the motorized division made rapid progress and by midnight on 13 May had cleared the west bank of the Garigliano right up to S Apollinare and the junction with the Liri, taking many prisoners. On the French Corps' left flank 4 Mountain Division had moved in round Castelforte, meeting a good deal of mortar and machine-gun fire on 12 May. The garrison held off early attacks but towards evening the Moroccans attacked in force and carried the town, although mopping up continued well into the night. The next day the attack was pressed forward to capture Mount Rotondo and Mount Ceschito, the two features which covered the road to Coreno. On 14 May Ausonia was captured and the French troops cleared all the country to the north between the town and the Liri.

In the coastal sector II Corps had met stiff resistance and determined counter-attacks particularly west of Minturno, where the 85 Division's attack made little progress until 14 May when the 94 German Infantry Division began to give ground. By this time 88 Division had taken Santa Maria Infante and was advancing towards Spigno. During these attacks HMS *Dido* and the two American cruisers, working on a rota basis, stood close inshore to bombard German battery positions which were out of range of Fifth Army artillery. This naval gun support was particularly valuable, as both American divisions were fighting their first engagement. By 14 May it was evident that Fifth Army had broken through the defences and that both German divisions had lost heavily. 71 Division was incapable of co-ordinated resistance and its shattered units were falling back towards the Liri. 94 Division had been badly mauled and found itself pushed back through the mountains towards Itri. This was the moment for which General Juin was waiting. Before, however, we follow the dramatic drive by the French into the mountains we must turn to the Cassino front, for in this sector the main effort was to be made by Eighth Army. Here the Monastery and the crossings of the lower Rapido were once again the scene of bitter fighting.

15
Roads to Rome

Eighth Army attacks: The Rapido bridgeheads: Phantom Ridge and
Albaneta: The Poles attack again: The Monastery taken: General Guillaume's Mountain Corps cross Aurunci Range: Kesselring attempts staged
withdrawal: Americans join up with Anzio beach head: Canadians break
through Hitler Line: Truscott attacks: Clark orders change of direction:
von Mackensen's mistake: Rome at last: Allied air co-operation described.

On Eighth Army front 1,060 guns pounded the German battery positions for forty minutes and then reverted to the special tasks allotted by their own Corps. The immediate objectives of General Kirkman's 13 Corps were bridgeheads across the Rapido on either side of S Angelo. 4 Division was on the right and 8 Indian Division on the left, each crossing on a two-brigade front. As the first boats were launched at 2345 hours 11 May a barrage from twenty-one artillery regiments, mostly of 25-pounders, crashed down on the forward German positions. The divisional machine-gun battalions joined in with their 4·2-inch mortars and Vickers guns and the rate of advance of the barrage was 100 yards in six minutes. From the very start the attacks ran into trouble. The current was exceptionally strong and many boats capsized and others were swept downstream. One of 4 Division's brigades lost forty boats during the night and the remaining five by the following afternoon. Orders had been given for the crossings to be screened by smoke from the German observation posts on Monte Cassino 1,500 feet above. The Germans, however, had plans to use smoke in a different way. Canisters had been dug into the river bank and fitted with trip wires and as the first troops landed they became enveloped in dense clouds of black smoke which marked the exact point of the attack. The German mortars and machine-guns opened up with devastating effect. In the low-lying ground the mist had now thickened and the bursting shells of the barrage threw up clouds of dust from the dry alluvial soil of the plain. Even away from the cloud of artificial fog visibility was down to two feet. These conditions were of little hindrance to the German machine-gunners firing on fixed lines but at the crossing points, where visibility was down to nil in places, the effects were serious and control became extremely difficult. 4 Division only succeeded in capturing very shallow bridgeheads and in daylight attempts to continue bridge-building operations had to be abandoned. Throughout 12 May two of the assault battalions suffered such heavy losses that the remnants had to be withdrawn to the east bank before dark and took no further part in the battle. On the whole divisional front only two anti-tank guns had been ferried across. At 8 Indian Division's crossings again many boats were swept downstream or holed by fire. At several crossings ropes were now attached to the few remaining boats, which were hauled backwards and forwards. In this manner a Gurkha battalion, moving up in reserve, crossed during the first night in just under three and a half hours with only four boats. The Germans were now firing phosphorous smoke shells to thicken up the artificial fog. Verey lights fired to locate a company lost in the 'fog' failed to burn in the smoke cloud and the Colonel had to tell the Company Commander over his wireless to get the men to shout in unison to show their position. In spite of heavy casualties several battalions succeeded in working forward and getting to grips with the entrenched German infantry. Although all the preliminary objectives were not reached, an advance below S Angelo was in sufficient depth partially to out-flank the village. In this area a tank-bearing bridge was completed by the Indian engineers by 0830 hours 12 May. An hour later and 1,000 yards to the south an astonishing feat now took place. A Sherman tank was seen moving up towards the river with a complete Bailey bridge on its back. Slowly the tank manoeuvred itself down the bank and into the stream, where it sank to the bed of the river but still with the bridge correctly poised on its back. As the crew 'bailed out', another tank came up from behind and pushed the bridge across the 50-foot gap—a fine combined operation by the Canadians and the Indian Engineers. In the face of heavy shelling at these two crossing points, four squadrons of Canadian tanks and some anti-tank guns crossed to the west bank during 12 May. Although both bridges were out of commission for short periods, the division was now able to bring forward strong infantry reinforcements and late in the afternoon 5 Royal Gurkhas, assisted by tanks, took S Angelo, although mopping-up operations continued well into the afternoon of 13 May.

The German Command still considered 13 Corps attack was only a feint and part of a deception plan, so only local reserves were committed on 12 May and the Germans relied more on their artillery to halt the attack. As the assault slowed up, the early advantage from the counter-battery programme was lost and the German gunners, who had been well dug in for months, quickly came back into the picture. 13 Corps bridgehead and crossings were now not only under heavy mortar fire but being shelled by batteries in the valley and also around Piedmonte, as well as by guns concentrated around Atina well tucked in to positions that were extremely difficult to hit from across the Rapido. Under this heavy shelling 4 Division's position became critical. The situation was saved by the Indian Engineers who, working under continuous shell fire, completed a Class 30 bridge overnight. The reserve brigade with tanks now crossed to lead a divisional attack. The situation in the entire Liri valley was now completely altered and by nightfall both 4 Division and 8 Indian Division had fought their way out from the initial bridgehead to a depth of between 1,500–2,500 yards. The machine-gun battalion of 1 Parachute Division, thrown in on Kesselring's orders against 4 Division, was severely handled and lost some twenty machine-guns and a number of prisoners. 8 Indian Division dealt firmly with a succession of counter-attacks made only at company strength by a battalion of 15 Panzer Grenadiers, whose strength was soon frittered away. The decision was now taken, late on 13 May, that 78 Division with a reinforced armoured brigade under command should pass through to take up the advance and make contact early on 15 May with the Polish Corps along Route 6.

The operations of 2 Polish Corps at Cassino resulted in some of the most bitter fighting of the whole war. Starving barefoot men released from camps in the Arctic region of the Soviet Union had marched halfway across Europe and Asia to join General Anders in Persia two summers before. These were the men who together with their compatriots from all over the free world formed the 2 Polish Corps. In the assembly areas north of Cassino conditions were extremely difficult. The slightest movement in daylight drew fire. No hot meals could be prepared and water was severely rationed but the Poles suffered these hardships willingly as they waited their chance to strike back. General Anders' order of the day opened with these words, 'Soldiers! the moment of battle has arrived. We have long awaited the moment for revenge and retribution over our hereditary enemy.' As already mentioned, the primary task of the Polish Corps was to isolate the area Monastery Hill–Cassino, so as to dominate Route 6 until a junction could be made with 13 Corps. This demanded the ultimate capture of Monte Cassino. It was decided that the attack must be made on a wider front than previously. Consequently, Monte Castellone would have to be held and the flank of the attack covered from German positions further west on Passo Corno. This would allow a broader sweep down from the north-west. Objectives were Colle S Angelo and the ridge leading through Point 575, beyond Snake's Head, to cover the main attack on Point 593 and Massa Albaneta. 5 Kresowa Division was given the task of holding Monte Castellone with one brigade and seizing Phantom Ridge, an intermediate feature, and Colle S Angelo. Simultaneously 3 Carpathian Division would assault Albaneta and Point 593 and then, only after Phantom Ridge had been taken, turn towards the Monastery itself. At this stage, two squadrons of tanks and a number of flame-throwers would be available. The tanks would move up by the same tank track used by the New Zealanders but now much improved by the Polish Engineers. As both divisions only had two brigades each, the two reconnaissance regiments and the armoured car regiment were to be dismounted and used as infantry, which would make up each division to the equivalent of seven infantry battalions. The only corps reserve would be a single infantry battalion and the remainder of the armoured brigade, which could hardly be used in country so unsuitable for tanks. Following the initial counter-battery programme some 300 guns would be available for the direct support of the attacks, plus fifteen heavy guns specially allocated to shelling the Monastery. Further close support would be given by seventy-two 4·2-inch mortars manned by men from anti-tank regiments. As the attacks could be observed from the Germans' observation posts on Mount Cifalco, vast numbers of smoke canisters were brought forward to be used in the upper Rapido valley. No less than 18,000 were discharged between 11 and 24 May. The success of the operation depended on two factors, the efficiency of the counter-battery programme and the early capture of Phantom Ridge to prevent 3 Carpathian Division being caught in cross fire at close range. The infantry assaults went in at 0100 hours 12 May and it soon became evident that the German gun positions were largely undamaged and that their communications had been quickly restored, probably through the laying of numerous alternative cable routes. Consequently the Kresowa Division suffered 20 per cent casualties before even reaching the foot of Phantom Ridge at 0230 hours, having taken twice as long as planned. Many wireless sets had already been damaged and control of the attack had become very difficult. On reaching the crest of the ridge the leading battalions came under such heavy fire that they could neither clear the ridge effectively nor hold a spur, some 300 yards beyond, that led to their final objective. In the midst of the confused fighting and with most of the ridge covered by cross fire, a reserve battalion advanced totally unaware of the situation, as all communications with the brigade had broken down. The subsequent withdrawal of this battalion, on the commanding officer's own initiative, from the congested and very limited foothold on the crest was misinterpreted by several other units which followed suit. 3 Carpathian division took Point 593 within twenty minutes of crossing their start line and pressed on round the 'elbow' to the next feature (Point 569) leading to the Monastery. On the right, however, the other forward battalion of the division had to clear a gorge, some 400 yards short of the farm, before reaching Massa Albaneta. Here the attack ran into serious trouble. The gorge was strongly held and covered by fire from Colle S Angelo. Engineers sent forward to clear minefields were virtually wiped out and more than a troop of tanks was lost and most of the second troop held down under heavy gun and mortar fire. On the left, close to the Monastery, the Germans emerged from their shelters at daylight and quickly mounted a series of counter-attacks. Seven of these attacks were beaten off but by 1130 hours Point 569 was lost. The German guns in the Belmonte–Atina area were now firing straight into the rear of the Polish attack with devastating effect. The situation had become critical and nothing short of a co-ordinated attack with fresh battalions supported by 13 Corps Artillery, in addition to that already available, could possibly succeed. While these plans were being prepared, it was learned that German reserves were assembling around Villa Santa Lucia and Piedmonte and it was evident that 13 Corps, who were struggling hard to maintain shallow bridgeheads, were in no position to achieve an early juncture with any Polish advance. General Anders had no option but to recall his troops to their start lines and General Leese issued instructions that any further attacks would have to await developments in the valley below and could not be before the afternoon of 13 May. Casualties on both sides had been very heavy. Owing to the Polish attacks coinciding with the arrival of the German reliefs, no less than nine

German battalions had been involved. This single factor may well have denied the Poles their chance of success but equally the German battle layout in LI Corps sector was dislocated as an unexpected high proportion of their infantry had been tied down in the Cassino sector.

Under the eyes of the German observation posts on Monte Cassino, 13 Corps struggled forward and it was not until early on 15 May that 78 Division was in position and ready to attack. The following day 1 Canadian Corps relieved 8 Indian Division and by 17 May 78 Division had penetrated almost halfway to the Hitler Line. The advance was through most difficult undulating country covered with long grass and trees and vines in full leaf and inter-sected by hedges, walls and innumerable ditches. During a sharp engagement that evening a number of prisoners were taken and these turned out to be men of the German 1 Parachute Division. Nearer Cassino 4 Division had already reached Route 6. This attack was one part of the co-ordinated attack to pinch out Monte Cassino and we must now turn again to the operations of the Polish Corps. During the four-day pause most of the Polish battalions had to be reorganised on a three company basis owing to losses. Active patrolling and the interrogation of prisoners meanwhile produced a good deal of information about the German positions. Lack of ground reconnaissance had in fact proved a serious handicap in the first attack. The German battery positions around Atina were now heavily attacked both by the Corps artillery and fighter-bombers. Loudspeakers from the German line blared out descriptions of conditions in Poland and propaganda on their 'betrayal' at Teheran and the Katyn massacres. The effect was only to make the Polish soldiers more anxious to resume the battle. Convinced that the choice of objectives had been correct, General Anders decided to stick to the same plan of attack, except that the Kresowa Division would attack in successive waves to reach Colle S Angelo. So as to co-ordinate with 13 Corps the assault would be made at 0700 hours 17 May after an hour's artillery preparation. Emphasis was placed on a rapid advance immediately the guns lifted. On the night before the attack a reconnaissance at company strength penetrated the Phantom Ridge positions and by dawn, after confused fighting, the ridge was captured. On 17 May Colle S Angelo was quickly reached, although the feature was not fully cleared until that evening. 3 Carpathian Division had been ordered to make a systematic reduction of the positions on their front, starting off with Point 593 and Massa Albaneta which were to be attacked simultaneously. Point 593 was captured by about 1130 hours after a heavy counter-attack had been beaten off but efforts to reach Massa Albaneta were frustrated. Firing from small steel pillboxes at close range, the defenders held out against all assaults by the Polish infantry and were also able to check the clearing of the minefields in the gorge. The pillboxes and dug-in tank turrets had been covered with earth, which was now overgrown with grass, making them virtually invisible. The only effective way of reducing these strongpoints was for them to be blown up by the direct application of 'beehive' mines to the steel casing. At nightfall the Poles were still 200 yards short of the farm, although they held Colle S Angelo and Point 593 to either flank. General Anders' Corps had again suffered heavily and his last reserve, made up of drivers and clerks, had been committed. The men were now exhausted. Throughout the night patrols were pushed forward and escape routes that the German paratroopers might use were shelled but the defenders were apparently sitting tight, at least in the forward positions. When the Poles advanced at dawn on 18 May only isolated pockets of resistance were met. The survivors of 1 Parachute Division were already moving west along the mountain paths towards Villa Santa Lucia, from where a final counter-attack was launched to check any follow up. At 1020 hours a patrol of Podolski Lancers entered the Monastery and raised their Regimental standard over the ruins. The devastation inside the Monastery was indescribable. Since it had been bombed, thousands of shells had poured down on to the ruins. The handful of wounded survivors 'looked like wild animals. Unshaven and unkept, they were half-starved and on the verge of madness.'[1] The dead lay everywhere. The battle for Monte Cassino was over and moving down the mountain side troops from the Carpathian Division made contact with 78 Division on Route 6 about noon on the same day. The losses of 2 Polish Corps at Cassino amounted to nearly 4,000 killed and wounded.

Overnight on 12/13 May, Major-General Guillaume concentrated the French Mountain Corps in a valley north of Monte Rotondo. His command was organized in three groups, each containing a Moroccan infantry battalion and a tabor of Goumiers. Guns, ammunition and a minimum of supplies were all carried by mules. Ahead lay the Aurunci Range, with Monte Revole rising over 4,000 feet in the centre of a treeless rocky mountainous mass, virtually inaccessible from the south or east, except by a steep shepherd's path climbing up from Spigno. With the fall of Ceschito the groups moved forward and, as soon as the Ausonia valley was clear, after Mount Maio had been captured, one group moved west from Ausonia to take Mount Fammera on 15 May, while the remainder of the Mountain Corps passed through the Americans at Spigno to capture Monte Castello. Climbing straight on up into the mountains, the main force marched and rode through the night, only halting for a short rest every four hours. By 0600 hours 16 May the leading column was on the crest of Monte Revole and a battery of guns was in position a mile behind. Forty tons of supplies were air dropped along the route. By late afternoon 17 May a battalion of mountain guns had been brought up and the force was established on a seven-mile front, within two miles or less of the Itri–Pico road between Serra del Lago and Mount Calvo. On 17 May a reinforced battalion from 15 Panzer Grenadiers had marched up in column of route towards Monte Revole. A 'noose' was set up by General Guillaume in person and under fire from both flanks and pounded by the

French batteries the column was annihilated. The German commander, who was captured, admitted that he had been told that no Allied attack in strength was expected in this sector for three or four days. The following night Monte le Pezze, three miles north of Itri and immediately overlooking the road, was taken in a surprise attack. To regain this vital point the Germans put in a further battalion of Panzer Grenadiers but the French beat back this counter-attack with accurate gun fire and a spirited bayonet charge. That night a young French artillery officer with two sections of Goumiers slipped un-observed through the German lines, scaled Mount Velle west of the road and, having overpowered the defences, settled down to direct the French batteries throughout the following day on to the German concentrations below. By nightfall the party was hard pressed and practically surrounded. This, however, was not the end of the saga of Sous-Lieutenant de Kérautem who not only slipped away with his men from his now untenable vantage point but succeeded in capturing and escorting back to his tabor the commanding officer, three officers and fourteen men of the Panzer battalion who, at that very moment, were attempting to mount a further counter-attack. Further north the third group of Goumiers and the remainder of the French Expedi-tionary Corps were sweeping round south of the Liri through S Giorgio and Castelnuovo, by which time their advance was opposed by elements of 90 Panzer Grenadier Division. By 17 May, however, S Oliva and Esperia had been occupied and two days later 3 Algerian Division, with 1 Motorized Division close behind, held Mount d'Oro and were within four miles of Pico. Linklater comments 'the Corps had made this very striking advance, in eight days, in manner that inevitably suggests the irresistibility of a flowing tide'.[2] The rapid advance of the Goumiers through country considered impassable by the Germans deserves special mention. With the fall of Cassino and the flank of the Hitler Line already turned, the Battle of the Liri valley was about to enter a new phase.

It took a long time for Kesselring to realize the extent of the Allied con-centration between Cassino and the sea. On 12 May his operational maps still showed only six Allied divisions on this front, including a single French division forward in the Garigliano bridgehead. There was no trace of the Canadians and he was convinced they had joined the 36 Division known to have been carrying out invasion exercises. Everything pointed to an amphi-bious landing in his rear. Two days later Kesselring angrily demanded identi-fications from every sector, 'as it was intolerable that troops could "be in fighting contact with the enemy for two days without knowing whom they were fighting" '.[3] The Canadians were in fact not identified until 16 May and that evening, after a brief discussion with von Vietinghoff on the telephone, Kesselring agreed to a general withdrawal to the Hitler Line. General Heidrich refused to abandon Cassino until he was personally ordered to do so by Kesselring himself. The next day von Senger arrived back at his headquarters at Pico to find von Vietinghoff and his staff also established there, having been bombed out of their own headquarters near Frosinone. Von Senger at once set off for Itri where a specially constituted machine-gun battalion from 44 Division, ordered forward by Kesselring, was attempting to stem the tide. He found the situation far worse than reported, with the machine-gunners in retreat and the Allies in hot pursuit. On 18 May Kesselring and von Vietinghoff met to discuss the situation and von Senger was asked to give his appreciation. With 15 Panzer Grenadiers split up and much of their strength already frittered away, there was no chance of mounting a proper counter-attack on XIV Corps front and von Senger had to recommend an immediate orderly withdrawal to prevent his Corps being cut off. As the architect of what was now called the Hitler Line, which he had designed specifically to guard against a penetration of the Gustav Line near the coast, von Senger was very outspoken about the situation. With LI Corps still holding on in the Cassino sector and his own Corps split down the centre and desperately struggling to maintain contact on their left, he saw little chance of the lay back position, that had been so carefully prepared, ever being properly manned. Kesselring, however, would not accept any suggestion of pulling right back. He was only concerned with establishing an intermediate line as far east of Anzio as possible. To achieve this he had already committed 90 Panzer Grenadiers to hold the Esperia defile, where they had arrived piecemeal and been roughly handled by the French, and had also brought up 26 Panzer Division to block the sector south of Pico. Part of 305 Infantry Division had already arrived in the Liri valley and Kesselring now sent for the remainder of the division and most of the 334 Infantry Division from the Adriatic coast, where they would be replaced by 278 Infantry Division from Istria. Von Vietinghoff undoubtedly saw the force of von Senger's argument and felt that the opportunity for an orderly withdrawal to the Hitler Line had been lost. Although that section of the line down as far as Pontecorvo was at that very moment being occupied, he was very worried about the situation south of Pico. If the French broke through here they might well reach Ceprano or Frosinone with disastrous results. 'Kesselring held a different view "regardless of whether we fight on the Senger barrier or have to withdraw, help for the right wing must be the primary consideration".'[4] Determined to restore the situation on the crumbling right flank, Kesselring (on 19 May) ordered 29 Panzer Grenadier Division forward to the Fondi area.

While Kesselring was attempting to regain a grip on the situation the Allies were making ground and the battle was becoming fluid. On 18 May a small armoured force of the Derbyshire Yeomanry, from 6 Armoured Division, just failed to carry Aquino, the key to the northern part of the Hitler Line in the valley, by a *coup de main* and the Canadian Corps were coming up fast on their left. After the capture of S Oliva the French now overlooked Pontecorvo, while down towards the coast II Corps took Itri and Gaeta on 19 May.

Alexander now decided to increase the pressure. 36 Division was dispatched to Anzio and Eighth Army were ordered to attack up the valley before the Germans could settle into the Hitler Line. Enveloping attacks were ordered by the French on Pico and by the Poles on Piedmonte. All these attacks would start on 19 May. On the right, the Poles took Villa Santa Lucia but the men of 1 Parachute Division held out in Piedmonte and on Mount Cairo for seven days of bitter and costly fighting. On the other flank, 26 Panzer and 90 Panzer Grenadier Divisions were equally determined to stand and fight it out and Monte Leucio was the scene of desperate fighting for two days, before it was finally recaptured by the French on 22 May. Pico eventually fell to 3 Algerian Division on the same day. In the valley, 78 Division with 1 Canadian Division on their left had come up against the main defences of the Hitler Line. These defences in many ways were even stronger than those of the Gustav Line in the valley and although they were weakly manned it became obvious that only a proper set-piece attack could succeed in breaking through. To give time for preparations and also for the move forward of 8 Indian Division and 6 Armoured Division over the now congested roads, General Alexander ordered that this co-ordinated attack should start on 23 May. The Canadian Corps would attack north of Pontecorvo while 13 Corps closed right up ready to debouch north of Aquino.

As Eighth Army was squaring up to the northern part of the Hitler Line, II Corps continued to make good progress. The transfer of 36 Division to the beach head had been spread over the four days 18–22 May so as not to draw attention to the move. General Clark, without sufficient landing craft to accelerate the rate of reinforcement by sea, now decided to make a determined effort to reach Anzio overland, taking advantage of the collapse of Tenth Army's right flank. Once Route 7 was open the supply problems at Anzio would be eased. The two divisions of II Corps were directed on Terracina and Fondi with orders to exploit down Route 7. These attacks north-west of Itri, which fell on 19 May, were to be pressed forward immediately. Kesselring expected 29 Panzer Grenadiers to reach Fondi on the morning of 20 May but when he got back to headquarters that evening he was told von Mackensen had protested against the removal of his last mobile division and that the 29 Panzer Grenadiers had not yet started to move south. Kesselring now ordered von Mackensen to take full responsibility for the threatened area on a line from Sperlonga on the coast through Fondi to Frosinone and Valmontone but it was too late. Fondi had been taken on 20 May and by 23 May an American advance guard was approaching Priverno. Elements of 29 Panzer Grenadiers reached Terracina on 22 May and delayed its capture for two days but the effort was too weak and too late. Terracina was abandoned overnight on 23/24 May and within twenty-four hours armoured patrols from the two wings of Fifth Army had advanced to meet each other on the coastal road near Lake Fogliano.

On 21 May Alexander issued orders for VI Corps' attack from the bridge-head to be launched on 23 May. The attack was timed for 0630 hours, just after the Canadian assault went in against the Hitler Line. 1 Armoured and 3 Infantry Divisions, plus the Special Service Force, would capture the area around Cisterna as a base and 36 Division would then 'pass through and advance to a line running across the valley below Velletri supported by 1 Armoured Division. Then reinforced by 3 Division it was to advance on Valmontone.'⁵ To counter any attempted breakout from Anzio, von Macken-sen had five divisions, reinforced by the arrival of 334 Infantry Division from the Adriatic, but with 26 and 90 Panzer Divisions transferred to Tenth Army his armour was reduced to the assault guns of 3 Panzer Grenadiers and a handful of tanks from the two independent Panzer Grenadier battalions. For over four months von Mackensen had been responsible for investing the Anzio beach head. At least these defensive operations had been remarkably successful. Now that the Hermann Göring Division was on its way south, he felt that his sector of the Caesar Line could be held without much difficulty. Deprived of air reconnaissance, however, neither Kesselring nor von Macken-sen had any real estimate of the Allied build up at Anzio. Constantly harassed from the air and forced to move at night as much as possible, the leading elements of the Hermann Göring Division had only reached Viterbo by 23 May. The battle of the Liri valley was about to reach its climax.

In Eighth Army sector opposite the Hitler Line 400 guns were settling down to soften up the German positions and on the night 19–20 May as many as 1,000 shells an hour were falling on known strongpoints. This softening up continued at varying rates of fire and timings until the 1 Canadian divisional attack on 23 May. By this date over 800 guns were in position to support the assault with a barrage on a 3,000-yard front and penetrating to the same distance. By noon 24 May Pontecorvo had been captured but with heavy losses on both sides. Continued resistance at Aquino and delays in getting the tail of 5 Canadian Armoured Division through the breach in the line, however, prevented 13 Corps from advancing until the following day. Mean-while a Canadian armoured brigade, led by the tanks of Lord Strathcona's Horse with the lorried infantry battalions of the Westminster Regiment, seized a crossing over the River Milfa on the afternoon of 24 May and held it overnight against counter-attacks by Colonel Baade's 90 Panzer Grenadiers. This penetration struck the junction point between the two German Corps and from captured orders it was subsequently discovered that 1 Parachute Division had never even received the order to hold the river line by the time the Canadians were across. On the other side of the valley the French Expeditionary Corps were making ground north-westwards towards the River Sacco and Ceccano.

At Anzio the Allied attack had penetrated, on 24 May, two miles north of Cisterna although the town itself had not yet fallen. The moment of decision had come for Kesselring; the left wing of Fourteenth Army was likely to crumble and might soon be under attack by the Americans coming up from the coast. The strong positions in the Alban hills could only act as a pivot for Tenth Army's withdrawal if Valmontone was held as a point of contact between the two armies and Routes 5 and 6 kept open as long as possible. The concentration of the Hermann Göring Division at Valmontone must be speeded up and the troops in the mountains around Belmonte pulled back. If the Caesar Line was to be occupied a general withdrawal by Tenth Army must start immediately. This withdrawal would be covered by XIV Corps, who would take command of all mobile troops in the valley. Over the next two days von Senger ordered his shattered infantry units to move north to an assembly point at Frosinone and dispatched 29 Panzer Grenadiers to check the French Expeditionary Corps' drive towards Route 6. Behind this armoured screen he gradually withdrew his armour northwards. In the mountains opposite 10 Corps, the Germans started their demolition programme on the night 24/25 May and by 26 May both the New Zealanders and the Italians had taken up the advance on the general axis of Atina–Sora–Avezzano. Progress against minefields, extensive demolitions and rearguards in the extremely difficult mountainous country, however, was very slow.

On 24 May General Truscott was holding 36 Division ready to pass through towards Cori and Artena but he represented to Clark, who had established a command post on the beach head, that von Mackensen might concentrate not only the Hermann Göring Division but also 3 Panzer Grenadier and 4 Parachute Division at Valmontone. He later wrote, 'Any such concentration might delay us at Valmontone long enough to permit the German main forces to escape. If there was any withdrawal from the western part of the beach head, I thought that an attack to the north-west might be the best way to cut off the enemy withdrawal north of the Alban hills. My staff was already preparing plans to meet this contingency. Clark agreed with my analysis and asked that I keep the plan up to date.'[6] The next day 3 Division took Cisterna and reached Cori. As the attack was going well Truscott held 36 Division back in reserve. A strong armoured force from 1 Armoured Division, supported by infantry, were now well through the valley past Velletri to within less than four miles of Artena. The Special Service Force were also making good progress through the mountains to protect the right flank of this thrust. Truscott's appreciation was that his troops would be astride Route 6 at Valmontone by the following morning and his corps had already taken 9,000 prisoners. When he got back to his command post late in the afternoon he found a staff officer from Fifth Army Headquarters waiting to tell him that Clark's orders were that the attack north-west would be mounted as soon as possible. Truscott was 'dumbfounded'. There was no sign of any withdrawal from the western part of the bridgehead; his attack was going well against light opposition and now, within a few hours of its success, he was ordered to turn and attack the strongest German positions head on. Truscott said he must first speak to General Clark personally but the reply was that Clark had already left the bridgehead and could not be reached even by radio. 'Such was the order that turned the main effort of the beach-head forces from the Valmontone Gap and prevented the destruction of the German Tenth Army.'[7] Truscott was now faced with extricating 1 Armoured Division (they were replaced by 36 Division) and switching it behind his front to come in on the left of 34 and 45 Divisions. These three divisions would now be directed on Campoleone and Lanuvio on a five-mile front. The Divisional Commanders were given their orders at 2300 hours 25 May and the attack started twelve hours later – a remarkable achievement in staff work. 'Clark's Chief-of-Staff, General Gruenther, was given the delicate task of explaining this unilateral decision to Alexander the next day after it had become irrevocable.'[8] To begin with the attack went well but the three German divisions, 3 Panzer Grenadiers, 65 Infantry and 4 Parachute Divisions, were falling back on well-prepared positions in the strongest part of the Caesar Line. After four days' hard fighting with heavy losses Campoleone was captured but on the right 34 Division was still a mile short of Lanuvio. With the support of a small tank force and the Special Service Force, 3 Division took Artena in the afternoon of 27 May but was unable to reach Route 6 two and a half miles beyond. Here the Hermann Göring Division were concentrating and had been joined by elements from the inexperienced 92 Infantry Division, brought down from north of Rome. Kesselring had expected the Hermann Göring Division to reach Valmontone by 24 May at the latest, but their march had been under constant air attack and the main body did not arrive until 27/28 May. Kesselring in fact had hoped that they would be brought into action forward of Artena in conjunction with the remnants of 362 and 715 Infantry Divisions.

On Eighth Army front Kesselring had one last opportunity of checking the advance. About Ceprano the River Liri came down from the north parallel to Route 82, while the valley of the River Sacco continued through Ceccano towards Valmontone. Arce could only be approached through a defile and defensive positions here and on the two river lines would protect the retreat of the remnants of Tenth Army both by Routes 82 and 6. On 26 May 8 Indian Division occupied Roccasecca but 6 Armoured Division was held up at Arce. 78 Division was now sent on 27 May across country towards Ceprano, ready to take up the advance up Route 6 as soon as the Canadians had forced a crossing. But it was clear that the German positions could not hold out much longer and that the withdrawal of Tenth Army by Route 6 and through the Simbruini mountains must be speeded up. All depended now on the Fourteenth Army. The French Expeditionary Corps, advancing in two columns in a north-westerly direction, were approaching Ceccano on 28 May, by which time Ceprano had fallen and a bridge had been constructed below the town. Although von Senger was getting worried about withdrawing

Crossing of the River Senio—8 Indian Division passes through, April 1945.

Fantails moving through floods towards Argenta, April 1945.

First pontoon
across the Po
on Eighth Army
front, constructed
in twelve hours,
April 1945.

General von
Vietinghoff in
Modena after the
surrender of Army
Group 'C', May
1945.

his Corps from Frosinone, he was even more concerned about the gap between the two armies and on 26 May he suggested to von Vietinghoff that the mobile divisions should be sent back as quickly as possible to hold Valmontone, which he considered the 'point of greatest threat to all German divisions standing south of the line Valmontone–Sora'.[9] Against overwhelming Allied air superiority the mountain roads east of Route 6 had become death traps and he feared that the main escape route through Subiaco to Tivoli would be cut by a thrust northwards across the head of the Sacco valley. The last chance of establishing contact with Fourteenth Army (after 26 May) and gaining time for the occupation of the Caesar Line, was to concentrate on this 'key point' at Valmontone where von Senger thought he could 'throw in' a division each day and possibly counter attack towards the Alban hills to prevent a breakthrough to Rome. Kesselring, however, was still relying on von Mackensen holding the 'hinge' positions around the Alban hills and left Tenth Army to make their way back as fast as they could. On 28 May 6 Armoured Division took the positions held by 1 Parachute Division on Monte Grande south of Arce, the denial of which had been vital to cover LI Mountain Corps' withdrawal toward Avezzano. The Canadians took Pofi on 29 May and entered Frosinone two days later, while 13 Corps advanced to Arpino and began to swing northwards. The French Expeditionary Corps were still making good progress and General Juin was not worried so much by the slowing down of Eighth Army's advance as by the situation developing on his own front, where he was about to run into a bottleneck and anticipated considerable congestion on Route 6, where his own Corps, the Canadians and possibly part of 13 Corps were likely to converge on Colleferro. On 28 May he suggested to Clark that Eighth Army's left flank should be on the axis Subiaco–Rieti–Terni, leaving him with a sector bounded to the left by the axis Prossedi–Gavignano–Tivoli. As he pointed out, the French Corps would then be well placed to take Valmontone from the east if von Mackensen continued to stand in front of Rome and he would also subsequently occupy 'sa place normale à l'est du Tibre dans les montagnes'.[10] Clark was much preoccupied with the battle south of Albano but agreed to the proposal. Alexander, however, still wanted Route 6 as one of the axes for the advance of Eighth Army and the result was that Juin was told to keep south of the Secco, while Clark concentrated 85 and 88 Divisions at Anzio and sent them with II Corps headquarters to take over the Artena sector, where 3 Division and the Special Service Force were still held down. In the Velletri–Lanuvio sector Clark now lined up 36, 34, 45 Divisions and 1 Armoured Division, with 1 British Division to protect the flank of his attack, while 5 Division held the coast sector. The attack by both II and VI Corps was ordered for 1 June. General Walker's 36 Division meanwhile had been pushing forward patrols east of Velletri and had found a gap in the German positions on Monte Artemisio. General Truscott immediately sent his corps engineers to help develop a tank track and before the main attack opened on 1 June 36 Division had reached the crest of Colle Laziali and cut the road west of Velletri. Von Mackensen's failure to close this gap resulted in his subsequent removal from command. This brilliant operation by 36 Division gave Truscott the key to the German positions astride the Alban hills. After a bitter fight Lanuvio fell on 3 June. 5 Division beat off a heavy counter-attack and the Germans were now being pushed back against the Tiber along the whole front. II Corps had been equally successful and captured Valmontone on 2 June and pushed on to Palestrina. The defeat of Fourteenth Army was complete. Racing down Route 6, II Corps turned down the left bank of the Tiber to enter Rome on 4 June, while 1 US Armoured Division of VI Corps entered the city by Route 7. While General Clark was being driven through the streets of Rome to take the formal surrender, the French Expeditionary Corps advance guards were working through the mountains close to Tivoli and 6 South African Armoured Division were leading the Canadian advance into Paliano. On the other axis of advance, 13 Corps were halfway to Subiaco and 10 Corps were south-west of Avezzano. On the Adriatic flank the Germans had no option but to conform to the retreat of the two defeated armies, now fleeing north from Rome on both sides of the Tiber.

Leaving 20,000 prisoners and probably well over half as many dead and wounded the two defeated German armies hurried northwards as best they could. The railways were still being cut by the Allied bombers and forced on to the roads the German transport columns came under relentless air attack. 'Their convoys were hemmed in by the mountains and ravines, and forced to keep to the highways. Fighters, fighter-bombers, and medium bombers caused fearful havoc in the columns of road transport. Their method of attack was to smash the head and tail vehicles of a convoy, and then deal with the centre at leisure. Burnt-out, battered, and wrecked vehicles of all kinds strewed the roadside, lay in ditches; the enemy casualties mounted, with no gain but only loss to show for their sacrifice.'[11] For the period 12–31 May the Tactical Air Force claimed 2,556 German motor vehicles destroyed and 2,236 damaged. Figures for the month of June were even greater by a third. With a superiority of over ten to one, the Mediterranean Allied Air Forces' aircraft had roamed the battlefield almost unopposed from the very start of the offensive. From 11–13 May the Strategic Bombers, after first attacking both Kesselring's and von Vietinghoff's headquarters, continued their attacks on the major marshalling yards and ports. On 14 May the airfields at Piacenza and Puggio Emilia were heavily bombed. No other major attacks on German airfields were necessary and the Luftwaffe never achieved more than an average of something over fifty sorties a day, with an occasional maximum effort of 200, for at least the next month. The Strategic Bombers now reverted to the POINTBLANK targets around Vienna, oilfields and concentrations in the Balkans, and to supporting Yugoslav partisans until the fall of Rome, when they once again intervened in attacking communication centres in the north. After the first three days of the offensive, the whole of the Tactical Air Force squadrons were employed in direct support of the land battle. Medium bombers attacked gun positions and strongpoints and bombed defiles and bridges to restrict the German movement behind the battlefield. Light and fighter-bombers were largely engaged in neutralizing the two main gun areas in the Liri valley and at Atina. Special mobile teams, equipped with VHF wireless equipment, worked direct with the ground troops. Linked by wireless with air headquarters and with squadrons on standby, or in the air circling in a 'cab rank', they were able to produce very quick results. Initially, vantage points such as Mount Trocchio were used by these 'Rover' teams allotted to supporting a particular formation. Later the teams moved forward close behind the advance and achieved excellent results. Full and effective air co-operation continued until the two fronts joined, by which time the medium bombers were attacking troop concentrations south of Rome and had also switched to attacking the railway lines leading down towards the battle area. The light bombers were now attacking dumps in and behind the battle area and the fighter-bombers had started armed reconnaissance sweeps to attack the reserves moving south and later to harry the retreating convoys and columns trying to escape along the congested roads. In the first seven days of the offensive, Mediterranean Allied Air Forces flew 20,500 sorties and during DIADEM 51,500 tons of bombs were dropped, largely as a follow up of the STRANGLE programme. The only significant German bomber operation was an attack on 12/13 May against airfields on Corsica where twenty-three Allied planes were destroyed and ninety damaged, an indication of Kesselring's preoccupation with the threat of an Allied landing in his rear. A few JU88s attempted to intervene at Minturno in a close support role, both by day and night, but these planes were withdrawn to France early in June. For the period 12 May to 22 June, Mediterranean Allied Air Force claims were 176 German aircraft destroyed with 44 probables and 93 damaged. Allied losses were 438 aircraft, practically all from flak. On the ground the Allied battle casualties amounted to 42,000 men. This figure was made up as follows:

Fifth Army	18,000
Eighth Army and the British Division with Fifth Army	14,000
French Expeditionary Corps	10,000

The battles of the Liri valley and for Rome bear the stamp of five commanders. On the German side we see Kesselring caught out by the threat of a landing in his rear and holding on too long at Cassino. Von Mackensen's parochial attitude brought near disaster to the Germans in the fight for Valmontone and his failure to stop the gap in his positions on the vital Colle Laziali feature lost him his command. Although Kesselring was completely deceived as to the point and strength of the Allied attack and unable to make proper use of his reserve divisions, it was his tenacity that saved much of both armies to fight again. Alexander stands out as a brilliant strategist; as the architect of an Allied victory that forced the Germans back to the Arno and beyond. The credit for the opening up of the Liri valley undoubtedly goes to Juin and the success of the French drive through the Aurunci mountains amply supports his earlier concept of avoiding head-on attacks against Cassino. Finally Clark's controversial decision to turn for Rome must be seen in the political context of his determination that that particular plum belonged to Fifth Army. The capture of Rome two days before the Allied Armies landed in Normandy was indeed a glittering prize but the occupation of an open city, even if it is the capital, is a poor alternative to the conventional object in battle – the destruction of the enemy's forces in the field.

16
The Strait Jacket

Kesselring reinforced: ANVIL debate drags on: Alexander's alternative discussed: Eisenhower's need for ports: Allied opinion divided: Churchill appeals to Roosevelt: Riviera landings: Fifth Army's strength halved: The pursuit slows up in central Italy: Lake Trasimene and Arezzo: Allies reach the Arno.

1944	
22 May	Wilson warns Alexander that he will lose seven divisions required for ANVIL during June and July.
Early June	German reinforcements arrive for Kesselring.
7 June	Alexander issues fresh orders for pursuit.
	VI Corps captures Civitavecchia.
9 June	Withdrawal of units from Fifth Army and FEC for ANVIL starts.
	General Truscott and VI Corps HQ leave to start planning.
14 June	Combined Chiefs of Staff select four possible areas for ANVIL – target date now 25 July.
17 June	Alexander proposes offensive through northern Italy as alternative to ANVIL.
19–22 June	Storms in English Channel. OVERLORD build-up slows down.
20–30 June	Battles for Trasimene Line.
23 June	Eisenhower supports ANVIL (on south of France) with target date 15–30 August.
27 June and 1 July	Churchill appeals to Roosevelt to support Alexander's proposals.
2 July	Chiefs of Staff directive orders ANVIL (on south of France) to be launched 15 August.
4–17 July	Battle for Arezzo.
18 July	Polish Corps takes Ancona.
By 4 Aug	Germans complete withdrawal behind line of River Arno.
6 Aug	Churchill proposes ANVIL (now DRAGOON) landing is made on west coast of France owing to changed conditions in battle of Normandy.
15 Aug	DRAGOON – Seventh Army lands on French Riviera.

Out of Kesselring's twenty-three divisions in Army Group 'C' eighteen had been committed in the battle for Rome. The Hermann Göring Division had suffered particularly heavy losses and 92 Infantry Division was so reduced in strength that it was disbanded. Three other divisions (71, 94 and 715) had virtually ceased to exist and the remainder had suffered heavily. Indeed Alexander's estimate of the German forces that would be available to hold the Pisa–Rimini line was the equivalent of ten divisions. In the northern Apennines the Germans had constructed what became known as the Gothic Line. These positions, some 200 miles in length, had been reconnoitred at the time of the Feltre conference nearly a year previously, when Hitler had told Mussolini that he was about to pull back to the northern Apennines. Now Kesselring's immediate task was to slow down the Allied pursuit of the remnants of Fourteenth Army, which was now under the Command of Lieutenant-General Lemelsen. Hitler had already seen the danger of a rapid Allied follow-up and two Luftwaffe Field Divisions (19 and 20) had already been ordered south from Denmark and Holland respectively. The 20 Luftwaffe Division, the first to arrive, together with 162 Turcoman Grenadier Division from Cecina were thrown in near Civitavecchia. The 356 Grenadier Division from Genoa and 16 SS Panzer Grenadiers from Hungary were also allocated to Fourteenth Army and hurried south, while 42 Jäger Division from the Balkans and 34 Infantry Division (from Russia) moved into Lombardy. Finally the OKW ordered forward a battalion of Tiger tanks from the central reserve in France and sent the whole of three divisions, that were forming in Germany, to fill up the establishment of the three infantry divisions that had been annihilated in the French breakthrough into the Liri valley and at Cisterna. These reinforcements, which totalled eight divisions, were supplemented by twelve battalions of Czechs and two Italian divisions which were used for guard and coastal defence duties in northern Italy. The dispatch of these reinforcements at the very time of the Normandy battle clearly show Hitler's determination to protect the southern frontiers of the Reich and contrast sharply with the development of Allied strategy that will now be described. It will be recalled that the directive given to General Wilson in the middle of April by no means closed the door on ANVIL and all that the American Chiefs of Staff would agree to was that the attack on southern France should be postponed to a target date of 10 July. While the decision to postpone ANVIL had given Eisenhower the much needed extra landing craft for OVERLORD and kept Wilson's forces intact for the DIADEM operations, it also re-focused the attention of both British and American planners on the relative value of ANVIL *vis-à-vis* a continued offensive through Italy. Given sufficient landing craft, the British saw little difficulty over the landing itself but felt that the Normandy battle would not benefit from a landing in the south of France, in accordance with the original ANVIL concept, as the Germans would be able to assemble nine divisions from central and southern France to check the advance inland by the ten Allied divisions it was proposed to land. With no certainty of decisive results in the Rhône valley, they saw the danger of the loss of initiative in Italy through the diversion of a number of Allied divisions and the fact that there could be no further immediate threat of another landing. The alternative seemed far more logical – to continue the offensive in Italy, drawing into the battle as many German divisions as possible, while at the same time maintaining the threat of a landing which would tie down further divisions on the long coastlines that the Germans must still guard.

The Americans, however, saw a landing in southern France as having an immediate and possibly decisive effect on the OVERLORD operation in the north. They now acknowledged that the offensive in Italy had absorbed a number of German divisions but felt that the situation might alter at a critical period of OVERLORD and that the Germans might take advantage of the pause before the opening of Alexander's spring offensive to switch many of their divisions to France. A fresh landing outside Italy, however, was a different matter. This must tie down German forces and have the further advantage that American troops would no longer be involved in 'the maintenance of the offensive in Italy for an indefinite period'.[1] Towards the end of March, General Roberts of the American Strategic Section, Operation Division wrote, 'if we cancel ANVIL completely, the following will be true:

(a) We get into political difficulties with the French.
(b) OVERLORD will lose at least ten fighting divisions.
(c) Our service forces continue to support the western Mediterranean.
(d) Our divisions and the French divisions will be committed to a costly, unremunerative, inching advance in Italy. The people of both the United States and France may or may not take this indefinitely.
(e) Once committed to Italy, we have our forces pointed towards South-Eastern Europe and will have the greatest difficulty in preventing their use for occupation forces in Austria, Hungary and southern Germany.'[2]

In mid-April the Joint Chiefs of Staff, in an attempt to keep ANVIL alive, had proposed diverting landing craft, that were due to leave for the Pacific in late May and June, to the Mediterranean. This, however, was conditional on the craft being used only for ANVIL and they went so far as to propose that the operation should be mounted by 10 July and take precedence over the operations aiming at the capture of Rome. In a tactfully worded message to

General Marshall on 16 April Churchill wrote: 'what I cannot bear is to agree beforehand to starve a battle or have to break it off just at the moment when success, after long efforts and heavy losses, may be in view. . . . The whole of this difficult question only arises out of the absurd shortage of LSTs. How it is that the plans of two great Empires like Britain and the United States should be so hamstrung and limited by a hundred or two of these particular vessels will never be understood by history.'[3] Alanbrooke's comment in his diary for 19 April was 'history will never forgive them for bargaining equipment against strategy. . . .'[4] Early in May, Wilson was called back to London to discuss the various alternatives for a major amphibious assault in support of OVERLORD. These were now seen as the seizure of a port in western France such as Bordeaux, or landing in the south as already proposed by ANVIL, in either case after OVERLORD was successfully under way; a 'left hook' in Italy, to aid or follow up the attack on Rome, and finally the capture of air bases across the Adriatic. Both Wilson and Eisenhower were against an assault on western France being mounted from the Mediterranean and on Wilson's suggestion four possible areas of attack all in the Mediterranean were chosen. These were Sete, Toulon, Genoa and possibly Civitavecchia 'if the course of the campaign demanded'. It was agreed that the (four) divisions not committed to DIADEM would start preparations immediately. This proposal met with the approval of the Joint Chiefs of Staff, who now arranged to send 19 LSTs, each carrying an LCT, to arrive in the Mediterranean between 20 June and 20 July. Within a few days, on 17 May, Wilson submitted his appreciation in favour of a landing in the south of France on the Riviera, rather than at Sete which had poor beaches and was out of effective fighter range from Corsica or Italy. At this time Churchill was continuing to press his preference for an assault on Bordeaux but meanwhile Wilson had to start planning and on 22 May sent Alexander the necessary directive. Alexander's task remained the destruction of the German forces in Italy and he would have a free hand up to the fall of Rome. Subsequently he 'should bear in mind the importance of the capture of the Ancona area', giving ports and airfields for operations across the Adriatic. After referring to the alternatives for amphibious operations, as set out above, Wilson gave Alexander warning that if the area chosen was outside the Italian theatre of operations, he would have to release three US infantry divisions and the whole of the French Expeditionary Corps. Subject to the capture of Rome, the earliest dates for these reliefs would be an experienced US Corps Headquarters by 1 June, two US divisions and one French division between 17 and 27 June, followed by the remaining divisions at longer intervals.[5]

Within a fortnight Rome had fallen and the Allies were pursuing the Germans northwards. Alexander now put in a strong plea for a further alternative – the continuation of the offensive in Italy at its present strength with the object of breaking through at Pistoia and Bologna by the middle of

August at the latest. Subsequently he would be free to turn towards Turin and Genoa as a base for operations in France, or towards Padua and Venice for operations into Austria. A less satisfactory alternative at this point would be to hold the Pisa–Rimini line and release 'substantial resources for operations outside Italy'. As the Joint Chiefs of Staff were visiting London and the Normandy bridgehead in a few days' time, these proposals were discussed almost immediately at two meetings on 11 and 13 June. Marshall was anxious to 'funnel the American divisions accumulating in the United States into the main front as soon as possible'.[6] Fifteen extra combat-loaders would be dispatched from America and he favoured a landing at Sete, followed by an advance through the Carcassone Gap to open up a port on the Bay of Biscay. An alternative, providing the Allied Armies had reached the River Loire, would be a direct landing in the Bay of Biscay and it was agreed that Eisenhower should be responsible for planning this particular operation. It seems evident that neither side realized the full import of Alexander's proposals, which was directly opposed to any diversion of troops from Italy. The Combined Chiefs of Staff generally agreed that Alexander's success should be exploited to the full but the Americans still wanted a three-division assault landing, probably in France, by the end of July. At the second meeting the Americans themselves pointed out that this might restrict Alexander's advance to the River Po. At this point the British Chiefs of Staff proposed that Alexander should halt on reaching the Pisa–Rimini line and possibly develop an amphibious assault on Istria 'to maintain the offensive'. Both King and Portal supported this proposal under the circumstances where the Russians launched an offensive towards the Balkans. Alanbrooke later wrote, 'Now at last we had put the south of France operation in its right strategic position. By the time we reached the Pisa–Rimini line, the Italian theatre should have played its part in holding German reserves away from northern France. We should then contemplate the landing in southern France to provide a front for French forces from North Africa and to co-operate on southern flank of OVERLORD operations. The Bay of Biscay landings did not attract me.'[7] On this note this particular part of the discussion concluded and the Combined Chiefs of Staff informed both Eisenhower and Wilson, on the following day, of their views concerning operations in the Mediterranean in the light of the success of DIADEM and the progress of OVERLORD. 'The over-riding necessity is to apply all our forces to the enemy at the earliest possible moment, in the way best calculated to assist the success of operation OVERLORD. We must complete the destruction of the German armed forces in Italy south of the Pisa–Rimini line. No Allied forces should be withdrawn from the battle that are necessary for this purpose.' The telegram continued by indicating that, after reaching this line, there was a choice of three amphibious operations against the south or west of France and at the head of the Adriatic but that the final choice depended on the progress of OVERLORD and the Russian offensive, which in fact opened in ten days' time, and of the German reaction to both. Meanwhile preparations must be pressed forward. The scale of the assault would be three divisions, plus an airborne division using such extra landing craft as Eisenhower could spare or the United States could provide. Without prejudice to the completion of operations to reach the Pisa–Rimini line, the target date should be 25 July. The Combined Chiefs of Staff were 'not inclined to favour landing in the area of Marseilles because of the strength of the coastal defences and the unprofitable line of advance up the Rhône Valley.' They felt the choice lay between a landing at Sete or a direct descent on the west coast of France, and planning and preparations would begin 'forthwith'.[8] The issue of this directive brought the whole question of Alexander's proposal to strike through the Gothic Line towards France or Austria, supported by small-scale amphibious attacks, as an alternative to any one of the proposed amphibious landings on France, right out into the open. At Wilson's request, Alexander presented his appreciation at Allied Forces Headquarters at Caserta on 17 June. Alexander's two armies, even allowing for recent losses, amounted to twenty-seven active divisions against an estimated fourteen German divisions. If Kesselring proposed to defend the Po valley he would have to be reinforced by between four and seven divisions and these could hardly come from the Russian Front or from the Balkans, where a major withdrawal might collapse that flank. At the worst, Alexander estimated he could reach the Po valley during August. A subsequent attack into France, he felt, would be of limited value to OVERLORD and restricted by the difficult terrain west of Genoa. 'A move to the east, on the other hand, would pass initially through easier country at the foot of the Julian Alps, would stimulate the partisans in Yugoslavia, and might result in a common front with the Russians against Germany's sensitive south-eastern flank. It was therefore likely to affect the whole position in Europe more powerfully than the apparently more direct move into France.'[9] Alexander considered eighteen divisions would be needed for this drive through the Ljubljana Gap but a reserve of six divisions was necessary to provide reliefs, which would bring the total requirements up to twenty-four divisions. The present proposals for landing on the south of France, however, would remove five to seven divisions, practically all from the Fifth Army, thus slowing down his advance and possibly causing a postponement of the attack on the Gothic Line. A continuation of his advance in strength, however, would draw German reinforcements to the Apennine positions at the earliest date. Up to this point Wilson supported the concept of a major assault landing to hold down the German reserves but now he inclined towards Alexander's view, which was generally supported by both the naval and air commanders and the administrative staff. Wilson saw, however, the difficulty of persuading the French to give up their hopes of a direct entry through the south of France and this point was taken up by General Rooks, his Deputy Chief of Staff, who thought that the land campaign in Italy could be continued satisfactorily without the French and the three American divisions already selected for an ANVIL operation. General Devers, Wilson's Deputy Commander, now objected to any operation except one on the south of France on the grounds that 'General Eisenhower needed not only a diversion of German troops from the northern front but a major port in France for the accommodation of supply services for the Allied Expeditionary Force there'.[10] Later that day Generals Marshall and Arnold arrived on a visit. Their discussion with Wilson was attended by Admiral Sir John Cunningham and Lieutenant-General Eaker, both of whom supported Alexander's proposals. Marshall took the view that the Germans might well pull right back and that the river line of the Adige and Piave would be easily defended. Thus Alexander would first be 'beating the air' and later fail to divert major German forces from other fronts. In any case Eisenhower needed an additional major port in France, as some forty or fifty US divisions were 'ready for action' and could not be handled, together with their supplies, through the present limited port facilities in France. Marshall concluded by stating that these reinforcements were only to be used in France. Wilson was now faced with a direct choice between ANVIL and Alexander's counter proposal, for, as he pointed out, there were insufficient troops to carry out both simultaneously.

Two days later Wilson called a further conference. General Eaker and Air Marshal Slessor were strongly opposed to splitting the air effort, as General Marshall had been prepared to do, as they saw the offensive in Italy petering out on reaching the Gothic Line. Admiral Cunningham similarly was opposed to a double offensive, as his naval forces could not supply both assaults 'on a sustained offensive basis'. The position of the French troops again raised difficulties. Wilson saw their removal from his command, without replacement, as prejudicing his ability to carry out the Combined Chiefs of Staff directive for completing the destruction of the Germans south of the Pisa–Rimini line. General Marshall, however, pointed out that General de Gaulle was pressing for French troops to make 'an early entry' into France but as they were untrained for amphibious operations the assault must be carried out by US divisions. Fully supported by his naval and air commanders, Wilson now sent a signal on 19 June to the Combined Chiefs of Staff and also to Eisenhower. His recommendation was that, from an overall strategic point of view and providing Eisenhower's beach head was secure, Alexander's proposal should be adopted. He saw a continued offensive in Italy as being more effective in drawing German reserves away from northern France and at an earlier date. An advance to the Ljubljana Gap, he felt, could bring the defeat of Germany in 1944 rather than in the first half of 1945. If on the other hand it became vitally necessary to seize another port, then the assault should fall on southern France but this could not be achieved before 15 August.

Such a decision, however, would involve a six weeks' halt in front of the Pisa–Rimini line, break up a first-class fighting machine and give the Germans a chance of recovering their balance. As the withdrawal of divisions for an ANVIL operation would have to start in less than ten days' time, he asked for an early decision and also sent his Chief of Staff to reach London on 21 June, so as to be available to discuss any details of his proposals.[11] Wilson's recommendation served to revive all the earlier arguments against ANVIL as, although the British Chiefs of Staff now agreed that a landing in the south of France was preferable to one near Bordeaux, they were anxious to explore the possibility of Alexander's plan which had been wholeheartedly supported by Field Marshal Smuts who attended their meetings on 21 June. On his way back to South Africa from the Dominion Prime Ministers' Conference, Smuts called on Wilson to discuss the matter further and on 23 June he telegraphed Churchill fully endorsing his earlier opinion. Meanwhile the English Channel had been swept by four days of serious storms (between 19–22 June) which had checked the build-up of OVERLORD and reduced the Allied air effort. An attack on Cherbourg had just been launched but Caen was still in German hands. The Mulberry artificial harbour in the American sector had been seriously damaged and, faced with a slowing up of his operations, Eisenhower became 'alarmed by the possibilities of a stalemate'.[12] Eisenhower now directly intervened in the debate, in a signal to the Combined Chiefs of Staff dated 23 June, and came out firmly in favour of ANVIL. He now saw little chance of a landing at Bordeaux and with much of his assault shipping damaged in the storm, felt it unlikely that he could spare any for the Mediterranean. The answer was to stick to the Combined Chiefs of Staff decision and get ANVIL under way by 15 August and not later than 30 August. Otherwise he wanted all the French and one or two US divisions transferred from Italy to Normandy as soon as possible, as, in his view, 'France is the decisive theatre'. What he wanted was the port of Marseilles as a means of opening a route to the Ruhr and he would only supply additional resources for this particular operation. The American Chiefs of Staff went further, recommending that General Wilson should make every effort to launch ANVIL by 1 August and that Eisenhower should release the necessary additional landing craft and support vessels between 1 and 10 July.

The debate had now reached deadlock. Churchill and the Chiefs of Staff were unwilling to sacrifice the campaign in Italy when they felt that means could be found to reinforce OVERLORD more directly than through Marseilles. The American Joint Chiefs of Staff 'were in complete disagreement . . . the desire is to deploy as many United States divisions in France and as quickly as possible. A successful advance by Alexander's force in Italy does not promote this possibility.'[13] Allied Intelligence had in fact just received a report that Hitler had issued orders for the Gothic Line to be held at all cost. This news, confirming Alexander's appreciation, spurred on the Chiefs of

Staff to reiterate their argument against ANVIL. Churchill now made a direct appeal to Roosevelt, following his telegram up with a memorandum (dispatched on 28 June) clearly and forcefully setting out the British argument. Three short extracts point to the nub of the whole debate.

In choosing points of landing or attack regard must be paid first, to their tactical relations with the main enterprise and battle proceeding under General Eisenhower in Western France, and, secondly, to the strain produced upon the Central Power of Germany, the OKW. The optimum is to combine both.

It is better to have two ventures than three, and there are certainly not enough LSTs etc available for more than two major ventures.

Let us resolve not to wreck one great campaign for the sake of another. Both can be won.[14]

Roosevelt's reply came the following day: the views of the Joint Chiefs of Staff were unaltered and he was backing them. Furthermore he could not agree to US troops being employed 'against Istria and into the Balkans' and saw difficulties with the French. He himself 'should never survive even a slight set back in OVERLORD if it were known that fairly large forces had been diverted to the Balkans'.[15] If agreement could not be reached the matter must be referred to Stalin. In a last appeal to the President, Churchill pointed out (on 1 July) that Roosevelt himself at Teheran had first proposed operations at the head of the Adriatic. As for Stalin's views he wrote:

I have considered your suggestion that we should lay our respective cases before Stalin. . . . I do not know what he would say if the issue was put to him to decide. On military grounds he might be greatly interested in the eastward movement of Alexander's Army which, without entering the Balkans, would profoundly affect all the forces there and which, in conjunction with any attacks he may make upon Rumania or with Rumania against Hungarian Transylvania, might produce the most far-reaching results. On a long-term political view, he might prefer that the British and Americans should do their share in France in this very hard fighting that is to come, and that East, Middle and Southern Europe, should fall naturally into his control. However it is better to settle the matter for ourselves and between ourselves.[16]

Churchill continued by saying that if the Joint Chiefs of Staff pressed the decision for ANVIL, His Majesty's Government could only accept the decision under 'a solemn protest. I need scarcely say we shall do our best to make a success of anything that is undertaken.'[17] The following day Roosevelt replied that the Combined Chiefs of Staff directive must be sent to Wilson. This ordered ANVIL for 15 August on a three-division assault basis, plus an airborne landing, building up to ten divisions. Eisenhower would supply the necessary additional resources. With his remaining resources Wilson was to carry out his present directive for operations in Italy. This decision, so long in the making and perhaps not entirely unexpected, came as a bitter disappointment to the Allied command in Italy and had a most profound effect on the Campaign, which was to drag on through another long and hard winter for ten more months.

By early August the situation in Normandy had changed drastically as the Western flank of the German forces around the bridgehead began to crumble. Granville and Avranches had been captured and a thrust southwards was about to reach the River Loire (on 6 August) cutting off the whole of the Brittany peninsula. The battle of the Falaise–Argentin pocket was about to open. Churchill made one more attempt to divert the assault landing (now called DRAGOON) to the west coast of France. Roosevelt was in the Pacific and Churchill signalled out to him suggesting that such a move, taking the shortest route across France, would be 'decisive for Eisenhower's victorious advance'.[18] Hoping that Harry Hopkins would influence the Joint Chiefs of Staff, he signalled out to Washington pointing out that Marseilles was 500 miles from the main battle front and that forces landed there were unlikely to influence the fighting in northern France for about ninety days. This forecast appears to have been based on the outline ANVIL plan discussed by Patch and Truscott in mid-June which gave D plus ninety as the date for the concentration of the DRAGOON forces on Eisenhower's right flank in the area Chalons-sur-Saône, Lyons, Vichy. Hopkins replied on 7 August that he was quite certain that Roosevelt would not agree and that in any case supply through the Brittany ports could not keep pace with this extra commitment. Churchill now travelled down to Portsmouth to see Eisenhower and try and persuade him to switch the landing to Bordeaux, a plan that now had the support of Bedell-Smith, Eisenhower's Chief of Staff, and the first Sea Lord Admiral Sir Andrew Cunningham, although Admiral Ramsay disapproved of any change of plan. Eisenhower firmly stood his ground and the following day a short message from Roosevelt clinched the matter.

Seven days later the DRAGOON assault went in, supported by six battleships and monitors, twenty-one cruisers, one hundred destroyers and 'the greatest air effort in the Mediterranean to date'[19] by the Mediterranean Allied air forces which flew 4,249 sorties on D-day alone. The D-day casualties in Patch's Seventh Army, amongst the three assault divisions and the 5,000 paratroopers, were 183 killed and wounded with 479 non-battle casualties.[20] Two German divisions had been thrown back with serious losses including 2,129 taken as prisoners. The landing owed its success principally to the overwhelming naval and air support but much credit was due to previous realistic training of the assault divisions and the speed and thoroughness with which the final staff work was carried out. As soon as the strength of the landing was fully appreciated, the Germans started an orderly withdrawal up the Rhône valley, somewhat hastened by the Allied bombers and harried by guerilla bands of the French Resistance. The advance of Seventh Army consequently was more rapid than expected and on 11 September had reached Dijon. Here a junction was made with elements from the US Third

Army, that had swept eastwards from the Normandy beach head through Orléans and Troyes. Patch's Seventh Army had advanced 300 miles in twenty-seven days but could hardly be said to have drawn off any German reserves from the main front. In fact the German divisions from the Riviera, although driven back with fairly heavy losses including the loss of 20,000 prisoners, now slipped into position on the left flank of the German forces holding the western frontier of the Reichland. By now the Normandy battle was over and 21 Army Group had swept forward across the plains to the Belgian frontier and beyond. In six days Second Army had advanced 250 miles to reach Antwerp, while the US First Army had reached the River Meuse above Sedan. The need for the port of Marseilles as a supply port had been the prime factor in the ANVIL decision and follow-up divisions were now landed. These consisted of an additional French division, three American armoured divisions and three infantry divisions. By April 1945 an Alpine division and five more infantry divisions had also been landed. The force was meanwhile organized as Sixth Army Group under General Devers. After joining up with Eisenhower's forces at Dijon, however, a further two months passed before General Devers mounted any major operations in his sector.

With the future of the Italian campaign very much in the balance, the warning order received by Alexander on 22 May to release seven divisions during June and July soon began to influence the pace of the pursuit north from Rome. Truscott had known since about the middle of March that he would be in command of the assault divisions in any ANVIL type operation and, within a week of the capture of Rome, VI Corps Headquarters was withdrawn to take part in the planning for the three possible operations, chosen by the Combined Chiefs of Staff on 14 June. It is of interest to note that Clark at this time supported Alexander's alternative strategy but 'thought there was little likelihood it would be approved by (the American) Chiefs of Staff'.[21] With the target date for the landing as 25 July the withdrawal of the American divisions for the assault, which Truscott was allowed to nominate, was speeded up. Consequently 45 Division came under command of Seventh Army immediately, to be followed by 3 Division on 17 June, 36 Division on 27 June and two French divisions between 24 June and the first week of July. A number of engineer and supporting units went with each division and the remaining two French divisions and a large proportion of the corps troops followed later. The removal of a complete corps, while actively engaged in the pursuit up the west coast, left Fifth Army seriously depleted. The loss of the French Moroccan Mountain Division and the Goumiers was particularly serious, as Alexander had hoped that they would be available for operations against the mountain positions of the Gothic Line. The balance in Italy was now beginning to swing against the Allies. While strong reinforcements were arriving for Kesselring, an equal number of Allied divisions were being drained off for DRAGOON at the very moment when they were required to

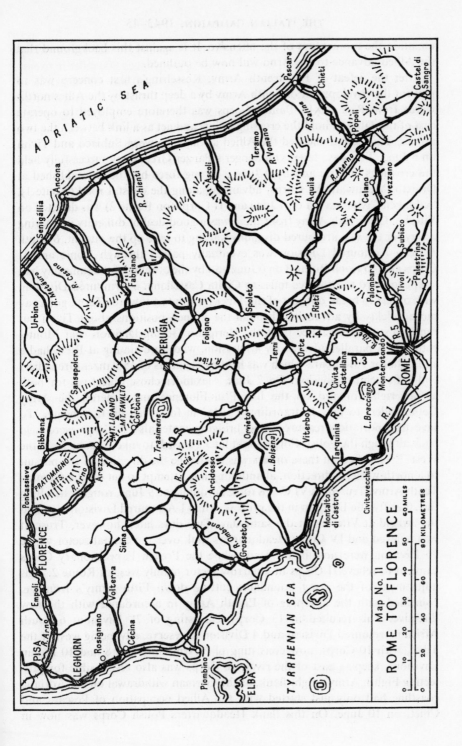

Map No. II

ROME TO FLORENCE

maintain the momentum of the offensive. It is against this background that the Allied advance to the Arno will now be outlined.

After the defeat of Fourteenth Army, Kesselring's first concern was to prevent the envelopment of Tenth Army by a deep thrust by the Allies northwards from Rome. XIV Panzer Corps was therefore employed to operate east of the Tiber to hold the crossing points and act as a link between the two armies. This action checked the Allied advance between Subiaco and Tivoli on 6 June. Two days later, von Senger's Panzer Grenadiers successfully held the crossings at Orte and by 9 June a strong force had been established at Orvieto. Meanwhile VI Corps, advancing along the coastal road (Route 1), had taken Civitavecchia on 7 June and II Corps (on Route 2) was directed on Viterbo. On Eighth Army front there was a good deal of difficulty in clearing a way for the two armoured divisions waiting to take up the pursuit. 6 South African Armoured Division was eventually passed through Rome and II Corps area to reach Route 3 on 6 June and by the evening of the same day had swept forward thirty-three miles to Civita Castellana. 6 Armoured Division, with orders to break out east of the Tiber on Route 4 towards Terni, got away more quickly by advancing through the French positions about Tivoli but ran into strong resistance from the Hermann Göring Division near Monterotondo. A parallel advance by 4 Division, who were aiming at Rieti, had a stiff fight for Palombara which was held by elements of 15 Panzer Grenadiers and 1 Parachute Division. On 7 June Alexander chose objectives for both armies right forward on the line Pisa–Florence and ordered the Army Commanders to take 'extraordinary risks' in following up the enemy. 'To save transportation resources and bridging materials'. 5 Corps were held back although the Polish Corps might later be used 'to take Ancona from the West'.[22] The effect of these orders was to change the direction of the pursuit to a north-westerly direction, abandoning any attempt to cut off the German Tenth Army. Truscott's VI Corps took Tarquinia on 9 June, roughly handling the 20 Luftwaffe Division in the process, while 1 Armoured Division captured the airfield at Viterbo on the same day. Two days later, however, Truscott was relieved and IV Corps Headquarters took over the coastal sector where 36 Division were now in the lead, while the French Expeditionary Corps came in to relieve II Corps in a narrow sector mainly west of Route 2. This adjustment of the army boundary, cutting down Fifth Army's frontage, coincided with the grouping of Eighth Army in accordance with the new directive. This resulted in 13 Corps, consisting of 78 Division, 6 South African Armoured Division and 4 Division in reserve, advancing west of the Tiber, with 10 Corps, now consisting of 6 Armoured and 8 and 10 Indian Divisions, keeping east of the river. 10 Corps was also responsible for protecting Eighth Army's right flank, as the German withdrawal on the Adriatic coastline had only just started with the Allied occupation of Pescara and Chieti on 10 June. On this flank Headquarters Polish Corps was now in command. The Canadian Corps, less 1 Armoured Brigade operating with 4 Division, were halted in the Upper Volturno valley in army reserve and for refit.

Having dispatched all the incoming reinforcements to Fourteenth Army sector and after achieving a junction between the two armies, Kesselring now set about slowing down the Allied advance. On 12 June, von Senger with Headquarters XIV Corps was dispatched to take charge of the newly arrived divisions in the centre of Fourteenth Army front, coming in between LIV Corps who were stationed along the coast and 1 Parachute Corps who were holding the junction between the two armies. When he reported to Army Headquarters he found Kesselring and Lemelsen in conference. Kesselring was very nervous about the coastal sector, as the state of training and general battle-worthiness of the reinforcing divisions was obviously low. In fact von Senger recommended a withdrawal to the Gothic Line, as he felt that the coastal sector was now the weakest part of the whole front. Against a strong attack by Fifth Army he saw no chance of holding the German right flank long enough to allow Tenth Army to complete the long swing back into line. Kesselring's orders, however, were to hold every inch of ground and protect the ports to his rear. So an early decision was taken to send 3 Panzer Grenadiers and Baade's 90 Panzer Grenadiers to rejoin XIV Corps, while 26 Panzer Division and 29 Panzer Grenadiers would follow as quickly as possible to stiffen up 1 Parachute Corps. Von Senger records the effect of this decision. 'Before these units arrived my more or less tattered divisions had been thrown back into the mountain terrain south-west of Siena by the enemy's northwards thrust from Grosseto. During twelve days following the capture of Rome on June 4, the Allied Fifth Army had moved forward 140 kilometres – a rate of advance that amounted to the pursuit of a defeated opponent. When XIV Panzer Corps took charge, the rate of advance was slowed down to 30 kilometres in the week from June 16 to 23 and to another forty kilometres during the subsequent three weeks.'[23] Kesselring's first main delaying position was on a line east and west through Lake Trasimene. Here the Germans stood with XIV Corps on the River Ombrone and 1 Parachute Corps behind the River Orcia, while LXXVI Panzer Corps was astride Lake Trasimene and up into the mountains. LI Mountain Corps held the Adriatic sector on the line of the River Chieti. West of the Apennines the Allies were up against this line on 20 June and the ensuing battles lasted for ten days. Further reinforcements were now joining Kesselring. 34 Infantry Division began to arrive from the Russian front and 16 SS Panzer Grenadiers came in behind von Senger's Corps in time to help inflict heavy losses on the US IV Corps, before the latter achieved a crossing of the River Cecina on 1 July. The French rather understandably did not press their attack, their relief to join the DRAGOON forces being due in a matter of weeks, but followed up the ultimate German withdrawal to reach Siena on 3 July. Attacking astride Lake

Trasimene the two British Corps came up against very stiff resistance, being 'opposed by their old enemies the Hermann Göring, 1 Parachute and 15 Panzer Grenadier Divisions, who were helped by sudden spells of wet weather. Both British Corps had to fight hard and were very relieved when they found early on 20 June that the Germans had withdrawn during the night.'[24] The brunt of the fighting fell on 13 Corps, as the mountainous area east of the lake prevented any attack by 6 Armoured Division who were sent over to assist.

Kesselring had now got a grip on the situation. He had reorganized the command structure and assembled some nineteen divisions in the line, although practically all of them were seriously under strength. In addition, he still had six divisions in reserve and three of these were working hard on the Gothic Line. At this point the Allied pursuit was being maintained with a forward strength of nine divisions. As the Germans withdrew north into the less wooded country north of Volterra and through the foothills towards Florence, the veteran panzer and mobile divisions, although seriously depleted, were able to put into effect their well-tried delaying tactics. Infantry rearguards at minimum strength were given improvised transport and supported by small groups of tanks and these small mobile groups were able to impose considerable delay on the Allied advance. Before withdrawing to the line of the River Arno, Kesselring chose to stand on one further main position which ran from just north of Cecina through Volterra and just south of Arezzo, thence over the mountains to include the port of Ancona. Here Kesselring once again forced the Allies to mount co-ordinated attacks. The concentration of German armour on their right flank in the coastal sector was particularly strong and the Allied attacks were now met with concentrated artillery fire, now supplemented by a number of 170-mm guns and numerous multi-barrelled *nebelwerfers*. In the coastal sector, the US 34 Division had a bitter struggle for the hill town of Rosignano (from 3 to 9 July), while 88 Division, which had relieved 1 Armoured Division, took Volterra on 8 July. Arezzo, overlooked by mountains on three sides, proved a particularly difficult position to attack. 13 Corps was now on a twenty-mile front and there were no reserves left. 4 Indian Division, who had just completed three weeks' training in mountain warfare, were shortly expected to join 10 Corps, but the natural approach to Arezzo was through a gap in the mountains southwest of the town in 13 Corps area. On 9 July the New Zealand Division was ordered forward from 1 Canadian Corps for an attack through this gap on 15 July. Meanwhile, the Germans put in a number of counter-attacks to try and regain the initiative west of the town. On 13 July 9 Gurkhas, from 4 Indian Division, captured Monte Favalto which was just west of the River Tiber and advanced through the mountains with the object of threatening Arezzo from the east. On the night 14/15 July the New Zealanders attacked Mount Ligano, which dominated the approach to Arezzo, from the south with 6 Armoured Division on their left. The attack was supported by maximum artillery fire and after dawn by a number of fighter-bombers. The New Zealanders captured the ridge before dawn and held Mount Ligano throughout the day. On their left 1 Guards Brigade, although held up in daylight, had succeeded in driving a wedge into the German positions west of the town. On the night 15/16 the Germans pulled out and 16/5 Lancers entered the town early the following morning. '2 Lothians after a dashing advance at full speed, were rewarded by the capture of an intact bridge over the Arno.'[25] With Florence as the next objective, the advance now started up again against increasing resistance from the German rearguards. Moving back by relatively short steps of perhaps ten miles at a time, the small mixed infantry and tank rearguards continued to force the Allies to develop attacks on successive positions which would be held according to their natural strength for up to three nights, when the defenders would slip away to the next position. The Allied advance was slow and laborious and the summer days began to run out. On the Adriatic flank General Anders' Polish Corps took Ancona on 18 July. By 4 August the Germans were back on the line of the River Arno running from Pisa through Florence where all the bridges had been destroyed, except for the Ponte Vecchio which was blocked by demolishing the houses at both ends. From Florence the German line ran across the Apennines to the river Metauro. With the Allied landing on the Riviera only ten days away, Fifth Army was now reduced to one armoured and four infantry divisions and had lost eleven out of its thirty-three corps artillery battalions. Alexander's original plan for the breaking of the Gothic Line would now have to be recast.

17

Summer Hopes Fade

Allied bombers reach forward: Mussolini visits Hitler: Partisan activities: Supplies for Warsaw: Gothic Line described: Alexander's plans: Coriano and the Rimini Gap: Kesselring commits his reserves: Clark strikes for Imola and Bologna: Air operations described: The weather breaks: Reinforcement policies compared: Balance sheet.

1944	Fifth Army	Eighth Army
4 Aug	Decision taken on Eighth Army assault on Adriatic front.	
		Re-grouping commences.
11 Aug		Polish Corps reaches River Cesano.
15 Aug	DRAGOON Landing by Seventh Army.	
16 Aug	Orders for assault of Gothic Line issued.	
18 Aug	13 Corps come under Fifth Army.	Eighth Army concentration complete.
		Poles cross River Cesano – reach River Metauro 21/22 August.
25 Aug	13 Corps attacks north from Florence.	Eighth Army attacks from line of River Metauro.
26 Aug	Port of Leghorn opened.	
31 Aug–1 Sept	Fifth Army follows up German withdrawal.	Eighth Army penetrates Gothic Line.
1 Sept	Germans commence withdrawal from Greece.	
3–15 Sept		Battle for Coriano.
12–16 Sept	Second Quebec Conference (OCTAGON) to plan defeat of Japan and occupation of Germany.	
13–18 Sept	II Corps assault on Il Giogo Pass.	
14–21 Sept		Assault on Rimini Line. Germans withdraw behind River Marecchia.
16 Sept	Russians enter Sofia. British Commandos land on Kythera.	
22 Sept	II Corps through Futa Pass.	5 Corps attack across River Marecchia.
25–26 Sept		Heavy fighting on River Uso.

1944	*Fifth Army*	*Eighth Army*
26 Sept	British Airborne troops withdrawn from Arnhem bridgehead. General Wilson gives instructions for re-occupation of Greece.	
27 Sept	II Corps halted by strong counter-attacks ten miles from Imola.	
27–29 Sept		Eighth Army cross River Uso, reach Fiumicino, now in spate, General McCreery assumes command, decides to continue offensive through foothills.
1–4 Oct	II Corps attack down Route 65 reaches Monghidoro.	
7 Oct		10 Indian Division capture Mount Farneto.
5–9 Oct	II Corps attack reaches Loiano.	
10 Oct		46 Division captures Longiano. Germans start withdrawal from Fiumicino.
10–14 Oct	II Corps attack on Livergnano escarpment.	
12 Oct	4 Division and Greek Brigade ordered to Greece, start to move 15 October.	
12–16 Oct	British Parachute troops and Commandos land at Athens and seize Piraeus followed by infantry reinforcements. General Scobie takes command.	
16 Oct		5 Corps and Canadians reach River Pisciatello.
20 Oct	Russians and Tito's Partisans take Belgrade. 88 Division captures Mount Grande.	Cesena entered. 4 Division bridgehead over River Savio on Route 9. Poles advance towards Forli through mountains.
23 Oct	Von Vietinghoff takes over command of Army Group C. 34 Division captures Mount Belmonte ten miles from Bologna.	
24 Oct		Germans withdraw from River Savio to River Ronco.
25 Oct	II Corps offensive halted at Vedriano four miles from Route 9.	
26 Oct	Heavy rains and floods halt operations Savio bridge swept away.	

When the advance beyond Rome started to spread out on a two-army front the Desert Air Force and XII Tactical Air Force moved forward in direct support of the two armies, using the same boundaries and with their head-quarters set up alongside those of Fifth and Eighth Armies. While the medium bombers remained under centralized control, concentrating on com-munications north of a line Pisa–Arezzo–Fano, the fighter-bombers of the tactical air forces continued interdiction operations on communications around Florence. Special attention was given by fighter wings from each air force to the coastal traffic at the head of the Adriatic and in the Ligurian Sea above the Pisa–Rimini line. Except for the period of bad weather at the end of June, when the two railway lines from Bologna to Pistoia and Prato were opened, these operations were very effective and all other railway links south of Florence remained cut. For instance, on 15 June seventy-eight effective rail blocks were reported. Working with and ahead of the advance the Allied fighters and fighter-bombers continued their attacks on transport and road communications. The Strategic Bombers took no part in this phase except to intervene on 21/22 June, when a successful night raid on the Ventimiglia yards, just east of Monaco, and a daylight raid by 580 heavy bombers protected by 513 fighters, dropped 1,400 tons of bombs on the main rail centres and bridges between the Po and the Arno, to counter the effect of repairs rushed through during the spell of bad weather. Otherwise the Strategic Air Force with nearly 2,000 aircraft and 81,000 personnel were fully engaged on the CBO Programme, except for a concentrated attack on 13 July against oil storage facilities and communications in northern Italy and attacks on 2/3 August on Genoa and the exits from the Brenner Pass below Bolzano.

XII Tactical Air Force completed the move of its units to Corsica by 18 July ready to support DRAGOON but for a while continued its attacks against communications in north-west Italy. The Desert Air Force now concentrated its efforts on the immediate battle front with the medium and light bombers stretching out for railway centres and bridges, as well as coastal shipping and supply centres that were serving Kesselring's positions in the Apennines. Since the middle of June the Air Commanders had been advocating the bombing of the bridges over the Po. These operations were first of all held up by the periods of bad weather and after the battle for the Trasimene Line Alexander still saw a chance of an early breakthrough to the Po valley and

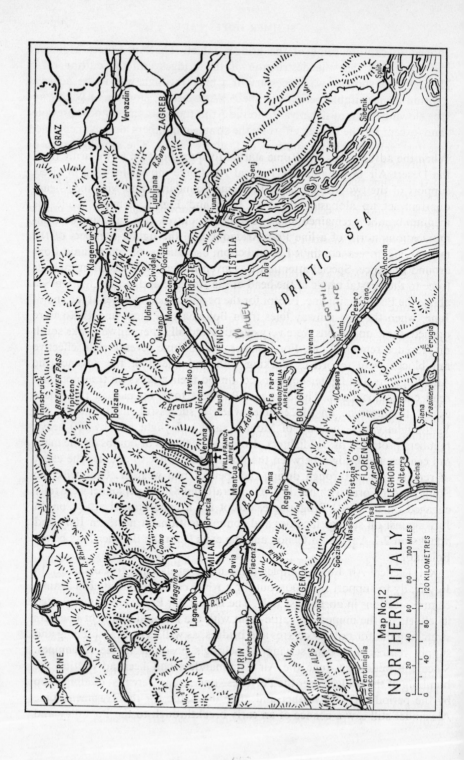

Map No.12

NORTHERN ITALY

0	40	80	100 MILES
0	40	80	120 KILOMETRES

hoped to capture some of the bridges intact. The Air Forces argument, however, was that the destruction of the bridges and the cutting off of Kesselring's supplies was necessary, if a breakthrough was to be achieved 'within a measurable period of time'.[1] With the decision on DRAGOON and the slowing down of the advance to the Arno these arguments now prevailed and, except for the limited effort by the strategic bombers already mentioned, the task fell entirely on the two tactical air forces. The attacks began on 12 July as a combined British and American operation.

At that time (including a few pontoon bridges) there were twenty-three bridges across the Po and the tributary Trebbia. Seventy-two hours later no bridge was usable. Pontoons lay derelict on the bank, miles downstream from their original crossing points. The sixteen permanent bridges all had one or more spans knocked out. Thereafter the nineteen German divisions south of the Po had to be supplied by ferry and pontoon bridges erected at night and dismantled and hidden by day.[2]

These operations were followed up by further attacks on bridges west of Piacenza to stop east-west traffic in the valley north of the Po. By 20 July there were ninety cuts in the railway system of all northern Italy. After 26 July all railway bridges over the Po east of Torreberetti were impassable; by 4 August Genoa was isolated and all railway lines from Milan to the south and east were cut. These results were achieved almost entirely by the medium bombers, as fighter-bomber attacks were quite ineffective against permanent structures and unsuccessful against pontoons, being only really effective against railway tracks, rolling stock and motor transport. Assisted by the Italian partisans, whose activities had steadily increased throughout the summer, this bombing programme undoubtedly created serious difficulties for Kesselring over the maintenance of his troops in the Gothic Line but failed to influence the main issue. Numerous Italian labour units were set to work on the continuous repair of bridges and rail and road communications. The number of pontoon bridges was increased and over fifty ferry points were established on the River Po. In all these operations Kesselring was considerably helped by the six-week check to air and ground attack on account of DRAGOON. Some American commanders indeed saw this pause continuing indefinitely. General Eaker in fact had completed plans by the end of July to move the XII Air Force into the south of France on the heels of Seventh Army and later, on 21 August, recommended to General Arnold that the remainder of Fifth Army should join what had now become General Devers's 6th Army Group. When later in the autumn the Allied offensive in Italy again lost its momentum, proposals for moving the whole of the American Air Forces out of Italy were seriously put forward. In spite of the fact that the Fifteenth Air Force's bases at Foggia were so well placed for the attack of industrial targets in Germany it was proposed that they too should move to France. The lack of airfields and the means of supporting the large numbers of additional units in France seems to have been the principal factor that determined that the Strategic Bombers should remain in Italy, at least throughout the winter months.

The fall of Rome had come as a grave blow to Mussolini's Republican Government operating from Salo on Lake Garda. Everywhere the Allied troops had been greeted as liberators. The local administrations based on the Fascist Party organization just ceased to function. The militia and armed police mostly went into hiding and the Allies found themselves not only having to feed the population of the cities but having to extend the Allied Military Government to cover over two-thirds of the country. As the Allies advanced north from Rome the partisan guerilla bands operating against the German communications grew bolder and it was obvious to Mussolini that his chances of holding what remained of his country depended not just on the Gothic Line defences but on the situation in northern Italy, where what was tantamount to civil war had broken out. During this period the Germans suffered quite a considerable number of casualties at the hands of the partisans and Kesselring estimated that 13,000 German soldiers were killed and about the same number wounded by the partisans between June and August 1944. Furthermore the sabotage of military installations, dumps and communications of all kinds was becoming more and more widespread. An order issued early in August to a newly arrived Grenadier Regiment shows the various methods used for dealing with the partisans. First of all their associates and relatives were to be arrested, all bicycles confiscated and telephone exchanges closed down. The local population would then further be discouraged by all men between the ages of seventeen and forty-five being sent for forced labour in Germany. The next stage was the shooting of hostages, if possible known Communists, chosen by the Fascist militia or Party officials. In any case of 'outstanding violence against German soldiers, an appropriate number of hostages will be hanged. In such cases the whole population of the place will be assembled to witness the execution. After the bodies have been left hanging for twelve hours, the public will be ordered to bury them without ceremony and without the assistance of any priest.'[3] While Kesselring ordered increasingly stern measures, which now included the burning of any village where a German soldier had been fired on, the Salo Government were powerless to prevent the spread of sabotage and waves of killing. 'Shortage of German manpower, and a deepening of suspicion by the German authorities as to the reliability of the Italian ally, bedevilled the scene.'[4] Towards the end of July Mussolini had travelled to Hitler's headquarters in East Prussia, ostensibly to review two Italian divisions formed from 'volunteers' out of the 600,000 Italian servicemen interned in Germany and made up with young conscripts from Italy. With some reluctance the Germans had equipped and trained four divisions but insisted that they should contain a strong German element and remain entirely under German command. The first two of these divisions to complete training had just returned to Italy. Mussolini was fully conscious of the fact that without any proper military forces of his own his Republican Government could not survive. The Militia, now reformed as Republican Guards, was totally unreliable and Mussolini's newly raised 'Black Brigades' of young conscripts were untrained and of unknown value. Mussolini arrived on 20 July only hours after the attempt on Hitler's life. After a brief exchange of greetings, during which Mussolini described Hitler's escape 'as a signal proof of divine intervention', the Fuehrer launched into his usual monologue and soon got round to the subject of manpower. Unless more Italian volunteers were forthcoming, he said, he would have to break up the two divisions still under training in Germany. At this point Mussolini was able to bring up the question of the deplorable state of the Italian servicemen interned in Germany and at the same time point out that he had already supplied some 130,000 workers to Kesselring and Richthofen and was now being asked to supply about a million more. He stressed that, in the present state of political unrest, what would make more difference than anything would be an improvement in the 'material position' of the internees held in Germany and their employment, according to their occupations and capabilities, 'for the process of German production'. Amidst the confusion and high tension at Hitler's headquarters the matter was quickly disposed of, as everyone present probably realized that without the two extra divisions Mussolini's puppet regime would quickly crumble. So it was decided that the Italian divisions would soon be sent to Mussolini and more internees would be put to work in Germany.

Encouraged by the Russian advances, the partisans in the Balkan countries had redoubled their efforts and in June 1944 General Wilson set up a special command to support their operations. Headquarters Allied Landforces Adriatic had already been formed and commando and naval units were engaged in carrying out raids on the coastal mainland and islands of western Greece, Albania and Yugoslavia. Now a Balkan Air Force was formed under the command of Air Vice-Marshal Elliot who also co-ordinated the inter-service planning of these operations. Between May and September 1944 the Germans made strenuous efforts to suppress Tito's forces in Yugoslavia and the Balkan Air Force was kept fully occupied supporting the partisans. During August 620 tons of supplies were flown out to Tito's divisions fighting in Montenegro and over 2,000 wounded men were brought back by air to Italy. The following month saw the collapse of Rumania and Bulgaria and Tito's partisans started a drive on Belgrade to join up with the advancing Russians. In aid of these operations the Balkan Air Force flew over 3,500 sorties and caused considerable damage to German communications and transport. On 1 August the Polish rising in Warsaw took place and a number of sorties were undertaken by the Polish squadrons serving in the Balkan Air Force, who made gallant attempts to drop arms and supplies to their countrymen fighting against steadily mounting odds. These missions were not only

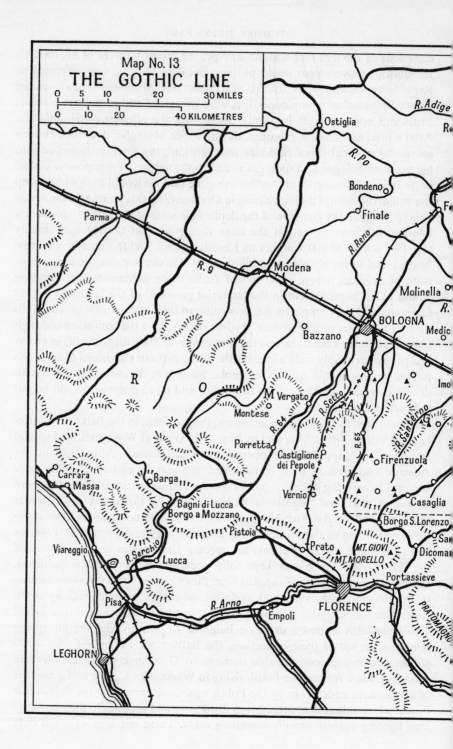

Map No. 13
THE GOTHIC LINE

0   5   10   20   30 MILES
0   10   20   40 KILOMETRES

R. Adige

Ostiglia

R. Po

Bondeno

Finale

Fe

Parma

Molinella

Modena

R. 9

R. Reno

BOLOGNA

Medic

Bazzano

R.

Imo

R

O

Vergato

M

R. Setto

A

R. Santerno

G

Montese

R. 64

R. 65

Porretta

Castiglione
dei Pepole

Firenzuola

Carrara

Massa

Barga

Vernio

Casaglia

Bagni di Lucca
Borgo a Mozzano

Borgo S. Lorenzo

Pistoia

Sa

Viareggio

R. Serchio

Prato

MT. GIOVI

Dicoma

Lucca

MT. MORELLO

Portassieve

PRATOMAGNO

Pisa

R. Arno

FLORENCE

Empoli

LEGHORN

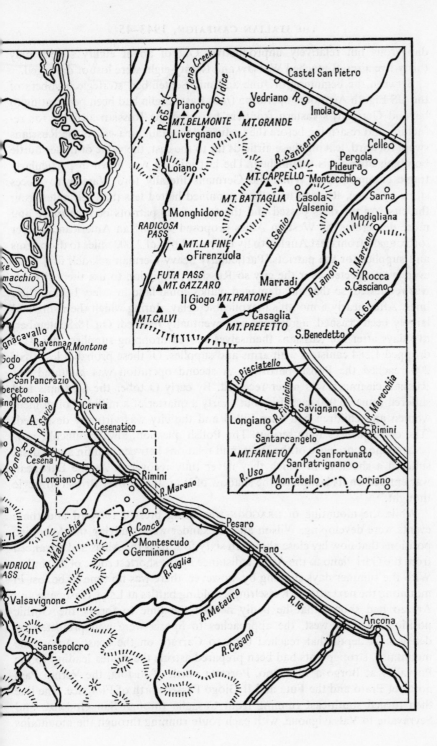

dangerous but relatively unproductive. Out of about eighty sorties only thirty-five aircraft reached Warsaw and twenty-eight were lost or damaged.

Between the beginning of June and mid-September, strategic bombers of the US Eighth Air Force operating from East Anglia had been penetrating to beyond Germany's eastern frontiers by using the Russian airfields for re-fuelling and re-arming before they returned via Italian bases. As the Russians swept forward, leaving these airfields far to the east, the value of these shuttle bombing operations diminished. The last mission was flown in particularly tragic circumstances. While the Germans literally tore Warsaw to pieces stone by stone, Russian units had remained halted less than ten miles from the city. As the days passed and the fate of the patriots became more and more desperate, the Western Allies proposed sending an American bomber force, again from East Anglia, to fly the round trip of 2,000 miles to drop arms and supplies for the patriots. Particularly heavy German ack-ack fire, however, was expected over the city so Russian permission to use their airfields was requested, so that any damaged planes could land in safety behind their lines. After nearly a month's inexplicable delay, during which the rising had largely been crushed, agreement was eventually reached. On 18 September, five days after the Russians themselves started dropping supplies, 107 B17s dropped 1,284 canisters with arms and supplies. Of these probably less than 200 reached the Polish partisans. A second operation was mounted but Russian clearance was never received. By early October the Germans had suffered some 25,000 casualties but nearly a quarter of a million Polish men, women and children had been killed and the city was virtually destroyed. 'The consequences were serious. The Polish question, always difficult, now became the conscience of the West, and relations between Britain and Russia suffered a shock from which they never fully recovered. As the European war entered on its last phase the shadow of Warsaw lay over British strategic thought.'[5]

While the mounting of DRAGOON was being pressed forward and these events were developing, Wilson and Alexander were studying the Apennine positions that now lay close ahead. In sixty-four days the Allies had advanced from the Garigliano to the Arno, a distance by the shortest route of 270 miles. With the summer days slipping by, however, there was no time to be lost in mounting the next attack. Kesselring's holding battles at Lake Trasimene and Arezzo had shown that he badly needed the time to fortify the Gothic positions. To the west, the approaches to Spezia were well protected by defences in depth that reached back to Carrara on the coast. Across the mountains, strongpoints had been prepared astride the routes leading to the Po valley at Borgo a Mozzano, Porretta north of Pistoia, the Vernio Pass north of Prato and the Futa and Il Giogo Passes north of Florence. The line then turned south-east running from Casaglia through San Godenzo and Sevravalie to Valsavignone, with each route running through the mountains again covered by strongpoints. The line now turned east and followed the River Foglia to Pesaro. This latter sector, covered only by low foothills, was well developed with anti-tank ditches, extensive minefields and the usual deep bunkers and dug-in tank turrets. On this flank coastal defences ran back as far as Ravenna. The southern face of the Apennines opposing the Allies rose sharply to high peaks but once the watershed was crossed the ground fell quite gradually down towards the valley of the Po. Alexander considered that the least difficult of the routes were through the Vernio and Futa Passes which linked Florence and Bologna. All the roads climbing through the passes, however, were particularly susceptible to demolition where they had been artificially constructed, by cutting into the sides of the valleys, to clear the high passes which were snowbound in winter. Kesselring's defensive positions on the Gothic Line ran for 200 miles coast to coast and all but about the last fifty-five miles on the eastern flank were sited in difficult mountainous terrain with many advantages to the defence. The work of fortifying the strongpoints already mentioned was largely completed and efforts were now being made to complete the construction of a line of connecting positions, which had already been carefully sited to form a continuous front. The only main road that did not have to climb over the formidable barrier of the northern Apennines was Route 16 on the Adriatic coast. Although 'on the flat' this approach was far from ideal as the low foothills and numerous rivers and streams, which were all liable to sudden flooding, struck across the narrow coastal plain at right angles to the line of advance. The whole area was indeed similar to that encountered earlier in the region of the River Sangro and the heavy soil quickly turned to mud after rain. Once through the narrow gap between the mountains and the sea at Rimini the plains quickly widened but the soft ground of the Romagna district is broken by a number of broad rivers flowing between embankments in a north-easterly direction, some of these flood banks being forty feet high. On the northern side of the Apennines, Route 9 passes close below the mountains from Rimini right through Modena to Pavia, giving the Germans an excellent lateral line of communication. Kesselring inspected the greater part of the construction work in August and expressed himself satisfied with the work done. He wrote 'most progress had been made between the Etruscan Apennines and the Adriatic, where the influence of Heidrich could be seen. I therefore contemplated an assault on the left wing, violent as it was sure to be, with a certain confidence. Everything hinged on the possibility of moving the divisions earmarked for the big battle into the battle zone in proper time.'[6] A report made on the defence work completed at the beginning of September lists 2,376 machine-gun posts, 479 anti-tank gun, mortar and assault gun positions, 120,000 metres of wire and many miles of anti-tank ditches. Only four out of thirty 88-mm Panther gun turrets ordered by the OKW in June, however, were in position. The balance of forces at about the time the battle for the Gothic Line opened was twenty-six German divisions including six Panzer or Panzer Grenadier divisions, plus about six Italian divisions, against twenty-one Allied divisions which included four Armoured divisions. The strength of the Luftwaffe in Italy had been reduced to forty single-seater fighters and forty-five reconnaissance aircraft of all types and thirty-five obsolete JU87s (Stukas), plus fifty Italian single-seater fighters. The Allies enjoyed complete air superiority.

The original plan for breaking the Gothic Line was based on a concentrated drive by four Corps totalling fourteen divisions in the centre on the axis Florence–Bologna. This plan presupposed the deployment of sufficient Allied strength on the two flanks to hold down Kesselring's formations away from the point of attack. Now Alexander had insufficient resources to achieve this and proposed shifting the main weight of the attack by nine divisions to the Adriatic flank, aiming initially at the narrow gap at Rimini. A secondary attack by five divisions would follow within the week through the central mountainous area towards Bologna, on which both attacks would now converge. As before, holding forces would be required on the left flank but the Allied right flank would be protected by the Adriatic. This new plan, known as OLIVE, largely resulted from General Leese's concern, shared by Alexander, that Eighth Army with no mountain divisions and no proper pack transport and little experience in mountain warfare would be better employed on the Adriatic sector, where it should be able to develop its superiority in artillery and armour. A lot, however, would depend on the assault being pressed through before the autumn rains. This plan suited one of Alexander's favourite strategies which he called 'the strategy of the "two-handed punch" or, more orthodoxly expressed, the strategy of attacking two points equally vital to the enemy (i.e. Ravenna and Bologna) either simultaneously or alternately in order to split the reserves available for the defence'.[7] The plan was agreed at a meeting on Orvieto airfield between Wilson, Alexander and Harding, his Chief of Staff, and the preparations were carried out in the greatest secrecy. No written orders were issued until immediately before D-day which was to be 25 August.

During the advance Fifth Army had been supplied from the dumps at Anzio and through the ports of Civitavecchia, Piombino and finally Leghorn. Eighth Army supplies had come forward by road and rail as far as Arezzo where a railhead was finally formed. To help out during the advance the Americans had agreed to a limited tonnage being landed for Eighth Army at Piombino. In mid-July Ancona on the Adriatic flank was captured but the capacity of the port was limited. The switch of most of Eighth Army to the Adriatic sector now required the use of both Arezzo and Ancona and urgent steps were taken to develop the port. Later when it became evident that the early capture of Bologna, which had been chosen as the advanced base, would not take place, as many base installations as possible were moved into the area around Ancona, which instead of being merely the port of entry now became the advanced base for Eighth Army. Fifth Army, including the large British element, continued to be supplied through the west coast ports. The port of Leghorn was captured on 19 July and salvage ships arrived eight days later. The dock area was heavily mined and booby-trapped and the quays were cratered. The entrance to the harbour was almost wholly blocked by sunken ships. Although the harbour remained under long-range gun fire for many weeks it was opened on 26 August and soon became the main supply port for Fifth Army.

The move eastwards across the Apennines of the equivalent of eight divisions, two Corps Headquarters and numerous corps troops involved some 80,000 vehicles. Only two mountain roads were available and each was largely one-way. Both roads had been heavily demolished and in addition to considerable reconstruction work the Royal Engineers had to build forty Bailey bridges before the roads could be opened. Eighth Army movement staff set up a special headquarters at Foligno and the whole move was completed in about fifteen days. The movement tables were complicated by the fact that priority had to be given to tank-transporters which were operating on a continuous shuttle service to complete the concentration of the tank brigades in time. The only reinforcements available to bolster up General Clark's Fifth Army were a Regimental Combat Team of 92 (Negro) Infantry Division which went into reserve in VI Corps area and an infantry regiment of the Brazilian Expeditionary Force. The 1 (US) Armoured Division, which was one-third under strength and had to be reorganized, also remained in reserve.

The original cover plan, which had already been put into operation, had been designed to draw the Germans away from the centre of the Gothic positions. Now Fifth Army were told to carry out 'ostentatious preparations' as for an attack in this very area, in the hopes that the Eighth Army attack towards Rimini would first appear to be a feint. Meanwhile Kesselring's order of battle had somewhat changed. The Hermann Göring Division had gone to East Prussia and was replaced by the 98 Infantry Division from Zagreb. Both the 3 and 15 Panzer Grenadier Divisions had gone to the Western Front and were not replaced until September. The preparations for DRAGOON had led Kesselring to fear an invasion on the Ligurian coast and 90 Panzer Grenadiers were sent first to Genoa and then, after the landing took place, to the Franco-Italian frontier to join 34 Infantry Division. Here they were reinforced by 148 Infantry and 157 (later renumbered 8) Mountain Division, which had fallen back on the Maritime Alps after being pinched out by the rapid advance into the Rhône valley. Guarding the coastline of the Italian Riviera between Spezia and Savona was 42 Jäger Division and two Italian Divisions. At the head of the Adriatic Kesselring retained 94 Infantry Division about Udine and 188 Reserve Mountain Division in Istria. The remainder of his force, amounting to some nineteen divisions, was deployed on and forward of the Gothic Line. Tenth Army held the eastern sector. LXXVI Panzer Corps was in the coastal sector with 278 and 71 Infantry Divisions (both at weak strength) and 5 Mountain Division in the line as far as San Sepolcro. 1 Parachute and 162 (Turcoman) Infantry Divisions were echeloned back in reserve and covering the coastline. LI Mountain Corps held the line as far as the inter-Army boundary, which ran back from just west of Pontassieve. This mountainous sector was held by five divisions, 114 Jäger, 44, 305, 334 and 715 Infantry Divisions. In army reserve near Bologna was the recently arrived 98 Infantry Division. Fourteenth Army held from Pontassieve across to the coast on the western flank with eight divisions. The central sector was held by 1 Parachute Corps with 356 Infantry, 4 Parachute and 362 Infantry Divisions. XIV Panzer Corps held from Empoli to the sea with 26 Panzer, 65 Infantry and 16 SS Panzer Grenadiers. In Army Reserve was 29 Panzer Grenadiers (north of Florence) and 20 Luftwaffe Field Division, made up from the disbanded 19 Luftwaffe Division, near Viareggio. This layout showed a certain preoccupation with the central sector with two of the three reserve divisions, including Kesselring's only mobile reserve, placed between Florence and Bologna. It is here that the mountain barrier is at its narrowest, being only fifty miles wide. The peaks however rise to 2,000 metres which is twice as high as in the narrow range of the Winter Line that had faced the Allies nine months previously.

During the night 10 August the Germans withdrew to the northern out-skirts of Florence and on the Adriatic coast the Polish Corps pressed forward to clear the high ground between the Cesano and Metauro Rivers. By 23 August the Poles held the right bank of the Metauro for some fifteen miles inland and were within about twelve miles of the main Gothic positions. In the Arno sector, however, the Germans still stood well forward of their main defence line. With as much of his strength as possible concentrated on the right flank Alexander was now ready to strike at Pesaro. 2 Polish Corps, which it will be remembered had suffered severe losses, were holding a front of seven miles and their sole task would be to capture the high ground north-west of Pesaro. 1 Canadian Corps (1 Infantry and 5 Armoured Divisions, plus a British Tank Brigade) was concentrated on a front of only two miles screened by the Polish troops. Their task was to gain the high ground west of Pesaro, make for Route 16 and attack towards Rimini. 5 Corps considerably strengthened and now consisting of 1 Armoured Division (plus an Armoured and a Tank Brigade) together with 4 Division, 4 Indian Division, 46 and 56 Divisions stood on a front of twenty miles ready to advance on an axis west of Rimini towards Bologna and Ferrara. The remainder of Eighth Army front right across to the high Pratomagno Range, which was halfway between Florence and Arezzo, was lightly held by 10 Corps with 10 Indian Division, an Armoured Brigade and dismounted Armoured Car Regiments, supple-mented by some infantry. In Army Reserve 2 New Zealand Division would shortly be joined by a Greek Mountain Brigade from the Middle East in the area around Iesi.

13 Corps had now joined Fifth Army and held the sector from the Pratomagno Range to just west of Florence with 6 Armoured Division, 8 Indian Division and 1 Division, with a Canadian Armoured Brigade in support. On their left was II Corps screened by 442 Regimental Combat Team holding a four-mile front. This Corps consisted of 34, 88 and 91 Divisions each with tank support and was held ready to deliver the second blow of 'the two-handed punch' towards Bologna, to be followed by an attack by 13 Corps towards Imola. The remainder of Fifth Army front was held by IV Corps with 6 South African Armoured Division, the reconstituted 1 (US) Armoured Division, 85 Division, part of 92 (Negro) Division and Task Force 45. This latter force, which was roughly of divisional strength, had been formed in a matter of weeks from American anti-aircraft, anti-tank and reconnaissance units supplemented by the units of a British anti-aircraft brigade. After a very short period of infantry training this force achieved fine results in holding extensive defensive positions. The Japanese American 442 Regiment was withdrawn on 3 September and sent to join Seventh Army.

An hour before midnight 25/26 August 2 Polish Corps together with 1 Canadian and 46 Divisions moved forward. The attack opened in silence but within an hour a barrage was laid down to cover the crossing of the River Metauro. By dawn five divisions were advancing well beyond the river against only weak resistance. Once again Kesselring had been completely surprised by Eighth Army's secret concentration. LXXVI Panzer Corps had in fact been caught in the middle of regrouping. In order to relieve 90 Panzer Grenadiers on the French Frontier with 5 Mountain Division, 278 Division was being withdrawn through 1 Parachute Division to fill the gap on the right flank of the Corps. The Germans were thus already moving back on the coastal sector and mistook the Polish attack for a normal follow-up to retain contact. Another three days passed before General Lemelsen realized that he had been caught out by the strength of the assault and on 30 August both 5 Corps and the Canadians were over the River Foglia into the advance positions of the actual Gothic Line. The next two days' fighting brought a further penetration over a twenty-mile front inland from the coast and 1 Parachute Division, which had suffered 50 per cent losses, only just managed to avoid being encircled in their withdrawal to the line of the River Conca. By 29 August a regiment from 26 Panzer Division was in action on the River Foglia and the remainder of the division plus 98 Division were rushed forward in an attempt to stem the Allied advance. 26 Panzer Division, however, was committed in small packets and both divisions suffered heavily. By 2 September the Canadians were over the River Conca and the two armoured divisions of 5 Corps were about to be launched in a drive to Rimini and beyond. Kesselring now committed his last mobile reserve, the 29 Panzer

Grenadiers from Bologna. Lying between the advance of the two Allied Corps was the town of Coriano standing high on a ridge which was to be the scene of some of the bitterest fighting of the whole campaign. Here and at Geminano some five miles to the south were now assembled 1 Parachute, 26 Panzer and 29 Panzer Grenadier Divisions and from 4-12 September they held their ground against all Allied attacks. Quite unexpectedly very heavy rain fell for three days at the start of this vital stand. The advancing Allied tanks and guns and vehicles were quickly bogged down and air support was seriously limited. The impetus of Eighth Army's attack had now been lost and the time had come to strike elsewhere.

As these battles developed and his reserves became committed, Kesselring soon appreciated that he could only hope to scrape up further reserves by drawing back to the well-prepared defences of the Gothic Line on the remainder of his front. Consequently on 30 August LI Mountain Corps started moving back followed up by 10 Corps. On the German extreme right flank XIV Corps also fell back on to the main positions and IV Corps were able to reach Lucca on 6 August and Pistoia on 12 August. 1 Parachute Corps, however, had good intermediate positions in the mountain immediately north of Florence and these were occupied on 3 September. This forward deployment was probably to make time for Kesselring to adjust the Army boundary and create the badly needed reserves. 20 Luftwaffe Division, from XIV Corps, and a Regimental Group from 90 Panzer Grenadiers were now brought in to reinforce the Adriatic Sector and 356 Division was taken out of 1 Parachute Corps as further reserves on this flank. Indeed a deep break-through by the Allies in the Adriatic sector would threaten the line of withdrawal north-eastwards of the whole of the remainder of Kesselring's forces. While full knowledge of these moves was still denied to the Allied Intelligence staffs, Alexander had already judged that the time was ripe to launch the Fifth Army attack. Clark's plan was for 13 Corps, using 8 Indian Division, to capture the line of hills from Monte Morello to Monte Giovi which covered the exits from Florence. II Corps would then advance through 13 Corps sector and attack straight towards Firenzuola with all four divisions and at the same time 13 Corps would advance on Faenza and Forli. The task of IV Corps would be to exert maximum pressure while 1 (US) Armoured Division came into Army Reserve ready to exploit any breakthrough. Fifth Army plans were complete by 8 September but the same day the Germans started to pull back from the forward positions north of Florence. 91 and 34 Divisions of II Corps followed up this withdrawal astride Route 65 and pressed the Germans back so successfully that by 12 September the strong positions on Mount Calvi had fallen and the Americans were hard up against the main Gothic Line at the strongly fortified position covering the Futa Pass.

Both Allied Armies were now poised for the renewal of the offensive. Attacking abreast on the night of 12 September the Canadians and 5 Corps reached the crest of the Corriano Ridge taking 1,000 prisoners on the first day. Geminano fell to 4 Indian Division on 15 September, by which date the Canadians were across the Marano and 4 Division had reached San Patrignano with 1 Armoured Division on their left and 46 Division was through Montescudo. The New Zealand Division was now moved forward ready to pass through the Canadians who meanwhile were engaged in a bitter fight for San Fortunato, a key position on a ridge some three miles from Rimini. The fight for San Fortunato continued for three days until the town was finally cleared on 20 September and the same night the Greek Mountain Brigade entered Rimini. This brigade, that fought well in their first engagement, was the only reinforcement that Eighth Army had received in response to General Wilson's urgent requests for reinforcements to the Combined Chiefs of Staff in July and early August. Again the weather intervened and under cover of torrential rain the Germans withdrew overnight across the 'broad and swollen' Marecchia River. The following day Allied patrols were across the river. Ahead lay the plains but across the line of advance the rivers were filling with the rain water pouring down from the mountains and under foot the heavy soil was starting to grip men and vehicles as they struggled forward through the narrow coastal strip below the mountains where Fifth Army's attack had already started. Overnight 21/22 September the New Zealanders took over from the Canadians and pushed on up Route 16 until checked by strong opposition on 25 and 26 September along the line of the River Uso and again by heavy counter-attacks on 29 September on the line of the Fiumicino. At this point their advance was held up by heavy rainstorms. On their left, 5 Canadian Armoured Division had also reached the Fiumicino against increasing resistance, being thrown back from a small bridgehead over the river on 29 September. 5 Corps were now struggling forward across the line of foothills further inland and were making slower progress. On the edge of the plain 56 Division, which had been continuously in action for three weeks, paused on 22 September for regrouping. Meanwhile 43 Gurkha Brigade took the heavily mined and booby-trapped village of Santarcangelo on the River Uso which was the key to a stop line running south-westwards to Montebello. 56 Division now relieved 1 Armoured Division and by 27 September drew up to the Fiumicino astride Savignano and by 29 September the eastern bank of the river in the plain had been cleared. The Germans were, however, still holding out in the foothills south of Route 9. Four days of torrential rain now made movement of vehicles off the roads quite impossible. Fords over the Rivers Marecchia and Uso became impassable and five bridges over the Marecchia were swept away. The Fiumicino, 'normally a shallow trickle, swelled to a width of thirty feet and its speed and depth made it impossible for infantry patrols to cross'.[8] 5 Corps struggled forward but it was nearly a week before 46 Division on their left reached the Fiumicino. Between the two armies 10 Corps pressed a German withdrawal up Route 71 and after a stiff fight for the Mandrioli Pass on 24 September crossed the watershed. The advance by 10 Indian Division on the long descent towards Cesena, however, was checked by four days of heavy rainfall and the armoured brigade was now switched to the Adriatic sector, being replaced by 1 Guards Brigade Group reinforced by the British Anti-Aircraft Brigade (from Fifth Army) fighting as infantry. By 6 October 10 Corps had reached within about 15 miles of Cesena.

The Fifth Army offensive was launched on 13 September simultaneously with the Eighth Army attack on Coriano. Clark's plan was to strike first at the Il Giogo Pass and through to the valley of the upper Santerno River, thus outflanking the strong defences at the Futa Pass on Route 65. A preliminary attack to hide this intention would be made astride Route 65 by 34 Division. The main thrust would then come from 85 and 91 Divisions assaulting the peaks that guarded the Il Giogo Pass from east and west respectively. 88 Division stood by to exploit any success and the left front of the attack was to be protected by 6 South African Armoured Division. The task of 13 Corps was to attack into the mountains and protect the right flank. 1 Division was given the axis of the road Borgo San Lorenzo–Faenza with 8 Indian Division on their right directed on Marradi, while 6 Armoured Division had the axis Dicomano–Forli. This combined British and American attack in fact straddled the German inter-army boundary which was now from Imola to east of the Il Giogo Pass. II Corps attack thus fell entirely on 4 Parachute Division and 13 Corps attack on 715 Infantry Division and the flank of 305 Infantry Division. After two days' heavy fighting, however, II Corps' attack had made little progress. On the highest part of the mountain range and east of the pass were the peaks of Mount Prefetto with beyond Mounts Pratone and Verruca and finally Mount Altuzza, which directly overlooked the Il Giogo Pass. In this area 13 Corps had more success and on 14 September 8 Indian Division was over the watershed and the following day 1 Division captured Mount Prefetto and started an attack towards Mount Pratone. At this point 85 Division took over the attack on Pratone, but were held 1,000 yards from their objective. The following night a battalion from 85 Division reached Mount Altuzza and held the peak throughout 17 September against strong counter-attacks. By that evening several other strongpoints and peaks had been captured and when 91 Division took Mount Montecelli on 17/18 September, II Corps was holding a seven-mile stretch of the Gothic Line on either side of the Il Giogo Pass. To stop this gap Kesselring ordered 362 Division across to cover Firenzuola and 44 Division was brought up from LI Mountain Corps to cover the road Firenzuola to Imola. This was a critical sector for the Germans as it was one of the few areas where artillery and transport could be deployed once they had crossed the watershed. Elsewhere the gradually falling ground towards the north-east was divided by rivers running in deep gorges and the terrain was rocky, broken and often precipitous, while the long mountain spurs which stretched out towards the plains below contained many isolated peaks which dominated the few and inadequate routes that slowly dropped down towards Route 9. Clark now decided to exploit forward on the road to Imola. On 21 September 85 Division captured Firenzuola and the strongly held position of Monte la Fine while to the east of the Imola road 88 Division, advancing over extremely difficult terrain, took Monte la Battaglia, a large mountain mass that dominated the valleys of the Senio and Santerno rivers below, on 27 September. The attack had now reached a point only ten miles from Imola itself. By this time, however, the Germans were mounting strong counter-attacks with elements of four divisions which now halted the advance. On Fifth Army's right flank, 13 Corps had captured San Benedetto and Marradi on 24 September but against increasing resistance could advance no further. On the left of II Corps, 91 Division had forced a passage of the Futa Pass through the capture of the dominant Mount Gazzaro and by 28 September had reached the Radicosa Pass. 34 Division had meanwhile advanced on the parallel road leading to Bologna and reached a point just short of Castiglione dei Pepole when they were relieved by 6 South African Armoured Division. To the west, the Allied line now ran from five miles north of Pistoia over the mountains to near Massa on the coast. In the last days of September the Germans abandoned the few remaining prepared Gothic Line positions except in the Ligurian Coastal Sector. As had been expected the major advance had been by Eighth Army, where a penetration of thirty miles in twenty-six days had been made.

On the Adriatic flank the Eighth Army were faced with a dozen or so river lines running directly across their line of advance to the Romagna district. The early and heavy autumn rain had brought both tracked and wheeled vehicles to a complete standstill anywhere off the few roads. This former swamp land that had been reclaimed and cultivated over centuries quickly became covered with the 'richest' mud met with in the whole campaign. With the rivers in spate and in the face of the violent rain storms at the end of September, the chance of any breakthrough in this area had gone but in spite of the worsening weather conditions and the growing exhaustion of Fifth Army there still seemed a chance of breaking clear of the mountains in the central sector up Route 65 to Bologna. 78 Division had just returned from the Middle East and was now sent, on 2 October, to reinforce 13 Corps. Alexander now issued orders for the renewal of the offensive. Fifth Army's drive towards Bologna would start on 1 October and Eighth Army's attack north and parallel to the Rimini–Bologna road would be launched by the Canadians and 5 Corps on the night 6/7 October. General Leese had been given the command of the Allied Land Forces in South-East Asia and was succeeded on 1 October by General McCreery. Having had recent experience in the mountains where 10 Corps had been acting as a link between the two armies, General McCreery felt the high ground was less of a barrier than the waterlogged plains. An attack by 10 Indian Division over the foothills succeeded in expanding a bridgehead over the River Fiumicino and Monte Farneto, which was only 8 miles south of Cesena, was captured on 7 October. The main attack north of Route 9, however, was held up owing to continued and violent rainstorms. Kesselring reacted immediately to the advance through the mountains and ordered 29 Panzer Grenadiers from north of Route 9 to protect Cesena. By 14 October, however, the Panzer Grenadiers were pulled out to help halt Fifth Army's attack on Bologna. In the meantime Eighth Army's main attack had started and on 16 October reached the line of the River Pisciatello and the following day 2 Polish Corps attacked through the mountains on the left of 5 Corps towards Rocca S Casciano, so as to open up communications with Fifth Army on Route 67. By 21 October both Galeata and Strada had been taken against stiffening resistance. By 20 October Cesena had been entered and bridgeheads seized over the River Savio, except down in the plain where the Germans still held Cervia on the coast. The Poles were now directed on Forli and 5 Corps started an attack from the Cesena bridgeheads. The Germans, however, held on for four days before voluntarily withdrawing to the line of the River Ronco. LXXVI Corps had in fact withdrawn 29 and 90 Panzer Grenadiers and 1 Parachute Division to reinforce the central sector where the situation opposite Bologna was critical. Consequently General Herr was forced to shorten his line in the foothills opposite Eighth Army. The weather by now had completely broken. Alexander later wrote, 'the rain, which was at that very time spoiling Fifth Army's attack on Bologna, now reached a new high pitch of intensity. On 26 October all bridges over the Savio, in our immediate rear, were swept away and our small bridgeheads over the Ronco were eliminated and destroyed.'[9] As will now be seen, the weather and the dogged determination of von Vietinghoff to hold on at all costs halted both Allied armies.

After 88 Division had been halted only ten miles from Imola, the German defensive line covering Route 65 was pulled back to the village of Monghidoro which stood on high ground astride the road. Behind this position streams, separated by ridge lines, drained northwards on both sides of the road. 'Transverse ridges and tributary streams, characterized by dominating hill masses and deep gullies, cut across this pattern at intervals of three or four miles.'[10] The Americans were now twenty-four miles from Bologna but three excellent defensive positions at Loiano, Livergnano and Pianoro covered the remaining fifteen miles of mountainous country. From the attackers' point of view the road communications were so limited that it was impossible to relieve divisions if the attack was made on a narrow front and Clark decided to advance with four divisions in line each holding back a regiment in reserve. The plan was to rotate the leading regiments about every five days so that the successive defence lines would be attacked by reasonably fresh or rested troops. The two divisions already in position would lead the attack; 91 Division astride Route 65, with 85 Division on its right. The left flank would be protected by 34 Division along the line of the Setta Creek and 88 Division would perform a similar task on the right flank, after being relieved by 1 Guards Brigade of 13 Corps on Mount Battaglia and by 78 Division on Mount Cappello. At 0600 hours on 1 October the attack by II Corps started on a sixteen-mile front. After early morning mist the day was clear and sunny, facilitating artillery and air supports. Opposite Imola strong counter-attacks were met but down Route 65 the advance started well. The following day brought fog and low cloud and a cold and driving rain which persisted for a week. The reduction of the Monghidoro line took four days, an average advance of about a mile a day and against stubborn delaying tactics the reserve regiments were now put in against the line of hills behind Loiano. By this time the American tanks and tank destroyers were having great difficulty in getting forward over the slippery muddy trails and the infantry attacks were also greatly hampered by the weather. There still seemed a good chance that II Corps would reach the Po valley before the rain turned to snow at the end of October but 16 SS Panzer Grenadiers were now moving eastwards against 34 Division on II Corps' left flank and there were indications that the whole of 65 Panzer Grenadier Division had also moved over from XIV Panzer Corps, to come in alongside 4 Parachute Division to block the road to Bologna. At the same time the German 98 Division, released from the Imola sector, was closing in on 88 Division. These moves brought the German strength opposing II Corps up to five divisions, plus elements from three other divisions, compared with a strength of one full division and elements of two others when the offensive started. Between 5 and 9 October the four American divisions struggled forward and forced the Germans to withdraw to the Livergnano escarpment. This position had great natural strength, the main barrier being a sheer rock wall some three miles long and in places nearly 1,500 feet high. Furthermore, the flanks were protected by the deep gorge of the Zena Creek to the east and a dominant hill mass to the west. Further hill masses lay astride the line of advance east of Route 65. The Germans were no longer prepared to give ground and an attack by 85 Division was held for three days by elements of no less than four German divisions. Between 10 and 15 October the weather improved considerably and now under heavy artillery and air attack the Germans were forced back from Livergnano, which they evacuated late on 14 October. Losses had been heavy on both sides but the reinforcement situation in II Corps was acute and the Germans still seemed to be able to find troops to fill the gaps. Elements of 29 Panzer Grenadiers had been identified north of Livergnano and the volume of German artillery fire had now doubled since the beginning of the month. Much of the credit for this must go to von Senger who, during the temporary illness of General Lemelsen, had been brought in to command Fourteenth Army on 15 October for about a week. During this time he succeeded in co-ordinating the defensive fire on the vital sector opposite Bologna and moved in further reserves from

317

his own Corps. Much of the German artillery was now concentrating on the American supply line up Route 65 and both here and to the west of the road the offensive had now been halted by the determined resistance of 16 SS Panzer Grenadiers and 29 Panzer Grenadiers. 13 Corps now took over more ground on the right flank to relieve 88 Division for the assault of Mount Grande in an attempt to widen the salient east of Route 65. With the assistance of 158 fighter-bomber sorties and 8,100 rounds of gunfire this feature was captured by dawn on 20 October, twenty-four hours before its fall was expected. The axis of II Corps attack was now switched to exploit this success but by this date 90 Panzer Grenadiers and 1 Parachute Division were in position covering the approaches to Castel San Pietro and Route 9. Attempts to take and hold the village of Vedriano on three successive nights between 22 and 25 October were finally frustrated by German counter-attacks. By the afternoon of 26 October, General Keys ordered 85 and 88 Divisions to dig in on the nearest defensive positions. 88 Division was halted only four miles from Route 9 and 34 Division to the east of Route 65 was halted ten miles from the centre of Bologna. The following day the whole of Fifth Army went over to the defensive.

Casualties on both sides had been extremely heavy. The appalling weather conditions, the difficulties of supply over inadequate roads and the lack of reinforcements all had contributed to the slowing down of the offensive and combined with the stubborn German resistance effectively prevented the exploitation of Alexander's success in breaking through the Gothic Line. The battle for the Gothic Line was fought between ground forces of relatively even balance. Allied Air supremacy, however, played a great part in deciding the issue. In the early stages of the battle, while XII Air Force was engaged on DRAGOON, the Desert Air Force had supported both Fifth and Eighth Armies. In fact the Desert Air Force had at this stage already taken over the interdiction programme from the River Po to the south between Pavia and the Adriatic. On 26 August the entire effort of the Desert Air Force was thrown in on Eighth Army front, with 664 sorties mainly against the defences about Pesaro. Day by day the fighters and fighter-bombers, directed by 'tentacles' manned by joint Army/Air staffs, struck at the German batteries, tank concentrations and positions and also stretched out to attack communication centres at Cesena and Rimini. By night, Bostons and Baltimores struck at communications between Rimini, Ravenna and Bologna. On the last three nights of the month medium bombers of the Strategic Air Force attacked Pesaro in support of the Polish attack. As Seventh Army advanced up the Rhône valley and passed beyond the range of the XII Air Force, its squadrons flying from Corsica switched some of their effort back to Italy and by early September three fighter groups and a medium bomber group were operating in support of Alexander's offensive. Prior to Clark's main attack these groups concentrated on communication targets and particularly the Po crossings and the rail bridges below Lake Maggiore, where all five bridges over the Ticino River were destroyed. After 9 September the medium bombers switched to attacking railway lines leading into Bologna and together with the fighter-bombers attacked targets immediately to the front of Fifth Army's advance. Between 9 and 20 September, when the weather broke, an average of 240 fighter sorties a day were flown, while on 9 and 11 September the medium bombers flew 337 sorties to attack positions on the Futa and Il Giogo Passes, followed by strong attacks on their northern exits on 12/14 September. After 16 September most of the medium bomber effort was switched to Eighth Army front. Here the Desert Air Force were making a tremendous sustained effort in support of the drive to Rimini. The peak came on 13 September when 900 sorties were flown and more than 500 tons of bombs were dropped. In the six days from 13 to 18 September, which included two days of bad weather, the Desert Air Force flew over 4,000 sorties. The medium bombers were now attacking the German positions on the Marecchia River but on 20 September the weather broke completely, bringing air operations to a virtual standstill for five out of the last ten days of the month. After the fall of Rimini the Desert Air Force had stretched out beyond the immediate battle-front to try and prevent the Germans regrouping and to attack the bridges over the River Savio and communications in the triangle Ferrara–Bologna–Ravenna, while medium bombers attacked the marshalling yards between Bologna and Cesena. When in early October the weather became steadily worse the scale of air operations fell sharply.

The Gothic Line battles cost the Germans 8,000 prisoners. On 15 September LXXVI Panzer Corps reported that, since the start of the battle, it had suffered 14,500 casualties. By 25 September over a third of Kesselring's ninety-two infantry battalions were down to less than 200 men each and only ten battalions had more than 400 men. In just over three weeks' fighting, up to 21 September, Eighth Army suffered over 4,000 casualties and lost some 210 tanks, with even more bogged down or beyond local repair. The Allied tank strength at the opening of the battle, excluding the relatively small number of American tanks with Fifth Army, and any held at the base ports, was 3,116. Three months later, in spite of the delivery of 363 'up-gunned' Sherman tanks, the figures stood at 3,014, showing an overall loss of 465 tanks, almost entirely in Eighth Army's sector. Between 10 September and 26 October, II Corps of Fifth Army had over 15,700 casualties amongst the four divisions involved in the drive on Bologna, a third of these casualties being in 88 Division. The accumulative effort of Allied losses since the fall of Rome may be judged from the following figures. Between 5 June and 15 August Fifth Army casualties in killed, wounded and missing had amounted to 17,959 and in the three months July to September Eighth Army had 19,975 battle casualties, of which 8,000 came in the period from 25 August to 9 September. The greatest losses were amongst the infantry units and in the Gothic Line battles British infantry regiments lost over 7,000 men. Drastic measures were forced on Alexander. 1 British Armoured Division had to be disbanded, 56 Division had a complete brigade reduced to a cadre and all British infantry battalions had to be reorganized on a three rifle company basis. Apart from the acute problem of the lack of reinforcements Alexander was also faced with extreme difficulty in replacing heavy weapons, tanks and vehicles. In this connection the work of recovery and repair may be illustrated by a brief survey of the activities of the Royal Electrical and Mechanical Engineer units who were working with 5 Corps. The period covered is from 27 August to 21 October.

	Recovered by Recovery Units	Received in Workshops	Repaired in Workshops
Tanks	335	592	308
Vehicles	2,900	6,877	5,192
Guns	49	302	239

Tank and Vehicle engines changed – 1,018, including 136 tank engines. The above figures apply only to 5 Corps.

As already mentioned, General Wilson had twice applied to the Combined Chiefs of Staff for reinforcements for the drive into northern Italy. In addition to asking for fresh US divisions and proper modern equipment for the Italian units that had come over to the Allied side, Wilson also asked for more Indian troops from the Middle East and reinforcements for the Polish Corps. No equipment was released for the Italian units and in the middle of August Wilson was told that 78 Division could be expected from the Middle East in September and that an Indian Infantry Brigade together with a Greek Brigade would arrive during August but that the maintenance of the Indian Brigade in protracted operations would be limited for lack of suitable reinforcements. A British Infantry Brigade was being formed from units already in the Mediterranean but would not be ready for some time. The Combined Chiefs of Staff went on to say that the release of US divisions must await developments in France but that 92 (Negro) Division and a Brazilian Division would be sent to Italy. Regarding reinforcements for the Polish Corps it was later discovered, in early September, that some 11,000 Polish soldiers had been screened out of the prisoners taken in Normandy and within a relatively short time 4,000 of these men, as a first contingent, were on their way to join the Polish Corps in Italy. Regarding Air Force reinforcements, the Combined Chiefs of Staff said that any increase in the Mediterranean could only be made at the expense of General Eisenhower's operations and that the matter would have to be argued out between the two theatres. Before this decision was announced, however, the Air Ministries in London had been able to redistribute squadrons within the Mediterranean so that eleven additional squadrons joined the Desert Air Force between the beginning of July and mid-August. At the end of August Alexander appealed directly to Alanbrooke but the latter could only reply, 'it is not possible to send reinforcements to the Mediterranean and you will have to continue to live on your own resources'.[11] In short, the result was that the only reinforcements that arrived in time for the Allied assault on the Gothic Line was the Greek Brigade, one Regiment of the Brazilian Expeditionary Force and a regimental combat team of 92 Division, so the battle had to be fought by the twenty Allied divisions many of which had been fighting for several years. Having lost seven divisions to Seventh Army, Alexander's strength was still five and a half divisions less than it had been at the fall of Rome. Early in October Clark appealed to Devers for reinforcements to continue the assault on Bologna but was turned down. At Alexander's personal request Eisenhower had 3,000 men flown from France, but owing to the stormy weather they arrived too late to influence the battle. Kesselring meanwhile had received strong reinforcements and the latest arrivals were 232 and 237 Infantry Divisions in replacement of 3 and 15 Panzer Grenadiers. These additions now brought his strength in Italy up to no less than twenty-eight German divisions of which twenty were committed south of the Po. At least two Italian divisions were already in the north of Italy and employed on internal security duties. The Allies had had to live on their own fat and while the conversion of anti-aircraft and other units had produced some 12,000 infantry reinforcements these were quite insufficient to make good the losses in the Gothic Line battles.

On 23 October Kesselring was on tour of the front when his car hit a 'long-barrelled' gun swinging out from a side road. He was in hospital for nearly three months and von Vietinghoff took over command of the Army group. There is no doubt that Tenth Army was taken by surprise by Eighth Army's rapid penetration of what Kesselring described as 'the first green line – with no equivalent position behind it in the whole depth of the Adriatic Sector'.[12] The OKW laid the blame on the local commanders and Jodl went on record as saying 'one of the worst and most momentous errors was to allow the left flank of the Apennines position to be pushed back as soon as the position was occupied'.[13] Kesselring had done his best to speed up the fortification and occupation of the Gothic Line but he was caught off-balance by the Eighth Army's offensive which developed in such unexpected strength. Prior to the landings on the French Riviera, Kesselring had feared an amphibious assault in the Genoa area and as Seventh Army advanced inland he became equally concerned about a possible Allied thrust over the Alpes Maritimes. After the German defeat in France and with the Allies sweeping forward through Belgium, Kesselring could expect no reinforcements and in fact was constantly being pressed to release formations for the Western Front. His plea for permission to withdraw to the Alps, in accordance with a plan called 'Autumn Mists' so as to shorten his line, was turned down out of hand. Hitler seemed far more concerned with the situation in the Balkans and when he finally came to the conclusion that Alexander was aiming at cutting Kesselring's communications through Carinthia and the Tyrol, the only solution that he could offer was the invariable order for static defence. This order that the Apennines must be held, not merely through the autumn but permanently, was not received until 5 October. By this date Clark's drive in the central sector had been switched towards Bologna, a move that Kesselring feared. Allied success at this point would cause a collapse of the whole of the eastern sector as far as the Adriatic. A fortnight earlier, when the Fifth Army assault on the Futa and Il Giogo Passes was developing, von Vietinghoff, whose troops were slowly being forced back from Rimini, had taken a more parochial view when he warned Kesselring, 'if he (Clark) gets the quite correct idea of moving to Imola instead of Bologna, we will be trapped in this pocket here'.[14] It was indeed fortunate for Kesselring that Route 9 gave him means for switching divisions so readily to meet the successive Allied threats. OLIVE had been planned primarily to hold down Kesselring's forces at a critical stage of the battle in France and the Low Countries where the blow that it was hoped would defeat Germany would be launched. Alexander achieved not only surprise at the opening of the offensive but the highest possible concentration of forces in the two vital sectors. The early and unseasonable break in the weather prevented Eighth Army from reaping the full benefit of their preponderance in armour and turned the Romagna into a sea of mud. In the plain the rivers were now broad and swollen and too deep to ford. The high flood banks gave the Germans not only observation but ready-made defensive positions. The depleted infantry units could no longer set the pace and the advance slowed down and was finally halted. In Fifth Army's sector the mountainous terrain was unsuitable for armour and restricted the deployment of artillery as well as creating great difficulties over supply. In the mountains the break in the weather brought fog and mist, driving rain and winds of gale force and the infantry suffered great hardship. The drawn-out fighting with no chance of relief and the endless small unit infantry actions brought progressive exhaustion and heavy casualties. The offensive that had been planned with such skill and launched with hopes of an Allied breakthrough had now become a battle of attrition, with both sides suffering excessively high casualties. Through the early onset of winter conditions the Allies were unable to reap the benefit of the main advantage they possessed, that of air supremacy. From the overall strategic point of view, Kesselring's forces had been held down and no German divisions left Italy for the Western Front. Alexander had gambled and nearly succeeded in breaking through. Kesselring had once more shown remarkable powers of recovery and just succeeded in holding a line in the Apennines. The weather held the balance.

18
Winter Trials

Pacific plans and OCTAGON: Winter campaign inevitable: Shortage of gun ammunition: Air and naval operations: Command changes: Eighth Army fights on: Mussolini's fling: Greek diversion: Canadians transferred: Winter tasks and training: Alexander plans spring campaign: von Vietinghoff's dilemma.

1944

12–16 Sept	Second Quebec Conference – OCTAGON.
early Oct	Alexander proposes operations across Adriatic.
24 Oct	Wilson warns Combined Chiefs of Staff that offensive cannot be maintained beyond mid-November.
early Nov	'Porterforce' operations towards Ravenna.
9 Nov	Poles enter Forli and capture Modigliana 12 November.
21–26 Nov	5 Corps and Poles converge on Faenza.
28 Nov	Alexander issues orders for final effort by both armies to reach Bologna, commencing with Eighth Army crossing the Santerno by 7 December.
2–5 Dec	Canadians capture Ravenna.
3–7 Dec	46 Division and Poles cross upper reaches of River Lamone.
10–12 Dec	Canadians cross lower reaches of River Lamone. Battle for Bagnacavallo continues until 21 December.
15–17 Dec	New Zealanders and 10 Indian Division reach River Senio.
16 Dec	43 Gurkha Brigade enters Faenza.
19 Dec–6 Jan	56 Division operations to clear east bank of Senio.
22 Dec	Fifth Army at 48 hours' notice to resume offensive. Intelligence reports of impending counter-attack in valley of River Serchio.
25 Dec	8 Indian Division sent to reinforce Serchio sector (followed by 85 Division and 1 (US) Armoured Division).
During Dec	4 Division move to Greece.
26/27 Dec	Germans and some Italians break through 92 Division positions in Serchio valley.
28/29 Dec	8 Indian Division recaptures lost ground and restores line in Serchio valley.

| 30 Dec | Alexander halts offensive. Heavy snow and weather conditions limit all operations. |

1945

2–5 Jan	Canadians and 5 Corps clean up area south of Lake Comacchio and River Senio.
early Jan	Alexander announces general plan of spring offensive.
During Jan	46 Division moves to Greece.
30 Jan	Combined Chiefs of Staff meet in Malta (en route for Yalta) and decide to transfer five divisions from Mediterranean to north-west Europe.
mid-Feb	General Truscott starts limited operations south-west of Bologna to gain elbow-room. Both Armies carrying out intensive training and other preparations for coming offensive.

By the end of August 1944 in pursuance of their 'Germany first' policy the United States had sent over two million men to the European theatre. Thirty-four American divisions and one hundred and three air groups were under Eisenhower's command, this was twice as many as were deployed in the Pacific. A further three-quarters of a million American troops were deployed in the Mediterranean and Middle East, the main commitment being the six divisions and forty-six air groups serving under General Wilson in Italy. A further four divisions were en route to join Eisenhower and the majority of the twenty-four divisions still stationed in the United States were also ear-marked to land in France. Determined to build up Eisenhower's forces as quickly as possible, the United States planners now proposed transferring the six American divisions in Clark's Fifth Army to France. This proposal was largely dictated by their 'guns and butter policy' and 'the concept of defeating Germany via a direct concentrated effort with a minimum of time, money and manpower'.[1] In Europe the Western Allies had reached Antwerp and were closing on the German borders and to the east the Russians were advancing into Poland and the Baltic States. Indeed the Western Allies expected the surrender of Germany by 1 December. In the Pacific, General MacArthur held most of New Guinea and Admiral Nimitz had seized the southern Marianas and a ring was steadily closing around Japan. When the British proposed another full-scale conference Marshall and the American planners felt there was little to discuss, as the pattern of future operations had already been decided and everything seemed to be going along according to plan. At Churchill's insistence, however, a meeting in Quebec was arranged for early September. The American planners considered that the two points most likely to be raised by their Allies were the question of the withdrawal of Fifth Army to France and British proposals for their participation in the Pacific war. Regarding the first point, the date of the move of Fifth Army would depend on the outcome of Alexander's attack on the Gothic Line but if Eisenhower decided he could not use the six divisions effectively the planners suggested they could be used in operations towards Vienna but not in the Balkans. On the other hand, if shipping and transport planes were available, there was no objection to their being used to support a British amphibious landing on the Istrian peninsula, the move that had been so ardently pro-posed as an alternative to ANVIL. On the first day out from the Clyde in the

Queen Mary the Chiefs of Staff held a meeting to discuss their line of approach at the coming conference. They agreed amongst themselves that, after Kesselring was defeated and driven back, the Italian theatre should become a secondary theatre of operations. Considerably less Allied troops would be required to oppose any German stand on the line of the Piave and all three Indian divisions and the landing craft in the Mediterranean would in any case be needed for the landing on Rangoon, which must be made before the monsoons in May 1945. According to a very tight schedule, which had to allow for the move to India, the reorganization, training and re-equipment of six divisions from Europe and the Mediterranean, the divisions from Italy would have to leave between mid-September and mid-November. Churchill, however, was looking further ahead than a mere holding operation in the north-eastern plains of Italy. He was far from convinced that the defeat of Germany was certain in 1944 and was also deeply concerned over the now barely concealed Russian intentions to dominate the Balkans and the whole of eastern Europe. He later wrote, 'If the Germans either evacuated Italy or retired to the Alps I much desired that Alexander should be enabled to make his amphibious thrust across the Adriatic, seize and occupy the Istrian peninsula, and try to reach Vienna before the Russians. It seemed much too early to start sending his troops to south-east Asia.'[2] It was agreed that there could be no question of any of Alexander's troops being withdrawn until Kesselring was driven back to the Piave, except for the first of the Indian divisions needed for the Rangoon operation. OCTAGON, the second conference at Quebec, lasted from 12–16 September and most of the time was spent discussing proposals for British participation in the defeat of Japan. Agreement on Italy was quickly reached. There would be no question of the withdrawal of the American divisions until the 'present offensive then under way to defeat Kesselring had been completed', and this would include 'the invasion of the Po valley'. Subsequently, if Eisenhower did not need the American divisions 'they should then be utilized to clear the Germans from Italy and to assist British forces in operation to the north-east and towards Vienna'. This decision applied equally to the Tactical Air Force and as regards the Fifteenth Strategic Air Force it was considered that it could 'best perform its mission by remaining at its Foggia bases'.[3] Regarding American landing craft in the Mediterranean, Admiral King agreed these could be retained providing a decision was reached by mid-October and General Wilson was therefore told to submit, by 10 October, his plans for the capture of the Istrian peninsula with the assault shipping already in the Mediterranean. The conference has been described as marking 'the summit of coalition warfare and the "golden era" of combined strategic planning'. Equally Churchill's warning of 'the political dangers of divergencies between the Soviet Union and the Western Allies with respect to Poland, Greece and Yugoslavia'[4] showed OCTAGON to be the forerunner of Yalta and Potsdam, when the urgent political problems of winning the peace could no longer be kept to one side.

While the Western Allies had been conferring in Quebec events in north-west Europe had been moving rapidly. Here Eisenhower had assumed command of the ground operations and in accordance with plans that had been made some time before the sudden collapse of the Germans in Normandy he ordered the advance of the five Allied Armies to continue on a broad front. With six divisions grounded in Normandy for lack of transport he still had fifty divisions, against which, at this point, Hitler could only produce some twenty-five disorganized and understrength divisions, pitifully weak in armour. Montgomery and Bradley were both calling for extra transport and orders to strike a concentrated blow in their sectors. But no re-allocation of transport or supplies was ordered and no concentrated blow was delivered. On 12 September a Combined Chiefs of Staff directive gave priority to the northern flank and extra transport was found to supply 21 Army Group. Ten more days, however, were to pass before the American thrust further south was turned northwards. But the German strength opposing Second Army had now doubled and the opportunity had passed. The battle at Arnhem was already lost and within twenty-four hours the surviving airborne troops were ordered back across the Rhine. The effect of this reverse and the need to drive the Germans from the Scheldt area and open the port of Antwerp had far-reaching results. Two months were to pass before Allied shipping could use the port and each day brought German reinforcements, scraped up from depots and training units, and time to form additional divisions by a ruthless combing of men from reserved occupations and the call-up of boys of sixteen. It was soon evident to the Allies that they now faced a winter campaign in north-west Europe and that the assault on the German frontiers must be postponed. In Italy Kesselring's troops took heart and clung with even greater determination to the Apennines positions.

It was about this time also that the Allies first began to feel the effect of having prematurely cut back on the production of certain types of gun ammunition. In mid-August Wilson had been warned that future supplies of ammunition would have to be revised, owing to a world-wide shortage that was developing. The different nature of the country and the reduction of the many fortified positions in the Gothic Line brought heavy expenditure of both field and medium gun ammunition. By the end of October, although production had restarted in the factories, the supply situation was critical and by mid-November had become a limiting factor in future operations in Italy.

Early in October Alexander's appreciation was briefly as follows. In order to support Eisenhower's decision to fight a winter campaign there appeared to be four courses of action. The direct transference of divisions to north-west Europe was at the moment unnecessary, as further American divisions were already on their way and from the supply point of view Eisenhower was already in difficulty. The second course envisaged a landing by Eighth Army in Yugoslavia to outflank Kesselring's remaining prepared positions in north-east Italy. This plan required the development of a base, using the ports of Split, Sibenik and Zara, to enable a rapid advance by at least six divisions to be made on Fiume and Ljubljana concurrently with a thrust by Fifth Army across the head of the Adriatic. For the time being, however, this plan would have to be shelved, as it would make no immediate contribution to Eisenhower's situation in north-west Europe. Any let-up in the present offensive, even if it was to enable a stronger blow to be made later, could easily result in veteran divisions being withdrawn from Italy and thrown into the battle in north-west Europe. The only course that could assist Eisenhower in his present predicament was for the offensive to be 'pressed on in Italy despite all the difficulties of climate and terrain, of deficient manpower and material'.[5] There were, however, serious limiting factors. Firstly, the weather would soon halt major operations in Italy. Secondly, there was the shortage of gun ammunition and lastly, if the Germans held out into 1945, it would be necessary to rest and reorganize the troops in preparation for an all-out spring offensive. The overall plan therefore emerged that the offensive in Italy must continue so long as the weather and the condition of the troops allowed. Following this there would be 'a period of active defence', when the maximum number of troops would be taken out for rest and to prepare for the Spring offensive. If meanwhile the Germans were driven back to the line of the River Adige, Eighth Army would plan and prepare the amphibious operation across the Adriatic already outlined. By the end of October Alexander realized that he could no longer hope to drive the Germans back to the Adige but he was still determined to capture Ravenna and Bologna before the offensive halted. Plans were therefore made for Eighth Army to continue their attack, with the object of reaching Ravenna by mid-November in the hopes of drawing off German divisions from Fifth Army, who would then make a final effort to take Bologna. On 24 October Wilson warned the Combined Chiefs of Staff that unless the line Ravenna–Bologna–La Spezia was reached by mid-November he would be forced to halt the offensive, even if Bologna had not fallen, through 'shortage of formations adequate to effect a breakthrough, the onset of winter conditions to offset our superiority in armour and in the air, as well as the replacement and ammunition situation'. At the same time he proposed, as an alternative, 'to continuing the frontal attacks against successive river lines'.[6] Assuming that he had captured Bologna, he proposed to halt and prepare to put into effect the outflanking attack across the Adriatic.

Throughout November Eighth Army struggled forward with 5 Corps attacking towards Forli, with the Polish Corps on their left directed on the high ground south of Faenza. After heavy fighting the Germans withdrew behind the Montone River and Forli was entered on 9 November. The advance was pressed forward through the foothills and by 12 November a strong force was over the river at Ladino and the Poles had reached the strongly fortified village of Modigliana. In the coastal sector of the Romagna plain, from which the Canadians had been withdrawn back into reserve, a composite force was operating under the command of Lieutenant-Colonel Horsburgh-Porter, Commanding 27 Lancers. 'Porterforce' was a mixed British and Canadian mobile force consisting of an armoured car and three armoured regiments, one of which was dismounted, with artillery and engineer supporting units and included the Desert Commando Force known as Popski's Private Army. In a series of skilfully conducted engagements 'Porterforce' reached the Fiumi Uniti immediately south-east of Ravenna. Here the banks of the river had been breached to increase the already considerable area of floods. Further inland and south of Ravenna, 12 Lancers advanced as flank protection to 5 Corps but were held up by strong opposition at Coccolia. This successful drive forward in the coastal sector had been greatly aided by a period of fine weather in the second week of November. The Desert Air Force also took advantage of better flying conditions and with the help of two medium bomber (B26s) wings some 900 sorties were flown against the German positions in the Forli area on 7 and 8 November. During the subsequent operations aiming at the capture of Faenza, medium bombers from Mediterranean Allied Tactical Air Force attacked the bridges at Faenza with 114 sorties between 16–19 November and 262 sorties against German battery positions in the same area between 21–24 November. During this latter period the Desert Air Force flew some 1,200 sorties in close support of 5 Corps. The attack on Faenza was made by 4 and 46 Divisions and was launched against fierce opposition early on 21 November. The assault was renewed the following day and on the night 23/24 November the Germans withdrew behind the lines of the Lamone and the Marzeno. By 25 November 4 Division was pursuing the German's rearguards through Scaldino and the following day 46 Division had crossed the Marzeno and reached Sarna. On the left the Poles had reached a point some six miles south of Faenza, where a strong German counter-attack retook and held the village of Converselle until it was recaptured by a fresh Polish Division on 21 November. Further into the mountains 13 Corps, on the right of Fifth Army, had kept pace with the Polish advance and 8 Indian Division had beaten off an attempt to retake Modigliana. A break in the weather now temporarily halted the advance.

Throughout November the Fifteenth Strategic Air Force had been making an all-out effort against oil installations, with subsidiary attacks now being made on Luftwaffe bases in Greece, Austria and northern Italy, rather than on aircraft production plants in southern Germany. In the middle of November fourteen heavy bombers returning from a raid on southern Germany had been lost in the Udine area. As some 100 German fighters were now reported on aerodromes at Aviano, Vicenza, Villafranca and Udine the Strategic Air Force made a concentrated attack on these four bases on 17–18 November.

Although by the last week of November (German) air operations had become almost non-existent, it was appreciated that perhaps the bad weather which was playing such havoc with Allied air operations prevented a fair evaluation of the enemy's air potential. But when clearing skies allowed a resumption of Allied air activity, the Luftwaffe was mostly absent. It would never again be a factor in the Mediterranean war.[7]

Meanwhile Mediterranean Allied Tactical Air Force continued the interdiction of the rail routes out of Italy and in particular attacked the Brenner route from Verona to Innsbruck and the bridges crossing the Brenta River. In early November the attacks were very successful and in fact the Brenner route was only open for about four days in the whole month. As the weather deteriorated, however, and the bombing became spasmodic and less accurate the German repair organization was able to catch up. During December attacks made on the Brenner bridges were no more successful than those directed against the bridges over the Brenta line and the other river lines in the north-east, which were cut for only about twelve days in the month. These failures were partly due to the transfer to north-west Europe of most of one of the American bomber wings and two fighter groups and the diversion of the Desert Air Force to the direct support of Eighth Army.

Towards the end of September the last three of the eleven German U-boats operating in the Mediterranean were sunk, two by American bombers in Salamis harbour and one off Crete, after a wisp of smoke from its 'schnorkel' had been spotted from the Polish-manned destroyer *Garland* at the astonishing range of eight miles. Sailings in convoy were now rarely ordered and many Allied warships were released for service in the Eastern theatres. Allied naval supremacy in the Mediterranean was now almost complete. In the last seven months of 1944 the Convoy and Routing Service handled 14,898 ships of which only five were lost. During the same period, taking the Mediterranean theatre as a whole, 378 German-controlled merchant ships totalling nearly 700,000 tons were sunk, in addition to a very large number of small vessels and naval auxiliaries. There were now six flotillas of Allied minesweepers, totalling thirty-nine ships, augmented by a large number of smaller vessels, engaged on clearing channels and harbours, both on the Italian and Yugoslav coasts, in what Admiral Cunningham claims to have been the biggest sweeping operation in the Mediterranean of the whole war. 'Between 1 September and 5 December over 2,000 mines were cleared.'[8] As far as the Dalmatian coast was concerned, by the end of 1944 the Germans only held the Istrian peninsula and the ports of Trieste, Fiume and Pola. British warships were now stationed at Split and Zara and further south, hard on the heels of the German withdrawal, food for the starving Albanians was being landed through the port of Valona.

The considerable German garrisons in Rhodes, Kos, Leros and other smaller Aegean islands were now cut off from all supplies and left to contemplate their inevitable fate. In 1945, as the Allies' air attacks on communications in northern Italy were stepped up, the Germans made renewed attempts to transport supplies by sea. A coastal convoy service was operating down the Ligurian coast between Savona or Genoa to Spezia. The naval escorts for these convoys were pitifully small and in February amounted to one destroyer, six torpedo boats or small escort vessels and about fifty assorted but heavily armed dual-purpose ferry/barges and other small craft. A similar convoy service was operating at the head of the Adriatic where a few cargo ships and a number of barges were crossing from Trieste to Venice, whence supplies were carried by barge to ports in the north of the Po delta. Some ships were still creeping down the opposite coast to supply the German forces operating in Yugoslavia. In the Adriatic there was one German destroyer, four torpedo boats, about forty E-boats and a large number of small landing craft, which could only be used close inshore.

In the western Mediterranean the principal Allied naval squadron consisted of three French cruisers and a number of British, French and American destroyers. This force, known as 'Flank Force', was principally engaged in bombardment duties on the Franco-Italian frontier but also supplied destroyers to support the Inshore Squadron operating against the Germans' supply convoys. This squadron was led by Commander R. A. Allan, RNVR, and operated from Leghorn. It consisted of British and American Motor Torpedo Boats and Landing Craft (Gun) trained to operate under Allan's control, using radar and radio from his own Motor Torpedo Boat, as 'a miniature battle fleet'. The squadron waged a constant battle against the German supply traffic in the Gulf of Genoa and its commanding officer received a warm tribute from Admiral Morse when it was finally disbanded in mid-April. Now that the U-boats had been eliminated, the Allied coastal aircraft were largely engaged in seeking out and destroying German supply vessels as they crept along the coast and in looking for fresh minefields sown to protect their routes. Between January and May of 1945 a further seventeen German merchant ships were sunk and when the campaign finished eighty-seven were reported as scuttled, captured or lost 'by other causes'. Captain Roskill writes 'though it is difficult to give an exact figure for his losses of auxiliary warships, it is almost certain they exceeded his losses . . . of merchantmen. The loss of virtually the whole of his merchant shipping undoubtedly contributed enormously to the failure of all the enemy's aims and purposes in this theatre.'[9] It was not, however, until the last few weeks of the campaign that these losses came near to stopping the flow of supplies by sea.

On 28 November Alexander issued his orders for what he realized would be the last major offensive before the spring of 1945. 4 Division was under orders to leave the theatre and its relief, 5 Division, was not due to arrive until January. The only reinforcement he had received was a second regiment of the Brazilian Expeditionary Force which needed a settling in period before being committed. By 5 December the four American divisions of 11 Corps would be ready but there was only enough American gun ammunition for fifteen days' full-scale operations and 13 Corps could only play a minor part in the offensive, as their divisions had had no relief or rest. Eighth Army had just about enough gun ammunition left for three weeks' operations. The first phase of the offensive would be an attack by Eighth Army to breach the line of the Santerno and then both armies would launch a concerted drive on Bologna. Fifth Army would attack straight up Route 65 with a subsidiary thrust at San Pietro and Eighth Army would attack north of Route 9. The date for the opening of this second phase of the offensive would be not before 8 December and would depend on favourable weather conditions. General McCreery's orders were for Eighth Army to attack with all three Corps up, the Canadians on the right and 5 Corps astride Route 9, with the Poles on their left continuing their advance through the mountains. Eighth Army had a formidable task; they first had to cross both the Lamone and the Senio and then seize bridgeheads over the Santerno by 7 December, if Alexander's earliest date for the general offensive was to be met. Only a day or so before the attack was due to start a reply was received from the Combined Chiefs of Staff to Wilson's proposals dispatched on 24 October. The reply was categoric – operations across the Adriatic were ruled out and the primary objective would be the immediate capture of Bologna, followed by the seizure of the line Ravenna–Bologna–La Spezia and the continuation of operations with a view to containing the German armies in Italy – in other words the mixture as before.

The German line opposite Eighth Army followed the Fiume Uniti and the Montone to three miles upstream from S Pancrazio, thence through Albereto and Scaldino to join the defences on the Lamone to Faenza and beyond. On the Adriatic coast a newly formed Corps headquarters, the LXXV, commanded the sector from the sea to about the switch line south-east of Russi with three divisions, including 90 Panzer Grenadiers who were sent over from Army Group Reserve behind Bologna before the end of the month. LXXVI Panzer Corps covered Route 9 and the ground to the south as far as the Santerno with four divisions, which included 26 Panzer and 29 Panzer Grenadier Divisions. The central sector opposing the Fifth Army salient near S Pietro and the approaches to Bologna by Route 65 was held by XIV Panzer Corps with five divisions and the south-western approaches to Bologna were covered by 1 Parachute Corps with three divisions. All four Corps came under Tenth Army. A further three to four divisions were held in Army Reserve in the Bologna area. The long western flank from Vergato to the sea was covered by Fourteenth Army with LI Mountain Corps containing two German and two Italian divisions. LXXV Corps of two German and one Italian division remained on the Franco-Italian frontier, while a further Italian division watched the Gulf of Genoa. Taking into account four weak divisions in north-east Italy, von Vietinghoff's Army Group now contained twenty-seven German and four Italian divisions, and included one Panzer and three Panzer Grenadier divisions. No less than fourteen German divisions were deployed to cover the front from Bologna to the Adriatic, with a further four in reserve behind Bologna.

Alexander's two armies contained sixteen infantry and four armoured divisions plus the equivalent of six infantry brigades and eight armoured or tank brigades. The contributions by the various Allies is summarized as follows:

	Infantry		Armoured	
	Divisions	Independent Brigades	Divisions	Independent Brigades
United States	5	Task Force 45	1	—
Great Britain	4 (a)	1	1	5 (b)
Canadian	1	—	1	1
New Zealand	1	—	—	1
South African	—	—	1	—
Indian	2	2	—	—
Polish	2	—	—	1
Brazilian	1	—	—	—
Italian	—	2 Combat Groups	—	—

Notes:
(a) Two of these divisions only had two brigades.
(b) Two armoured brigades and three tank brigades.

The three Corps of Eighth Army involved in the first phase of the new offensive comprised a total of six infantry divisions and 43 Indian Lorry Brigade and two armoured divisions, plus three armoured brigades and a tank brigade. In the second phase, the double thrust on Bologna, the whole might of II Corps (four infantry and one armoured division) of Fifth Army would be added.

In November Sir John Dill died in Washington and early in December Wilson was appointed to take his place as head of the British Joint Staff Mission and Churchill's personal military representative in the United States. Field Marshal Alexander* was appointed Supreme Allied Commander Mediterranean on 12 December and at Churchill's request Clark took over command of the Allied Armies in Italy, while General Truscott was recalled from France and given command of Fifth Army. In Greece civil war was

---

* Alexander's promotion to Field Marshal had been announced on 5 December, but was back-dated to 4 June, the date of the capture of Rome.

flaring up and 4 Division left Italy in the middle of the month to join 4 Indian Division in the Athens area, where General Scobie had taken over control.

On 1 December 1 Canadian Corps took over from 'Porterforce' and prepared to attack through 10 Indian Division who were holding the area between the two rivers opposite the German switch line near Albereto. The Germans were believed to be comparatively weak in this sector and the plan was to make a sudden surprise attack to cut Route 16 west of Ravenna and to capture the town. Striking at Russi and S Pancrazio on 2 December, the Canadians opened a gap between the 114 Jäger and 356 Infantry Divisions near Govo, through which their armour advanced to cut Route 16 at Mezzano. By dawn on 5 December Ravenna had been taken. The 28 Garibaldi Brigade played a significant part in the capture of the town by attacking the Germans from the rear. This force, consisting of several hundred partisans, was commanded by an Italian officer known as 'Major Bulow' who was actively co-operating with Canadian Corps headquarters. They were supplied with arms by air drop and extra small-arms ammunition had been delivered to them by 'row-boat' patrols of Popski's Private Army. By 6 December the Canadian Armoured Division had reached the Lamone on a five-mile front south from Mezzano. On the night of 3/4 December 46 Division and 3 Carpathian Divisions launched a joint attack across the Lamone south of Route 9. A bridgehead extending to Pideura and Montecchio was secured against stiffening resistance by 7 December. Von Vietinghoff now committed one of his reserve divisions against 46 Division who, on 9 December, were being relieved by 10 Indian Division but this 'violent counter-attack (was) repulsed with great skill and determination'.[10] This German repulse might have been turned to good account but 46 Division, already much reduced in strength, could not follow up their advantage. Faenza was still firmly held by the Germans and there was only one very poor road for the maintenance of the two divisions across the Lamone. By 13 December, however, a second bridge had been built by the New Zealanders and a regiment of tanks had crossed. 'By the following day re-grouping had been completed in the bridgehead, with 10 Indian Division on the left and the New Zealanders straddling the river south of Faenza. North of Faenza, 56 Division's sector was comparatively quiet.'[11]

Meanwhile General Foulkes, Commanding the Canadian Corps, had been preparing a co-ordinated attack by both Canadian divisions to force a crossing over the lower reaches of the River Lamone but the meteorological report, forecasting storms in the mountains, was so bad and the rivers had become so swollen that the attack was postponed until the evening of 10 November. A surprise attack by the Canadian Armoured Division was launched without previous artillery support and was followed on the left by an attack by three Infantry battalions from 1 Canadian Infantry Division, using artificial moonlight and full artillery support. Both attacks made ground during the night

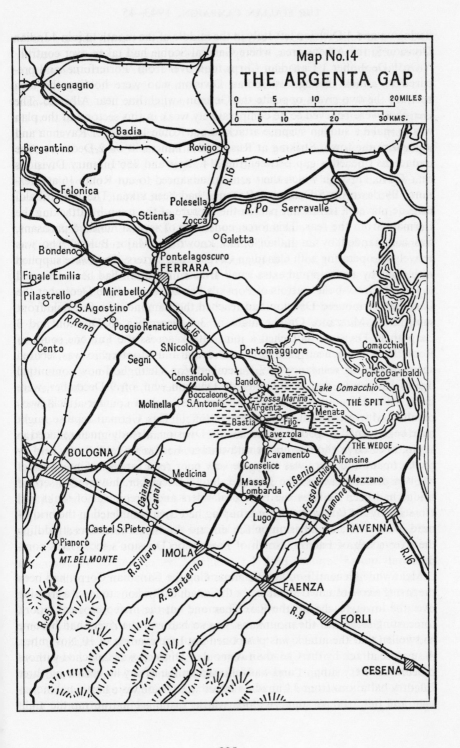

and on the following day received excellent support from the Desert Air Force which flew 312 sorties, its biggest effort for any single day in December. Von Vietinghoff was still reluctant to reduce his reserves near Bologna and formed a scratch counter-attack force by grouping local reserves, amounting to three weak battalions and about twenty tanks, from the three left-hand corps. This battle group was launched early on 11 December against the northern end of the Canadian Armoured Division's bridgehead. Three separate attacks were beaten off by the Westminster Regiment. By 12 December the Canadian engineers had tank bridges across the Lamone and the infantry had reached the Fosso Vecchio, with the Germans holding the sector north and south of Bagnacavallo on the line of the Canale Naviglio, whose twenty-foot-high banks were only some 5–700 yards away across the flat and treeless fields. At this point the remainder of 98 Division, which had already supplied a battalion for the earlier counter-attacks, was hurried across from von Senger's sector to hold Bagnacavallo and a specially heavily armed machine-gun battalion (named after Kesselring) was allotted to the 114 Jäger Division in the sector north of the town. When the Canadian Corps attacked on the night 12/13 December on either side of Bagnacavallo, to seize bridgeheads across the Naviglio, they met fierce resistance and heavy counter-attacks from 98 Division and several groups of tanks. North of the town the fighting was particularly fierce and one German counter-attack, supported by six regiments of artillery and two mortar regiments, was only driven off with the aid of the concentrated artillery fire from both Canadian divisions and a number of fighter-bombers. Further south, between Bagna-cavallo and Crotignola, in a particularly difficult area where the advance was overlooked both from Bagnacavallo and also from the high banks of the Senio, three days' fighting ended with the leading Canadian Brigade still east of the Fosso Vecchio, after being thrown back from a shallow bridgehead. The Corps Commander then decided to put in a co-ordinated attack north of the town where the armoured division had established a firm bridgehead. Here a series of skilful attacks resulted in the Canadians reaching the line of the Senio by 21 December, on which day the Germans were forced to with-draw from Bagnacavallo. South of the town the Germans held on for several days but by 4–5 January both 1 Canadian Division and 56 Division had closed up to the east bank of the river. Colonel Nicholson records that in the first three weeks of December the Canadian Corps had forced the passage of three strongly defended water lines and cleared 145 square miles of territory. During the advance to the Senio the corps and divisional artillery had fired 184,000 rounds and 1,670 Germans had been taken prisoner. 'But the cost had been great. In the twenty days since the offensive began on 2 December 1 Canadian Corps had suffered casualties of 548 officers and men killed, 1,796 wounded and 212 prisoners of war. These were heavy losses and averaged only six per day less than those sustained in the Gothic Line fighting.'[12] On the night of 14 December, 5 Corps and the Poles resumed their attack to outflank Faenza by a thrust from Pideura down to Route 9 west of the town. This move was bitterly contested and during the first day 90 Panzer Grenadiers lost 500 men killed and prisoners. On the inner flank the New Zealanders captured Celle on 15 December and reached the Senio the following day. On their left 10 Indian Division secured Pergola and by 17 December had two small bridgeheads over the river. Further into the mountains the German 715 Division lost heavily and were unable to prevent the Poles from drawing level. 26 Panzer Division, now reduced to 1,000 men, holding Faenza now found themselves outflanked and 43 Indian Lorry Brigade entered the town with little difficulty on 16 December. The Panzer troops, however, hung on to a switch line between the Senio and Lamone Rivers, which ran immediately behind the north-eastern outskirts of Faenza and successfully beat off the Indians' attack the following day, before being relieved by 29 Panzer Grenadier Division brought over from von Senger's sector. Difficulties of supply and heavy casualties to both Allied divisions prevented any full-scale attack, at least until new bridges could be built at Faenza. On the night 19/20 December 56 Division continued the attack northwards from Faenza and by 6 January had cleared the east bank of the Senio to link up with the Canadians near Cotignola. This was a period of bitter fighting with the Germans contesting every yard of ground. By now the winter weather had truly set in with blizzards and heavy snow in the mountains and snow also falling in the plain.

The Eighth Army offensive had not drawn off as many German reserves as had been hoped but there had been a shifting of strength away from the Bologna sector during the fighting for the Lamone crossing and the advance to the Senio. Since 20 November von Senger's XIV Panzer Corps had been ordered to send three divisions to help this flank, one to LXXV Corps and two to LXXVI Corps. Two of these divisions, however, had been replaced from local reserves and, to compensate for the loss of a third, his front had been somewhat shortened. A further division, 90 Panzer Grenadiers, which had been in Army Group reserve behind XIV Corps' front, had already been committed and von Vietinghoff took good care to hang on to the remainder of his central reserve. Furthermore Hitler was not prepared to weaken the Apennine positions and when in November von Vietinghoff sent two infantry divisions to meet a crisis in Hungary they were immediately replaced from Hitler's meagre reserves. One of the replacement divisions travelled non-stop from Norway to reach Italy in mid-December.

In a final attempt to reach Bologna before the winter conditions put a stop to operations in the mountains, Alexander decided that the attack by Fifth Army could not wait for the Eighth Army to reach the line of the Santerno. So, still hoping for the necessary spell of reasonable weather, Fifth Army were put at forty-eight hours' notice from 22 December to resume the offensive. The ammunition situation, however, had now become a dominating factor in the Allied timetable. The combined offensive would probably last a further three weeks and if it started after about 25 December the whole of the January allocation of ammunition would be used up by the middle of the month. Not only would the Allies be unable to deal with any major counter-attack but there would be insufficient time to build up adequate stocks for a spring offensive. In the end Mussolini introduced yet another factor which forced the issue. Seeking a 'spectacular' success for his newly formed divisions, he persuaded von Vietinghoff to co-operate in an attack against the left flank of Fifth Army. The Monte Rosa Division who were on the spot were joined by the newly arrived and highly spoken of Bersaglieri Division the 'Italia'. Von Vietinghoff had been asked to match this force with two German divisions but decided against any further diversion from the Bologna front and only allocated 148 Division, plus two independent mountain battalions. The Allies had never attempted to penetrate far into the mountains in the western sector, being satisfied to hold the southern slopes at a sufficient distance to cover the port of Leghorn, through which the whole of Fifth Army was being maintained. On the left of IV Corps, 92 Division was holding an extended but very quiet sector from Bagni di Lucca for about twenty-five miles to the sea. Running down through this area was the 'wild and romantic' valley of the River Serchio which dropped down through Lucca into the valley of the Arno. An attack in strength down this valley would be very dangerous to the Allies if it threatened the supply base and port of Leghorn. About 22 December reports of an impending attack in some strength from this direction began to arrive and it was feared that von Vietinghoff might commit a major part of his reserves in a desperate blow, as had just been attempted in the Ardennes offensive in north-west Europe. The interrogation of prisoners from 16 SS Panzer Grenadiers, who spoke of a move westwards to take part in an attack, tended to confirm this possibility. The threat was too real to be ignored and 8 Indian Division, less one brigade, was dispatched from 13 Corps to hold a reserve position in the Serchio sector. The Indian troops arrived on 25 December and dug in behind 92 Division. The following day the first attack came in astride the river and the American outposts were driven back, in some cases in disorder. East of the river the defence gave way and a reinforced German battalion quickly drove into a gap, with the result that the whole of the forward positions on both sides of the river were over-run by the afternoon of 26 December. Following up this success the Germans captured the second line of defences twenty-four hours later, by which time the thoroughly disorganized units of 92 Division were flowing back through 19 Indian Brigade. By now 8 Indian Division had assumed command of the sector and after nightfall on 27 December Indian patrols moved forward and were soon in contact with the Germans. The Germans brought forward reinforcements the following day but meanwhile 8 Indian Division had set up an attack with strong air support and within twenty-four hours had re-captured the town of Barga and two days later all the lost ground had been recovered and the line restored. It subsequently transpired that rather more than five battalions had been committed in the attack down the Serchio valley, the majority of the troops being German. Described by one captured German officer as a reconnaissance in force, the attack was probably launched for political and propaganda reasons. The result, however, was that three of Fifth Army's divisions were switched from the main battle area, as Truscott had ordered 85 Division with strong tank and artillery supporting units to the vicinity of Lucca as an immediate reserve and on 28 December moved 1 (US) Armoured Division into the same area. As has already been noted, heavy snow was now falling in the mountains and on 30 December Fifth Army's attack on Bologna was called off and Alexander issued orders that both armies should pass to the defensive.

In Eighth Army sector both the Canadians and 5 Corps launched limited attacks to drive the Germans back from their remaining positions east of the Senio. Near the southern end of Lake Comacchio the River Senio joins the Reno and skirting the lake itself crosses the narrow strip of land to the east to enter the Adriatic. This water line was considered vital to the protection of the Canadians' right flank. Taking advantage of a bright spell of weather and hard frost and using a strong force of tanks and full air support the Canadians cleared the area from north of Ravenna to the Reno at the southern tip of Lake Comacchio between 2–5 January, in spite of persistent counter-attacks by 16 SS Panzer Grenadiers. This division had in fact been brought over from Bologna in the hopes of launching a counter-attack to recapture Ravenna and the Canadian attack just succeeded in getting in first. 5 Corps made a similar limited attack on their front using armoured infantry carriers, known as 'Kangaroos', for the first time in the theatre and by 5 January the only major German foothold on Eighth Army's front east of the Senio was a strongly held redoubt at Alfonsine. By 7 January Eighth Army had settled down as best they could in the severe winter conditions to hold the line of the Senio. Kesselring, fully recovered from his accident, had now returned to take over command of the Army Group and seeing that the main threat to Bologna was now from the east carried out a regrouping of his forces. The Parachute Corps was re-formed to include both parachute divisions (at Göring's request) and put into the line between XIV and LXXVI Corps. Two divisions were sent to reinforce the Lake Comacchio and lower Senio sector and four divisions were allocated under von Senger to cover the approaches to Bologna. The reserves, however, in this latter area were now very much depleted and as we shall soon see both Kesselring and Alexander were about to lose several divisions to other fronts.

By the end of the year the Civil War in Greece was causing a major diversion of troops from the Eighth Army as over 51,000 Allied troops, including both 4 Indian and 4 Division had by then been sent to Greece to prevent the Communists from seizing power on the withdrawal of the Germans. By mid-January the whole of 46 Division had also been sent from Italy. As a result of Churchill's personal intervention, during a flying visit to Athens over Christmas, the political leaders, including those of ELAS, the People's National Army of Liberation, were brought together and a truce was arranged. By the middle of January the six weeks' war was ended but right through to March over 80,000 Allied troops were involved in supporting the new Government under the Regent, Archbishop Damaskinos, with General Plastiras as Prime Minister. The only division that returned to Italy was 46 Division and this was not until 11 April. At the time of Churchill's intervention Alanbrooke wrote, 'and what are we to get out of it all? We shall eventually have to withdraw out of Greece and she will then become as Communist as her close neighbours consider desirable. Meanwhile the campaign in Italy stagnates.' Later he commented 'Greece was saved from Communism. I do not think that I realized sufficiently the vital importance of preventing Greece from giving Communism a door into the Mediterranean.'[13]

By now Churchill was beginning to realize that there was little chance of operations mounted from Italy reaching Vienna and he began to talk of using some of Alexander's divisions on the main Western Front, after Kesselring had been driven back to the Adige. With Hitler's decision to stand on the line of the Apennines and after the diversion of Allied divisions to DRAGOON, the opportunity to reach Vienna had passed. Stalin's recognition of the Communist 'Lublin Committee' as the provisional government of Poland had unmistakably underlined his intentions for the occupied territories. With the urgent need to review the post-war structure of Europe a meeting of the three Allied war leaders had already been proposed by the Western Allies and finally took place at Yalta at the beginning of February. At Churchill's suggestion the Combined Chiefs of Staff met at Malta, prior to the arrival of the President by sea, for a short conference before the whole party flew on to meet Stalin. The German counter-offensive in the Ardennes had just been driven back and the inevitable post mortems had brought doubts as to whether 'in the absence of a more effective overall control of the ground forces the offensive in the north would receive either the concentration or the sense of urgency needed for its success'.[14] The coming meetings at Malta would be an opportunity of trying to persuade the American Chiefs of Staff of the necessity of reorganizing the higher direction of SHAEF and meanwhile, if more British troops could be found for Montgomery's 21 Army Group, the more chance there would be of an advance in strength across the Rhine in the north, a strategy that the British felt would be most likely to lead to the early defeat of Germany. As far as Alexander was concerned this would require the earliest possible withdrawal of troops from Greece and the transfer of British divisions from Italy and elsewhere in the Mediterranean to France.

Alanbrooke's opinion at this time was that the campaign in Italy had by now served its purpose in containing the German reserves. In Malta most of the Combined Chiefs of Staff's discussions were taken up with the strategy for the Western Front. As regards Italy, the Americans agreed to leave their own troops there but Alexander would have to send three divisions to France immediately and two more as soon as the political situation in Greece would allow. Alexander was now given a fresh directive to hold the present front and 'by means of such limited offensive actions as may be possible and by the skilful use of cover and deception plans to contain the Germans and take advantage of any weakening or withdrawal of their forces'.[15] At about this time Churchill was proposing that Alexander should be sent to France as Eisenhower's deputy and it was not until the end of February and after the Prime Minister's return from Yalta that Alexander was finally told that he would remain in Italy. Meanwhile in accordance with the new directive and to meet the wishes of the Canadian government, the Canadian Corps was withdrawn from Italy and dispatched to France. The withdrawal and move was carried out without the Germans in either theatre realizing what had taken place and was completed by about mid-April. During this time two fighter groups were also transferred to France. In the middle of February 5 Division began to arrive in Italy from the Middle East but was immediately sent straight on to France. By the end of March, however, the Combined Chiefs of Staff had decided that no more divisions were needed from the Mediterranean and 46 Division, which was on the point of leaving Greece for France, was diverted in time to take part in Alexander's spring offensive. Mention has already been made of two German divisions (44 and 71 Divisions) having left for Hungary in November and December and in each of the following months the OKW withdrew to Germany in turn 356 Division, 16 SS Panzer Grenadiers and 715 Division. On the other hand the two Parachute divisions were brought up to a combined strength of 30,000 men and the majority of the remaining divisions in Army Group C were given sufficient reinforcements to bring them up to strength by the end of the winter.

The pause in operations in the new year brought some relief to the Allied formations holding the line on which they had been forced to halt. As soon as the forward defences had been extended in depth, units were relieved in rotation for rest and training. Under the severe winter conditions the maintenance of the forward units, however, became a constant fight against the forces of nature. Mention has already been made of many bridges being swept away on the Eighth Army front by the sudden spates following the late autumn rains. Low level or floating bridges, built immediately behind the advance, had to be replaced by Bailey bridges in order to get the tanks and heavy equipment forward. The expenditure of Bailey bridges had been immense and the rate of supply to Eighth Army alone was two to three a day and in the whole campaign the Allied engineers built 2,494 Bailey bridges.

There was never enough of this invaluable equipment and in order to maintain the advance, or prepare for an offensive, the Bailey bridges had to be replaced with other types of construction as quickly as possible, to release the equipment for use further forward. The Americans, who were skilled in log cutting and had ample transport to carry the timber, generally constructed timber bridges for this purpose. The Royal Engineers built with brick, stone or concrete, often using Italian labour and reopening quarries and brickworks, as well as providing all the transport and supervising the jobs. In the mountains the work of bridging and of road construction and repair was never ending. The magnitude of the problem may be illustrated by taking the story of Eighth Indian Divisional Engineers. In November the Division was based on Marradi with routes stretching forward to Modigliana, Fognano and Casola Valsenio. The Engineers' task was to open and maintain these routes and build jeep and mule tracks and even aerial ropeways for the supply of the forward troops. The number of Indian engineers was about 30 officers and 850 sappers, assisted by six or so small anti-aircraft or other units at battery or troop strength, half an Italian pioneer company and up to a hundred and twenty Italian labourers.

Between the 5th of November and the 27th of December these troops carried out the following tasks: construction of twenty-three Bailey bridges with a total length of two thousand, nine hundred and eighty feet; construction of two bridges with folding boat equipment; construction of six timber bridges; dismantling of seven Bailey bridges; opening of thirty-four miles of road, and maintenance of sixty-four miles. Most of the bridges crossed mountain ravines, and Bailey piers up to seventy feet high were built.[16]

Although a few more snow ploughs were available than in the previous winter, these were almost exclusively used in the forward area and as the winter progressed the task of keeping the roads open depended on the never-ending labour of thousands of soldiers and civilians and the constant efforts of the Engineers in carrying out and supervising road repairs. While many of the troops in the forward areas were thus engaged in keeping the supply routes open, the Services to the rear were building up stocks in the supply depots, while in the ordnance workshops, lorries and heavy equipment were being repaired and in many cases completely rebuilt in preparation for the coming offensive. At long last the latest equipment began to reach Italy. The new 'Kangaroo' armoured personnel carriers, which were in fact converted Sherman tanks, have already been mentioned and were joined by the Duplex Drive amphibious tanks, the 'DDs' that swam ashore on to the Normandy beaches, and 'Fantails'. These latter had been developed in the Pacific and had been used by the Canadians in Belgium, where they were known as 'Buffaloes' and were tracked landing vehicles designed to operate in shallow water. Some 400 of them were promised for use in the Lake Comacchio and nearby flooded areas.

The armoured regiments were re-equipped with flame-thrower tanks, up-gunned Sherman and Churchill tanks, and with tank-dozers. Some of their tanks were fitted with widened 'Platypus' tracks to enable them to move over the soft fields of the Romagna. New armoured engineer equipment was also produced within the theatre for rapidly bridging ditches, canals and rivers. All these new equipments and devices needed specially trained crews to man them and new tactical techniques. In the rear areas, particularly round Lake Trasimene, intensive experimental work and training went on throughout the winter.[17]

The training carried out by an infantry division may be illustrated by taking examples from 78 Division. From the beginning of November until the middle of February this division had been fighting in the mountains with Fifth Army and was now assembled once more under Eighth Army in the plain around Forli. Cyril Ray writes:

Training began almost at once – exercises for testing communications, in river crossings, in street fighting and, above all in co-operation with armour. 2 Armoured Brigade . . . was affiliated to the Division for these exercises . . . it was the first time in Italy that 78 Division had lived, trained, and held the line with the armour with which it was later to carry out full-scale operations: this was the genesis of the splendid team work between tanks and infantry soon to be shown in the final battle. The new types of equipment were many and varied. The assault sappers produced the Arks and AVRE (Armoured Vehicles Royal Engineers), bridge-laying tanks; each battalion had four Wasp flamethrowers as well as Life-buoys (portable flame-throwers carried on a man's back), and there were Crocodiles, which were Churchill tanks towing an armoured flame-fuel container behind them.[18]

In less than a month the division moved up to relieve 56 Division on the banks of the Senio. While the reserve brigade and even the reserve units of the forward brigades continued to carry out training with the armour and Kangaroos, the forward troops faced the Germans across the 'narrowest of no-man's-lands. At this point the Senio was only a narrow stream some three to four feet deep between steep muddy banks about eighteen feet apart and six feet high. On both sides were additional flood banks ten feet high with a wide base and a flat top about nine feet wide.' The Germans held the west flood bank and controlled the river bed, using numerous specially built footbridges and rafts. Some positions on the east bank were only ten yards from those held by 78 Division.

While Fifteen Army Group was methodically building up stocks of ammunition and making every possible preparation for the resumption of the offensive, Army Group C was equally busy hoarding supplies of all kinds and particularly petrol and strengthening a number of defensive positions in depth. By the end of the winter Kesselring's strength had been cut down but he still had three mobile divisions, two particularly strong parachute divisions and eighteen mountain, Jäger and infantry divisions, plus four Italian divisions and SS units. Little of his present line was of his own

343

choosing and much of its 130 miles were the temporary positions and river lines that his troops were occupying when the fighting had died down. With the ground rapidly drying out there were many sectors which could hardly be held against a strong co-ordinated attack. In the Alps a considerable force of German 'fortification specialists' with Italian labour had been feverishly working on the southern defences of what Hitler had named as the National Redoubt. This 'Alpine Fortress' as it was also called was later described by General Halder, Chief of the German General Staff until 1942, as 'nothing more than a phantom in Hitler's brain',[19] as it never contained any supply bases nor means of producing weapons or ammunition for its garrison. The defences on the River Adige were being similarly developed under the direction of General Jordan as the forward line of defences on this part of the sector. It must have been obvious to Kesselring that, in spite of Hitler's orders to hold what was left of the Apennine line at all costs, he had an equal responsibility to ensure that as much of his army as possible reached the Venetian line on the River Adige intact, if only to protect the frontiers of Germany itself. Kesselring's earlier plan for a withdrawal back to this line now had to be revised, as Eighth Army stood dangerously close to the hinge of his present line on the Adriatic side and Fifth Army were poised very close to the valley of the Po in the centre of his sector. When he had previously tried to get Hitler to agree to his 'Autumn Mist' plan for a deliberate withdrawal he had been far better placed to extricate his divisions and now he would undoubtedly have to fight his way back, holding every possible water line. Consequently, his troops spent their winter not only strengthening the 'Ghengis Khan' line on the River Idice and the 'Irmgard' and 'Laura' lines on the Senio and Santerno but also in preparing the 'Paula' line on the Sillaro and of course defences on the Reno, which had become an integral part of all these positions. Not content with these preparations, Kesselring also ordered defences to be built on the River Po, more to assist a withdrawal than in the hope of holding such an extended front. Kesselring certainly was not worried about the morale of his troops. Allied propaganda had made little impact and his two armies still contained some of Germany's best divisions, which were now up to strength and thoroughly rested. On the other hand, he believed there was a definite threat of an Allied landing operation on his Adriatic flank and under conditions of complete Allied supremacy in the air he had considerably less chance of getting his troops back intact across the Po than six months previously when the weather had started to break. Kesselring later wrote:

The stage was set for the decisive battle. Whether our defence now took the form of a delaying action or of a retreat it was at least secured by prepared sectors and positions manned against surprise. This forbade the acceptance of a decisive battle south of the Po. Meanwhile the transfer of divisions to other fronts continued, and the indispensable flow of supplies was seldom fully maintained. Notwithstanding

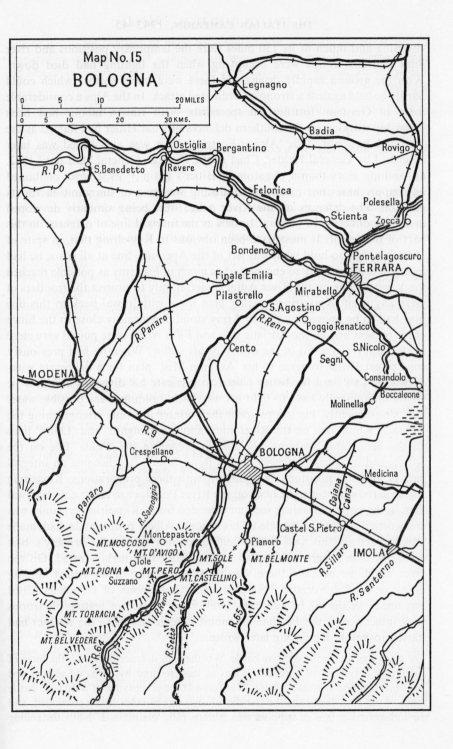

Map No. 15

BOLOGNA

0   5   10   20 MILES

0   5   10   20   30 KMS.

Legnagno

Ostiglia   Bergantino

R. Po   S. Benedetto   Revere

Badia

Rovigo

Felonica

Polesella

Stienta   Zocca

Bondeno

Pontelagoscuro

FERRARA

Finale Emilia

Mirabello

Pilastrello

S. Agostino

R. Panaro   R. Reno

Poggio Renatico

S. Nicolo

Cento

Segni

Consandolo

MODENA

Boccaleone

Molinella

R. 9

Crespellano

BOLOGNA

Medicina

Montepastore

R. Panaro   R. Samoggia

Castel S. Pietro

Gaiana Canal

MT. MOSCOSO

Pianoro

MT. D'AVIGO   MT. SOLÉ   MT. BELMONTE

R. Sillaro

IMOLA

MT. PIGNA   MT. PERO   Tole

R. Santerno

Suzzano   MT. CASTELLINO

R. Reno

R. 65

MT. TORRACIA

R. 64   R. Setta

MT. BELVEDERE

345

all this Hitler could not at first be prevailed upon to readjust his orders to the altered situation. But as the weeks went by without a veto on my plans I believed that at the crucial moment, as before, I could handle the situation as should be necessary.[20]

Alexander's plans for the Spring offensive were now ready and in his report he writes:

A question which very much exercised us at the time, when considering enemy dispositions, and intentions, was how much credence should be given to the reported plan of a national redoubt . . . undoubtedly there was such a plan – because there could be no other plan – and it seemed likely that the forces of Army Group C were intended to play an important part in it. If they could withdraw intact into the southern face of the redoubt it would be extremely difficult to dislodge them. It was more than ever necessary, therefore, to destroy them south of the Po.[21]

In the middle of March Kesselring was appointed Commander-in-Chief West and on 23 March von Vietinghoff (urgently recalled from Latvia) took command of Army Group C. Hitler's orders were still to hold every yard of ground and von Vietinghoff, with perhaps less imagination than Kesselring, was certainly unlikely to question the Fuehrer's orders.

In mid-January Clark discussed the Spring offensive with each of his Army Commanders. One of these discussions is recorded by Truscott:

Clark told me he had discussed the spring offensive strategy with McCreery. Since the British had three times as many divisions in Italy as did the Americans at the time, McCreery wanted Clark to concentrate his whole effort on the Eighth Army front in the Adriatic plain. Clark, however, did not agree, and contended the Fifth Army should make a strong effort west of Highway 65 while the Eighth made its main effort along Highway 9. I suggested to Clark we should consider throwing the weight of the Fifth Army west of Highway 64 because the German defense was much less fortified there than on the front of the II Corps along Highway 65 south of Bologna. Clark replied that he would never agree to a main attack west of Highway 64.[22]

Two weeks afterwards the news came of the withdrawal of divisions from Eighth Army and this strengthened Clark's plan which was 'to have the Fifth make the main effort of the Spring offensive west of Highway 65, while the Eighth Army would relieve the Fifth Army on Mount Grande and make as strong an effort in the Po valley as would be possible'.[23] Truscott's reactions are of interest. To avoid a head-on attack against the very strongly fortified defences south of Bologna, he wished to attack west of Route 64 to isolate Bologna, while a holding attack only was made down Route 65. To get a suitable jumping off position for the main attack he proposed using the newly arrived 10 (US) Mountain Division in limited operations to secure Mounts Belvedere and Torraccia and if possible the peaks immediately beyond. As regards the Eighth Army, he agreed with Clark that their best line of attack would be north from Mount Grande on the immediate right flank of Fifth Army. Clark, however, was still very much against the main attack by Fifth Army being made west of Route 64. In fact the ground on both sides of Route 64 presented grave problems to XIV Panzer Corps who were responsible for its defence. Any penetration from the east would quickly break into the broad valley at the junction of the Rivers Setta and Reno and on the west side of the route there were no mountains suitable for defence where 'the hills being flat and without cover favoured armoured operations'.[24] The German rearward defences against a penetration along Route 9 were based on the River Idice which joined the Reno at Bastia just north of Lavezzola. Behind Bologna, however, the Reno formed a great loop. For almost half its length it flowed northwards past the western outskirts of the town and then, within only ten miles of the Po, turned south-east to flow past Argenta and round the southern shore of Lake Comacchio to the Adriatic. The rivers from the Senio westward which blocked the advance of Eighth Army all flowed into the Reno in this latter part of its course. While a concentrated attack at Bologna could split the German forces, it would not necessarily prevent an orderly withdrawal of those divisions that were east of the town back towards the lines of the Po and the Adige. Alexander was determined not only to break through but to destroy the Germans before they reached the Po and the plan emerged for Eighth Army to strike across the Reno close to Lake Comacchio thus avoiding the river lines further west. The axis for exploitation would be Ferrara–Rovigo–Padua on Route 16. Meanwhile Fifth Army would attack west of Route 64, so as to avoid the 'fortress' of Bologna and exploit north to Modena–Ostiglia and Verona. These thrusts would not only cut the principal escape routes to the north-east but should 'encircle important enemy forces in the loop of the Reno'.[25]

Between mid-February and early March Truscott put in two limited attacks to get elbow-room west of Route 64. In succession, 10 Mountain Division took Mount Belvedere and Mount Torraccia, while the Brazilians captured Mount Castello and a second attack carried IV Corps line forward until it was almost level with II Corps' salient on their right. Unwilling to show his hand too much, Truscott halted the attacks about twenty miles south of the Po valley. Meanwhile Eighth Army was making careful preparations for their preliminary moves against the 'hinge' of the whole German line. Along the south-western shores of Lake Comacchio the Germans had cut the dykes and floods extended to within two miles of Argenta and parallel to Route 16. West of Route 16 the banks of the Reno had similarly been breached to flood the whole area between the Bastia bridge and Argenta and for some nine miles to the south-west. The first practicable crossing point over the Reno therefore lay twenty miles inland at the Bastia bridge but ahead, up Route 16, was only the narrow 'Argenta Gap' between the two flooded areas. This key position would obviously be well protected from frontal attack.

The shallow muddy waters of Lake Comacchio and the flooded fields were, however, less of a barrier to the Allies than the Germans had hoped. Fantails had been successfully used by the Canadians in the flooded Scheldt area in Holland and 400 of these armoured amphibious troop carriers, designed to operate in mud or shallow water, had been promised. It was therefore decided to plan an outflanking attack against Argenta across the Lake in support of the main attack from the south.

The timing for the offensive had to be closely linked with Allied plans in North-West Europe. Here the continuation of the offensive throughout the winter was beginning to produce dividends and in the six weeks following the Battle of the Ardennes Eisenhower's seven armies had cleared the whole of the west bank of the Rhine and a bridgehead at Remagen had been seized by US First Army. By the end of March Patton's Third Army had crossed the Rhine near Mainz and both armies were striking north to join up with Montgomery's British Second and US Ninth Armies who were across the Rhine astride Wesel. With these successes still in the making it had been obvious that if the offensive in Italy was to hold down von Vietinghoff's forces it must come as soon as the ground and weather conditions would permit. The troops were rested, sufficient ammunition had been delivered and the only shortage might be in the number of Fantails delivered, but this would have to be accepted. The date finally chosen for the opening of the offensive was 9 April. Again the method would be a two-handed punch, first against the German's eastern flank to draw off his reserves, followed by a sudden blow west of Bologna. The cover plan was a simulated concentration, including the whole of II Corps behind Eighth Army's right flank for an amphibious landing north of the Po delta. These deceptive measures would at the same time disguise the true object of Eighth Army's preparations to cross Lake Comacchio.

Although a major landing immediately north of the Po was completely impractical from a naval point of view, owing to poor gradients and numerous sandbars, and virtually all the Allied landing craft had already been withdrawn, von Vietinghoff appears to have accepted the threat and made his dispositions accordingly. On his eastern flank the German Tenth Army, under General Herr, held from the Adriatic to Monte Grande with eight divisions which included 26 Panzer Division, in addition 29 Panzer Grenadiers and 155 Infantry Divisions were posted in Army Reserve in the area Venice–Treviso. Two further infantry divisions were stationed in north-east Italy round the head of the Adriatic as far as Fiume. The western part of the front from south of Bologna to the Tyrrhenian Sea was held by Fourteenth Army, under General Lemelsen, with eight German and one Italian division. The approaches to Bologna were given to XIV Panzer Corps with four German divisions, assisted by LI Corps with three of its four German divisions concentrated in the narrow sector from west of Montese to Vergato.

The rest of the front was held by the remaining German division and one Italian division. With one Italian division and a German battle group watching the Gulf of Genoa and two German and two Italian divisions tied down on the Franco-Italian frontier, von Vietinghoff had only a single mobile division (90 Panzer Grenadiers) in Army Group Reserve. This he placed near Modena. Discounting two further Italian divisions and some SS troops, which were fully occupied with the growing activities of the partisans, whose potential strength had reached 50,000 by the end of March, von Vietinghoff's overall strength was 23 German divisions and 4 Italian divisions. Of the German divisions, ten were committed on his eastern sector and a further seven were concentrated south and west of Bologna. Von Vietinghoff found himself in an unenviable position. Without aerial reconnaissance his chances of discovering the Allied intentions were slender and few Luftwaffe planes could hope to penetrate the Allied fighter screen. He certainly could not afford to let Fifth Army reach Bologna with its network of roads reaching out across the plains and now the threat of a landing stretched his line to the limit of his meagre reserves. As far as the Tenth Army sector was concerned, it seemed evident from the position of 26 Panzer and both Parachute divisions astride and south of Route 9 that General Herr was concerned more with the Senio and Santerno lines than with his left flank towards Comacchio.

18

Spring Sunrise

19

Spring Sunrise

Balance of forces: The 'Spit' and the 'Wedge': Diversion at Massa: Senio aflame: Fantails on Comacchio: Eighth Army converges on Bastia: Truscott attacks: Argenta – the battle for the gap: German front collapses: The pursuit to the Po: The Surrender: Comments on the Spring Campaign.

1945	*Fifth Army*	*Eighth Army*
1–6 Apl		Commandos and 56 Division's operations Lake Comacchio, expansion of bridgehead over Reno.
5–11 Apl	92 Division attacks towards Spezia.	
9 Apl		Main offensive opens with 5 Corps and Polish attack with maximum air and artillery support. Crossing of Senio.
10–12 Apl		Operations across Lake Comacchio and advance on Bastia.
12 Apl	Fifth Army waiting for good flying conditions.	New Zealanders reach Massa Lombarda. 13 Corps HQ and 10 Indian Division move into the plain. 78 Division directed on Bastia.
13 Apl	Russians enter Vienna.	
13–21 Apl		Battle of Argenta Gap. 13 Corps and Poles cross Sillaro and fight on towards Bologna.
14 Apl	Von Vietinghoff seeks permission to withdraw to Po. Told on 17 April to fight on present line. IV Corps opens attack. 10 Mountain Division makes good progress.	

1945	*Fifth Army*	*Eighth Army*
14–19 Apl	II Corps attacks towards Bologna with maximum air and artillery support.	Battle of Argenta Gap continues.
17 Apl		Argenta captured.
17–19 Apl		13 Corps and Poles capture Castel S Pietro and cross Gaiana canal.
18–20 Apl	US Armoured Division heavily engaged south-west of Bologna.	German counter-attacks at Argenta beaten off.
18 Apl		6 Armoured Division advances into gap ready to break out.
19 Apl	Truscott prepares for advance by-passing Bologna	
20 Apl	Elements of 10 Mountain Division cross Route 9.	Fierce fighting for Consandolo.

Von Vietinghoff issues orders for general withdrawal to Po.

21 Apl	Bologna entered – Americans advance on a broad front. Elements of 10 Mountain Division cross Panaro 21 April and Po 23 April.	6 Armoured Division and 5 Corps break out from Argenta Gap.
23 Apl	Armoured forces from both Armies join up at Finale.	
24 Apl		6 Armoured Division and New Zealanders cross the Po.
27–28 Apl	88 Division reach Vicenza.	Crossing of the Adige.

28 Apl Mussolini executed by Partisans.

28–29 Apl German plenipotentiaries sign instrument of surrender at Caserta.

29 Apl 6 South African Division joins up with Eighth Army at Padua.

30 Apl	91 Division reaches Treviso.	New Zealanders cross Piave and in contact with Tito's forces at Monfalcone. 6 Armoured Division thrust towards Udine.

1 May Hitler commits suicide.

2 May Surrender of all remaining German and Italian forces of Army Group C.

Russians occupy Berlin.

8 May Unconditional surrender of Germany.

In great secrecy both Allied armies completed their concentrations. Virtually the whole strength of Eighth Army was assembled between Lake Comacchio and Route 9 with 5 Corps on the right and the Polish Corps on the left. 10 and 13 Corps held the remainder of the mountain positions, their combined strength being a single division, 10 Indian, the recently arrived Jewish Brigade and two Italian combat groups. General Kirkman, commanding 13 Corps, was warned that he might be required to move his headquarters and 10 Indian Division in between 5 Corps and the Poles, taking the New Zealanders under command. In the Comacchio area 56 Division, plus 9 Armoured Brigade, 2 Command Brigade and the Garibaldi Birgade were given the preliminary task prior to D-day of capturing in turn the 'spit' of ground east of the lake, the islands in its centre and the 'wedge' of land on its southern shores, in preparation for the amphibious flank attack. The main offensive would open with the 5 Corps attack on 9 April, when 8 Indian and 2 New Zealand Division would cross the Senio astride Lugo and the Polish Corps would cross north of Route 9. The objectives would be bridgeheads over the Santerno, after which the Poles would exploit towards Medecina and Castel S Pietro, while 8 Indian Division and the Italian Cremona Group started clearing up enemy pockets south of the Reno. At this point 56 Division on the extreme right flank would cross Lake Comacchio and in the centre 78 Division would debouch from the Santerno bridgeheads and strike north-wards to Bastia, with their left protected by the New Zealanders who would be in a position to move either north or west. Eighth Army reserve would be 6 Armoured Division and 2 Parachute Brigade. Fifth Army would first make a diversionary attack on the extreme left in the direction of Spezia on D-day−4, using the reconstituted 92 Division. The actual date for the main attack by Fifth Army would be chosen by General Clark but would probably be on D+3. The plan was for IV Corps (10 Mountain, 1 Armoured Division and the Brazilians) to attack towards Bazzano. Thirty-six hours later II Corps would strike northwards between Route 64 and the River Idice, with 34, 88, 91 Divisions, 6 South African Armoured Division and the Legnano Group. The Army reserve (85 Division) was held back in IV Corps' area and Truscott's intention was to cross Route 9 west of Bologna and then advance on Bondeno and Ostiglia, thus completing the encirclement of the Germans south of the Po, while subsequent exploitation towards Verona would cut off all German troops to the west. It will be seen from the tables at Appendix G giving the broad organization of the opposing armies that the German and Allied strength on the ground was very evenly balanced. Fifteen Army Group, in fact, was at its lowest strength since the invasion of the Italian mainland and it was only the threat to his coastline and the need to hold the frontiers and protect his rear areas as far as possible from the partisans that prevented von Vietinghoff concentrating a superior force against the Allies on his main front. Alexander's hand, however, contained several trump cards. He now had received a reasonable quantity of the latest assault weapons and equipment. His cover plan and secret concentration of Eighth Army appeared to have deceived the Germans and forced a diversion of their reserves, as well as setting up Eighth Army attack so that the maximum use could be made of their superiority in artillery to support a set-piece attack on a narrow front. In the hot sun the ground had now dried out, at last producing favourable conditions for his superior armoured forces. Above the battlefield in clearing skies the Allies' planes roamed at will. Alexander could now play his ace card. The whole strength of the Allied air forces, amounting to 258 squadrons totalling 4,000 aircraft, would first be used on the Eighth Army front and then switched to support Fifth Army's attack. Thereafter the two Tactical Air Forces would revert to the close support of their own armies, while the medium and heavy bombers would return to their long-range strategic missions.

Between 1–6 April Commando and Special Boat Service units had captured the 'spit' alongside Lake Comacchio and also the islands in the centre. The opening attack was launched in spite of inumerable difficulties. Reconnaissance of the lake had been extremely difficult and several weeks of drought had lowered the level of water and the southern end of the lake was found to be too shallow for the storm boats to be launched from the shore. In the end, each of these boats, weighing three-quarters of a ton, had to be carried out by eighteen men for some 500 yards before it could be floated, although its draught empty was only nine inches. Another seven men were needed to carry the outboard engines and equipment and the boats had then to be pushed a further 1,000 yards before they could be fully loaded and paddled several hundred yards further before the engines could be properly lowered. The initial assembly of forty-five storm boats and thirty-five assault boats, to reach a starting point over half a mile distant through six inches of mud and slime, had to be covered by tank and aircraft noise and loudspeakers bellowing propaganda and Wagnerian music across the Reno on the flank. Fantails had already been tried out on the lake but had failed to climb back over the river bank, where they had to lie up under camouflage in full view of the Germans. The plan was for the Fantails to tow the other boats but when on the night of 1/2 April the Commandos moved forward to their assembly point the Fantails refused to move and their crews had to be transferred to the storm and assault boats. 'For hours men heaved and dragged and pushed unwieldy craft across more than a mile of sticky glutinous mud. By the time they reached deeper water and could be floated, the individual units of 2 and 9 Commando were inextricably mixed.' The Brigade Major described the scene as, 'a nightmare mixture of Venice by moonlight and the end of the Henley Regatta. The night hours were slipping by, and presently the commanding officers asked that the assault might be postponed.'¹ Brigadier Cobb, however, relying on the support of 350 guns, ordered the operation to continue. Meanwhile the two Royal Marine Commandos made a pincer attack across the Reno near its outlet to the sea to clear the south-eastern corner of the 'spit'. The Germans mistook the right hand of these attacks for the main assault and in spite of the earlier difficulties and a good deal of dispersion the two Commandos crossing the lake reached the far dyke unobserved, being partially covered by mist and the smoke from the artillery bombardment. Two days' fighting brought 950 prisoners and the virtual destruction of three German battalions and their supporting units and a firm occupation of the whole of the 'spit'. There had been considerable concern when the Fantails stuck in the mud of the shallow lake but when 56 Division successfully attacked the 'wedge' of land across the Reno the Fantails proved their value and crossed the flooded fields and inundations without difficulty. Fifth Army's diversionary attack followed straight on and was remarkably successful. The 92 Infantry Division had been reconstituted by two of its three coloured regiments being replaced by 442 Japanese-American Regiment and 473 Regiment, formerly Task Force 45. On 5 April the Division attacked towards Massa and good progress was made by 442 Regiment through the mountains. In the narrow coastal strip, however, 370 Regiment were checked by German counter-attacks and eventually had to be withdrawn. 473 Regiment was now brought forward and Massa fell on 9 April and Carrara two days later. The battle had now drawn in all the German and Italian troops in the coastal area and when Fifth Army's main attack developed on 14 April at least a battalion from 90 Panzer Grenadiers had been sent to reinforce the hard-pressed 148 Division.

The Allied air forces had also been carrying out preliminary operations in preparation for the Spring offensive. Throughout March the two Tactical Air Forces had concentrated on communications north of the Po and on attacks against the Po bridges themselves. The Combined Bombing Offensive programme was nearly at an end and more and more squadrons of Fifteenth Strategic Air Force were now pounding away at the railway routes leading out of Italy, so that by D-day every major railway line north of the Po was cut in many places. General Spaatz in fact called off the Combined Bomber Offensive in the middle of April and the whole weight of the heavy bomber force was then thrown in to support the land battle. Towards the end of March much of the effort of the Tactical Air Forces was devoted to attacks on the German supply dumps that had been built up throughout the winter and these attacks were intensified right up to the last moment.

Just after mid-day (on 9 April) formations of heavy bombers droned northwards over the Adriatic, to all intents and purposes bound for some distant communications target. But upon reaching Cesenatico, on the east Italian coast, the flights turned west over the mainland and unloaded their bombs on the enemy's Senio river position. The final battle for Italy was on. . . . In two days 1,673 heavy bombers, aided by a carefully worked out system of navigational aids which included a bomb line of smoke shells in the sky from 3·7 inch anti-aircraft guns, completely drenched specific target areas opposite British 5 Corps and Polish 2 Corps, concentrating first on guns and troops opposing the establishment of a bridgehead over the Senio and turning on the second day to crossing sites on the Santerno River.[2]

At the same time 624 medium bombers attacked defences and troop concentrations back towards the Santerno, while XXII Air Support Command attacked headquarters and command posts and the Desert Air Force concentrated on gun positions and strongpoints in the immediate battle area. Attacks on dispatch riders and by as many as fifteen planes on a single tank were gloomily reported back to von Vietinghoff as an indication of the overwhelming degree of air superiority. In an hour and a half on the afternoon of 9 April the heavy bombers had in fact dropped 125,000 fragmentation bombs on the German gun positions and reserve areas in front of each assaulting Corps. At 1500 hours the forward troops were withdrawn 600 yards back from the river and at 1520 hours 5 Corps' artillery and mortars opened fire for forty-two minutes, this was immediately followed by a ten-minute attack by fighter-bombers strafing the German defences on the Senio and particularly the positions dug in to the western flood banks of the river. This continued for four hours. At 1900 hours:

The Crocodiles, Wasps and the leading infantry with its boats and kapok bridges were formed up within 200 yards of the river ready for the assault. Just as the last rounds of the guns burst on the enemy forward positions and the flame-throwers and infantry advanced, fighter-bombers appeared and in the strange silence following the hours of bombardment made a dummy attack at low level, designed to keep the enemy's heads down until the attack crossed the river. A few minutes later the first flame-throwers sent out a spurt of flame and then the whole front seemed to burst into lanes of fire.[3]

The Germans in the forward positions had been under almost continuous air or artillery attack for over six hours. In the failing light and in the clouds of dust and smoke it was now an infantry battle for the crossings. In places the Germans succeeded in holding on for some time and one of the Indian Brigades on the right, as well as the Poles, had a bitter struggle to capture the western flood bank in their sectors. Overnight several bridges were completed and armour and anti-tank guns crossed. As daylight returned the sky again filled with planes and both the New Zealanders and the Poles were making good progress. Lugo was taken and the Cremona Group crossed and started a sweep through Fusignano towards Alfonsine. At about noon the heavy bombers flew in to lay their second 'carpet', this time along the Santerno. Unfortunately both the Indians and the New Zealanders suffered a number of casualties from bombs falling short. By the evening, however, the New Zealanders were within a thousand yards of the Santerno and their attack at dawn on 11 April, followed by fierce fighting throughout 12 April, brought them to the outskirts of Massa Lombarda before dusk. Here they were joined by 8 Division whose leading troops had waded the river waist deep under murderous enfilade fire. On the right flank the North Irish Horse, using Fascine bridge-layers, had made a spirited advance in their tanks of over 6,000 yards without infantry support. A feature of this opening phase of the battle was the New Zealanders' success in completing no less than three low and two high level tank bridges across the Senio by between 0130 and 0630 hours on 10 April. At this early stage the Indian Division only had one tank bridge and the Poles had none at all across the river. This remarkable achievement of the New Zealand engineers was due to the experimental work previously carried out by the CRE of the division, Colonel Hanson. The method involved dumping the equipment on the near side of the flood bank and carrying it forward as soon as conditions permitted. Girders were then assembled and launched by supporting them on a folding boat raft, which was pushed across the gap as the construction continued. Once the girders were in position the bridge could be rapidly completed. 'Alternatively [the bridge] was completely built *in situ* with a folding boat or some other form of raft or trestle to act as a supporting platform during the building work.'[4] The complete construction of bridges from forty to fifty feet long was achieved in from thirty-five minutes to an hour. 'The blowing or dozing of the near flood banks progressed while the bridge was being built, and the first vehicle to cross was an armoured dozer to prepare an exit on the far bank.'[5] This method proved not only remarkably fast but very economical in equipment. In the battle of the River Senio 98 and 362 Divisions lost over 2,000 prisoners in three days' fighting and the five battalions on the front opposing 13 Corps attack had been virtually destroyed. The New Zealand drive across the Santerno now threatened the northern flank of 26 Panzer Division which was forced to withdraw and 4 Parachute Division in the foothills pulled back in conformity. There was still, however, no move by 90 Panzer Grenadiers who again were concentrated behind Bologna.

While the Battle of the Senio had been raging the flank attack on Bastia and Argenta was launched. Two brigades of 56 Division and a Royal Marine Commando were involved. On the south-western face of Lake Comacchio the dyke, having been breached by the Germans, now stood between the lake and a wide flooded area. This bank was about thirty yards wide and heavily mined. Under cover of darkness on the night 10/11 April the Commandos advanced straight along the dyke. A thirty-foot gap was crossed by joining assault boats but the far side of the gap had been extensively mined. Working as quickly as possible the engineers cleared a hundred and fifty mines but time was now getting so short that it was decided only to cut the trip wires and to press forward through the remainder of the minefield. The objective was the bridge at Menata and the pumping station alongside. Dawn came with the Marines just short of their objective and in a very exposed position. An attempt to rush the bridge brought heavy casualties and it seemed that nothing would now prevent the demolition of the bridge. At the critical stage of the attack the fire from a Bren gun cut the wires connecting the charges and a pre-arranged strike by dive bombers brought the momentary opportunity for launching an attack towards the pumping station by a party of Marines, who had swung themselves across a canal on a line made from toggle ropes. The sudden arrival, across the flooded fields from a totally unexpected direction, of several Fantails from the main force threw the defence into a panic and clinched the matter and the bridge was captured intact. These Fantails, which had arrived at such an opportune moment, were the advance guard of one of the battalions of 169 Brigade which had embarked from the 'wedge' and sailed across the floods, screened by smoke from the Germans on the Reno. The defenders of Menata itself, already shaken by a heavy air attack, were completely taken by surprise and were soon surrounded. While this attack was developing, 167 Brigade attacked from the 'wedge' along the north bank of the Reno towards Bastia with the object of joining up with the flank attack. Although this attack was at first checked by heavy fire, the two brigades joined up by dawn 12 April and throughout that day the advance continued against light opposition, both across the Menata bridge and towards Filo, halfway between Menata and Bastia, while 167 Brigade thrust along the banks of the Reno almost to 'the confluence of the Santerno before being halted by minefields and self-propelled guns'.[6] Beyond Menata, however, the advance was now getting beyond the range of the supporting artillery and there was a pause while a battery of twenty-five pounders was brought up in Fantails.

The critical point of the battle had now been reached, and the decision was made to bring 13 Corps Headquarters across, together with 10 Indian Division, with the object of developing an attack westwards by the New Zealanders and the Poles. General McCreery had now decided that the breakthrough would be on 5 Corps front northwards through the Argenta gap and in the early afternoon of 12 April 78 Division was ordered forward to the Indian Division's bridgehead across the Santerno. Meanwhile the flanking attacks on Argenta were continued. On 13 April part of 24 Guards Brigade embarked to cross the floods and attack towards Bando and Argenta from the north-east. An unexpected underwater obstacle, however, forced the

Fantails to turn off short of their landing point and they came under heavy fire from a regiment of 29 Panzer Grenadiers and suffered heavy casualties. Von Vietinghoff had at last realized that there could be no major landing by sea north of the Po delta and the 29 Panzer Grenadiers had been rushed forward to reinforce the Bastia–Argenta area, where 42 Jäger Division was now reduced to three battle groups of about 200 strong. Initially 78 Division made a rapid advance but the leading brigade was checked at Conselice, where the Germans made a determined stand for twenty-four hours before withdrawing behind the Sillaro. A special striking force had, however, been built round the Irish Brigade who were supported by the majority of 2 Armoured Brigade, two regiments of field guns, together with Crocodile tanks, medium machine-guns, heavy mortars and assault engineers with bridging equipment. Part of this strong force was entirely mounted on tracked vehicles, with an infantry battalion in 'Kangaroos' and placed under the command of Brigadier Combe, Commander 2 Armoured Brigade, which became known as 'the Kangaroo Army'. The Irish Brigade successfully fought their way up the west bank of the Santerno and Brigadier Combe's vanguard of 'Kangaroos' and tanks reached Cavamento in the late afternoon of 13 April, just in time to see the charges blown on the bridge carrying the main road to Bastia. The demolition, however, was only partial and two troops of tanks were able to cross. The following day 78 Division reached Highway 16 south-east of Bastia. By this time 56 Division had taken Filo; the Germans, however, still held the village of Bastia in strength, though their perimeter in front of the road and rail bridges, which had now been virtually destroyed by shelling and air attacks, could not be maintained. By now 26 Panzer Division had been moved to Ferrara to counter the obvious intention of a break-through with armour at Argenta, which threatened to cut off the entire Army Group, and as we shall now see von Vietinghoff was about to fritter away his only remaining mobile reserve – 90 Panzer Grenadiers.

Fifth Army's attack had been planned for 12 April but the date was to depend on flying conditions and poor weather caused two twenty-four-hour postponements. Early on 14 April, however, the weather was clearing and the decision was taken to launch the attack. By 0845 hours fighter-bombers were attacking the Mount Pigna area and following a thirty-five minute artillery preparation 10 Mountain Division launched their attack. The Germans re-acted sharply but the mountain troops worked steadily forward and by 15 April had captured Mount Pigna, while on their right 1 Armoured Division took Mount Pero and Suzzano. The Strategic Bombers meanwhile had been launched against targets south of Bologna and along Route 9 and flew 2,052 sorties between 15 and 18 April, while the medium bombers continued to attack the rear areas north of Bologna. These heavy air attacks were mainly concentrated on II Corps' front but XXII Tactical Air Command continued to support both Corps flying 1,500 sorties between 16–19 April. This effort by the Mediterranean Allied Air Forces totalled up to the greatest sustained air attack of the whole of the campaign. II Corps' attack opened overnight 14–15 April and seventy-five thousand gun and tank shells were pumped into the German positions in thirty minutes, but the South Africans and 88 Division, attacking towards Mount Sole and Mount Rumici, were met by a storm of machine-gun fire. The German positions were in fact exceptionally strong and had been well prepared to withstand heavy shelling and air attacks. It was in the first hour and a half of this attack that the South African motorized brigade scored a spectacular success. Second Lieutenant Mollett, a platoon commander of the Royal Durban Light Infantry, with five men attacked straight through a large minefield only 500 yards short of the crest of Mount Sole and rushed the positions on the crest, where the defenders were still sheltering from the artillery fire. By dawn three counter-attacks had been beaten off and Mount Sole was secure. The defences south of Bologna were so strong that II Corps' attacks made very slow progress and on 17 April, with gains of only one or two miles at the most, there was no sign of any serious break in the German line. The situation on IV Corps' front, however, was quite different. 10 Mountain Division had thrust deep between LI Mountain Corps and XIV Panzer Corps. Von Vietinghoff had previously sent a regiment from 90 Panzer Grenadiers to open the roads south from Parma and Reggio, where strong bands of partisans had assembled, and now committed the remainder of the division in an attempt to stop the gap between the two Corps. The Panzer Grenadiers were launched piecemeal in support of 334 Infantry Division, on the left flank of LI Mountain Corps, but the advance of 10 Mountain Division had already started to swing north-eastwards and was unhinging 94 Division, who were soon in an untenable position. Both these German divisions had committed their reserves early on 15 April and had each lost over 1,000 prisoners. With 10 Mountain Division holding Montepastore and the Brazilians on Mount Moscoso, the whole German position between the Reno and the Samoggia was now beginning to crumble. General Truscott at this point brought forward his reserve division to maintain the impetus of the attack on the right of IV Corps due north from Mount d'Avigo, while 1 Armoured Division was switched westwards across the front to attack from Tole down into the valley of the Samoggia. On 18 April substantial progress was made by the armoured columns but a strong concentration of anti-tank guns north of Savigno checked their advance that night and for two days 1 Armoured Division fought it out with the tanks of 90 Panzer Grenadiers. By the early hours of 21 April, however, the American tanks were in Crespellano and both 85 Division and 10 Mountain Division were driving the shattered formations of XIV Panzer Corps out of the foothills and across Route 9. A company of 86 Mountain Infantry had in fact crossed Route 9 at noon on 20 April.

On II Corps' front there had been deadlock on 16 and 17 April but the following day there were signs that the dogfight was ending. Deserters surrendering to the South Africans spoke of a withdrawal and by the evening South African patrols were close to Praduro, while 91 Division entered the ruins of Pianoro, which was found to be heavily booby-trapped. 34 Division at last captured the Sevizzano ridge beyond Belmonte and the Legnano group was advancing west of the Idice. This sudden change in the fortunes of II Corps had not only been brought about by the advances of IV Corps west of Bologna, as without waiting for 10 Indian Division the New Zealanders had forced a crossing over the Sillaro on the night 13/14 Apri., while the Poles took Imola and drew level. In this sector 98 Division and 26 Panzer Division had suffered severe casualties and were now out of the line. On the night 15/16 April 13 Corps and the Poles attacked, inflicting heavy casualties on 278 Division, and in spite of all the efforts of the two parachute divisions both Medicina and Castel S Pietro fell on 17 April and both the Allied Corps had closed right up to the Gaiana Canal. 10 Indian Division had now come in on the right of 13 Corps directed on Molinella, but in the mud and minefields of the flooded plain south-west of Argenta the Indians could only make very slow progress. The New Zealanders and the Poles, however, stormed the line of the Gaiana on the night of 18/19 April and swept forward to find the bridges over the Idice destroyed but the river line undefended. The German withdrawal had already started and the remnants of 65 and 305 Divisions were making for Cento, to attempt a stand on the Reno and 278 Division was moving back to the northern arm of the Idice, as a pivot for the withdrawal of the two parachute divisions north-eastwards. At General Clark's suggestion a Polish Brigade moved straight down the remaining five miles of Route 9 into Bologna, where they reached the centre of the town unopposed at 0600 hours on 21 April and were soon joined by the leading elements of both 91 and 34 Divisions and the Legnano Group. As soon as he sensed the German resistance slackening south of Bologna, Truscott ordered the remainder of II Corps to make for Route 64 and by-pass the town to the west. Here IV Corps had already broken out into the valley of the Po.

On 20 April von Vietinghoff issued orders for a general withdrawal to the Po but the fate of his armies was already sealed. On 14 April he told the OKW that only a withdrawal behind the Po and the Ticino could save his armies but that Tenth Army would still have to hold out for two weeks after the order had been given, to enable the remainder of his forces to reach their positions. His telegram was dispatched before the Fifth Army main attack went in but the hinge to his whole position and escape route to the north-east was already threatened, for by 14 April Eighth Army had crossed the Santerno and turned in strength towards Argenta. The reply from Hitler came on 17 April and was signed by Jodl. It could hardly have been more insulting A short homily on 'defeatist attitudes' included the usual order 'the Fuehrer expects now as before the utmost steadfastness in the fulfilment of your present mission, to defend every inch of the north Italian areas entrusted to your command' and ended in an unusually threatening sentence pointing out the 'serious consequences' awaiting commanders of any rank who failed to carry out the Fuehrer's orders. Von Vietinghoff hesitated for three days before finally authorizing the withdrawal that had already started. On 19 April, however, General Keightley had issued his orders for the advance by 5 Corps and the completely fresh 6 Armoured Division through the Argenta Gap and it is this battle for the Argenta Gap, that had already started by 16 April, that sprung the noose that Alexander had so carefully cast towards the broad and fast-flowing river in the plain, now so close behind the battle line.

On the morning of 14 April 78 Division, the Cremona Group and 56 Division were all converging on Bastia. The narrow two-mile gap running north past Argenta was the most heavily mined area that any of the Allied troops had met in the whole of the campaign. North-eastwards of Argenta the Fossa Marina ran diagonally across the north end of the gap. This was not a particularly wide water obstacle but its approaches were heavily mined and it was now held by strong elements of 29 Panzer Grenadiers, the last remaining German troops available for its defence. The Panzer Grenadiers had already halted the flank attack in Fantails made by the Buffs on a vital bridge over the Fossa Marina and were strongly resisting the advance of the remainder of 24 Guards Brigade to join up with this last and least successful of the amphibious flank attacks. When the Irish Brigade of 78 Division reached the now demolished road and railway bridges over the Reno south of Bastia, infantry had crossed behind a smoke-screen but had been thrown back and the division now crossed the Reno on a bridge built by 56 Division further to the south. The two divisions were now faced with attacking through an extremely restricted area of waterlogged ground with no room to manoeuvre, few roads and innumerable minefields. 56 Division's attack began at dawn on 15 April and made some progress, except on the right flank where the Guards Brigade met very heavy fire, which also destroyed all their assault boats. The following day Bastia fell to 56 Division and 78 Division pushed the Irish Brigade through towards Argenta, now a smouldering mass of ruins after two days' heavy bombing. Both divisions were now hard up against the Fossa Marina. On the right, the Guards Brigade, after four days' fighting, had achieved a bridgehead and a battalion with tanks had penetrated about half a mile beyond the canal. On the left, the Irish Brigade reached the canal after darkness but met most violent opposition and bitter fighting around a minute bridgehead continued all night. This attack had caught the forward German troops being relieved by 29 Panzer Grenadiers and the German casualties from shell fire were particularly heavy, as many men were caught in the open. On 17 April the bridgehead was expanded and two battalions were now firmly established across the canal, while an attack on Argenta supported by Crocodile flamethrowers succeeded in clearing the town before dark.

The town was a hideous heap of rubble, the civilian dead piled in pathetic masses, and Germans still holding out in cellars and strongpoints. The Northamptons cleared it by nightfall only to be counter-attacked from the north in the early hours of April 18. The counter-attack, of company strength, with tank support, was not only beaten off but driven into the arms of the Inniskillings working round to the north of the town.[7]

West of the town, 2 Commando worked up the west bank of the Reno but were driven back by a determined counter-attack. While these counter-attacks were in progress, a fresh brigade of 78 Division was passed through east of Argenta to strike north-westwards towards Boccaleone and Cons-andolo on Route 16. The Germans were still desperately trying to retake Argenta and to prevent the use of Route 16. At 0200 hours 18 April the attack against Boccaleone 'struck straight across the network of ditches, fences, wire and minefields'.[8] This assault was shortly followed by an attack on Consandolo further up the road. These two attacks caused a good deal of confusion to the Germans who by dawn had been driven back from Argenta and had lost control of Boccaleone. Consandolo now became the scene of a bitter struggle. The attacking battalions lost several tanks in the first rush and quickly became involved in fighting at extremely close quarters, while the whole of their area was subjected to heavy artillery and mortar fire. Several bayonet charges were made and the divisional artillery was often unable to fire without endangering their own troops, owing to the closeness of the fighting. Across the Reno the Royal Marine Commandos had taken over the attack and were now advancing against increasing opposition to come level with the little village of S Antonio, just north of Argenta on Route 16. In S Antonio itself a small force of Germans, with their backs to the river and surrounded on three sides, were holding out with great determination and in spite of a heavy attack by fighter-bombers succeeded in halting part of the reconnaissance regiment of 56 Division who were sent to clear the village. That night 6 Armoured Division started moving forward towards the narrow Argenta Gap, where clouds of dust hung over the few inadequate roads already congested by vehicles and guns of the two infantry divisions, and by the afternoon of 19 April were passing through 78 Division. Their objective was Bondeno, while 56 and 78 Divisions were to continue the attack towards Ferrara and the Po crossings north of the town. 8 Indian Division was ordered to protect the left flank of the armoured division's advance. By the following day 20 April, the day that von Vietinghoff ordered a general with-drawal, Porto Maggiore had fallen and 5 Corps were advancing on a three-divisional front, only some fifteen miles short of Ferrara. This was one of the crossing points where it was planned to drop the Parachute brigade. Reports of a particularly heavy concentration of anti-aircraft guns caused the opera-tion to be cancelled. Although many drops were planned the brigade was never used in its airborne role, as in the latter stages of the offensive the ground over which the advance took place was unsuitable for a landing. The battle was now moving forward from the gap and although the country was flat and fairly open from an infantry point of view it was intersected by many canals and irrigation ditches, often with high banks and the extensive fruit orchards, which were already in leaf, further seriously affected the view of the advancing tanks. The remnants of LXXVI Corps were now supported by elements from 26 Panzer Division, as well as the whole of 29 Panzer Grenadiers who were fighting hard to delay the advance which now directly threatened the principal escape route for all the German troops from the Bologna area. 6 Armoured Division was now swinging to the west and was up against firm resistance both at S Nicolo and Segni and it was not until the afternoon of 21 April that the hoped for breakthrough came. Working round to the west of Segni, hard against the high flood bank of the Reno, the 17/21st Lancers, followed by a battalion of the Rifle Brigade, broke through the flank of the German position and, advancing with considerable dash, reached Poggio Renatico before dark.

At Corps and Army headquarters, the victory was now assured, but in the dark, under the walls of Poggio Renatico the Regiment felt very insecure. There had been very heavy expenditure of ammunition on a large number of targets and possible enemy positions during the advance, petrol was down to below twenty-five miles, and there was no prospect of replenishment until the route was cleared of the enemy.[9]

While waiting for the supply echelon which arrived about noon, an infantry attack was launched before dawn on 22 April and the whole force moved in to clear the town, where they were heavily attacked by mortar fire throughout the day. The Germans, however, still held the bridge over the Reno a short way to the south. By now 6 Armoured Division held Mirabello and had reached Bondeno, where an attempt to rush the bridge over the Panaro failed by a hair's breadth. The following day saw the junction of Eighth and Fifth Armies.

During the night, orders came for the Regiment and one company to advance at first light to S Agostino, five miles to the west, leaving the rest of the infantry to hold the town until relieved. 7th Rifle Brigade were to capture the Reno Bridge at Poggio before first light. This they did at 4.15 am, clashing with a patrol from the New Zealanders advancing from the south. An officer was at once sent to contact the New Zealand Division and to inform them about the position and intentions of our own troops. At 6.30 am the advance was begun, and S Agostino was soon reached without opposition. A Squadron got into position on the banks of a dry canal known as the Cavo Napoleone, and shot-up transport moving northwards, including three heavy guns. B Squadron at the south end of the town were soon in contact with the New Zealand advance, and C Squadron were sent westwards for two or three miles to find the South African Armoured Division. At Pilastrello, the leading troop saw tanks coming up the road from the south and a seventeen-pounder shot was fired at them. Fortunately it missed, since they were American, and for the Regiment it was the last shot of the war. Contact was soon made, just in time to prevent the Americans from launching a full-scale attack with artillery barrage on Finale in Emilia, already in the hands of the 16th/5th Lancers. The rest of the day was spent in collecting prisoners. . . . Organized resistance south of the Po ceased two days later on April 25, and the German Corps Commander asked to surrender.[10]

General Truscott's orders for the pursuit to the Po was given out on 19 April and implemented immediately. Bologna was entered on 21 April. 'The two Corps each with one armoured division and two infantry divisions were to press on boldly and rapidly, seize the line of the Panaro River, and then press on to the Po to secure crossing sites and cut off German forces still south of the river.'[11] General Crittenberger ordered IV Corps to advance almost due north, using 85 Division and 10 Mountain Division and keeping 1 Armoured Division and the Brazilians to protect the left flank. A task force of 10 Mountain Division with armour crossed the Panaro twenty miles north-west of Bologna on 21 April and the remainder of the division had reached S Benedetto by midnight 22/23 April, where a crossing of the Po in assault boats was made against some opposition on the following day. General Keyes put the South African Armoured Division in the van of II Corps' advance, followed by 91 and 88 Divisions abreast. German rearguards, however, fought hard on the Panaro and delays in bridging the river prevented the early crossing of the South African Division, which was now directed on Felonica on the army's right flank, which was reached on 24 April, by which time the infantry were on the line of the Po as far west as Revere. Meanwhile on Eighth Army's front, 8 Indian Division was already across the Po west of Ferrara having taken the town. Further east, 78 Division was engaged in a fierce battle with rearguards of 29 Panzer Grenadiers for the villages of Galetta and Zocca, while 2 Armoured Brigade was driving westwards along the river bank towards Pontelagoscuro, which was the main crossing point for Highway 16 over the Po north of Ferrara.

All afternoon and evening and far into the night, under brilliant moonlight and among fiercely burning fires, a mobile battle raged until the Germans had clearly lost all control; when the Armoured Brigade was ordered to turn at right angles to its previous direction, and drive into the disorganized remnants of the German divisions. Dawn discovered a scene of extraordinary desolation and fearful carnage. There was no longer any coherent resistance, and along the river lay the ruins of a German army. On April 25th resistance also ceased before the 56th Division's advance to the Po, and by dusk the Vth Corps had cleared the ground on a stretch of twenty-five miles from Stienta to Serravalle except for a little pocket south of Polsella.[12]

On 24 April 6 Armoured Division and the New Zealanders, both under 13 Corps, crossed the Po and the next day 56 and 8 Indian Division, under 5

Corps, were also over the river and both Corps now raced for the Adige. By 25 April Fifth Army had five divisions across the Po and the following day 10 Mountain Division entered Verona, while 88 and 91 Divisions turned towards the Adige. At dawn on 27 April the New Zealanders and 56 Division forded the crossings of the Adige at Badia and Rovigo, while the two American infantry divisions crossed higher up at Verona and Legnano and advanced on Vicenza. 10 Mountain Division had meanwhile been dispatched up the east side of Lake Garda to seize the Brenner Pass and a small force in DUKWs had crossed the lake in an abortive attempt to capture Mussolini. While the advance on the Adige was developing, Truscott had dispatched 1 Armoured Division to seize the northern escape routes as far west as the Swiss border at Lake Como, towards which the two German divisions of LXXV Corps were now making their way harried by large partisan bands. 34 Division was sent via Bresica and Milan in support of the armoured division and the Brazilians were kept south of the Po to cut off the remainder of LI Mountain Corps, who were withdrawing before 91 Division in the coastal sector. In the first fourteen days of the offensive the Germans' casualties were around 67,000 of whom 35,000 were made prisoner, the majority surrendering to the Americans. The total Allied casualties from 9 April to 2 May were 16,747 of which 5,258 were in 5 Corps. Between 14–25 April Fifth Army's casualties were 5,027. During the whole period of the Spring campaign the Germans had been under continuous air attack. In the week immediately before the capture of Bologna, the Tactical Air Forces flew nearly 12,000 sorties and between 22 and 26 April a further 2,122 sorties were flown, principally in attacks on the line of the Po and the now utterly disorganized German troops attempting to cross. General von Senger describes his experiences at this stage of the battle.

On the night of April 22nd I had to decide whether to be taken prisoner with my Corps HQ Staff while still south of the Po, or whether to cross the river. I decided to attempt the crossing. My HQ Staff was dissolved into separate groups. At dawn on the 23rd we found a ferry at Bergantino. Of the thirty-six Po ferries in the zone of Fourteenth Army, four only were still serviceable. Because of the incessant fighter-bomber attacks it was useless to cross in daylight. As the level of water in the Po was low, many officers and men were able to swim across. The access road at Revere was blocked by many columns of burning vehicles. I had to leave my cars behind. In the morning twilight we crossed the river, and together with my operations staff I marched the twenty-five kilometres to Legnano. We were unable to establish any communications. Major General von Schellwitz, who after General Pfeiffer's death had assumed command of the remnants of 65 and 305 Infantry Divisions, was captured south of the river.[13]

General Heidrich, commanding I Parachute Corps, escaped by swimming but as the now disorganized mass of troops streamed back almost all their tanks and guns and such vehicles as had not already run out of petrol had to be abandoned. After the Po the Allies were pursuing a routed enemy. The result of Hitler's orders of 'no retreat' to von Vietinghoff had been catastrophic. General Warlimont comments as follows:

The result of adherence to this principle was that when on 9 April 1945, the Allies loosed their last great attack, reached Bologna on 21 April and so laid open the whole plain of the Po, the entire Army Group, which by then had no fuel and was practically immobile, disintegrated. OKW thereupon issued orders for withdrawal to the southern foothills of the Alps, but these were too late. Supreme Headquarters had then split and on 26 April issued appeals for 'fanatical determination to fight' and 'fanatical resistance' – but there was no one to hear them. There were encouraging exhortations to concentrate in the 'bulwark of the Alps Keep' but they bore no relation whatsoever to reality. On 2 May the Commander-in-Chief on his own initiative brought the unequal struggle to an end by an armistice agreement for which preparations had long since been made.[14]

The story of the secret negotiations for the German surrender, originally given the code name SUNRISE, starts in February 1945 in the offices of the American Intelligence mission in Switzerland run by their Office of Strategic Services. By a quirk of fate the key figure was Hitler's personal representative and commander of all the SS in Italy, a certain General Wolff and it was he who followed up the early overtures with the Americans by a personal visit to their headquarters in Switzerland early in March. Kesselring certainly knew something of what was going on and allowed the secret discussion to continue but his replacement by von Vietinghoff put a temporary brake on the negotiations. Von Vietinghoff was strictly a non-political soldier and unlikely to be easily persuaded, so for the time being he was kept out of the conspiracy and Wolff continued to try to get Kesselring to act. Kesselring, however, had much on his plate and was difficult to contact in the midst of the battle on the Western Front. One meeting between Wolff and Kesselring took place and Kesselring appeared to support the idea of a surrender in Italy but Wolff now feared that Himmler had guessed what was going on and the negotiations with the Allies inevitably slowed down. On 14 April Wolff was galvanized into action by the hopelessness of the situation at the front in Italy and approached the two Army Commanders, Herr and Lemelsen, who both agreed on the necessity to end the fighting. The principal stumbling blocks now were that von Vietinghoff would inevitably refuse to break his oath to Hitler and the other senior commanders would not act without Kesselring's authority. At this critical point Wolff was recalled to Berlin for a meeting with Himmler, who himself, it subsequently transpired, was already involved in secret negotiations with the Allies through Count Bernadotte. While he was in Berlin, Wolff was called to two meetings with Hitler and was considerably relieved to discover that Hitler had only the vaguest idea that some contact had been made with the Allies in Zürich, about six weeks previously, and knew nothing of the subsequent moves. Wolff did not reach Lucerne to report these conversations until 24 April and the next few days were ones of high drama. The first positive move was made by Graziani who asked Wolff to negotiate the surrender of the Italian forces and about the same time the Combined Chiefs of Staff authorized Alexander to send for German envoys to sign an unconditional surrender. On 28 April Mussolini and his mistress, Claretta Petacci, were caught by partisans and shot near the shores of Lake Como. The bodies were taken to Milan and 'hung from the girders of an un-finished building in the Piazza Loreto, at a site of a reprisal shooting of partisan hostages by Fascist units the year before'.[15] When Wolff returned to Bolzano he found that von Vietinghoff had been won over and had agreed that Wolff and two envoys should go to Caserta with full powers to arrange a capitulation. The wording of von Vietinghoff's authorization, however, was too vague for the Allies and two further days passed, during which American agents had to be sent to rescue Wolff from a partisan band that attacked his headquarters. Meanwhile the Combined Chiefs of Staff agreed to the German plenipotentiaries being received, in the hopes that a formula could be reached and between 28 and 29 April an instrument of surrender was drawn up and signed at Caserta. Kesselring meanwhile had sent for von Vietinghoff to meet him in Innsbruck and, in spite of von Vietinghoff's report of the hope-lessness of the situation and arguments for an immediate surrender, now announced that while Hitler was alive he himself could not agree to a sur-render. On the evening of 30 April Kesselring, who now was Commander-in-Chief of all the German armies in the South and thus immediately respons-ible for Army Group C, heard the terms of the surrender and immediately relieved von Vietinghoff and his Chief of Staff, General Roettiger, of their appointments and ordered them to be court-martialled. Generals Schultz and Wentzell were sent to take over. Time was now very short, as the cease fire was due to be implemented at 1400 hours on 2 May. Wolff and Roettiger, who had managed to stay at the headquarters on the excuse of having to hand over, now decided on desperate measures and the following morning moved in with a detachment of military police to arrest both Schultz and Wentzel. Most of the day was taken up with persuading these two generals to join the conspiracy and they finally agreed, providing Kesselring would authorize the surrender. That evening about a dozen of the German generals and the few senior staff officers who were also in the know assembled and it was quickly agreed that Kesselring should be telephoned immed-iately. Both Wolff and Schultz put through calls but at this crucial moment Kesselring could not be reached and the evening dragged on. At about 2230 hours General Herr suddenly turned to a staff officer and gave the order that Tenth Army would cease fire on the following day, in accordance with the agreement that had already been signed. The remaining commanders quickly followed his lead and Wolff sent a wireless signal to Alexander's headquarters confirming that the surrender would take place. A few minutes later news of Hitler's death was announced over the radio and the German generals now expected to have Kesselring's approval, but his vacillations nearly wrecked their plans. Within the hour orders from Kesselring arrived for the arrest of several of the senior officers in the surrender plot and the meeting quickly dispersed. About two hours later, early on 2 May, Kesselring telephoned Wolff at his headquarters, outside which SS and Wehrmacht tank units were facing each other in an uneasy confrontation. Kesselring 'showered on Wolff the most severe accusations' while Wolff 'pleaded for an end to the senseless fighting'. The call, on a bad line and with many interruptions, went on for nearly two hours with General Westphal, Kesselring's Chief of Staff, and Major Wenner, Wolff's adjutant, joining in. Wolff's final argument is reported as:

and it is not only a military capitulation in order to avoid further destruction and shedding of blood. A cease fire now will give the Anglo-Americans the possibility of stopping the advance of the Russians into the West, of countering the threat of the Tito forces to the port of Trieste and of a communist uprising which will seek to establish a soviet republic in northern Italy. . . . Since the death of the Fuehrer has released you from your oath of loyalty, I beg you as the highest commander of the entire Alpine area devoutly and with the greatest sense of obedience to give your retroactive sanction to our independent action which our consciences impelled us to take.[16]

Half an hour later Kesselring phoned again, giving his approval to the surrender. That afternoon the cease fire brought hostilities to an end.

From an administrative point of view the final campaign was characterized by several factors. Firstly, much of the planning that had already been done for the winter offensive, which was subsequently cancelled, was of value in the planning for the final offensive and in addition an unusually long space of time was available for the preparations. Secondly, there was the need for stockpiling ammunition throughout the winter and for a great deal of effort being devoted to the repair of vehicles and much of the heavy equipment that would be required. Thirdly, there was the acceptance of a number of calculated risks connected with the availability of ammunition, petrol and transport, based on the assumption that a relatively short campaign would be mainly fought in the Po valley. Three main problems had to be tackled, the maintenance of the army, the occupation of northern Italy and the disposal the enemy forces after surrender. It was decided that twelve British divisions could be maintained as far as the Adige but that, until a railway from Leghorn to Bologna could be completed, only four American divisions could be maintained on the Po, unless a breakthrough and subsequent German collapse took place. As regards future development of the lines of communication into Austria, it was planned that Eighth Army would be maintained through Bologna and the Brenner. The careful hoarding of ammunition through the winter and the dumping of the whole of the allocation for April and May allowed the Allied artillery to give full support right up to the end of the campaign. The situation, however, had arisen by 20 April that, at the rate of expenditure of the first week's fighting, a shortage of field-gun ammunition would arise by 7 May and of medium-gun ammunition even earlier. The situation regarding petrol was also fairly tight owing to the limited capacity of the ports and the move of an additional bomber wing and two fighter groups into the Ancona area brought the question of petrol supplies to a head. The move forward of a further fighter group in fact had to be delayed. Initially the quantity of transport available for the maintenance of both armies was sufficient but by 25 April the situation had deteriorated and there was nothing left in reserve. This was principally due to the now urgent need to start moving supplies forward for the liberated areas. The shortage was overcome by making the maximum use of captured vehicles. Early agreement with Tito on the opening of the port of Trieste could not be reached and air supply to the Udine area started on 7 May with a lift of 200 tons, reaching a peak of 2,000 tons by the middle of the month. In spite of difficulties in unloading and clearing the supplies from the airfields, this airlift averted a crisis at a time when the more normal sea and land communications were lagging far behind.

The battle of the Po valley demonstrated for the last time the folly of Hitler's 'rigid defence' tactics. Von Vietinghoff entered the ring for the final round of the campaign like a boxer with his bootlaces tied together. The order to fight where he stood denied him any chance of conducting either a mobile defence or a properly phased withdrawal. When retreat was forced on him it was too late to save his army and having already lost the majority of his mobile troops and used up his meagre stocks of petrol he had no proper rear-guards capable of preventing the withdrawal turning into a rout. Alexander's plans for the final offensive had a classic quality, achieving both surprise and concentration at the vital 'hinge' to the German line and was yet another example of his favourite tactic, the 'two-handed punch'. The execution of the plan was faultless and resulted in the destruction of Army Group C and the subsequent unconditional surrender of nearly a million German and Italian troops in Italy and Austria. As we have seen the Allies enjoyed no numerical superiority of ground forces but complete air supremacy, combined with the intervention of strong bomber forces in the land battle, together with the Allied superiority in both armour and artillery more than made up the weight to tip the balance in favour of the attack. Furthermore, months of effort by the Mediterranean Allied Air Forces against the communication system in northern Italy had kept the German divisions short of supplies and the destruction of the Po bridges and many of the ferries prevented the crossing of practically all their heavy equipment and vehicles, as well as many thousands of men trapped against the River line. Highlights of the encircling armoured thrust to the Po have already been recounted, but the employment of specially trained and equipped troops to overcome the problems of attacking through two completely contrasting types of terrain, through which these thrusts were mounted, deserve special mention. Except for the French mountain troops employed against the Gustav Line, 10 Mountain Division was the first specially trained and equipped Allied mountain formation to be employed in the theatre and their successes west of Route 64 were spectacular. In Eighth Army's attack against the 'hinge' at Argenta both Commandos and 56 Division, using the newly arrived Fantails and other special equipment, attacked through an area which the Germans thought quite impassable and tribute should be paid to the skill and determination both of the 'professionally' trained Commandos and the more conventionally trained and equipped infantry units, whose flank attacks through the mud and slime of Comacchio and the floods alongside opened up the road to Ferrara. But after the strategists and tacticians have had their say above all this was a soldiers' battle. Carefully laid plans, air superiority, new and special equipment all take their various places on the stage, but it was the courage and the skill of the sailors, soldiers and airmen of many nations fighting side by side that won this last and quite decisive battle of the campaign.

20
The Pacemakers

Austria occupied: Difficulties with Tito: Stalin's Foreign Policy: Strategic and tactical factors of the campaign reassessed: Some lessons of amphibious, naval and air operations: Balanced forces: Artillery: Administration: Allied Military Government: Hitler's Balkan strategy: Commanders' views in retrospect.

On 13 April Russian troops occupied Vienna and further south, in the valley of the Sava, Red Army divisions were a hundred miles west of Belgrade. In Yugoslavia Tito's forces had advanced to Senj and were about to take Fiume in their advance on Trieste. On 2 May Russian troops completed the occupation of Berlin and six days later occupied Dresden and moved south to take Prague. In Austria the Russian advance had now reached Graz, where contact was made with Patton's Third Army. The US Seventh Army advancing through Innsbruck had already joined up with elements of 88 Division on the Brenner at Vipiteno, a few miles north of Bolzano, on 4 May. Further east, 6 Armoured Division thrust through Udine to reach Caporetto ahead of Tito's troops, who were already established in Cividale. Meanwhile the New Zealanders had made a forced march to reach Trieste on 2 May and took the surrender of the German garrison in the face of Tito's partisans, who had entered the town three days previously and were set on seizing as much Italian territory as possible. Clark immediately sent 91 Division as reinforcements and General Harding, 13 Corps commander, to take command of the two divisions, with responsibility for completing the occupation of the province of Venezia Giulia and to make certain that port facilities were available for the support of the Allied advance into Austria. 56 Division, which had enjoyed six days' respite in and around Venice, were moved forward to the line of the River Isonzo and to occupy Gorizia and Monfalcone. The surrender of the remaining German forces in Europe was signed the next day. Meanwhile a very explosive situation was developing between the Allies and the Yugoslavs over the latter's claims to Trieste and the surrounding Italian territories. Alexander now sent his Chief of Staff, General Morgan, to meet Tito in an attempt to get an amicable temporary agreement to leave the question of national boundaries to the forthcoming peace conferences. Tito, however, was not to be fobbed off so easily and took a very firm line, saying that his forces had liberated Yugoslavia and that Trieste, which he had occupied in advance of the Allied troops, would not be given up. Churchill's correspondence with President Truman over Trieste and his instructions to Alexander to advance, 'as far and as fast as you can into former enemy territory and until you form contact with Russian or Yugoslav forces', show his fears that any weakness by the Western Powers at this stage could lead to 'uncontrollable land-grabbing'[1] by their allies with far-reaching consequences. Truman at first supported Churchill's firm line but by the

375

middle of the month he made it clear that only if Tito's forces attacked the Allied positions could he agree to American troops being involved. Although he sent Churchill the text of a joint instruction to be issued to Eisenhower and Alexander for a show of force, in the hope of dissuading Tito from any precipitate action, his telegram made it clear that any delay in the move of American troops to the Pacific was not acceptable. General Morgan, however, eventually got agreement for a line of demarcation in the Trieste area, to which Tito's partisans were persuaded to withdraw. Meanwhile the thoroughly practical local approach to the crisis is well illustrated by the following account of the experiences of a battalion of the Queen's Regiment in 56 Division:

On arrival at Sutta we at once began to dig in and were not in the least surprised to see the Slavs do likewise. It was not unusual to find opposing weapon pits so close together that, in the event of trouble, the occupants would scarcely have needed weapons – they could have punched each other on the nose. Not that relationships between the two sides were unfriendly; the troops talked together, exchanged cigarettes and treated the whole affair as a storm in a teacup. It was, however, a most explosive situation and the implications, had hostilities broken out might have been world shaking. On 6th June we were particularly on the *qui vive* as intelligence reports suggested a possible move by the Yugoslavs. However, two companies of Slav troops from a nearby camp saw a battalion exercise in which 'Wasps' flamethrowers were employed. The Yugoslavs seemed rather put out by what they saw and later in the morning their Political Officer complained to Brigade that the exercise had been 'put on to demoralise his troops'. However, nothing untoward happened and, in the evening when a Mobile Cinema Unit arrived to show 'Crystal Ball', about fifty Yugoslav troops and many civilians were in the audience. Gradually tension eased until, on 11 June, it was announced that a line (the Morgan Line) had been agreed upon and that all Slav troops would move behind it by 0900 hours on 12th.[2]

On arrival in their new area the Commanding Officer explained the presence of the battalion in a proclamation, as the inhabitants were not only frightened but hostile, having absorbed a good deal of anti-British propaganda. The friendly attitude of the British troops who wandered round the villages unarmed made an immediate impact,

but a real change was noticeable a few days later when practically the whole battalion pulled out to attend one of our periodic dances in Monfalcone: the local girls began to realise that they were missing something and took active steps to ensure that if anything good was to be had in future, they were going to have their full share.[3]

Churchill, faced with the probability of a General Election within a matter of weeks, was already pressing for a conference between the three heads of state, Truman, Stalin and himself, to resolve the political problems that, now hostilities had ceased, could no longer be shelved. With the 'melting' away of the forces of the Western Allies he felt Stalin would be left 'all powerful in Europe'. At the beginning of July American troops drew back to the boundary of their occupation zone that had been originally proposed three years previously, and later agreed at Quebec in September 1944, and the Russian troops now stood on a line from Lubeck to Linz and occupied a third of Austria. Vienna, like Berlin, was to be an international zone but owing to disputes with the Russians over a number of technicalities, the 'Western Allies were unable to move their headquarters into Vienna until 23 August. This was four months after the Soviet Army had full control of the city.'[4] By the end of July, however, Stalin's virtually unassailable position had been clearly demonstrated at the Potsdam conference and Churchill was no longer Prime Minister of Britain.

The basic Soviet demand at Potsdam was for the immediate and unconditional recognition of the Soviet-dominated regimes in Hungary, Rumania and Bulgaria. . . . Stalin made the Soviet position clear when he stated that 'any freely elected government would be anti-Soviet and that we cannot permit'. . . . The strong American stand at Potsdam and London in favour of free elections in East Central Europe threw a few handfuls of grit into the grinding wheels of the Soviet power-machine but it could not stop their turning.[5]

Work on the various peace treaties met endless delays at the hands of the Soviet negotiators and as months dragged on the Soviet grip on the territories occupied by the Red Army tightened, and soon, of the Balkan states, only Yugoslavia and Greece remained outside the Soviet communist bloc. Yugoslavia's independence had largely been won through the efforts of Tito and his strong partisan forces and Greece had been saved from a communist domination by British and Commonwealth troops. Could an earlier advance by the Western Powers into other countries in the Balkans and Eastern Europe have fostered or directly brought about similar results? While Stalin may have had no firm blueprint for Eastern Europe in 1944, one thing is clear, he did not want any country on the frontiers of Russia to emerge after the war with a government that was hostile to Soviet Russia. Once the Red Army was in occupation he certainly would not give up control unless this condition was met and he soon discovered that, 'the only way he could ensure undisputed Soviet influence in Eastern Europe was to apply controlled revolution from above'.[6]

It has been suggested that the Western Powers failed to act when the writing was on the wall and that as early as the October conference in Moscow in 1943 the Soviet attitude towards the East Central European countries had become clear. Any question of an extension of the war in the Mediterranean by the Western Allies towards the Balkans, however, must be related to several important factors. Overall would be the difficulty of breaking through the barrier of mountains that guarded the occupied territories of South-

Eastern Europe, with the attendant problems of lengthy and complicated lines of communication. Secondly, the requirements of OVERLORD were being given absolute priority both in men and assault shipping. This latter factor determined the course of the diversionary operations in the Aegean, and there is no evidence that they were planned to be otherwise than diversionary, which Churchill hoped would also influence the Turks. Later proposals for stepping-up the scale of operations in northern Italy, or for a landing at the head of the Adriatic, aimed directly at extending the battle of attrition in Italy at this crucial stage of the war in Europe. By now nearly five hundred ships and landing craft and strong air and ground forces were assembling for DRAGOON, but any proposal for their use elsewhere in the Mediterranean was completely contrary to the American viewpoint on how best to defeat Germany and at the same time achieve a quick conclusion of the war in Europe. Regarding the deployment of American troops or resources in the European or Mediterranean theatres at this time, it was the view of Marshall and Eisenhower that counted and what they wanted was the port of Marseilles and the maximum number of American divisions in France. Any change of plan at this stage could also adversely affect the time-table of operations planned to bring about the early defeat of Japan and place a further strain on the American economy. Finally, the difficulties attending any attempt to break through to Vienna through the confined and readily defended mountainous 'gap', which could only follow on a German defeat or withdrawal, would still have been immense. As Professor Howard points out, in his recently published *The Mediterranean Strategy in the Second World War*, at this late stage in the war the post-war balance of power in South-East Europe could hardly have been influenced by such an operation, 'even if successful'. For Stalin the formulation of strategy and indeed of Russia's post-war policies was a good deal less complicated.

By November 1943 he could see victory ahead and as regards his foreign policy was able to revert to the party line. It is true to say that the appalling losses of nineteen million soldiers and civilians killed, with a further three million disabled and twenty-five million rendered homeless, together with the loss of two-thirds of Soviet Russia's pre-war economic wealth made the internal restoration of his country his first concern in May 1945, but the vast territories that the Red Army had occupied gave 'brilliant opportunities . . . for a power that had always taken advantage of economic and social disaster to implement its foreign policy'.[7]

A well-known United States military historian has written: 'With the Americans still innocent concerning ultimate Soviet intent, guilty over the long postponement of the Second Front, and desirous in any event of Soviet participation in both the Pacific war and the United Nations, after 1944 Stalin had only to cope with the resistance of his British ally to his policy in Europe.'[8]

It is perhaps axiomatic to say that in the Allied decision to withdraw landing craft from the Mediterranean, even before the attack on the mainland of Italy got under way, there was a self-imposed denial of the most obvious advantage of naval and air superiority in operations against any country with such extended coastlines, that is the development of amphibious assault in the rear of the enemy's defences. It is equally true to say that the Germans, forced to fight a purely land campaign with diminishing air support and involving a never-ending series of delaying actions and withdrawals, made a skilful and maximum use of the physical features of the peninsula throughout the whole campaign, right up to the final stand on the Gothic Line and in the Romagna. On the Adriatic flank, the Allies were forced to assault a seemingly endless series of river lines, while the mountainous spine of the Apennines, with its spurs running down towards the Tyrrhenian Sea, constricted the movement and deployment of the more mechanized and more heavily armoured Allied forces. Much of the fighting thus devolved upon the infantry, who were called on to force a passage over the river lines or assault a whole series of mountain peaks that dominated the roads in the plains below. By making full use of the natural barriers of mountains, rivers and inundations, the Germans were able to concentrate considerable effort on fortifying such critical areas in their defences as were unprotected by natural means, such as the Liri valley or the eastern coastal sector of the Gothic Line. The heavy casualties that resulted from head-on attacks against such heavily fortified areas and the key mountain positions that covered them, such as on the Rapido and Monte Cassino positions, led the Allies to seek less obvious and costly lines of attack. The brilliant successes of the French mountain troops in their attacks both to the east of Monte Cassino and through the Aurunci mountains and also of the American 10 Mountain Division west of Route 64, demonstrate the great value of properly trained and equipped mountain troops in such a theatre of operations. The removal of the French Expeditionary Corps to take part in DRAGOON could not have come at a worse time and their use against the Gothic Line might well have resulted in the hoped-for breakthrough in the autumn of 1944 that could have had far-reaching military and political effects. The sacrifices of the Gurkha regiments at Cassino underline this point that the lack of mountain formations with appropriately equipped supporting troops and supply columns had a stulti-fying effect on Allied tactics. At Cassino these incomparable mountain troops were committed in conventional attacks on extremely narrow fronts in an area which offered no tactical latitude. Again in the battle for the Gothic Line, 43 (Lorried) Gurkha Brigade was employed in the coastal sector and the Romagna and never in the mountains. Just as the North African deserts favoured the employment of armoured formations, so conditions in Italy required mountain formations capable of independent action. The retention in the United Kingdom of the British 52 Mountain Division, eventually employed in the flooded Scheldt area in Holland, is in retrospect difficult to justify.

The pattern of road and rail communications running up the length of the peninsula has already been described. As the Germans could readily anticipate, the principal axis of advance for the Allies ran up through the coastal plains. The paucity of road and rail communications gave the German engineers a considerable advantage, as they were able to effect a concentrated demolition programme in considerable depth. Furthermore, the considerable areas of mountainous terrain gave the German engineers tremendous scope for road-blocking and bridge-blowing, which they carried out with great skill and economy of effort. The result, as we have seen, is that a combination of skilfully sited demolitions and light covering forces in the numerous mountainous areas imposed very considerable delays on the Allied advance. The German decision to stand south of Rome on the successive lines of the Volturno, the Winter Line and the Gothic Line, brought an increasing use of mines, both in conjunction with road and bridge demolition and to cover approaches to vital points in the defensive positions. The mining of Cassino town, out of the ruins of which half a million mines were lifted after its capture, and of the Argenta Gap, which was even more heavily sown with mines, illustrate this point.

One of the paradoxes of the Italian Campaign is that after the fall of Sicily the Germans were in almost daily fear of an Allied amphibious landing in their rear, while the Allies were forced, by a shortage of landing craft, to fight their way up the long peninsula against the grain of the country. The success of the Allied air and sea assault on Sicily undoubtedly made a deep impression on the German High Command and their failure to develop decisive counter-attacks, both at Salerno and at Anzio, only confirmed their belief that, in the absence of naval and air forces to attack the convoys at sea, future Allied landings must be fought off on the beaches themselves. There is no doubt that the adoption by the German High Command of this tactical doctrine in their defence of the French coastline once more dispersed and weakened their counter-attack forces, much to the benefit to the Allies.

HUSKY and OVERLORD were the two largest amphibious assaults of the whole war and the experience gained in the mounting and launching of HUSKY was of incomparable value to the planners of OVERLORD. The essential difference between the two operations, apart from the fact that one involved long sea passages and the other a short approach across the Channel, was in the size of the subsequent build-up. The initial stages, however, of a combined operation are critical and the Allied planners for the cross-Channel assault had the great benefit of being able to study in detail all the problems of mounting and launching an operation of comparable strength. Many lessons had emerged from the Sicily landings and the operations at Salerno and Anzio brought further practical experience. Techniques in naval and air support, in the mounting of airborne operations, requirements for special assault craft and equipment, together with the whole complex task of allocating priorities for loading and deciding the exact scale of vehicles and equipment to be carried in various flights, all these could be studied in the light of actual experience. Furthermore, units and formations in all three services had gained actual fighting experience in what is the most complicated and difficult of all operations in war. The successful development of beach maintenance in Sicily, supplemented by the brilliant concept of the MULBERRY artificial harbour, made OVERLORD independent of the seizure of a major port, while the Build-up Control Organization for the follow-up forces was entirely based on experience gained in Sicily. One of the most positive results of HUSKY, however, and one which was fostered by the remainder of the Italian campaign, was a real and growing awareness of the benefits and vital importance of inter-service co-operation. The launching of HUSKY, the largest amphibious assault of the whole war, set the stage and brought practical experience in co-operation between all three services and the operations that followed in Italy continued to receive the whole-hearted support of both the Allied navies and air forces. Unlike the Wehrmacht, who for long periods h. d to fight in Italy with practically no air support, the Allied armies were never without aerial reconnaissance and an increasing degree of air support. Having gained air superiority before the launching of HUSKY, the Allies enjoyed its fruits to the end of the campaign. This air superiority made possible the landings both at Salerno and at Anzio, where the navy in their turn demonstrated the effectiveness of naval gunfire against land targets. As the advance continued up the peninsula and ports were captured, army engineers and naval ratings moved in to work side by side to clear the harbours and open the ports for the supply ships already waiting offshore. The driving back of the Luftwaffe from Sicily and southern Italy opened the sea route through the central Mediterranean. The sailing of the great convoys for HUSKY, the bombardments at Gella, and Salerno, the dash for Taranto were highlights in a period of growing domination by the Allied navies in the Mediterranean, which culminated in the surrender of the Italian fleet and the hunting down by air and naval forces of the remaining German U-boats. The British naval losses in the Dodecanese, however, demonstrated the continued danger to ships operating within range of land-based aircraft without adequate air cover. It is curious that Kesselring anticipated Allied amphibious landings in his rear in areas which were in fact far beyond the range of Allied land-based fighters. Admittedly the Germans constantly over-estimated the Allied capacity to carry out amphibious operations but equally their intelligence certainly failed to discover the complete absence of a carrier force after its withdrawal from Salerno. With the withdrawal of the Luftwaffe from Greece Allied naval supremacy became effective throughout the whole of the Mediterranean and while the task of mine clearance continued unabated, the need for escorting supply ships in convoy became unnecessary. It must not be forgotten that the task of transporting the men and materials and supplies for the Allied armies and air forces in Italy was a round-the-clock task that continued for nearly two years and was faithfully discharged by the sailors of many nations who crossed the Atlantic and Indian oceans to reach the Mediterranean ports and anchorages.

One of the objectives of the Allies in the assault of the Italian mainland was the seizure of the Foggia airfields, The contribution of the Fifteenth Strategic Air Force which subsequently operated from these airfields was considerable. Many targets which otherwise could not have been bombed in eastern and southern Germany were now within reach of the Allied bombers, and from this point onwards the strategic bombing offensive became increasingly effective. As regards the Allied air forces taking part in the campaigns in Sicily and on the Italian mainland several points emerge. The establishment of Allied air supremacy well before the launching of HUSKY set the pattern for subsequent operations both at Salerno and Anzio, but whereas in Sicily it was possible to seize and bring into use airfields at an early stage for local air defence, this was not possible on the other two occasions. At Salerno the carrier-borne squadrons were soon seriously reduced in strength and the distance the land-based aircraft had to fly to reach their patrol areas both at Salerno and Anzio limited the effectiveness of the air cover. If the Luftwaffe had not first been driven back from their advanced bases, heavy air attacks against the beach heads and assembled shipping would have been inevitable and difficult to counter. As regards tactical air support, the Desert Air Force had already developed this to a high degree but the Americans were slow to adopt comparable techniques. It was not until the slowness and inefficiency of their methods for calling for air support had been demonstrated at Gella, Salerno and Anzio that they set up an organization comparable to the British joint army-air command and communications system used in Eighth Army. In the latter part of the campaign the Americans made a great success of their 'Rover' organization for calling for direct air support.

The success of the aerial assault on Pantelleria led to a too optimistic assessment of the value of bombing attacks against modern fortifications. The lesson was one of morale, and misunderstood; certainly if the island had been held by Japanese or German troops it would not have been taken without a long and bloody struggle. Consequently, Allied bombers were often launched against fortified towns or villages and mountain positions. The failure of the 'obliteration' attacks on Cassino town and the Monastery cannot be explained away by pointing to delays by the ground troops in following up the aerial bombardment. Similarly, the heavy bombing of the German mountain positions south of Bologna did not prevent the follow-up infantry attacks being halted by small arms and mortar fire from the very weapon pits and embrasures that had just been pounded by heavy bombers, who were operating with complete freedom from interference and under favourable weather conditions. In each of these instances the Germans had time to fortify their positions and provide protection for their troops by shoring up cellars or improving or blasting caves into the mountainside or, where conditions permitted, constructing particularly deep dug-outs. In each case battle-seasoned and thoroughly reliable troops held the defences. The Germans expected heavy bombing and prepared for it and were determined to repulse any follow-up attack. Consequently they suffered less casualties and withstood the heaviest bombing raids with less loss of morale and fighting capacity than was anticipated. In the attack on Cassino town the bombing indeed created serious problems for the advancing infantry and tanks, who now met enormous craters and found every passage through the town filled with huge mounds of rubble. To a lesser degree the same problem was often encountered in hill villages that had been attacked by medium, or even fighter-bombers, where fallen masonry became as effective a road block in the narrow streets as that produced by the German engineers with their demolition charges. The effectiveness of concentrated heavy bomber attack in a defensive role, however, was demonstrated by the attacks at Salerno and Anzio on the communication centres of Battipaglia and Campoleone, which in both instances were assembly points for the German counter-attack forces. During the campaign the Allied air forces carried out an almost continuous policy of attacking enemy communications. The paucity of the air effort against the German evacuation across the Straits of Messina has already been discussed, but it should be remembered that the air preparations for an Allied advance to the mainland were already in full swing and that the bombing of air bases to destroy and drive back the Luftwaffe, together with attacks on communications to stop the move south of reinforcements, would automatically be given top priority by the Air Commanders who would be thinking a good way ahead of the land battle. Before the spring offensive that led to the capture of Rome and again right through the battle for the Gothic Line to the Spring offensive of 1945, the Allied air forces made serious attempts to 'interdict' the German rear communications and thereby strangle their supply lines and prevent as far as possible the movement of reserves and reinforcements. The changes in target priorities and the various methods employed have already been discussed and we see in Italy, in miniature, the bombing pattern that was applied before OVERLORD and in the battle for Normandy. In fact the Allied air forces in Italy had a very difficult task. Whereas in north-western Europe the industrial centres, principal marshalling yards and main railway communications were fairly concentrated and relatively near to the battle front and had been under heavy bomber attack for a long time, the rail communications in Italy were extended and far less concentrated and presented a number of small and widely dispersed targets. This complicated the task of the Allied air forces and facilitated the German repair organization. In the battle for Rome the Germans suffered not so much from a shortage of supplies but from the difficulty of moving reinforcements and counter-attack formations south in the face of air attack, particularly in daylight. The battle for the Gothic Line posed a somewhat different problem. Whereas the rail communications into northern Italy were clearly defined, the bombing of the Brenner and other passes proved inconclusive. Attacks on the Po bridges were more successful, but the Germans quickly built a large number of ferries, which were skilfully hidden during daylight and enabled them to keep their supply organization going. During the winter, when flying conditions often prevented air attack, the Germans in fact were able to build up sufficient supplies south of the Po, not only to fight on through the winter months but in preparation for the inevitable Allied spring offensive. When the spring offensive opened the Germans were only really short of petrol, but this was a shortage which applied to all their fronts. In the long-term view, the interdiction programme had undoubtedly created difficulties for the Germans but throughout the winter they had had plenty of time to make their preparations and to move forward reinforcements and supplies. The crux came in the twenty days' campaign in the valley of the Po, when in good flying conditions the whole strength of the Allied air forces, including the strategic bombers, were thrown into the battle. The crossing points over the Po were now under intensive attack and many of the ferries were damaged or sunk and the movement of counter-attack forces became extremely difficult. When the moment came for withdrawal, much of the German transport and heavy equipment had to be abandoned south of the river and few of the forward troops from the Bologna sector escaped except by swimming. This final air offensive achieved the isolation of the battlefield and demonstrated, under the perhaps somewhat exceptional circumstances of complete air supremacy, the power of the air arm to turn a withdrawal into a rout. In Italy the Allied commanders enjoyed the benefits accruing from well-balanced forces and in particular their sea and land forces enjoyed a high degree of air cover and air support. This was a direct result of the establishment, before the start of the campaign, of Allied air superiority and its maintenance to an increasing degree right up to the end. Conversely, the Wehrmacht, during their long withdrawal up the peninsula and in their final stand on the Apennines, were increasingly on their own. One of the most serious facets of this situation was their inability to 'see over the hill' and it was this lack of adequate aerial reconnaissance that put Kesselring at such a grave disadvantage in the DIADEM and OLIVE operations, in both of which Alexander's secret concentrations achieved complete surprise. The fact that the Germans withdrew their bombers and practically all of their fighters from Italy as the campaign progressed, is not an indication that the theatre was unimportant in their eyes but rather that they chose to employ their diminishing bomber forces elsewhere and, in the end, were forced to concentrate their fighters in defence of Germany itself. Furthermore, the German High Command probably took the view that the Gustav and Gothic Lines, both of which had great natural strength, could be held quite adequately by ground forces alone. Had the Germans attempted any counter-offensive, such as the recapture of the Foggia airfields, they undoubtedly would have attempted to assemble a strong air component in support of the ground attack, as was done to a lesser degree in their all-out counter-attacks at Anzio. By the early summer of 1944, however, the Luftwaffe was fighting a losing and largely defensive battle. Although German aircraft production was expanding, particularly in single-engined fighters, the Allied bombing offensive against aircraft factories was bringing heavy losses in trained pilots, apart from causing some destruction and dispersal of the industrial plant itself. The Allied bombing attacks in the late spring and summer of 1944 on the German fuel production plants resulted in an increasing shortage of aviation fuel and a most unwise decision to restrict the training of replacement pilots. 'The German High Command was then shown the full extent of its mistakes, for its pilots, whose training had been skimped in an effort to save oil, were unable to make use of the huge production of aircraft to stop the destruction of the remaining oil supply.'[9] As has already been mentioned the operations of Fifteenth Air Force, particularly against the Ploesti oil refineries, made a major contribution to this situation.

The question of balance also became a factor in the equipping and employment of artillery. Since El Alamein and through the North African campaign the Allied artillery had shown its superiority over that of the Germans. HUSKY and the advance to the mainland of Italy brought special conditions and problems. Assault landings required mobile or lightweight equipment and the small number of 3·7-inch howitzers, the mountain artillery 'screwgun', used on the British beaches proved invaluable, as did self-propelled guns that came into action at the water's edge, even before the beach was cleared. The development of support landing craft helped to fill the gap immediately before the assault craft touched down and the rocket craft in particular had a considerable morale effect. The fighting around Etna showed the difficulty of finding suitable positions for twenty-five pounders in mountainous terrain and after the advance to the mainland some 'pack-portee' 3·7-inch howitzers and American 75-mm howitzers were issued to field regiments as an alternative gun for mountain conditions. In the autumn of 1943 the decision was taken to form mountain artillery regiments but these did not reach the theatre until July of the following year, when three regiments and additional pack transport companies joined 10 Corps, later to be employed in the support of 10 Indian Division in the Apennines. As the Allies came up against the strong fortifications of the Winter and Gustav Lines, more and more medium and heavy guns were required, not only to deal with the concrete emplacements but also to give increased range, at a period when direct air support was less highly developed than later on in the campaign. By this stage of the campaign the Germans had demonstrated the value of their mobile guns, which had been successfully employed to check the advance from the toe of Italy and at Salerno, and also were employing large numbers of mortars and *nebelwerfers* in their main defensive positions. These latter proved so effective that at the crossing of the lower Garigliano Allied medium and heavy guns were used to neutralize the German close support weapons, including machine-gun emplacements, before turning to their counter-battery tasks. Meanwhile the Germans were making great efforts to increase the number and effectiveness of their own artillery and in the Gothic Line most of the Allied casualties were caused by enemy shell fire. In both winter campaigns the effectiveness of the Allied strength in tanks and aircraft was seriously limited by the weather and increasing reliance was placed on the artillery. Unfortunately both periods were also marked by a shortage of gun ammunition which, as has already been shown, became acute in the latter stages of the battle for the Gothic Line. In the final offensive of 1945 the Allied artillery outnumbered that of the Germans by nearly two to one in field and medium guns and over five to one in heavy guns. Fortunately, sufficient ammunition had been accumulated for this superiority to be fully exploited. During the progress of the campaign, co-operation between the air force and the artillery became highly developed, not only in techniques for artillery reconnaissance and spotting by aircraft, but in the linking of aerial bombardment with the artillery barrage, as at the crossing of the River Senio. This co-operation became highly sophisticated and had notable success, a simple example being the technique developed for fighter-bombers attacking German battery positions while the artillery neutralized the German flak defences. In set-piece co-ordinated attacks, such as at the Sangro and at the opening of the DIADEM offensive, the Allied artillery so dominated the battlefield that infantry casualties during the assault phase were greatly reduced, while at Anzio they demonstrated how concentrated defensive fire could erode the most determined counter-attacks the Germans were capable of mounting.

The administration of the Allied forces in the early stages of the campaign involved a number of headquarters; Allied Force Headquarters in Algiers; General Headquarters Middle East Forces in Cairo, and Headquarters 15 Army Group which subsequently moved to Sicily and on to Italy. 15 Army Group, however, did not perform the full administrative function of a Force Headquarters, as Eighth Army was maintained by a special headquarters known as 'Fortbase', which also provided an advanced base both in Sicily and in southern Italy. In accordance with the normal American system, the Services of Supply North African Theatre of Operations continued to arrange for the supply of the American forces as they had done throughout the North

African campaign. Lack of co-ordination in the overall administrative plan for the maintenance of the troops advancing into Italy, on the heels of the German withdrawal from Sicily, led to many difficulties and the need for a great deal of improvization. Eighth Army in particular could only be supported on a hand-to-mouth basis. The inadequacy of such *ad hoc* arrangements was soon apparent and General Robertson was sent in late October 1943 to establish an advanced administrative echelon of Allied Force Headquarters to support 15 Army Group and the Mediterranean Allied Air Forces. By the end of March 1944 the base organizations and lines of communication in Italy were functioning smoothly. General Wilson had meanwhile taken over from Eisenhower with the additional responsibility for areas formerly under General Headquarters Middle East and General Robertson's administrative headquarters was married up with Headquarters 15 Army Group, which now became Headquarters Allied Army in Italy. Later in July 1944 Allied Force Headquarters moved to Italy and assumed executive administrative control, so that Alexander's headquarters could concentrate on the operations in northern Italy. This arrangement greatly facilitated the administrative co-ordination between the two armies that in the early stages of the campaign had been far from satisfactory.

The administration of the occupied enemy territories in Sicily and Italy posed a completely new problem to the Americans and it was 'the first British operation involving the occupation of any but Colonial enemy territories'. The precedents established would obviously 'set the pattern for later operations in Europe'.[10] Well in advance of the Sicily landings Eisenhower set up a completely integrated Anglo-American organization known as Allied Military Government of Occupied Territories. Officers and men were provided on a fifty-fifty basis by the Americans and British. By June 1943, 440 officers and 460 other ranks had been recruited and formed into small teams, ready to move in behind the invading forces. This establishment was increased after the decision to advance to the mainland was taken and the combined requirements for Allied Military Government officers and for the Control Commission was raised to nearly 1,500 officers to cover Italy south of the Po valley. This proved an under-estimate as by the end of the campaign 1,400 officers were employed on the Control Commission alone. After the Italian surrender King Victor Emmanuel and Marshal Badoglio fled to Brindisi where they were joined by an Allied Military Mission flown in from Algiers. The civil administration of the four provinces, known as 'King's Italy', in the heel of the country being under the new Italian Government, it was decided that so long as the Allied Forces obtained all the facilities and assistance they required these areas should continue to be administered by the Italians under the direction of the Allied Control Commission. This pattern was gradually extended to Sicily and the remainder of the country, except for the operational zones and enclaves around the vital ports and supply centres of Naples and the Pisa–Leghorn areas. These latter remained under Allied Military Government control until December 1945. After February 1944 the administration of Sicily and southern Italy was gradually handed back to the Italians and by the end of October 1944 when the Allies were fighting in the Apennines and Romagna the whole of Italy south of a line Teramo–Rieti and Viterbo, except for the Naples enclave, was being administered by the Italian Government under the Control Commission.

The most pressing task of Military Government had been found to be the feeding of the civilian population, particularly in cities such as Naples and the industrial area of northern Tuscany. In both cases a serious emergency arose which required the dispatch of supplies, regardless of the operational situation, to save the population from starvation and the ravages of disease. In the final phase of the campaign careful plans were made to deal with similar problems in the heavily populated industrial areas of northern Italy, but due to the sudden ending of the campaign a shortage of transport became the key factor. The most urgent task of Allied Military Government on the conclusion of hostilities, however, became the maintenance of public safety and the disarming of the partisans. All neo-Fascist forces and the Black Brigades were treated as prisoners of war. The 'Popular' Tribunals formed for the punishing of Fascists and collaborators were difficult to eliminate and illegal executions continued in secret for some time. The setting up by Allied Military Government of Special Courts of Assize did much to prevent outbreaks of popular vengeance. Throughout the whole campaign the administration of justice by the Allied Military Government Courts was in several respects a notable and possibly unique achievement. No less than 150,000 cases were tried and 'from the point of view of the general public perhaps the most impressive feature was the procedure of permitting defence by enemy lawyers in a court-martial by an occupying force'.[11] The overall achievements of Allied Military Government were impressive. The 'completely integrated' organization avoided national zones of occupation and succeeded in maintaining law and order behind the fighting front, in preventing the action of civilians from endangering or impeding the operations of the armed forces, and in ensuring that [except on two occasions connected with food shortages] neither the resources nor the attention of military commanders were distracted by the necessity of attending to problems caused by civilian disease or unrest.[12]

The Allied campaign on the mainland of Italy was fought under conditions of restraint and frustration that have given rise to arguments as to its conception, strategy and importance. The capture of Sicily opened the Mediterranean at a critical stage in the battle of the Atlantic, the invasion of the mainland achieved the immediate purpose of holding down German divisions from employment elsewhere, seized airfields from which the strategic bombers could attack southern Germany and increased the Allied control of the Mediterranean. At this point, however, decisions taken by the Western Powers and by Hitler determined the strategic pattern for the remainder of the campaign. At the QUADRANT Conference in late August 1943, OVERLORD became the 'primary' effort against the Axis in Europe. The 'diversionary' landing in the Toulon–Marseilles area, in conjunction with OVERLORD, came on the drawing board, and operations in the Balkans were limited to supplying the partisans and to minor Commando raids. The role of the Allies in Italy, after the capture of the airfields at Foggia and around Naples and the islands of Sardinia and Corsica, was defined as 'unremitting pressure on the Germans in the north'. The implication is clear; a quick advance to Rome and beyond was expected and the Allies would then force the Germans to deploy troops to protect the northern industrial areas and the obvious exits to the north-east, while the Allies prepared to launch the 'diversionary' attack against southern France. The campaign during this latter stage would be subordinated to the requirements of OVERLORD. Hitler, however, made a different appreciation, contrary indeed to the current plans of the OKW. The day before the Salerno landing took place, Goebbels noted 'the most urgent problem is to get Tenth Army and the Luftwaffe out of southern Italy' and two days later he wrote in his diary,

naturally we shall not be able to hold southern Italy. We must withdraw northwards beyond Rome. We shall now establish ourselves on the defence line that the Fuehrer has always envisaged, namely the line of the Apennine mountains . . . the aim of our military operations must be to free a number of divisions for the Balkans. Without a doubt the spearhead of the Anglo-American invasion will be pointed in that direction in the immediate future.

Orders from the OKW for the occupation 'of the shortest possible front on the Apennines' were already going out and on 25 September Hitler had agreed to the appointment of Rommel to take command of this sector with twenty-one divisions. What then made Hitler change his mind and decide to make a stand south of Rome contrary to the advice of all his military commanders except Kesselring? The Italian surrender, combined with growing unrest and partisan activities, focused his attention on the Balkans. There were now insufficient German troops to hold both the long coastline and the interior of this enormous area. Hitler's staff tried to insist that 'the defence of the Albanian–Montenegrin–Dalmatian coastline must be a basis for all plans in the area'[13] and the theatre commander considered Greece and the islands only as 'an outpost'. Both strongly recommended the flank should be held on a line east and west through Salonika. Hitler, however, spoke continually of the vital Balkan mineral resources and of the Rumanian oil supplies and the need to maintain a threat to keep Turkey out of the war. Hitler and the OKW were convinced that the Allies would next strike in the

Balkans and Admiral Dönitz's appreciation that they would use southern Italy as a springboard had electrifying results. Brushing to one side all advice to abandon the island outposts and concentrate on a shorter line, more appropriate to the strength of his forces, Hitler made a snap decision, 'not merely to hold "the entire south-eastern area" but to continue to oppose the enemy in southern Italy'.[14] This obsession over the Balkans and the campaign in Italy, now firmly linked in Hitler's mind, continued to the end of the war. Aided by Jodl, he supervised every detail of the operations in Italy and the Western Front was milked to furnish reinforcements for that theatre. General Warlimont comments:

Hitler's Mediterranean strategy threw a far greater strain upon the German war potential than the military situation justified and no long-term compensating economies were made in other theatres. . . . Hitler's large scale demands for the Mediterranean meant that all possibilities of further reinforcements had been exhausted and the plan for the construction of an 'East Wall', which Zeitler had at last managed to get through after much effort, were overtaken by the increasingly rapid advance of the Red Army.[15]

At the end of July 1944, when the Allied armies were closing on the Arno and the defence of the Apennine position was given top priority, Hitler ordered the construction of positions in considerable depth to protect his southern flank and, in particular, to guard against any penetration into Austria through the Udine basin. These included the 'cross line' on the Adige and Piave and the continuation of the 'Alpine defences' eastwards on the southern slopes of the Julian Alps through Trieste to the Gulf of Fiume.[16] Six weeks later, when the battle for the Gothic Line was at its height, the construction of a further rearward position against attack from the Adriatic coast was ordered. This was a continuation of the 'Alpine' line from Colmein (north-east of Udine) to the River Sava near Ljubljana, then eastwards on the line of the river, before swinging up to Varazdin on the River Drava. Six days later, similar orders were issued for the fortification of Slovakia against the impending Russian advance in the east, which soon was to force the German withdrawal from Greece and Albania.[17] Hitler's Mediterranean policy, as regards the holding of the Balkans, had collapsed but to the last he ordered 'fanatical resistance' in Italy. To Hitler, the Allied campaign in Italy had meant a continued threat to the Balkans and an increasing threat to the southern frontiers of the Reich, resulting from a thrust either through Istria or the Udine basin.

As we have seen, Alexander was forced to fight the campaign in Italy with a minimum of troops and resources compatible with his task of holding down the maximum number of German divisions. The Allied success was highlighted by the fact that, except for the brief period of DIADEM in the summer of 1944, the Germans were always in greater strength on the ground. Major-General Jackson gives the following comments:

At the critical points of the campaign the relative divisional strengths were:

	Allied	German
Advance to the Volturno	19	19
Autumn battles of the Bernhardt Line	11	18
Winter battles of the Gustav Line	21	23
DIADEM offensive	25	24
Fall of Rome and Normandy landings	25	26
Autumn battles of the Gothic Line	20	26
Final offensive	17	21

At the moment when Eisenhower's landings began in Normandy, the number of German divisions drawn into Italy reached the peak figure of 26 divisions and was held at that figure throughout the summer months of 1944 when stalemate could so easily have engulfed the Allied main effort in North-West Europe.[18]

Field Marshal Alexander has underlined the salient factors. In the face of the difficulties of the terrain and most determined German resistance, the Allies were always the attackers and during the critical period before OVERLORD 'drew off to that remote quarter forces that might have turned the scale in France', while during the Normandy battle the Germans 'found themselves forced to divert eight divisions to this secondary theatre'. This was not, however, the complete picture as Alexander continues:

at that time when the value of our strategic contribution was at its greatest, fifty-five German divisions were tied down in the Mediterranean by the threat, actual or potential, presented by our armies in Italy. The record of the comparative casualties tells us the same story. On the German side they amounted to 536,000. Allied casualties were 312,000.[19]

In any account of the campaign it is this wider view that must predominate.

Hitler's Mediterranean policy stemmed from a real fear of an Allied landing in the Balkans, even before the Allies advanced to the Italian main-land, and after the war General Westphal summed up the effect of the Italian Campaign as follows. The strategic bombing of southern Germany and south-east Europe 'had a direct effect on the course of the war' and the tying down of forces in Italy, Yugoslavia and Greece (estimated at a fifth of Germany's total ground forces) 'made a large contribution to the final decision'.[20] Kesselring rather naturally takes a more parochial view, being concerned, it seems, with justifying his conduct of the campaign, although the main decisions were invariably made by Hitler. Firstly, he saw a with-drawal to the line of the Alps as giving 'the enemy untrammelled freedom of movement in the direction of France and the Balkans, having meant sacrificing an indispensable deep battle zone and unleashing the air war on the whole of southern Germany and Austria'. Early withdrawal to the Apennines he suggests, 'would not have resulted in any saving of men and materials, nor have appreciably lessened the danger of sea or air borne landings or the extension of the air war'. He concluded that the battle for Italy, based of course on his 'forward' policy, was not only 'justified but even imperative' and assessed the value of the campaign in terms of his own successes in holding down Allied forces that 'might have powerfully influenced events in the east or in the west adversely for Germany, and the sparing of southern Germany from 'the sufferings of war in every aspect, the effect of which in terms of our capacity to resist was immeasurable'.[21]

General Clark has written, 'in the Italian Campaign we had demonstrated how a polyglot army could be welded into a team of allies with the strength and unity and determination to prevail over formidable odds'.[22] It should equally be acknowledged, however, that the lengthening of the odds was the result of a deliberate policy of employing minimum forces to achieve a calculated result and that the role of fighting battles of containment and attrition is both unenviable and frustrating. The role of pacemaker, in a long and gruelling struggle to draw off and wear down one's opponents and create the conditions for a breakthrough by the rest of the team, brings no glittering prize but only the knowledge of having played a vital part in the final victory. This account of the campaign attempts to set the political and strategic factors side by side within the frame of global war, but above all it is the story of the men of many nations who crossed the oceans to strike at Hitler's southern frontiers and, in spite of the courage and the determination of the Germans and the great mountain barriers and the rivers in the plains below, claimed their own and quite conclusive final victory in the valley of the Po.

Appendix A

CODE NAMES

ACCOLADE   Operations in the Aegean

ACHSE   German plans for dealing with the collapse of Italy

ANVIL   Allied landing in the south of France, August 1944 – later named DRAGOON

AVALANCHE   Allied landing at Salerno, September 1943

BAYTOWN   Allied crossing of the Straits of Messina, September 1943

BUCCANEER   Proposed Allied operations against the Andaman Islands

DIADEM   Allied spring offensive, May 1944

DRAGOON   Landing by Seventh Army in the south of France, August 1944 – originally called ANVIL

EUREKA   Conference at Teheran, November 1943

GOOSEBERRY   Artificial breakwater used for MULBERRY harbours and offshore anchorages

HUSKY   Invasion of Sicily, July 1943

MULBERRY   Artificial harbour used for the Normandy landings

OCTAGON   Second Quebec Conference, September 1944

OLIVE   Eighth Army's assault on the Gothic Line, August and September 1944

OVERLORD   Invasion of Normandy, June 1944

PHOENIX   Concrete caisson for MULBERRY breakwaters

POINTBLANK   The Combined Bomber Offensive against Germany 1943–5

QUADRANT   First Quebec Conference, August 1943

RICHARD   German anti-invasion plans covering Anzio area

SEXTANT   Conference at Cairo, November and December 1943

SHINGLE   Allied landing at Anzio, January 1944

STRANGLE   Allied air attacks on communications prior to DIADEM in spring of 1944

SUNRISE   Original code-name for the secret negotiations for the German surrender in Italy

SYMBOL   Conference at Casablanca, January 1943

TORCH   Allied invasion of French North Africa, November 1944

TRIDENT   Third Washington Conference, May 1943

CHIEFS OF STAFF COMMITTEES

Chiefs of Staff   The British Chiefs of Staff, responsible to the Prime Minister, as Minister of Defence, and the War Cabinet.

Joint Chiefs of Staff — The American Chiefs of Staff, responsible to the President, who was also Commander-in-Chief of the United States Armed Forces.

Combined Chiefs of Staff — A committee consisting of both the British and American Chiefs of Staff. As meetings could only take place occasionally, a special headquarters was set up in Washington where the British were represented by a Joint Staff Mission under Field Marshal Sir John Dill and later by Field Marshal Sir Henry Maitland Wilson.

ABBREVIATIONS

CBO — Combined Bomber Offensive. The strategic bombing offensive against Germany (1943–5) by the Royal Air Force and United States Army Air Force (later called POINTBLANK)

CIGS — Chief of the Imperial General Staff

DUKW — American amphibious truck

FEC — French Expeditionary Corps (also CEF)

LSI — Landing ship infantry. For other landing ships and craft see Appendix F

OKW — German Supreme Command (Ober Kommando der Wehrmacht)

Appendix B

DIVISIONAL ORGANIZATIONS

British Infantry Divisions consisted of Divisional Headquarters; three Brigades, each of three Infantry Battalions; a Reconnaissance Regiment and a Machine-Gun Battalion. The Divisional Artillery was three Field Regiments (72×25 pr gun/hows), an Anti-Tank Regiment (32×17 pr and 16×6 pr anti-tank guns) and a Light Anti-Aircraft Regiment. Engineer, Signal, Medical, Supply and other units make up a total strength of 18,347 all ranks and 4,330 vehicles. Each Infantry Battalion and the Reconnaissance Regiment included an Anti-Tank Platoon equipped with 6 pr Anti-Tank guns of which there were 78 in the Division. The Divisional Artillery, Royal Engineers, etc., were so organized that they could be centrally controlled or sub-allotted under command of the Brigades.

American Infantry Divisions were organized into three Regiments, each of three Infantry Battalions. Each Battalion included a heavy weapons company with anti-tank guns and heavy machine-guns, the latter could also be used in an anti-aircraft role. The Divisional Artillery consisted of three Medium Batteries (12×155 mm hows) and three Light Artillery Regiments (54×105 mm gun/hows).

Auxiliary units included a Reconnaissance Troop, an Engineer Battalion, Signals Company, etc., on about the same scale as the British Infantry Division, except that supplies were centrally controlled and the Division itself had no supply echelons within its own establishment. The divisional organization facilitated the grouping of Artillery and other units under command of the Infantry Regiments (which corresponded to British Infantry Brigades) to form Regimental Combat Teams. At full strength the Division had 14,037 all ranks and 2,113 vehicles. The lesser number of vehicles, compared with the British Infantry Division was owing to the centralized supply system mentioned above.

British Armoured Divisions contained one Armoured Brigade (of three Armoured Regiments) and a Motor Battalion (motorized infantry), an Armoured Reconnaissance Regiment, an Infantry Brigade and an Independent Machine-Gun Company.

The Divisional Artillery consisted of two Field Regiments (one towed, one self-propelled, total 48×25 prs) an Anti-Tank Regiment, (48×17 prs) and an Anti-Aircraft Regiment (40 mm eqpt).

RE, R. Signals, RAMC, RASC, RAOC and REME units made up a war establishment of 14,964 all ranks. In May 1944 the tank strength was raised from 244 tanks (plus 34 AA tanks) to 310 tanks (plus 8 for Artillery Observation and 25 AA tanks). Each Armoured Regiment had 55 cruiser tanks and 11 light tanks. The Armoured Reconnaissance Regiment had 40 cruiser tanks and 30 light tanks, exclusive of Command and AA tanks in each case. In addition the Division had

390 tracked vehicles, 490 scout and other cars and over 2,000 lorries and trucks. The total number of vehicles (incl 853 motor cycles) was 4,267.

In 1944 *Independent Armoured Brigades* contained three Armoured Regiments, each of about 690 all ranks and 78 tanks. Some Armoured Brigades included a Motor Battalion.

Tank Brigades which were designed for co-operation with Infantry also contained 240 tanks organized in three battalions.

1 *American Armoured Division* consisted, in April 1945, of Divisional Headquarters and two Combat Command Headquarters, 1, 4 and 13 Tank Battalions; 6, 11 and 14 Armoured Infantry Battalions; 27, 68, 91 Armoured Field Artillery Battalions (54×105 mm self-propelled hows) and 81 Cavalry Reconnaissance Squadron. Together with Signal, Engineer, Medical and Ordnance units, the effective strength was 11,304 all ranks. Standard equipment was 195 medium tanks, 77 light tanks and about 450 other tracked or half-tracked vehicles. The total of vehicles in the Division was about 2,650.

Mobile anti-tank guns from a Tank Destroyer Battalion, extra tank battalions, mine-clearing companies, etc., were added from Fifth Army, according to the requirements of a particular operation.

German Divisions. In general terms there were no set war establishments for the various types of German Divisions which fell into three main categories. Infantry Divisions, some of which were given the honorary title of Grenadier Division, mobile or Panzer Grenadier Divisions, and armoured or Panzer Divisions. Within each group establishments varied according to the theatre and type of operations for which the Division was raised. Schutzstaffel or SS units originally contained only selected members of the Nazi party and in spite of dilution, as to political or racial 'purity' continued to contain the most fanatical fighting troops right up to the end of the war.

German Infantry or Grenadier Divisions. Wolf Keilig in *Das Deutsche Herr 1939–45* gives an establishment for an 'average' Infantry Division in 1944. This consisted of Divisional Headquarters, three Grenadier Regiments each of two Infantry Battalions, a Fusilier or Reconnaissance Battalion and an Anti-Tank unit (9 to $12 \times$ 75 mm towed or self-propelled guns). The Divisional Artillery consisted of an Artillery Regiment (about 30×105 mm gun/hows and 9×150 mm hows). Signal and Engineer Battalions and Divisional Services made up a strength of 12,772 all ranks, which included a reinforcement unit. The significant difference between German and Allied Infantry Divisions was the inclusion, within the German Infantry Regiment, of 6×75 mm and 2×150 mm Infantry guns, plus 3×75 mm mobile anti-tank guns, and within the Infantry Battalion of a Heavy Support Company, containing both medium and heavy machine-guns and heavy mortars. German Infantry Regiments and Battalions were thus largely self-contained as regards close support weapons. This organization gave great flexibility and it was common practice for battle groups to be formed, under a named Commander with Infantry, Tank and Artillery units allocated according to the requirements of a particular situation. These 'Groups' remained in being for long periods.

The types of transport and degree of mechanization of the German Infantry Division varied considerably. One authorized scale of transport, quoted by Keilig, for an Infantry Division in 1944, is as follows, and is set alongside the transport establishment of a British Infantry Division.

	German Infantry Division (at strength 12,772)	British Infantry Division (at strength 18,347)
Motor Cycles	168	983
Bicycles	678	—
Motor Cars	136 (mostly with cross-country performance)	558 (incl Armoured and Recce cars)
Tracked Vehicles	60 (about) (plus 10 Assault guns)	205
Small Tracked Vehicles (incl Infantry Carriers)	—	595
Buses	9	—
Lorries and Trucks	370	1,937
Trailers	40	226
Horse Drawn Vehicles	1,375	—
Riding Horses	802	—
Draught Horses	3,177 (incl 1,767 for Artillery Regt)	—

German Parachute Divisions were the strongest and best equipped Infantry Divisions in the German Army. With an authorized strength of 16,000 carefully selected and highly trained officers and men, and a larger allocation of machine-guns, they were particularly suited for defensive operations. Only a proportion of the men were trained as parachutists.

Panzer Grenadier Division. This was a motorized Division with two motorized (Panzer Grenadier) Infantry Regiments, an Armoured Reconnaissance Unit and/or a Tank Battalion, together with a number of assault guns, an Artillery Regiment (30 × 105 mm gun/hows, 18 × 150 mm hows and 6 × 150 mm rocket projectors) and an Anti-Tank Regiment (43 × 75 mm guns and 12 dual-purpose light AA/Anti-tank guns). Signal, Engineer and Services units made up a strength of about 14,000 all ranks with up to about 3,500 vehicles of all types.

During 1944, 105 and 150 mm assault guns were introduced to replace many of the 75 mm long tank guns previously issued. The normal equipment of a Panzer Grenadier Division included a number of heavy mortars, *nebelwerfers* and flame-throwers.

Panzer Division. This contained a Panzer Regiment, two Panzer Grenadier Regiments, an Armoured Reconnaissance Unit, an Armoured Artillery Regiment and an Anti-Tank Battalion, plus Signals, Engineers, etc. The Tank Regiment usually consisted of two Tank Battalions (Panther or Panzer IV tanks) with a tank strength of about 200 tanks, but Tiger tanks and Assault guns were often added. In addition to the armament of the tanks the number of guns in the Division was about the same as in a Panzer Grenadier Division except that Panzer Divisions usually had an additional 30 × 88 mm dual-purpose guns. At full strength a Panzer Division could have something over 14,000 all ranks and 4,000 vehicles of all types.

In outline the above examples of German Divisions are based on details given by

Keilig for 44 (Hoch und Deutschmeister) Infantry Division, 3 Panzer Grenadier Division and 16 Panzer Division. It must be stressed, however, that the scales of equipment, etc., were those authorized but not necessarily implemented.

INFANTRY WEAPONS

In this short survey it has not been possible to give details of unit organizations and equipment. A note, however, is appropriate on infantry weapons. An Infantry Battalion, in any Army of this period, depended for its main fire effect on the light machine-gun, the main weapon of every infantry section. The British used the Bren Light Machine-Gun (·303 in calibre), the Germans the MG34 machine-gun (·31 in) and the Americans a combination of the ·30 Light Machine-Gun and the ·30 Automatic Rifle.

At platoon level a 2-in (50 mm) mortar was common to the British and Germans, while the Americans used a comparable, but slightly larger, 60 mm mortar. At battalion level an establishment of 6 × 3-in (or equivalent calibre) mortars was common to all three Armies.

As regards infantry anti-tank weapons, as distinct from the anti-tank guns already mentioned, the British Projectile Infantry Anti-Tank (PIAT) was issued on a wide scale, 436 in an Infantry Division and 302 in an Armoured Division, while the American Anti-Tank Rocket Launcher (the Bazooka) was issued on the more lavish scale of 558 to a US Infantry Division and 607 to the Armoured Division. The Germans used both Anti-Tank rifles and recoil-less grenade dischargers and were quick to copy the Bazooka in their 88 mm *Raketen Panzerbüchse* 43, often known as the *Ofenrohr* or 'stovepipe', which fired a hollow charge rocket. The inclusion of heavy machine-guns and heavy mortars in both the American and German Infantry Battalions has already been mentioned. In British Infantry Divisions these were provided on a lesser scale by the Vickers machine-guns and 4·2-in mortars of the Machine-Gun Battalions.

Appendix C

Name	Weight (tons)	Gun
Allies		
Churchill VII (introduced 1944)	40	75 mm (a)
Sherman US–M4A 1	30	75 mm
Sherman US–M4A 3—76 mm	32	76 mm (b)
German		
Panzer IV	22	75 mm
Panther	44·8	75 mm
Tiger I	56	88 mm
Tiger II (introduced 1944)	68·7	88 mm

Notes

(a) Prior to 1944 an earlier version of the Churchill was in use—38·5 ton and 6 pr gun.

(b) Some Sherman tanks were re-armed with the British 17 pr gun.

The British Churchill tanks were used in an infantry support role. Both British and American Armoured Divisions were equipped with American Sherman tanks. The Sherman 75 mm gun, however, could not penetrate the frontal armour of either the German Panther or Tiger tank at any range. It was only towards the end of the campaign that the 'up-gunned' Shermans with 76 mm guns achieved any degree of parity with the Panther or Tiger tanks and then only at a range of 600 yards or less. At longer distances the German tanks continued to outrange and dominate the Sherman, but in close country and amongst the vineyards and orchards of the Romagna and the Po valley this advantage was largely offset. For further details see Orgill, *The Gothic Line*, Howe, *The Battle History of 1st Armoured Division*, and von Senger, *Die Kampfpanzer von 1916–1966*.

Appendix D

Outline organization of the Allied Air Forces
July 1943 and March 1945

OUTLINE ORGANIZATION MEDITERRANEAN AIR COMMAND JULY 1943

Air Chief Marshal Sir Arthur Tedder

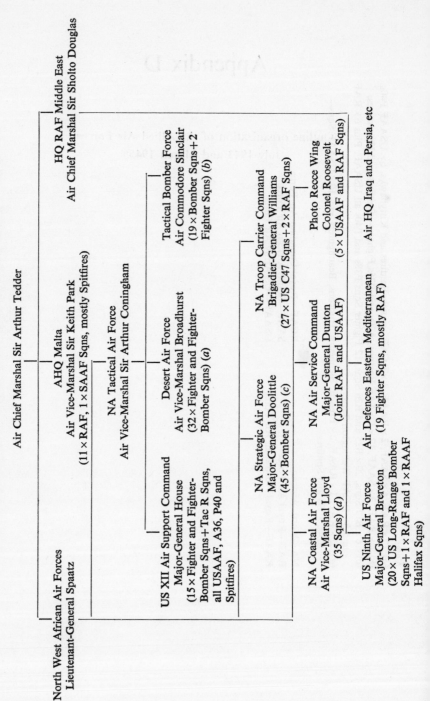

- North West African Air Forces
  Lieutenant-General Spaatz

- HQ RAF Middle East
  Air Chief Marshal Sir Sholto Douglas

AHQ Malta
Air Vice-Marshal Sir Keith Park
(11 × RAF, 1 × SAAF Sqns, mostly Spitfires)

NA Tactical Air Force
Air Vice-Marshal Sir Arthur Coningham

Desert Air Force
Air Vice-Marshal Broadhurst
(32 × Fighter and Fighter-Bomber Sqns) (a)

Tactical Bomber Force
Air Commodore Sinclair
(19 × Bomber Sqns + 2 Fighter Sqns) (b)

NA Troop Carrier Command
Brigadier-General Williams
(27 × US C47 Sqns + 2 × RAF Sqns)

Photo Recce Wing
Colonel Roosevelt
(5 × USAAF and RAF Sqns)

US XII Air Support Command
Major-General House
(15 × Fighter and Fighter-Bomber Sqns + Tac R Sqns, all USAAF, A36, P40 and Spitfires)

NA Strategic Air Force
Major-General Doolittle
(45 × Bomber Sqns) (c)

NA Air Service Command
Major-General Dunton
(Joint RAF and USAAF)

Air Defences Eastern Mediterranean
(19 Fighter Sqns, mostly RAF)

Air HQ Iraq and Persia, etc

NA Coastal Air Force
Air Vice-Marshal Lloyd
(35 Sqns) (d)

US Ninth Air Force
Major-General Brereton
(20 × US Long-Range Bomber Sqns + 1 × RAF and 1 × RAAF Halifax Sqns)

Notes:

(a) 17 × RAF, 6 × SAAF, 2 × RAAF, 1 × RCAF—mostly Spitfires and Kittyhawks. 6 × USAAF P40s.

(b) 4 × RAF, 3 × SAAF, 12 × USAAF Bostons, A30s and B25s Fighters—Spitfires and Hurricanes.

(c) 16 × B17 Sqns, 20 × B25 and B26 Sqns, 12 Fighter Sqns P38s and P40s all USAAF. Plus 6 × RAF and 3 × RCAF Wellington Sqns.

(d) 22 × RAF, 1 × RAAF, 2 × French, Blenheims, Hudsons, Beaufighters, etc. 10 × USAAF Sqns—B24s, P39s and Spitfires.

NA—North African
RAF—Royal Air Force
RAAF—Royal Australian Air Force

RCAF—Royal Canadian Air Force
SAAF—South African Air Force
USAAF—US Army Air Force

OUTLINE ORGANIZATION OF MEDITERRANEAN ALLIED AIR FORCES MARCH 1945

Air Chief Marshal Sir Guy Garrod

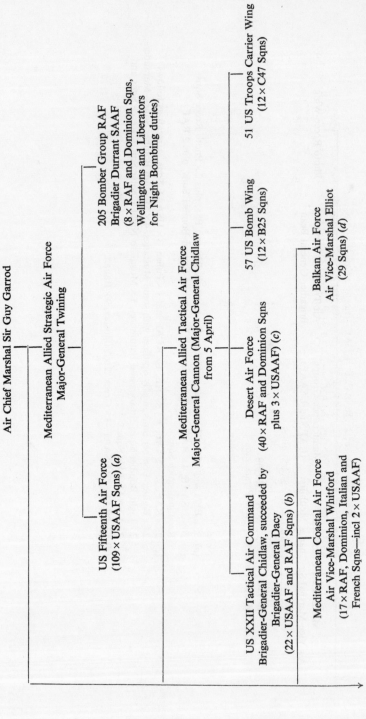

Mediterranean Allied Strategic Air Force
Major-General Twining

US Fifteenth Air Force
(109 × USAAF Sqns) (a)

205 Bomber Group RAF
Brigadier Durrant SAAF
(8 × RAF and Dominion Sqns,
Wellingtons and Liberators
for Night Bombing duties)

Mediterranean Allied Tactical Air Force
Major-General Cannon (Major-General Chidlaw
from 5 April)

Desert Air Force
(40 × RAF and Dominion Sqns
plus 3 × USAAF) (c)

57 US Bomb Wing
(12 × B25 Sqns)

51 US Troops Carrier Wing
(12 × C47 Sqns)

US XXII Tactical Air Command
Brigadier-General Chidlaw, succeeded by
Brigadier-General Dacy
(22 × USAAF and RAF Sqns) (b)

Mediterranean Coastal Air Force
Air Vice-Marshal Whitford
(17 × RAF, Dominion, Italian and
French Sqns—incl 2 × USAAF)

Balkan Air Force
Air Vice-Marshal Elliot
(29 Sqns) (d)

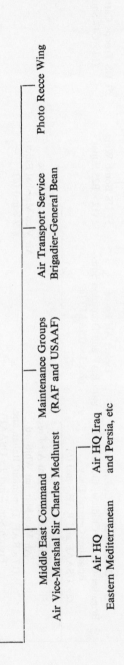

Middle East Command
Air Vice-Marshal Sir Charles Medhurst

Air HQ Eastern Mediterranean

Air HQ Iraq and Persia, etc

Maintenance Groups (RAF and USAAF)

Air Transport Service Brigadier-General Bean

Photo Recce Wing

Notes:

(a) 85 × B17s and B24s, 22 long-range Fighter Sqns, mostly P38 and P51, plus 2 × Photo Recce Sqns.

(b) 16 × USAAF, 4 × RAF and Dominion, all Fighter and Fighter-Bomber Sqns, plus 2 RAF Reconnaissance Sqns.

(c) 23 × RAF, 12 × SAAF, 3 × RAAF, 1 × RCAF and 1 × Polish, 3 × USAAF Sqns. Aircraft as follows: 24 × Fighter-Bomber Sqns mostly Spitfires with some Mustangs. 4 × Medium Bomber Sqns—Marauders. 7 × Light Bomber Sqns, Bostons and Baltimores, 1 × Mosquito Night Fighter Sqn, 4 Recce Sqns and 3 × USAAF P47s Sqns.

(d) 13 × RAF, 2 × USAAF, 3 × Greek, 2 × Yugoslav, 9 × Italian.

405

Appendix E

PRINCIPAL AIRCRAFT USED IN THE ITALIAN THEATRE OF OPERATIONS

RAF, DOMINION AND USAAF

	Maximum Speed mph	Service Ceiling feet	Range and Bomb Load miles	lb	Armament
Bombers (four-engined)					
Fortress, B17	295 at 25,000	35,000	1,100	6,000	13 × ·50 in or 12·7 mm
Liberator, B24	270 at 20,000	27,000	2,290 or 990	4,000 12,800	10 × ·50 in
Bombers (twin-engined)					
Wellington	255 at 20,000	18,250	1,855 or 1,325	1,500 4,500	6 × ·303 in
Boston, A20	320 at 11,000	24,500	1,570 or 710	2,000 4,000	5 × ·50 in
Baltimore, A30	302 at 11,000	22,000	950	2,000	10 × ·30 in 4 × ·303 in
Mitchell, B25	292 at 15,000	20,000	1,635 or 950	4,000 6,000	6 × ·50 in
Marauder, B26	305 at 15,000	28,000	1,200	4,000	11 × ·50 in

	Maximum Speed mph feet	Service Ceiling feet	Range and Bomb Load miles / lb	Armament
Fighter and Fighter-Bomber (single-engined)				
Hurricane	330 at 18,000	32,500	420 — 2×250 (B) or 2×500 (B)	2×40 mm, 2×·303 in
Spitfire	400 at 11,000	43,000	434 — 2×250 (B) or 1×500 (B)	2×20 mm, 4×·303 in or 2×·50 in or 4×20 mm
Airacobra, P39	385 at 11,000	35,000	675 (with external tank) — 1×500 (B)	1×37 mm, 4×·50 in
Kittyhawk, P40	364 at 20,000	35,000	610 — 1,600 or 2×500 (B)	4 or 6×·50 in or ·303 in
Thunderbolt, P47	420 at 26,000	35,000	590 — 2×1,000 (B) plus 1×500 (B)	8×·50 in
Fighter and Fighter-Bomber (twin-engined)				
Lightning, P38	414 at 25,000	over 35,000	460 — 1,600	1×20 mm, 4×·50 in
Long-Range Fighter and Fighter-Bomber (twin-engined)				
Mosquito	380 at 13,000	33,000	1,270 — 4×250 (B) or 8×60 lb RP	4×20 mm, 4×·303 in
Beaufighter	320 at 10,000	19,000	1,400 — 1×1,650 or 2,127 (T) or 8×60 lb RP or 2×500 (B) and 2×250 (B)	4×20 mm

Long-Range Fighter and Fighter-Bomber
(single-engined)

Aircraft					
Mustang, A36 and P51	445 at 24,000	over 40,000	1,000	2 × 500 (B) or 10 × 5 in RP	4 × ·50 in or 4 × 20 mm
Coastal, etc Albacore (Fleet Air Arm) (single-engined, 2/3-seater Torpedo Bomber and Recce)	161 at 4,500	20,700	930	6 × 250 (B) or 4 × 500 (B) or 1 × 1,610 (T)	1 × ·300 in 2 × ·303 in
Hudson, A28, A29 (twin-engined, General Recce)	257 at 8,000	24,500	2,800	1,400 (bombs or depth charges)	7 × ·303 in
Transport Dakota, C47 (twin-engined General and Para Transport also Glider Tow)	229 at 7,500	23,200	1,500	—	—
Albemarle (twin-engined Bomber as Para Transport and Glider Tow)	250 at 10,500	—	1,350	—	2 × ·303 or ·50 in
Halifax (four-engined Bomber as Para Transport and Glider Tow)	270 at 10,500	—	3,000	—	2 × ·50 in

GERMAN

Bomber and Reconnaissance

	Maximum Speed mph feet	Service Ceiling feet	Range and Bomb Load miles	Range and Bomb Load lb	Armament
Junkers (JU) 87 Single-engined, two-seater Dive Bomber	255 at 13,500	18,500	720	2,200	4 × 7·9 mm
Junkers (JU) 88 Standard twin-engined general purpose aircraft as Bomber, Recce, Torpedo Bomber or Fighter	370 at 26,000	35,000	700	1,980	1 × 13 mm 1 × 7·9 mm
Heinkel (HE) 111 Twin-engined bomber, often used for convoy attacks and minelaying	240 at 14,000	26,000	1,510	2,200	7 × 7·9 mm **2 × 20 mm**
Heinkel (HE) 177 Four-engined Bomber	305 at 20,000	21,000	2,650	2,200	5 × 13 mm 4 × 20 mm
Dornier (DO) 217 Bomber/Transport (DO) 217E5 was specially equipped to carry radio-controlled glide bombs	305 at 18,000	21,500	1,170	4,400	4 × 7·9 mm 4 × 13 mm 1 × 15 mm

Fighter and Fighter-Bomber

	Speed	Ceiling (ft)	Range (miles)	Bomb load / weight	Armament
Junkers (JU) 88	295 at 17,500	27,000	1,900 with maximum fuel / 650 with maximum bomb load	4,400	7 × 7·9 mm 3 × 20 mm
Focke-Wulf (FW) 190	402 at 18,000	36,000	950	1,122	2 × 20 mm or 4 × 7·9 mm
Messerschmitt (ME) 109	400 at 22,000	39,750	350	1 × 550 (B)	2 × 7·9 or 13 mm 3 × 20 mm
Messerschmitt (ME) 110 2/3-seater twin-engined Day and Night Fighter and Fighter-Bomber	340 at 21,000	36,800	1,300 with maximum fuel	2 × 1,100 (B)	6 × 7·9 mm 4 × 20 mm 1 × 37 mm
Messerschmitt (ME) 210 2-seater twin-engined Fighter-Bomber	370 at 21,000	35,000	1,200	1 × 1,100 (B) or 2 × 550 (B)	2 × 20 mm 2 × 13 mm 2 × 7·9 mm

Transport

	Speed	Ceiling (ft)	Range (miles)	Bomb load / weight	Armament
Junkers (JU) 52 Three-engined general purpose transport aircraft	165	—	18,000	800	—	1 × 13 mm 2 × 7·9 mm

Note: (B) Indicates specified bombs   (T) Torpedo   RP—Rocket Projectile.

411

These tables are only intended to give general details for the principal aircraft employed in the campaign and do not attempt to take account of the variation in performance of different versions or 'marks' of the aircraft listed. The RAF name for an Allied aircraft is given first followed, where appropriate, by the USAAF designation.

The maximum speed is given for comparative purposes only, as this speed could only be maintained for very short periods. The figure given for range, i.e. the maximum distance the aircraft could fly in still air, assume that the sortie was at the 'most economical cruising speed', which could vary between 55 to 80 per cent of the 'maximum speed'.

In the planning of operations account must also be taken of weather conditions, tactical manoeuvring, navigational errors, etc. These factors reduced the range by about 25 per cent.

As regards fighter aircraft the figures quoted are based on the 'built-in' fuel capacity. While the fighter's range could be increased by using drop tanks, the performance of the aircraft was reduced, as indeed occurred when the aircraft was employed as a fighter-bomber and fitted with bombs, rocket projectiles or smoke canisters.

The tables are mainly based on Richards and Saunders, *Royal Air Force 1939–45* and *Jane's All the World's Aircraft*, both of which authorities give many additional details.

Appendix F

LANDING SHIPS AND CRAFT

The following notes give the characteristics of the main categories of landing ships and craft used by the Allies.

Landing Ships

Landing Ship Infantry – LSI. Often referred to by the Americans as combat loaders. These were passenger ships and cargo liners converted to carry troops. An average size was about 12,000 tons, although large liners often had to be used in the Mediterranean, owing to the shortage of smaller ships. The troops were landed by assault craft carried in the ships' davits in place of lifeboats.

Landing Ship Tank – LST. These specially constructed ocean-going ships of nearly 1,500 tons had a ramp door in the bow. They carried fifty tanks in the hold and on the upper deck, plus 150 soldiers. If the beach was fairly steep the tanks could land straight off the ramp, otherwise LCTs or Rhino ferries had to ferry the tanks ashore.

Major Landing Craft

Landing Craft Infantry (Large) – LCI (L). These craft of about 200 tons had a speed of fifteen knots. They were designed to carry 200 men in covered accommodation for periods of up to twenty-four hours. The troops landed from long ramps which were carried on the craft. The craft was too vulnerable to be used early in the assault.

Landing Craft Tank – LCT. This craft of 123 or 143 tons had a hinged ramp door and carried five tanks, or ten to twelve fully loaded vehicles, which were discharged straight on to the beach over the bow ramp.

Minor Landing Craft

Landing Craft Assault – LCA. An armoured craft of ten tons with silent engines and a low silhouette, carrying thirty-six men and their personal weapons who were landed over a bow ramp.

Landing Craft Vehicle and Personnel – LCVP. This was the American version of the LCA, being of the same size, somewhat faster but unarmoured. Either men or a small vehicle could be discharged over the bow ramp.

413

Support Craft

These were LCTs or other craft adapted to carry guns, mortars or rockets. For instance, a Landing Craft Tank (Rocket) carried 800–1,000 five-inch high-explosive rockets and a Landing Craft Support (Large) carried a tank gun in a turret, two machine-guns, two Oerlikon anti-aircraft guns and a mortar for firing smoke.

Rhino Ferry

This was a self-propelled raft constructed of steel pontoons and was invaluable for unloading LSTs in deep water.

Appendix G

Outline organization and dispositions of the
opposing Armies, 9 April 1945

OUTLINE ORGANIZATION AND DISPOSITION OF THE OPPOSING ARMIES 9 APRIL 1945
FIFTEENTH ARMY GROUP

Corps and Sectors	Infantry Divisions and additional Brigades or equivalent	Armoured Divisions and Brigades
Eighth Army		
5 Corps Adriatic to south of Lugo	56 Division (incl 24 Guards Brigade)	2 Commando Brigade and Garibaldi Brigade	9 Armoured Brigade
	8 Indian Division 2 New Zealand Division	21 Tank Brigade 4 NZ Armoured Brigade
	78 Division	Cremona Group*	2 Armoured Brigade
2 Polish Corps Astride Route 9	3 Carpathian Division	43 Lorried Gurkha Brigade	2 Polish Armoured Brigade
	5 Kressowa Division (each incl a newly formed Brigade)	7 Armoured Brigade
10 Corps Upper Senio to south of Imola		Jewish Brigade Friuli Group*	
13 Corps South of Imola to Mt Grande	10 Indian Division	Folgore Group*	

416

Army Reserve
Behind right flank
2 Parachute Brigade
6 Armoured Division

Fifth Army
II Corps
Mt Grande to Route 64
Legnano Group*
34 Division
88 Division
91 Division
6 South African
Armoured Division

IV Corps
Route 64 to east of
Bagni di Lucca
10 Mountain Division
1 Brazilian Division
Two RCTs from 92 Division (as flank protection
west of Mt Belvedere)
1 US Armoured Division

Under Army Command
Tyrrhenian coast area
92 Division
(incl 442 RCT Jap/American and 473 RCT—
formerly Task Force 45)

Army Reserve
Poretta area
85 Division

Total for both armies
Fourteen Infantry Divisions plus six Brigades or equivalent.
Three Armoured Divisions plus six Armoured or Tank Brigades.

* *Note.* The four Italian Combat Groups each had two Infantry Regiments (US organization).

ARMY GROUP C

Corps and Sectors	Infantry Divisions	Panzer or Panzer Grenadier Divisions
Tenth Army XCVII Corps N-E Italy and Fiume	118 Mountain Division 237 Infantry Division (Both these divisions were transferred to Army Group E when Eighth Army Offensive opened)	
LXXIV Panzer Corps Adriatic to north of Route 9	162 (Turkoman) Infantry Division (North of Lake Comacchio) 42 Jäger Division 362 Infantry Division 98 Infantry Division	
1 Parachute Corps Route 9 to Mt Grande	4 Parachute Division 278 Infantry Division 1 Parachute Division	26 Panzer Division
Army Reserve Area Venice–Treviso	155 Infantry Division (also Cossack Division near Venice)	29 Panzer Grenadier Division
Fourteenth Army XIV Panzer Corps Mt Grande to Route 64	305 Infantry Division 65 Infantry Division 8 Mountain Division (formerly 157) 94 Infantry Division	

418

LI Mountain Corps

334 Infantry Division
114 Jäger Division
232 Infantry Division
These three divisions were concentrated from west of
Montese to Vergate
'Italia' Infantry Division
148 Infantry Division

Holding remaining mountainous
area and coastal sector

Army Group Reserve
Near Modena

90 Panzer Grenadier Division

Corps Lombardy
Gulf of Genoa

San Marco Infantry Division
Battle Group Meinhold

LXXV Corps
Franco-Italian Frontier

34 Infantry Division
5 Mountain Division
Littoria Infantry Division
Monte Rosa Mountain Division

Total for main front
Sixteen Infantry Divisions and one Italian Division.
Three Panzer or Panzer Grenadier Divisions.
Committed on Frontiers, etc
Five Infantry Divisions and three Italian Divisions.

Alexander, Field Marshal Earl: The Allied Armies in Italy from 3 September 1943 to 12 December 1944 (London Gazette Supplement), 1950

Alexander, Field Marshal Earl: The Conquest of Sicily 10 July to 17 August 1943 (London Gazette Supplement), 1948

Alexander, Field Marshal Earl: Report by Supreme Commander, Mediterranean, to the Combined Chiefs of Staff on the Italian Campaign 12 December to 2 May 1945 (HMSO), 1951

Alexander, Field Marshal Earl: The Alexander Memoirs 1940-1945, Cassell, 1961

Aris, G.: The Fifth British Division 1939-1945, London, 1959

Bader, W. B.: Austria between East and West 1945-55, Stanford University Press, 1966

Badoglio, P.: Italy in the Second World War, O.U.P., 1948

Blake, Lieutenant-Colonel R. L. V. ff.: A History of the 17th/21st Lancers, 1922-1959, Macmillan, 1962

Blumenson, M.: Anzio: the Gamble that Failed, Weidenfeld and Nicolson, 1963

Bohmler, R.: Monte Cassino, Cassell, 1964

Bradley, General O. N.: A Soldier's Story, Eyre and Spottiswoode, 1951

Bryant, A.: The Turn of the Tide 1939-1943, Collins, 1957

Bryant, A.: Triumph in the West 1943-1946, Collins, 1959

Ballin, R. H.: History of the 27th Battalion ... Royal ... 1939-1945, printed by Besley, Exeter, 1958

Ballin, W. C.: The Great Globe Itself, Macmillan 19..

Churchill, W. S.: The Second World War, Vol V The Hinge of Fate, Vol VI Closing the Ring, Vol VI Triumph and Tragedy, Cassell, 1951 ...

Clark, General M.: Calculated Risk: His personal story of the war in North Africa and Italy, Harrap, 1951

Cody, J. F.: New Zealand Engineers in the Middle East (Official History of New Zealand in the Second World War), Wellington, 1961

Connell, C.: Monte Cassino, the Historic Battle, Elek, 1963

Craven, W. F., and Cate, J. L.: The Army Air Force in World War II, Vol 2 Europe: Torch to Pointblank August 1942 to December 1943, Vol 3 Europe: Argument to VE Day January 1944 to May 1945, University of Chicago Press, 1949 and 1951

Crew, F. A. E.: The Army Medical Services Campaigns, Vol III, Sicily, Italy, Greece, HMSO, 1959

Deakin, F. W.: The Brutal Friendship, Weidenfeld and Nicolson, 1962

Denneboom, I.: Italia ... P Rise of Metropolis, O.U.P., 1947

Dulles, A.: The Secret Surrender, Weidenfeld and Nicolson, 1967

Dearnford-Slater, Brigadier J.: Commando, Kimber, 1953

Bibliography

Alexander, Field Marshal Earl: The Allied Armies in Italy from 3 September 1943 to 12 December 1944 (London Gazette Supplement), 1950

Alexander, Field Marshal Earl: The Conquest of Sicily 10 July to 17 August 1943 (London Gazette Supplement), 1948

Alexander, Field Marshal Earl: Report by Supreme Commander, Mediterranean, to the Combined Chiefs of Staff on the Italian Campaign 12 December to 2 May 1945 (HMSO), 1951

Alexander, Field Marshal Earl: *The Alexander Memoirs 1940–1945*, Cassell, 1962

Aris, G.: *The Fifth British Division 1939–1945*, London, 1959

Bader, W. B.: *Austria Between East and West 1945–55*, Stanford University Press, 1966

Badoglio, P.: *Italy in the Second World War*, O.U.P., 1948

Blake, Lieutenant-Colonel R. L. V. ff.: *A History of the 17th/21st Lancers, 1922–1959*, Macmillan, 1962

Blumenson, M.: *Anzio, the Gamble that Failed*, Weidenfeld and Nicolson, 1963

Bohmler, R.: *Monte Cassino*, Cassell, 1964

Bradley, General O. N.: *A Soldier's Story*, Eyre and Spottiswoode, 1951

Bryant, A.: *The Turn of the Tide 1939–1943*, Collins, 1957

Bryant, A.: *Triumph in the West 1943–1946*, Collins, 1959

Bullen, R. E.: *History of the 2/7th Battalion the Queen's Royal Regiment 1939–1946*, printed by Besley, Exeter, 1958

Bullitt, W. C.: *The Great Globe Itself*, Macmillan, 1947

Churchill, W. S.: *The Second World War*; Vol IV The Hinge of Fate, Vol V Closing the Ring, Vol VI Triumph and Tragedy, Cassell, 1951–54

Clark, General M.: *Calculated Risk*. His personal story of the war in North Africa and Italy. Harrap, 1951

Cody, J. F.: *New Zealand Engineers in the Middle East* (Official History of New Zealand in the Second World War), Wellington, 1961

Connell, C.: *Monte Cassino, the Historic Battle*, Elek, 1963

Craven, W. F., and Cate, J. L.: *The Army Air Force in World War II*, Vol 2 Europe: Torch to Pointblank August 1942 to December 1943, Vol 3 Europe: Argument to VE Day January 1944 to May 1945, University of Chicago Press, 1949 and 1951

Crew, F. A. E.: *The Army Medical Services Campaigns*, Vol III, Sicily, Italy, Greece, HMSO, 1959

Deakin, F. W.: *The Brutal Friendship*, Weidenfeld and Nicolson, 1962

Deutscher, I.: *Stalin, A Political Biography*, O.U.P., 1967

Dulles, A.: *The Secret Surrender*, Weidenfeld and Nicolson, 1967.

Durnford-Slater, Brigadier J.: *Commando*, Wm. Kimber, 1953

Ehrman, J.: *History of the Second World War*, United Kingdom Military Series, Grand Strategy Vol V August 1943–September 1944, Vol VI October 1944 – August 1945, HMSO, 1956

Eisenhower, General D. D.: *Crusade in Europe*, Heinemann, 1948

Feis, H.: *Churchill – Roosevelt – Stalin. The War They Waged and the Peace They Sought.* Princeton University Press, 1957

Fergusson, B.: *The Watery Maze.* The Story of Combined Operations. Collins, 1961

Garland, Lieutenant-Colonel A. N., and Smyth, H. McG.: *Sicily and the Surrender of Italy* (United States Army in World War II), Washington, 1965

Gibbs, Lieutenant-Colonel D. L. A.: *Apennine Journey*, Gale and Polden, n.d.

Greenfield, K. R. (ed): *Command Decisions*, Methuen, 1960

Halder, F.: *Hitler as War Lord*, Putnam, 1950

Harris, C. R. S.: *Allied Military Administration of Italy 1943–45*, HMSO, 1957

Hinsley, F. H.: *Hitler's Strategy*, C.U.P., 1951

Howard, M.: *The Mediterranean Strategy in the Second World War*, Weidenfeld and Nicolson, 1968

Howe, G. F.: *The Battle History of the 1st Armoured Division*, Combat Forces Press, Washington, 1954

Hunt, Sir David: *A Don at War*, Wm. Kimber, 1966

Jackson, Major-General W. G. F.: *The Battle for Italy*, Batsford, 1967

Juin, Maréchal: *Mémoires – Alger, Tunis, Rome*, Paris, 1959

Keilig, W.: *Das Deutsche Herr 1939–1945*, Bad Nauheim, n.d.

Kennedy, Major-General Sir John: *The Business of War*, Hutchinson, 1957

Kesselring, Field Marshal: *The Memoirs of Field Marshal Kesselring*, Wm. Kimber, 1953

Kippenberger, Major-General Sir H.: *Infantry Brigadier*, O.U.P., 1949

Knapp, W.: *A History of War and Peace 1939–65*, O.U.P., 1967

Leahy, Fleet Admiral W. D.: *I Was There*, Victor Gollancz, 1950

Lee, Wing Commander A.: *The German Air Force*, Duckworth, 1946

Liddell Hart, Captain B. H.: *The Rommel Papers*, Collins, 1953

Linklater, E.: *The Campaign in Italy*, HMSO, 1951

Lochner, L. P. (ed): *The Goebbels Diaries*, Hamish Hamilton, 1948

Macmillan, Captain N.: *The Royal Air Force in the World War*, Vol III, Harrap, 1949

Majdalany, F.: *Cassino, Portrait of a Battle*, Longmans Green, 1957

Martineau, G. D.: *A History of the Royal Sussex Regiment*, Moore and Tillyer, Chichester, n.d.

Matloff, M.: *Strategic Planning for Coalition Warfare 1943–1944* (United States Army in World War II), Washington, 1959

Matloff, M., and Snell, E. M.: *Strategic Planning for Coalition Warfare 1941–1942* (United States Army in World War II), Washington, 1953

Montgomery, Field Marshal: *El Alamein to the River Sangro*, Hutchinson, 1948

Morison, S. E.: *The Two-Ocean War, A Short History of the United States Navy in the Second World War*, Little, Brown, 1963

Morison, S. E.: *Sicily–Salerno–Anzio. January 1943–June 1944* (History of United States Naval Operations in World War II, Vol IX), Little, Brown, 1951

Mowat, R. C.: *Ruin and Resurgence 1939–65*, Blandford Press, 1966

Muggeridge, M. (ed): *Ciano's Diary 1939–1943*, Wm. Heinemann, 1947

Murphy, W. E.: *2nd New Zealand Divisional Artillery* (Official History of New Zealand in the Second World War), Wellington, 1966

Nicholson, Lieutenant-Colonel G. W. L.: *The Canadians in Italy 1943–45* (Official History of the Canadian Army in the Second World War, Vol 2), Queen's Printer, Ottawa, 1957

Orgill, D.: *The Gothic Line. The Autumn Campaign in Italy, 1944*, Heinemann, 1967

Owen, R.: *The Desert Air Force*, Hutchinson, 1948

Pal, Dr D.: *The Campaign in Italy 1943–45* (Official History of the Indian Armed Forces in the Second World War), Combined Inter-Service Historical Section (India and Pakistan) and Orient Longmans, 1960

Pethybridge, R.: *The Development of the Communist Bloc*, Heath and Co, 1965

Puttick, Lieutenant-General Sir E.: *25 Battalion* (Official History of New Zealand in the Second World War), Wellington, 1960

Ray, C.: *Algiers to Austria. A History of 78 Division in the Second World War*, Eyre and Spottiswoode, 1952

Richards, D., and Saunders, H. St G.: *Royal Air Force 1939–1945*, Vol II The Fight Avails, Vol III The Fight is Won, HMSO, 1954

Roskill, Captain S. W.: *The War at Sea 1939–1945*, Vol III The Offensive, Pts. I and II, HMSO, 1960 and 1961

Royal Engineers in the Italian Campaign, GHQ Central Mediterranean Forces, n.d.

Saunders, H. St G.: *The Green Beret*. The Story of the Commandos, 1940–1945. Michael Joseph, 1949

Saunders, H. St G.: *The Red Beret*, Michael Joseph, 1950

Senger und Etterlin, General F. von: *Neither Fear nor Hope*, Macdonald, 1963

Stacey, Colonel C. P.: *The Canadian Army 1939–1945*. An Official Historical Summary. King's Printer, Ottawa, 1948

Starr, Lieutenant-Colonel C. G.: *From Salerno to the Alps. A History of Fifth Army 1943–1945*, Infantry Journal, Washington, 1948.

Stevens, Lieutenant-Colonel G. R.: *Fourth Indian Division*, McLaren, n.d.

Stimson, H. L., and Bundy, McG.: *On Active Service in Peace and War*, Hutchinson, n.d.

Tedder, Lord: *With Prejudice*. The War Memoirs of Marshal of the Royal Air Force Lord Tedder, GCB, Cassell, 1966

Trevelyan, R.: *The Fortress. A Diary of Anzio and After*, Collins, 1956

Trevor-Roper, H. R. (ed): *Hitler's War Directives 1939–1945*, Pan, 1966

Truscott, Lieutenant-General L. K.: *Command Missions – A Personal Story*, Dutton, 1954

United States Army Department, Historical Division (American Forces in Action Series): *Salerno. The Anzio Beachhead*, Washington, 1944 and 1947

Vaughan-Thomas, W.: *Anzio*, Longmans, 1961

Warlimont, W.: *Inside Hitler's Headquarters 1939–45*, Weidenfeld and Nicolson, 1964

Westphal, General S.: *The German Army in the West*, Cassell, 1951

Wilmot, C.: *Struggle for Europe*, Reprint Society, 1954

Wilson, Field Marshal Lord: Report by the Supreme Allied Commander to the Combined Chiefs of Staff on the Italian Campaign. Parts II and III 10 May to 12 December 1944, HMSO, 1948

Wilson, Field Marshal: *Eight Years Overseas 1939–1947*, Hutchinson, 1948

Wiskemann, E.: *The Rome-Berlin Axis*. A Study of the Relations between Hitler and Mussolini. Collins, 1966

Young, Lieutenant-Colonel P: *Storm from the Sea*, Wm. Kimber, 1958

As regards Divisional and Regimental Histories, only those from which extracts have been quoted are included in the above list.

Notes to Chapters

NOTES TO CHAPTER 1 BETWEEN PAGES 1 AND 16

1 Ciano, *Diary 1934–43*, 521 and 535
2 Hinsley, *Hitler's Strategy*, 222
3 Ibid, 243
4 Ciano, 544
5 Ibid, 548
6 Ibid, 549
7 *Spectator*, article by Alan Bullock, 14 May 1965
8 Mowat, *Ruin and Resurgence 1939–64*, 56
9 Churchill, *Second World War*, Vol IV, 241–2
10 Ibid, 451
11 Matloff and Snell, *Strategic Planning for Coalition Warfare, 1941–42*, 334
12 Ibid, 335
13 Jacob, Sir Ian, *Diary*, entry for 15 Aug 1942
14 Bryant, (I) *The Turn of the Tide 1939–42*, 471
15 Ibid, 537
16 Jacob, *Diary*, entry for 13 Jan 1943
17 Matloff and Snell, 21
18 Jacob, *Diary*, entries 14–18 Jan 1943
19 Bryant (I), 551
20 Churchill, Vol IV, 620
21 Ciano, 551
22 Churchill, Vol IV, 634–5
23 Bryant (I), 571
24 Matloff, *Strategic Planning for Coalition Warfare, 1943–44*, 120
25 Churchill, Vol IV, 724
26 Eisenhower, *Crusade in Europe*, 185
27 Ibid, 186
28 Matloff, 155

NOTES TO CHAPTER 2 BETWEEN PAGES 17 AND 35

1 Hunt, *A Don at War*, 184
2 Kennedy, *The Business of War*, 292
3 Garland and Smyth, *Sicily and the Surrender of Italy*, 46
4 Roskill, *The War at Sea*, Vol III Pt I, 120
5 von Senger, *Neither Fear nor Hope*, 126
6 Ibid, 127

7 Kesselring, *Memoirs*, 158
8 von Senger, 130
9 Kesselring, 161
10 Richards and Saunders, *The Royal Air Force 1939–45*, Vol II, 304
11 Ibid, 300
12 Hunt, 186

NOTES TO CHAPTER 3 BETWEEN PAGES 37 AND 54

1 Garland and Smyth, 16
2 *Alexander Dispatch* (I) *Conquest of Sicily*, 1017–18
3 Hunt, 187
4 Craven and Cate, *The Army Air Force in World War II, Vol* II, *Europe: Torch to Pointblank*, 438
5 Ibid, 439
6 Roskill, Vol III Pt I, 120
7 Roman numerals are used for American and arabic numerals for British Corps. Eg: (US) II Corps, (British) 13 Corps
8 Eisenhower, 190
9 Craven and Cate, Vol II, 447
10 Garland and Smyth, 117
11 Ibid, 176
12 Ibid, 177
13 Craven and Cate, Vol II, 454
14 Garland and Smyth, 184

NOTES TO CHAPTER 4 BETWEEN PAGES 55 AND 75

1 Wiskemann, *The Rome–Berlin Axis*, 351
2 Kesselring, 163
3 Garland and Smyth, 213
4 Saunders, *Red Beret*, 128
5 Richards and Saunders, Vol II, 313
6 Alexander Dispatch (I), 1020
7 Ibid, 1020
8 Ibid, 1021
9 Montgomery, *El Alamein to the River Sangro*, 89
10 Eisenhower, 194
11 *Rommel Papers*, 431
12 Ibid, 432
13 Garland and Smyth, 292
14 Ibid, 293
15 *Rommel Papers*, 438
16 Ibid, 440
17 Roskill, Vol III Pt I, 146

18 Ibid, 148
19 Tedder, *With Prejudice*, 454
20 Ibid, 451
21 Liddel Hart, *Other Side of the Hill*, 355
22 Roskill, Vol III Pt I, 139
23 Montgomery, 92
24 Eisenhower, 196–7
25 Roskill, Vol III Pt I, 151
26 Crew, *Army Medical Services – Campaigns Vol* III – *Sicily, Italy, Greece*, 52
27 Ibid, 54
28 Kesselring, 164
29 von Senger, 148
30 Ibid, 151
31 Garland and Smyth, 553

NOTES TO CHAPTER 5 BETWEEN PAGES 77 AND 96

1 Matloff, 177
2 Roskill, Vol III Pt I, 47
3 Ehrman, *Grand Strategy*, Vol V, 26 and 27
4 Matloff, 183–4
5 Bryant (I), 671
6 Ehrman, 73
7 Bryant (I), 673
8 Trevor-Roper (ed), *Hitler's War Directives*, 210
9 Churchill, Vol V, 52–4
10 Ibid, 35
11 Bryant (I), 682
12 Alanbrooke, *Notes on my Life*, 828–30
13 Stimson and Bundy, *On Active Service in Peace and War*, 224
14 Bryant (I), 674
15 Ibid, 693
16 Matloff, 211
17 Ibid, 212
18 Ibid, 213
19 Stimson and Bundy, 228–9
20 Matloff, 215
21 Ibid, 216
22 Churchill, Vol V, 68
23 Bryant (I), 702
24 Churchill, Vol V, 74
25 Bryant (I), 703
26 Matloff, 220
27 Ibid, 221
28 Bryant (I), 706
29 Matloff, 223

30 Bryant (I), 707–8
31 Matloff, 224
32 Ibid, 225
33 Ehrman, 9 and 10
34 Bradley, *A Soldier's Story*, 196
35 Churchill, Vol V, 85
36 Ibid, 86–7
37 Trevor-Roper, 215
38 Greenfield (ed), *Command Decisions*, 232
39 Ibid, 235
40 Ehrman, 65
41 Hunt, 216–17
42 Ibid, 217

NOTES TO CHAPTER 6 BETWEEN PAGES 97 AND 114

1   Alexander Dispatch (II) *The Allied Armies in Italy*, 2880
2   Ibid, 2882 and note 2881
3   Ehrman, 59
4   Ibid, 60
5   Alexander Dispatch (II), 2883
6   Ehrman, 63
7   Alexander Dispatch (II), 2885–6
8   Ibid, 2887
9   Ibid, 2880
10 Ibid, 2891
11 Richards and Saunders, Vol II, 327
12 Craven and Cate, Vol II, 504
13 Tedder, 464
14 Ibid, 458
15 Ibid, 462
16 Hunt, 219
17 Roskill, Vol III Pt I, 185
18 Ibid, 157
19 Ibid, 162
20 Ibid, 159
21 Churchill, Vol V, 98
22 Montgomery, 103
23 Ibid, 103
24 Morison, *Sicily–Salerno–Anzio*, 234
25 Eisenhower, 205
26 Hunt, 224
27 Garland and Smyth, 507
28 Alexander Dispatch (II), 2895
29 For the full argument see Mavrogordato's, Hitler's Decisions on the Defence of Italy in *Command Decisions* (Chap 10)

NOTES TO CHAPTERS

NOTES TO CHAPTER 7 BETWEEN PAGES 115 AND 136

1 'State of Alarm I' indicated the possibility of invasion, 'II' warned that an invasion fleet was at sea, destination unknown and all units to be ready to move at short notice. 'III' indicated a landing on the formation's sector was imminent.
2 Alexander Dispatch (II), 2895
3 Roskill, Vol II Pt I, 171
4 Morison, 276
5 Starr, *From Salerno to the Alps*, 16 and 17
6 Roskill, Vol III Pt I, 175
7 Ibid, 264
8 Starr, 19
9 Roskill, Vol III Pt I, 175
10 Morison, 269
11 Kesselring, 186
12 Linklater, *The Campaign in Italy*, 69
13 Craven and Cate, Vol II, 526
14 Alexander Dispatch (II), 2896
15 Ibid, 2897
16 Morison, 285
17 Clark, *Calculated Risk*, 195
18 Historical Division, War Department, Washington, *Salerno*, 65
19 Ibid, 67
20 Morison, 291
21 Ibid, 292
22 Craven and Cate, Vol II, 535
23 Tedder, 465
24 Roskill, Vol III Pt I, 178
25 Alexander, *Memoirs*, 115
26 Churchill, Vol V, 129
27 Kesselring, 187
28 Alexander, *Memoirs*, 116
29 Roskill, Vol III Pt I, 183
30 Montgomery, 107
31 Alexander, *Memoirs*, 114
32 See Mavrogordato, *Command Decisions*, Chap 10

NOTES TO CHAPTER 8 BETWEEN PAGES 137 AND 156

1 Churchill, Vol V, 167
2 RIIA, *Bulletin on International News* (2 Oct 43), 889
3 Gibbs, *Apennine Journey*, 61–2
4 Mavrogordato, 239
5 Wiskemann, *The Rome–Berlin Axis*, 364
6 Starr, 36
7 Morison, 310
8 Ibid, 312

9 Alexander Dispatch (II), 2901
10 Ray, *Algiers to Austria*, 85
11 Durnford-Slater, *Commando*, 163
12 Kesselring, 188
13 Ray, 90
14 Ibid, 91
15 Alexander Dispatch (II), 2901
16 Linklater, 82
17 Kesselring, 187
18 Starr, 51
19 Kesselring, 183
20 Linklater, 133
21 Craven and Cate, Vol II, 367
22 Ibid, 561
23 Tedder, 489

NOTES TO CHAPTER 9 BETWEEN PAGES 157 AND 169

1 Alexander Dispatch (II), 2902
2 Montgomery, 115
3 Aris, *The Fifth British Division 1939–45*, 158
4 Alexander Dispatch (II), 2903
5 Ray, 97
6 Montgomery, 117
7 Ibid, 118
8 Ray, 98
9 Craven and Cate, Vol II, 579
10 Alexander Dispatch (II), 2905
11 Montgomery, 124
12 Alexander Dispatch (II), 2905
13 Montgomery, 131
14 Starr, 58
15 Clark, 228
16 Starr, 65–6
17 Ibid, 69

NOTES TO CHAPTER 10 BETWEEN PAGES 171 AND 186

1 Ehrman, Vol V, 81
2 Ibid, 97–8
3 Eisenhower, 211
4 Ehrman, Vol V, 113
5 Ibid, 110
6 Ibid, 117
7 Bryant (II), *Triumph in the West*, 75

8 Wilmot, *Struggle for Europe*, 149
9 Matloff, 360
10 Hopkins, *White House Papers*, Vol 2, 774
11 Ehrman, Vol V, 104
12 Bryant (II), 92
13 Ehrman, Vol V, 181
14 Ibid, 182
15 Matloff, 366
16 Bryant (II), 97
17 Ibid, 90
18 Werth, *Russia at War*, 754–5
19 Matloff, 371–2
20 Ehrman, Vol V, 187
21 Matloff, 381 (note)
22 Alexander Dispatch (II), 2909

NOTES TO CHAPTER 11 BETWEEN PAGES 187 AND 198

1 Majdalany, *Cassino*, 6
2 Ibid, 34–5
3 Starr, 83
4 Blumenson, *Anzio: The Gamble that Failed*
5 Craven and Cate, *The Army Air Force in World War II, Vol* III *Europe: Argument to VE Day*, 345
6 Aris, 181
7 Starr, 87
8 von Senger, 192
9 Starr, 95
10 von Senger, 193

NOTES TO CHAPTER 12 BETWEEN PAGES 199 AND 222

1 Morison, 339 and note
2 Roskill, Vol II Pt I, 300
3 Ibid, 301
4 Clark 257
5 Ibid, 256
6 Starr, 130
7 See Linklater, 189
8 Craven and Cate, Vol III, 351–3
9 Kesselring, 194
10 Bohmler, *Monte Cassino*, 170
11 Alexander Dispatch (II), 2913
12 Clark, 282
13 Linklater, 193

14 Starr, 135
15 Vaughan-Thomas, *Anzio*, 105
16 Starr, 141
17 Linklater, 199
18 Ibid, 200
19 Bohmler, 197
20 Starr, 151
21 Ibid, 161
22 Vaughan-Thomas, 172
23 Ibid, 174
24 Ibid, 182
25 Crew, 237
26 Morison, 281
27 Roskill, Vol II Pt I, 317
28 Morison, 231 and see also Truscott, *Command Missions*, 353–5
29 Craven and Cate, Vol III, 361
30 Alexander Dispatch (II), 2909–10
31 Blumenson: *General Lucas at Anzio* in Greenfield, *Command Decisions*, 271
32 Alexander Dispatch (II), 2913
33 Greenfield, 271
34 Kesselring, 194
35 Westphal, *The German Army in the West*, 158
36 Alexander, *Memoirs*, 125–6
37 Westphal, 160–1

NOTES TO CHAPTER 13 BETWEEN PAGES 223 AND 244

1 Starr, 100
2 von Senger, 195
3 Kippenberger, *Infantry Brigadier*, 353
4 von Senger, 195–6
5 Alexander Dispatch (II), 2914
6 Alexander, *Memoirs*, 121
7 von Senger, 203
8 Martineau, *History of the Royal Sussex Regiment*, 271–2
9 Majdalany, 140
10 Bohmler, 179–80
11 Majdalany, 148
12 Ibid, 149
13 Murphy, *2nd New Zealand Divisional Artillery*, 567
14 Stevens, *Fourth Indian Division*, 305

NOTES TO CHAPTER 14 BETWEEN PAGES 245 AND 260

1 Wilson Dispatch, *The Italian Campaign*, Part II, 3
2 Kesselring, 198
3 Craven and Cate, Vol III, 384

4 Clark, 317
5 Linklater, 210
6 Truscott, 368
7 Clark, 323
8 Alexander Dispatch (II), 2921
9 *Revue Historique de l'Armée – Mai, 1967*, 89

NOTES TO CHAPTER 15 BETWEEN PAGES 261 AND 278

1 Connell, *Monte Cassino: the Historic Battle*, 152
2 Linklater, 253
3 Nicholson, *The Canadians in Italy 1943–45*, 407
4 Bohmler, 273
5 Alexander Dispatch (II), 2936
6 Truscott, 374
7 Ibid, 375
8 Greenfield, 280
9 von Senger, 249
10 Juin, *Mémoires Alger, Tunis, Rome*, 323
11 Macmillan, *The Royal Air Force in the World War*, Vol III, 247–8

NOTES TO CHAPTER 16 BETWEEN PAGES 279 AND 296

1 Ehrman, Vol V, 250
2 Matloff, 225
3 Churchill, Vol V, 453–4
4 Bryant (II), 184
5 Wilson Dispatch Pt II, 27–8
6 Matloff, 468
7 Bryant (II), 211
8 Ehrman, Vol V, 269
9 Ibid, 247
10 Wilson Dispatch Pt II, 33
11 See Wilson Dispatch Pt II, 34–5 and Ehrman, Vol V, 348–9 which conflict with Matloff, 470, the latter placing emphasis on the need for a port.
12 Ehrman, Vol V, 349
13 Ibid, 352
14 Churchill, Vol V, 656 and 662
15 Ibid, 664
16 Ehrman, Vol V, 356
17 Ibid, Appendix X gives the full text
18 Churchill, Vol VI, 59
19 Craven and Cate, Vol III, 430
20 Truscott, 415
21 Ibid, 382
22 Alexander Dispatch (II), 2932

23 von Senger, 261
24 Jackson, *The Battle for Italy*, 260
25 Alexander Dispatch (II), 2938

NOTES TO CHAPTER 17 BETWEEN PAGES 297 AND 322

1 Craven and Cate, Vol III, 403
2 Macmillan, Vol III, 248
3 Extract from an order issued to 117 Grenadier Regiment of 98 Infantry Division at Rimini, 9 Aug 1944
4 Deakin, *The Brutal Friendship*, 725
5 Ehrman, Vol V, 376
6 Kesselring, 211
7 Alexander Dispatch (II), 2943
8 Ibid, 2950
9 Ibid, 2953
10 Starr, 344
11 Bryant (II), 287
12 Kesselring, 212
13 Warlimont, 473
14 Nicholson, 562

NOTES TO CHAPTER 18 BETWEEN PAGES 323 AND 350

1 Matloff, 522
2 Churchill, Vol VI, 131
3 Ehrman, Vol V, 510
4 Matloff, 515
5 Alexander Dispatch (II), 2953
6 Wilson Dispatch, *The Italian Campaign*, Pt III, 84
7 Craven and Cate, Vol III, 471
8 Roskill, Vol III Pt 2, 111
9 Ibid, 248
10 Nicholson, 623
11 Linklater, 412
12 Nicholson, 640
13 Bryant (II), 372
14 Ibid, 379
15 Ibid, 399
16 *Engineers in the Italian Campaign 1943–45*, 45
17 Jackson, 293–4
18 Ray, 191–2
19 Halder, *Hitler as War Lord*, 68
20 Kesselring, 221
21 Alexander Dispatch (III) *The Italian Campaign 12 Dec 1944–2 May 1945*, 28–9
22 Truscott, 476
23 Ibid, 477

24 von Senger, 281
25 Alexander Dispatch (III), 33

NOTES TO CHAPTER 19 BETWEEN PAGES 351 AND 372

1 Saunders, *Green Beret*, 313
2 Craven and Cate, Vol III, 484
3 Puttick, *25 Battalion*, 590
4 Cody, *New Zealand Engineers in the Middle East*, 685
5 *Royal Engineers in the Italian Campaign*, 49
6 Linklater, 430
7 Ray, 210
8 Ibid, 211
9 ffrench Blake, *History of the 17/21 Lancers*, 222
10 Ibid, 223–4
11 Truscott, 491
12 Linklater, 464
13 von Senger, 300–1
14 Warlimont, 505
15 Dulles, *The Secret Surrender*, 218
16 Ibid, 236

NOTES TO CHAPTER 20 BETWEEN PAGES 373 AND 392

1 Churchill, Vol VI, 483
2 Bullen, *History of 2/7th Battalion The Queen's Royal Regiment 1939–46*, 152
3 Ibid, 153
4 Bader, *Austria between East and West 1945–55*, 26–7
5 Mosely, *Stalin at Yalta and Potsdam – the development of the Communist Bloc*, 12–13
6 Pethybridge, *A History of Postwar Russia*, 38
7 Ibid, 13
8 Higgins, *Hitler and Russia: The Third Reich in a Two Front War 1937–43*, 283
9 Craven and Cate, Vol III, 63
10 Harris, *Allied Military Administration of Italy, 1943–45*, 1
11 Ibid, 368–9
12 Ibid, 367
13 Warlimont, 382–4
14 Ibid, 385
15 Ibid, 287–8
16 Trevor-Roper, 255–62
17 Ibid, 278–9
18 Jackson, 318
19 Alexander Dispatch III, 48
20 Westphal, 167
21 Kesselring, 222–3
22 Ibid, 461

Acknowledgments

My grateful thanks are due to the following authors (or their executors, trustees or representatives) and publishers for their kind permission to include passages from the undermentioned works:

History of the Second World War – Grand Strategy Vol V by John Ehrman; *The War at Sea 1939–45* Vol III Part I by Captain S. W. Roskill; Field Marshal Earl Alexander's dispatch, *The Allied Armies in Italy* (*3 September 1943 to 12 December 1944*) and *The Campaign in Italy* by Eric Linklater, all published by Her Majesty's Stationery Office; *Strategic Planning for Coalition Warfare 1943–45* by Maurice Matloff and *Sicily and the Surrender of Italy* by Lieutenant-Colonel A. N. Garland and H. McG. Smyth, both published by the Office of the Chief of Military History Department of the Army, Washington; *The Second World War* Vol V by Sir Winston Churchill, published by Messrs Cassell and Co; *Crusade in Europe* by General Eisenhower, published by Messrs William Heinemann Ltd; *El Alamein to the River Sangro*, by Field Marshal Lord Montgomery, published by Messrs Hutchinson and Co; *The Turn of the Tide* and *Triumph in the West* by Sir Arthur Bryant, published by Messrs Collins and reprinted by permission of A. D. Peters and Co; *A Don at War*, by Sir David Hunt, and *The Memoirs of Field Marshal Kesselring* translated by Lynton Hudson, both published by Messrs William Kimber and Co, and *Neither Fear nor Hope* by General von Senger und Etterlin, published by Messrs Macdonald and Co. I also wish to acknowledge my use of passages from Lieutenant-Colonel C. G. Starr's *From Salerno to the Alps – A History of the Fifth Army 1943–45*, published by the Infantry Journal, Washington.

Amongst the many who have helped me in the preparation of this book I am particularly indebted to:

Lieutenant-General Sir Ian Jacob, GBE, CB, for his kindness in allowing me to use and quote from his unpublished Diaries; Mr D. W. King, OBE, Chief Librarian, the Ministry of Defence; Miss R. E. B. Coombs, Librarian of the Imperial War Museum; Group Captain W. J. Stuchbury, Librarian, RAF Staff College, for their most valuable assistance over research and the loan of material.

The Photographic Librarian of the Imperial War Museum, Mr J. F. Golding; Mr L. Willey, whose cartographic skill is self-evident; Mrs E. R. Dobson and Mrs E. A. Steele who generously gave much time and attention to typing the manuscript.

My many friends of all three services at Sandhurst, whose encouragement and assistance over points of detail have been of the greatest support, particularly James Taylor and David Chandler for kindly reading the typescript and for their most helpful suggestions, and Michael Wright for his invaluable work on the index.

Brigadier Peter Young for his generous advice and guidance, and finally my wife, but for whose patience and support these words would not have been written.

436

Index

437

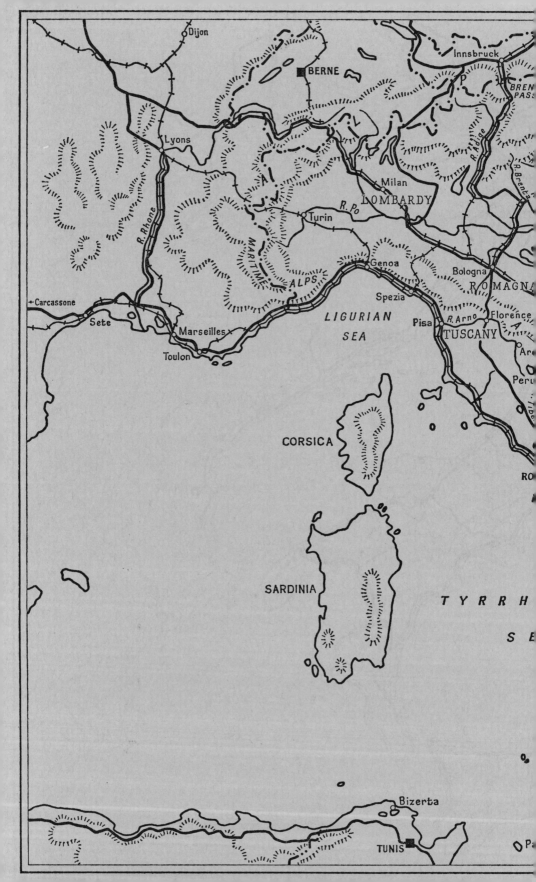